PENGUIN  CL

ON WRITING HISTORY
FROM HERODOTUS TO HERODIAN

JOHN MARINCOLA WAS born in Philadelphia in 1954, and was educated at Swarthmore College, the University of Pennsylvania and
Brown University. He is the Leon Golden Professor of Classics at
Florida State University. His main interests are Greek and Roman
historiography and rhetoric. He is the author of *Authority and
Tradition in Ancient Historiography* and *Greek Historians*, and
has edited *A Companion to Greek and Roman Historiography*
and *Oxford Readings in Greek and Roman Historiography*, among
other books.

On Writing History

From Herodotus to Herodian

Translated with an Introduction and Notes by
JOHN MARINCOLA

PENGUIN BOOKS

PENGUIN CLASSICS

UK | USA | Canada | Ireland | Australia
India | New Zealand | South Africa

Penguin Books is part of the Penguin Random House group of companies
whose addresses can be found at global.penguinrandomhouse.com

This edition first published in Penguin Classics 2017
003

Translation and editorial material © John Marincola, 2017
All rights reserved

The moral right of the editor has been asserted

All rights reserved

Set in 10.25/12.25 pt Sabon MT Pro
Typeset by Jouve (UK), Milton Keynes
Printed and bound in Great Britain by Clays Ltd, Elcograf S.p.A.

ISBN: 978-0-141-39357-5

Contents

3. Antiochus of Syracuse

4. Thucydides

5. Ctesias of Cnidus

6. Xenophon

7. Ephorus of Cyme

8. Aristotle

9. Theopompus of Chios

10. Callisthenes

11. Timaeus of Tauromenium

12. Duris of Samos

13. Cato the Elder

14. Agatharchides of Cnidus

15. Polybius

16. Sempronius Asellio

17. Cicero

29. Tacitus

30. The Younger Pliny

31. Arrian

32. Appian

38. Herodian

39. Ammianus Marcellinus

40. Anonymous Evaluation
of Historians

41. Anonymous Commentary
on Thucydides

Preface

This volume gathers together many of the explicit remarks made by Greek and Roman historians and critics concerning the writing of history. The authors, whether practising historians or critics, are arranged in chronological order (to the best that this can be determined), and the passages range in length from brief remarks of only a sentence or two to independent and self-contained essays on particular authors or on the writing of history in general. The passages are all newly translated and I have provided them with notes to guide the reader in understanding the traditions that were established or assumed by those who wrote and read histories in classical antiquity. The notes are historiographical rather than historical in nature: by 'historiographical' I mean having to do with the actual writing of history rather than with the events themselves as described in the histories, which I would consider 'historical'; I have limited comments on the actual historical situation to that which is necessary for understanding individual passages. Nearly all the historians and critics in this volume have excellent commentaries that deal with the historical issues raised by their works and I have cited these in my notes if readers are interested in pursuing such issues. My task in this volume is to look at the literary and methodological conventions surrounding the writing of history in antiquity, and the notes are designed mainly to provide background information, context or references to similar discussions in other authors.

The difficulties of translation are well known and I do not need to rehearse them here. Suffice it to say that I have tried, to the best of my ability, to offer translations that are faithful to the original Greek and Latin while maintaining the normal idiom of modern

English. I would, however, point out to readers a number of features of my translations that might seem unusual or unique.

I have tried to maintain to the extent possible the same translation for the same Greek and Latin words across different works, especially where these words have a semi-technical sense. This is not always possible, of course, but where it is, I hope the reader will be able to see how similar ideas recur sometimes in the same, sometimes in different contexts. I have tried as well to maintain metaphors where they occur, so that (again) the reader can see some similarity of approach across the centuries.

I have also followed the ancient convention of using the first-person singular and plural exactly as the ancient writers themselves do. This can sometimes seem jarring, but as I have no reason to think that a first-person plural would have read differently to ancient ears than it does to modern, I have kept this feature so that readers can follow the alternation (common in some authors) between 'I' and 'we', sometimes in the same sentence. I am not certain that there is any significance in the use of one or the other, but more perceptive readers than I might see some.

One of the salient characteristics of ancient historiographical criticism (as of ancient criticism in general) is the way in which it is personalized. Some translations gloss over this by using abstract nouns which read more easily in English, but I have maintained the 'personal' tone; so, for example, not 'Ephorus' method seems absurd' but rather 'Ephorus seems absurd', just as the ancient writers express it.

Other issues present other challenges. When Dionysius is discussing Thucydides' style or word order, for example, it is virtually impossible to get this across in English, given the differences between a highly inflected language such as Greek (or Latin) and a very lightly inflected language such as English. But I have done my best in trying to convey the difficulties that Dionysius saw in Thucydides by translating the latter in as literal a manner as possible. Similarly, I have tried to reproduce the workmanlike prose of Polybius, with its repetitiveness of language and style, and have deliberately avoided injecting a kind of variation that is not to be found in the original.

Finally, the reader should be aware that I maintain ancient

usage in referring to the Spartans (in the texts, at least) as Lacedaemonians. Authors sometimes used 'Spartiates' to indicate the
'peers', the elite level of Spartan society, but in general they refer
to them as Lacedaemonians and their city as Lacedaemon.

The notes are many, though I have tried to keep them within
reason. (Not all will judge that I have succeeded.) I try to cite primarily English-language scholarship, but also occasionally call
attention to standard or important treatments of topics done in
other languages. I trust that the latter will be of use to more
advanced students.

It remains to thank those who have offered guidance and assistance in the writing of this book. My longest-standing debt is to
Charles Fornara, who first taught me how to read the Greek and
Roman historians and whose example I have tried, however
imperfectly, to follow. Christopher Pelling was an early and enthu-
siastic supporter of the project, and he also kindly read over some
of the translations and made many helpful suggestions. I thank
also Scarlett Kingsley, Jonathan Master, Jeffrey Rusten and Tim
Rood either for reading over material or offering corrections and
comments or both. To Tony Woodman I owe very special thanks
indeed, since he examined my Latin translations with his usual
gimlet eye, saving me from more errors than I care to recall, and
making the translations themselves much more readable. None of
these people, of course, should be held responsible for the errors
and infelicities that remain.

I have benefited as well from the support and kindness of several people and institutions. Katherine Dundas and William
Fulkerson provided a *locus amoenus* for beginning the project in
summer 2014. I made further progress in 2014–15 during an academic leave, for which I thank Sam Huckaba, the Dean of Arts
and Sciences at Florida State University. The Institute for
Advanced Study, Princeton, provided a stimulating atmosphere
for work and discussion, and St Anne's College, Oxford, honoured me with a Plumer Fellowship for Trinity Term 2015. I thank
also Worcester College, Oxford, for naming me a Visiting Fellow,
and for their wonderful hospitality during Trinity Term in 2016
and 2017. Closer to home, my colleagues at Florida State have

been supportive throughout, and have allowed me to bother them repeatedly with my thoughts and questions. I consider myself fortunate to be surrounded by such fine people. I am indebted as well to the Interlibrary Loan staff of Strozier Library for their unfailing helpfulness and astonishingly swift ability to procure even the most obscure books and articles. At Penguin Books I thank Jessica Harrison, who originally accepted the project and allowed me to shape it in the way I thought best, as well as Henry Eliot, Anna Hervé and especially my copy-editor, Alison Tulett, who put an ungainly manuscript into excellent shape.

Above all, I thank my wife, Laurel Fulkerson, who has been there throughout this project and many others, and who has never failed to encourage and inspire me. This volume is dedicated to her – with no regrets.

J. M.
Tallahassee, June 2017

Textual Notes

For the reader's convenience I give here the editions used in the translations which appear in the volume. Listed (where appropriate) are those places where this edition's translation departs from the standard text. The fragmentary Greek historians are cited from *FGrHist*, and the fragmentary Latin historians from *FRHist* unless otherwise noted.

Words within angled brackets are not in the ancient text as it has come down to us but have been suggested (with varying levels of confidence) by scholars. An ellipsis within angled brackets (< . . . >) indicates a gap in the text.

Authors are given here in the order in which they appear in the volume.

Herodotus: N. G. Wilson (Oxford, 2015)

Thucydides: G. A. Alberti (Rome, 1972–2000)

Xenophon: E. C. Marchant (Oxford, 1900)

Aristotle's *Poetics*: L. Tarán and D. Gutas (Leiden, 2012)

Callisthenes: D. Whitehead and P. H. Blyth, *Athenaeus Mechanicus: On Machines* (Stuttgart, 2004)

Agatharchides: R. Henry (Paris, 1974)

Polybius: Books 1, 2, 5 and 12: P. Pédech (1969, 1991 [2nd edn.], 1977 and 1961 respectively); Book 3: J. de Foucault (1971); Books 7–9: R. Weil (1982); Books 10–11: E. Foulon and R. Weil (1990); Books 15–16: E. Foulon, R. Weil and P. Cauderlier (1995), all published at Paris; for Books 20–39: T. Büttner-Wobst (Stuttgart, 1889–1905), except for:

7.7.1: reading αὐτοῦ (Schweighäuser) instead of αὐτοῖς

12.6b.10: reading συνηθεστέρας ἤ (Bekker) instead of συνήθειαν, μὴ

15.35.1: reading καθάπερ εἶπα, τῷ δ᾽ Ἀγαθοκλεῖ (Büttner-Wobst) instead of καθάπερ, εἴποι τις ἄν, Ἀγαθοκλεῖ (Dindorf)

29.12.10: τοῖς τῆς λέξεως σχήμασι (Heyse) for τοῖς τῆς λέξεως ῥήμασι (Büttner–Wobst)

36.1.1: reading ἀγωνίσματι for ἐν ἀγωνίσματι

Sempronius Asellio: P. K. Marshall (Oxford, 1968) except for:

5.18.9: reading *segniores ab re perperam faciunda* (Woodman) instead of *segniores ad rem perperam faciundam*

5.18.9: reading *introierit quae<que> in bello gesta sint* (Woodman) for *introierit, et eo libro, quae in bello gesta sint.*

5.18.9: reading *non praedicare aut interea* (Woodman) instead of *non praedicare autem interea*

Cicero: *Letters to Friends*: D. R. Shackleton-Bailey (Cambridge, 1977), except for:

5.12.5: reading *reditu* for †*reditu*

On the Orator: K. Kumaniecki (Leipzig, 1969) except for:

2.47: reading *inest in ratione* for *est in rationem rerum*
2.54: reading *colorum* for *locorum*
2.57: reading *rhetorum* (Müller) for *rhetoris*

On the Laws: J. G. F. Powell (Oxford, 2006); *Brutus* and *Orator*: A. S. Wilkins (Oxford, 1903)

Diodorus: Book 1: P. Bertrac (Paris, 1993); Book 5: M. Casevitz (Paris, 2015); Book 10: A. Cohen-Skalli (Paris, 2012); Book 11: J. Haillet (Paris, 2001); Book 16: D. Gaillard-Goukowsky (Paris, 2016); 18: P. Goukowsky (Paris, 1978); Books 4, 13, and 20: F. Vogel and C. Th. Fischer (Leipzig, 1888–1906)

Sallust: L. D. Reynolds (Oxford, 1991)

Strabo: S. Radt (Göttingen, 2002–5)

Dionysius of Halicarnassus: *On Thucydides*: H. Usener and L. Radermacher (1899–1929), except for:

1: reading ὁρώσης instead of θηρώσης
5.2: reading <ὁ Κυζικῆνος καὶ ὁ> Βίων (Jacoby)
9.7: reading καταλήγει (Usher) instead of καταλείπει
9.10: reading <ὁδοὺς καὶ εἰωθυίας> (Reiske) instead of < ὁδοὺς καὶ δυναμένας>

18.7: reading <τοὺς δ' ἐν Σικελίᾳ πεσόντας> – τῶν γὰρ ἐκ καταλόγου (Aujac) instead of <τοὺς δ' ἐν Σικελίᾳ πεσόντας, ἐν οἷς>**, τῶν δ' ἐκ καταλόγου (Usener–Radermacher)

46.2: reading τά τε γὰρ 'φρονήματα' <καὶ τὰ 'καταφρονήματα'> 50.4: reading ἡ διάλεκτος <αὕτη συνήθης τε καὶ γνώριμος . . .>. χρήσιμος δ' οὗτος (Aujac) instead of ἡ διάλεκτος *** χρήσιμος οὗτος

Letter to Pompeius Geminus: Usener–Radermacher as above; *Roman Antiquities*: Book 1: V. Fromentin (Paris, 1998); all others: C. Jacoby (Stuttgart, 1885–1925)

Livy: Books 1, 4: R. M. Ogilvie (Oxford, 1974); Books 6, 8: C. F. Walters and R. S. Conway (Oxford, 1919)

The Elder Seneca: M. Winterbottom (Cambridge, Mass, and London, 1974)

Pompeius Trogus: O. Seel (Leipzig, 1956)

The Younger Seneca: H. M. Hine (Stuttgart/Leipzig, 1996), with the following exception:

4b.3.1: reading *se negant* <*sed audisse*> instead of *se negant*.

Quintilian: M. Winterbottom (Oxford, 1970).

Josephus: B. Niese (Berlin, 1887–9).

Plutarch: *On the Malice of Herodotus*: G. Lachenaud (Paris, 1981); *Alexander, Theseus, Pericles*: K. Ziegler (Leipzig, 1964–73); *On the Glory of the Athenians*: W. Nachstädt (Leipzig, 1935) with the following exception:

347A: accepting Nachstädt's conjecture ἐναργείας <οὐχ ὑστεροῦσιν ἀλλ' ὁμ>ως εἰ for his ἐναργείας <****> ως εἰ

Tacitus: *Histories*: K. Wellesley (Leipzig, 1989); *Annals*: H. Heubner (Stuttgart, 1983) with the following exception:

16.16.2: reading *oderint* (L) for *oderim* (M)

The Younger Pliny: R. A. B. Mynors (Oxford, 1963)

Arrian: A. G. Roos and G. Wirth (Leipzig, 1967)

Appian: P. Viereck and A. G. Roos (Leipzig, 1905–39)

Fronto: M. P. J. van den Hout (Leipzig, 1988)

Lucian: *How to Write History*: M. D. Macleod (Warminster, 1991 = his Oxford 1980 edn with corrections)

Granius Licinianus: N. Criniti (Leipzig, 1981)

Sextus Empiricus: J. Mau (Leipzig, 1958)
Cassius Dio: U. P. Boissevain (Berlin, 1895–1931)
Herodian: C. M. Lucarini (Munich, 2005)
Ammianus Marcellinus: W. Seyfarth (Stuttgart, 1999)
Oxyrhynchus Papyrus 4808: A. G. Beresford, P. J. Parsons and
M. Pobjoy, 'On Hellenistic Historians', *P.Oxy.* 71 (2007) pp.
27–36, with the new readings of F. Landucci and L. Prandi,
'P.Oxy. LXXI 4808: Contenuto e Problemi', *Rivista di Filologia
e di istruzione classica* 141 (2013) pp. 79–97 at p. 82.

Abbreviations

Frequently cited ancient authors and works are abbreviated as follows in the notes:

Cic. Cicero
D.H. Dionysius of Halicarnassus
    Pomp. Letter to Pompeius
    Rom. Ant. Roman Antiquities
    Thuc. On Thucydides
Diod. Diodorus
H. Herodotus
L. Lucian
    Hist. How to Write History
P. Polybius
Pl. Plutarch
    Malice On the Malice of Herodotus
T. Thucydides
X. Xenophon

Standard collections, frequently cited modern works and journals are abbreviated as follows in the notes:

AJPh American Journal of Philology
ANRW W. Haase, ed., *Aufstieg und Niedergang der römischen Welt* (Berlin and New York, 1972–)
ATAH J. Marincola, *Authority and Tradition in Ancient Historiography* (Cambridge, 1997)
BNJ I. Worthington, ed., *Brill's New Jacoby.* Online publication, updating *FGrHist*, following that work's method of citation

BTP G. Parmeggiani, ed., *Between Thucydides and Polybius*
  (Washington, D.C., 2014).
CC T. P. Wiseman, *Clio's Cosmetics: Three Studies in Greco-
  Roman Historiography* (Leicester and Totowa, N.J., 1979)
CCRH A. Feldherr, ed., *Cambridge Companion to the Roman
  Historians* (Cambridge, 2009)
CGRH J. Marincola, ed., *A Companion to Greek and Roman
  Historiography*, 2 vols. (Malden, Mass., and Oxford, 2007)
CJ *Classical Journal*
CPh *Classical Philology*
CQ *Classical Quarterly*
CT S. Hornblower, *A Commentary on Thucydides*, 3 vols.
  (Oxford, 1997–2008)
EGM R. Fowler, *Early Greek Mythography*, 2 vols. (Oxford,
  2000–2013)
F, FF Fragment, Fragments
FGE D. L. Page, ed., *Further Greek Epigrams* (Cambridge, 1981)
FGrHist F. Jacoby, et al. *Die Fragmente der griechischen
  Historiker*, 15 vols. in 3 parts (Berlin and Leiden, 1923–58;
  Leiden, 1994–) Each historian is assigned a number, followed
  by T(estimonium) or F(ragment): thus 70 F 9 means historian
  no. 70 (Ephorus), fragment 9
FLP E. Courtney, ed., *The Fragmentary Latin Poets* (Oxford,
  1993)
FRHist T. J. Cornell, ed., *The Fragments of the Roman
  Historians*, 3 vols. (Oxford, 2014). Citation follows the
  method of *FGrHist*, assigning a number to each historian
  followed by T or F
GH J. Marincola, *Greek Historians* (*Greece & Rome* New
  Surveys in the Classics, no. 31, Oxford, 2001)
GRBS *Greek, Roman and Byzantine Studies*
HCP F. W. Walbank, *A Historical Commentary on Polybius*, 3
  vols. (Oxford, 1957–79)
HCT A. W. Gomme, A. Andrewes and K. J. Dover, *An
  Historical Commentary on Thucydides*, 5 vols. (Oxford,
  1945–1980)
HSCPh *Harvard Studies in Classical Philology*
ICS *Illinois Classical Studies*

*IEG*² M. L. West, ed., *Iambi et Elegi Graeci*, 2 vols., 2nd edn
(Oxford, 1989–1992)
JHS *Journal of Hellenic Studies*
JRS *Journal of Roman Studies*
LatHist C. S. Kraus and A. J. Woodman, *Latin Historians*
(*Greece & Rome* New Surveys in the Classics, no. 27; Oxford,
1997)
LH A. J. Woodman, *Lost Histories: Selected Fragments of
Roman Historical Writers* (*Histos* Supplement 2; Newcastle,
2015)
LIMC *Lexicon Iconographicum Mythologiae Classicae*
(Zurich, 1981–99)
LSG Avenarius, *Lukians Schrift zur Geschichtsschreibung*
(Meisenheim am Glan, 1956)
Nature C. W. Fornara, *The Nature of History in Ancient
Greece and Rome* (Berkeley, Los Angeles and London, 1983)
*ORF*⁴ H. Malcorati, *Oratorum Romanorum Fragmenta Liberae
Rei Publicae*, 4th edition (Turin, 1953)
ORGRH J. Marincola, ed., *Greek and Roman Historiography*
(Oxford Readings in Classical Studies; Oxford, 2011)
PCG R. Kassel and C. Austin, eds., *Poetae Comici Graeci*
(1983–)
PEG A. Bernabé, ed., *Poetae Epici Graeci*, 4 vols. (1987–2007)
PMG D. L. Page, *Poetae Melici Graeci* (Oxford, 1962)
PMGF M. Davies, *Poetarum Melicorum Graecorum
Fragmenta*, vol. 1 (Oxford, 1991).
PRHW F. W. Walbank, *Polybius, Rome and the Hellenistic
World: Essays and Reflections* (Cambridge, 2002)
Polybius F. W. Walbank, *Polybius* (Berkeley and Los Angeles,
1972)
Purposes H. Verdin, G. Schepens and E. deKeyser, eds.,
*Purposes of History: Studies in Greek Historiography from
the 4th to the 2nd Centuries BC* (Leuven, 1990)
RE A. von Pauly, G. Wissowa and W. Kroll, *Real-encyclopädie
der classischen Altertumswissenschaft*, 84 vols. (Stuttgart,
1894–1978)
RICH A. J. Woodman, *Rhetoric in Classical Historiography:
Four Studies* (London, Sydney, and Portland, 1988)

SIG[3] W. Dittenberger, *Sylloge Inscriptionum Graecarum*, 4
   vols., 3rd edn (Leipzig, 1915)
SP F. W. Walbank, *Selected Papers* (Cambridge, 1985)
T, TT Testimonium, Testimonia
TAPhA *Transactions and Proceedings of the American
   Philological Association*
Topoi E. Herkommer, *Die Topoi in den proömien der
   römischen Geshichtswerke* (diss., Tübingen, 1968)
TrGF B. Snell et al., eds., *Tragicorum Graecorum Fragmenta*, 5
   vols. in 6 parts (Göttingen, 1986–2004)
TrRF W.-W. Ehlers et al., eds., *Tragicorum Romanorum
   Fragmenta* (Göttingen, 2012–)
VS H. Diels and W. Kranz, *Die Fragmente der Vorsokratiker*,
   6th edn, 3 vols. (Berlin, 1951–52)

Introduction

1. Sources and Limitations

It has often been noted that in the ancient Greek and Roman world there was no separate discipline which concentrated exclusively on history, nor were there professional historians, so to speak, of the sort that one would expect today, that is, people who had followed a course of study and learned skills particular to discovering and describing what happened in the past. Instead, the historian was a man (or, more rarely, a woman) of letters, one schooled in the same rhetorical education as those who went on to be orators or poets, or indeed any who aspired to a public career. Although we hear of some 'theoretical' works with the title *On History* or the like, these have been lost, and our only surviving essay on the writing of history as a whole is Lucian's *How to Write History*.[1] The other independent treatises dealing with historiography which survive are Dionysius of Halicarnassus on Thucydides and Plutarch on Herodotus. These two works are representative of a popular type of criticism in antiquity, one which discussed an author's strengths and/or weaknesses, not infrequently with the aim of correcting that historian's account. All three essays come comparatively late in the tradition. Lucian's treatise, for example, was written about 166 CE when Greeks and Romans had been writing history for some seven centuries. Scholars sometimes begin with this essay in the belief that it summarizes and incorporates a good deal of the 'theory' of the previous centuries, but even though much of the essay contains material from earlier times, it would be a mistake to give it too normative a role in articulating the tradition of historiographical criticism, or indeed to see any of these essays as in some way authoritative or canonical. The evidence for the practice of historiography in antiquity is piecemeal, scattered, far from uniform and subject to varying interpretations.[2] The reader should always be aware that in order to 'reconstruct' ancient theory about the writing of history, we focus mainly on a series of extracts, that is, detached snippets where an author seems to offer some generalizing remark or remarks. Yet in doing so we wrench such remarks from their context, which is often integral to understanding and interpreting the passage.[3]

For our knowledge of the ancient approach to history, we rely on two strands of information. First, there are remarks made by the historians themselves in the course of their work; these constitute the bulk of our material, and they might seem particularly valuable since they come from those who practised history rather than simply discussing it in an abstract or theoretical way. Second, we have a number of remarks by critics or writers in other genres, either in the course of their discussions of literary topics in general or (much more rarely) in works devoted solely to particular historians. There is some overlap between the two groups, as one would expect, but in many ways the contrast between these two sources is notable: certain topics discussed by one group are rarely if ever discussed by the other. This is not only because historians, in fashioning a narrative, focused on deeds and largely eschewed theoretical analysis of most sorts, but also because literary critics were interested (not surprisingly) in the literary qualities of narrative history, and the ways in which those narratives engaged or failed to engage their audiences. To take only the most prominent example: the ancient critics speak at length on the appropriate style for history, while the historians themselves rarely mention this aspect and when they do, it is in a cautious and circumscribed way.[4]

It is important to remember as well that the vast majority of classical historiography is lost to us; there were thousands of historians in antiquity, but their works have perished over the centuries, and even for some of the important historians who survive – Polybius, Livy, Tacitus – a great (in some cases the greater) part of their work is lost.[5] In addition, although it is clear that much of what survives was deemed by the ancients to have been of high quality and worthy of imitation, we cannot be sure that what survives is reliable as a guide to what there actually was. The accidents of survival are just that – accidents. Finally, it seems very clear even in this shipwreck of classical historiography that there were several approaches to the writing of history in antiquity, and within rather generous norms,[6] there was significant and vibrant disagreement about how history should be written.

The methodological remarks made by the historians themselves seem to have been 'codified' early on (no doubt largely under the influence of the early historians who became canonical), and they remain thereafter remarkably consistent, such that historians writing centuries after Herodotus and Thucydides often say virtually the same things as their illustrious predecessors. It might be tempting then to see the remarks made by most historians as little more than clichés, uttered because authors knew they were expected by their audiences, but not meant in any serious way. Indeed, when we are confronted with obvious falsehoods in a history claiming 'truth' or obvious bias in a work claiming impartiality, this can seem the right approach. Yet these claims played their part in an overarching strategy by the historian to situate himself with regard to both his predecessors and his contemporaries, and to lay claim to a particular place within a long and distinguished tradition. An important aspect of writing history in the ancient world was the emulation of predecessors, and this helps to explain both the general cast of ancient historical works and the similarity of situation and treatment that we encounter over much of the classical historiographical tradition.[7] Emulation could show itself as mindless imitation that took over material from predecessors wholesale and without imagination: one can see this in the historians castigated by Lucian who simply copied out language and situations from Herodotus and Thucydides; but at the other end was the notion that one could more creatively reimagine situations in the light of one's great predecessors. Because of the largely imitative nature of ancient literary creation, then, we find in history (as in other genres) variations on the same few themes played over and over. Yet their continued enunciation indicate that they were in fact expected of a historian.[8]

The other issue that affects the way in which we read a historian's methodological pronouncements has been already hinted at, and that is context. Many statements about methodology are enunciated in a polemical context, where the historian presents himself as embattled or at odds with either named or unnamed adversaries. This distinctive feature of classical historiography is evident already in the proto-historian Hecataeus of Miletus, who castigates the ridiculous and contradictory accounts of unnamed 'Greeks' (F 1a), and it is carried on by Herodotus and virtually all the historians after him. Historiographical polemic comes to us as neither disinterested nor abstract, but as already entangled in the matrix of claims made by individual historians and often aimed at increasing the renown of the historian who offers such criticism. Not infrequently, it serves to advance the polemicizing author's particular interpretation of events, a feature that is well worth keeping in mind when reading these methodological remarks.[9]

The literary critics offer no separate treatment of historiography; instead, their criticism is integrated within their larger focus on prose writing, and history often gets short shrift. This is not surprising since ancient literary criticism began from engagement with the poets (Homer and Hesiod especially) and then the tragedians, and so was always more focused on poetry than prose; and indeed when it did turn its attention to prose, it was oratory that dominated the critics' interests, because the usual career for any upper-class young man involved engagement in the civic life of his state and carried with it the need for him to be able to speak persuasively before his audiences. It is thus perhaps no coincidence that history is so often weighed against poetry on the one side and oratory on the other, and that it is often found wanting on both counts.[10]

2. Definition, Subject Matter, Audience

The subject matter of history was greatly influenced by Homeric epic[11] and was determined largely by Herodotus and Thucydides, the former taking as his topic the 'great and marvellous deeds, some displayed by Greeks, some by non-Greeks' (*preface*), and tracing within his work the rise and fall of earlier empires, with the climax the successful contests fought by the Greeks in 490–479 BCE against the Persian empire. Herodotus had wider interests as well, including geography and ethnography, but his successor Thucydides narrowed the focus of his work nearly exclusively to political and military events, and concentrated on one particular war, the twenty-seven-year conflict between Athens and Sparta known as the Peloponnesian War (431–404 BCE); and, although Herodotus had his adherents in later times, it was Thucydides and his approach which dominated the rest of antiquity.

Within this orientation, the idea of what was 'worthy of account' or 'worthy of memory' (the terms most often employed) remained key for determining the subject matter of history. History aspired to be a 'high' genre, like epic or tragedy, and emulated epic in concerning itself with larger-than-life figures, destructive wars and outstanding achievements. Great men and their accomplishments, conquest and empire, sieges and sufferings, contrivances and constitutional upheavals – these were history's concerns.[12] Along with this came a tendency to magnify the importance of one's subject matter: many historians claim that theirs is the greatest conflict ever known, a boast that goes back to Herodotus' enumeration of forces in the Persian Wars and Thucydides' remark that the Peloponnesian War was 'more worthy of account than all previous wars'.[13] Not surprisingly, authors engaged in polemic will often fault others for writing histories of events which they dismiss as minor or insignificant. Polybius, for example, says that Timaeus made too much of Sicilian history, while centuries later Lucian satirizes historians who use history to tell of humble people and everyday events. Tacitus freely admits that some portions of his history may lack the 'greatness' and drama of his predecessors', though in his case he seeks to alert the reader to the importance of the events he chronicles and what can be learned from examining them.[14]

One reason for exaggerating the deeds was that the historian's renown was closely tied to the subject matter of his history. It was difficult to be considered a great historian without a great subject. Claiming such renown is not something the historians usually do in an overt way, but we can see from literary critics and others that the aspiration to write history involved not only chronicling worthy events but also winning fame and repute for the chronicler. Although Sallust treads carefully and says that the glory of the doer and the recorder is not equal, he also observes that the deeds of the Athenians are considered to be greater than they probably deserve because of the genius and talents of Athenian writers.[15]

Since innovation and experimentation were always to be found in literary endeavours in antiquity, there were subtle and gradual changes in history's subject matter as time went on. The fourth century BCE was a time of ongoing historiographical innovation,[16] and Xenophon is an important figure here. In his *Hellenica*, he shows signs of desiring to expand history's purview: he wants to speak of people's natures and characters (not just their deeds) and he wants to memorialize the achievements of smaller cities, those usually passed over in the 'great' histories. There is a connection between these two, since Xenophon's increased and persistent interest in morality meant that he was on the lookout for noble deeds wherever they occurred. History never lost its interest in noble and base actions – far from it – but thanks to Xenophon the moral evaluation of the character of individuals and states was to become a hallmark of classical historiography, influencing both the Greeks and the Romans.[17]

In addition to the expansion of interests in history, other types of history began to be written as the genre developed in the fourth century BCE and thereafter.[18] Thucydides, as noted, concentrated on a war, and war remained a fundamental category for historians. Herodotus' early interest in peoples and customs ensured that ethnographical description often had a place in historical works. Historians might focus their histories on contemporary inter-Greek conflict, producing works entitled *Hellenica* (*Greek Affairs*), a type of writing that recurs in the fourth and third centuries BCE, or they might look more narrowly at the history of a particular city-state or region, a form sometimes referred to as 'local history', the best known representative of which is the so-called *Atthis*, the local history of Athens.[19] There were also chronographical works from early on, but these seem never to have had a narrative form.[20]

Xenophon again plays a key role in contemporary historiography. In his *Hellenica*, a history of Greek affairs from 411 (where Thucydides' unfinished history broke off) to 362 (the inconclusive battle of Mantinea), Xenophon continued the practice of contemporary history, but focused now not on a particular conflict such as the Peloponnesian War with beginning, middle and end, but on a particular period of time. Such histories of particular eras, which the Romans referred to as *historiae perpetuae* ('continuous histories'), became popular thereafter, and quite a number of Greek and Roman writers began their history where a predecessor left off and were themselves in turn continued by a successor.[21] Xenophon's other work, the *Anabasis*, narrated the self-contained story of the adventures of a group of Greek mercenaries, trapped within the Persian empire after their defeat, as they fought their way back to Greece and freedom, and this more monographic treatment of self-contained events, where one might distinguish a beginning, middle and end, remained popular thereafter.[22]

Other writers made similarly important contributions. Ephorus of Cyme wrote a 'universal' history of the Greeks, both those of the Greek mainland and those of the western Mediterranean (where the Greeks from the seventh century had established colonies in Italy, Sicily and Africa). Ephorus began with the return of the descendants of Heracles to the Peloponnese (*c.* 1200 BCE) continued down to his own day, ending in the year 340 BCE.[23] At roughly the same time Theopompus of Chios took a step that was to have wide-ranging consequences: initially embarking on a *Hellenica* of his own times, he ended that work and decided to continue his contemporary history by now orientating his work around the dominant figure of Philip II of Macedon: his individual-centred *Philippica* (*Affairs of Philip*) was to have many imitators, and proved an especially useful way of writing history under kings and dynasts, not least for Philip's son, Alexander the Great.[24]

In one of his many polemical passages Polybius divides history by its subject matter and focus into three groups: the treatment of genealogy; the accounts of foundations and colonies; and the actions of nations, cities and monarchs. By the first he means the accounts (originally poetic) of the heroes and their descendants (of importance because many noblemen in both Greece and Rome claimed descent, however distant, from heroes and even gods); by the second he indicates the earliest history of Greece, when cities were being founded and colonies were being sent throughout the Mediterranean; and with the third he is thinking of more recent history and the wars and upheavals that formed history's basic subject matter from Herodotus and Thucydides on. His categories might be somewhat tendentious, since Polybius wants to make the argument that only the third type really deserves the name of history, but his distinction, based as much on periods of time (early, middle, more recent) as on actual form or subject matter, calls attention to the peculiar challenges posed to the ancients when they attempted to narrate very early history.[25]

The categories of Roman historical writing eventually mapped fairly closely on to those of the Greeks, but the Romans also had a type of native historiography in their *Annales Maximi*, records kept by the chief priest (the Pontifex Maximus), which recorded events such as famines, eclipses, and the like. These records do not seem to have been narratives, though much about these *Annales* is obscure and contested. They may have influenced the early tradition on Rome, and possibly the first historians of Rome, but even this is not certain. The earliest Romans who wrote on Roman history composed not in Latin but in Greek and the fragmentary evidence hinders our understanding of the exact nature of these works.[26] The first Roman historian to write in Latin, Cato the Elder, explicitly rejected the subject matter of the *Annales* as inappropriate for history (F 80). He, however, does follow the basic orientation of Roman historians, namely a more narrow focus on their own city and its history, somewhat akin to Greek local history, but with an increasingly wider focus as Rome came to dominate the Mediterranean.

A common way of writing Roman history was to start at its very beginning ('from the foundation of the city' as it's often phrased, or 'from Remus and Romulus') and bring the account up to the author's own day, usually increasing in detail as the writer approached his own times. The most famous (and the last) of this type of historian in Rome was Livy writing in the late first century BCE.[27] But the Romans too wrote works focused on an individual war or series of wars (Sallust's two monographs, the *Catiline* and the *Jugurtha*, are examples of this, as was the elder Pliny's (lost) *History of the German Wars*), or they composed *historiae perpetuae*, treatments of particular periods (as did Sisenna and Sallust in their individual *Histories*). The Romans, ever generically adventurous, might combine different elements in their histories: Tacitus began his literary career with a work on his father-in-law which combined history and biography in innovative ways, while his historical narratives, the *Annals* and the *Histories*, are also generically something of a hybrid, combining a type of continuous history with individual-centred history, since they focus on a particular period of Roman history (the *Annals* cover the years 14–68 CE, the *Histories* 69–96) but orientate events largely around the reigning emperor.[28] Whatever the form, however, the subject matter of Greek and Roman historiography remained strikingly consistent, and historians were often careful to distinguish their genre from neighbouring ones such as biography, geography or ethnography.[29]

In his distinctions of genre mentioned above, Polybius not only delineates different types of history; he also assigns a putative audience to each: the earliest genealogical material appeals to one who 'likes hearing a story'; the treatment of colonies and foundings appeals to the 'curious and lover of the recherché'; while actions of peoples and cities attract 'the statesman'. These categories should not be taken to be authoritative, but they do raise the question of the audience for history in the classical world. It seems clear that many of the histories that have come down to us on both the Greek and the Roman sides, with their refined language and careful composition, were meant primarily for an elite audience that could appreciate them properly. There are certainly indications that history was enjoyed by all classes, though we must remember as well that the sources for the knowledge of the past, whether in Greece or Rome, will always have been more numerous than simply narrative histories: orators, poets, painters and sculptors also claimed to represent great men and great events, and indeed for the non-elite these may have been far more frequent sources of knowledge about the past than Thucydides or Tacitus. However that may be, the excerpts and essays in this volume were most probably directed towards like-minded men of the upper class who had the time, education and training to evaluate and appreciate these carefully constructed works.[30]

3. Eyewitness and Inquiry

Both Homer and Hesiod make reference to the Muse or the Muses as their inspiration or source for their songs,[31] but despite the influence of early poetry on history, this was one place where the genres parted ways. Beginning with Hecataeus' individualistic claim that he wrote his account 'as it seems to me to be true' (F 1a), the historians eschew poetic inspiration for the more prosaic path of investigation. For remarks about the research needed to find out what had happened in the past (or in the contemporary world), the historians themselves are the main source. The literary critics are, not surprisingly, uninterested in this. In the three complete essays in this volume, discussion of research plays virtually no role: it is unmentioned by Plutarch in his attack on Herodotus; mentioned only in passing in Dionysius' essay on Thucydides; and given one paragraph in Lucian's treatise.[32]

In the historians themselves, by contrast, professions of eyewitness and inquiry abound. Herodotus refers to his work as a 'display of inquiry' (*preface*) and he means this in two senses: first, he displays the results of his inquiries, the material he writes up, including that portion which is historical narrative; second, he himself as the inquirer is consistently on display, addressing, guiding and occasionally cajoling readers, to draw their interest and attention to the work. Later historians, beginning with Thucydides, make only occasional remarks in the history itself and usually reserve their professions of inquiry for the preface.

Thucydides is the first who elaborates a methodology for the writing of contemporary history. After a long preface in which he attempts to show (amongst other things) that most people are careless in their investigations of the past, he explains how he composed both the speeches and the deeds of his history. There remain quite a few uncertainties about the exact meaning of much of what Thucydides writes here, but the important point is that he outlined a way of writing history, and he bequeathed to his successors both a method and a vocabulary for examining and narrating the past. For the speeches, he says, he observed a hybrid method, making the speakers say what the occasion demanded, but also holding himself as closely as possible to the general purport of what they actually said;[33] deeds he did not compose as he

thought they might have occurred, nor from any random informant, but instead only after testing out with exactness the reports
he heard from others who were present, and subjecting even his
own recollections to the same process.[34]

Later writers add some things to this but hew fairly carefully to
the Thucydidean approach: Polybius, for example, says that eyewitness of events is far and away the most superior form of
knowledge; but as it is impossible for one person to be present at all
important events, inquiry of participants is the next best thing; one
cannot simply inquire of anyone, however, but must seek out reliable people, including those who played a leading role in the events
being considered; and one must make allowance for the bias of
individual informants when comparing accounts (12.4c.4). Over
the many centuries that Greeks and Romans wrote history, this
remained at bottom their methodology, at least for contemporary
history. Documents, archives and records, even when they existed,
were used sparingly.[35]

Those who wrote non-contemporary history, by contrast, usually presented themselves as basing their works on earlier or
authoritative predecessors and writings. Herodotus' slightly
younger contemporary, Antiochus of Syracuse, for example,
claimed that his history of early Italy was composed using 'the most
trustworthy and most reliable material from ancient accounts'
(F 2), and later non-contemporary historians portray themselves as
having done exhaustive research, mainly by familiarizing themselves with the works of their predecessors (i.e. narrative historians
such as themselves), whose accounts they subjected to examination and comparison, occasionally bringing in information from
elsewhere,[36] but mainly employing their critical skills to discern
the truth in earlier accounts. Often they will cite variant versions,
but they rarely try to reconcile them, or even indicate a preference
for one or the other: most of the time they consider their task to be
accomplished just by bringing the variant traditions to light and
showing their readers that they themselves are aware of the relevant traditions: resolution they do not see as one of their tasks.[37]
In addition, we find no example of a historian going back and
reinvestigating events of long ago *de novo* or departing radically
from the tradition before him. Instead, recording the tradition

and improving upon it[38] were what was expected of the historian of non-contemporary events. In some cases the historians lacked the tools that would have allowed them to make new discoveries about the past (other than discoveries in earlier texts); in other cases, pragmatic issues, such as the difficulties, dangers and expense of travel in the ancient world, would have stood in their way.[39]

Sometimes a historian proffered a superior version by claiming to be using a special source for the first time: this was probably the case with the Roman historian Gaius Licinius Macer writing in the first century BCE. He claimed to have discovered 'linen books', which he then used as a basis for his (sometimes quite different) account of Roman history.[40] It was also common for those writing histories of foreign lands to aver that they were basing themselves on native records. The claim is encountered first in Herodotus' reliance on the Egyptian priests 'reading out' to him native accounts of earlier pharaohs (2.100.1), but it is best seen in authors such as Ctesias of Cnidus who said he used chronicles of the Persians themselves, and it became more common in the Hellenistic era as we can see from Manetho of Egypt and Berossus of Babylon, who claimed that their works were based on native records; this is the claim likewise of Josephus in his *Jewish Antiquities*.[41]

4. Effort

Whether writing contemporary or non-contemporary history, another persistent theme, one shared both by historians and by critics, is that of the effort involved in composing a history. Thucydides first introduced the notion but he applied it specifically to the difficulty of disentangling contradictory accounts (1.22.3). Polybius follows this line in seeing the investigative aspects of writing history – the travel, participation and examination of witnesses – as the difficulties inherent in the genre (12.25e–f), and Lucian seems to support this, however brief his own remarks on the subject (*Hist.* 47). Such emphasis on this type of effort does not disappear from later historians, but it either has a slightly different emphasis or is overlaid with other types of difficulty. With non-contemporary history, for example, the effort involved seems to become largely the tasks of reading, sifting through and making sense of one's predecessors' works. Some talk of the 'difficulty' of investigating and making sense of 'mythical' accounts, and they likewise seem to mean mainly the comparison of accounts, now with the added need for applying consistent rationalizing methods to stories encrusted with poetic exaggerations.[42]

Many writers, however (and here the historians and critics are united), see the difficulty of history elsewhere, specifically in composing an account worthy of the events being described, that is, in the task, as it is so often phrased, of deeds needing to be matched by words. This claim, found in both Greek and Latin historians, refers to the challenge of crafting an account in language that will do justice to the loftiness and importance of the events embraced by one's history, and it shows the ongoing interest in finding an appropriate historiographical style. Another 'difficulty' of history that requires the historian's efforts is that of convincing readers of the truth of one's account, especially when the deeds are great and people's natural jealousy makes them reluctant to believe what is being written. This issue of 'believability' arose originally in a rhetorical context where the difficulties attendant specifically on praising people were discussed, because those writing encomia needed to be aware of how to make their accounts acceptable and credible.[43]

5. Truth

Historians insist that their material is true, and truth claims (again, beginning with Hecataeus) are some of the most common professions found in prefaces. Timaeus demands that truth is the standard by which history should be judged (F 151) and Polybius states concisely and clearly that 'the aim of history is truth' (34.4.2). Historical truth is often contrasted with falsehood or lies, or with pretence, or with what is incredible or exaggerated, or merely gives pleasure. All of these suggest aspects of what we might think of as our own notion of truth in history.[44]

Truth claims, however, are amongst the hardest to evaluate in the ancient historians. When ancient historians refer to truth, do they in fact mean fidelity to the actual events that happened, as we might expect for a historical account? The answer may seem self-evident but it is far from being so. There are, of course, numerous places where historians correct their predecessors on matters of detail and substance, and this would seem to argue for an interest in what actually happened. Yet at other times the term 'truth' seems something decidedly different. It is noteworthy that the terms for falsehood in Greek and Latin (*pseudos* and *falsum*, respectively) can range from simple unconscious error to deliberate falsification, while the words for truth (*alētheia* and *veritas*) mean 'what actually happened' but also 'real life'. The latter term suggests an account more probable than true. An excellent example is Dionysius of Halicarnassus faulting Thucydides for attributing a speech to Pericles which Dionysius claims is not 'true', and he means by this 'not the kind of speech someone in that situation would give': here probability is the yardstick rather than whether or not Pericles actually said what Thucydides claims he did.[45]

One finds much condemnation of 'lying' historians by both other historians and critics; indeed, the mendacity of historians is proverbial in antiquity.[46] Even so, there are various forms of lying envisioned by ancient authors: deliberate falsehood, of course;[47] unintentional error; lies of omission; lies of commission; lying by exaggeration; tendentiousness arising from bias; tall tales and/or supernatural events ('the mythical element', as the ancients called it: see below, §9); and illegitimate elaboration.[48] All these forms of lying are attacked by ancient historians and critics, although one recurs insistently and above all: the charge of bias.

6. Bias and Impartiality

Ancient historians, both Greek and Roman, tend most often to oppose 'truth' to 'bias',[49] such that a claim of truth by the historian should mean not that he is necessarily claiming that his account is a faithful representation of historical reality, but rather that he himself is not biased and has brought the proper mental disposition to his work, that is, not choosing sides but treating all the events and characters in his history fairly. Looked at in this way, a claim of truth concerns the historian's *character* rather than the nature of the material he narrates, and a 'true' account, therefore, is one which is unbiased, not necessarily accurate as to historical details. There is much to recommend this view, certainly in terms of the space given over to bias in ancient discussions of historiography. In contrast to Lucian's single chapter on investigation (above, §3), bias, by contrast, is mentioned early on and harped on from start to finish. And the accusations of bias made against historians both by fellow practitioners and by other critics dwarf complaints about faulty or incomplete investigation and research.

That said, there is of course a relationship between bias and the actual events of history. Accusations of bias, as they appear in our sources, are closely allied to the ways in which characters or events are praised and blamed. Now the teachings of rhetoric as far back as Aristotle made it clear that praise and blame needed to be based on evidence, which in historiography would, of course, be the events themselves. Thus a biased historian would think nothing of altering some facts or ignoring those facts which were at odds with his interpretation; nor would he scruple to invent material that bolstered the way in which he wished to present his characters. In this way, truth and impartiality were closely connected with the events themselves.[50]

In any case, ancient writers make it clear that impartiality was essential to the writing of history, and indeed one would not go far astray in observing that impartiality was of paramount importance to both author and audience: it is an overriding concern of most historians to assure their readers that they are impartial, and the readers of ancient histories in antiquity seem to have been particularly on the lookout for traces or indications of bias.[51] Interestingly enough, the earliest historians did not address this issue head-on, although they were well aware of it. Herodotus, for example, unlike nearly all his successors, makes no explicit claim to be impartial, but already in his story of the meeting of the wise man Solon with the Lydian king Croesus, Herodotus says that Solon, asked by the king to give his opinion, offered a true answer rather than a flattering one (1.30.3), inaugurating here an extremely common theme in later writers, namely the difficulty of speaking truth to power, and the desire to substitute flattery for truth. Elsewhere Herodotus is aware that stories grow up around figures of power, and he explicitly rejects those accounts of the rise of Cyrus

which sought to magnify the king (1.95.1). Finally, his own care-
fulness in recounting the conflicting traditions of various peoples,
many of which were clearly self-serving and partial (in both senses
of the word), might be said to reveal his fundamental understanding that truth is difficult to discern in the partiality so prevalent
amongst mankind.[52] Thucydides identifies the favouritism of his
informants as something that he needed to test, but his mention of
those same informants' occasional imperfect memory suggests
that he may have envisioned bias both as intentional favouritism
and as an unintentional forgetting of inconvenient truths (1.22.3).
In later historians, by contrast, beginning with Polybius, the issues
of favouritism and hostility are placed front and centre, and they
are envisioned as the main reasons why history became corrupted
and betrayed the cause of truth. Polybius uses his first major digression to discourse on the essential role of impartiality in history.[53]

Indeed, it can hardly be denied that many ancient historians
used their works to embellish and praise their subjects to such an
extent that the works became more encomium than history: this is
abundantly clear from Lucian and others.[54] The opposite side of
the coin, vituperative attack, seems to have been just as common;
particularly when writing about autocrats, whether Sicilian
tyrants or Roman emperors, historians seem to have employed all
the tools of their trade to besmirch rulers' reputations and achievements after their deaths. Historians who wrote favourably about
rulers were assumed to have done so for material gain or some
advantage, whether that be enhanced status or monetary reward.
Those who wrote hostile accounts against rulers were believed to
have used history to avenge themselves on those who had wronged
them, or perhaps also as gratification of the current ruler who
occasionally wished to blacken the reputation of his predecessor.
It is sometimes suggested in the sources that the dead are beyond
the realm of fear and favour: Quintilian recommends using historical examples from the past because there can be no question of
bias about them (10.1.34); and Lucian offers a particularly striking
example (*Hist.* 40) when he says that some believe that Homer's
account of Achilles, despite its exaggerations and 'mythic' nature,
is reliable, because Homer wrote long after Achilles and could thus
expect no reward from him for his encomiastic account!

The demand that the historian be impartial (whatever the reality was) would be realized in the history itself in several ways. First, the historian needed to focus on and evaluate the antagonists independently and fairly: as Polybius says, he must sometimes praise his enemies and criticize his friends. It also meant that he was not to spend all of his time just on one side, but rather was to move between the two sides. He was expected to keep his language moderate so as to observe a kind of narrative impartiality: the narrative itself was not the place to vilify one's opponent or exalt one's own forces or allies. In addition, the historian was expected to play fair with the evidence: we have a number of statements in which a particular historian is faulted because in his praise he neglected the negative aspects of his subject or in his criticism he failed to speak of his subject's good deeds. This is lying by omission, the concealment of evidence being as false as its invention.[55]

The reasons why bias and favouritism loom so large in ancient histories are perhaps several. First, beginning with Xenophon and Theopompus in the fourth century, explicit evaluation of the figures in one's history became pronounced,[56] and history began to be much more concerned with the moral dimensions of actions and actors (see below, §8). Characters were judged not only for their activities in the public realm but also for their private qualities. And, given that from Herodotus onwards one of the purposes of history had been to bestow glory, the combination of praise and blame together with the recognition that history could immortalize people (or conversely doom them to eternal ignominy) made it more difficult to abstain from taking a particular side. Second, history in antiquity was never written as a disembodied 'academic' subject but was almost always closely connected with the life of the state, whether that was a small Greek city-state or the vast Roman empire. In addition, it is clear that political figures wished their status enhanced by a favourable portrait in history, as one can see from the letters of Cicero, Pliny and Lucius Verus.[57] There was also the strong desire of some to use history to settle scores: Timaeus' highly critical account of the tyrant Agathocles is often ascribed by critics to his hatred of the man who exiled him, while Tacitus mentions that his predecessors who wrote of the Julio-Claudian emperors employed flattery when their subjects were alive and displayed hatred in accounts written after their deaths. Finally, in order even to be able to write history, especially in societies which were ruled by a monarch, an aspiring historian needed access to the centres of power since it was the great and the mighty who formed the subject of his work, and this very necessity put the historian in a bind, since no sole ruler was likely to welcome anything other than a favourable account of his actions.[58] We might say, then, that this persistent emphasis in the historians and literary critics on bias represents very well the actual conditions under which history was written in classical antiquity.

7. Utility, Pleasure and Purpose

One of the most frequent claims made by historians is that their work will be useful, and this utility is often contrasted with other works written simply for pleasure. The historians here were partaking a long-enduring debate that went back to the very beginnings of ancient literary criticism and that originally focused on poetry and its value. For some, poetry's sole purpose was pleasure and one did not need to look to it for any form of usefulness or learning: in Eratosthenes' words, 'every poet strives for amusement, not instruction'.[59] The centrality of Homeric poetry in Greek society, however, whereby Homer was thought to be supreme in everything and a nearly infallible authority, made this a difficult point to maintain, and many critics came to poetry's defence and argued that Homer composed both for utility and for pleasure.[60]

Herodotus does not concern himself specifically with the question of his work's utility. His bequest to later historiography is the belief that one of history's functions is to ensure that things are not forgotten in time and that glory or renown be assigned to great deeds: the concern with glory (*kleos*) harks back to Achilles in the *Iliad* (9.189) singing of the 'glorious deeds of men' (*klea andrōn*), but also to the odes for athletic victors as we know them from Pindar and Bacchylides, and his concern thus connects historiography with epic and epinician poetry in their desire to immortalize and praise great deeds. Herodotus' other contribution (which can be connected with what he saw as his work's utility) was to ally history with the study of causes: his preface ends with the remark that his history will show the reasons why Greeks and Persians came into conflict. For later critics, Herodotus was the example of a historian who desired to praise and who wrote a history that moved and motivated readers by its focus on glorious events; and in this he found many followers, some of whom make even more explicit than he their desire to 'immortalize' the great deeds of the past or of their own times. In this approach, history's purpose is to ennoble great deeds (and men), and in so doing to inspire emulation in others: this attitude is found in authors as disparate as Polybius, Diodorus, Dionysius, Livy and Arrian.[61]

It is Thucydides who first addresses the subject of utility head-on. In his famous methodological statement (1.22) he observes that 'the lack of a mythical element' in his work may seem less pleasurable to his readers, but that the work's utility lies in informing his audience accurately and vividly about events that happened in the past and that will recur in the same or similar ways in the future. Thucydides will, of course, have been very familiar with the debates of his time surrounding Homeric poetry[62] and with poetry in general, and the claim of choosing utility over pleasure is pointed, staking out a particular kind of territory for what was still a young genre. For Thucydides the utility of his history is closely bound up with the knowledge of events that is to be gained by reading his work, which will also contribute to understanding what will happen again in the future in similar ways.

Here, as with so much else, his influence was paramount, and his successors all claim a role for the utility of their histories and profess themselves unconcerned with pleasure, suggesting that any pleasure in their work is merely incidental. Yet these later historians' notions of history's utility, whatever they might owe to Thucydides, begin to differ from his in important ways. Polybius claims (1.1.1) that virtually all of his predecessors praised history because it was a training and education for public life and the best teacher of how to bear nobly the inevitable changes of fortune in our lives – which may well be true but which is not stated by Thucydides. Polybius also says explicitly (15.36) that history should provide both utility *and* pleasure, but he sees the latter as arising from an accurate account of the deeds and a focus on what is noble in historical figures and can be emulated by readers. This notion of emulation can be found as well in Diodorus, who in his history makes consistent connections between those in the past who have benefited mankind and his readers who are to imitate and emulate such great men, thereby striving to do similar great things for their own communities and what he calls 'our common life'. Such a notion of motivating readers in the public sphere is one that is also deeply ingrained in Roman historiography: Sempronius Asellio in the first century BCE implied that his own style of history, which focused on causes and circumstances, would make good men more likely to benefit their country and bad men less likely to do wrong (FF 1–2), and Tacitus two centuries later thought that amongst the benefits of history was its ability to record virtuous action and simultaneously to keep people from wrongdoing by the fear of eternal condemnation (*Annals* 3.65.1). Tacitus may be said to be part of a tradition which goes back to Theopompus in the fourth century BCE, where history's utility is seen not in conferring glory on great deeds but rather in shining a spotlight on immoral and corrupt behaviour, and so to impress upon readers the power of history to ensure everlasting condemnation.[63]

In contrast to assertions about utility, ancient historians are much more guarded about making statements concerning the pleasure that could be offered by their histories. Just as they rarely discuss style or language (except to suggest that it is unimportant), so too they are chary of claiming pleasure in their work, unless it be of the sort that Polybius suggested. They generally see any pleasure arising from their history as ancillary and a function of the events themselves, not the result of a conscious manipulation of those events to achieve a desired response in the audience. Lucian explicitly says that any pleasure must be congruent with a truthful account, and can only arise from the language in which the history is written, not from the wholesale invention of events (*Hist.* 13).

One important exception to the reticence of historians about pleasure was Duris of Samos in the fourth century BCE, who explicitly claimed that his predecessors, Ephorus and Theopompus, took no thought for the representation and pleasure inherent in narrative (F 1). We must assume that Duris offered some explanation of what he thought the pleasure of history was, and how it ought to be achieved. It is generally assumed that he was referring to style and the elaboration of events rather than to the kind of pleasure mentioned by Polybius. Yet caution is necessary since Duris' remark is quoted by a later author, lacks context and is by no means completely clear in its intention; even so, it has loomed large in discussions of the writing of history. The term that Duris uses for representation is *mimesis*, a key term in Aristotle's *Poetics* for the function and purpose of tragedy. Because of this, a connection is made with Polybius' criticism of the historian Phylarchus, who is charged with confusing the purposes of history and tragedy (2.56), and with a passage of Diodorus (20.43.17) in which Diodorus, speaking of the difficulty of narrating simultaneous events, says that historical narrative represents (*mimeisthai*, the verb related to *mimesis*) events but falls short of their truthful disposition. Scholars have combined these three passages to suggest that there were historians who tried to replace history's proper pleasure with that of tragedy, and wrote a kind of 'tragic history' so that the reader would be more emotionally engaged in reading of events.

In Polybius' critique of Phylarchus, he says that this historian tried to make the audience 'sympathetic' to the events being narrated; employed a vivid style in which sufferings were 'placed before the eyes' of the reader; and focused on reversals of fortune (2.56.6–8). All of these, it is maintained, are characteristic of tragedy, and so Phylarchus, possibly taking his cue from Duris, must have written in a 'tragic' manner. Now while it is true that some historians (including Duris) are often criticized by ancient critics for tragic writing, it is not at all clear that what is meant by 'tragic' really corresponds to the characteristics just mentioned. Briefly stated, engaging the audience's sympathies, vivid writing and an interest in reversals of fortune are characteristic also of history, Polybius' no less than others. A different reading of the Polybius passage might suggest that what exercises Polybius most is that Phylarchus' account (or so he argues) is untrue, and this accords with remarks made by Polybius elsewhere indicating that he thinks of tragedy and the stage as the realm of falsehood.[64] Polybius goes so far as to say elsewhere (15.36.7) that tragedy offers neither pleasure nor utility, because it focuses on irrational reversals of fortune rather than those reversals embraced by history which, being real, can be of actual benefit to readers. Though this may seem a simplistic, if not obtuse, approach to literature, there is nonetheless plenty of evidence that for historians 'tragedy' and 'tragic' were synonyms for 'falsehood' and 'false'.[65] Dionysius and Plutarch use the term 'theatrical' similarly to refer to material that is overly dramatic or false, rather than to something vivid or emotional. Whether or not Duris' remark can be made to support the kind of theoretical approach that some scholars have suggested will no doubt continue to be discussed; it is, however, good evidence that the ancients were interested in how and to what extent a historical narrative could approach or reflect the experience of real life, and in what ways a historical narrative could provide pleasure.

Although emotional engagement was expected in a history, it was not the case that any form of it was acceptable. Just like a speaker in the assembly or courtroom, a historian too could bring before the eyes of his readers the events in all their detail and pathos, but he was expected to exercise his talent reasonably and appropriately. Agatharchides of Cnidus criticizes emotional presentations that do not supply the reasons for events and he gives much attention to the language in which one should describe emotional scenes.[66] Polybius, by contrast, as we noted, criticized emotional scenes in Phylarchus, but he faults the emotional scenes not because they are emotional or seek to draw the reader's pity, but because Phylarchus attempted to raise the emotions in the wrong context and for events which did not deserve such a reaction. That Polybius does not abjure the employment of emotional narrative is clear both from what he does elsewhere and even from his criticism of Phylarchus, where he states (2.56.13) that without a knowledge of causes and circumstances, one can feel neither appropriate pity nor reasonable anger.

8. Moralism

A prevalent feature of classical historiography is its concern with moralism. We mentioned above that Xenophon first offered explicit and frequent moral evaluation in his work, and this could concern not only characters' public activity (as, for example, Thucydides did for Pericles) but also their private virtues and vices.[67] Both Ephorus and Theopompus in their different ways carried Xenophon's approach further: Ephorus by his 'amplification of the narrative'[68] and Theopompus by his overt (and often condemnatory) judgements made throughout his *Philippica*. We do not know whether there was an explicit theoretic that justified this increased moralism or whether it was a natural development from its hints in Herodotus and Thucydides, and its more explicit appearances in Xenophon.[69] The fact that history had clearly become more didactic may have encouraged a greater appeal to pronouncements on the character of figures in history, although it is important to remember that an 'ethical' approach is a hallmark of ancient literary criticism from its inception, and the ancients thought it entirely appropriate to evaluate and judge a person's, or even an entire people's, character.[70]

Naturally this feature, like others, could be taken to extremes, and it is clear from the criticism levelled against historians such as Theopompus and Timaeus that they used their histories to engage not so much in moral evaluation of their characters but rather in full-scale attacks, including by the use of innuendo and salacious rumours. Such relentless criticism would suggest a lack of impartiality, and could gain its author a reputation for bitterness or malice, since it was thought to transgress the historian's obligation to be impartial and to evaluate both sides fairly (see above, §6).

It is usually assumed that a more explicitly moralistic historiography was responsible also for the development and importance of historical examples (Greek *paradeigmata*, Latin *exempla*) in classical historiography. Historical examples are as old as the *Iliad*, and occur whenever speakers invoke the past behaviour of great men to motivate their audience to act in the same or similar ways. When, for example, Achilles' old tutor Phoenix tries to encourage him to rejoin the battle, he tells the story of the earlier hero Meleager who, like Achilles, withdrew in anger from his people, but in the end suppressed his feelings and came to the aid of his city: Achilles, says Phoenix, should behave likewise (*Iliad* 9.524–605). In Athenian courtroom speeches of the fourth century, the use of historical examples is ubiquitous.[71] Exemplarity in historiography reveals itself in two ways: first, characters in the narrative use examples from the past to motivate their audiences; this generally presents no problem and is thought to mirror actual practice. The second form, however, is thought to be problematic because some historians selected certain figures as models of good or evil behaviour and then manipulated their material to make the characters conform to types. This procedure is often held to be antithetical to truth and representative of the general cast of 'unhistorical thinking' in antiquity.[72] It is not clear, however, that exemplarity in historiography must be at odds with an accurate account. In Polybius the importance of examples can hardly be doubted, yet Polybius is at pains to emphasize the importance of truth to the historian: it seems clear that for him, at least, the great value of history was that from it readers could draw a supply of *true* historical examples. This is not to deny that at the same time, of course, the use of historical examples could and did lead many a historian to stereotypes and clichés, where any tyrant portrayed would be expected to have all the negative qualities that tyrants everywhere have. Yet, whether the examples were true or not, their use was seen as one of the most important components that history wielded in support of its pedagogical claims.

9. Myth

We noted above that the ancients do not seem to have developed a methodology for the writing of non-contemporary history, although they recognized particular challenges when trying to write about the distant past. Ephorus, at least, thought that detailed accounts of the distant past were not credible (F 9), and other historians were aware that much of what happened in the past was lost or shrouded in uncertainty. There was the additional challenge that much of what had come down from early times involved the gods and all sorts of miraculous or superhuman achievements, and this 'mythical' material presented an ongoing challenge to writers of the distant past. Indeed, for the earliest times, the Greeks and Romans recognized that they had an extensive tradition but little accurate knowledge. In Greece the earliest writers who made inquiries into this area, the so-called mythographers, tried to bring order to the mass of material, mainly by trying to eliminate contradictions and rationalize the stories from Homer, Hesiod and others that had obvious exaggerative qualities.[73] The word we usually translate as 'myth', *mythos*, had already been used by Herodotus to denote something that is unverifiable and improbable. Yet as in other areas, the dominant influence on the way the historians approached mythical material was Thucydides, who in two places in his preface introduced and then rejected from history what he called 'the mythical component' (*to mythōdes*). Like Herodotus, he associates this with exaggeration and unverifiability, and says it will have no part in his work, even though its lack might seem to some to make his history less pleasurable.[74] And, indeed, throughout his history, even when he treats early times, he avoids anything that seems supernatural or strains credulity, preferring human explanations and motivations instead.[75]

From Thucydides onwards, then, the mythical has two related features: it is allied with the earliest times of history, and it is associated with legendary or fantastic material. Some historians emphasize the former aspect, some the latter. Both aspects can be seen in Polybius who rejects such mythical stories and claims that the purpose of myth is simply pleasure (34.4.3). While he no doubt has Thucydides in mind, he is also perhaps relying on theories of narrative which had developed in the Hellenistic world and which divided narratives by their nearness or distance from truth and probability.

In this arrangement, narratives (both poetic and prose) were divided into three categories: (1) history (*historia* both in Greek and Latin); (2) what we might call fiction (*plasma* or *argumentum*); and (3) myth (*mythos* or *fabula*). The distinction is made on the basis of whether or not the events they recount are (respectively) true, like the true, or false. In the pseudo-Ciceronian *Rhetoric to Herennius* (written sometime in the first century BCE) we find history described as an account of things done, while fiction comprehends events that are not true but have verisimilitude, and myth comprises events that are neither true nor probable. To the extent that each of these was associated with a genre, the first was assigned to history, the second to comedy and mime, and the third to tragedy.[76] That might seem a very straightforward delineation, but it is not as clear-cut as it may appear. For as we can see from the fuller account of Sextus Empiricus (late second century CE) but ascribed to the much earlier Asclepiades of Myrlea (first century BCE), the category of 'history' might admit much that was not actually historical. Here the term 'history' comes with particular adjectives attached: 'true' history, 'false' history and 'as if true' history; that, at least, is clearly part of the same schema found in the *Rhetoric to Herennius*, but matters are further complicated by the division of 'true' history into that of (1) gods, heroes and men; (2) places and times; and (3) actions.[77] The fact that gods and heroes are in the first category of 'true' history is a reflection of the fact that for the Greeks and Romans their legendary figures from the past were thought of as having lived and done, if not everything ascribed to them, then certainly the greater part. Jettisoning them would in their eyes have been losing a part of their 'history', so, despite poetic exaggeration, there was still some value for ancient writers in holding on to the earliest accounts, whatever their shortcomings.

To return to the mythical, then, we find that most historians reject it as being inappropriate for their work, but it is also the case that some wished to have their cake and eat it. Whether because in writing an account of earliest times they had only 'the mythical element' or because they knew that their audience might expect and enjoy some fantastical material, historians regularly found themselves wandering in the realm of the mythical. In Diodorus' early books, for example, he commits himself to telling of the 'deeds' of heroes, and this inevitably involves him in treating matters that portray events and characters far greater in scale and number than in his own contemporary world. Dionysius' solution is to give the poetic account but then balance it by offering a rationalized version of the same story, such that he reveals to his audience that he is aware of the limitations of the material. Livy similarly recognizes that some early events in the history of Rome are 'more suitable to the mythical',[78] and he compensates by a sophisticated narrative manner which shows at every turn that he is aware of the challenges and limitations in working with such early material.[79] Several centuries later Lucian has harsh words for those who would introduce myth – by which he means both exaggerative encomia of emperors and stories of fantastic places or occurrences – into history. The former he demands be completely banned from history, while the latter can be included but the historian should express no opinion on the truth or falsity of the account (*Hist.* 60).

10. *Rhetoric and Embellishment*

Herodotus in the fifth century lived in a milieu that began to be pervaded by the systematic study of language and argumentation, and this was to become a defining feature of ancient literary criticism for as long as the ancients looked at literature. The art of speaking well was necessary in a society in which men in public life would need to be able to address and persuade both their colleagues and the people at large. Numerous rhetorical treatises survive in Greek and Latin, and, despite their differences, the consistency with which they treat the subject is noteworthy. Rhetoric is important for classical historiography both because it conditioned the way the ancients read narratives in general, including narrative histories, and because its rules formed the backbone of education and were thus, in the absence of a 'profession' of history, implemented regularly by historians.[80]

To be sure, every narrative history is a rhetorical creation by definition, and were one to think of rhetoric as the technique of speaking or writing a well-organized and persuasive account, then one would not necessarily need to see any conflict between that portion of the historian's activity which had to do with research (in either contemporary or non-contemporary history) and that portion which had to do with 'writing up' the results of one's research. Gibbon's history, for example, is rhetorical but this says nothing necessarily about its accuracy or reliability. This is not, however, what most scholars mean when they talk about the influence of rhetoric on historiography. Rather, they believe that with the rise of rhetorical composition there was a simultaneous devaluation of research, and that the orator's reliance on invention and probability *replaced* a concern with inquiry and 'truth'.[81]

The term 'rhetoric' today is likely to suggest an excessive concern with words, and is often contrasted with action or with the 'real' world: 'empty' is as likely an adjective as any to precede the word. The ancients knew this meaning of 'rhetoric' and could often use the terms 'rhetoric' and 'rhetorically' disparagingly, but it must be emphasized that more often the term comprehends not merely the use of fancy words that sound good but also the appropriate understanding of a situation, the conception and deployment of the most effective arguments, the anticipation of objections (logical and otherwise) to one's argument, and the best ways in which to involve one's audience intellectually and emotionally in the matters one discussed or wrote about. Rhetoric was for the Greeks and Romans a systematic study devoted to the best ways of integrating content and form, with a love for the power and beauty inherent in language: in this sense it involved critical thinking and imaginative reconstruction, qualities that one might still expect a historian to display. Ancient education was indeed rhetorical but it should be kept in mind just how much was comprehended by that term.

Naturally, given the ways in which an ancient historian was expected to do research (see above, §3), the deployment of rhetoric could be significantly different if one were writing contemporary or non-contemporary history. All events, of course, can be rhetorically embellished, but it might be the case that for certain events, especially those of the distant past, the historian had very little information, such that in order to compose a continuous and engaging narrative of events he would by necessity have to use his imagination to a great extent; in that case, the result might be more what we would think of as historical fiction than history, more based on imagination and probability than on accurate knowledge and a desire to know the truth. For contemporary history, on the other hand, when facts might be better known or more capable of being established, rhetorical adornment might play something of a different role, either in the exaltation and denigration of the historical characters or in the way in which information was given or withheld, or the way in which rhetorical *color* (a Latin term not entirely dissimilar to contemporary 'spin') might be applied. As in a courtroom trial, even where the facts are established, different interpretations can be advanced. Here the ancient historian might have more closely resembled what today would be a journalist, writing up events on the spot but without the use of documents, archives and other ancillary material that we would expect of an 'historical' account.[82]

One quality especially prized in the narrative was vividness (Greek *enargeia*, Latin *evidentia*), something thought to be present in all great literary works, and which consisted of envisioning and presenting the scene in such as way as to bring events 'before the eyes' of readers.[83] Thucydides' work was especially praised for this quality, and the scene that he paints of the final naval battle in the harbour at Sicily in 413 BCE was considered a masterpiece, imitated by other historians and explicitly praised by Plutarch.[84] Polybius, on the other hand, while praising vividness in narration, ties it closely to his more pedagogical aims, so that his employment of vividness enabled his readers to envision and thus understand the matters that he expounds.[85] He emphasizes as well that only the man of experience can write a vivid narrative, because only such a man really knows whereof he speaks. This seems a different approach, however, from most of the writers who treat this subject, who are instead working in the rhetorical tradition and are encouraging the writer to imagine for himself the situation, and then creatively recast this for his audience. That the results were often stereotypical or hackneyed seems not to have discouraged writers from the attempt.[86]

The main controversy amongst scholars today is to what extent we should regard the ancients' rhetorical approach to history as affecting the reliability of the narratives that have come down to us. One viewpoint is that, while rhetoric was pervasive, it consisted mostly of a kind of adornment of the facts that one can, with patient attention, remove so as to get to the 'hard core' of the material: in a famous analogy, this would be like removing the icing from a cake. For such scholars, ancient historians are seen as like their modern counterparts, only better stylists. The other viewpoint maintains that rhetoric cannot so easily be separated out from historical 'fact' and is rather part of the cake itself: rhetoric structured and shaped the ancients' entire approach to the past, from the invention of plausible detail to their borrowing of epic and poetic motifs, their emulation of predecessors and (perhaps most obviously) the long and detailed speeches which they ascribe to their characters.

11. Speeches

Nowhere is the influence of rhetoric more pronounced in ancient historiography, and nowhere are modern readers more likely to be confused, than in the practice by Greek and Roman historians of composing speeches for their historical characters. These speeches may range from brief, conversational dialogues to full-scale orations that go on for pages, and they may be offered in direct or indirect discourse. The inclusion of speeches is an inheritance of historiography from Homeric epic, and speeches can be found in all surviving historians, even if the ratio of speech to narrative differs greatly from one author to the next. Some historians, it is true, complained about over-long or frequent speeches in history, but none entirely eschewed the practice.[87] Whether in direct or indirect discourse, speeches fulfilled important functions in a history: they explained the motivations and reasons why particular actions were taken; they offered background to actions, especially when a speaker cited previous history; they provided a form of explanation in a genre more directed towards narrative than analysis; and they served to characterize the speakers themselves. Herodotus employs brief conversations and debates of moderate length, whereas Thucydides first introduced lengthier debates, especially those with two speakers holding antithetical viewpoints and presenting them before the public. His speeches have a high level of abstraction and detailed argumentation, and move regularly between the specifics of the current situation and appeals to general and widely believed truths.

Only a few historians discuss how they composed speeches, the most important being Thucydides himself. In his methodological remarks he distinguishes between the recording of deeds and words, stating that for the former he wrote not as it seemed to him nor from random informants but rather only after examination and comparison of the accounts given to him, whereas for the latter he composed the speeches by maintaining closely the general purport of the speech while having the speakers say what the occasion must have demanded (1.22.2). To say that much ink has been spilt on this passage would be a serious understatement.[88] To some it seems that Thucydides is contradicting himself (I made them say what they had to say but I kept closely to what they did say), whereas others think that he is outlining a flexible approach, maintaining the arguments or viewpoints which were generally known (this would have been easier in public matters, of course) while allowing himself to assume, where he did not know or have an accurate report, the kinds of argument that must have been made in the situation. So ubiquitous and pervasive are our modern tools for recording that it is difficult to imagine a world in which speech, once uttered, vanished for ever. Even when a written version remained (and this would not have been the case for the vast majority of speeches recorded by historians), one could not be certain that this was what the speaker actually said on the occasion, since orators were known to polish up (and sometimes drastically alter) in publication the speeches which they had previously delivered. Thus there is never the question of a historian reporting the very words of the speaker (except perhaps for short utterances which were remembered and might even become proverbial), and some element of creative reconstruction was absolutely essential, even for the most public of speeches. Here, of course, a historian's rhetorical training would have come to the fore.

That many historians wrote up the speeches in their history without consideration for what was actually said can hardly be denied. Polybius' long attack on Timaeus' speeches (12.25a–b), which he compares to schoolboy exercises, is (for all its polemical tone) an important piece of evidence. Polybius reiterates and expands Thucydides' methodological reflections, carrying them even further by saying that the historian's duty is to report the actual words of the speaker. In other cases, of course, especially for early history, it would have been impossible to know what was said. Yet historians still gave speeches, sometimes of great length, to historical characters of old, and they too could only have done this by following the rules of rhetoric, imagining the scene for themselves and reckoning what was appropriate to the occasion. Indeed, Lucian says as much when he offers that the historian must make sure that his speaker speaks words appropriate to his character and the situation (*Hist.* 58), a notion that probably has its origins many centuries earlier in a remark by the Alexander-historian Callisthenes (F 44). It can hardly be doubted that many

of the speeches in classical historiography were composed in just
this way, especially in that for early times no accurate recording of
the words spoken would have existed. In this case the historian
reconstructs what the circumstances and the character of the
speaker would have demanded. Much revolves around the ancient
conception of 'invention'. The term we translate as 'invention' – in
Greek *heurēsis*, in Latin *inventio* – means in fact 'discovery',
because the arguments were thought to be inherent in the case, and
the historian's task (like that of the orator) was to 'discover' the
most effective ones and then employ them. This is what Thucydides
means when he says that he made his speakers say 'what was necessary', that is, necessary in their particular situation.[89] It may seem
that once again what is at issue here is not actuality but appropriateness, not 'truth' as much as 'real-life', but the ancients were assisted
in this by their belief in the general continuity of character and situation, the fact that the past was much like the present, and so such
'timeless' arguments were universal and capable of being deployed
whenever an appropriate situation presented itself.[90]

12. Style

We noted at the outset that whereas literary critics discuss almost
nothing except literary form, the historians within the body of
their work rarely say anything about this aspect of their histories,
or if they do, they suggest that it is of slight or no concern to them;
not infrequently they criticize their predecessors for caring too
much about style and this is always, it is suggested, at the expense
of truth.[91] It would be foolish, however, to take historians at their
word and to assume that they really did not care about their style
or spend much effort on it; rather, historiographical conventions
seem to have dictated their procedure. Dionysius provides a per-
fect example: in his many writings about literature, and in his
essays on Thucydides and on the proper historians to imitate, he
concerns himself greatly with questions of word-arrangement,
style, figures, adornment, periods and the like, yet in the preface
of his actual history, the *Roman Antiquities*, not a word about
these is said and he emphasizes instead his devotion to truth, the
accuracy and reliability of the authors whom he has chosen to

follow, the content of his work, and the use that he hopes his history will have to the audience.

As we mentioned above, poetry was almost always the main concern of literary critics, whereas prose held second place. For Aristotle the distinction between the two, aside from the obvious one of metre, lay in the uniqueness of each form's virtues: prose was less grand than poetry, and its excellence consisted in the virtues of correctness, clarity, pomp and propriety; it should, of course, make use of rhetorical figures such as antithesis and metaphor; and it should have vividness. [92] His pupil Theophrastus first systematized these and proposed that a speech should have four virtues: purity, clarity, propriety and ornamentation. Some suggest that he is also responsible for the delineation of three styles – plain, middle and grand – which we find in Cicero (and which were to have long-lasting influence) but this is less certain. [93]

The virtues of historiographical style were not divorced from those of prose in general, although it was necessary to fix history relative to the other genres, especially oratory, whose narration (Greek *diēgēsis*, Latin *narratio*), the part of the speech where the facts of the case were recounted, had an obvious affinity with historical narrative. [94] Words should be equal to the deeds, as we saw above (§4), but not all agreed on what that meant for actual style. Dionysius and Lucian both claim that the language of history should be neither artificial nor everyday, [95] whereas Cicero desired that history be written in a fluid and bountiful style, and he is followed in this by Quintilian. [96] For Cicero, only someone with this full style could exploit the possibilities inherent in history and could take full advantage of the fact that it was an *opus oratorium maxime*, a work more suitable for the orator – who could employ all the techniques he had learned from oratory – than for any other. [97] Many critics agreed that history's style demanded grandeur and an elevated diction which was appropriate to the treatment of great deeds. [98] Lucian, by contrast, suggests that history should be elevated only at times, for example in descriptions of battles, when a 'poetic wind' could blow over one's normally plain account. Even when it was not elevated, however, history, like other literary forms, had need of figures and tropes. [99]

Others preferred a plain style for history. Although Diodorus equated an unadorned account with the uselessness of narratives about the mythical, some saw the plain, unadorned style as indicative of the 'unvarnished' or 'unadorned' truth. Polybius, for example, criticizes the literary working-up of events which are small and unimportant, while at one point he even asks pardon for his very lack of style in using the same figures and words again and again.[100] It is not unlikely that Polybius is here playing on an idea that goes back to the very beginning of Greek literature, namely, that words are charming and deceptive, and that the purpose of rhetoric was to beguile, not enlighten, the listener. Precisely because of this, some writers eschewed the ornate style and chose one that was pared down.[101] Still others preferred a disjointed, even harsh, style, and this is especially well seen in Thucydides, Sallust and Tacitus.[102]

In his comparison of Herodotus and Thucydides, Dionysius distinguishes between the 'necessary' and the 'ancillary' virtues in literary composition: the former are purity of language (correct Greek speech), lucidity and conciseness, while the latter are vividness, imitation of character and emotions, grandeur and impressiveness, force, intensity, pleasure, persuasion, delight and, most important of all, propriety.[103] He praises variety also as a quality both beautiful and attractive, one which can be achieved by the use of digressions, timely variations and figures of different kinds.[104] Lucian, for his part, emphasizes clarity as the historian's main aim, and this virtue recurs again and again in discussions of the narratives of the ancient historians.[105] Clarity is frequently associated with purity of diction, a purity that consists above all in choice of language and the avoidance of unusual or uncouth words.[106]

The one element of style that was commonly discussed by historians was arrangement – not of words, but of material, with particular attention to the unity of events and the use of digressions. Polybius assumes that because of his regular alternation of geographical venue, some will fault the 'disconnected' nature of his narrative, but he offers as a defence of his procedure that our senses prefer change, and so in this way his method conforms to nature.[107] Polybius also frequently interrupts his narrative to elucidate a point or a methodology to his reader, and his remark in at least one place shows that he assumed that the reader expected a continuous narrative.[108] The main justifications offered for a certain type of arrangement are coherence, the ease of the reader and a desire to convey the impressiveness of events. Diodorus addresses the problem in several places in his history, and notes that a historical narrative can never have 'the true arrangement' that one finds in life. Elsewhere he faults Timaeus for untimely and lengthy censures of others, while praising (and claiming to follow) Ephorus who was a model of good arrangement. Diodorus says that historians should include the actions of cities or kings whenever they are self-contained from beginning to end, since those which are not interrupt the reader's enthusiasm,[109] and other historians as well suggest that they will give events each in their own place lest in moving back and forth they confuse the reader.[110]

A frequent explanation for the insertion of descriptions and digressions is to offer the reader 'relief' from the more arduous parts of history. Digressions were much favoured by Herodotus,[111] but are rare in Thucydides, occurring fewer than half a dozen times in his work.[112] Here proportion was thought necessary, both in the employment of digressions and in their length;[113] but there was no single way in which historians dealt with digressions, for here, as in other areas of historiographical criticism, debate was rife and differing viewpoints were held even on the most important and essential topics.

This rapid overview of historiographical procedure can only scratch the surface of the subject, and there is, of course, more to be said. Many of the relevant testimonia appear in the essays and extracts that make up this volume. And while the lack of uniformity may be disappointing for those looking for a 'science' of ancient historiography, the variety of viewpoints on offer amongst the ancients provides continuing food for thought even for moderns who debate how history should be written.

NOTES

1.   Lost works on history are attributed to Theophrastus (Cic. *Orator* 39), the Peripatetic philosopher Praxiphanes (F 18 Wehrli) and the Roman polymath Varro (Gellius 16.9.5). For the historian's studies, Nicolai (1992) pp. 156–64.

2. See the Introduction to L. for the context of *Hist.* For the piecemeal nature of historiographical theory, cf. the useful discussion of Moles (1993) pp. 116–18 on the contradictory nature of the testimonia.

3. On the care needed when analysing lost historians and isolated remarks see P. A. Brunt, 'On Historical Fragments and Epitomes', *CQ* n.s. 30 (1980) pp. 477–94; Pitcher (2009) pp. 167–74.

4. See below, §12.

5. See H. Strasburger, 'Umblick in Trümmerfeld der griechischen Geschichtsschreibung', in id., *Studien zur alten Geschichte III* (Hildesheim, 1990) pp. 169–218; there is no comparable survey on the Roman side, but a glance at the contents of *FRHist* will show just how many Roman historians have been lost.

6. There were, however, some historians who seemed beyond the pale even to the ancients: Ctesias, for example (below, p. 19), is virtually always criticized as a liar, and Hegesias of Magnesia is universally condemned for his artificial and frigid style: see Agatharchides, *On the Red Sea* 5.21.

7. D.H., for example, makes it very clear that *Thuc.* is designed for those who wish to imitate the historian and need guidance in distinguishing his good traits from his bad: see 1.2. On the canon of historians see Nicolai (1992) pp. 250–340.

8. On emulation see D. A. Russell, 'De Imitatione', in D. West and A. J. Woodman, eds., *Creative Imitation and Latin Literature* (Cambridge, 1979) pp. 1–16; L. *Hist.* 15–19 for mindless imitators; for emulation of historiographical predecessors, *ATAH* pp. 13–19.

9. On historiographical polemic see *SP* pp. 262–79; *ATAH* pp. 225–36.

10. For a good introduction to ancient literary criticism, D. A. Russell, *Criticism in Antiquity* (London and Berkeley, 1981) and the essays in A. Laird, ed., *Ancient Literary Criticism* (Oxford Readings in Classical Studies; Oxford, 2006).

11. This is taken for granted by ancient literary critics; for modern studies of what historiography owes to Homeric epic see H. Strasburger, 'Homer und die Geschichtsschreibung', in id., *Studien zur alten Geschichte II* (Hildesheim, 1982) pp. 1057–97; *Nature* pp. 62–3, 76–7; *RICH* pp. 26–38; D. Boedeker, 'Epic Heritage and Mythical Patterns in Herodotus', in E. J. Bakker et al., eds., *Brill's Companion to Herodotus* (Leiden, 2002) pp. 97–116; Marincola (2007); id., 'Historians and Homer', in M. Finkelberg, ed., *The Homer Encyclopedia* (Malden, Mass., 2007) vol. 2, pp. 357–9.

12. For the rhetoricians' very different method of classifying history see below, §9.

13. H. 7.20.2 with Moles (1993) pp. 97–8; T. 1.1.1.

14. On historians' augmentation of their subject, see *ATAH* pp. 34–43; for Tacitus' remarks see *Annals* 4.32.

15. Sallust, *Catiline* 8.1–3. See Callisthenes' remark (T 8) that Alexander's fame depended on him, something strongly suggested as well by Arrian, *Anabasis* 1.12.5.

16. See the essays collected in *BTP*.

17. For X. see the passages below, p. 23. On moralism see below, §8.

18. On the development of Greek and Roman historiography, Jacoby (1909) is fundamental; *Nature* pp. 1–46 summarizes and improves on Jacoby. The ancient view is somewhat different: see D.H. *Thuc.* 5 with notes there.

19. At least half a dozen 'Atthidographers' are known to us and their works are often quoted by later writers. Jacoby (1949) is fundamental, though dense and for specialists; for more accessible treatments see P. J. Rhodes, *Purposes* pp. 73–81; P. Harding, *CGRH* pp. 180–88; id., *Androtion and the Atthis* (Oxford, 1994); Harding has also translated and annotated their fragments in *The Story of Athens* (London and New York, 2008). For local history in general see K. Clark, *Making Time for the Past: Local History and the Polis* (Oxford, 2008); R. Thomas, *BTP* pp. 239–62.

20. On chronography see Jacoby (1909) pp. 12–14; *Nature* pp. 28–9; Potter (1999) pp. 138–44; P. Christesen, *Olympic Victor Lists and Ancient Greek History* (New York and Cambridge, 2007); there is much of value on Greek and Roman chronography in D. Feeney, *Caesar's Calendar: Ancient Time and the Beginnings of History* (Berkeley and Los Angeles, 2007).

21. On continuators see *ATAH* pp. 237–57, 289–92.

22. The term 'monograph' is used by modern scholars but is not ancient; for them a work is usually referred to by its subject matter, e.g. a 'war' or 'conspiracy', or the like.

23. On universal history see Jacoby (1909) pp. 39–44; *Nature* pp. 42–6; J. M. Alonso-Núñez, *Purposes* pp. 173–92; id., *The Idea of Universal History in Greece* (Amsterdam, 2002); J. Marincola, *CGRH* pp. 171–9; P. Liddel and A. Fear, eds., *Historiae Mundi: Studies in Universal Historiography* (London, 2010); Scanlon (2015) pp. 176–9.

24. For individual-centred history, Jacoby (1909) p. 41, who sees it as a type of *Hellenica*, which indeed it is; but cf. *Nature* pp. 34–6 for a better appreciation of the importance of Theopompus' step; cf. Scanlon (2015) pp. 179–86.

25. For P.'s categories, 9.1.1–3 with *PRHW* pp. 178–92; for the challenges of early history, see below §9.

26. The *Annales Maximi* are a vexed issue: see Cato, F 80 with n. 7; Cic. *On the Orator* 2.52 with n. 49. On the development of Roman historiography, Leeman (1963) pp. 67–90; E. Badian, 'The Early Historians' in T. A. Dorey, ed., *Latin Historians* (London, 1966) pp. 1–38; *Nature* pp. 23–8; *LatHist* pp. 1–5; N. Purcell, 'Becoming Historical: The Roman Case', in D. Braund and C. Gill, eds., *Myth, History and Culture in Republican Rome* (Exeter, 2003) pp. 12–40; T. P. Wiseman, *CGRH* pp. 67–75. For Romans writing in Greek, J. Dillery, *CCRH* pp. 77–107.

27. A distinction is sometimes made between Romans who treated their history from its origins to contemporary times and those who wrote up their own era exclusively; the former are often referred to as 'annalists', the latter 'historians' (see. e.g. *Nature* pp. 24–6; cf. *CC* pp. 9–26), but this terminology is problematic: see G. P. Verbrugghe, 'On the Meaning of *Annales*, On the Meaning of Annalist', *Philologus* 137 (1989) pp. 192–230. Nearly all Roman historians wrote in an annalistic manner, i.e., following events year by year. See Sempronius Asellio FF 1–2 for a distinction between history and annals based on content.

28. On Tacitus' arrangement see B. Walker, *The Annals of Tacitus* (Manchester, 1952) pp. 13–77; on the tension between form and subject matter in Tacitus' work see J. Ginsburg, *Tradition and Theme in the* Annals *of Tacitus* (Salem, NH, 1981).

29. See e.g. P. 10.21.2–8 and Arrian, *Anabasis* 5.5.1–2.

30. On the audience for ancient historiography, A. Momigliano, 'The Historians of the Ancient World and their Audiences: Some Suggestions', in id., *Sesto Contributo alla Storia degli studi classici e del mondo antico* (Rome, 1980) pp. 361–76; R. Nicolai, *CGRH* pp. 13–26.

31. *Iliad* 1.1; *Odyssey* 1.1; *Iliad* 2.484–92; Hesiod, *Theogony* 1, 24–34.

32. See L. *Hist.* 47 with n. 156.

33. See further, below, §11.

34. See T. 1.22 with notes there.

35. Potter (1999) pp. 81–4; P. J. Rhodes, *CGRH* pp. 56–66; Pitcher (2009) pp. 50–57.

36. Sometimes 'official' sources are cited (as in Tacitus) or monuments are investigated (Timaeus, Cato, Livy), but these are occasional additions and could never be the basis for the *narrative* account expected of ancient historians, which needed always, unless it was invented wholesale, to be based on the accounts of predecessors.

37. It is, in fact, somewhat more complicated than this. The explicit
     comparison of accounts (x says this but y says this) can be found in
     most historians, and it is in these cases that they rarely choose. But
     we can tell sometimes by comparison of accounts that historians
     have omitted particular variants in the sources that we know they
     used, and sometimes even have followed sources whom they do not
     cite or even name.

38. Including especially in the style: see below, §12.

39. On method in non-contemporary history see *ATAH* pp. 95–117;
     A. B. Bosworth, 'Plus ça change . . . Ancient Historians and their
     Sources', *Classical Antiquity* 22 (2003) pp. 167–98.

40. On Macer and the Linen Books see *FRHist* vol. 1, pp. 324–6
     (S. P. Oakley).

41. For Ctesias see below, p. 19; for Near Eastern records, Potter (1999)
     pp. 95–102; for Manetho and Berossus, J. Dillery, *CGRH* pp. 221–
     30 and, more comprehensively, *Clio's Other Sons* (Ann Arbor,
     2015).

42. On both types of effort see *Topoi* pp. 169–74; *ATAH* pp. 148–58;
     on myth see below, §9.

43. On the difficulty of praising others see Isocrates 4.6, Demosthenes,
     Funeral Speech 14, Nepos, *Chabrias* 3.3 and especially Pseudo-
     Cicero, *Rhetoric to Herennius* 4.50, Quintilian 11.1.15–16.

44. For truth in history, *LS* 40–46; *RICH*, *passim*, cf. Index, s.v.
     'truth'; Moles (1993); Potter (1999) pp. 12–19; J. Marincola,
     '*alētheia*', *Lexicon Historiographicum Graecum et Latinum* II
     (Pisa, 2007) pp. 7–29.

45. See D.H. *Thuc.* 45–6 with notes there.

46. See e.g. Seneca the Younger, *Pumpkinification of Claudius* 1.1–2.

47. P. has much to say about this: see 1.14.2 with n. 17.

48. See Wiseman, *ORGRH* pp. 314–36, for the varieties of lying in
     historiography.

49. The evidence for this is overwhelming: see *RICH*, *passim*, esp. pp.
     71–4, 79–80, 83–6; fundamental on the topic is T. J. Luce, *ORGRH*
     pp. 291–313.

50. See further *ATAH* pp. 158–74.

51. Luce, *ORGRH* pp. 301–7; *LSG* pp. 49–54.

52. See D. Lateiner, *The Historical Method of Herodotus* (Toronto,
     1989) pp. 76–90.

53. See P. 1.14.

54. See L. *Hist.* 7; Fronto's correspondence with Lucius Verus; and
     Ammianus 16.1.3.

55. P. 12.15.10; Cic. *On the Orator* 2.62; Diod. 21.17.2; Pl. *Malice* 4.

56. Not absent previously but done implicitly (Herodotus on Xerxes) and/or briefly (T. on Pericles and Alcibiades); see below, n. 67.

57. See Cic. *Letters to Friends* 5.12; Pliny, *Letters* 7.33; Fronto, *Letters to the Emperor Verus* 1.2.

58. On the difficulties attendant on access to power see *ATAH* pp. 86–95.

59. See Agatharchides, *On the Red Sea* 1.8 with n. 7; Meijering (1987) pp. 6–7, 58–60.

60. On the pleasure/utility debate see *LSG* pp. 22–9; *Nature* pp. 120–34; Rutherford (1994); D'Huys, *Purposes* pp. 267–88; *PRHW* pp. 231–41.

61. On explanation in historiography, Pelling (2000) pp. 82–111; for the 'encomiastic' slant in H.'s work see Moles (1993) p. 94; for the disposition of the historian as favourable or hostile see *RICH* pp. 40–47.

62. He himself actually engages in Homeric criticism in his preface: see T. 1.9–11 with *HCT* I.108–16 and *CT* I.31–7.

63. This is not to say that there is no praise in Theopompus or Tacitus, but it is sparing, and the overwhelming cast of the age, whether fourth-century Greece or first-century Rome, is one of corruption.

64. I have made this argument in 'Polybius, Phylarchus and "Tragic History": A Reconsideration', in B. Gibson and T. Harrison, eds., *Polybius and his World* (Oxford, 2013) pp. 73–90.

65. The notion of the stage as full of falsehoods is Platonic and is embraced strongly by both P. and Pl. See P. de Lacy, 'Biography and Tragedy in Plutarch', *AJPh* 73 (1952) pp. 159–71; L. van der Stockt, *Twinkling and Twilight: Plutarch's Reflections on Literature* (Brussels, 1992) pp. 162–9. P.'s notion (3.48.8–9) that historians who write improbable accounts resemble tragic poets and have need of the crane may also be in play here. It should be added, of course, that historians also use the word 'tragic' as we do in English, to indicate something that is particularly sad or pitiable (see e.g. P. 5.48.9) with no suggestion of the stage or of the genre of tragedy. See also below, n. 78.

66. Agatharchides, *On the Red Sea* 5.21.

67. Compare T. 2.65 on Pericles, largely limited to his character as displayed in his public office, with X.'s long evaluations of the personal qualities, public and private, of the commanders Clearchus, Proxenus and Menon (*Anabasis* 2.6).

68. See P. 12.28.10 and n. 234.

69. Some suggestions in *Nature* pp. 106–9.

70. See above, n. 10.

71. See M. Nouhaud, *L'utilisation de l'historie par les orateurs antiques* (Paris, 1982).

72. For *exempla* see Nicolai (1992) pp. 32–60; Pownall (2004); M. Roller, *CCRH* pp. 214–30; A. Gowing, ibid., pp. 332–47; see also J. Chaplin, *Livy's Exemplary History* (Oxford, 2000); on *exempla* in historical speeches, Rutherford (1994) pp. 59–62, 67–8; for 'unhistorical thinking', *CC* pp. 41–53.

73. The fragments of the early mythographers are in *EGM*; for myth in historiography see A. Wardman, 'Myth in Greek Historiography', *Historia* 9 (1960) pp. 403–13; M. Pierart, 'L'historien ancien face aux mythes et aux légendes', *Les Etudes Classiques* 51 (1983) pp. 47–62, 105–15; P. Veyne, *Did the Greeks Believe in their Myths?* (Chicago, 1988); *ATAH* pp. 117–27; S. Saïd, *CGRH* pp. 76–88.

74. T. 1.21, 1.22.4. On pleasure see above, §7.

75. On T.'s rationalizing see V. J. Hunter, *Past and Process in Herodotus and Thucydides* (Princeton, 1982) pp. 17–49, 107–15; W. R. Connor, *Thucydides* (Princeton, 1984) pp. 20–32; J. de Romilly, *The Mind of Thucydides* (Ithaca and London, 2012) pp. 144–84.

76. *Rhetoric to Herennius* 1.13. For the absence of the novel (which we would consider the most obvious example of fiction) in this categorization, see J. R. Morgan, 'Make-believe and Make Believe: The Fictionality of the Greek Novels', in Gill and Wiseman (1993) pp. 175–229 at 175–93. There was also a two-category distinction (Meijering (1987) pp. 75–6) but the threefold is the most common.

77. Compare this to P.'s generic distinctions, above, §2.

78. Livy, *preface* 6; his language of *fabula* (which can also refer to a play) recalls the falsehood often associated with tragedy: above, n. 65.

79. R. B. Steele, 'The Historical Attitude of Livy', *AJPh* 25 (1904) pp. 15–44.

80. On rhetoric, R. Volkmann, *Die Rhetorik der Griechen und Römer in systematischer Übersicht* (Leipzig, 2nd edn, 1874) is still valuable; see also Kennedy (1963) and (1972), and Leeman (1963) pp. 19–42. On rhetoric and historiography see D'Alton (1931) pp. 491–524; *CC* pp. 1–8, 27–53; C. Macleod, 'Rhetoric and History (Thuc. 6.16–18)', in id., *Collected Essays* (Oxford, 1983) pp. 68–87; *RICH*, *passim*; Nicolai (1992) pp. 89–138; Moles (1993) pp. 114–21; Pelling (2000), *passim*, especially pp. 1–43, 61–81; M. Fox and N. Livingstone, 'Rhetoric and Historiography', in I. Worthington, ed., *A Companion to Greek Rhetoric* (Malden, Mass., S and Oxford, 2007) pp. 542–61; C. Damon, 'Rhetoric and Historiography', in W. Dominik and J. Hall, *A Companion to Roman Rhetoric*

(Malden, Mass., and Oxford, 2007) pp. 439–50; A. Laird, *CCRH* pp. 197–213.

81. For 'invention' see below, §11. For probability in historical accounts, Pitcher (2009) pp. 94–102.

82. For an overview of recent attitudes towards classical historiography see *LatHist* pp. 1–6; *GH* pp. 3–8; see also Moles (1993) pp. 114–21.

83. On *enargeia/evidentia* see Meijering (1987) pp. 29–52; Nicolai (1992) pp. 139–55; Zangara (2007) pp. 55–89, 229–78; R. Webb, *Ekphrasis, Imagination and Persuasion in Ancient Rhetorical Theory and Practice* (Farnham and Burlington, 2009) pp. 87–106.

84. P. *On the Glory of the Athenians* 347A; cf. L. *Hist.* 51.

85. See J. Davidson, 'The Gaze in Polybius' Histories', *JRS* 81 (1991) pp. 10–24.

86. For P.'s vividness, G. Schepens, '*Emphasis* und *Enargeia* in Polybios' Geschichtstheorie', *Rivista Storica Italiana* 5 (1975) pp. 185–200; for the latter, more 'rhetorical' approach see G. M. Paul, ' "Urbs Capta": Sketch of a Literary Motif', *Phoenix* 36 (1982) pp. 144–55.

87. On speeches see *LSG* pp. 149–57; Walbank, *SP* pp. 242–61; *Nature* pp. 142–68; R. Brock, 'Versions, "Inversions" and Evasions: Classical Historiography and the "Published" Speech', *Papers of the Liverpool Latin Seminar* 8 (1995) pp. 209–24; A. Laird, *Powers of Expression, Expressions of Power* (Oxford, 1999), especially pp. 116–52; Pelling (2000) pp. 112–22; J. Marincola, *CGRH* pp. 118–32; Pitcher (2009) pp. 103–11.

88. Cf. Moles (1993) p. 104: 'No passage in Greek literature has generated greater interpretative controversy . . . '

89. D.H. *Thuc.* 35.2 praises T.'s speeches specifically for their 'invention'.

90. See above, §5, for D.H.'s criticism of T.'s speech as not congruent with real life.

91. P. 16.17.9 on Zeno; Josephus, *Jewish War* 1.1.1, *Jewish Antiquities*, preface 2 on unnamed predecessors.

92. Aristotle, *Rhetoric* 1404b; 1407a.

93. On Theophrastus see Kennedy (1963) pp. 278–82 and (more sceptically) Grube (1965) pp. 107–8. The three styles: Cic., *Orator* 75–99.

94. See L. *Hist.* 55 for the explicit connection.

95. D.H. *Thuc.* 51; L. *Hist.* 43, 46.

96. Cic. *On the Orator* 2.58, 2.64; *Orator* 66, 207; Quintilian 9.4.18, 129; cf. 2.4.2–3.

97. Cic. *On the Laws* 1.5.

98. D.H. *On the Arrangement of Words* 4; Pliny, *Letters* 5.8.9–11.

99. L. *Hist.* 45; 43; 55.

100. P. 29.12.4–10; cf. 16.17.9–11.

101. See J. de Romilly, *Magic and Rhetoric in Ancient Greece* (Cambridge, Mass., 1975); the pared-down style was most often associated with 'plain-speaking' military men, where such plain speech is equated with truth: see Livy 3.56.3, 10.24.4; Sallust, *Jugurtha* 85.31; and cf. Cicero, *Brutus* 262 on the commentaries of Julius Caesar.

102. *RICH* pp. 119–96 is fundamental on this topic.

103. D.H. *Pomp.* 3.16–21.

104. D.H. *On the Arrangement of Words* 19.

105. Aristotle *Rhetoric* 1404b; 1407a; L. *Hist.* 44, with *LS* pp. 61–2.

106. Hermogenes (*On Forms* 411) praises Hecataeus for being 'pure and lucid', Dionysius calls Theopompus' style 'pure, usual and clear', and elsewhere claims that the pre-Herodotean historians gave their efforts and attention solely to being clear, ordinary, pure and concise (D.H. *Pomp.* 6.9; *Thuc.* 5.4; L. *Hist.* 44).

107. P. 38.5.1–6. 7.

108. See 6.2.1.

109. The three passages are (respectively) Diod. 20.43.7, 5.1.1–4 and 16.1.1–3.

110. See n. 109 and also D.H. *Thuc.* 9.4–10; L. *Hist.* 50; Ammianus 26.5.15. The issue is also addressed by the first-century BCE Roman historian, Sisenna, who writes (*FRHist* 26 F 130), 'My literary treatments of a single season's accomplishments in Asia and Greece have been juxtaposed purposely so that I do not hobble my readers' attention by writing twitchily or jumpily' (A. J. Woodman's translation; see his discussion, *LH* pp. 51–3). On arrangement see Pitcher (2009) pp. 127–37.

111. See H. 4.30 and 7.152.3, the latter quoted by Pl. *Malice* 28.

112. T. 1.89–118, 126–138; 2.96–101; 6.1–5, 54–59: cf. D.H. *Pomp.* 3. 11–12.

113. See further P. 12.28.10; Pl. *Malice* 3; L. *Hist.* 57; Ammianus 26.1. 1–2 for a complaint about overlong digressions.

ON WRITING HISTORY
FROM HERODOTUS TO HERODIAN

I

HECATAEUS OF
MILETUS

Hecataeus of Miletus was born around 560 BCE; little is known of his life, although he seems to have been an important statesman: Herodotus (5.36) shows him amongst a group of leading Ionians in 499 BCE, counselling them not to revolt from the Persian king. Hecataeus improved on Anaximander's map of the world and wrote two important works: *Journey around the Earth*, an account of the peoples and customs of the lands (Greek and non-Greek) that border on the Mediterranean Sea, and *Genealogies*, an attempt to bring order and some level of rationalization to the many widespread and contradictory Greek accounts of heroes and their offspring, a not insignificant effort and one with political consequences since very often leading families claimed descent from gods and heroes partly as justification for their pre-eminence. Nearly 400 fragments of his works survive, but many of these are little more than single-word quotations from the *Journey* which are preserved in a later work on geographical place-names. Although not considered a historian himself, he is an important influence on Herodotus, and the words below, probably from the preface of the *Genealogies*, embody the nascent exploratory and critical spirit that would eventually lead to historical narrative.[1]

Preface

(*FGrHist* 1 F 1a = *EGM* F 1)

Hecataeus of Miletus speaks thus: 'I write what follows as it seems to me to be true; for the stories of the Greeks, as they appear to me, are numerous and ridiculous.'[2]

2

HERODOTUS

Herodotus was born in Halicarnassus (modern Bodrum) in Asia Minor (the western coast of modern-day Turkey) *c.* 485 BCE. According to the biographical tradition he was exiled from his native city and went to Samos, returned to Halicarnassus but was again forced to flee, and this time went to Athens and eventually joined in the foundation of Thurii (444/3 BCE), a pan-Hellenic Athenian-led colony in southern Italy, and he is said to have died there or in Pella in Macedonia. The date of his death is uncertain, perhaps sometime in the late 420s.

Considered the father of history both in ancient and in modern times, Herodotus does not expound a methodology for the writing of history in any single place (as Thucydides was to do), and indeed may not have followed a consistent method, given the different types of material that his history embraced. It is clear, however, that much of his method is founded on his personal investigations, using eyewitness and inquiry from knowledgeable sources. Because he lived at a time when records and documents were scanty, there was no substitute for travel and examination of different witnesses.[1] Although much criticized by later generations for a variety of faults, especially bias and fable-mongering, Herodotus was nonetheless considered one of the great historians, and was much imitated by later writers in both style and substance.[2]

The first passage below gives some sense of Herodotus' purpose in writing; the ones that follow try to give a representative selection of remarks on his methodology.

Preface to the *Histories*

Herodotus of Halicarnassus displays his inquiry in what follows, so that human achievements may not become faded in time, and so that great and marvellous deeds, some displayed by Greeks, others by barbarians,[3] may not be without their glory;[4] and especially to show the reason why the two peoples fought against each other.[5]

What is Worthy of Record

(1.14.4 + 1.177 + 5.65.4)[6]

When he took the throne he [Gyges] made an expedition against Miletus and Smyrna, and he captured the citadel of Colophon. But we shall pass over him, having mentioned only these, since he accomplished no other great deed in his reign of thirty-eight years.

177   While Harpagus was depopulating the lower parts of Asia, Cyrus was depopulating the upper parts, conquering every nation and passing over none. Now we shall omit most of his deeds, but I will record those which gave him the most trouble and are worth describing.

5.65.4   In this way, then, Athens was freed from her tyrants. I shall now recount everything that they did or suffered which is worth describing once they were freed and before Ionia revolted from Darius and Aristagoras of Miletus came to Athens asking for assistance.[7]

Choosing an Account

(1.95.1)

From here my account examines who this Cyrus was who brought the reign of Croesus to an end, and how the Persians came to rule Asia. Now there are some Persians who do not wish to magnify

events that have to do with Cyrus,[8] and it is in accordance with
these that I shall give the actual account, even though there are
three other courses my narrative could take.

Inquiries Concerning Heracles[9]

(2.43.1 + 2.44.1–45.1)

I heard that Heracles was one of the twelve gods; about the other
Heracles, the one whom the Greeks are familiar with, I heard
nothing anywhere in Egypt . . . Wishing to get some clear know- 44
ledge about these matters to the extent it was possible, I sailed to
Tyre in Phoenicia and I learned that there was a temple there
sacred to Heracles. I saw it richly adorned with many dedications, 2
including especially two pillars, one of refined gold, the other of
emerald which shone at night with a great radiance. I conversed
with the priests of the god and asked them how long ago the temple had been built. I discovered that these too did not agree with 3
the Greeks, for the priests said that the temple had been built at
the same time that Tyre was founded and that was 2,300 years
before the present. I saw in Tyre another temple of Heracles called
'the Thasian'. I went also to Thasos where I found a temple built 4
by the Phoenicians who had founded Thasos when they had sailed
off in search of Europa. And these events occurred five generations before Heracles the son of Amphitryon appeared in Greece.
My researches reveal clearly then that Heracles is an ancient god. 5
And I think that those Greeks who have two temples and two
cults for Heracles are acting most correctly: they offer sacrifice to
the one as a god and call him 'the Olympian', while the other they
venerate as a hero.[10] But the Greeks say many other things without 45
examining them.[11]

Sources for the Egyptian Account

(2.99.1, 2.147.1)

Up to this point[12] it is my observation, my reasoning and my inquiry that recounts these things; from here on I shall give the Egyptian accounts, speaking in accordance with what I heard; and I shall add to this something of my own observation . . .

(*At the end of this account, Herodotus summarizes:*)

147   These things, then, the Egyptians themselves say.[13] In what follows I shall relate those things about which the Egyptians and everyone else agrees; and I shall add something of my own observation.

Treating What Has Not Been Treated Before

(3.103 + 6.55)[14]

Because the Greeks are familiar with the appearance of the camel, I shall not write that down, but I shall speak of something they do not know: in its hind legs the camel has four thighs and knees, and its genitals point backwards through its hind legs.

6.55   Since the actions they [sc. the descendants of Heracles] took to seize the kingdoms of the Dorians has been noted by others, we shall pass over them; but I shall record what others have not found.

Intentional Silence

(4.43.7)

A eunuch in the service of this Sataspes, as soon as he found out that his master was dead, escaped to Samos with a great deal of money. A man of Samos took possession of this money; I know his name but I deliberately forget it.[15]

Inability to Give Accurate Information

(6.14.1)

At that time, then, the Phoenicians sailed out against them and the Ionians for their part sailed out in line to meet them.[16] But as to what happened when they came to close quarters and grappled with each other, I cannot record accurately who of the Ionians were cowards and who were brave men in the sea battle: for they all blame one another.[17]

Recording the Tradition

(7.152.3)

I am obligated to recount these traditions,[18] but I am in no way obligated to believe them; and this may be held to apply to my entire work.

3

ANTIOCHUS OF SYRACUSE

Antiochus belongs to the last third or last quarter of the fifth century BCE, and was a younger contemporary of Herodotus and an older contemporary of Thucydides. He wrote a *Sikelica (Sicilian Matters)* in which he traced the history of Sicily in nine books from its origins and first king of the Sicanians, Kokalos, to the year 424 BCE. He also wrote a work *On Italy* in one book. For both works he would have been dependent on oral sources, and his remark below suggests that he sifted through such oral accounts and applied criteria of probability to them, perhaps much as Hecataeus had done with earlier Greek tradition in general.[1]

From the Preface of *On Italy*

(*FGrHist* 555 F 2):

Antiochus, the son of Xenophanes,[2] composed the following about Italy, the most trustworthy and most reliable[3] material from ancient accounts.

4
THUCYDIDES

Considered the greatest historian in ancient (and often in modern) times, Thucydides was born sometime in the 450s BCE. Of his early life nothing is known, but it is a good inference that he was an active citizen, since he was elected by the Athenians as one of their ten annual generals for the year 424 during the Peloponnesian War (431–404). He himself mentions that he had mining concessions in Thrace (4.105) and tells us of his assignment during the year of his generalship to save the strategically important city of Amphipolis in the north; he arrived too late to keep it from falling into the hands of the Spartan commander, Brasidas, and was subsequently exiled. His exile, he says, afforded him the possibility to conduct inquiries for his history from all sides (see 5.26). His work breaks off in mid-sentence during his narrative of the year 411, and it is usually assumed that he died before he could complete it.

Thucydides inaugurated the writing of contemporary history, an account of the author's own time. He is the first ancient historian to give a detailed explanation of his method, and he emphasizes the specific benefits of writing contemporary history, especially the ability to see events for oneself and to talk with those who were actually there. For Thucydides the Peloponnesian War was a way of exploring issues of power, empire, civic responsibility and human choice, and he saw this war as paradigmatic (though not in the simple sense of imitative *exempla* that one was to find in later writers): from his one war, readers could draw lessons of universal validity. Although it is often imputed to him, he does not, as Polybius was later to do, suggest that a knowledge of history will allow readers to avoid the mistakes of the past; rather, he emphasizes above all that his history will bring clarity, both for the events that occurred during the war and for those that will occur in a similar fashion in the future.[1]

His influence in antiquity was enormous, as can be seen from the number of imitators (some fairly inept) who tried to write a work like his, and from the remarks that are found in later critics and historians: Dionysius of Halicarnassus must apologize for criticizing even a few aspects (see *Thuc.* 2.2); and his spirit and approach (though in a slightly different register) are to be found throughout Lucian's essay, *How to Write History*.[2]

Preface

(1.1.1–2)[3]

Thucydides of Athens composed the war of the Peloponnesians and Athenians,[4] how they fought against each other, beginning as soon as the war broke out, and expecting that it would be a great war and more worthy of account than those which had gone before,[5] taking as evidence the fact that both sides went into the war at their peak in every aspect of their preparation, and seeing that the rest of the Greek world was siding with one or the other, some right away, others intending to do so. This was the greatest 2 upheaval for the Greeks and for some portion of the non-Greek world, and one might even say for the majority of mankind. It was impossible to discover clearly events before this and events even older than those because of the amount of time that had passed. Yet, from the pieces of evidence that I have examined as far back as possible and that I find trustworthy, I do not think that those events were great either as regards their wars or the rest.[6]

Investigating Early Times and Method in Composing the Present History

(1.20.1–21.3 + 1.22.1–4)[7]

Early times, then, I have discovered to be such,[8] even though it is difficult to trust every single piece of evidence put forward in the traditions about them. For people accept from one another the reports of earlier events in a similarly uncritical spirit, even if the traditions are their own.[9] For example, the majority of Athenians think that 2 Hipparchus was tyrant when he was killed by Harmodius and Aristogeiton, and they do not know that it was Hippias, as the eldest of the sons of Peisistratus, who ruled, while Hipparchus and Thessalus were his brothers[10] ... The rest of the Greeks also have 3 incorrect notions about many other things, including contemporary events, not just those which have been forgotten because of time:

examples would be that each of the Lacedaemonian kings gets to cast not one vote but two or that the Lacedaemonians have a Pitan-ate regiment – something which has never even existed.[11] The search for truth is done with so little effort by the majority of people, and they turn instead to what is ready to hand.

21   Nevertheless, one would not err if one considered the evidence I have supplied, and from it supposed that these events were such as I have described them. One should not trust either the poets who celebrate these events by adorning them to make them greater, or the prose-writers who have composed their works to make them more attractive to hear rather than more truthful, given that the majority of these events cannot be refuted because of time, and they have won their way into the realm of the myth-ical[12] so as to be incredible. But one would not err if one considered that these events, as I have recounted them, have been sufficiently researched using the clearest evidence, at least in light of their antiquity . . .

22   And as for all the things[13] which each said in speech[14] either when they were about to make war or when they were already in it, it was difficult to remember with precision exactly what was said, both for me, regarding the things I myself heard, and for those reporting to me at one time or another from elsewhere. I have written the speeches as I thought that each would say espe-cially what was necessary[15] for the given occasion, holding as closely as possible to the general purport of what was truly said.[16]

2   But as for that part of the war's actions that had to do with deeds, I did not deem it worthy to write those having learned of them from some chance informant, nor as I thought, but instead I went through each matter in detail – both those at which I was present and those that were reported to me by others – with the greatest

3   accuracy possible. This kept revealing itself to be a difficult matter since those present at each of the events did not give uniform accounts, but gave them as each was affected by partiality for one

4   or the other side, or by their memory. And in the hearing perhaps the lack of a mythic element will seem less pleasurable; but if all those who wish to examine the clarity of events – both those that occurred and those that will occur at some time or another in the same or similar ways in accordance with human nature – will judge this

useful, that will be sufficient. The work has been composed as a possession for all time rather than as a competition piece to be heard in the present.[17]

The 'Second Preface'

$(5.26)^{18}$

The same Thucydides of Athens has written these things as well, as individual events occurred, by summers and winters, up until the Lacedaemonians and their allies put an end to Athenian power and captured the Long Walls and the Piraeus. The total period of the war was twenty-seven years. If one does not deem it proper to 2 consider the agreement in the middle of it to be part of the war, then one is not judging correctly: for let him consider how that period is characterized in terms of its actions, and he will find that it is not reasonable that it should be called peace, since during that time they neither gave back nor received everything that they agreed to in their truce, and apart from this, both sides committed infractions in the Mantinean and Epidaurian wars and in other matters, the allies in Thrace continued to behave in no less a hostile manner, and the Boeotians kept promulgating ten-day armistices. And so 3 with the first war of ten years' duration, the suspect cessation of hostilities after it, and the war that later resulted from this, one will find, calculating by the seasons, that the war lasted as many years as I said, with a few additional days. And for those who trusted in any way to oracles, this one alone turned out to be reliable. For I remember how on every occasion, both when the war 4 was starting and until it ended, many proffered that it was fated to last 'thrice nine years'.

I lived through the whole of the war, of an age to perceive it and 5 applying my mind so that I might have some exact knowledge of it. It so happened that I was in exile from my own country for twenty years after my generalship in Amphipolis, and because I was present at events on both sides (and no less Peloponnesian events because of my exile), I could better perceive something of them at my leisure. So then I shall narrate the conflict after the ten years, the rupture of the truce and the subsequent events of the war.

Difficulty of Narrating a Night Battle

(7.44.1)[19]

And it was here now that the Athenians were in serious disorder and at a great loss, and it was not easy to learn from either side in what way each of the events transpired. In the daytime, things are clearer, though even here those present know hardly anything except what is going on with their own particular situation.[20] But in a battle at night – and this is the only one between two great armies, in this war at least – how could anyone know anything clearly?

5

CTESIAS OF CNIDUS

Ctesias, the son of Ctesiarchus, was born in Cnidus in most likely *c.* 440 BCE, and like his father he was a physician. At some point he became a prisoner of war of the Persians and we are told that because of his medical skill the Persian king Artaxerxes II (ruled 405–359/8 BCE) kept him at court for seventeen years.

Ctesias was best known for two works, a *Persian Matters* (*Persica*) and an *Indian Matters* (*Indica*). The former, in twenty-three books, was a history of the ancient Near East starting from the Assyrian rulers Ninus and Semiramis, and progressing through the Median Empire before coming to the Persian history proper, and ending with the year 398/7. Ctesias was involved in the events of later Persian history, though Plutarch says that he consistently exaggerated his activities and influence. The *Indica* in a single book was an account of the marvels to be found in that land. As can be seen from the prefatory remarks below, Ctesias claimed both to base his work on native sources and to refute Herodotus on many matters. Despite these assurances, he was already famous as a liar in antiquity, both because of his exaggerations about his activities in Persia and for the fabulous accounts he offered of Indian flora and fauna.[1]

The Work and its Sources

(*FGrHist* 688 T 8 = Photius, *The Library* 72, pp. 35b35–36a6)

I read the book[2] of Ctesias' entitled *Persian Matters*, which is in twenty-three books. In the first six he treats Assyrian history and all the events preceding the rise of the Persians. In Books 7, 8, 11, 12 and 13, he goes through the affairs of Cyrus, Cambyses and the Magus, Darius and Xerxes. His history contradicts Herodotus' in nearly everything, and he seeks to refute Herodotus as a liar in many places, and he calls him a fable-monger. (He lived in fact after Herodotus.) He says that he wrote his history having been an eyewitness of the majority of the events he describes, and where it was not possible for him to be an eyewitness he heard of events from the Persians themselves. In his history he not only contradicts Herodotus; he also disagrees on some points with Xenophon, the son of Gryllus.[3]

The Historian's Investigations

(*FGrHist* 688 T 3 + F 5 = Diod. 2.32.4)

Ctesias of Cnidus lived at the time of the expedition of Cyrus against his brother Artaxerxes.[4] Ctesias was a prisoner of war and had been engaged by the King, and he spent seventeen years at his court, receiving honours from him. Ctesias says that he investigated all the details to be found in the royal parchments, in which the Persians, following some custom or other, preserve in written form their deeds of old; and that when he had composed his history, he published it for the benefit of the Greeks.[5]

6

XENOPHON

Xenophon was born in Athens c. 430 BCE. Of his early life we know little, but coming from a well-to-do family, he was almost certainly a member of the cavalry. He also associated with Socrates and was later to write about him. In 401 he joined a group of Greek mercenaries in the service of the Persian Cyrus, who wished to contest the throne against his brother, Artaxerxes. The Greeks marched inland but at the battle of Cunaxa, in the autumn of that year, Cyrus was killed and the Greek mercenaries were left to find their way back home, a story that Xenophon himself, who became their leader, tells in the *Anabasis*. Afterwards, he accompanied the Spartan king Agesilaus on his campaigns in Asia Minor in 394 (he had been exiled by Athens a few years before this), and he was later given an estate in Scillus in the Peloponnese to which he retired and where (most likely) he wrote many of his works. In 371 he was forced to leave his estate and although his exile was rescinded at Athens, there is no evidence that he returned there. He died sometime after 355.

Besides the *Anabasis*, Xenophon wrote a *Greek History* (*Hellenica*), an account of Greek affairs from 411 (where Thucydides' history broke off) to the inconclusive battle of Mantinea in 362 BCE. Amongst the many other writings of his that survive in addition to his historical works are: the *Memorabilia* (*Conversations of Socrates*, whose pupil he was); the *Defence of Socrates*; the *Education of Cyrus*, a work on leadership with the Persian king Cyrus the Great as the spokesman; *On Horsemanship*; a work on household management; a laudatory biography of the Spartan king Agesilaus; and a work on the finances of Athens.

He was considered one of the great historians of antiquity and his works were much imitated by later writers, though some considered him more of a philosopher than a historian. He nowhere elucidates a historical methodology (indeed, his historical works lack even the standard kind of preface: see L. *Hist.* 23, 52) and we only occasionally get glimpses of how he viewed history, as in the remarks below, made in the course of the *Hellenica*, which show him seeking to enlarge what was up to his time considered the appropriate material for history.[1]

Inclusion of Non-traditional Material

(*Hellenica* 2.3.56)

These, then, dragged Theramenes away through the marketplace,[2] and he was crying out in a loud voice about all that he was suffering. When Satyrus told him he would be sorry if he did not remain silent, Theramenes replied, 'And if I do keep quiet, won't I also be sorry?' And when he was compelled to die and was drinking the hemlock, they say that he threw the dregs as if he were playing *kottabos* and remarked, 'Let this be for the fair Critias.'[3] Now I am not unaware that these remarks are unworthy of account;[4] but I think the man admirable because with death near at hand he lost neither his wits nor his wit.

Events Worthy of Remembrance

(*Hellenica* 4.8.1)

The war on land, then, was fought in this way.[5] I shall now narrate events that occurred by sea and against the cities on the coast, events that took place at the same time as the war on land. I shall write up those actions that were most worthy of remembrance, and I shall omit those not worthy of account.[6]

Contemplating Teleutias' Accomplishments

(*Hellenica* 5.1.3–4)

After this, the new admiral Hierax arrived from the Lacedaemonians and took over the fleet.[7] Teleutias sailed home with the most splendid good fortune: as he was making his way to the sea, not a single soldier failed to shake his hand. One even put a garland on his head, another a fillet. Others, who arrived too late to

see him off (for he had already departed) threw garlands into the
4   sea, praying that he would be attended by many blessings. Now I
know that in recounting these matters I am narrating no expense,
danger or contrivance that is worthy of record;[8] but by God, I
think it's worth someone's while to contemplate what it was that
Teleutias could possibly have done to make those under his command so disposed towards him. For this is a deed of the man's that
is more worthy of account than many expenditures or dangers.[9]

Including the Actions of Small Cities no less than Great

(*Hellenica* 7.2.1)

. . . the people of Phlius were especially hard pressed, and were
short of necessities; even so they remained firm in their alliance
with the Lacedaemonians.[10] Now if one of the great cities has done
something noble, all the historians commemorate it; but it seems to
me that if some city which is small has done many noble deeds, that
is even more worthy of being made known.

Conclusion of the *Hellenica*

(*Hellenica* 7.5.27)

Let it be written by me, then, up to this point. Events after this
may perhaps be the concern of another.[11]

7

EPHORUS OF CYME

Ephorus was born around 400 BCE in Cyme in Asia Minor. Little is known of his life; he and Theopompus were considered students of the rhetorician Isocrates,[1] though this was perhaps only an inference made on the basis of their subjects and their styles. He wrote a number of works including a history of his home town Cyme, but his most important work was his *Histories*, an account of the deeds of western and eastern Greeks (and non-Greeks to the extent that they interacted with the Greeks) in a unified treatment, beginning with the return of the descendants of Heracles to the Peloponnese (*c.* 1200) and ending in his own day with the siege of Perinthus in 341/340 BCE. He was the first to divide his history into separate books, and he gave each one a preface. His structure was topical, rather than strictly annalistic, dealing with particular areas one at a time. His early history was based on predecessors' accounts, and it is thought that even his contemporary portions were based on written sources. If that is the case, then Ephorus might be the first historian who did not engage in the kind of eye-witness and inquiry practised from Herodotus onwards.[2]

Contemporary versus Non-contemporary Events

(*FGrHist* 70 F 9)

Ephorus . . . in Book 1 of his history . . . says that for contemporary events we consider most trustworthy those who speak most exactly, while for events of long ago we consider least trustworthy those who narrate them in this way, because we suppose that it is improbable, given the great distance in time, that all the deeds or the majority of the speeches would be remembered.[3]

Truth and Myth in History

(*FGrHist* 70 F 31b = Strabo 9.3.11)

Ephorus . . . a man worthy of consideration, seems to me to do the opposite sometimes of his intention and his promises at the beginning [sc. of his history]. For although he praises truth and finds fault with those who are fond of myth in the writing of history, he adds to his account of this oracle [sc. of Apollo at Delphi] a solemn pledge that while he considers truth to be everywhere the best thing, it is especially so in this matter: 'for it would be absurd', he says, 'if we follow this procedure in other matters but when speaking about this oracle, which is the least false of all things, we use accounts which are so untrustworthy and false'.[4]

Eyewitness in History

(*FGrHist* 70 F 110 = Pol. 12.27.7)

Ephorus says that if it were possible for historians to be present at all events, this would be much the best form of knowledge.[5]

8

ARISTOTLE

The *Poetics* of Aristotle (384–322 BCE) has been enormously influential throughout the centuries. Although it is mainly concerned with poetry and is not actually about historical methodology, it has two passages in which history is discussed, and which were almost certainly influential on later discussion of historiography. To give just three examples: (1) Duris of Samos (see below, p. 40) may have been influenced by Aristotle's notion here of representation (*mimesis*) to demand something similar in history; (2) Polybius in his criticism of Phylarchus (see below, p. 58) is likely to be answering Aristotle's claims about the superiority of poetry to history; and (3) Polybius may also be answering Aristotle's thoughts on the randomness of historical events in the preface to his history where he argues for the unity of his topic.

History and Poetry

(*Poetics*, chapter 9, 1451a36–b11, b27–32)[1]

It is evident from what has been said[2] that it is the task of the poet to speak not of what has happened, but of the sorts of things that might be expected to happen, i.e. that which is possible in accordance with probability or necessity. For the historian and the poet differ not in the use of metre or lack of metre (the writings of Herodotus could be put into verse and they would no less be history with metre than without),[3] but in the fact that one speaks of what has happened, the other of the sorts of things that might be expected to happen. Because of this, poetry is both more philosophical and more serious than history. For poetry speaks more of universal things,[4] history of each individual thing. The universal is the kind of thing a certain kind of person might say or do in accordance with probability or necessity – this is what poetry aims at, even if it uses individual names;[5] the specific is what Alcibiades did or had done to him.[6]

. . . It is clear then that the poet must be more a maker of plots than of verses, to the extent that he is a poet in respect to representation,[7] and he is representing action. Even if it happens that he treats actual events, he is no less a poet; for nothing prevents some actual events from being probable and possible, and it is in accordance with this that the poet is their maker.

Randomness of Historical Events

(*Poetics*, chapter 23, 1459a17–29)

Concerning the narrative art and that which is representative in verse,[8] it is evident that one must, just as in tragedy, compose plots that are dramatic and concern a single action which is unitary and complete, having beginning, middle and end, so that it effects its proper pleasure, just as with a single living creature.[9] It should not be like historical compositions, in which an exposition is necessarily made not of a single action but of a single time period and all that happened in this period to one or more people,[10] and in which each of the actions is related to the other by chance. For just as the naval battle at Salamis and the battle of the Carthaginians in Sicily happened in the same time period, but they in no way tended to the same goal,[11] so also in successive periods of time one thing sometimes follows after another, but there is no particular goal.

9

THEOPOMPUS OF CHIOS

Theopompus was born in Chios *c.* 378 BCE; exiled with his father, Damasistratus, for pro-Spartan leanings, he was restored to his homeland *c.* 333, thanks to the influence of Alexander the Great. After Alexander's death in 323 Theopompus was again forced to leave Chios and he took refuge in Egypt at the court of Ptolemy I, who wished to have him executed for being a troublemaker but was dissuaded by his friends. He probably died shortly after 320.

Theopompus wrote an epitome (summary) of Herodotus' history and also a *Greek History* (*Hellenica*), in twelve books, covering events from 411, where Thucydides left off, to the Spartan naval defeat at the battle of Cnidus in 390; but his importance for Greek historiography rests on his *Affairs Concerning Philip* (*Philippica*), a history of Greek and non-Greek events now centred around the figure of Philip II of Macedon, the father of Alexander the Great. The *Philippica* was an enormous work, fifty-eight books, and comprised all sorts of material, including history, geography, ethnography, myths and marvels. He and Ephorus were both considered pupils of Isocrates, but this may have been no more than inference made on the basis of their subjects and styles (see above, p. 25). Theopompus was known for his harsh appraisals of contemporaries and earlier historical actors, and for a persistent strain of moralism throughout his history; for later generations he was known above all for his bitterness and harshness.[1]

The first passage below is not a direct quotation from Theopompus but comes from Dionysius' evaluation, and is assumed to be based on what Theopompus actually said, most likely in the preface of his *Philippica*.

Preparations for Writing History

(FGrHist 115 T 20a = D.H. Pomp. 6.2–3)

For it is evident, even if he had not written anything about it,[2] that he prepared himself by the greatest preparation for the work and incurred the greatest expense in its composition. In addition, he was an eyewitness of many things and met and spoke with many of the leading men of his time – generals, popular leaders, philosophers – all for the sake of his history. For he did not, like some, consider the writing of history to be a secondary activity but rather an activity most necessary of all.

Eyewitness and Experience

(FGrHist 115 F 342 = Pol. 12.27.8–9)

Theopompus says that he who has been present at the greatest number of battles is best in war, while he who has had the greatest share of political struggles is most effective in speech, and the same is true for skill in medicine and navigation.[3]

Narrating Myths in History

(FGrHist 115 F 381 = Strabo, 1.2.35, p. 43C)[4]

And Theopompus recognizes this, when he says that he will also tell myths in his history – and by explicitly saying so, he behaves better than do Herodotus, Ctesias, Hellanicus and the writers on India.[5]

10

CALLISTHENES

Callisthenes was born in Olynthus and was raised by his uncle Aristotle, with whom he composed a list of victors at the Pythian games and a list of the supervisors (*agonothētai*) at that same festival; the inscription set up to honour them for their work still survives. Callisthenes wrote a *Greek History* (*Hellenica*) covering the years 387/6–356 BCE and a separate monograph on the so-called Third Sacred War (356–346 BCE; the war was significant not least because it brought Philip of Macedon into Greek affairs permanently). Alexander the Great invited Callisthenes to accompany him on his campaigns, and Callisthenes' *Deeds of Alexander* reached to at least the year 330. He quarrelled with Alexander over the latter's demand for obeisance in the manner of a Persian king (something abhorrent to Greeks since whatever its exact nature, it resembled an act one would perform only before a god), and perhaps because of this he was implicated in a conspiracy against Alexander, arrested and executed. For later writers in antiquity he was often faulted for being the first of a long series of flattering court-historians.[1]

The first passage below speaks of propriety in history; the second, from Arrian's *Anabasis*, is perhaps apocryphal but is useful in indicating the relationship between a historian and his subject matter.

Appropriateness in History

(FGrHist 124 F 44 = Athenaeus, *On Machines* 6–7 Schneider)

I do not suppose it is proper to work on them for so long that one cannot employ them in their intended use.[2] This happened to Isocrates with his advisory letter written to Philip: the war was over before Isocrates finished writing up his advice[3] . . . Furthermore, it
7   seems to me that it is right to trust those who give correct advice about such matters. The historian Callisthenes says that 'one attempting to write anything must not fall short of the character but must assign words that are appropriate to the person and to the deeds';[4] but every treatise on a technical matter needs concision and clarity, whereas rhetorical precepts are not appropriate to it.[5]

Relationship between the Historian and his Subject Matter

(FGrHist 124 T 8 = Arrian, *Anabasis* 4.10.1–2)

. . . I think that Callisthenes was not being reasonable when he said (if in fact the story that's recorded is true)[6] that Alexander and
2   Alexander's deeds depended on him and his history, and that he had come not to win renown from Alexander but to make Alexander famous amongst mankind.[7] He said also that Alexander's divine nature came not from the false story that Olympias had invented about his birth[8] but rather from what he himself would write about Alexander and publish to the world.

TIMAEUS OF
TAUROMENIUM

Timaeus was born in Tauromenium (modern Taormina) in Sicily *c*. 350 BCE. His father Andromachus was an active participant in Sicilian politics and a strong supporter of Timoleon, the Corinthian who in the 340s had liberated the Sicilian cities from their tyrants. Timaeus was exiled sometime *c*. 315, probably because of his hostility towards Agathocles, the military leader and virtual tyrant of Syracuse who had taken power in 319/8 and had subsequently seized Tauromenium. Timaeus went into exile at Athens and remained there for fifty years, writing his historical works: (1) *Olympic Victors*, which synchronized Spartan, Athenian and Argive events with the victors at the Olympic games; (2) *Sicilian Matters* (*Sicelica*), also called *Histories*, which treated Sicilian history in thirty-eight books from earliest times to the death of Agathocles in 289/8; and (3) *Wars against Pyrrhus*, an account, separate from his main history, of events surrounding the military adventurer from Epirus, including his famous wars and 'Pyrrhic victories' against the Romans, ending with the year 264.

Timaeus' history comprised many different kinds of information, including mythical, geographical, ethnographical and cultural. He treated Sicily's wars with Carthage and remained an important source for both Greeks and Romans on the history of the West. He was pilloried by later historians and critics, who gave him the nickname 'Fault-finder' (*Epitimaios*, a play on his actual name) for the merciless way in which he corrected and chastised his predecessors (nor did he limit himself to historians); one critic wrote an entire work in twelve books entitled *Against Timaeus*. He is the main subject of Polybius' Book 12, where he is faulted for being pedantic, carping, inaccurate and in general an armchair historian who took no part in actual events. Despite Polybius' criticisms and despite Timaeus' obvious captiousness he was praised by some (especially the Romans) for his learning and full historical style.[1]

The two methodological passages given here are both from Polybius Book 12 (they can be found in context there) and should be read with a certain amount of caution given Polybius' enormous dislike of the man.

On Truth in History

(*FGrHist* 566 F 151 = Polybius 12.11a–12.2)

Timaeus says that the greatest fault in history is falsehood. He also exhorts those whom he refutes as having written falsely in their treatises to find another name for their books, any name other than history. For he says it is just like a carpenter's ruler: we call it a ruler even if it is shorter in length or deficient in width, but nonetheless has the specific quality that makes it a ruler; but if it lacks straightness and all that conforms to straightness, then one must call it anything rather than a ruler. So too for all historical works that are at fault in style or in treatment or in any other detail: if they nonetheless cling to truth, those books merit, he says, the name of history; but whenever they go astray from truth, they must no longer be called history.

History and Epideictic Oratory

(*FGrHist* 566 F 152 = Polybius 12.28.8–9 + 12.28a.1–3)

In the preface of his Book 6,[2] he [Timaeus] says that some suppose that the genre of epideictic speech requires greater natural ability, effort and preparation than does history,[3] and he adds that these sentiments were known to Ephorus earlier, but Ephorus was unable to refute those who held this view; and so he, Timaeus, would attempt to decide the matter by a comparison of history with epideictic rhetoric ... Wishing nonetheless to extol history, he says first that the difference between history and epideictic oratory is as great as that between real buildings or constructions and the theatre decorations that show landscapes and scenes. Second, he says that gathering material for history[4] is a greater task than the entire composition of epideictic speeches. He himself, for example, had undergone such great expense and hardship in gathering records of the Tyrians and investigating the customs of Ligurians and Celts and the Iberians as well, that neither he nor those others who reported these matters would be believed.

DURIS OF SAMOS

Duris was born *c.* 340 BCE and is said to have been a student of Theophrastus, Aristotle's successor as head of the Peripatos. From about 300 to his death in 270 he was tyrant of Samos. He wrote a number of works of literary criticism, including one on Homer; a local history of his home island, *Samian Annals*; and a history of the Sicilian tyrant Agathocles (ruled 316–288 BCE) in four books. His main historical work was entitled *Macedonian Affairs* (*Makedonica*), which reached at least twenty-three books and covered the period from 370/69 to 281 BCE. It seems to have had an anti-Macedonian slant. The much-discussed remark below came from the preface of this work. It is notable both as the earliest example of an ancient historian comparing himself with predecessors by name and as an explicit attempt to demand certain literary qualities in the writing of history.[1]

Representation and Pleasure in History

(*FGrHist* 76 F 1)

Duris of Samos in the first book of his *Histories* writes as follows: 'Ephorus and Theopompus fell very far short of events; for they employed neither any kind of representation nor pleasure in the recounting, but concerned themselves solely with the writing itself.'[2]

13

CATO THE ELDER

Marcus Porcius Cato was one of the most distinctive figures of the Roman Republic. Born at Tusculum in 234 BCE he was raised in the Sabine country. Serving with distinction in the Second Punic War (218–201), he found a patron in Lucius Valerius Flaccus and rose rapidly through the *cursus honorum*, achieving the consulship in 195 and the censorship of 184. He was famous for his frugality and strict way of life, and in later life was an inveterate foe of Carthage, whose destruction he famously demanded on every occasion. He died in 149 or early 148.

Cato is generally regarded as the father of Latin prose literature, and was a prolific writer, composing works that included such topics as agriculture and military tactics; he published many of his speeches (Cicero knew of more than 150: see *Brutus* 65). His historical work, the *Origins* (*Origines*), was the first history of Rome written in Latin,[1] and, in keeping with the unique nature of Cato himself, it followed a path that was new and (so far as we know) never thereafter imitated. In Book 1, he treated the origins of Rome, and in Books 2 and 3 the origins of the Italian city-states that were allied with Rome. These early books explain the work's title. The last four books treated Roman history from the First Punic War (264–241 BCE) to events of Cato's own time, and in these books Cato himself was a prominent character, and he even included speeches that he himself had delivered. His unusual procedure of not naming military commanders in the field (see T 1) was not followed by any later historian, but his style was very popular with some, especially Sallust and the archaizing writers of the early Empire.[2]

FF 1 and 2 come from the preface of the whole work, F 80 from the preface of Book 4.

Omission of Commanders' Names

(*FRHist* 5 T 1 = Nepos, *Life of Cato* 3.3–4)

In the fourth book is the First Punic War, in the fifth book the
4 Second. These events are described summarily. The remaining
wars he went through in the same way, ending with the year in
which Servius Galba, who plundered the Lusitanians, was praetor
[151 BCE]. The commanders in these wars he did not name, but
identified events without names.[3]

Delight in Recording History

(*FRHist* 5 F 1 = Sergius, *Grammatici Latini* IV.502 + Pompeius, *Grammatici Latini* V.208)

Cato also begins his *Origins* like this: 'If there are any men who
delight in recording the deeds of the Roman people . . .'[4]

From the Preface

(*FRHist* 5 F 2 = Cicero, *On Behalf of Plancius* 66)

For I have always thought that what Marcus Cato wrote in the preface to his *Origins* was splendid and brilliant: it was necessary that
for distinguished and important men a satisfactory account should
exist of their free time no less than of the time they spent in public
business.[5]

The Ligurians' Ignorance of their History

(FR Hist 5 F 34b = DServius on Aeneid 11.715–17)

They themselves [sc. the Ligurians], having lost the memory of their origins, are illiterate and liars, and they scarcely remember the truth.[6]

Subject Matter of the History

(FR Hist 5 F 80 = Gellius, Attic Nights 2.28.6)

The words of Cato from the fourth book of his Origins are these: 'I have no desire to write what is on the tablet at the house of the Pontifex Maximus: how often grain was expensive, how often darkness or something obscured the light of the moon or sun.'[7]

14

AGATHARCHIDES
OF CNIDUS

Agatharchides was born around 215 BCE in Cnidus (in south-western Asia Minor), but spent most of his life in Alexandria. We are told that he was a Peripatetic philosopher and that he was in the service of Heracleides Lembus, a fellow historian and states-man at the court of Ptolemy VI Philometor (ruled 180–145 BCE). Agatharchides wrote three historical works, all of which combined historical, geographical and ethnographical material: (1) *Asian Affairs*, in ten books; (2) *European Affairs*, in forty-nine books; and (3) *On the Red Sea* (the term in antiquity for what comprises the Indian Ocean, the Red Sea and the Persian Gulf) in five books, which, despite its title, was most likely a history rather than a geography; this was his final work before his death, which occurred sometime after 145.

In the first passage below, from Book 1 of *On the Red Sea*, Agatharchides rejects myth for history while conceding that it has a place in poetry, for the latter aims at pleasure. The second passage comes from the prologue of Book 5 and is directed against Hegesias of Magnesia, a third-century historian and orator who wrote a *History of Alexander*, and whose florid and rhythmical style was universally condemned in antiquity. Agatharchides takes Hegesias to task especially for the inappropriate language he used in his descriptions of the sufferings of people, and this was most likely in connection with Agatharchides' own account, which followed and described the pitiable condition of those who worked the gold mines in Nubia. The final passage comes from the end of the work and explains why the author can no longer write history.[1]

On Myth in History

(*On the Red Sea*, 1.8 = Photius, *Library* 444b)[2]

He [sc. Agatharchides] says that he has made himself responsible for refuting any who would transfer the freedom accorded to the writers of myth to the description demanded by a factual account.[3] If one removes that refutation, no more worthless genre will remain, since its trustworthiness will have been destroyed.[4] 'But then why do I not reprove Homer,[5] who speaks of the quarrel of Zeus and Poseidon, something which is impossible for him as a human being to prove? Why do I not find fault with Hesiod for daring to narrate the birth of the gods? Why do I not reproach Aeschylus who told many falsehoods and wrote much that one would not permit? Why do I not accuse Euripides for ascribing to Archelaus the deeds of Temenos, and for bringing on stage Teirisias who had lived more than five generations?[6] And why do I not fault the rest of the poets who in their dramas fashioned impossible situations? It is because every poet strives for pleasure more than for truth.'[7]

On Describing Disasters in History

(*On the Red Sea*, 5.21 = Photius, *Library*, 445b–447a)

Many statesmen and poets are at a loss as to how extremes of fortunes are to be narrated properly by one who is himself not in danger. There would be no very clear way of doing this unless one were to give a reason that conforms with what is being narrated.[8]

446a

Alexander and Philip plundered and razed to their foundations two renowned cities, Olynthus and Thebes.[9] The terrible nature of this destruction which occurred beyond all expectation raised great anxiety amongst many of the Greeks for their whole situation,[10] and it furnished an opportunity for many speakers to narrate these events in a way appropriate to the suffering. Some, then, have spoken of this event in an allegorical way and, it seems, in unrestrained language. Others have spoken in a more serious manner, not avoiding regular expressions and using words for the terrible events in their proper sense. We shall offer you examples of each kind so that you may consider their styles by comparison and thus discover from these examinations who spoke well and who did the opposite.[11]

To begin with, Hegesias, who often makes mention of the destruction of cities, is worthless. For he is unwilling to speak in a manner appropriate to the circumstances,[12] but always seeks compulsively, even when the subject is grave, to make a display of his skill, and although he accomplishes his personal goal to a certain extent, he does not strive to match the dignity of the underlying events; he is caught in the act, as it were, in such remarks as these: 'We took a name, leaving a city.' Examine this: it arouses not the least bit of emotion, but directs one's attention to the expression and makes one ask what it is that he's saying. For whenever one injects uncertainty about the meaning, one removes the power of the expression. Why? Because what can be clearly understood in expression brings with it an emotional reaction, while that which lacks clarity also falls short in force.[13]

He then says something similar about Thebes: 'The misfortune has left speechless the place that spoke so loud.' And again of Olynthus: 'I left a city of innumerable men, and when I turned around I saw it no more.' Indeed, what were you looking for? The words, fallen into such a manner of expression, have made our thoughts stray from the subject. The one who wishes to inspire pity must dispense with *bons mots* and must indicate the event for which the emotion is appropriate, if he wishes not to embellish it by his language but rather to attend to the reason for the misfortune.

Let us move on to another one. 'Alexander, consider that Epaminondas,[14] looking on the remains of the city, is here beside me joining in my plea.' The demand is childish and the metaphor is harsh, but the grimness of the deed is unspoken. Here is another: 446b 'Tripped up by a king's madness, the city became more pitiable than a tragedy.' This seems to have been composed for anything else rather than what was appropriate for a skilled speaker, since it does not even come close to grasping its subject. I think it is difficult to overlook mocking language used in difficult circumstances.

Here is another: 'Why should I speak of the Olynthians and Thebans, all that they suffered dying in their cities?' Another one, close to undignified flattery[15] and foolishness:

> What a thing you have done, Alexander, destroying Thebes! It is as if Zeus had taken the moon from its place in the sky. I reserve the sun for Athens. These two cities were the eyes of Greece. And so I am in fear now for the other. For one of the eyes, the city of Thebes, has been plucked out.

It seems to me that this clever speaker with these words is ridiculing, not lamenting, the fate of the cities, and seeking how he could most quickly end his discourse, not how he might through vivid representation bring the disaster[16] before our eyes.

Here is another one like it: 'The neighbouring cities bewailed the city, seeing that the one previously there was no longer there.' Now if someone said this to the Thebans and the Olynthians at the moment their cities were taken, expressing their sympathy in such periods,[17] I think they would have laughed at the writer and would have considered him more wretched than themselves.

Let us move on to a different type of expression in the same speaker. 'It is terrible that the land that bore the Sown Men[18] should be unsown.' But that is not how Demosthenes (whose expression Hegesias has changed for the worse) expresses it: he writes that it is terrible that Attica, which first gave to everyone else cultivated crops, had become pasturage for sheep.[19] By contrast Hegesias, in saying that it was terrible that the land that bore the Sown Men should be unsown, created an opposition from the words, not from the actual circumstances. And so he demonstrates the utmost frigidity, just as when Hermesianax[20] in his encomium of Athens says: 'It is appropriate that having sprung from the head of Zeus she should be at the head of happiness.'[21] Here is one of the same sort:[22] 'Who could consider a gift of Cyrus a gaffe?'[23] And this is similar: 'How could this place be inviolate when violets are all around?'[24] All such remarks, Agatharchides says, are worthless. But if Hegesias said them as a way of *not* arousing pity, then he came close to what is appropriate; but if he thought them appropriate for every form of discourse, he showed incorrect judgement[25] . . .

447a

He [sc. Agatharchides] nevertheless cites other similar expressions, bringing the same criticism to these, for example: 'The Thebans, more than 10,000, were killed in battle against the Macedonians.' What a fine description, so many men unexpectedly killed! Again: 'When the city had been razed, the men endured the misfortunes of their children, the women were transported to Macedonia, having in some way buried the city.' Another: 'The phalanx of the Macedonians, forcing its way with weapons inside the wall, killed the city.'[26] In the earlier passage there is the grave of the city, in this one its death. It remains only to have the funeral and to carve the epitaph and the business is done. So, Agatharchides says, we have gone through most of this author's 'refinement' (if I[27] said 'madness' I would seem too bitter).[28]

Conclusion

(*On the Red Sea* 5.112 = Photius, *Library* 460b)

So then we have composed carefully in five books this material on the tribes that lie towards the south as they were in our time. As for the islands in the sea that were later discovered, the people that dwell beyond these, and the fragrances that grow in the land of Troglodytice,[29] we may ask for indulgence in giving up writing about them at all, since our age cannot undergo the similar effort needed,[30] and we have already composed much about Europe and Asia, and because we could not examine accurately the memoranda because of the revolts in Egypt.[31] But one who has acquainted himself with affairs in that part of the world has fashioned words worthy of history,[32] and has a disposition capable of pursuing renown by his efforts will not shy away from this task.[33]

POLYBIUS

Polybius was born in Megalopolis in the Peloponnese *c*. 200 BCE, a town which was part of a federation of Achaean states that had been revived in the century before Polybius' birth; in the generation or so before him its power grew rapidly under the leadership first of Aratus of Sicyon and then Philopoemen, also of Megalopolis. Polybius' father, Lycortas, was much involved in the affairs of the League, and the young Polybius followed in his footsteps, carrying Philopoemen's ashes in his funeral procession in 182 and serving as cavalry commander of the League in 170/69. The Achaean League was divided about how to deal with the rising power and influence of Rome, and in 168 Polybius was amongst those denounced at Rome by his fellow Achaean Callicrates. He and a thousand others were deported to Rome. Polybius was fortunate in befriending there Lucius Aemilius Paullus, and he became friends with Paullus' son, Scipio Aemilianus. In 150, nearly two decades after they had been deported, the exiles were allowed back home. Polybius travelled with Aemilianus and was present with him at the destruction of Carthage in 146 BCE. In that same year Corinth too was destroyed, and the Romans asked Polybius to arrange affairs in Greece in the aftermath of that conflict. We do not know when he died but one source tells us it was at the age of eighty-two when he fell from his horse.

His works include a biography of the Achaean statesman Philopoemen, a work on tactics and one on fire-signals, as well as a separate monograph on the Numantine War (143–133 BCE). His fame, however, rests on the forty-book history that he composed about Rome's rise to hegemony in the Mediterranean, beginning with the year 264 BCE and going down to 146. Only the first five books survive entire; the rest are fragmentary. Even so, no historian from antiquity speaks so often and so passionately about the proper way to write history. Although the breadth of his interests in the writing of history is noteworthy, he nonetheless returns again and again to the same themes: the importance of autopsy, inquiry and experience; the need to give causes and consequences of events; the value and benefit of 'universal' history and its superiority to individual histories; the importance of treating both sides fairly and avoiding partisan bias; and the appropriateness of concentrating on actual historical deeds, ignoring legendary, mythical and any kind of material meant to startle or merely entertain the reader. Even as a 'fragmentary' author he offers the most comprehensive approach of anyone from antiquity on the proper way to write history.[1]

Praise of History and of Universal History

(1.1.1–6 + 1.2.7–8 + 1.3.1–6 + 1.4.1–11)

If it were the case that our predecessors who wrote up events had omitted the praise of history, it would perhaps have been necessary for me to encourage everyone to choose and accept such histories as these, because there is no readier means of correction than the knowledge of past deeds.[2] But all my predecessors, not 2 some,[3] and not just to a certain extent, but from beginning to end, one might say, have claimed both that the truest education and training towards a career in public life is the knowledge that comes from history, and that the most vivid and indeed only teacher of the ability to bear changes of fortune nobly is the recollection of the reversals of others;[4] and so it is clear that it would be 3 fitting for no one, least of all me, to repeat things that have been said well and by many. In my case, the very unexpectedness of the 4 events about which I have chosen to write is sufficient to encourage and incite everyone, young and old, to the study of my treatise. Is there anyone in the world so worthless or lazy by nature who 5 would not wish to know how and with what kind of constitution nearly everything in the known world, in less than fifty-three years,[5] fell under the sway of a single empire, that of the Romans – a thing which cannot be found to have happened before? And is there any- 6 one so passionate about another spectacle or study that he would consider something else more useful than this understanding?

Polybius now compares the Roman empire with previous ones, arguing that in size and length of rule there had never been one like it. He then summarizes:

But the Romans have conquered not some portions but nearly 2.7 all of the inhabited world, and they have left behind a preeminence of power that cannot be resisted by contemporaries or surpassed by posterity. One can learn from my work why they 8 have attained universal domination, and similarly how and how greatly helpful political history[6] is for those who love learning.

Our treatise will begin in the 140th Olympiad,[7] with the follow- 3 ing events: in Greece the so-called Social War, the first which

Philip, the son of Demetrius and father of Perseus, waged together with the Achaeans against the Aetolians; in Asia the war for Coele-Syria which Antiochus and Ptolemy Philopator fought
2 against each other; and in Italy and Africa the war between the Romans and the Carthaginians which most people call the Hannibalic War.[8] These events follow on the final parts of Aratus of Sicyon's treatise.[9]

3   Now in previous eras, it happened that the events of the inhabited world were, so to say, scattered, since all of the events were separate in their attempts, still more in their completions, and especially
4 in their locations. But, beginning with the above date, history becomes, as it were, organic, and Italian and African affairs are interwoven with those in Asia and in Greece, and everything
5 becomes aligned towards one goal.[10] That is why we have begun
6 our account with these times, since it was in the aforementioned war that the Romans, having defeated the Carthaginians, considered that they had accomplished the main and greatest part in their attempt at universal conquest, and so at that time were first emboldened to stretch their hands towards what remained, and to cross with military forces into Greece and the lands of Asia.[11]

Polybius then explains that he will use Books 1 and 2 to sketch for readers the background material that they will need to appreciate his actual commencement of events in Book 3. He then continues:

4   What is unique in my treatise and amazing about the times in which we live is this: that just as Fortune[12] has made nearly all the affairs of the known world incline in one direction and compelled everything to bend towards one and the same goal, so likewise it is necessary, by means of history, to bring for my readers, within a single purview, this accomplishment of Fortune, which she has
2 employed in her fulfilment of all affairs. It was this, more than anything else, that challenged and encouraged us in this attempt at history, and in addition the fact that no one of our contemporaries has attempted a treatise of universal history. If they had, I
3 would have been much less eager to take on this task. As it is, I saw that many had written treatises on individual wars and some of the events connected with them, but that no one, at least to our knowledge, had even attempted to examine the general and comprehensive

disposition of events, that is, when and whence they started and how they ended; and so I assumed that it was absolutely necessary 4 neither to omit nor to allow to pass without study this most attractive and simultaneously most useful work of Fortune. Although she 5 herself makes many innovations and constantly contends with the lives of men, she has by no means ever accomplished such a deed or put on such a show-piece as she has in our lifetime.[13] And this is the 6 very thing that cannot be envisaged from the works of those who write individual histories. It would be as if someone were to travel through the most famous cities one by one or even, by God, were to look at separate pictures of each and then should immediately presume that he perceived both the form of the whole inhabited world and its entire setting and arrangement – which is in no way likely.[14]

In general, those who have persuaded themselves that they can 7 envisage the whole by means of individual histories are, I think, under the same illusion as people who, seeing the dismembered limbs of a creature that had been alive and beautiful, thought that in this way they had sufficiently been eyewitnesses of the creature's vitality and beauty. Yet if someone could straightaway put 8 the creature back together, give it its perfected form in both its shape and the beauty of life, and then showed it again to those people, I think that they themselves would quickly agree that they had been very far from the truth and had been like dreamers. It is 9 possible to get an idea of the whole from a portion, but impossible to acquire knowledge and accurate understanding. And so one 10 must generally consider that individual histories contribute only a little to the knowledge and trustworthiness of the whole. When 11 all events are woven together, however, and placed side by side, and their similarities and differences are compared, only then, by such an examination, might one attain this knowledge and be able to derive what is useful and pleasurable from history.[15]

Bias in History

(1.14.1–8)

Polybius says that his account of the First Punic War is essential background for his main story of the rise of Rome to world power. The war was also the greatest in terms of its length, preparations, battles and changes of fortune; and both states were equal in strength and at the height of their character. He then explains how he will use his sources:

I was impelled to pay attention to this war no less for the aforementioned reasons than also because the two men who have the reputation of having written about it with the greatest competence, Philinus and Fabius, do not seem to me to have stated the truth

2 about it as they ought.[16] Judging from their life and principles, I do not suppose that these men falsified deliberately;[17] but they do seem to me to have suffered something very similar to what happens to lovers: Philinus, because of his partisanship and his consistent favouritism, thinks that the Carthaginians did everything wisely, well, bravely, while the Romans did the opposite; Fabius thinks exactly the

4 reverse. Now in the rest of life one would perhaps not exclude such an attitude: a good man should indeed love his friends and his country, and he should share in his friends' hatreds and alliances.[18]

5 But whenever someone takes up the character appropriate to history, he must forget all such things, and he must often speak well of his enemies and adorn them with the greatest praises, when the events demand this, while he must often reproach and reprove severely those closest to him, whenever their failures of conduct

6 deserve such treatment.[19] For just as a living creature deprived of its eyes becomes completely helpless, so when history is deprived of

7 truth what remains is a useless narrative.[20] One must, therefore, not shrink from accusing one's friends or praising one's enemies; nor must one hesitate sometimes to find fault with, at other times to praise, the same people: for it is not probable that those who are engaged in political affairs should always succeed or continuously

8 fail. In history, therefore, one must keep some distance from the actors, and instead apply to the deeds themselves the opinions and judgements that are appropriate.

The Experience Afforded by History

(1.35.1–10)

Polybius has just narrated events surrounding the figure of Marcus Atilius Regulus, who had been sent to Sicily as commander of Roman forces and had been victorious, but had treated his captives harshly. The Carthaginians then appointed Xanthippus of Sparta (the 'one man and one mind' referred to below) to the command; he engaged Regulus, soundly defeated him, and took him prisoner. Polybius here reflects on this reversal of fortune:

In this particular event, one who examined rightly would discover many things conducive to the improvement of human life. The idea that one should distrust Fortune, especially in success,[21] 2 seemed absolutely manifest to everyone, thanks to the calamities of Marcus. For he who just a little before gave neither pity nor 3 pardon to the defeated almost immediately afterwards was himself led away to beg for these very things to assure his own survival. Indeed, that remark of Euripides, long admired, that 'one wise 4 counsel conquers many hands' was at that time proven by these very events.[22] For one man and one mind destroyed a multitude 5 that seemed invincible and difficult to overcome, and strengthened and restored both a state that was utterly fallen and the demoralized spirits of its military forces.

I have mentioned these matters to instruct those who read this 6 history. There are two ways for all men to make a change towards 7 the better: through one's own mishaps and through those of others.[23] The change that comes through one's own reversals of fortune makes a greater impression, while that which comes through others' does less harm. So we should never choose the for- 8 mer willingly, since its instruction is accompanied with great toils and dangers, while we should always seek the latter, since it is possible to envision in it the better course free from harm. Reflecting 9 on this, one must consider that the finest education for real life is the experience that comes from political history,[24] since this alone 10 makes us, without hurt to ourselves, real-life judges of the better course of action on every occasion and in every situation.

Criticisms of Phylarchus

(2.56.1–16, 58.9–61.12)[25]

*This digression comes in connection with Polybius' narration of
the Social War (220–217 BCE), where a coalition of Greek forces
in alliance with Philip V of Macedon waged war against Aetolia,
Sparta and Elis. The immediate occasion for this digression is the
Spartan king Cleomenes' capture of the city of Megalopolis, and
Phylarchus' account of it, which Polybius repudiates; in his refutation of Phylarchus, Polybius focuses on the former's account of
the capture of Mantinea in 223 and uses it to enunciate some general observations on the writing of history:*

Amongst those writers who were contemporaries of Aratus,
Phylarchus, who in many places offers different opinions from and
2 contradicts Aratus, is thought worthy of approval by some.[26] Now,
since we have chosen to follow Aratus' account of the Cleomenean
War,[27] it would be useful, or rather it would be necessary, not to
leave unexamined this portion of his history, lest we allow falsehood to have equal strength with truth in historical writings.

3 To begin with, this writer in general throughout his entire
work has made many statements at random and without due con-
4 sideration.[28] For now it is not necessary perhaps to criticize and
correct all the other remarks he has made, but it is necessary that
we give a careful examination of those that are directly related to
the occasions that we are writing about, that is, the events sur-
5 rounding the Cleomenean War. These will suffice completely for
understanding his intent and the competence of his work.

6 Wishing to make clear the savagery of Antigonus and the Macedonians, and with them that of Aratus and the Achaeans, he says
that, when the Mantineans were defeated, they were encompassed
by great misfortunes, and this most ancient and greatest of the
cities of Arcadia was brought low by such sufferings as to elicit the
7 concern and tears of all the Greeks. Eager to incite the pity of his
readers and make them sympathetic to the events being recounted,
Phylarchus brings on women clinging to one another, with their
hair dishevelled and baring their breasts, and in addition to this,

the tears and wailings of men and women as they are being led away, together with their children and aged parents. He does this 8 throughout his history, always trying in each of the events to place terrors before our eyes.[29]

Let us leave aside his ignoble and womanish disposition,[30] and 9 instead examine what is appropriate and at the same time useful in history. Now then the historian must not, by relating marvels 10 throughout his history, frighten his readers nor must he, like the writers of tragedy, seek after men's probable utterances[31] or enumerate the possible consequences of the events under consideration, but instead simply record what was truly said and done, even if such things happen to be very modest. For the purpose of history 11 is not the same as that of tragedy but rather its opposite. Tragedy must startle and entertain its listeners in the present moment by using the most persuasive words, while history must teach and persuade for all time those who love learning, by means of actual deeds and words. In tragedy the ruling principle is whatever is 12 persuasive, even if it is false, so as to deceive those looking on; in history it is truth, so as to benefit those who love learning.[32]

Apart from this, Phylarchus narrates the majority of the revers- 13 als of fortune in his history without suggesting the reason and the purpose of actions, and without these it is impossible to feel pity reasonably or anger appropriately in each particular event.[33] For example, who does not consider it terrible to strike a free 14 man? But if that man was the first to commit unjust action, then we judge that he has suffered this justly. And if one strikes with the aim of correction and instruction, then someone who strikes a free man will also be judged worthy of honour and gratitude. To 15 take another example: the killing of citizens is considered the greatest impiety, deserving of the greatest punishments; and yet a person who kills a thief or an adulterer is not punished, and someone who kills a traitor or a tyrant receives honours and privileges amongst all people. Thus in every case a final judgement of these 16 matters lies not in the actions themselves but in the reasons and the intentions of those doing the actions, and the differences between them.

The next four chapters give the details of the events surrounding the capture of Mantinea. Polybius says that Aratus got hold of

the town a few years earlier, and that the Mantineans accepted
him and the Achaeans in friendship, but asked for a garrison to
defend them in case of hostile action by the Lacedaemonians.
When an insurrection arose in the town, the Mantineans sum-
moned the Lacedaemonians and handed over the city to them,
putting to death the garrison sent by the Achaean League. This
was treachery beyond belief:

58   What punishment would have been considered fitting for them
to suffer? One might perhaps say that they should have been sold
into slavery with their wives and children since they had been
10   defeated in war.[34] This is something that the customs of war allow
even for those who have not committed such an impious act. They
were worthy, therefore, of some greater and more complete pun-
11   ishment, so that even if they had suffered what Phylarchus claims,
it was not reasonable that it should have elicited pity from the
Greeks but rather praise and approval for the men who by their
12   actions punished such impiety. But even though nothing more serious accompanied the Mantineans' change of fortune than the
plunder of their property and the selling of their free men into
slavery, the historian, all for the sake of sensationalism,[35] had
recourse not only to a complete lie but to an improbable lie at
13   that.[36] And because of Phylarchus' excessive ignorance he was not
even able to pay attention to a parallel situation, namely that when
these same Achaeans at the same time captured Tegea by force,
14   they did nothing of the sort that they did to Mantinea. Yet if the
savagery of the perpetrators was the cause, it is logical that Tegea
would have suffered the same things as another city captured at
15   the same time. If Mantinea alone was treated differently, it is clear
that there was necessarily a different reason for the Achaeans'
anger.

59   Phylarchus then says that Aristomachus of Argos,[37] a man who
came from the noblest house, had been tyrant over Argos and was
himself descended from tyrants, fell into the hands of Antigonus and the Achaeans, and was taken away, tortured and put to
death, having suffered most terribly and unjustly of all men.
2   Maintaining in this action too his particular talent, the historian
invents some cries that fell upon the neighbours' ears during the
night as the man was being tortured, and he says that some of

them were astonished at the crime, others could not believe it, and still others, aggrieved by what was happening, ran to his house. Let us say no more about Phylarchus' sensationalism since it has been suitably demonstrated before. I maintain that Aristomachus was worthy of the greatest punishment, even if he had committed no other crime against the Achaeans, because of his character throughout his life and his lawless acts against his own country. And yet this writer, wishing to increase Aristomachus' renown and move his audience to a greater compassion for him and what he suffered, says not only that Aristomachus was a tyrant but also that he was descended from tyrants! It would be difficult to formulate any accusation greater or more bitter against the man: for the very word 'tyrant' gives the impression of the greatest impiety and comprehends all injustices and crimes among mankind. If Aristomachus had suffered the most terrible punishment, as Phylarchus says, he would nevertheless not have paid a sufficient penalty for his actions on that one day when Aratus and the Achaeans entered the city and endured great battles and dangers on behalf of the Argives' freedom, but finally had to withdraw because none of those in the city who had agreed to fight with them dared to make a move because of their fear of the tyrant; Aristomachus used this occasion and pretext to charge eighty leading men of the city with being party to the admission of the Achaeans, even though they had done no such thing, and after torturing them before the eyes of their relatives, put them to death. I pass over all the crimes that he and his ancestors committed throughout their lives, because it would be a long story.

And so it must not be considered a terrible thing if Aristomachus suffered something similar to what he had inflicted. It would have been far more terrible if he had *not* experienced this and had died without having paid the penalty. Nor must one charge Antigonus or Aratus with a crime because they tortured and killed a tyrant whom they had captured in war, since right-thinking men praise and honour those who punish and kill tyrants even in peacetime. What should Aristomachus have suffered when, apart from the matters mentioned, he also broke faith with the Achaeans? He had abdicated the tyranny not long before, being in straitened circumstances after the death of Demetrius, but then

was saved unexpectedly, protected by the lenience and generosity
5 of the Achaeans, who not only did not make him pay for the
crimes he had committed as a tyrant, but also took him into their
federation and gave him the highest honour, making him their
6 leader and general. But he quickly forgot the aforementioned generosity: seeing greater hopes for his future in Cleomenes, Aristomachus
withdrew himself and his favour from the Achaeans, and at the
7 most crucial moment he joined with their enemies. When he
became the Achaeans' prisoner they should not have tortured and
killed him in Cenchrea, as Phylarchus reports, but should have led
him around the whole Peloponnese and made their vengeance a
8 spectacle, and in that way have put an end to his life. But despite
being such a man, he experienced nothing more terrible than
being drowned by the magistrates at Cenchrea.

61   Aside from this, Phylarchus has narrated for us the misfortunes
of the Mantineans with exaggeration and elaboration,[38] evidently
supposing that it is fitting for historians to point out only lawless
2 actions, while he has not even made mention of the nobility which
3 the Megalopolitans displayed in these events, as if it were more
appropriate for history to enumerate the errors of men than to
point out deeds that are noble and just, or as if those who read
histories will be less instructed by honest deeds worth emulating
than by criminal actions that should be shunned.[39]

4   Now Phylarchus, wishing to show Cleomenes' magnanimity
and his moderate behaviour towards his enemies, has revealed to
us how he took the city, and how he, while ensuring that it was not
ravaged, immediately sent messengers bearing a letter to the Megalopolitans in Messene,[40] asking them to take his side since he was
5 keeping their city unharmed. Phylarchus has revealed further how
the Megalopolitans, while the letter was being read out, did not
even allow it to be read to the end, but came close to stoning the
6 messengers. So much he has made clear. But he has eliminated
what followed and that which is the peculiar function of history,
namely the praise and the honourable mention of worthy conduct.
7 And yet it was there to hand. For if we consider to be good men
those who by word and decree undergo wars for their friends and
allies, and if we assign to those who have endured the destruction
of their territory and the siege of their city not only praise but also

the greatest thanks and gifts, what judgement should we have   8
about the Megalopolitans? Must it not be the most reverential and
best? First, they abandoned their territory to Cleomenes; next   9
they lost their country because they chose the side of the Achaeans; finally, when the possibility was offered to them – unexpectedly   10
and contrary to expectation – to get back their country unharmed,
they chose to be deprived of their territory, graves, temples, their
country and possessions – everything, in a word, that men consider dearest – all for the sake of not betraying their faith with
their allies. Has there ever been or could there ever be a nobler   11
deed? To what could a historian better call the attention of his
readers? Through what deed could he more encourage his readers
to maintain their pledges and share the enterprises of an honourable and well-established state?[41] But Phylarchus has made no   12
mention of these things, blind, so it seems to me, to deeds which
were fairest and particularly appropriate for a historian.

Causes, Pretexts, Beginnings

(3.6.1–7 + 3.7.4–7)

Some of those who have written the history of Hannibal,[42] wishing to indicate to us the reasons why the aforementioned war
between the Romans and the Carthaginians occurred, declare the
first reason to be the siege of Saguntum by the Carthaginians, and   2
second, their crossing, contrary to the treaty, of the river that the
natives call Ebro.[43] I would say that these were the *beginnings* of   3
the war, but in no way would I agree that they were the *causes*. Far   4
from it – unless someone will say that the crossing of Alexander
into Asia was the cause of his war against Persia, or the arrival of
Antiochus at Demetrias was the cause of his war against the Romans:
but neither of these is probable or true.[44] Who could consider these   5
to be the causes, when Alexander had made many preparations (and
his father Philip, while he was still alive, had made some too) for the
war against the Persians, and likewise the Aetolians had made plans
for war against Rome before the appearance of Antiochus? Such   6

beliefs are characteristic of men who cannot distinguish how and to what extent a beginning differs from a cause and a pretext, and how the latter two come first of all, while the beginning comes

7 last. I assert that the beginnings in each case are the first attempts and the first actions arising from decisions already made, while the causes are the events which guide our purposes and decisions, that is, thoughts, dispositions and the reasonings about these things, by which we are led to decide and execute something.

Polybius next gives an extended account of the causes of the war between Antiochus and Rome.

7.4   I have expanded upon these matters not in order to fault histor-

5 ians but to instruct students. For what benefit can come to the sick from a physician who is ignorant of the causes of the body's conditions?[45] What benefit can come from one engaged in political affairs who cannot reckon how, why and whence each event has

6 begun? It is not likely that the former could ever prescribe the necessary treatments for the body nor that the statesman, without a knowledge of what I have mentioned above, could take matters in

7 hand as needed. And so one should pay attention to and investigate nothing so much as the causes of each event, given that the greatest matters sometimes arise from chance occurrences, and it is easiest in every matter to remedy initial impulses and decisions.[46]

Uses of History and the Benefits of Universal History

(3.31.1–32.10)

Some people who examine such things uncritically might say that

2 we have extended our discussion unnecessarily. But I would say this perhaps: if anyone thinks he is self-sufficient in every circumstance, then the knowledge that comes from history would be

3 good for him but not necessary. But if no one who is human would dare to maintain such a thing, either in his personal affairs or in public matters (since no sensible person, even if he is fortunate in the present, could ever have a secure expectation of a similar state

4 in the future),[47] then I would say that the knowledge of past events

is not only good but also necessary. For how would anyone find 5
allies to bring assistance if he himself or his country were injured?
How could anyone who desired to acquire some possession or ini-
tiate hostilities rightly urge his allies on to some enterprise? How 6
could he justly incite those who would be likely to secure the success of his own principles and preserve the status quo when he is
pleased with the current situation, if he had no recollection of past
events for each of these situations? All men, because they adapt 7
themselves somehow to the present and play a role, always speak
and act in such a way as to make it difficult to detect the intention
of each, and often the truth is very much in shadow.[48] But past his- 8
tory allows us to judge more certainly from the events themselves,
displays truly the principles and intentions of each, and reveals
from whom we can expect gratitude, benefactions and aid, and
from whom the opposite of these things. From this it is possible 9
often and in many cases to discover who will take pity on us, who
will share our outrage, and still more who will join with us in taking vengeance. And these things are of the greatest assistance both 10
in our private and public lives. That is why neither writers nor 11
readers of history should pay attention so much to the narrative of
events as to what happened before, during and after the events. 12
For if you remove from history the study of why, how and for what
purpose each thing was done, and whether the outcome was reasonable, what remains is a competition piece, but not a means of
instruction, and while it gives delight for the present, it is entirely
devoid of benefit for the future.[49]

Now those who think that our history, because of its size and 32
the number of its books, is difficult to acquire and difficult to read
are mistaken. How much easier is it to acquire and read through 2
forty books, as if woven thread by thread,[50] and thus follow
clearly events in Italy, Sicily and Africa from the time of Pyrrhus[51]
to the capture of Carthage, and events in the other part of the 3
inhabited world from the flight of Cleomenes the Spartiate continuously to the battle of the Achaeans and Romans at the
Isthmus,[52] than it is to read or acquire the treatises of those who
write on each of these events individually? Aside from the fact that 4
those are many times the size of our history, readers cannot
acquire anything certain from them, first because the majority

5 give conflicting accounts of the same events; second, because they
omit events in parallel, and it is from the comparison of these that
people may examine and judge them together and so come to evaluations that differ from a partial notion; and finally, because those
partial histories are completely unable even to touch upon the
6 most important matters.[53] For we maintain that the most necessary
parts of history are the consequences of events, their concomitant
7 circumstances, and above all their causes. We see that the war with
Antiochus took its beginnings from the war with Philip, while the
war with Philip began from the war with Hannibal, and the war
with Hannibal from the war over Sicily, and that events between
these had many varied circumstances but were all tending towards
8 the same end.[54] It is possible to know and learn all of this from
those who write universal history, but not from those who write
about individual wars such as the Persian War or the war with
9 Philip. It would be as if someone supposed that by reading only
the accounts of the battles written by those authors, he knew
10 clearly the management and plan of the entire war. But this is in
no way the case. Our history, I think, differs from those individual
treatises to the same extent that learning differs from merely
hearing.[55]

Errors Made by Historians of Hannibal

(3.47.6–9 + 3.48.8–12)

Some of those[56] who have written of this crossing [sc. of the Alps],
wishing to startle their readers with accounts of marvels[57] in the
aforementioned regions, fall unawares into two things that are
most alien to history: they are compelled to tell falsehoods and to
7 contradict themselves.[58] For example, having presented a Hannibal who is an inimitable general in his daring and forethought,
8 they then admittedly show him to us as completely irrational; at
the same time, because they have no conclusion or exit for their
9 falsehood, they introduce gods and heroes into a political history.
They suppose that the Alps are so inaccessible and rugged, that

not even light-armed troops could cross them, much less horses and armies accompanied by elephants; likewise they describe for us this area as so deserted that all Hannibal's men would have lost the way and perished, unless some god or hero had met up with Hannibal and showed him the paths; in this way they admittedly fall into the two faults that we mentioned . . .

From this, as one would expect, they fall into a state like that of 48. 8 the writers of tragedy, who all need the *deus ex machina* for the resolution of their dramas, because their first assumptions are false and irrational.[59] Historians must of necessity be in a similar 9 situation when they make gods and heroes appear, since they too have made beginnings that are false and improbable. For how is it possible to have a reasonable ending when the beginnings are irrational? Hannibal, of course, executed his plans not as these 10 authors state, but in a very practical way: he had clearly investi- 11 gated the fertility of the land which he was invading and the opposition of the inhabitants there to the Romans, and in the difficult areas in between he used native guides and scouts who shared in his hopes.[60] We can confidently assert these things 12 because we made inquiry about these events from those who were present on those occasions, and we inspected the terrain and made the same passage through the Alps so that we could know and see for ourselves.[61]

Writers who Claim to Write Universal History

(5.33.1–8)

And yet I am not unaware that many other historians make the same claim that I do, namely that they write universal history and have undertaken a work greater than any that has gone before.[62] 2 Asking Ephorus' pardon (for he was the first and only one to attempt to write a universal history)[63] I shall avoid saying much about them or remembering any of them by name, and instead note only this: 3 that some contemporary historians, having narrated for us the war of the Romans and Carthaginians in three or four columns,[64] claim

₄ to have written universal history. Yet who is so ignorant as not
to know that very many great deeds were done at that time in
Spain, Africa and still more in Sicily and Italy? And that everyone
was compelled to pay attention to the war with Hannibal – the
most famous and the longest aside from the war for Sicily – on
₅ account of its greatness, and in fear of the result to come?⁶⁵ Some
authors, nonetheless, claim that they have compiled all events in
the Greek and non-Greek world, even though they have recorded
events not even to the extent as those who on public authority set
up memoranda of occasional happenings in chronological records
₆ on walls.⁶⁶ The reason for this is that it is perfectly easy to claim
in words the greatest deeds, but in practice it is not easy to achieve
₇ anything excellent. It is open to anyone and common to all, one
might say, to be able to make claims only, but the accomplishment
₈ is extremely rare and falls only to a few in this life. I was led to
make these remarks because of the bravado of those who make
arrogant claims for themselves and their own histories.

On Sensationalism in History

(7.7.1–8)

Some historians who have written on the fall of Hieronymus⁶⁷ have
made a long account of it, and have inserted much sensationalism,⁶⁸
narrating, for example, the signs that appeared before his rule and
₂ the misfortunes of the Syracusans, writing in a tragic mode about
the savagery of his character and the impiety of his deeds, and on top
of it all the unexpected and terrible nature of the circumstances surrounding his fall, with the result that no tyrant, not Phalaris or
₃ Apollodorus,⁶⁹ was harsher than he. And yet he was a boy when he
began to rule and he departed from life no more than thirteen
₄ months later. In that time it is possible that one or two people were
tortured and some of his friends and other Syracusans were put to
death, but it is not probable that there was excessive lawlessness and
₅ extraordinary impiety. It has to be said that his character was especially reckless and lawless but he cannot be compared with either of

the tyrants just mentioned. I think, rather, that those who write indi- 6
vidual histories, whenever they choose themes that are limited and
insignificant, are compelled, for want of material, to make small
things big and to expend many words on matters not even worthy of
mention. Some fall into a very similar state through a lack of judgement.[70] How much more sensible it would be for writers to apply 7
that amplification of the narrative, which they use merely in padding
out their books, to Hiero and Gelon,[71] and dispense with Hieronymus. This would be more pleasant for those who are fond of listening 8
and entirely more useful to those who love learning.

Benefits of Universal History

(8.2.1–11)

I believe that something I often said in the beginnings of our treatise[72] has now been confirmed in truth by the deeds themselves. I 2
said that it is not possible to examine together the development of
events as a whole through those who write partial histories. For 3
how is it possible for someone who reads the separate history of
Sicilian or Spanish affairs to know and learn either the greatness
of the deeds or – the most important thing – how and with what
form of constitution Fortune accomplished in our lifetime the
most unexpected deed,[73] namely the bringing of all the known 4
portions of the world under one rule and governance, something
which is not seen to have happened before?[74] It is not impossible, 5
from partial histories, to know even a little how the Romans took
Syracuse or came to possess Spain; but without a universal history 6
of events it is difficult to apprehend how they acquired hegemony
over everything and what worked against their far-reaching
attempts in particular cases, and in turn what worked for them
and on what occasions. For the same reasons it is not easy to 7
understand the greatness of the Romans' deeds or the power of
their constitution. For to say that the Romans had designs on 8
Spain or on Sicily and campaigned against them with infantry and
naval forces would not in itself be amazing; but when we see that 9

these events and many others like them happened at the same time
and from the same power and state, and that the people who had
all this on their hands were also undergoing wars and dangers in
10 their own land, only then would the events be clear and marvellous, and, most of all, only in this way would someone give them
11 the attention they deserve. Let this be what we have to say, then,
to those who suppose that they can impart by means of separate
histories the knowledge that comes from universal and world
history.[75]

On Writing about Monarchs

(8.8.1–11.8)

When he arrived in Messenia, Philip devastated the countryside in a
2   hostile spirit, acting with more passion than reason.[76] He expected, I
think, that those who were being treated badly would never be angry
3   or hate him even while he was continuously harming them. I was
led, both now and in the previous Book, to expound somewhat more
clearly on these matters not only for the reasons I mentioned formerly,[77] but also because of the fact that some historians have
4   completely omitted events in Messenia, while others, in general
because of their favouritism towards monarchs or, on the contrary,
their fear,[78] have informed us that Philip's impiety and lawlessness
towards the Messenians were not wrong but the opposite: a virtuous
5   action worthy of praise. One can see them doing this not only concerning Philip's actions against the Messenians but similarly with
6   the rest of his deeds, and the result is that their treatises no longer
have the form of history but of encomium.[79]

7   Now I assert that one needs neither to slander nor to praise
monarchs falsely, as many have done; instead, one should con-
struct an account which always coheres with what has previously
8   been said and which is fitting to the characters of each. Yet this is
perhaps easy to say but exceedingly difficult to do, because conditions and circumstances are many and varied, and in yielding to
these, men in the course of their lives cannot say or write what

they really think. For this reason pardon should be granted to 9
some, but not to others.

One would especially find fault with Theopompus[80] in this matter 9
because he says in the beginning of his treatise about Philip that
what especially spurred him on to attempt his history was that
Europe had never before produced such a man as Philip, the son of
Amyntas,[81] but almost immediately after this in the preface, and 2
throughout his entire history, he shows Philip as someone who had
no self-control towards women, so that he ruined his own house by
his desire and addiction to this sort of thing; who was most unjust 3
and most wicked in the forming of friendships and alliances; who
enslaved and betrayed a very great number of cities using guile and
force; who was so passionate and immoderate in drinking that even 4
during the day his friends could often see that he was clearly drunk.

If someone wished to read the beginning of Book 49 of Theo- 5
pompus' history, he would be completely amazed at the inconsistency
of the historian, who, apart from everything else, has dared to say
the following (and we cite the very words that he has used):[82]

Any among either Greeks or barbarians who were studs[83] or outra- 6
geous in their character, all these gathered together at the court of
Philip in Macedonia and were called the king's 'Companions'. In 7
general Philip rejected those who were orderly in their habits and
who took care for their private life, while he honoured and pro-
moted those who were very wealthy and who spent their lives
drinking and gambling. He made sure further not only to encourage 8
them in these vices but also to make them competitors in every
other form of injustice and shamelessness. What shameful or hor- 9
rible thing did they not possess? What fine or noble quality did they
not lack? Some of them continued to shave and depilate themselves
even as adults, and others dared to fornicate with adult men.[84] Two 10
or three used to lead around men prostituting themselves, and these
would render their same services to others. One would more justly 11
call them not companions but courtesans, not soldiers but common
prostitutes. Men-slayers by nature, they were men-layers in their 12
behaviour.[85] To sum up, lest I go on at length, especially as there are 13
so many matters pressing upon me, I consider that those who were
called Philip's friends and companions had the character of wild

beasts, worse than the Centaurs of Mount Pelion or the Laestrygonians who inhabit the plain of Leontini or any other creatures of
that sort.[86]

10 Who would not reprove the bitterness and unrestrained nonsense
2 of this writer?[87] He deserves to be reproved not only because he
contradicts here what he said about his intent in writing, but also
because he has falsely accused the king and his friends, and not
least because he has promulgated this lie coarsely and inappropri-
3 ately.[88] If someone were giving an account of Sardanapalus[89] or
one of his companions, even here he would hardly dare to use such
vulgar offensive language. And we can infer *his* character and
4 licentiousness in life from the inscription on his tomb,[90] which
reads:

These I yet possess: the meals I ate, the outrages I committed, the
pleasures I took in love.

5 But to return to Philip and his companions, one would hesitate
not so much in speaking of effeminacy and cowardice, still more
of shamelessness; on the contrary, one would hesitate because if
one tried to heap praise on them, one could never speak worthily
of the aforementioned men's bravery, industriousness and, in a
6 word, virtue. It was clearly they who by their efforts and daring
fashioned Macedon from the smallest kingdom into an empire
7 that was the greatest and most famous. In addition to the deeds
done by Philip, those accomplished by Alexander after Philip's
death gave the Macedonians a reputation for bravery that every-
8 one agrees on. Perhaps one should assign the greatest portion of
credit for Macedon's pre-eminence in the world to Alexander,
even though he was only a young man, but no less credit must go
9 to his accomplices and friends, who conquered their enemies in
many extraordinary battles, and endured many risky battles, dangers and hardships. And when they had made themselves masters
of enormous wealth and could enjoy the fruits of their labours for
any and all desires, they never because of this were diminished in
bodily strength, nor did they practise anything unjust or immod-
10 est in accordance with their impulses, but virtually all of them,

while they associated with Philip and after him with Alexander, proved themselves to be kingly in their magnanimity, their self-control and their daring. No one of them needs to be mentioned by name. In their struggles after Alexander's death over the great- 11 est parts of the inhabited world, they won a reputation that has been handed down in many histories.[91] So while we can admit 12 that the bitterness that Timaeus employed against Agathocles the Sicilian, even though it seems to be excessive, is justified (he was, after all, accusing an enemy, a wicked man and a tyrant),[92] the bitterness of Theopompus does not even deserve consideration.

For having proposed that he was going to write about a king 11 who was naturally disposed towards virtue, he then omits no shameful or terrible act. It follows then that either the historian is 2 manifestly a liar and a flatterer in the beginning and the introduction of his treatise or that he is thoughtless and childish in his individual assertions if he supposed that he himself would seem more trustworthy by his foolish and exaggerated slander, and that his encomiastic assertions about Philip would be deemed more worthy of acceptance.[93]

Furthermore, no one would approve of the arrangement of the 3 aforementioned historian, since he undertook to write of Greek actions, following from where Thucydides left off, but when he was approaching the times of the battle of Leuctra and the most renowned of Greek accomplishments,[94] he cast aside Greece and her efforts, and changing his subject, he decided to write of Philip's actions. And yet it would have been more respectable and 4 more suitable to encompass Philip's deeds within a history of Greece rather than Greece's deeds within a history of Philip.[95] For 5 no one, not even one who had been previously captivated by royal power, would hesitate when the opportunity arose of transferring the title and chief role in his work to Greece; likewise, no one who had begun with an account of Greece and had made some progress with it would have exchanged this for the regal pomp and biography of a king – at least not if he had an uncontaminated mind. And what indeed could it have been that forced Theopom- 6 pus to overlook such great contradictions, unless, by God, it was that the purpose of the earlier treatise was noble, while that of the account of Philip was advantageous?[96] Now as regards this mistake 7

of his, he might perhaps have been able, if someone asked him, to
8 give a reason why he changed his subject. But, as for the abuse that
he employed against Philip's friends, I do not think that he would
have been able to render any account of it, and he would have had
to agree that he deviated very much from what was fitting.

Types of History and their Audiences

(9.1.2–2.7)

I am not unaware that our history, because of the uniformity of its
composition, is somewhat dry, and is meant for, and will win the
3 approval of, only one class of reader. Nearly all other historians,
or at least the majority, by employing all the types of history,
4 attract many to the reading of their works. The genealogical type
attracts one who likes hearing a story, while that which deals with
colonies, foundings and kinship relations attracts the curious and
the lover of the recherché (as Ephorus also says somewhere),[97]
while the type that deals with actions of peoples, cities and dynasts
5 attracts the statesman.[98] In directing our efforts only to this last
type and dedicating our entire arrangement to this, we have, as I
said before, properly fashioned it towards one kind of reader, and
6 made it unappealing for the greater number. We have spoken elsewhere and at length as to why we eschew the other types of history
and have chosen to write political history,[99] but nothing prevents
us now from reminding our readers briefly what we said by way of
explanation.
2   Since many writers have in many ways enumerated matters concerning genealogies, myths and colonies, and in addition kinship
2 ties and foundations, it follows that he who concerns himself with
these at the present time must either pass off other people's work as
his own (which is the most disgraceful thing of all) or, if he is
unwilling to do this, he must obviously labour in vain in composing and caring about things that have been suitably demonstrated
3 and handed down to posterity by previous authors. Such material,
4 then, I omitted, for these reasons and many others. I chose the type

concerned with political history, first, because new events are constantly occurring and need new narratives (since the ancients could not narrate for us events in their future); second, because it is the 5 most useful of all genres: this was so even in times before ours but it is especially the case in our time, when the arts and sciences have advanced to such a degree that those who love learning can deal scientifically, one might say, with any emergency that arises. It is 6 for this reason that we have aimed not so much at enjoyment as benefit for those who attend to our work,[100] and dispensing with all that other material, we have been led to this one type. Those who 7 give their careful attention to our writings will furnish the surest evidence of what I say here.

On the Difference between History and Biography

(10.21.2–8)

Now that we have the occasion in our history to treat the deeds of Philopoemen,[101] we consider it appropriate to do something similar for him as we have attempted to do for other notable men, namely to indicate his upbringing and his character. For it is 3 odd that historians should offer detailed narratives of how, when and by whom cities were founded, and in addition the circumstances and difficulties of the operations, but yet pass over in silence the upbringing and the ambitions of the men who were in charge of it all, even though such matters are more profitable. For 4 to the extent that it is more possible to imitate living men rather than lifeless buildings, to the same extent is it probable that an account of such men would be more important for the improvement of the reader.

Now if we had not composed a separate treatise about Philo- 5 poemen, in which we revealed his nature, his ancestry and the kind of upbringing he had when he was a young man, it would have been necessary to offer an account of each of these things.[102] 6 But since we have written an account of him in three books and separate from the present work, where we revealed his youthful

7 upbringing and his most brilliant deeds, it is clear that in this present work it would be appropriate to omit the detailed treatment of
his youthful training and his youthful ambitions, and instead to
include a detailed account of the deeds he accomplished in his
8 prime, which we treated in that earlier work only summarily. For
just as that genre, which is encomiastic, demanded a summary and
amplified account of his deeds, so the genre of history, which dis-
penses praise and blame equally, seeks an account which is true
and which demonstrates the reasons for praise or blame in each
case.[103]

On Tables of Contents versus Introductions

(11.1a.1–5)

Some might ask why we have not, like our predecessors, given a
table of contents in this book, but instead an introductory survey
2 giving the events of each Olympiad.[104] Now I think that a table of
contents is useful, since it makes those who wish to read attentive,
while it excites those who come to the work and induces them to
read it.[105] In addition, one can with such a table readily find any-
3 thing one is looking for. But when I saw that for many reasons
(even insignificant ones) these tables are held in little account and
4 get destroyed, I was led to write introductory surveys. An introduction is not only equally as effective as a table, but in fact
somewhat more effective, and simultaneously its place is more
5 assured because it is interwoven with the treatise itself. For this
reason, then, we considered an introductory survey to be more
useful for our entire history except in the first six books, where we
composed tables because surveys would not have been very suitable for them.[106]

Errors Arising from Insufficient Inquiry

$(12.3.1-4.4)^{107}$

Everyone would marvel at the fertility of the land [sc. Africa], but 2
one would have to say not only that Timaeus had made no inquiries about Africa but that he also was childish, wholly illogical and
excessively beholden to the ancient reports that he had received,
which said that Africa was sandy throughout and dry and sterile.
His account is the same for animals there: the multitude of horses, 3
cattle and sheep, and goats in Africa cannot be found, I think, anywhere in the rest of the known world, and this is because many of 4
the African tribes do not cultivate crops but live with their animals
and gain their livelihood from them. Who has not read of the mul- 5
titude and strength of the elephants, lions and panthers there, and
the beauty of the antelopes and the size of the ostriches? Not a one
of these can be found in Europe but Africa is full of them. Yet 6
Timaeus, because he made no inquiry about these, has given an
account that is, almost deliberately, the opposite of what is truly
there. And just as he makes random remarks about Africa, so like- 7
wise does he do so concerning the island called Corsica. Making 8
mention of that island in his second book, he says that there are
many wild goats and wild cattle and sheep in it, and further that
there are deer, hares and wolves, and some other kinds of animals,
that the men there spend their time in hunting these, and that this
is their sole occupation.[108] But in the aforementioned island there 9
is not a single wild goat or cow nor a single hare, or wolf, deer or
any other such animal except for foxes, rabbits and wild sheep. 10
(Seen from afar, the rabbit looks like a small hare, but when one
captures it, one can see that it differs greatly in its appearance and
taste. It lives underground most of the time.)

All the animals on the island nevertheless *seem* to be wild for 4
the following reason. The herders cannot follow their animals 2
into the pastures because the island is thickly wooded, rocky and
rough. So whenever they wish to gather their flock, they stand at
an appropriate place and with a trumpet they summon the animals, and each one, without error, runs towards its own trumpet. 3

Hence whenever people land at the island, and see goats or oxen pasturing without a guardian and wish to seize them, the animals will not approach them because they are unfamiliar, and instead

4 flee. And whenever the shepherd sees the new arrivals to the island, he sounds the trumpet, and the animals rush headlong and run in the direction of the trumpet; and it is this that gives the impression that they are wild. But these matters Timaeus has treated superficially, because his inquiry was poorly made and cursory.[109]

Niggling Criticisms and Pedantry

(12.4a.1–4d.8)

Furthermore, who could pardon such errors especially when it is

2 Timaeus, who latches on to such trifles in others? For example, he charges Theopompus with having Dionysius sail from Sicily to Corinth in a merchant boat whereas he actually made the journey

3 in a warship.[110] And he in turn falsely accuses Ephorus, claiming that Ephorus said that Dionysius the elder began to rule at age 23,

4 was tyrant for 42 years, and departed life at 63. Now no one would say that this is the writer's own error, but rather all would agree that

5 it is the scribe's.[111] Ephorus must have been stupider than Coroebus and Margites[112] if he could not calculate that 42 and 23 equals 65,

6 but since no one would believe this of Ephorus, two things are obvious: the error is the scribe's; and no one could approve of Timaeus' love of fault-finding and making accusations.

4b   Furthermore, in his account of Pyrrhus,[113] Timaeus says that the Romans, still to this day, as a way of commemorating the fall of Troy, shoot down a war horse on a certain day in front of the city in the area called the Campus Martius, doing so because the fall of Troy was accomplished through the famous wooden horse –

2 a remark more puerile than any other.[114] For we would then have

3 to say that all the barbarians are descendants of the Trojans, since nearly all of them, or at least the majority, whenever they begin a war or engage in a particularly decisive battle, sacrifice a horse

beforehand and immolate it, interpreting the future from the way in which the animal falls.

In this matter, Timaeus seems to me to display not only ignor- 4c ance of such foolishness, but even more a great deal of pedantry: because the Romans sacrifice a horse, he immediately supposes that it's because Troy was said to have been captured by a horse. But 2 from this it is evident that he has made inquiries poorly in matters pertaining to Africa, to Sardinia and especially to Italy, and that in 3 general the part of his history that has to do with personal inquiry has been done in a wholly careless way; and yet this is the most important thing in history: for since events occur at the same time 3 in many places, and it is impossible for the same person to be present in many places at the same moment, and likewise for one man to be an eyewitness of all the places in the known world and the distinctive features in these lands, what remains is to inquire from 5 as many people as possible, to trust those who are worthy of trust, and to be a good judge of the things that one hears.[115]

In this matter Timaeus, although making a great display, seems 4d to me to have fallen far short of the truth. So far is he from exam- 2 ining accurately the truth through others that not even for those places where he has been an eyewitness and those lands he has visited, not even about these does he report to us anything sound. 3 This will be clear if we show that he is ignorant even about the things he describes in Sicily. For it would hardly require any more 4 words about his false accounts if he is shown to be ignorant and in error concerning the places where he was born and raised, and indeed in the most celebrated of those places.[116] 5

Now then, he says that the spring Arethusa in Syracuse has its source in the Peloponnese from the Alpheius river which flows through Arcadia and Olympia;[117] this river, going underground 6 and running 4,000 stades beneath the Sicilian sea, comes up again in Syracuse;[118] and this is evident, he says, from the fact that on 7 one occasion, when torrential rains fell at the Olympic games and the river flooded the areas of the sacred precinct, a great quantity 8 of dung gushed forth from Arethusa and this was from the cattle that had been sacrificed at the festival; and the spring also disgorged a golden bowl which was recognized as an object from the sacrifice by the people who extracted it.[119]

The Differing Accounts of Timaeus and Aristotle on the Origins of the Epizephyrian Locrians

(12.5.1–12a.3)[120]

It so happens that I have in fact travelled many times to the city
2 of the Locrians and rendered them important services,[121] and
through my agency they were excused from participating in the
campaign in Spain and against the Dalmatians, even though their
3 treaty required them to assist the Romans with naval forces. Thus
freed from trouble, danger and considerable expense, they paid us
back with honours and privileges. And so I ought much more to
4 speak well of the Locrians than the opposite.[122] Nevertheless, I
have not hesitated to affirm in speech and in writing that the
account of their foundation as a colony which Aristotle has transmitted is in fact more truthful than the one recorded by Timaeus.[123]
5 For I know that the Locrians agree that the tradition about their
founding which they received from their fathers is the one that
Aristotle, not Timaeus, has recorded.

6   These are the proofs they were citing:[124] first, that amongst
them all hereditary nobility derives from women, not from men,
for example, those considered to be their nobility, the ones said to
7 be 'from the hundred houses'. The hundred houses were selected
by the Locrians before the colony was sent out, and it was from
these that the Locrians, in accordance with the oracle, were sup-
8 posed to choose the virgins to be sent to Troy.[125] Some women
from these families went out with the colony, and their descendants are still today considered to be the nobility and are called
9 'those from the hundred houses'. Then there is the matter of the
woman they call the 'cup-bearer', about whom some account
10 like this has been handed down: at the time when the Locrians
expelled the Sicels who possessed that part of Italy,[126] they themselves adopted and preserved many of the Sicels' customs because
they had none of their own, and one of these was this cup-bearer,
who was a boy from the most renowned and noblest families who
11 marched at the head of sacrificial processions; but the Locrians
altered one thing only, namely, that the cup-bearer chosen was

not a boy but a girl, because nobility for them descended from women.

There were no treaties between them and the Locrians in 6 Greece, nor were there said to be any in their possession. But all knew of treaties with the Sicels, about which they offered the fol- 2 lowing account: when the Locrians first appeared and surprised the Sicels who possessed the territory which the Locrians now inhabit, the Sicels were petrified and because of their fear accepted them and made a treaty with them, each side swearing to be well- 3 minded towards the other and to hold the land in common so long as they walked on this earth and bore their heads on their shoulders. Now the story is that when these oaths were being sworn, 4 the Locrians threw dirt into the soles of their shoes and hid heads of garlic on their shoulders, and in this way they swore their oaths; 5 after taking the oaths, they shook out the dirt from their shoes, cast off the heads of garlic, and not much later, when an opportunity arose, drove out the Sicilians from their land.[127] This, then, 6 is what is said by the Locrians.

Timaeus of Tauromenium in the ninth book of his history says 7a it was not the custom amongst the Greeks formerly to be served by purchased slaves, and he writes, 'they blamed Aristotle generally for having been wrong about the Locrians' customs: for the law was that the Locrians could not even possess slaves'.[128]

Reckoning from this, one would rely more on Aristotle than 6a on Timaeus. And indeed what follows in Timaeus is entirely absurd. He suggests that it was not probable that the slaves of 2 these Lacedaemonians' allies would maintain the same goodwill as their masters towards the friends of those masters. But this is a foolish supposition: when those who are slaves unexpectedly have 3 the good fortune to gain their freedom, and time has passed, they try to appropriate not only the friendships their masters had but even the relations of hospitality and kinship, even more so than those who are related to them by birth; and they are keen to do 4 this so as to wipe out their former inferiority and shame by wishing to appear as their masters' descendants rather than as their freedmen.

And it is especially probable that this would have been the 6b case with the Locrians. Far removed from those who knew about

their past, and with time as their helper, they were not so foolish as to pursue behaviours that would lead to the revival of their own inferiority, but rather quite the opposite: they would much more
2 conceal it. Thus it was natural that they named their city after the women, and they pretended that their descent went according to women and further, that they renewed their ancestral friendships and alliances with the people who were descended from their
3 women. And the fact that the Athenians ravaged their territory[129]
4 is no indication that Aristotle has spoken falsely. For it follows from what has been said above that even if the Locrians were slaves ten times over, the men who set sail from Locri and landed in Italy would have feigned friendships with the Lacedaemonians; and it was reasonable also that the Athenians' enmity towards the Locrians was not so much because they had looked into the Locrians' past as because the Locrians sided with the Lacedaemonians.
5 But, someone might object, how was it that the Lacedaemonians themselves once sent back to their homeland men in the prime of life so that they might father children, and yet did not allow the
6 Locrians to do something similar?[130] Each of these situations dif-
7 fers greatly, however, not only in probability but in truth: the Lacedaemonians were not intending to prevent the Locrians from doing what they themselves had done (that would have been absurd), nor were the Locrians intending to behave in entirely the same way as the Lacedamonians, even if the latter had ordered
8 them to do so. The reason is that amongst the Lacedaemonians it was an ancestral custom that three or four men (or even more if they were brothers) would have one wife, and the children were held in common, and when a man had sired a suitable number of children, it was an honourable and customary thing to give her to
9 one of his friends.[131] But because the Locrians were not bound by the same imprecations and oaths as the Lacedaemonians had sworn – namely, that they would not return home until they had taken Messenia by force – they naturally did not partake in a col-
10 lective return, but making their returns in groups, and then only rarely, they gave their wives time to become more intimate with their slaves than with their original husbands, and even more was this the case for the unmarried women. This, then, was the reason for their emigration.

Timaeus records many falsehoods, not because he is wholly 7
inexperienced in such matters but because he is blinded by quarrelsomeness, and, when once he has proposed either to blame or,
conversely, to praise someone, he forgets everything, and he often
departs from what is fitting. But let this suffice to defend Aristotle 2
and the sources he relied on in his discussion of the Locrians. 3
What I am now going to say will be a response to Timaeus and his
whole work and in general to what is appropriate for those who
practise the writing of history. Everyone, I think, would agree 4
from what has been said that both Timaeus and Aristotle based
their accounts on probable reasoning but that the greater probabilities are in Aristotle's account. It will be objected, however, that
it is impossible to separate out the truth in each of these matters. 5
Well, then, let us assume that Timaeus' account is more probable:
is this a reason why those who report a less probable account in
their histories must necessarily hear every kind of insult and abuse
and only just evade a sentence of death? Certainly not.[132] We said 6
that those who write up false accounts through ignorance deserve
to receive friendly correction and pardon, while those who do so
from deliberate choice deserve inexorable prosecution.[133]

One must show, then, that Aristotle in the account we just now 8
gave concerning the Locrians said what he did trying to curry
favour, or for some gain, or from some personal enmity,[134] or if
one dare not say this, then it must be conceded that those who use
against others the kind of hostility and bitterness that Timaeus
used against Aristotle are ignorant and deluded. Timaeus says 2
that Aristotle was arrogant, unscrupulous and rash, and in addition that he has behaved utterly recklessly against the city of the
Locrians, saying that their colony was made up of runaway slaves,
menial servants, adulterers and kidnappers. Aristotle wrote this, 3
he says, with such assurance as to seem to be one of the generals
who had through his own strength just conquered the Persians in
battle at the Cilician Gates, and not a pedantic and hateful sophist 4
who had just now locked up his renowned pharmacy.[135] He adds
that he leapt into every court and general's tent and moreover that
he was a glutton and a gourmand, led on by his mouth in everything. Such things, I think, would scarcely be tolerable in a 5
vagabond or one recklessly hurling abuse in a law court. Such a 6

man does not seem moderate in his speech. But no writer of general history and no historian of the first rank would dare think in his heart, let alone write, such a thing.[136]

9   Let us examine now Timaeus' own character and let us judge the remarks he has made about this same colony, comparing the two point by point, so that we may know which of them will be 2 deserving of such accusation. Timaeus says in this same book that he investigated the matter of the colony no longer using arguments based on probability but himself going to the Locrians in 3 Greece. They first showed him written treaties, still preserved, made with those who were sent off, on which the following begin-4 ning had been inscribed: 'as parents to children'; in addition, there were decrees according to which the citizens of the one city were citizens of the other. And that in general when they heard Aristotle's account of the colony, they marvelled at that writer's effrontery. 5 Then going to the Locrians in Italy, he says that he found their laws and customs congruent not with the recklessness of slaves but with 6 a colony of free men, and they assuredly had penalties for kidnappers and likewise for adulterers and runaway slaves; and that none of this would have existed if they had known that they were descendants of such men.

10   First off, one would be at a loss as to which of the Locrians he 2 visited and asked about these matters. If it were the case that the Locrians in Greece had one city, as do the Locrians in Italy, then 3 one would not wonder and the matter would be clear. But since there are two people called Locrians in Greece,[137] to which group did he go, and which of the cities, and in whose possession did he 4 find the inscribed treaties? He clarifies none of this for us. And yet I think everyone knows that this is a peculiarity of Timaeus', the thing in which he outdoes the rest of historians and for which he has won favour: I mean his display of accuracy when treating chronology and public records and his special care in these mat-5 ters. It is worth wondering, then, why he has not made clear to us the name of the city and the people among whom he found it, nor the place where the treaty is inscribed, nor the magistrates who showed him the inscription, nor the people with whom he spoke, so that there would be no uncertainty but rather, with the place and the city specified, it would be possible for those in doubt to

discover the exact state of the matter. But as he has omitted all 6
this, he is manifestly conscious of deliberately lying, since Timaeus
would have omitted nothing of this if he had discovered it, but
would have, as the saying is, held fast with both hands. This is
evident from the following: would the man who bases himself on 7
Echecrates, mentioning him by name, and saying that he spoke
with him about the Italian Locrians and learned about them from
him, and who adds besides, lest he seem to have spoken with 8
someone at random, that Echecrates' father had previously been
deemed worthy by Dionysius of being an ambassador – would this 9
man, getting hold of a public record, or a commemorative inscription, have kept silent about it?[138]

This is the author who makes comparisons, going back to the 11
earliest time, of the ephors with the kings in Lacedaemon, the
archons at Athens and the priestesses at Argos, aligning them
with the Olympic victors, while refuting the errors of those cities
in their public inscriptions when there is a difference of three
months![139] It is this Timaeus who has discovered inscribed pillars 2
in back rooms and treaties of friendship on the doorposts of temples. One could not believe that *he* would have been ignorant of 3
anything of that sort if it existed, nor that, having discovered it, he
would have failed to mention it; nor could one in any way pardon
him if he has lied. For since he is a bitter and implacable fault- 4
finder in others, it is only reasonable that he meet with implacable
accusation in his turn. And there is no question that he is lying 5
here when, passing over to the Locrians in Italy, he says first that
their constitution and the rest of their culture were similar for
both Locrians, and then that Aristotle and Theophrastus[140] had
made false allegations against the cities. I am not unaware that in 6
delineating and establishing definitely these matters I shall be
forced to digress in this part of my work. But I deferred my account 7
of Timaeus all to one place so that I am not too often compelled
to neglect my duty.[141]

Timaeus says that the greatest fault in history is falsehood. He 11a
also exhorts those whom he refutes as having written falsely in
their treatises to find another name for their books, any name
other than history. For he says it is just like a carpenter's ruler: we 12
call it a ruler even if it is shorter in length or deficient in width,

but nonetheless has the specific quality that makes it a ruler; but if it lacks straightness and all that conforms to straightness, then one

2   must call it anything rather than a ruler. So too for all historical works that are at fault in style or in treatment or in any other detail: if they nonetheless cling to truth, those books merit, he says, the name of history; but whenever they go astray from truth they must no longer be called history.[142]

3   I quite agree that truth must play the leading role in works of this kind, and I myself have spoken in this way somewhere in my work, remarking that just as a living creature when deprived of its sight is wholly useless, so too if you take truth from history what

4   is left is a useless narrative.[143] We have also said, however, that there are two types of falsehood, one done through ignorance, the

5   other by deliberate choice, and one must pardon those who go astray through ignorance of the truth, but be irreconcilably

6   opposed to those who lie by deliberate choice.[144] If we agree with these principles, I imagine that there is a great difference between the error committed through ignorance and the one committed through deliberate choice, and that the one merits pardon and kindly correction, but the other should rightly receive implacable

7   accusation. And it is to the latter that one would especially find Timaeus liable. And this is now the occasion to examine this.

12a   For those who do not keep their contracts we apply the proverb, 'The Locrians their agreements'.[145] Who does not know what historians and everyone else agree on, namely that when the Locrians had promised, during the return of the Heracleidae,[146] to raise fires announcing the enemy if the Heracleidae happened to invade via Rhion rather than via the Isthmus (so that they might know

3   beforehand and guard against their incursion), the Locrians did not do this but rather the opposite: they raised friendly signals when the Heracleidae were at hand, and so it happened that the Heracleidae made their crossing in safety whilst the Peloponnesians were neglectful and received their enemy into their country all unawares because they had been betrayed by the Locrians.

Timaeus' Criticisms of Callisthenes, Demochares and Agathocles

(12.12b.1–15.12)

<...> to criticize and <...>[147] of those who are divinely pos-
sessed in their histories. But all those who have put much of this
sort of nonsense into their works should be delighted if they do
not escape condemnation for it rather than accuse others of it, as
is the case with Timaeus. For he says that Callisthenes is a flat- 2
terer for writing what he does, and says that he is very far from
being a philosopher, paying attention to ravens and raving women,
and that he received a just punishment at the hands of Alexander
because he had corrupted Alexander's mind to the extent that he
could.[148] He praises Demosthenes and the other orators who flour- 3
ished in that era and says that they were worthy of Greece because
they consistently spoke out against divine honours for Alexander,
while that 'philosopher', who adorned a mortal with the aegis and
thunderbolt, received his just deserts from the 'divinity'.[149]

Timaeus says that Demochares[150] so prostituted the upper parts 13
of his body that he was unworthy to blow the sacrificial flame,
and that in his pursuits he excelled the writings of Botrys and
Philaenis and the other writers of obscenities.[151] This slander and 2
these presentations are not the sort of thing that would be made
by a cultured man nor even by any of those who traffic in their
body in a brothel. Timaeus, so that he may seem reliable in his 3
slander and the rest of his shamefulness, makes false accusations
against Demochares, citing in additional evidence some comic
poet of no repute.[152] What makes me infer that he has lied? First, 4
that Demochares was well born and well brought up, being the
nephew of Demosthenes; second, that he was judged by the Athen- 5
ians worthy not only of the office of general but of the rest of his
honours as well, none of which would have fallen to his lot if he
had had to contend with such shameful charges. So it seems to me, 6
therefore, that Timaeus is accusing not so much Demochares as
the Athenians if they advanced such a man and entrusted him
with their country and their individual lives. But none of this is 7

the case. For the comic poet Archedicus would not have been alone
8 in saying such things about Demochares, but would have been
joined by many of Antipater's friends – given that Demochares
had spoken bluntly and bitingly against not only Antipater but
also his successors and his friends – as would many of Demochares' political opponents, including Demetrius of Phalerum.[153]
9 Against Demetrius Demochares has made no commonplace accusations in his histories, claiming that when leader of his country
he took the kind of pride in his arrangement of the state that a
10 common tax collector would, and that his pride arose from the
fact that food was plentiful and cheap throughout the city, and the
11 necessities of life were abundantly available. Demochares says
also that a mechanical snail spitting out saliva went at the head of
his procession, and in addition donkeys were led throughout the
theatre; and that his country, having yielded to others all the
moral virtues of Greece, was following the orders given by Cassander. And Demochares says that Demetrius felt no shame in
12 doing all this.[154] Yet neither Demetrius nor anyone else has made
any such charge against Demochares as Timaeus has.

14   And so, because I consider the testimony of Demochares' country to be more reliable than Timaeus' bitterness, I am emboldened
2 to assert that Demochares' life was guilty of no such disgrace. Yet
even if there were some such disgrace attaching to Demochares,
what occasion or what action compelled Timaeus to insert this into
3 his history? When sensible people wish to avenge themselves against
their enemies, they do not begin by considering what their adver-
sary deserves to suffer but rather what they consider a fitting action
4 for themselves; in the same way when we are dealing with slanders
we must first consider not what is suitable for our enemies to hear
5 but what is fitting for us to say.[155] With those who reckon everything
by their own passions and ambitions we must suspect everything
6 and distrust everything that is said beyond measure. That is why in
this case we should with all probability reject what Timaeus has
7 said against Demochares. Timaeus could not reasonably be granted
pardon or trust from anyone since he has so clearly, because of his
inherent bitterness, gone beyond what is appropriate.

15   Nor do I approve of his slander against Agathocles, even if he
2 had been the most impious of all men.[156] I am referring to the place

where, at the end of his history, he says that Agathocles in his
early youth was a common prostitute, at the ready for all the most
debauched, a jackdaw and buzzard, forward with his rear for any
who wished. In addition he says that when Agathocles died his   3
wife mourned him and wailed as follows: 'What did I not do to
you? What did you not do to me?'[157] One would not only say again   4
what we said before about his treatment of Demochares, but
would also be amazed at this excess of bitterness. For it is evident   5
from Timaeus' own narrative that Agathocles had great natural
superiority. Given that he came to Syracuse at eighteen, having   6
fled the wheel, the smoke and the clay,[158] and that from such a   7
modest condition he became shortly thereafter master of all Sicily,
and that he encircled the Carthaginians with the greatest dangers,
and at last growing old in power he ended his life with the title of
king – well, now, isn't one forced to say that there was something   8
great and admirable in Agathocles, and that he was endowed with
great gifts and capacity for political life? In regard to these mat-   9
ters, it is necessary that the historian narrate for posterity not
only that which has to do with slander and accusation but also
that which redounds to the man's praise; for this is the proper
function of history.[159] But Timaeus, blinded by his own bitterness,   10
has described for us Agathocles' faults expansively and in a hostile
manner, but has completely omitted his successes, not knowing   11
that in history to <conceal> what has actually been done is no less a
lie <than to> write <about things that never happened>.[160] Whereas   12
we, for Timaeus' sake, have avoided going on beyond measure concerning his hostility, but we have not omitted anything that is
germane to our purpose.

Criticism of Callisthenes' Battle Narrative

(12.17–22)[161]

So that we may not seem to be claiming credence for ourselves at
the expense of such men, we shall mention one battle which happens to be both famous and not far distant in time, and most

2 importantly one at which Callisthenes himself was present. I refer
to the battle in Cilicia between Alexander and Darius, in which
Callisthenes says that Alexander was already making his way
through the narrows and the so-called Cilician Gates while Darius, using the pass through the Gates called Amanid, descended
3 with his forces into Cilicia.[162] Learning from the natives that Alexander was proceeding in the direction of Syria, Darius, he says,
followed, and drawing near to the Cilician Gates, encamped
4 alongside the Pinaios river. The width of this spot was not greater
than fourteen stades[163] from the sea to the foot of the mountain,
5 and the river flowed through it at right angles to the sea and hills.
In the immediate area where it flowed from the mountains, it was
bordered by ravines, and where it flowed through the plain to the
6 sea, there were precipitous hills impossible to climb. This is the
scene he sets, and then says that when Alexander faced about and
was marching against Darius' forces, Darius and his commanders
decided to arrange their entire phalanx in the camp in its original
position and to use the river for protection since it flowed along-
7 side the camp itself. After this, he says, they stationed the cavalry
alongside the sea and the mercenaries next to them along the
length of the river and side by side the slingers stretching all the
way to the mountains.

18   It is difficult to understand how he arranged the men in front of
the phalanx given that the river flowed alongside the camp itself,
2 and moreover given that the number was so great: for Callisthenes
himself says that the cavalry numbered 3,000 as did the mercenaries, and it is easy to determine how much space each of these
3 needed. For a regular engagement, cavalry are arranged eight
deep at the most and between each of the troops there must be a
space in the line equal to the front of a troop in length to allow for
4 ease in wheeling and facing about. It follows then that a stade can
hold 800 cavalry, ten stades 8,000, and four stades 3,200, such
5 that an area of fourteen stades would hold 11,200 cavalry. But if
Darius had drawn up the entirety of his 30,000 cavalry, he would
have had to arrange the cavalry alone at nearly three times their
6 usual depth. And where then would the mercenaries have been
stationed, unless, by God, behind the cavalry? But this is not
what happened, Callisthenes says, since the cavalry engaged the

Macedonians at the beginning of the action. From which one is ⁊
obliged to conclude that the corps of cavalry held the half of the
ground nearest to the sea, the mercenaries the half nearest to the
mountains. From this it is easy to calculate how great the depth of 8
the cavalry was and how far distant the river was from the camp.
After this, Callisthenes says that when the enemy approached, 9
Darius himself, who was commanding the centre, called the mercenaries from the wings to himself. One is at a loss to understand 10
what Callisthenes is saying here. Since the conjunction of the cavalry and mercenaries must of necessity have been in the middle,
such that Darius would have been amongst the mercenaries, then
where, why and how did Darius summon the mercenaries? Finally, 11
Callisthenes says that the cavalry on the right wing charged and
attacked Alexander's cavalry but that the latter received the
charge valiantly, counter-attacked, and the battle was fierce. He 12
has forgotten that there was a river between them, a river he himself has just described.

Similar to this is his treatment of Alexander's forces. He says 19
that Alexander made the crossing into Asia in command of 40,000
infantry and 4,500 cavalry, and that an additional 5,000 infantry 2
and 800 horse came to him from Macedonia when he was about
to invade Cilicia. Now if one should deduct 3,000 infantry and 3
300 horse, making a generous allowance for losses in previous
campaigns, that would still leave 42,000 infantry and 5,000 cavalry. This being the case, Callisthenes says that Alexander learned 4
of Darius' entry into Cilicia when he was 100 stades distant from
him when Darius had already marched through the passes. Alex- 5
ander, therefore, turned around and marched back through the
pass putting the phalanx in front, the cavalry after them and at
the rear the baggage train. As soon as he came to open ground, he 6
altered this deployment and gave the order to all to form the phalanx, and make it thirty-two deep, but afterwards he made it
sixteen deep, and finally as he got nearer the enemy eight deep.
These absurdities are greater than the previous ones. For when 7
the depth of the line is sixteen men, then a stade will hold – when
men are on the march and allowing for six feet between them –
1,600 men, from which it is obvious that ten stades will hold 8
16,000 men, and twenty twice that. From this one can easily see 9

that at the point at which Alexander arrayed his forces sixteen deep, the width of ground needed would of necessity have been twenty stades, and still all of the cavalry and 10,000 of the infantry would have been left over.

20   After this, Callisthenes says that Alexander was leading his forces in line while he was still forty stades away from the enemy.
2 A greater absurdity than this would be hard to find. For where would one find such ground, especially in Cilicia, that one could lead a phalanx – and one wielding the long Macedonian pike at that – in line for forty stades, all the while having twenty stades in
3 width?[164] It would be difficult even to enumerate how many obstacles there were to the employment of such a formation. One of them, mentioned by Callisthenes himself, will serve as sufficient
4 proof: he says that the torrents coming down from the mountains had made so many ravines throughout the plain that the majority of the Persians as they fled were said to have been destroyed in
5 such hollows. But one might object that Alexander wanted to be
6 ready when the enemy appeared. Yet what could be more unprepared than a phalanx that is marching in line yet separated and thrown into confusion? How much easier would it have been to form the line from marching order into battle order than to put a separated and confused force which was marching in line into that same order and prepare it for battle on wooded and broken
7 ground? It would have been much better, therefore, to lead his force in double- or quadruple-phalanx formation where it was possible to find the ground for marching and easy to form the troops up swiftly, given that he would be able to learn long in advance from scouts when the enemy was at hand. But apart from
8 other blunders, Alexander did not even place his cavalry in front while he was leading his forces in line on level ground, but placed them in line with the infantry.

21   But here is his biggest mistake of all: he says that when Alexander was nearing the enemy, he formed his men in position eight
2 deep. In that formation the length of the phalanx would have had
3 to be forty stades. But if they had stood in close order, such that they 'pressed close to each other', as the poet says,[165] even so they
4 would have needed a place twenty stades wide; but Callisthenes
5 himself says that it was less than fourteen stades. <. . .> and some

portion of this alongside the sea, and half on the right;[166] <. . .>
and further that the whole line must have maintained a suitable
distance from the mountains as a way of preventing attacks
against themselves by the enemy who possessed the foothills. We   6
know that against these men Alexander stationed his troops at an
angle. Even here we are leaving out of our calculations the 10,000
infantry more that Alexander's plan required. And so the result   7
from such calculations is that for the length of the phalanx eleven
stades at most are left, according to Callisthenes himself, and in
this space it would have been necessary for the 32,000 men to be
pressed together shield-to-shield and thirty deep. Yet he says that   8
the battle took place with the men arrayed eight deep. One can   9
offer no defence for such errors as these: the physical impossibility
convinces us of this straight away. Whenever writers give the   10
spaces between the men and the total area of the place, as well as
the numbers of men, any falsehood is inexcusable.

It would take too long to tell of all Callisthenes' absurdities, so
I shall mention a very few. He says that when drawing up his line   2
Alexander was eager that he himself should fight opposite to Darius, and that Darius also in the beginning likewise wished to be
opposed to Alexander, but later changed his mind. Yet Callis-   3
thenes omits to say how each of them knew where the other was
stationed in his own line or where Darius went when he changed
his position. And how did a phalanx mount the bank of the river   4
which was precipitous and overgrown with thorns? This too is
illogical. Now, then, we must not attribute such absurdity to   5
Alexander – since everyone agrees with what has been ascertained
about his experience in warfare and his training in it from
childhood – but rather to the historian because he could not, on   6
account of his own inexperience, distinguish in these matters the
possible from the impossible. This, then, is what we have to say   7
about Ephorus and Callisthenes.

Timaeus' Criticisms of Other Writers

(12.23)

Timaeus has made his greatest attack against Ephorus, although
2 Timaeus himself is guilty of two failures, first that he bitterly
attacks others for things of which he himself is guilty, and second
that in offering such assertions in his history and in instilling such
opinions in his audience, he reveals that his own mind has been
3 thoroughly corrupted. But if one admits that Callisthenes 'reasonably' lost his life because he engaged in flattery, what would Timaeus
deserve to suffer?[167] The divinity would more justly take vengeance
4 on him than on Callisthenes. Callisthenes wished to deify Alexander, while Timaeus sought to make Timoleon[168] greater than the
5 most illustrious gods; Callisthenes was dealing with a man who all
6 agree had a soul greater than human in its nature, while Timaeus
dealt with someone who not only had no reputation for doing something great but did not even attempt anything great, and made but
a single move in his life – I mean the one from his home town to
Syracuse – and this can hardly be considered of any consequence in
7 view of the enormity of the known world. But Timaeus believed,
I think, that if Timoleon, who sought fame in Sicily (a saucer, so
to speak) could be made to seem comparable to the most distinguished of heroes, then he himself, who wrote only on Italy and
Sicily, would be deemed worthy of comparison to those who composed treatises on the whole inhabited world and works of universal
8 history.[169] Let this treatment be sufficient, then, for Timaeus'
attacks on Aristotle, Theophrastus and Callisthenes, and further
on Ephorus and Demochares, and likewise for those who are persuaded that he is an author who speaks truth impartially.

Timaeus' Character and Disposition

(12.24–5)

One must not be in doubt about Timaeus' character. He says that 2
poets and prose-writers reveal their own natures in those places
where they give excessively full treatment, saying that Homer thus
reveals himself to be a glutton, as it were, by showing feasting
everywhere in his poetry, and Aristotle, who often describes rich
food in his writings, shows he is a gourmet and a lover of dainties;
similarly, the tyrant Dionysius' nature was revealed in his interest 3
in the ornamentation of couches and his continuous research into
the qualities and embroideries of woven robes.[170] Well then, one 4
must necessarily make a judgement on Timaeus consistent with
his own methods, and be annoyed with him in his conduct, since
he shows great harshness and boldness in his accusations against
others while in his own narrative he is full of dreams, prodigies
and unbelievable mythical material, and, in short, ignoble superstition and a womanish love of the marvellous.[171] Nevertheless, it
is obvious from what I have said and from what has happened
with Timaeus, that many writers sometimes, on account of inexperience and poor judgement, though present, are, as it were, not
present, and do not see what they see.[172]

There was a bronze bull which Phalaris had had constructed at 25
Acragas, into which he threw people and then lit a fire beneath,
and took such vengeance on his subjects that as the bronze became 2
red-hot and the man inside, who was perishing by being slowly
roasted all over, would in his immense agony cry out; and because
of the way in which the bull had been constructed, those listening
heard a sound similar to the lowing of a bull.[173] When the Cartha- 3
ginians were masters of Sicily this bull was brought from Acragas
to Carthage and although the door between the shoulder blades
(which was where the victims were thrown in) is preserved and
although no other reason at all can be discovered why such a bull
would have been constructed at Carthage, nevertheless Timaeus 4
attempts both to demolish the common account and to expose the
remarks of poets and prose-writers as false, claiming that no bull

from Acragas existed at Carthage nor had any such bull existed at
5 Acragas; and he has composed a long discussion on this topic.[174]

What word or phrase must we use when speaking of Timaeus'
disposition?[175] His manner seems to me to deserve all the extremely
6 bitter expressions he employs against others. That he is fond of
quarrels, a liar and reckless has been sufficiently shown from my
words above. But it will be equally evident from what I am about to
7 say that he is uncultured and in general uneducated. In his Book 21
towards the end he says the following in Timoleon's speech of
exhortation: 'the earth lying beneath the heavens being divided into
8 three portions, which are called Asia, Africa and Europe'. Nobody
would believe that even the proverbial Margites would say such a
9 thing, much less Timoleon.[176] For who is so ignorant, and I don't
just mean of those who deal with history . . . [177]

On the Composition of Speeches in History

(12.25a–b)

Just as the proverb says that one drop from the largest vessel is
sufficient for knowing the whole content, in the same way we must
2 judge now concerning the subject at hand. Whenever one or two
falsehoods are discovered in treatises and this is deliberate, then it
3 is clear that nothing said by such authors is reliable or certain. In
order that we may change the minds of those disposed somewhat
more generously towards Timaeus, we must speak about his
method and in particular his method in his addresses to the
people, his exhortations to the soldiers, and further his own
ambassadorial speeches and in general this entire genre, seeing
that speeches are, as it were, the summation of the actions, and
4 they hold together the entire history.[178] Which of his readers would
not know that Timaeus has recorded these in his history contrary
5 to truth, and that he has done this by design? For he has not written what was said nor the true sense of what was said, but instead
offers what he thinks should have been said, and enumerates in all
these speeches the concomitant details[179] like someone at school

trying his hand at a set theme; as if he were making a display of his own ability but not offering an account of what was truly spoken.

What is unique to history is, first, that one must learn the words 25b that were truly spoken, such as they were, and, second, that one must inquire into the reason why what was done or said failed or succeeded, since a bare statement of what happened beguiles us 2 but offers no benefit. When explanation is added, however, the study of history becomes fruitful.[180] For if we transfer similar cir- 3 cumstances to our own times we then have starting points and mental pictures for foreseeing the future, and sometimes in imitating the past we shall behave more cautiously while at other times we shall face what confronts us somewhat more boldly.[181] But the writer who passes over in silence the speeches that were 4 actually given and the causes, and in place of these offers false rhetorical compositions, destroys the peculiar virtue of history. Timaeus especially does this, and we all know that his books are full of this kind of thing.

Criticism and Credibility

(12.25c)

One might wonder, perhaps, how, if Timaeus is such as we have shown him to be, he has been accorded such approbation and reliability by some.[182] The reason for this is that his fault-finding and 2 slander against others is so expansive throughout his own work that he is viewed not from his own work nor his own remarks, but from his accusations of others, a kind of writing at which I think he took great pains and in which he displayed superior talent. In 3 this he was similar to Strato, the writer on nature.[183] Whenever Strato tries to pick apart and prove false the opinions of others, he is marvellous; but whenever he offers something of his own and goes through his own ideas, those who are experts see him revealed as much stupider and duller than he seemed. What happens with 4 writers, I think, is quite similar to what happens in our everyday life: it is in fact easy to find fault with our neighbours but hard to 5 conduct ourselves without fault; and nearly always, one might say, we observe that those who are readiest to find fault with others are those who most often make mistakes in their own lives.

The Experience Necessary for Writing History

(12.25d–28a)

Aside from what has already been written, there is something else about Timaeus. Having resided for nearly fifty years at Athens[184] and having access to the writings of his predecessors, he supposed that this provided him with the greatest qualification for writing 2 history, and in this he was quite ignorant, I think. For history and medicine have something in common: each has three principal divisions, and the dispositions of those who devote themselves to 3 these pursuits are similar to each. Thus medicine has a part concerned with theory, a part with diet, and a part with surgery and drugs.[185] <. . .> entirely <. . .> make false accusations against the 4 practice <. . .> and the theoretical part which chiefly began in Alexandria with the school of Herophilus and Callimachus,[186] in some respect has a controlling hold on medicine, and in their ostentation and in the claims they make, these practitioners give themselves such an air of superiority as to make none of the others 5 seem to have mastery of the subject. Yet when you try to recall these men to reality and entrust a sick person to them, they are found to be as deficient of any real use as those who have never read a medical treatise. Indeed, some who have entrusted themselves to such men because of their power at speaking put their lives in danger, 6 even though there was nothing seriously wrong with them. These theoreticians are in truth like someone who tries to pilot a ship relying on a book. Yet they visit different cities with great fanfare and whenever they gather crowds together, they reduce those doctors who have shown real skill in practice to confusion, singling them out by name, and inducing the contempt of the audience, because the persuasiveness of their speech often vanquishes a 7 judgement based on actual facts. The third branch, the one that is concerned with providing true skill in each professional treatment, is not only found rarely but also is often overshadowed by idle chatter and recklessness because the multitude lack judgement.[187]

In the same way, political history has three parts: the first has   25e
to do with the study of written histories and the comparison of material made from these; the second has to do with the visual examination of cities and places, rivers and harbours, and in general the peculiar characteristics and distances on land and sea; and the third has to do with political activity.[188] Similarly to medi-   2
cine, many aspire to write this kind of history because of the esteem in which it has been held,[189] but the majority of those writing it bring to the task nothing to justify themselves except negligence, boldness and laziness, courting favour like sellers of drugs and always adapting their material to the occasion, with a view towards currying favour and for the sake of earning a living through these. About them we need say no more. Some who seem   4
to be justified in attempting to write history, like the theoretical physicians spending their time in libraries and generally gaining the great experience that comes from books, persuade themselves that they are capable of the task, and to outsiders they seem to have applied themselves sufficiently <although they clearly bring only one> part, I think, to the writing of history. It is useful to   5
study the writings of predecessors so as to know the opinions of the ancients and the notions which they formerly held about some places, peoples, governments and actions, as well as to comprehend the situations and the fortunes which they experienced in earlier times. For past events naturally make us attentive towards   6
the future, if someone has actually made investigations concerning individual events. But it is completely foolish to believe, as   7
Timaeus persuaded himself, that if one relies on this method one can write more recent history well; it is as if one thought oneself a capable painter and a master of the art because one had viewed the paintings of artists of old.

What I am saying will be made still clearer from what follows: 25f
for example, what happens to Ephorus in certain places in his history.[190] In military matters I think Ephorus has some notion about naval matters to a certain extent, but in land battles he is completely inexperienced. Thus when one examines closely his accounts of the   2

naval battles of Cyprus and Cnidus, in which the Persian king's generals fought against Euagoras of Salamis and the Lacedaemonians respectively, one can marvel at the author's descriptive force and his competence, and can take away much useful material for
3 similar situations.[191] But when we look at, or examine in detail, the battle formations and the subsequent changes in the formations in his narration of the battle of the Thebans and Lacedaemonians at Leuctra, or those same combatants' battle at Mantinea when Epaminondas lost his life, Ephorus appears absurd, completely lacking in experience, and he seems never to have seen such things.[192]
4 Now the account of Leuctra, which was a simple battle and engaged only a part of the army, does not reveal the historian's inexperience too much, but his account of Mantinea, while giving the appearance of being complex and technical, is in fact incoherent and
5 completely incomprehensible. This will be evident if one first makes an assessment of the topography and then makes a true measure-
6 ment of the movements he describes. This same thing happens to Theopompus[193] and especially to Timaeus who is our present sub-
7 ject. Where these historians treat such matters summarily, they can get away with it, but where they wish to develop and explicate something of this kind in detail, they wind up looking exactly like Ephorus.[194]

25g   It is not possible for one who has no experience of what happens in war to write well about military actions, nor can one write of matters of state if one has no experience of such events and
2 circumstances.[195] Because nothing can be written with experience or with vividness from books, the account that results is without usefulness for readers: for if one removes from history the part that
3 can benefit us, what remains of it is dreary and useless.[196] What is more, whenever such historians try to write individual works about cities and localities in detail but are not practised in such experience, something similar must necessarily happen, and they pass over many things worthy of account and write at great length about
4 many things that are not worthy.[197] And this happens especially to Timaeus because he has not seen things for himself.

25h   Timaeus says in his Book 34, that having lived away from home for fifty years continuously at Athens, he had, admittedly, no experience of military service nor again of personal inspection of

topography.[198] It follows that when you come to one of these por-   2
tions of his history, he is ignorant of many things and he makes
many false statements. If he ever does touch on the truth, he is similar to those painters who make their sketches from stuffed dummies:
with these the outline is sometimes preserved, but the impression   3
and the vividness of actual living creatures is missing,[199] and it is
this which is the particular function of the art of painting.[200] The
same thing happens to Timaeus and in general to those who begin
from this bookish habit. For the impression made by the events is   4
lacking in their work since this can only come from the personal
experience of the writer. And so those who have not taken part in
public affairs cannot engender genuine enthusiasm in their audience.[201] Here our predecessors thought that histories should have   5
such vividness that when the narrative treated political matters,
the audience would say that the writer must have taken part in
political life and had experience of its circumstances; again, if he
treated wars, that he must have been a soldier and taken part in
battle; and even when it treated private life, that he had had children and lived with a wife.[202] And likewise with the other areas in
life. It is reasonable that one would find this only in those histori-   6
ans who have had experience in public affairs and who have made
this part of history their own. Now it is perhaps difficult to be the
agent and the actor for everything but it is necessary at least for
the most important actions and those that occur most frequently.
Homer furnishes a suitable example for trusting that what I say is   25i
not impossible, since one sees in him much of this sort of vividness.[203] From this everyone would reasonably agree in concluding   2
that detailed work with written sources makes up but a third part
of history and holds third place.

The political speeches, military exhortations and ambassador-   3
ial speeches that one finds in Timaeus would show most clearly
that what I am now saying is true.[204] There are few occasions that   4
provide an opportunity to set out all possible arguments;[205] most
occasions require only brief arguments and only some of those
one thinks of, and of these some are appropriate to contemporaries, others to an earlier generation, some to Aetolians, others to
Peloponnesians and others to Athenians.[206] To go through all pos-   5
sible arguments uselessly and inopportunely on every occasion, as

Timaeus does, inventing ingenious arguments on every subject, seems wholly untruthful, puerile and pedantic; and this is why for
6   many he is guilty of failure and deserving of contempt. Since there is no rule which and how many of the possible arguments the statesman should use on each occasion, we historians need an unusual degree of attention and clarity of principle if we are to
7   benefit and not harm our readers. What the situation demands can hardly be reduced to rules in every case, but it is certainly not impossible to be led to an idea of it from precepts based on personal experience and practice.[207] In the present case, one would
8   best understand what I am saying from the following: if writers indicated the occasions, the aims and the circumstances of those who are deliberating, and then, by setting forth the arguments that were truly spoken, made clear to us the reasons why the speakers failed or succeeded, we would then have a true idea of the matter and we would be able always to be successful in our enterprises, by distinguishing what was successful from what failed, and by transferring the situation to similar circumstances.
9   But identifying causes is, I think, difficult, while phrase-mongering in books in easy; speaking briefly and opportunely and discovering the rules governing this can be attained by only a few, while composing at length and uselessly is within reach of anyone and open to all.[208]

25k   In order to confirm our judgement about Timaeus in this matter also, just as we did for his ignorance, and then for his deliberate writing of falsehoods, we shall bring forward a few of those speeches which are incontestably his, giving the name of the
2   speaker. Of those tyrants who ruled in Sicily after the elder Gelon, history informs us that the most capable rulers were Hermocrates, Timoleon and Pyrrhus of Epirus, and one would least ascribe to
3   these men puerile and pedantic arguments.[209] Yet in his Book 21, Timaeus says that at the moment when Eurymedon arrived in Sicily and was inviting the cities to join the war against Syracuse, the people of Gela, being hard pressed by the war, sent to the people of
4   Camarina to ask for a truce.[210] The latter eagerly agreed and both sides subsequently sent ambassadors to their respective allies, urging them to send reliable men to come to Gela and discuss a cessation of hostilities and what was in the best interests of all.

Once the delegates arrive and the deliberation begins, Timaeus 5
brings on Hermocrates who uses some such arguments as these: he 6
praises the people of Gela and Camarina, first because they themselves made peace, second because they were responsible for
holding a debate about the peace, and third because they had had
the foresight not to entrust such a debate to the multitude but
rather to those who were the foremost men in their states and who
knew well the difference between war and peace. After this he 7
makes two or three practical proposals and then says that if they
give their attention to him, they will learn how great a difference
there is between war and peace – even though he said a little before
this that he was thankful to the people of Gela for holding the debate not among the commons but in a council that knew well such
differences![211] From this Timaeus would seem not only to be defi- 8
cient in political ability but even to fall short of rhetorical school
exercises. For surely all think that it is necessary to offer one's lis- 9
teners proofs for those points that are uncertain or open to doubt,
but it is entirely useless and puerile to invent arguments <for what
is either agreed upon or known>. But Timaeus, quite apart from 10
the complete mistake of constructing the greater portion of the
speech around matters that had absolutely no need of being discussed, has used such arguments as no one could believe spoken by 11
even a common schoolboy, much less by Hermocrates, a man who
fought alongside the Lacedaemonians at the naval battle of Aegospotami and who captured the Athenian forces to a man and their
generals in Sicily.[212]

Timaeus is the one who thinks that, first, the delegates to the 26
congress should be reminded that in war trumpets awaken sleep-
ers in the morning while in peacetime it is roosters. And after 2
this he says that Heracles established the Olympic games and
armistice as an indication of Heracles' own character and that he
harmed all those with whom he fought out of necessity or because
he had been ordered; and he was the cause of evil to no man willingly. Next he says that Homer portrays Zeus as angry with Ares 3
and saying,

> Most hateful to me are you of the gods who hold Olympus,
> For strife is always dear to you, and wars and battles.

4 Similarly he has the most intelligent of the heroes say,

> without brother, without law, without hearth is that man
> who passionately desires horrid civil war,

5 and Euripides agrees with the poet in the lines where he says,

> O peace, deep in riches,
> most beautiful of the blessed gods,
> I am eager for you as you tarry.
> I fear that old age will overtake me
> before I see your graceful season
> and the beautifully danced songs
> and your garland-loving revels.[213]

6 In addition to this he says that war is very like sickness, peace very
like health, for the one heals even the sick while the other destroys
7 even the healthy; in peace the old are buried by the young as nature
8 intended, but in war the opposite holds true, while the greatest
thing is that in war there is no safety even where there are walls,
while in peacetime there is safety even on the frontiers – and much
9 more like this. I wonder what other words or utterances would be
used by a boy newly introduced to school exercises and the study
of history books, and who wished to make up an essay according
to the rules containing everything appropriate to the character of
certain historical figures. For the remarks that Timaeus has Hermocrates make seem to be no different from these.[214]

26a   And again, what of when Timoleon in the same book, encouraging the Greeks to battle when they are almost at the point at
which the actual fighting will begin, and against an enemy far
more numerous than themselves, tells them first to look not at the
2 multitude of the enemy but at their lack of courage? For (he continues) although Africa is inhabited end to end and teems with
men, we nevertheless use the phrase 'emptier than Africa' when
we wish to emphasize something's emptiness, and in this we are
not taking account of actual barrenness but of the inhabitants'
3 lack of courage. In brief, he says, who would fear men who hold
their hands – the very thing that nature has given men as a mark

that distinguishes them from the rest of the animals – idly inside
their tunics their entire lives?[215] Most of all, men who under their   4
tunics wear undergarments so that whenever they are killed in
battle, they may not be exposed to their enemies <. . .>[216]

When Gelon announced to the Greeks that he would send as   26b
assistance 20,000 infantry and 200 decked ships if they would agree
to his commanding either land or naval forces,[217] they say that the
representatives in Corinth gave an extremely effective reply to
Gelon's ambassadors: they said that Gelon should come in assis-   2
tance with his forces but that events would entrust the command to
the bravest of men. This is a reply made not by men who had fled to   3
whatever hope could be offered by Syracuse but of men who had
confidence in themselves and were inciting whoever wished to take
part in a contest for bravery and a crown for valour. But Timaeus   4
on each of the aforementioned things goes on at length[218] and displays great zeal to make Sicily the most magnificent part of all
Greece and more beautiful than all the rest of the inhabited world,
to make her men the most distinguished in wisdom, to make Syracuse's men of affairs the greatest and the most godlike commanders,
such that he leaves no possibility of being surpassed by those boys
employing paradoxical arguments in the schoolroom disputes and
commonplaces when they attempt to praise Thersites or defame
Penelope or some other thing of that sort.[219]

The result of this is that because of his excesses in paradox he   26c
exposes the men and the actions that he wishes us to prefer not to
serious comparison with others but to ridicule, and he very nearly
falls into a practice like those in the Academy who have trained
themselves in extreme readiness of speech.[220] In fact, some of them,   2
wishing to lead their interlocutors into doubt concerning those
things which are manifestly perceptible and those which are not,
employ such paradoxes and pile up such probabilities that one cannot tell whether it is possible for those who are in Athens to smell
eggs that are being cooked in Ephesus;[221] or they doubt whether
somehow, at the very moment they are engaged in dialogue at the
Academy on such subjects, they are not in fact composing their
speeches while awake, but rather are asleep at home. The result is   3
that because of this excess of paradox they have brought the entire
sect into such disrepute that they have come to be distrusted by

4 men, even where there are justifiable doubts. And quite apart from their own thoughtlessness, they have instilled in young men such zeal for this that they give not even passing thought to ethical and political issues, through which those who study philosophy acquire benefit; instead, they waste their lives in the vain pursuit of inventing useless and paradoxical arguments.

26d The same thing has happened in history to Timaeus and his imitators. Being full of paradox and fond of quarrelling on any subject, he has absurdly dazzled the majority of people and has compelled them to pay attention to him through his appearing to speak the truth, and some he has even won over to himself, giving the impression that he will persuade them with demonstrative

2 proof. He has especially made his reputation from his assertions

3 about colonies, foundations of cities and genealogies. In these he creates such an appearance by his use of minute detail and the bitterness of the refutations that he deploys against others, that on these topics all other historians seem to have slept through events and made random statements about the inhabited world, while he alone examined the details and judged traditions rightly in each case. In fact, much that he says on these matters is sound, but

4 much is actually false. Nevertheless, if someone points out to those who have spent more time with his earlier books (which is where his accounts of the aforementioned matters appear) and who have come to place confidence in him whenever he professes an excess of assurance, that Timaeus is himself guilty of the same faults towards which he is so bitter when others commit them (as we have just established him to be in error in the matter of the

5 Locrians and what followed), they become contentious, quarrelsome and intransigent, and for those who have most diligently attended to his histories this is, one might say, the only benefit

6 they get from their reading.[222] Those who give their attention to his public speeches and to his detailed arguments in general become themselves puerile and pedantic and wholly untruthful for the reasons which I just now stated.

27a The political part of his history[223] comprises all his errors, and

2 we have now gone through most of them. But we shall now explain the reason for his error which seems improbable to most people but which will be found to be the truest of the accusations against

Timaeus. He seems on the one hand to have been provided with a   3
capacity for detailed research and a disposition for painstaking
inquiry, and in general to have approached the writing of history
with great industriousness. Yet on the other hand, in some mat-   4
ters no historian of renown appears more inexperienced or more
careless. What follows will make this clear.

Although we possess from nature two instruments, as it were,   27
sight and hearing, with which we inquire about and investigate
everything, and although sight is more truthful not by a little as Heraclitus says (for eyes are more accurate witnesses than ears),[224]
Timaeus took the more pleasurable but the lesser of these roads in   2
inquiry.[225] He shrank entirely from inquiries made though eyewit-   3
ness and exerted himself only for those made through hearing.[226]
And even though this kind of inquiry has two parts, Timaeus eagerly
latched on to the kind done through books, but he carelessly turned
away from that based on oral examination of witnesses, as we have
shown above.[227] It is easy to determine why he made this choice: 4
material from books can be investigated without danger and hardship if one has taken forethought for having either a city with a
multitude of books or a library in the vicinity. All that remains then   5
is to look into what you are examining while reclining, and compare
the errors of previous historians, free of all hardships. Investigation,   6
on the other hand, requires much exertion and expense, but it contributes greatly to, and is the most important part of, history, and   7
this is evident from those who themselves have written history.
Ephorus says that if it were possible for historians to be present at all
the events, this would be the best form of knowledge.[228] Theopom-   8
pus says that he who has been present at the greatest number of
battles is best in war, while he who has had the greatest share of political struggles is most effective in speech, and the same is true for   9
skill in medicine and navigation.[229] Homer has spoken still more   10
emphatically than these others on this aspect. Wishing to show us
what sort of person the man of affairs should be, he puts forward the
example of Odysseus, saying 'Tell me, Muse, of the much-turned
man who wandered greatly'; and right after this:

> He saw the cities of many men and came to know their minds,
> and many were the pains he suffered in his heart at sea;

and again, 'cleaving his way through the wars of men and the grievous waves'.[230]

28   I think that the dignity of history demands such a man. Plato
2   says that human affairs will prosper when either philosophers are
3   kings or kings are philosophers.[231] And I would say that history will prosper when men of affairs set their hand to writing history –
4   and not as they do now, treating it as a pastime, but rather considering it to be the most necessary and fairest of professions, applying themselves unceasingly to the task through their whole
5   lives – or when those who attempt to write history consider the experience that comes from actual events to be necessary for history. Until then, there will be no end of the ignorance of historians.

6   I cannot understand how he has the reputation of being in the front rank of historians since he gave not the slightest thought to these things, but settled down in one place as an exile, and denied himself (almost of set purpose) the active personal experience in military and political affairs that comes from travel and from see-
7   ing things for oneself. It is easy to show that Timaeus is such as I
8   have described him, since he confesses as much. In the preface of his Book 6,[232] he says that some suppose that the genre of epideictic speech[233] requires greater natural ability, effort and preparation than does history, and he adds that these sentiments were known
9   to Ephorus earlier, but Ephorus was unable to refute those who held this view; and so he, Timaeus, would attempt to decide the matter by a comparison of history with epideictic rhetoric, thereby
10   doing the most absurd thing. First, he has made a false charge against Ephorus: for Ephorus who throughout his entire history is admirable in his style, composition and invention of arguments, is at his most forceful in his digressions, his personal reflections and
11   in general in his amplification of the narrative.[234] As it happens, he has treated most charmingly and most persuasively the compari-
12   son between historians and speechwriters. Timaeus, however, lest he seem to repeat what Ephorus said, has, in addition to bringing a false charge against him, condemned everyone else, and Timaeus supposed that no one alive would observe that matters which had been suitably treated by others are dealt with by him at length, obscurely and worse in every particular way.

28a   Wishing nonetheless to extol history, he says first that the

difference between history and epideictic oratory is as great as that
between real buildings or constructions and the theatre decorations that show landscapes and scenes. Second, he says that 2
gathering material for history is a greater task than the entire composition of epideictic speeches. He himself, for example, had 3
undergone such great expense and hardship in gathering records of
the Tyrians and investigating the customs of Ligurians and Celts
and the Iberians as well, that neither he nor those others who
reported these matters would be believed. One would happily ask 4
this historian which matter he supposed required greater expense
and hardship: gathering treatises and making inquiries about the
Ligurians and Celts whilst sitting in town, or trying to be an eyewitness of the greatest number of people and places? Learning 5
about battles, sieges and naval encounters from those who were
present at the dangers, or getting experience of wars and their
attendant circumstances by being present at the actual events?

I do not think that the difference between real buildings and 6
theatre decorations or that between history and epideictic rhetoric
is as great as that between historical works written from one's
own participation or personal experience and those narratives
that are composed from oral report or some written treatise.
Because Timaeus is entirely without experience of this, he natur- 7
ally assumes that for those writing history what is slightest and
easiest of all – I mean comparing written sources and inquiring
from those who know the events in each case – is the biggest and
most difficult thing.[235]

Yet even here, in inquiring about battles, it is necessary that 8
those without experience will make serious errors.[236] For how
could such a person judge well about a battle, siege or naval combat? How could such a person understand those who are giving
detailed reports when he himself has no conception of such things?
The inquirer contributes no less to the narrative than his inform- 9
ants, since the very recollection of the concomitant details guides
the informant from point to point.[237] For this reason the man 10
without experience is not capable of properly judging those who
were present, nor when present himself does he know what is happening, but even if he is present it is manifest that in a certain
sense he is not really present.

Sensationalism in History

(15.34.1–36.10)

I am not unaware of the sensationalism and the elaborate descriptions which some who have written about these events have used to shock their readers, producing a narrative which offers more than is really necessary for an adequate account of the events.[238]
2 Some have ascribed all events to chance, placing before the reader's eyes how fickle fortune is and how difficult to guard against,[239] while others in trying to provide reasons for the unexpected nature of the events, have tried to ascribe reasons and probable
3 causes to what happened. I myself, by contrast, chose not to use this method[240] for the aforementioned events because Agathocles[241] showed neither daring in war nor distinguished ability, nor was his management of affairs successful or worthy of imitation.
4 Nor in the end did he have that shrewdness and distinctive wickedness of the courtier, which Sosibius and many others employed throughout their lives, managing one king after another – in fact, quite the opposite of this happened in Agatho-
5 cles' case. For he obtained his remarkable position because of
6 Philopator's inability to rule, but once having obtained it, and with a favourable opportunity after the death of that king for maintaining his power, he lost simultaneously control of both his affairs and his life because of his own cowardice and laziness, and in a very short time he came to be despised.

35   And so, as I said, one must not give an extended account of such men as these; one should instead speak of Agathocles and Dionysius of Sicily, and certain others who have been renowned in
2 their management of affairs.[242] For Dionysius arose from common and humble origins, while Agathocles, as Timaeus (who is trying to be critical) says, was a potter who left behind the wheel and the
3 mud and the smoke, and came as a young man to Syracuse. First, each in his own era became tyrant of Syracuse, a city which in those days had the greatest reputation and had secured for itself
4 the greatest wealth. Second, both were recognized as kings of all
5 Sicily and controlled even some parts of Italy. And Agathocles

not only attempted to conquer parts of Africa but also died still in
possession of his power. That is why Publius Scipio, the first con-   6
queror of the Carthaginians,[243] when asked which men he thought
were most pragmatic but also showed daring combined with intelligence, said the Sicilians Agathocles and Dionysius. So it is fitting   7
to draw our readers' attention to such men as these, and I suppose
too we can make mention of fortune, and of human affairs, and
generally add some instructive remarks – but not for Agathocles
of Alexandria and his associates.

For these reasons, then, we have omitted an elaborate account   36
of Agathocles, and above all because all shocking changes of for-   2
tune[244] deserve our attention only when they are first presented to
us; but afterwards not only is it the case that seeing and hearing
about them conveys no benefit but also the vivid representation
of such things brings a certain disgust. For since there are two   3
purposes, utility and pleasure,[245] towards which all those who
investigate something (by either hearing or seeing) should direct
themselves – and this is especially appropriate in the case of
history – an overabundance of shocking events contributes to neither. For who would wish to emulate abnormal reversals of   4
fortune? No one takes any consistent pleasure in seeing and hearing about things that are contrary to nature and the general
opinion of mankind. It is true that at first we are interested in   5
hearing and seeing such things once and for all, just so that we
might know that what seemed to be impossible is in fact possible;
but once convinced that it is possible, no one enjoys lingering on   6
things that are contrary to nature, and no one would wish at all to
encounter this same thing again and again. And so what is written   7
should either excite emulation or provide pleasure, and excessive
treatment of an event which does neither of these is more appropriate to tragedy than to history.[246] But perhaps one should pardon   8
those who pay attention neither to natural events nor to those that
generally occur in the world, because they think that the greatest   9
and most marvellous events are those that they themselves have
encountered (since they happened to be present), or events that
they have learned from others, and which hold their attention.
And so they are unaware that they are extending their account   10
more than is appropriate for events that are neither new (since

they have been narrated by others before) nor capable of giving pleasure or benefit.

Criticism of Zeno and Antisthenes

(16.14.1–10 + 16.17.8–18.3 + 16.20.1–9)

Since some writers of individual histories have also treated these events, those of Messenia and the aforementioned sea battles,[247] I
2 wish to say a few things about them. I address these remarks not to all but only to those I think worthy of mention and discussion,
3 and I mean the Rhodians Antisthenes and Zeno.[248] I consider them worthy for quite a number of reasons, namely that they were contemporaries of the events, they were men who took part in political life, and in general they wrote their treatises not for gain but for renown and to accomplish their duty to men in public
4 life.[249] Since they have written about the same events as we have, it is necessary that we not pass them over in silence, lest students follow them rather than us because of their country's renown and the Rhodians' reputation for being most familiar with naval matters.[250]
5   Now then, both of them declare that the naval battle of Lade was not less important than that of Chios, but more violent and more hazardous; and they say that the Rhodians were victorious
6 in the individual engagements and in its general outcome. Now I would agree that historians should give their countries an important role, but in no way must they make statements that are the
7 opposite of what actually happened.[251] Quite enough are those errors made by writers through ignorance, something which is
8 difficult for us as human beings to avoid. But if we deliberately write false accounts either for the sake of our country or our friends or to gain favour, how do we differ from those who write
9 for a living? For just as such writers, measuring everything by profit, write treatises that are unworthy of themselves, so too statesmen who are led by their hatreds or sympathies often end up
10 in the same way as those mentioned above. And so each group

must be careful: readers should be on their guard about it and writers should guard against it.

Polybius then offers a detailed criticism of the accounts of Zeno and Antisthenes concerning the battle of Lade and the events at Messene.

I think that all of these, however, are errors, but errors that one 17 could excuse or pardon. Some occurred through ignorance, while those about the naval battle through affection for one's country. 9 But is there something for which we might reasonably find fault with Zeno? Yes, because he gave greater effort to stylistic elegance than to inquiry of the events and the organization of his material, and it is clear that he often takes pride in this, as have indeed many other renowned historians.[252] Now I admit that one must give some 10 thought and effort to how one should narrate deeds as needed (for it is evident that this makes not a small but a large contribution to history), but in no way should this be the leading or first objective for reasonable men. Far from it. There would be other parts of a 11 history that a man in public life could better take pride in.

The following might make my meaning especially clear. The 18 aforementioned writer, in narrating the siege of Gaza and the bat- 2 tle that took place between Antiochus and Scopa at Panion in Hollow Syria,[253] has clearly made such efforts in his manner of expression that he has left no possibility of exceeding his sensationalism even to those who write display pieces intended to shock the multitude, while for the actual events he has taken so little 3 care that the negligence and careless of this historian could likewise not be exceeded.

Polybius details the errors in Zeno's account of the battle itself, then states:

I think that this narrative and in general these kinds of mis- 20 takes bring shame upon historians. One must especially try to 2 master all the components of history, for that would be best. But if this is not possible, one must give the greatest attention to those parts that are most necessary and most important.[254]

I was led to make these remarks because I see that today, in his- 3 tory as in other arts and professions, what is true and capable of being useful is neglected, while what is ostentatious and done for 4 appearance's sake is praised and emulated. Such work is easier to

5 compose but the approval won is of less value. Now because of the magnitude of his errors caused by his ignorance of the topography
6 of Laconia,[255] I did not hesitate to write to Zeno himself, and I did this not because I think that one should consider another's faults to be one's own virtues,[256] but because we should take thought for and correct the errors of others, to the extent that we can, for the
7 sake of our common benefit. When Zeno received my letter and realized that he could not change his account because his history had already been published, he was very saddened, but he could do nothing. But at least he accepted our behaviour in a friendly
8 spirit. I would likewise call upon contemporaries and posterity to behave in the same way towards me, and if someone discovers that I have deliberately lied in my history and neglected the truth, then
9 criticize me without pity, but if I have erred through ignorance, then pardon me, especially given the magnitude of our history and the comprehensive treatment of events.[257]

The Value of Eyewitness

(20.12.8)

It is not the same to judge events from hearsay and from being an eyewitness, but rather there is a great difference; for the reliability that is based on the evidence of one's eyes contributes greatly in each matter.[258]

Causes, Pretexts, Beginnings

(22.18.6–7)

I assert that it is of the greatest importance for historians and students to know the causes from which individual events arise and grow. Yet these things are confused by the majority of writers because they do not distinguish in what way a pretext differs from
7 a cause and the beginning of a war from its pretext. But since now

these very circumstances remind me, I am compelled to repeat again what I said before.²⁵⁹

On Writers of Individual Histories

(29.12.1–12)

... others in turn concerning the Syrian War.²⁶⁰ The reason for this we have explained before at length.²⁶¹ Whenever they take up 2 topics that are simple and uniform and they wish to be considered historians and to make such an impression not because of the events they narrate but because of the number of books that they write, they must necessarily make small things great, and elaborate and go on at length about things spoken briefly,²⁶² and they 3 must develop incidental deeds and actions by constructing contests and narrating battles in which sometimes ten men (or perhaps a few more) died and even fewer cavalrymen. And one could not 4 express adequately the extent to which they work up sieges and descriptions of topography and such material, all because of a lack of actual events. The situation is the opposite for those who 5 write universal history. And so one should not criticize us for 6 omitting deeds whenever we at times pass over events that were treated at length and elaborately by some, or at other times we narrate them just briefly, but one should trust that we have in each case assigned an account that is fitting. For throughout their 7 whole work those authors, whenever they write about the siege of Phanote or Coronea,²⁶³ and <. . .>, they are compelled to set out all the plans and acts of daring and features of the siege, and in 8 addition <. . .>²⁶⁴ to waste time on the capture of Tarentum, or the siege of Corinth, Sardes, Gaza, Bactra and above all Carthage,²⁶⁵ and to make elaborations of them and they do not at all appreciate it if we simply offer an account of those matters that is itself true and suitable. Our opinion is the same concerning battle narratives, 9 speeches and similarly all the other parts of history. In all these, even 10 in the narratives that follow, we might be justly pardoned, <if>²⁶⁶ we are seen to employ the same arguments, the same arrangement of

11   material or even the same mode of speech, and in addition if I
somehow err in my naming of rivers or mountains or in my description of particular features of places; for the scale of my work makes
12 it appropriate for me to ask this in all these matters, unless of
course we are detected telling falsehoods deliberately or for some
advantage: in that case it would be unsuitable to ask, just as we
have often warned about this aspect in our history.[267]

On Homeric Poetry and History

(34.3.12–4.4 = Strabo 1.17, 25C)

And [Polybius] says that the situation of Meninx[268] agrees with
4   what is said about the Lotus-Eaters. But where the details do not
agree, he says that the reasons can be changes over time, the poet's
ignorance or poetic licence. The last comprises of history, rhetorical
2   elaboration and myth. The aim of history is truth, as in the Catalogue of Ships when the poet gives appropriate descriptions of
places, calling one city 'rocky', another 'at the furthest edge',
3   another 'abounding with doves' and another 'by the sea'.[269] The
aim of rhetorical elaboration is vividness, as when the poet brings
4   on men fighting. Myth's purpose is pleasure and amazement. But
wholesale fabrication by Homer is neither plausible nor characteristic of him.

On Speeches in History

(36.1.1–7)

Some might ask why it is that we have not availed ourselves of a
performance-piece, by offering the individual speeches, now that
2   we have taken up such a subject and so great an action.[270] This is
what the majority of historians do, proffering all the inherent
3   arguments on both sides.[271] Now I have made clear in many parts
of my history that I do not renounce this part of history, having

reported speeches before councils and assemblies as well as the compositions of statesmen. But it will now be manifest that I do 4 not choose to do this under all circumstances, since it is not easy to find a more renowned topic or greater subject matter for comparison. Indeed, nothing could be easier for me to fashion. But I 5 think it's fitting for statesmen not to invent arguments and give 6 detailed explanations for every decision being discussed but rather on every occasion to use those arguments appropriate to the specific occasion; likewise, historians should not practise on their 7 audiences and make a display of their own powers, but should simply make clear what was truly spoken to the extent that they have investigated this, and even of these remarks only the most important and most effective.[272]

On Narrative Arrangement
(38.5.1–6.6)[273]

I am not unaware that some will find fault with my treatise and claim that our narrative of events is incomplete and broken up, seeing that we, for the sake of our account, attempt to treat the 2 siege of Carthage, but then abandon this and interrupt ourselves and change course for Greek affairs and from there Macedonian or Syrian or some other events. They say that students seek con- 3 tinuity and long to hear the conclusion of the subject being treated; and that in this way whoever gives their attention to these matters finds that pleasure and utility coincide. But it seems to me just the 4 opposite, and I would call to witness nature herself, who is not pleased when any of our senses remains on the same things consistently, but is always prone to change, wishing to come back to the same things only after a pause and some contrast.

What I am referring to would be clear first from our sense of 5 hearing, which is not pleased to remain consistently on the same strains, either in music or in the delivery of speeches; rather, it is 6 stirred by a variable manner and in general anything that is broken up and has great and numerous changes. Similarly, one would find 7

that our sense of taste is incapable of repeatedly eating the richest
foods; instead it is repelled by this, and pleased by a change, and
often finds simple dishes more pleasant than rich ones, simply on
8 account of their difference. One would see that this is true also in
the case of sight. It is least able to hold its gaze fixedly on
one thing, but is excited by variety and a change of scenery.
9 And one would see that this happens most of all in the case of the
mind. For here changes of observation and attentiveness are like
rest for hard-working men.

6   That is why, I think, the most renowned of older historians
inserted places of rest in this manner, some using mythical or
descriptive digressions and others factual digressions, shifting the
scene not only when treating places throughout Greece but even
2 when they treated foreign lands.[274] For example, when they narrate events in Thessaly and the deeds of Alexander of Pherae, they
intersperse the activities of the Lacedaemonians in the Peloponnese as well as those of the Thebans, and even affairs in Macedon
and Illyria. Having dwelt on these matters they then speak of Iphicrates' campaign against Egypt and the illegal acts performed by
3 Clearchus in Pontus.[275] From this one would discover that all writers use this kind of arrangement, but whereas they do it in an
4 irregular manner, we do it in an orderly way.[276] For when they
narrate how Bardyllis, the king of the Illyrians, and Cersobleptes,
the king of the Thracians, acquired their kingdoms,[277] they do not
add what followed, nor do they come back to the sequel after an
interval, but treating them as if they were episodes in a poem, they
5 then go back to the subject with which they began. But we have
kept separate all the most renowned lands of the inhabited world
and the events that occurred in them, and we consistently keep to
one and the same method in our arrangement of our division; we
have, furthermore, strictly delineated the parallel events that
6 occurred in each year, and thus we leave to our readers a clear
way of carrying their minds back to the continuous narrative and
the constantly occurring interruptions, so that my audience will
find nothing left incomplete or deficient in the matters I have
mentioned.

The Type of Man Required by History

(39.1.1–12)

Aulus Postumius[278] deserved criticism for the following reasons. He came from a distinguished house and family, but he was in his nature wordy, talkative and an excessive braggart. From his youth he was eager for Greek learning and the Greek language, and he was deeply interested in these, and because of this and his Greek manner, he was offensive to the older and most renowned Romans. In the end he set his hand to writing a poem and a political history; in the preface to the latter he entreated those who encountered his work to grant him pardon if he was not able, as a Roman, to master the Greek language and the Greek way of treating the subject. I think Marcus Porcius Cato[279] answered him appropriately: he said that he was amazed at whatever reason he had for making this request. For if the Amphictyonic council[280] had ordered him to write a history, perhaps it would have been necessary for him to propose this and ask to be excused; but given that he willingly and with no compulsion wrote this history, it was markedly absurd to ask for indulgence if he should make errors in the Greek, as absurd as that of a man who signed up for an athletic contest (boxing, say, or the pankration),[281] and when he entered the stadium where he had to fight, asked for pardon from the spectators if he was unable to endure the effort or the blows.[282] It is evident that such a man would reasonably incur ridicule and immediate punishment, as should such historians, so that they not disregard the proprieties. Likewise in the rest of his life he emulated what is worst about the Greeks, for he loved pleasure and hated work. This will be evident from what actually happened: when he first went into Greece at the time of the battle in Phocis,[283] he feigned illness and made his way to Thebes so as not to take part in the danger. When the battle was over, he was the first to write to the Senate about the victory, giving additional details as if he himself had taken part in the contests.

16

SEMPRONIUS ASELLIO

Sempronius Asellio served as a military tribune in 134 BCE under Scipio Aemilianus at Numantia in Spain, and he seems to have been the first Roman to write contemporary history. His work, in at least fourteen books, began possibly in 146 BCE (the year in which Rome destroyed both Corinth and Carthage) and extended at least as far as 91 BCE. He is explicitly attested as having recorded the events at Numantia. We owe these two quotations from his preface to the second-century-CE writer Aulus Gellius, whose work, *Attic Nights*, comprises a miscellany of various topics and themes. The quotations from Asellio begin properly at 5.18.7, but included here are the preliminary remarks that Gellius himself makes, since they possibly also derive from Asellio and are in any case relevant and important in their own right.[1]

History and Annals

(*FR Hist* 20 FF 1 + 2 = Aulus Gellius, *Attic Nights* 5.18.1–9)

Some think that 'history' differs from 'annals' in that, although each is a narration of things accomplished, the term 'history' is nevertheless only appropriate for those events for which the narra-
2 tor himself participated in their accomplishment.[2] Verrius Flaccus in the fourth book of his *On the Significance of Words* reports that this is the opinion of some. And indeed while he says that he for his part is doubtful about this, nevertheless he thinks there could be some apparent reason for their opinion since *historia* in Greek indicates the investigation of[3] present-day accomplish-
3 ments.[4] But we are usually told that annals are histories in every
4 respect, but that histories are not annals in every respect, just as a
5 human being is by necessity an animal but an animal is not necessarily a human being.
6 Thus they say that 'histories' are either the narration or the description (or whatever term is to be used) of things accomplished, while 'annals' are when accomplishments of many years are written up in succession, maintaining the order of each year.
7 On the other hand, when events are written not by year but day by day, that kind of history in Greek terminology is called *ephēmeris*, and its Latin translation is written in the first book of Sempronius Asellio; from this book we have attached some additional words so that we might simultaneously show what he said the difference was between accomplishments and annals. He says:

8 But the chief difference above all between those who wished to leave behind annals and those who tried to write in detail of the accomplishments of the Romans[5] was this: books written as annals described only what deed was done and in what year it was accomplished,[6] that is, like those who write a diary (which the Greeks call *ephēmeris*). I see that it is not enough for us only to proclaim what the deed was but also to demonstrate with what intention and for what reason things were accomplished.

A little later in this same book Asellio likewise says:[7]   9

> For books written as annals cannot in any way move the more eager
> to defend their country nor the more idle from doing something
> wrong.[8] To write, moreover, in whose consulship a war was begun
> and in whose it ended, and who entered the city in triumph, and to
> recount what was accomplished in the war, but not to declare[9] what
> the Senate decreed meanwhile or what law or what bill was passed,
> nor to recount with what intentions things were done – this is telling
> stories to children, not writing history.[10]

17

CICERO

Marcus Tullius Cicero was born at Arpinum in 100 BCE. He received an excellent education at Rome and Athens, and made his name in Roman politics in 70 by successfully prosecuting Gaius Verres for malfeasance as governor of the province of Sicily, a victory not least notable for the fact that Verres was being defended by Quintus Hortensius, the acknowledged leader of the bar at Rome. Propelled by his oratory and his connections, Cicero made his way through the *cursus honorum*, the rungs of magistracies, reaching each in the first year he was eligible. The capstone came with his election to the consulship in 63 BCE. In that year, a conspiracy of noblemen led by Lucius Sergius Catilina (Catiline, as he is traditionally known in English) attempted to assassinate the consuls and take over the state. Cicero received word of the plot through his sources, but, as part of his measures to defend Rome, he had the conspirators, though Roman citizens, put to death without a trial, ignoring the right of appeal from a capital charge that Roman citizens possessed. The Senate approved his action, but as that was an advisory, not a legislative body, they could offer no support when Cicero's opponents brought before the people in 62 a bill denying fire and water to any who had executed Roman citizens without a trial. Cicero went into exile but was again restored to Rome in the following year. He now found his actions overshadowed by the great military men of the late Republic, especially Marcus Licinius Crassus, Gnaeus Pompeius (Pompey) and (eventually) Julius Caesar. When these three formed an agreement for the mutual advancement of their interests in 60, Cicero was effectively shut out of politics.

Although Cicero never composed a history proper,[1] he was

very much interested in how to write history, and he returns to the subject regularly throughout his vast oeuvre. For many scholars he is the single most important theorist of historiography at Rome. He has a particular interest in the style and structure of history, i.e. its artistic elaboration, and although his comments on historiography often come in dialogues where characters express opposing views, it seems clear that he endorsed the 'grand' style for history and had little time and less appreciation for those who failed to write history using what he considered the appropriate language and figures.[2]

The first passage is a letter, written by Cicero in April 55 BCE, addressed to his friend, Lucius Lucceius. Lucceius unsuccessfully prosecuted Catiline in 64 BCE for crimes committed during the proscriptions of Sulla, and he later tried for the consulship in 60 (jointly canvassing with Julius Caesar), but was here also unsuccessful. He was later a partisan of Pompey's but was pardoned by Caesar in 46 BCE in the aftermath of the battle of Pharsalus, after which we hear nothing more of his life. Preserved are a letter of 45 BCE from him to Cicero encouraging him to return to Rome and public life in the aftermath of the death of his daughter, Tullia, and Cicero's reply (*Letters to Friends* 5.14–15). Of his historical work the following letter is the sole testimonium. From it we can tell that he was writing a history of the Social War between Rome and her allies (91–88 BCE) and intended to continue it down at least to his own time.

Request to Lucceius for an Account of Cicero's Deeds

(Letters to Friends, 5.12)[3]

Marcus Cicero sends greetings to Lucius Lucceius, son of Quintus.

Although I have often tried to discuss these matters with you in person, a certain shame, almost unsophisticated, has prevented me, but now, since I am not in your presence, I shall disclose them to you somewhat more boldly: a letter, of course, won't blush.

I burn with an unbelievable desire (and it is not, in my opinion, one that should be censured) that our name be illuminated and extolled by your writings. And even though you have often indicated to me that you will do this, I would nevertheless like you to forgive this impatience of mine. For although I had been energetically awaiting your kind of writing, it has nevertheless defeated my expectation, and so captured or rather inflamed me that I desire that our achievements be entrusted to your record as soon as possible. And it is not only posterity's remembrance and a kind of hope for immortality that seizes me but also the desire that, while still alive, we may enjoy the weighty authority of your testimony, the token of your goodwill, or the charm of your talent.

Nor was I unaware, when writing this, how weighed down you 2 are with the burden of the events you have undertaken and already begun. But because I saw that you had nearly completed your history of the Italic and Civil Wars, and you had told me that you were embarking on the remaining events,[4] I did not want to let myself down but remind you to think whether you would prefer our deeds to be woven in with those remaining events or do what many Greeks have done, for example, Callisthenes in his *Phocian War*, Timaeus in his *War of Pyrrhus* or Polybius in his *Numantine War*: all these separated out these wars I've mentioned from their continuous histories.[5] You too could likewise detach the domestic conspiracy from external wars with the enemy. As regards our renown, I do not see that it makes much of a difference; but it makes some difference to my impatience if you do not wait until you come to that topic, but immediately grasp the whole subject and period. At the same time, if your entire thought is focused on one theme and on one person, I can already see in my mind how much richer and more embellished everything will be.[6]

Even so, I am not unaware how brazenly I am acting, first in placing such a burden on you (though your current obligations can deny me) and then demanding that you embellish me. What if those events don't seem to you worthy of embellishment? Well even so, once one has crossed over the bounds of modesty, it's fitting that one be well and truly shameless. And so I simply ask you ever more urgently that you embellish these events more forcefully even than you perhaps feel, and, in doing so, that you neglect the laws of history, not spurning that favouritism which you wrote about so charmingly in one of your prefaces – you said you could no more be swayed by it than Hercules by Pleasure in the famous Xenophon passage[7] – if it recommends me to you rather more forcefully; and give in to your affection for me a little bit more than the truth will allow.

If we can induce you to take this on, there will be material (I firmly believe) worthy of your ability and your eloquence. It seems to me that a modest volume could be composed, starting with the beginning of the conspiracy and ending with our return:[8] here you can employ that special knowledge of yours about civic upheavals, whether you are explaining the causes of revolution or the remedies for such troubles, when you censure whatever you consider should be criticized and you set out reasons for approving whatever is pleasing. And if, as is your custom, you think a more outspoken discussion is required, you will make mention of the treachery, the traps, the betrayal of many against us. Our experiences will also offer you great variety in your writing, full of a pleasure which will be able, with you as the author, to hold the minds of men forcefully as they are reading. For nothing is more appropriate for delighting the reader than the changes of circumstances and the vicissitudes of fortune. Even if we did not desire them when we experienced them, they will nonetheless be delightful when we read about them; for the remembrance in safety of past pain gives pleasure.[9] When one has experienced no trouble of one's own but can look at the situations of others without any pain, then even pity itself is delightful.[10] When the famous Epaminondas dies at Mantinea, for example, which of us does not experience pleasure along with a certain pity? He at length orders the javelin to be pulled out from his body only when he has inquired and been told that his shield is safe, so that despite the pain of his wound he would die with praise and with his mind at ease.[11] Whose readerly interest is not aroused and held by the exile and return of Themistocles?[12] The very sequence of annals holds our attention only a little,[13] as if it were the listing of a calendar; but the uncertain and varied experiences of a pre-eminent man often provide wonder, expectation, joy, distress, hope, fear; and if the experiences conclude with a striking ending, the mind is filled with the most delightful pleasure in reading.[14]

And so I will find it even more welcome if you are of the opinion 6 that you could detach from your connected writings, in which you embrace a continuous history of events, this drama, as it were, of our actions and their outcomes: it has various acts and many changes of both plans and circumstances.[15] And when I indicate that I wish to be embellished and extolled by you more than anyone else, I am not afraid of seeming to snare your favour by some piece of flattery. For you are not a person who does not know your own worth, or one who would judge that those who do not admire you are jealous rather than that those who praise you are flatterers; nor, however, am I so mad that I wish to be commemorated in everlasting glory by one who will not also win glory for his own talent in commemorating me.[16] When the famous Alexander 7 wanted to have his image painted by Apelles and sculpted by Lysippus more than any others, it was not as a mark of favour towards them but because he thought that their art would redound to both their glory and his own.[17] And these artists were making images of his body known to those who did not know them; but even if those images did not exist, famous men would in no way be more obscure. Nor is the well-known Spartiate Agesilaus, who did not allow any likeness of himself to be painted or sculpted, to be less talked about than those who have exercised themselves concerning this genre.[18] For that one little book of Xenophon's, with its praises of that king, easily surpassed all those paintings and statues of the rest.

And it would be preferable, both for the joy of my spirit and the dignity of my memory, if I appear in *your* writing rather than anyone else's, not only because your talent will have been at my disposal – just as Timaeus' was for Timoleon or Herodotus' for Themistocles – but also the authority of a man who is himself most renowned and distinguished, known and esteemed in the greatest and most serious matters of state; and so I would have not only publicity, as Alexander, when he was at Sigeum, said Achilles had from Homer, but also the weighty testimony of a distinguished and great man. For I approve of Naevius' Hector who is not only delighted 'to be praised' but also adds, 'by a man who is himself praised'.[19]

8   But if my request to you does not succeed, that is, if something prevents you (since I don't think it's possible not to obtain from you anything I ask), I shall perhaps be forced to do what some often criticize: I shall write about myself, albeit following the example of many eminent men.[20] But (and this will not escape you) there are problems with this type of writing: those who write about themselves must necessarily do so in a more restrained way when praise is required, and they must pass over whatever requires criticism; additional factors too are that the trustworthiness of the account becomes less, and its authority also: many, in a word, find fault with it and say that the heralds at athletic events act with greater restraint: for although they place the crowns on the victors' heads and proclaim their names in a loud voice, nonetheless when they themselves are awarded a crown at the end of the games, they bring in another herald so as not to proclaim themselves victors in 9 their own voice.[21] It's *these* problems that we desire to avoid, and, if you take up our case, we shall avoid them: we ask that you do.

If by chance you are wondering why we are now begging this from you so strongly and at such great length, when you have often indicated to me that you would entrust the intentions and outcomes of our own times most carefully to written form, it is that desire for speed which inflames us, the one I mentioned at the beginning, because we are eager both that others will come to know us from your books while we are still alive and that we ourselves, in our lifetime, may enjoy some small bit of glory.

10   Please write back to me, if it's not troublesome, to tell me what you are going to do in this matter, for if you take on the case, I shall copy out notes about everything;[22] if, however, you put me

off for another time, I shall speak with you in person. You, in the meantime, must not give up: put the finishing touches on what you have begun. And continue your regard for us.

Towards the end of the same year, 55 BCE, with his political fortunes still uncertain, Cicero published his dialogue On the Orator, *in three books. Cicero had written a work,* On Invention *(treating the first part of the standard rhetorical system where the orator chose the arguments that he would use in his case), when he was seventeen but now (1.5) he disavows that work for this much more comprehensive treatment. The dialogue is set in 91 BCE, and the main expounders of the arguments are Marcus Antonius (143–87 BCE) and Lucius Licinius Crassus (140–91), who were considered the two greatest orators of their day and who both guided Cicero's development as a speaker. Over a two-day conversation they examine what oratory is, what attributes and skills are needed to be an excellent orator, and what technical matters must be mastered by the successful orator. We pick up the dialogue on the second day, when Antonius is offering a praise of the power and scope of oratory. Although the actual discussion of historiography does not come until section 51, the earlier part here translated helps to give the context in which Antonius' remarks are to be understood.*

The Need for an Orator to Write History

(On the Orator 2.28–64)[23]

Then all turned their eyes to Antonius and he said, 'Listen, by all 28 means, listen, for you will hear a professional, educated by a teacher and learned in Greek literature, and I shall speak more confidently because Catulus has come as one of the listeners:[24] not only are we accustomed to grant him subtlety and refinement in the Latin language but also the Greeks themselves in their own tongue. But 29 seeing that all this, whatever it is – whether a system or merely a pursuit of speaking – can be nothing without a mouth,[25] I shall teach you, students, something that I myself have not learned, namely, what I think about every branch of speaking.'

30   After everyone laughed at this,[26] he then said, 'Oratory seems to me to be something distinguished for its potential but ordinary in terms of skill; for an art has to do with things that are known,[27] whereas the entire activity of the orator consists in opinions, not knowledge: for we speak in front of the ignorant and speak about things of which we ourselves are ignorant. And so our audience feel and judge the same things one way at one time, another way another time, and we for our part often argue contrary cases, by which I mean not only does Crassus sometimes speak against me and I against Crassus (where it is necessary that one of us must be speaking falsely), but also that each of us defends one thing at one time, another at another concerning the same issue (where more than one cannot be true). I shall speak, therefore, as far as one can about a subject of this kind, which relies on falsehood, which does not often attain to knowledge, and which lays traps for the opinions and often the errors of humans – if, that is, you think there is a reason for you to listen.'

31   Catulus said, 'Truly we *do* think so, and in fact strongly, all the more so because I think you are not going to show off. You did not begin boastfully, but more from the truth as you conceive it rather than from some high valuation of oratory.'

32   Antonius said, 'So then although I have confessed that the genre itself is not a very great art, nevertheless I assert that certain precepts *can* be given which are very shrewd for manipulating people's feelings and gaining their sympathy. If anyone wishes to say that the knowledge of this matter is a great art, I will not take exception; for indeed although many speak on cases in the forum carelessly and with no method, while some do this more skilfully because of practice or habit, there is no doubt that, if one were to attend to the reason why some speak better than others, one would be able to identify it. And so whoever did this over the whole subject would find, if not

33   plainly an art, then something like an art. And how I wish I could explain to you how those things I think I see in the forum and the law courts are acquired! But that will be my concern later.

'Now I put forward an idea of which I am convinced: that although oratory is not an art, nonetheless there is nothing more splendid than a thoroughly accomplished orator. For quite apart from the use of oratory, which exercises sovereignty in every peaceful and free state, delight in the actual ability of speaking is such that men's ears and minds can perceive nothing with greater pleasure. What song can be found that is sweeter than a well- 34 balanced speech? What poem is better composed than an artistic period?[28] What actor in his imitation of real life is more pleasurable than an orator who takes on a real-life case? And what is more subtle than frequent and pointed ideas?[29] What is more admirable than some matter which is illuminated by the brilliance of words? What is richer than a speech that is piled high with every manner of topic? No subject is alien to the orator, provided that it should be spoken elaborately and with dignity. It is his task 35 when giving advice about the most important matters[30] to explicate his ideas with dignity; his is the task of urging on the people when they are faint-hearted and restraining them when they are unbridled.[31] By that same ability of his, men's dishonesty is called to destruction and their probity to safety.[32] Who can more ardently exhort the people to virtue, who can more sharply recall them from mistakes? Who can more bitterly find fault with evil-doers, who can more elaborately praise good men? Who can more forcefully crush passion by his accusations? Who can more mildly alleviate sorrow by his consolations? In what voice other than the 36 orator's can history − witness of the ages, light of truth,[33] life of memory, mistress of life, herald of antiquity − be entrusted to immortality?[34]

'For if there is any other art which professes knowledge of creating or choosing words; or if anyone other than the orator is said to compose a speech and give it variety and brilliance by certain distinctions (so to say) of words and ideas; or if there is any method handed down other than this one alone for arguments or ideas or lastly for division and arrangement, then let us admit either that what this art claims really belongs to some other art or that it shares something in common with some other art. But if that method and 37 teaching resides in this art alone, then it is the property of this art alone, and this is no less so if any who are proficient in other arts have spoken well. But just as an orator is best able to speak about those matters that belong to other arts, provided he has acquainted

himself with them (as Crassus was saying yesterday),[35] so men proficient in other arts can speak about their own subjects more
38 elaborately if they have learned something from this art. For it is not the case that if a particular farmer can write or speak articulately about agricultural matters or even a doctor about diseases (and many doctors have done so)[36] or a painter about painting, then one must think for this reason that eloquence belongs to their particular art. It is because there is great strength in human talents, that many men in all professions and arts, even without instruction, achieve some success in it. But even if what belongs to each can be judged from your observation of what each one teaches, nevertheless there is no more convincing proof than this: all other arts can perform their tasks without eloquence, but the orator cannot be called an orator without it. Whereas the rest, if they are eloquent, have something from him, he cannot obtain a "supply" of speaking from elsewhere if he has not equipped himself with provisions drawn from his own stores.'

39   At this Catulus said, 'Even though your speech should not be impeded at all by an interruption in mid-course, Antonius, nevertheless allow it and forgive me. For "I cannot keep from crying out", as that character in *Trinummus* says.[37] You seemed both to explicate subtly the essence of the orator and to praise it most fully; and it is fitting that an eloquent man should be best at praising eloquence, since he ought to bring to his praise of eloquence that very thing he is praising. But go on; I agree with you that speaking skilfully belongs entirely to you orators, and if anyone employs it in another art, he is using an advantage that he has taken from elsewhere, and is not his own; and one that does not belong to his subject.'

40   Crassus said, 'The night has polished you up, Antonius, and has returned you to us a human being. For in our conversation yesterday you had described the orator to us as "a man of only a single task of some sort, a rower or porter", in the words of Caecilius, a person lacking in culture and unrefined.'[38]

     Then Antonius said, 'Yes, because yesterday I had the notion that I might draw these students away from you if I refuted you. But now, with Catulus and Caesar as our audience,[39] I think I should not so much fight with you as say what I myself feel.

'Since the person we are discussing must be established in the   41
forum and before the eyes of the citizens, it follows that we should
envision what task we are going to give him and with what responsibility we wish him to be entrusted; for Crassus yesterday (when
you, Catulus and Caesar, were not present) in classifying the art
set it down briefly in the same way as many Greeks have done, and
he revealed not indeed what he himself felt but what was said by
them:[40] that there are two sorts of questions with which eloquence
is concerned, one indefinite, the other specific. He seemed to me to   42
say that the indefinite was that in which the question was general,
on the order of "should eloquence be pursued?" or "should offices
be pursued?". The specific, however, is something in which the
questions concern individuals and in a fixed and particular
matter – these are the sorts of things which have to do with public
life and the legal cases and disputes of citizens: I think these are   43
defined as pleading a case or giving advice. The third type, which
was also touched on by Crassus and which was added, I hear, by
the famous Aristotle himself (who more than any other elucidated
these matters), even if it is needed, is less essential all the same.'

'Are you referring to speeches of praise?' said Catulus. 'For I see
that that is considered the third type.'[41]

'Precisely,' said Antonius, 'and in that type I know that I and   44
everyone who was present were forcefully pleased when you
praised your mother, Popilia, who was the first woman, I think, to
be granted this honour in our state.[42] But I don't think that everything we speak of must be reduced to an art and to rules; for one   45
can adorn a speech of praise just as well from the sources from
which precepts are derived for all our ornamentation of speech,
nor do we require those basic principles which no one passes on,
since who is there who does not know what things to praise in a
person? If one bases oneself on those things which Crassus said in
the beginning of that famous speech of his[43] which he delivered
while censor against his colleague – namely, that he could endure
with an untroubled mind being surpassed in those things given to
men by nature or fortune, but could not in those things which
men can acquire by themselves – then the speaker who intends to
praise someone will first understand that he is to enumerate those
goods we acquire from fortune. These are lineage, wealth, family,   46

friends, resources, health, physical beauty, strength, talent, and
the rest of those things that either have to do with the body or
come from outside us; if the person being praised has these things,
the speaker will say that he used them well; if he does not have
them, that he behaved wisely without them; if he lost them, that
he bore their loss with moderation. Next he will say that the person being praised either did or endured everything wisely, proudly,
bravely, justly, grandly, piously, graciously, humanely, or in short
with some virtue. He who wishes to make a speech of praise will
easily see these things and things of this sort; and for a speech of
blame, he will do the opposite.'

47   'Why,' said Catulus, 'do you hesitate to make this a third type
of speech since it is inherent in the nature of things? It should not
be excluded from the group just because it is rather easy.'

'Because,' he said, 'I do not wish to treat everything, however
slight, which falls somehow into the orator's purview, as if it can-
48   not be spoken without its own rules. Often testimony must be
given and sometimes even rather carefully, as I had to do once
against Sextus Titius, a seditious and violent citizen.[44] In giving
that testimony I explained all the policies in my consulship with
which I resisted him as tribune of the plebs on behalf of the state
and I enumerated everything that he had done that I judged contrary to the state's benefit. I was kept there for a long time, listening
to many things and giving many replies. Now surely it is not the
case, when you are giving instructions in eloquence, that you must
hand down some rules on the giving of testimony as if it were a
part of the art?'

'No, of course, there is no need for that,' said Catulus.

49   'What about when, as often happens with men who hold the
highest offices, messages must be explained, either in the Senate
from a commander in the field or from the Senate to some commander or king or people: surely you would not hold that because
one must proceed more carefully in cases of this kind, this branch
of cases must also therefore be enumerated and supplied with its
own precepts?'

'No, indeed, not at all,' said Catulus, 'for a learned man will
not lack the ability, which he will have obtained from other matters and cases, to speak in matters of this sort.'

'It is just the same,' said Antonius, 'with those things that often 50
must be treated skilfully and which I, when I was praising eloquence a little before,[45] said were the province of the orator – they
do not have any place of their own in the division of the parts of
the subject nor a fixed set of rules: I am referring to reprimand,
exhortation, consolation, all things which demand the greatest
adornments of rhetoric and must be treated no less carefully than
matters spoken in court; but the matters themselves do not have
any need of rules taken from the rhetorical art.'

'I wholeheartedly agree,' said Catulus.

'Come now,' said Antonius, 'tell me, what kind of an orator and 51
how great a speaker do you think one should be to write history?[46]

Catulus replied, 'If you mean as the Greeks wrote it, then an
orator of the greatest kind; but if you mean as our own writers
have done it, there is no need for an orator at all; it's enough not
to be a liar.'

'But you must not disparage our writers so,' said Antonius,
'since the Greeks themselves in the beginning also wrote just like
our Cato, Pictor and Piso.[47] History was nothing other than a 52
compilation of annalistic records; it was for the sake of this and
for the preservation of the public record that the Pontifex Maximus, from the beginning of Roman history up to the time when
Publius Mucius was Pontifex Maximus,[48] committed to writing all
the events of individual years, copied them out onto a white board,
and placed the tablet in front of his house, so that the people would
have the ability to learn of events; and these even today are called
the 'Annales Maximi'.[49] Many have followed this kind of writing, 53
and have left behind without any adornment only the records of
dates, persons, places and actions. And so just as the Greeks had
Pherecydes, Hellanicus, Acusilaus[50] and many others of this sort,
so we have Cato, Pictor and Piso, who do not possess the means
by which a speech is to be adorned – for such means have only
recently been introduced here – but think that, so long as one can
understand what they say, the sole virtue of speaking is brevity.
That excellent man Antipater,[51] a friend of Crassus, raised him- 54
self up a little and added a greater tone to history; but the rest
were only narrators, not embellishers, of events.'

'Yes,' said Catulus, 'you are right. But even that Coelius of yours did not himself embroider his history with any variety of colouring nor did he give a finishing polish to his work by the arrangement of words or by a placid and uniform drawn-out style. But as a man neither learned nor especially suited for speaking, he hewed it into shape as best he could; and yet, as you say, he did surpass his predecessors.'

55   'But it's not at all astonishing,' said Antonius, 'if that subject has still not been elucidated in our language; for no one of our people seriously studies eloquence except that he may shine in court trials and in the forum; whereas amongst the Greeks it was the most eloquent men, uninvolved in courtroom affairs, who applied themselves both to other distinguished subjects and especially to writing history: for tradition tells us that even the famous Herodotus, who was the first to adorn the genre, was entirely without experience of the courtroom. And yet his eloquence is such as to delight me, at

56   least to the extent that I understand Greek writings. And after him Thucydides, in my opinion, easily surpassed everyone in his skill at speaking: he is so dense with a mass of material that the number of thoughts nearly keeps pace with the number of words, and further he is so exact and concise with words that you don't know whether the subject matter is illuminated by the language or the words by the ideas.[52] And yet not even of him do we hear that he was one of those who pleaded cases, even though he participated in public life: and he is said to have written those books of his when he was uninvolved in public life and indeed had been exiled, something that customarily happened to every excellent

57   man at Athens.[53] He was followed by Philistus of Syracuse, who, although he was in the most intimate circle of the tyrant Dionysius, spent his free time in writing history and, it seems to me, imitated Thucydides most of all.[54] After this, Ephorus and Theopompus, two men pre-eminent in talent, coming from the most brilliant factory (so to say) of rhetoricians, were influenced by their teacher Isocrates and applied themselves to history: they had

58   nothing at all to do with legal cases.[55] Finally, setting out from philosophy, first Xenophon, a student of Socrates, and then Callisthenes, a pupil of Aristotle's and companion of Alexander, wrote history, the latter indeed almost in the manner of a rhetor.[56] The former, however, employed a somewhat more placid tone,

and one which does not have the impulse of an orator, perhaps less forceful, but is (at least in my opinion) a little more charming. Youngest of all of these was Timaeus,[57] but, to the extent that I can judge, he was far and away the most learned, fullest both in the abundance of material and in the variety of ideas; not unpolished in the arrangement of words, he brought great eloquence to his writing, but no courtroom experience.'

When Antonius had said this, Caesar asked, 'What do you say 59 to this, Catulus? Where are the people who say that Antonius does not know Greek? How many historians he named! How knowledgeably, how appropriately he spoke about each one!'

Catulus said, 'Although I admired it, by God, I am no longer amazed at something which used to amaze me even more, namely, that this man has such ability at speaking although he does not know these things!'[58]

'And yet, Catulus,' said Antonius, 'I am accustomed to read their books and some others, when I have the leisure, not because I'm on the lookout for some practical help at speaking but for the sake of pleasure. Is there anything else? I confess that there is 60 something. For just as, when I walk in the sun, even if for some other reason, it naturally happens that I take on some colour, so, when I read those books rather attentively at Misenum (since it is scarcely permitted me at Rome),[59] I feel that my speech, because of contact with those books, takes on some colour as it were. But so you don't think this has a wider bearing, I understand in Greek books merely what the writers wished to be generally understood. If I ever come upon your philosophers,[60] misled by the titles of 61 their books, which are nearly always about well-known and famous matters such as virtue, justice, honour and pleasure, I understand not one single word; they are so bound up with narrow and elliptical arguments. The poets I don't even attempt to touch, since they speak, as it were, a different language. I entertain myself with those who, as I said, have composed histories or speeches which they themselves have delivered, or those who speak in such a way that they evidently wanted to be friends to those of us who are not very learned.

'But I return to my point. Do you see how great a task history is 62 for the orator? For fluency and variety of speech, it may be the

greatest; but I do not find history anywhere furnished separately
with rules established by the rhetors; for these rules are obvious.
Everyone knows that the first law of history is not to dare to say
anything false and that the second is not to dare to omit anything
that is true; that there be no suspicion of favouritism or animosity
63 in the writing. These foundations are, of course, known by all.

'The superstructure itself, however, is in the content and the
style. The treatment of content requires chronological order and a
description of topographical locations.[61] And since with reference
to deeds that are great and worthy of memory, there is an expectation of first the plans, then the actions, and afterwards the
outcomes,[62] it also requires an indication of what the writer
approved of in the plans; and for the events a statement not only
of what was done or said but also of how, and, when the outcome
is discussed, that all the causes are explained, whether the result
of chance, wisdom or recklessness; and for the men themselves
not only their deeds, but also, for those who are most prominent
in renown and reputation, the way of life and character of each.
64 The treatment of style, however, and the type of speech to be followed is that which is expansive and drawn out, flowing with a
certain regular placidity, without the harshness of the law court
or the barrister's barbed maxims.[63]

'Do you see that the rules for these matters, numerous and
important as they are, are found nowhere in the handbooks of the
rhetoricians?'

On the Laws, *written in the late 50s, is modelled on Plato's* Laws.
The characters are Cicero (Marcus), his brother Quintus and Cic-
ero's friend Titus Pomponius Atticus. The opening scene portrays
the three, before they get down to the business of discussing the
best laws for a state, in a conversation about the relationship
between poetry and history. The starting point for the discussion
is Cicero's poem, the Marius, *written probably in the 50s, which*
treated in epic hexameters the great general of the early first cen-
tury BCE, *Gaius Marius, a 'new man' like Cicero and from the*
same home town, Arpinum. Only a few fragments survive and it
seems that the poem was mainly concerned with Marius' exile
and return to Rome.[64]

History and Poetry

(*On the Laws* 1.1–10)[65]

Atticus. That is the grove and here I recognize the oak of the Arpinates which I have often read about in the *Marius*. If that famous oak tree still exists, this is certainly it, since it is decidedly ancient.

Quintus. It truly does exist, my dear Atticus, and will always exist: for it was sown with inspiration. No farmer could cultivate a plant more long-lasting than can be sown by a poet's verse.

Atticus. How in the world do poets sow, Quintus? And what sort of thing do they sow? You seem to me, in praising your brother, to be canvassing on your own behalf.[66]

Quintus. That may be so, but nevertheless, as long as Latin literature shall have a voice, this place will always have an oak known as 'Marian', and, as Scaevola says of my brother's *Marius*, it 'will grow grey in the countless centuries to come'.[67] But you surely can't think it's the case that your Athens has been able to maintain an everlasting olive tree on its citadel or that the palm that they point out today on Delos is the same 'tall and slender' palm that Homer's Ulysses said he saw there; and many other things in many places survive longer in a written record than they could ever have existed in nature. And so let this be that famous 'acorn-bearing oak' from which there once flew out 'the tawny messenger of Jove, seen in its amazing form'.[68] And when time or age has worn it away, there will still be in these places an oak which they call Marius'.

Atticus. That I don't doubt. But I want to know now not from you but from the poet himself: have your verses planted this oak or did you believe that Marius acted as you have written?

Marcus. I will answer you, of course, but not before you yourself, Atticus, answer me whether Romulus, while walking about in a spot not far from your house after his 'departure', said to Julius Proculus that he had become a god and was called Quirinus, and ordered that a temple be dedicated to himself at that spot; and also whether it is true that at Athens, likewise not far from that ancient house of yours there, the north wind abducted Orithyia: for that's what has been handed down.[69]

4   *Atticus.* What is your point in asking that?

Marcus. No point at all, other than that one should not inquire too diligently into matters that have been handed down in this way.

Atticus. And yet quite a few people want to know whether many things in the *Marius* are invented or true, and they demand the truth from you because you were dealing with a period of recent memory and with a man of Arpinum.

Marcus. And by God I have no desire to be thought a liar! But those 'quite a few people' of yours, my dear Titus, are behaving like novices, demanding truth in this 'trial' as if from a witness not a poet. I don't doubt that these same people think Numa spoke with Egeria and that an eagle placed a crown on Tarquinius.[70]

5   *Quintus.* I understand, brother, that you think different laws are to be observed in history and in poetry.

Marcus. Yes, of course, since in the former <everything> must be judged according to truth while in the latter almost everything must be judged according to pleasure – although both in Herodotus, the father of history, and in Theopompus there are countless tall tales.[71]

Atticus. I now have an opportunity I have consistently wished for and so I won't pass it up.

Marcus. And what may that be, Titus?

Atticus. For a long time now there has been the request, or rather the demand, that you write history. For people think that if you take this in hand, the result could be that in this genre also we will concede nothing to Greece. And so that you know my own feeling, I think you owe this duty not only to the desires of those who are delighted by your literary compositions but also to your country, so that she who was saved by you[72] should likewise be embellished by you.

For history is absent from our literature, as I myself think, and as I have often heard you say. You, however, can certainly give satisfaction in this, since the task, at least so you are accustomed to think, is the one task more than any other suited to an orator.

6   And so undertake this, we beg you, and find time for this matter which up to now has been either overlooked or abandoned by our people. For after the annals of the chief priests (nothing can be

drier than these),[73] when you come to Fabius or to your own favourite Cato, or Piso, Fannius or Vennonius,[74] even though one of them has more force than another, nevertheless what could be thinner than all of them? Antipater,[75] who was of Fannius' era, blew a little more forcefully, and he had certain rustic and uncouth strengths, without elegance and dexterity; but he nevertheless could urge the rest to write more meticulously.

The writers who followed these, Gellius, Claudius and Asellio, were nothing in comparison with Coelius but rather had the feebleness and ignorance of earlier writers. And why should I even 7 mention Macer?[76] His garrulity possesses some cleverness in the use of words, yet it's not drawn from that abundant learning of the Greeks but from their Latin copyists, and in his speeches[77] it shows many absurdities and reaches a peak of shamelessness. Sisenna, his friend, easily surpassed all the writers up to our own day (unless there are any by chance who have not yet published their work and whom we thus cannot judge): he, however, was never considered an orator in your and your colleagues' class, and in his history he consistently goes after childish effects. He seems to have read only Cleitarchus[78] and no other of the Greeks besides, and to wish to imitate only him; and even if he had been able to attain *his* level, he would still have been some distance from the best. And so this task is yours, it is expected of you; unless perhaps Quintus thinks differently.

Quintus. Not I, certainly: indeed we have often discussed it but 8 there is a slight disagreement between us.

Atticus. And what is that?

Quintus. With which era he should begin his narrative. My opinion is that he should start at the very beginning, since accounts of it have been written in such a way that no one even reads them; but he himself demands an account contemporary with his own time, so that it may cover events in which he himself took part.[79]

Atticus. I for my part agree with him: for very great events have taken place in living memory and in our own era. He will, moreover, be able to embellish the praises of Gnaeus Pompey, his dearest friend; he will also run into that memorable year of his own. I would prefer he treat these events rather than from Remus and Romulus (as they say).

Marcus. I understand, Atticus, that there has long been a demand for such a work by me; and I would not refuse it if I were granted any time that was unoccupied and unclaimed. For so great a task cannot be undertaken when one's efforts are already engaged and one's mind is encumbered; there are two preconditions: I must be free from care and business.

9   *Atticus.* What about all those other things you've written, more than any of us? What free time, I ask you, had been yielded to you for those?

Marcus. Some odd moments are encountered which I do not allow to be wasted, with the result that any days I am given in the country are adapted to the number of things I am writing. But history cannot even be begun unless free time has been planned in advance, nor can it be completed in a brief amount of time.[80] I am usually in mental suspense when, having begun something, I transfer to something else. And it's not as easy for me to make the connection with things that have been interrupted as to complete in one go something I've begun.

10   *Atticus.* What you say surely demands some embassy or any respite of that sort from activity, which would offer freedom and free time.

Marcus. I was trusting rather to the exemption granted my age, in spite of the fact that I would not decline to sit in the chair and in the manner of our fathers give counsel to those who asked for legal advice, and discharge the pleasant and honourable function of a not inactive old age. In that way I would have the opportunity to give as much attention as I wished to that work that you desire and to many others that would be more beneficial and greater.

The Brutus *was written in the early months of 46* BCE. *It is a comprehensive survey of the famous orators from Rome's past, all of whom Cicero discusses and evaluates. The characters in the dialogue are Cicero himself, Atticus and Marcus Brutus, a renowned orator in his own right, but better known, of course, as one of the chief assassins of Julius Caesar in* 44 BCE. *The four excerpts below reveal important aspects of Cicero's thoughts on history and historiography. In the first, he points out the liberties taken by orators when speaking of historical events; in the second,*

Cicero notes the false documents which contaminate the writing of accurate and authentic history; the third offers praises of Cato's style in the Origins; *and the fourth praises the simple style of Caesar's* Commentaries, *and offers a useful contrast with the discussion of style in* On the Orator *and* On the Laws.

Liberties of Orators in the Use of History

(*Brutus* 41–4)

(*Cicero is speaking*) 'In the next century Themistocles followed him,[81] and while he is for us Romans very ancient, for the Athenians he is not very old at all. He lived when Greece was already an empire, whereas our state had not long been freed from the domination of kings. For that greatest war of ours against the Volscians, in which Coriolanus took part as an exile, occurred at nearly the same time as the Persian War,[82] and the fortunes of the leading men were similar, in as much as each man, despite being a distinguished citizen, was driven out by the unjust conduct of an ungrateful people and went over to the side of the enemy; and each put an end to the impulses of his passionate anger by death. Now even if things are different in your work,[83] Atticus, do nevertheless grant me to side with this kind of death.' 42

He laughed and said, 'It's your choice, since it is indeed conceded to orators to speak falsely about historical incidents so that they may make a more pointed argument. For just as you now fashioned a story about Coriolanus, so too did Cleitarchus and Stratocles[84] about Themistocles. Whereas Thucydides, a native 43 Athenian and of the highest birth and one who lived only a little after Themistocles,[85] wrote only that the latter died of illness and was buried secretly in Attica, but added that there was a suspicion that he had committed suicide by poisoning, those writers of yours say that he sacrificed a bull, drank its blood from the libation saucer, and from that drink fell dead. This sort of death they could embellish in a rhetorical and tragic manner, but the ordinary death gave them no material for embellishment. So, then,

since it suits you that everything be equal with Themistocles and
Coriolanus, you may have the saucer from me and I'll throw in the
sacrificial victim, so that Coriolanus can manifestly be another
Themistocles.'

44   And I said, 'By all means, then, let it be as you please for Themistocles. And I from now on will approach history more carefully
when you are listening – you whom I can praise as the most scrupulous author of Roman history.'

Funeral Orations and History

(*Brutus* 61–2)

Cethegus was followed in that era by Cato, who was consul nine
years after him.[86] We consider him to be very ancient; he died
when Lucius Marcius and Manius Manilius were consuls, exactly
eighty-six years before I was consul.[87] Truly I don't think the writings of anyone earlier can be put forward for consideration unless
someone takes delight in the actual oration of Appius Claudius
62   about Pyrrhus and perhaps some funeral eulogies.[88] And by god,
those do indeed exist; the families themselves preserved them as
ornaments and reminders, for use whenever one of their clan died,
and to remember the house's distinctions and as illustrations of
their own nobility. And yet the accounts of our history have become
more faulty because of these orations,[89] since written in them are
many things that did not occur: false triumphs, additional consulships, even false clans and adoptions into plebeian families, when
men of lower station were blended into another family of the same
name, just as if I were to say that I was descended from that Manius
Tullius, the patrician who was consul with Servius Sulpicius ten
years after the kings were driven out.[90]

Excellences of Cato

(*Brutus* 65–6)

But who of our orators, at least those alive today, reads Cato?[91] Who is familiar with him at all? And yet good god, what a man! I leave aside the citizen, senator and general, for we are looking here for an orator. Who is weightier when he praises, more bitter when he criticizes, who is more pointed in his maxims, or subtler in exposition and proof?[92] Of the 150 speeches of his which I have found and read, all are replete with an illustrious style and content. Extract from these whatever is worthy of notation and praise: all the virtues of oratory will be found in them. And truly what 66 adornment or flash of eloquence does his *Origins* not have? And yet he has no devotees, just as many centuries earlier was the case with Philistus of Syracuse and Thucydides himself. For both of them, with their crabbed maxims (which in their brevity and excessive subtlety are sometimes not even sufficiently clear), were eclipsed by Theopompus' lofty and elevated style – Demosthenes did the same to Lysias – and so too the high-flown oratory of later writers has, almost like a tall building, obstructed Cato's light.[93]

Caesar's *Commentaries*

(*Brutus* 262)

Then Brutus said, 'His [sc. Caesar's] speeches I commend most strongly indeed. I have read quite a number of them; and also the commentaries[94] which he wrote of his own actions.'

'Yes indeed,' I said, 'they should be commended; for they are stripped, erect and graceful, with all ornament of speech laid aside, as with a garment. But while he wanted others to have available the material from which those who wished to write history could select, he perhaps obliged only those foolish enough to apply their curling irons to that material; sensible men he certainly deterred from writing: for nothing is sweeter in history than unadorned and lucid brevity.'

Later in 46, Cicero wrote another work on oratory, the Orator, *the last of his works on the subject. It takes up some of the themes of his earlier writings, particularly on rhetorical theory, and makes his strongest case against the 'Atticists'.*[95] *These writers claimed to hark back to a pure and simple style and modelled themselves especially on the Greek orator Lysias. Cicero, who desiderated a fuller and more ornate style, was hostile to this approach and ascribed to the Atticists the belief that one should speak in 'a rough and unpolished style, provided only that it is precise and discriminating in thought' (Orator 28). He does not wish to deny Lysias his status as an Atticist but he argues that others, including Aeschines and Demosthenes, are also Attic orators and that their 'ornate, vehement, and eloquent language' should also be considered Attic. The four passages below are valuable for the stylistic judgements they offer on Greek historians as well as Cicero's insistent belief that orators must have as their influences writers who are appropriate for oratory, and that history is not an appropriate genre for the orator to employ.*

Thucydides an Inappropriate Model for the Orator

(Orator 30–32)

But look now, here are some who claim to be 'Thucydideans', a novel and unknown tribe of ignoramuses. Those who claim to follow Lysias at least are following an orator, not one who is impressive and lofty, but nonetheless exact and skilful and who can famously hold his ground in court cases. Thucydides, on the other hand, narrates historical events and wars and battles, with dignity of course and ably, but nothing from him can be applied to what's needed in a court or civic gathering. Those famous speeches of his have so many obscure and hidden expressions that they can scarcely be understood – and this is pretty much the greatest fault

in civic discourse. How perverse would it be for men to continue ₃₁
to eat acorns once grain had been discovered? Could only men's
diet, not their oratory, be improved by the Athenians' gift?[96] What
Greek rhetorician, moreover, ever took anything from Thucydides? 'He is praised by everyone.' I agree, but he is praised as an
expounder of events who is sagacious, serious, dignified; he is not
praised as one who has handled cases in the courts, but as a narrator of wars in history, and so is never numbered among the
orators. Nor would his name still be known if he had not written ₃₂
history, even though he held public office and was a nobleman.
Even so, no one ever imitates the impressiveness of his language
and sentiments; instead, when they've uttered some truncated and
disjointed phrases, which they could just as well have composed
without a teacher, each of them thinks that he's a genuine Thucydides. I've even encountered a man who wished to be like
Xenophon: his style is indeed sweeter than honey, but who could
be farther removed from the clatter of the courtroom?[97]

Epideictic and History

(*Orator* 37–9)

There are numerous categories of speeches and they are different
and cannot all be reduced to one type. I shall not treat here the type
that includes eulogies, histories, the sort of exhortations Isocrates
offers in his *Panegyric* (and which many others called sophists composed), and all the other kinds of compositions, which have nothing
to do with the conflicts of public life, and that whole category which
is called 'epideictic' in Greek, because they are composed, as it
were, to be viewed critically, for the audience's enjoyment.[98]

This is not to say that this type of speech should be ignored,
since it can be the nurse, so to speak, of that orator whom we wish
to fashion and about whom we are striving to say something more
detailed. By that type both the supply of words is nourished and
their arrangement and the rhythm enjoy a certain freer licence.
Indulgence is given to symmetry in sentences; periods clearly cut, ₃₈

well defined and rounded off are permitted; and this is all worked out deliberately, not in any insidious manner but openly and without concealment. The result is that words correspond to words as if measured out and parallel; inconsistencies are often brought together, and contrasting things are compared; and clauses are made to conclude in the same way and with the same sound. In the real world of the courtroom we do such things much more rarely and certainly more covertly. In the *Panathenaicus*, by contrast, Isocrates admits that he sought such effects eagerly, for he had written not for a trial in the courts but for the pleasure of his audi-

39 ence. They say that Thrasymachus of Calchedon and Gorgias of Leontini first treated such matters, and then Theodorus of Byzantium and many others, whom Socrates in the *Phaedrus* calls 'cunning speech-wrights'.[99] They have many pointed expressions, which seem as if they are only just being born, stunted, resembling mere verselets and decked out with excessive ornamentation.

And so Herodotus and Thucydides are even more to be admired, for although they lived in the era of the men I named above, they themselves nevertheless kept a long way off from such niceties or rather from such insipidity. Herodotus flows along without any roughness like a tranquil river, while Thucydides is carried along more vigorously and in his description of wars he even, one might say, sounds the trumpet for the attack.[100] These two were the first, as Theophrastus says, who roused history to dare to speak with greater richness than their predecessors, and with greater adornment.[101]

Sophistic Style and Historical Style

(*Orator* 65–6)

This rhetorical style must also be distinguished from the similar style of the Sophists whom I mentioned above, all of whom wish to pursue the same flowers that the orator brings to bear in his cases. But they are different because although their aim is not to stir the minds of their audience but rather to soothe them, and they wish more to persuade than to delight, they do so more openly and more frequently than we do. They seek out sentiments that are ingenious rather than persuasive, they often wander from the subject, they weave in tall tales, they use far-fetched metaphors, and they arrange them as painters arrange their various colours; they use balanced clauses and antitheses, and they very often end their sentences in a similar way.

History closely resembles this category, for in history the narrative is embellished, and often a region or battle is described; speeches and harangues are often interspersed, but even for these the style is drawn out and flowing, not compact and vehement. The eloquence which we seek must be kept separate from that of the historians no less than from that of the poets. 66

Why the Orator Should Know History

(*Orator* 120)

And when he is acquainted with divine matters, I would not have him be ignorant of human affairs as well: he should grasp civil law, which is needed daily in the courts. What is more disgraceful than taking up the role of defender in legal or civil disputes when you are ignorant of both the statutes and the civil law? He should also be familiar with the sequence of historical events and ancient tradition, of our own community most of all, but also of imperial peoples and renowned kings. The efforts of our own Atticus have lessened the effort needed here, for he has gathered together in one book the history of 700 years, with the dates strictly observed and specified and omitting no famous event.[102] Not to know what happened before you were born is to remain always a child.[103] What is the life of a man if it is not woven into the life of his ancestors by that memory of ancient events? Moreover, the recollection of ancient times and the bringing forth of exemplary models[104] give authority and reliability to a speech together with the greatest pleasure.

18
DIODORUS

Diodorus was born probably *c.* 90 BCE in Agyrion (modern Agira) in Sicily. His history in forty books covered the origins of the world to 60 BCE, though he intended to carry it down to 46. Fifteen of the original books survive, the remainder are fragmentary. He has wide interests and includes much legendary and ethnographical material, especially in the first six books. Diodorus claimed to write 'universal' history by which he meant not the type that Polybius had, but one that treated all eras and many of the lands bordering on the Greco-Roman world. He called his work (uniquely) *Historical Library*, and he has usually been assumed to be a 'scissors-and-paste' historian, copying out whole sections of his predecessors though writing it all in his own style. For this reason the various parts of his history have been deemed only as good as the source he used (where this can be determined or conjectured). More recently, some scholars have argued that Diodorus was not a mindless copyist, but instead creatively adapted his sources and followed themes throughout his history which mirrored his own interests. As will be seen from the passages that follow, he has much to say about the ways in which one should write history, though (not surprisingly in light of scholars' evaluation of his work) the extent to which they are Diodorus' own musings or those of his sources remains contested.[1]

Praise of History and of Universal History; Contributions of History to Human Life

(1.1.1–5.2)

1 It is right that all men give the greatest thanks to those who have laboured at universal histories, because they have endeavoured to benefit our common life by their individual labours. In offering an education without danger in what is beneficial, they furnish their

2 readers with the finest kind of experience.[2] The learning which each man has from his own experience, which is accompanied by many toils and dangers, makes us discern in each case what is useful, and that is why the most experienced of heroes with great misfortunes 'saw the cities of many men and came to know their mind'.[3] But the understanding of others' failures and successes that comes through history offers an education without experi-

3 ence of misfortunes. These historians have further endeavoured to bring all men, who share a kinship with one another even though they are separated in time and place, into one and the same treatise, becoming as it were ministers of divine Providence.[4] For just as that Providence, which brings the arrangement of the visible stars and the natures of men into a common relationship, continuously encircles every era, apportioning to each that which has been assigned by destiny, so those who have composed the events of the entire inhabited world as if it were one city have made their works a single account and common treasure-house of events

4 from the past. For it is a fine thing to be able to use the ignorance of others as examples for the improvement of ourselves, and to have at our disposal for the varied happenings throughout our lives not an analysis of the present but the imitation of previous successes. When decisions need to be made, we all prefer older men to younger men, because of the experience they have gained over time. But we recognize that the experience that comes from history surpasses individual experience in the same measure as history itself is superior by the abundance of events that it embraces. And so one would consider that a knowledge of history is most useful in all life's circumstances.

History gives the young the understanding of the old, whilst for ₅ the old it multiplies the experience they already have; it makes private citizens worthy to command, and it incites commanders to attempt the fairest of deeds through its promise of renown; it also makes soldiers more prepared to undergo dangers for their country because of the praises they will receive after death, and it dissuades wicked men from attempting evil by the fear of eternal condemnation.[5]

In general because history commemorates that which is noble,[6] ₂ some have been inspired to found cities, others to introduce laws which encircle our common life with safety, and many others have endeavoured to investigate the sciences and arts for the benefit of mankind. Since our happiness has been fulfilled by all these things, we must give the first of our praises to history, which is most responsible for this. We must think of history as the guardian ₂ of good men's virtue, witness of evil men's wickedness, benefactor of the common life of mankind.[7] For if it is the case that the myths told about the underworld, despite their fictitious nature, contribute to men's piety and justice, how much more must it be supposed that history, the mother-city as it were of all philosophy, can mould men's characters to noble action?[8] All human beings because of ₃ the weakness of our nature live only for a very short moment of eternity, and are dead for the rest of time. For those who have done nothing worthy of account while they were alive, everything perishes together with their bodies; but those who have won renown for themselves through their virtue have their deeds remembered for eternity, proclaimed by that most divine voice of history. And I ₄ think it is a fine thing for intelligent men to take in exchange for their mortal toils an immortal renown. Heracles, for example, is agreed to have undergone willingly great and continuous labours and dangers all the time that he was amongst men, so that he might obtain immortality from his benefactions to the human race. Amongst other good men some have received honours befitting heroes, some honours equal to the gods, and all have been deemed worthy of the greatest praises: and it is history that has immortalized their achievements.[9] All other remembrances last ₅ only a short time, and are destroyed by all sorts of circumstances; but the power of history, extending over the whole known world, holds time – which destroys everything else – as the guarantor of its eternal transmission to future generations.

6   History also contributes to the power of speech, and one could not easily find anything finer than that. It is this that makes Greeks superior to barbarians, and the educated to the ignorant; and in addition it is only through speech that one man can prevail over the multitude. In general every proposal manifestly corresponds to the power of the speaker who proposes it, and we call good men 'worthy of speech'[10] because they have won the finest reward for

7 their excellence. The art of speaking is divided into several branches: it happens that poetic speech seeks more to please than to benefit,[11] while the composition of laws seeks to punish, not teach; in a similar way all the other types of speaking contribute nothing towards happiness, since they contain harmful things mixed in with beneficial ones, and some even falsify the truth. History alone, in having the deeds harmonize with the words,[12] embraces in its writing all

8 the other benefits. It can be seen urging men towards justice, condemning the wicked, heaping praise on the good,[13] and in a word providing its readers with the greatest experience.

3   And so we, seeing that writers of history receive an approval that is deserved, were impelled to a similar eagerness for this task that they had. When we gave our careful attention to our predecessors, we approved without reservation their intention, but we thought that their works did not attain to the benefit and power

2 that they might have. Although readers benefit from the greatest number and variety of circumstances, the majority of historians have composed self-contained accounts of the wars of only one people or city.[14] A few have attempted to compose accounts of common actions from earliest times to their own day,[15] but some of them did not properly align the dates and the events, others passed over the deeds of the barbarians, still others rejected ancient mythical accounts because of the difficulty of the material,[16] while others had their lives cut short by fate and thus did not complete the task

3 they had set themselves. Of those who did complete their works, none brought his history down to any later time than the era of Macedon: some went as far as Philip's accomplishments, some to Alexander's, and some brought their accounts down to the Diadochs and the Epigoni.[17] Although many great deeds after this

time and up to our own day have been neglected, no historian has attempted to gather them into a single treatise because of the magnitude of the task. Given that the times and the deeds are to be 4 found in many treatises and in different authors, it turns out to be difficult to embrace all the events and difficult to perpetuate their memory.

So then having made careful examination of the arrangements 5 of each of these writers, we have decided to compose a historical treatise that is capable of conveying to our readers the greatest benefit and the least trouble. For if one should, to the best of one's 6 ability, write up the deeds of the whole world which have been handed down to memory from the most ancient times to one's own era, the author would of course need to expend enormous labour on the work, but he would be composing a work of the greatest utility for those who love to read.[18] For it will be possible that each person 7 will readily take what is useful for his own purpose, as if drawing from a great spring.[19] But if people attempt to go through the his- 8 tories of so many writers, they find first of all that it is not easy to procure the books that they need; second, because of the lack of uniformity and the multitude of works, the totality of events becomes absolutely difficult to grasp and difficult to understand; whereas a treatise which contains a connected account of events within the compass of a single work provides a convenient account while offering comprehension of the actions that is complete and easy to follow.[20] One must in general consider that a work of this sort is more useful than all the others to the same degree that the whole is more useful than the part, the connected more useful than the fragmentary, and an exact chronology more useful than an ignorance of the period in which particular events occurred.

Seeing that such a task would be most useful but would also 4 require great labour and time, we have spent thirty years on this work,[21] and we have travelled through Asia and Europe encountering much distress and many dangers, all so that we might be an eyewitness of the greatest and most important places.[22] Many errors in topography have been made not only by ordinary historians but also by some of those who have the reputation of being in the first rank. For this enterprise we have had as our starting point 2 above all our enthusiasm for the task, which allows all men to

complete a task that seems impossible, and next the supply of
3 materials pertaining to our work that are found in Rome: the
greatness of this city, which extends its power to the ends of the
earth, has furnished us (who have long been resident here) with
4 the most numerous and most accessible resources.[23] We originally
came from Agyrion in Sicily, and because of the frequent contact
with the Romans on that island, we acquired understanding of the
Latin language, and we have been able to acquire an accurate
knowledge of all their deeds preserved over many years in their
5 records. We have decided to begin our history from those mythical events recorded by Greeks and barbarians, examining, to the
extent of our ability, what has been recorded by both groups
about ancient times.

*Diodorus now gives the outline of his work and the periods
that it embraces, from mythical times through the foundation of
the Olympic games and up to the beginning of the Celtic War (c.
60 BCE). He then concludes:*

5.2   We have delineated these matters in detail to give our readers
an idea of the whole project, but also to discourage compilers of
books from mutilating the treatises written by others.[24] May we
not be envied for whatever has been well written throughout this
work, and may our errors receive correction from those more cap-
2 able.[25] Having explained the reasons for our choices, we shall now
attempt to fulfil in our work the promises we have made.

On the Inclusion of Myth in History

(4.1.1–4)

I am not unaware that those who have compiled ancient mythical
accounts are in many ways at a disadvantage in their writing.[26]
The antiquity of the events makes them difficult to discover and
this often leaves writers at a loss; nor does the attempt to establish
dates lend itself to any kind of accurate proof, and this makes readers look down on such a history. In addition, the variety and the
multitude of those heroes, demi-gods and the rest whose lineage

we are trying to establish makes the narration of them difficult to comprehend. The most problematic and strangest thing of all is that those writers who have compiled the most ancient deeds and mythical accounts do not agree with one another. That is why 2 those historians of the first rank have kept away from ancient mythical material because of its difficulty, and have attempted instead to compose accounts of more recent events. Ephorus of 3 Cyme, a student of Isocrates, who undertook to write up world events passed over ancient mythical stories and made the beginning of his history the return of the Heracleidae, writing up events from that time onwards.[27] Similarly Callisthenes and Theopompus, who were Ephorus' contemporaries, kept away from ancient myths.[28]

But we hold the opposite opinion to these men, and we have 4 undergone a great deal of effort in our composition of this, and have taken every care over ancient accounts. For the greatest and most numerous deeds have been accomplished by heroes, demigods and many other good men, and on account of the benefits they brought to all alike, later generations have honoured them with sacrifices, some receiving those that are equal to the divine, other those appropriate to heroes. And history has sung of all of them for all time with the appropriate praises.[29]

On Arrangement in History

(5.1.1–4)

Those who compose histories must give special thought to everything in their writings that will be useful, but especially the arrangement of the individual parts of the work.[30] For this contributes not only to the preservation and increase of our property in private life but also offers writers many advantages in their histories. Some who are justly praised for their style and their 2 expertise in the deeds they have composed nonetheless have failed in their attempts at good arrangement, and so while their labours and their care have received approval from readers, the order of

3 what they have composed deservedly receives censure. Timaeus, for example, gave the greatest attention to establishing an exact chronology and cared about the breadth of experience gained from history, but he is rightly faulted for his inopportune and extensive criticisms, and has even been given the nickname 'Fault-finder' by
4 some because of his excessive criticism.[31] Ephorus in his composition of universal history has been successful not only in his style but also in his arrangement. For he made each of his books treat events topic by topic.[32] And because we judged this way of handling material preferable, we too are embracing this principle to the extent possible.

Praise, Criticism and Future Generations

(10.12 = 10.27 Cohen-Skalli)

Composing the lives of men of the past creates difficulty for historians but benefits our common life in no small measure. For by revealing with complete freedom of speech what was done well and what poorly, it exalts good men and diminishes bad ones by assigning the appropriate praises or criticisms that are due to each. Praise is, one might say, a reward for virtue but without cost, whereas criticism is vengeance taken against wickedness but with-
2 out physical punishment. And it is a fine thing for future generations to keep in mind that one will be deemed worthy of a memory that is in keeping with the sort of life that one chose while alive, so that they should be preoccupied not with setting up memorials in stone – which, after all, reside only in one place and are subject to rapid decay – but rather with reason and all the other virtues, which thanks to their renown go everywhere. Time, which destroys all other things, preserves these as immortal: as time itself grows
3 older, it makes these younger. What we have said is evident in the case of these men:[33] for although they lived long ago, they are remembered by all just as if they were alive now.

History's Treatment of the Good and Wicked

(11.38.6)

It is just and beneficial for our common life that through history those in power who have behaved wickedly should be strongly rebuked, while those who have been benefactors should receive immortal remembrance. For in this way it will especially come about that many in future generations will direct their efforts towards the common good.

Deliberate versus Accidental Falsehood

(13.90.6–7)

I was impelled to speak about this rather more at length because Timaeus, who accused writers before him most bitterly and indulged in no leniency towards historians, is here caught in the act of inventing precisely in those matters about which he claimed he was speaking most accurately. It is necessary, I think, that histor- 7 ians be pardoned in errors arising from ignorance because they are human beings after all, and the truth about previous eras is difficult to discover, while those historians who deliberately offer inaccurate accounts must appropriately receive criticism whenever they slip away from the truth because they are flattering someone or are attacking someone too bitterly because of personal animosity.[34]

Arrangement and 'Self-Contained' Events

(16.1.1–2)

In all historical treatises it is fitting that historians treat in their individual books the deeds of cities or kings which are complete in themselves from beginning to end. For in this way especially we

determine that history will be clear and easy to remember for
2 readers.[35] Half-finished events, where the end is not contiguous
with the beginning, impedes the interest of those who love reading, while arrangements which preserve the continuity of the
account up to the end offer a narration of events that is complete.
Whenever nature itself cooperates with historians, then one must
not in any way deviate from this principle.

History's Value in Changing Circumstances

(18.59.4–6)

All marvelled at the fickleness and unexpected nature of fortune,
when they saw that the kings and the Macedonians had condemned
Eumenes and his friends to death just a little before this, but now
had forgotten their own judgement and had not only let him go
without punishment but had in fact handed over to him command
5 of the entire kingdom.[36] And it was reasonable that all those who at
the time beheld the reversals of Eumenes experienced such feelings.
For who could have considered the inconstancy in human life and
not been struck by the way in which fortune flowed back and
forth? What person, experiencing good fortune, would trust in his
6 abundance and have thoughts greater than human weakness? Our
common life, as if steered by some god, moves in a circle throughout time alternately between good and evil. And so it is not
unusual if *one* unforeseen event happens; what is unusual is that
everything which happens is not unexpected. And so one would
fittingly approve of history, since by the irregularity and constantly changing nature of events it corrects both the arrogance of
the fortunate and the despair of the poor.[37]

Speeches in History

(20.1.1–2.2)[38]

One might justifiably find fault with those historians who insert into their histories over-long speeches or employ frequent rhetorical display-pieces. For not only do they break up the continuity of the narrative by their inopportune insertions, but they also impede the desire of those who are eager to know about the deeds.[39] And yet for those who wish to display their rhetorical ability it is possible to compose private addresses to the people, speeches of ambassadors, speeches of praise and blame, and all other such compositions.[40] For if they were to observe the classification of genres and worked out their compositions in each separately, they would reasonably be held in high esteem in both types of composition. But as it is, some writers have made their entire history an appendage of political discourse by going on at length in their rhetorical passages. And one finds offensive not only what is badly written but also that which seems to have achieved its goal in everything else but strayed completely from the topics and occasions of its proper disposition of subject matter. And so some of those who read such histories pass over the speeches even when they seem to have achieved their goal perfectly, while other readers, because of the writer's verbosity and inappropriateness, find their spirits worn out and stop reading altogether. Their experience is not inexplicable since the genre of history is simple, cohesive, completely like a living body: when it is torn apart, it loses its living charm, but when it maintains its necessary connection, it is appropriately preserved; and by the cohesiveness of the entire composition it makes the reading pleasurable and clear.[41]

We do not, however, entirely reject rhetorical speeches or completely cast them out of a historical account. Since history should be embellished with variety, it is necessary in some places to avail oneself of such speeches – and I would not wish to deprive myself of this opportunity – so that whenever a situation demands an ambassadorial speech or an assembly speech or some other kind, the writer who does not boldly go down and join in the contest of

2   words would himself be blameworthy. One could discover many
reasons why rhetoric would often be necessary. Since many have
spoken well and sagaciously, we must not pass over what has been
said that is worthy of memory and possesses a usefulness blended
into the history;[42] and when the topics are great and renowned, we
must not allow our speech to appear inferior to the deeds;[43] and
sometimes, when the end is beyond our expectation, we shall be
compelled to use words appropriate to the topic so that we might
explain something otherwise inexplicable.[44]

Narrating Simultaneous Events

(20.43.7)[45]

And here[46] one might in fact find fault with history, when one
observes that although in life many different actions come to fruition
at the same time, those who write history must necessarily interrupt
their narrative and, contrary to nature, break up the times of events
which happen simultaneously. The result is that while the actual
events contain forceful emotion, the written account, deprived of
similar power, represents what has happened but falls very short of
the way events occurred in real life.

Bias in History

(21.17.1–4 = 21.30 + 31 Goukowsky)[47]

This historian [sc. Timaeus], who refutes the errors of his predecessors with the greatest bitterness, gave the greatest attention to
truth in all the rest of his history, but when treating the actions of
Agathocles, often made false accusations against the tyrant
because of his personal hatred towards him.[48] For in as much as he
had been exiled from Sicily by Agathocles, and could take no vengeance while the tyrant was alive, he defamed him after his death
2   for all time by means of his history. The historian generally adds

to the actual misdeeds of the king many others of his own invention, and he takes away his successes and transfers his failures – not only those that were the result of Agathocles' own agency but also others which should be ascribed to fortune – to one who was not in any way at fault.[49] And although it is agreed that Agathocles had the good sense of one who was skilled in command and was accomplished and bold in his daring in the midst of dangers, Timaeus in his history never ceases calling him unmanly and cowardly. And yet who is unaware that of the rulers of that time no one began with lesser resources and acquired so great a kingdom? Because of his poverty and the obscurity of his lineage, he was a craftsman in his youth, but that later, because of his own virtue, not only did he become master of nearly all Sicily but he also conquered in arms much of Italy and Africa.[50] One would be amazed at the carelessness of Timaeus, who throughout his whole work heaps praise upon the bravery of the Syracusans, but says that when they were conquered by Agathocles they exceeded all mankind in cowardice. From such contradictions it is clear that the historian abandoned the love of truth which is a part of history's free speech because of his private hatred and quarrelsomeness. It is for this reason that one could not rightly accept the last five books of his history in which he treated the deeds of Agathocles.

Callias of Syracuse properly and fittingly is deserving of criticism.[51] For when he was supported by Agathocles and given great gifts by him, he offered him history, the prophetess of truth, in exchange and never ceased heaping praise unjustly upon his paymaster. For although Agathocles did much that was impious towards the gods and lawless towards men, the historian says that he was much superior to the rest in piety and humanity. And just as Agathocles stole the property of the citizens and unjustly gave as a present to the historian things that were not his to give, so this amazing historian throughout his history gave his ruler all good qualities. It would be easy, I think, for the historian, in exchange for those favours, not to allow his praises to fall short of the bribery coming from the royal family.[52]

19

SALLUST

C. Sallustius Crispus was born in 86 BCE. His family came from the Sabine town of Amiternum, and he was a senator from at least 55 or 54 BCE, taking part in a fair share of the dangerous and violent events of the late Roman Republic. From about 50 BCE or so he was a partisan of Julius Caesar's. Expelled from the Senate in 50 (probably because of his alliance with Caesar) he returned in 48, and in 46 he served in Caesar's African campaign, after which he was rewarded with the governorship of Africa. He was charged in 45 with extortion while governor but was prevented from standing trial by Caesar's intervention. With Caesar's death in 44, however, opportunities for Sallust's continued advancement disappeared, and he retired from public life. Three historical works by him are known: the *Conspiracy of Catiline* (the earliest), the *War with Jugurtha* and the *Histories*. Although the first two take the form of monographs on individual topics, the *Histories* followed in the tradition of continuous histories (see Intro. §2), and began with events in 78 BCE. It comprised five books but we do not know where Sallust intended to stop (the latest datable event is 67 BCE), and it survives today only in fragments. He had a significant influence on later Roman historiography. The passages that follow are taken from the prefaces of each of the three works.[1]

How the Historian Came to Write History

(*Conspiracy of Catiline* 3.1–4.5)

It is a fine thing to serve your country well by deeds, and even to serve it by speech is by no means inappropriate: one can become famous in peace or in war. Both those who have done deeds as well as those who have written of the deeds of others are praised

2 in great numbers. But even though it is hardly the case that an equal glory follows the writer and the doer of deeds, nonetheless it seems to me at least an especially difficult task to write history: first, because the deeds must be matched with words;[2] second, because many people will think that what you criticize as wrong is said because of malice and jealousy, and when you make mention of the great virtue and glory of good men, each person will accept calmly those things he thinks would be easy for himself to do, but anything beyond that he will consider false, as if invented.[3]

3 As a young man, I at the beginning, like very many, was carried by eagerness towards public affairs, but many things were opposed to me there.[4] For in place of modesty, in place of restraint, in place

4 of virtue, there flourished recklessness, bribery, greed. And although my spirit, unfamiliar with evil practices, spurned such things, nonetheless among such vices my frail youth was led astray

5 and held by ambition. And although I dissented from the evil behaviour of the others, still the desire for distinction troubled me

4 with the same reputation and jealousy as the rest. And so when my spirit had settled down after many afflictions and dangers, and I had decided that I would live the rest of my life far from the public sphere, it was not my plan to waste my valuable free time in inactivity and laziness, nor was I going to lead my life occupied with agriculture or hunting or concerned with the duties of slaves.[5]

2 Rather, I would return to that undertaking and pursuit from which evil ambition had kept me back. I decided to compose a detailed account of the deeds of the Roman people, selectively, about whatever things I thought were worthy of memory,[6] the more so because my mind was free from expectation, fear and the political factions of the state.[7]

And so I shall set forth briefly an account of the conspiracy 3
of Catiline as truthfully as I can; for I think that that event was 4
especially memorable because of the novelty of the crime and
danger.[8]

History's Ability to Inspire

(*The War with Jugurtha* 4.1–9)

But amongst other tasks which employ the mind, the recording of
2 past deeds is especially of great use. Since many have spoken of its
value, I think I can omit this, and also so that no one thinks that
I, through lack of moderation, am extolling my pursuit by prais-
3 ing it.⁹ I do believe, moreover, that because I have decided to live
my life away from political activity, some will give the name of
idleness to this labour of mine, a labour so great and so useful:
certainly that will be the case for those whose notion of great
industriousness is to court the common people and seek their
4 favour with dinner parties.¹⁰ But if they will reflect what sort of
men were unable to achieve magistracies at the time when I
attained them, and then afterwards the kinds of men who came
into the Senate, then they will certainly judge both that I changed
my mind from good motives rather than from a lack of spirit, and
that greater benefit will come to the state from my free time than
from the activities of others.

5 I have often heard that Quintus Maximus, Publius Scipio¹¹ and
also other distinguished men of our state used to say that when
they gazed upon the images of their ancestors,¹² their spirit was
6 most violently kindled towards virtue. They did not mean, of
course, that the wax or the figure had such power in itself, but
rather that by the memory of great deeds that flame grew in the
breasts of exceptional men and would not die down until their
own virtue had equalled the fame and renown of their predeces-
7 sors.¹³ Today, on the other hand, with our morals, is there anyone
who does not compete with his elders in wealth and extravagance,
rather than in honesty and hard work? Even new men,¹⁴ who previously were accustomed to surpass the nobility through virtue, now
strive for commands and offices with secret arrangements and ban-
8 ditry rather than through good practices – as if praetorships,
consulships and all other things of that sort were distinguished
and ennobling in themselves, rather than depending on the virtue
9 of those who hold the office. But I have gone on rather more freely

and at rather greater length in giving vent to my revulsion and weariness with current morals. I now turn to my subject.

Profession of Impartiality

(*Histories* 1.6)

Nor has my being on the opposing side in the civil wars dislodged me from the truth.[15]

20

STRABO

Strabo of Amaseia (modern Amasya in Turkey, just south of the Black Sea) was born *c.* 64 BCE, and is today best known for his massive *Geography* in seventeen books, but he also wrote a history (or historical 'memoranda', since he calls them *hypomnēmata*) in forty-seven books, which continued that of Polybius; only fragments remain. The passages below, all from the *Geography*, offer some important methodological remarks about history.[1]

History's Audience and its Subject Matter

(*Geography* 1.1.22–3, C13–14)

In short, this work [sc. the *Geography*] is meant to be both for the man in public life and useful to the common people, just as was my history.[2] We said there that by 'man in public life' we meant not one who was entirely uneducated but one who had a share in the usual curriculum studied by free men and philosophers. One who cared nothing for virtue or thought and compositions directed towards such things would not be able to criticize well or praise well, or judge what things from the past are worthy of memory. And so, when we had composed our *Historical Treatise* to be useful (as we supposed) for moral and political philosophy, we decided to set beside it the present treatise. For it is similar in form and directed towards the same men, and especially those in power. And just as in that earlier work, only that which concerned distinguished men and lives was remembered, while the trivial and the insignificant were omitted, so too here we must leave aside what is small and obscure, and spend time instead with what is renowned and great, or which has practical use, or is easily remembered, or affords pleasure.[3] For just as in colossal works of art we do not seek accuracy in every detail, but pay attention more to the work in general and whether the whole is well done, so too one must judge this work. For this is a kind of colossal work and deals with big things and the way they are, and with entireties, except when some small thing can stir a man in public life or someone who loves knowledge.[4]

23

C14

Early Historians and their Prose Style

(*Geography*, 1.2.6, C18)

One might say that prose – I mean artistic prose – is an imitation of poetic speech. For poetic elaboration came onto the scene at the very beginning and was esteemed. Then Cadmus, Pherecydes and Hecataeus composed their works in imitation of poetry, abandoning the metre, but keeping all the other poetic elements. Those who came after them continually removed one or another of these elements, and brought it to its present form, just as one might say that comedy took its form from tragedy but then stepped down from tragedy's loftiness and came to its present so-called conversational form.[5]

Writers of Myth in History

(*Geography*, 1.2.35, C43)

There are some who move Ethiopia to what we know as Phoenicia, and they say that Andromeda's adventures occurred in Iope.[6] But surely these things are said not in ignorance of the actual place but rather because they are told in the form of myth.[7] This is true also for the material that Apollodorus[8] cites from Hesiod and the rest, not knowing in what way he is comparing these things with those of Homer. For he compares what Homer says about the Black Sea and Egypt, and charges him with ignorance because he wanted to relate the actual situation but did not do so, and instead because of ignorance stated as the actual situation what was not the actual situation. Yet one would not charge Hesiod with ignorance when he speaks of 'half-dog men' or 'long-headed men' or 'pygmies', nor should one charge Homer when he tells such mythical stories (one of which is in fact about the pygmies) nor Alcman, when he speaks of 'web-footed men', nor Aeschylus when he talks of 'Dog-headed men', 'men with eyes in their chests' or 'one-eyed men',[9] since in any case we do not give much attention even to writers who compose in the form of history, and even when they do not explicitly state that they are writing myths. One can see at once that they are deliberately weaving myths into their history, not because of ignorance of reality but because they wish to fashion impossibilities for the sake of spouting marvels and giving pleasure. They appear, however, to be acting in ignorance, because they can then recount such mythic material about what is unfamiliar and unknown in an especially persuasive way. And Theopompus recognizes this, when he says[10] that he will also tell myths in his history – and by explicitly saying so, he behaves better than Herodotus, Ctesias, Hellanicus and the writers on India.[11]

Falsifications by Alexander's Historians

(*Geography* 11.5.5, C505–6 + 11.6.2–4, C507–8)[12]

Those things that are commonly said about his [Alexander's] renown are not agreed upon by all, and the fabricators were those who took care to flatter rather than speak the truth.[13] For example, they moved the Caucasus from the mountains that lie above Colchis and the Euxine Sea to the Indian mountains and the eastern sea that lies near those mountains. The Greeks call these the Caucasus mountains and they are more than 30,000 stades from India.[14] It was here that they told the myth of Prometheus and his chain, because these were the furthermost eastern regions known to the men of that time.[15] But the expedition of Dionysus and Heracles to India seems like a later mythical account,[16] since Heracles was said to have freed Prometheus a thousand years later. And it was more glorious that Alexander conquered Asia as far as the Indian mountains than that he went only to the inlet of the Euxine and the Caucasus. But the reputation and name of the mountain, and the belief that Jason and his men had completed their extremely long expedition all the way to the area of the Caucasus, and the story handed down that Prometheus was bound at the ends of the C506 earth in the Caucasus <. . .>[17] they supposed that they would in some way gratify the king by transferring the name of the mountains to India . . .

6.2   But they have written nothing accurate as regards the truth of these matters, and the ancient history of the Persians, Medes and Syrians is not of great trustworthiness because of the naïveté of 3 historians and their love of myths. For when these historians saw that those who wrote myths openly won renown, they thought that they too would offer a treatise that gave pleasure if they narrated in the form of history things which they had never seen or heard (or at least not from those who knew), and they cared only that their work was pleasurable and astonishing to their listeners. One would more easily trust Homer and Hesiod when they give heroic genealogies, or the tragic poets, than Ctesias, Herodotus, Hel- C508 lanicus, and others like them.[18]

Nor would it be very easy to trust the many historians who have 4 written on Alexander. These behave negligently because of Alexander's reputation and because his campaigns occurred at the ends of Asia, far from us. And what is far off is difficult to refute. The Roman empire and the Parthian empire have revealed something more than was previously handed down by tradition. For historians who write of the lands and peoples where events occurred now speak more credibly than their predecessors, and that is because they have examined things more closely.

DIONYSIUS OF HALICARNASSUS

Like Herodotus, Dionysius hailed from Halicarnassus (modern Bodrum) in Asia Minor (the western coast of modern-day Turkey). What little we know of his life comes from his own writings, and he tells us that he came to Rome when Augustus had put an end to civil disturbances, in the middle of the 187th Olympiad (*Rom. Ant.* 1.7.2), thus about the year 30 or 29 BCE. From internal indications in his writings, he appears to have been born in the late 60s or early 50s. He was most likely a teacher of rhetoric in Rome, and his remarks suggest that he knew many of the leading literary lights of his day, both Greek and Roman. We do not know the date of his death, although it will have been at some time after 7 BCE, the date at which his history of Rome appeared (*Rom. Ant.* 1.3.4).

With Dionysius of Halicarnassus we are in the unique position of having an author of both critical essays on literature and an actual history treating the early years of Rome. In the former, Dionysius covers a variety of topics including arrangement and imitation. There are several essays on the Attic orators, including Lysias and Demosthenes, and (most relevant for our purposes) a long treatment of Thucydides and his history. Dionysius is a perceptive critic, even if not all his judgements will win approval. In particular his discussion of aesthetics and aesthetic responses to literature is one of the most sophisticated to have come from the ancient world. In language, Dionysius was a strong proponent of what is called the Attic style; though the term might mean different things to different writers, it most usually refers to the language used by the great fifth- and fourth-century prose writers. Dionysius rejected utterly Hellenistic rhetoric and composition, which he saw as beginning at the death of Alexander the Great in 323 BCE

and lasting up to his own times. He saw such rhetoric as both politic-
ally and aesthetically inferior, and he believed that just as Rome had
ushered in a new era of peace and stability, so too Greek literature,
thanks to Rome, could now flourish by observing an appreciation
and imitation of the great writers of the classical era.[1]

The *On Thucydides* is sometimes held to be an excellent
example of Dionysius' strengths and weaknesses as a critic. Dionysius gives great effort to trying to place Thucydides in his
historical milieu, showing where he comes in the development of
Greek historiography and what was original and exceptional in
his approach. He praises Thucydides' commitment to truth, the
efforts he made in composing his history and his impartiality. He
finds fault, however, with Thucydides' division and arrangement,
which he deems to be unacceptable: Thucydides begins in the
wrong place, has inappropriate digressions and breaks up events
of each year instead of telling individual incidents from their beginning to end in one place. As to his style, Dionysius offers criticism of
Thucydides' strained language and syntax where he sees him often
striving for effects but writing obscurely and in a manner unnecessarily difficult to understand. He praises some speeches as beyond
imitation and condemns others as inappropriate and obscure. Last
but not least, he argues that Thucydides' later influence was important, especially on the great orator Demosthenes.[2]

Following the *On Thucydides* are excerpts from Dionysius'
Letter to Pompeius Geminus, in which he offers a comparison of
Herodotus and Thucydides along with capsule summaries of
some of their fourth-century followers. The comparisons have
been criticized as somewhat mechanical, and many scholars find
it difficult to accept Dionysius' final decision that Herodotus is a
greater historian than Thucydides.[3]

The final excerpts, from the *Roman Antiquities*, contain two of
Dionysius' prefaces in which he explains his reasons for and aims
in writing history. His history of early Rome, beginning with the
city's foundation in 753 and concluding in the year 264 (where
Polybius' history began), originally comprised twenty books, of
which 1–10 survive in whole, 11 in large part, and the rest in fragments. The work was written, he says, in thanks for the benefits
he had received from the city, and his purpose was to refute the

hostile treatments of Rome by her detractors, and to argue that from its very beginnings Rome was a Greek city and its inhabitants performed great deeds and displayed nobility of character. For a long time modern scholars saw the work as little more than rhetorical history, containing elaborated and frequently fictive episodes punctuated by long and (at least to moderns) wearying speeches; more recent approaches have been more sympathetic to what Dionysius was trying to accomplish, taking seriously his claim that the work is meant both for those engaged in philosophical reflection and political activity, and seeing, even in the speeches, a recognition of the important role played in the state by persuasion of one's fellow citizens.[4]

On Thucydides

In my treatise *On Imitation*,[5] which I published previously, my dear Q. Aelius Tubero,[6] I went through those poets and prose writers whom I considered to be the most distinguished, and I revealed briefly what good qualities in terms both of subject matter and of style each of them contributes, and I noted where each writer's failings are especially pronounced, either because his plan did not envisage everything with the most exact reckoning or

2 because his talent was not successful in all parts of the work. I did this so that those who seek to write and speak well might have noble and proven standards, starting from which they could compose their exercises on individual topics, not by imitating everything they find in these men but by following their good

3 qualities and guarding themselves against their faults.[7] When I treated prose writers I revealed my opinions about Thucydides, treating him briefly and summarily, not because of disdain or laziness or for want of arguments that could strengthen my assertions, but because I was aiming at an appropriate scale for my topic, as in fact I had done with the rest of those authors. For it was not possible to give a detailed and thorough exposition for each of these men since I had chosen to compose my treatise as concisely as I

4 could. But when you wished me to compose an individual treatise on Thucydides which would comprehend everything that requires discussion, I promised to postpone the treatise on Demosthenes[8] on which I was working, and do as you requested. Having fulfilled my promise, I present the work here.

2 Since I am about to engage in a detailed analysis, I wish to preface this with a few remarks about myself and this kind of treatise, and this is not for you, by God, nor those like you who judge matters from the highest standard and consider nothing more estimable than truth, but for those others who love greatly to find fault either because of their envy of the writers of old or from their disdain for those of their own time, or for both of these reasons,

2 since both are feelings common to human nature. I suspect that some of the readers of my treatise will find fault with us because we dare to declare that Thucydides, the greatest of all historians,

makes errors sometimes in his choice of subject matter and some-times shows weakness in his powers of expression. For this reason it has occurred to me that we shall be thought the first and only one to come up with new and unexpected arguments if we should attempt to criticize some of the things written by Thucydides, and in doing so we should thereby not only oppose the *communis opinio* – which everyone acquired a long time ago and now main-tains unshakeably – but also doubt the individual testimonies of the most renowned philosophers and rhetoricians who hold the man to be the yardstick of historical narrative and to represent the ultimate in the forceful style of deliberative oratory. But neither are their principles solid <. . .>.[9]

Since I wish to acquit myself of these accusations of fault- 3 finding which have something theatrical about them and attract the masses,[10] it will be enough for me to say only this about myself: that throughout my life and up to the present day I have guarded against such contentiousness, quarrelsomeness and carping at random against anyone, and have never published a work in which I attacked anyone, except for one treatise which I composed to defend political philosophy against those who inveighed against it unjustly; nor would I now for the first time have attempted to dis-play against the most distinguished of historians a malice which is neither appropriate to the character of free men nor a part of my nature.[11] I could have said more about the nature of this compos- 4 ition but I shall be satisfied with these few remarks. You and the other students of language will judge if the words I have chosen are true and appropriate to myself.

My intention in this treatise is not an attack against Thucyd- 3 ides' choice of subject or his talent, nor is it a selection and disparagement of his faults, nor the sort of thing in which I would have decided that his successes and virtues were of no account and instead grasped on to whatever passages were not written in the best manner. This work is instead an analysis of his style which considers everything, both those features that he shares with other writers and those in which he differs from others. To do this 2 it is necessary that not only his virtues be discussed, but also the vices which adjoin them.[12] For no self-sufficient human nature is without fault either in words or deeds, but the best is the one that

most often succeeds and least often fails. And so let each reader keep in mind my purpose as he reads what follows, not condemning my choice but being instead a fair-minded examiner of the
3 particular effects of his style. I am not the first to have attempted this, and many writers of old and in our own day have chosen to produce treatises that are written not in a spirit of quarrelsomeness but of seeking the truth, and although I could produce countless witnesses to this, I shall content myself with two alone:
4 Plato and Aristotle. Aristotle does not believe that everything said by Plato is excellent (on the forms, for example, the nature of the good, or the ideal state), and Plato himself wishes to demonstrate that Parmenides, Protagoras and Zeno and quite a number of the other natural scientists were wrong. And so no one finds fault with him just for this, because people take seriously that the aim of philosophical inquiry is the knowledge of truth and that from
5 this the purpose of life becomes clear. So then if no one blames those who differ in philosophical doctrines for their choice when they do not praise everything in their predecessors, then who would find fault with critics who try to make clear an individual's distinctive style simply because they do not vouch for all the qualities (including those that it does not possess) which earlier critics had claimed for them?[13]

4   I still need to make one remaining part of my defence against a jealous sort of accusation and one that is delightful to the masses, but easily refuted as being unsound, namely, that if we fall short of Thucydides and other authors, we have not thereby lost the
2 right to study them. For those who do not have the same talents as Apelles, Zeuxis, Protogenes and the other renowned painters are not prevented from judging them, any more than judging the works of Phidias, Polyclitus and Myron is forbidden to those who are
3 not as great craftsmen.[14] I need not say that for many works an individual is no worse a critic than the craftsman, since such things are perceived through irrational perception and by means of the emotions; and every form of art aims at these standards, and from these takes its beginning.[15] Let this be a sufficient prologue for me lest I unwittingly spend my entire treatise on these matters.

5   Before I begin my study of Thucydides, I wish to say a few

things about the other historians, both those older than he and his
contemporaries. From this, both the man's choice of subject, in
which he differed from his predecessors, and his talent will be
clear. To begin with, there were many historians of old in many   2
places before the Peloponnesian War, among whom were Eugeon
of Samos, Deiochus <of Cyzicus, Bion>[16] of Proconnesus, Eudemos
of Paros, Democles of Phygele, Hecataeus of Miletus, Acusilaus of
Argos, Charon of Lampsacus and Melesagoras of Chalcedon;[17]
those who were a little before the Peloponnesian War and who
lived to Thucydides' time were Hellanicus of Lesbos, Damastes of
Sigeum, Xenomedes of Ceos, Xanthus of Lydia, and many others.[18]
These men employed a similar choice in their selection of mater-   3
ials, and their talents did not differ much from one another. Some
composed Greek histories, some the histories of non-Greeks, and
they did not connect these with each other but divided them
according to people or city and produced them separately from
one another, observing one and the same aim: to publish, just as
they had found them, and neither adding anything to them nor
taking anything away, whatever oral traditions were preserved
amongst the local inhabitants (whether peoples or cities) and
whatever writings had been stowed away in places sacred or pro-
fane, so that they would be known to all.[19] In these were some
myths which had been believed from far in the past and certain
theatrical reversals of fortune which seem to people today to contain much foolishness. All those who wrote in the same dialect[20]   4
also employed for the most part the same style, which was clear,
ordinary, pure and concise, suitable to the events and showing no
artistic elaboration. And yet a certain charm and grace runs
through their writings, some more, some less, and this is why
their works survive.

But it was Herodotus of Halicarnassus, who was born a little   5
before the Persian Wars and lived up to the time of the Peloponnesian War, who brought to his choice of subject matter something
greater and more distinguished. He chose not to write up a history
of one city or one people but to bring together within the purview
of one work many different events from both Europe and Asia;
beginning from the Lydian dynasty he brought his history down
as far as the Persian Wars, comprehending in one treatise all the

distinguished events that occurred, whether of Greeks or non-Greeks, in 220 years,[21] and to his style he gave those qualities that had been neglected by the historians before him.[22]

6   Thucydides, coming after these, wished neither to limit history to one place, as writers such as Hellanicus had done, nor to bring together into one treatise the deeds that had been accomplished by Greeks and barbarians from every land, imitating Herodotus. He disdained the former because it was paltry and humble, and could
2   not much benefit the reader, while the latter was greater than human reckoning could examine in the most accurate way. Instead, he chose one war, which the Athenians and Peloponnesians fought against each other, and he devoted his energy to
3   writing this up. He was strong in body and of sound mind, and he lived through the whole of it; he composed the deeds not by relying on chance reports but rather from his own experience for events at which he himself was present, and by inquiry from those who knew best for events where he was not present on account of
4   his exile.[23] He surpassed historians before him first in choosing a subject that was neither wholly one-sided nor divided into many
5   disconnected topics, and second, in including in his history no mythical material[24] and in not directing his writing to the deception and bewitching of the multitude, as all before him had done, when they told, for example, of the Lamian women rising up from the earth in woods and glens, or amphibious Naiads coming up from Tartarus, swimming through the sea, half fish, half women, and having intercourse with men, from which unions of mortal and divine a race of demi-gods was produced – and other such stories which are incredible to us today and seem to contain much silliness.[25]

7   I was led on to say these things not to find fault with those writers but rather with great sympathy for them in their treatment of these mythical fictions when they produced their histories of
2   peoples and places. For as I said, among all mankind both collectively in villages and individually in cities such memories were preserved, and children received these oral accounts from their fathers and took care to hand them on to their children: those who wished to make these traditions available thought it appropriate to write them up as they had received them from men of old. These

writers, then, had of necessity to embroider their local treatises with mythic accounts.[26] Thucydides, by contrast, chose one set of [3] events, at which he himself was present, and did not see it as appropriate to mix theatrical charms[27] into his narrative nor did he fashion it for the deception of his readers (as those earlier treatises had naturally done) but rather for their benefit, as he himself has revealed in the preface of his work, writing as follows (and here I quote):[28]

> And in the hearing the lack of a mythic element will seem less pleasurable; but if all those who wish to examine the clarity of events – both those that occurred and those that will occur at some time or another in accordance with human nature in the same or similar ways – will judge this useful, that will be sufficient. The work has been composed as a possession for all time rather than as a competition piece to be heard in the present.

All philosophers and public speakers, or, if not all, the majority, [8] testify that Thucydides took the greatest care over truth – and we desire history to be the priestess of truth[29] – neither adding anything that was not justified nor taking anything away; he did not give himself free rein in the writing but kept his method blameless and pure from every kind of jealousy and flattery, especially in his opinions of great men.[30] For example, when he mentions [2] Themistocles in Book 1, he has treated unstintingly the virtues that the man had, and where he treats the policies of Pericles in Book 2, he has pronounced an encomium worthy of that man's celebrated reputation. When he has to speak about the generals Demosthenes, Nicias, the son of Niceratus, Alcibiades, the son of Cleinias, and the rest of the generals and public speakers, he has made clear everything that was due to each.[31] I do not need to fur- [3] nish examples of these for those who have gone through these accounts. These, then, one would say are successfully done by the historian and are fine and worthy of imitation.[32]

Where he has fallen somewhat short and is blamed by some is [9] in the more artistic part of his work, which is called 'arrangement' and which must be sought after in all writings, whether someone chooses philosophical or rhetorical subjects. This has to do with

2 division, order and elaboration.³³ I shall begin with division, pref-
   acing it by noting that although writers before him divided up
   their treatises either by area or by era so as to be easy to follow,
3 Thucydides approved of neither of these. He did not make his
   divisions guided by the places where the events took place, as had
   Herodotus and Hellanicus and some other writers before him, nor
   by chronology, as those who produced local histories had chosen,
   dividing their works up either by the succession of kings or of
   priests or by Olympiads, or by those magistrates appointed to
4 annual offices.³⁴ Wishing rather to set out on a new path untrodden
   by the rest, he divided his history following the seasons, by summers and winters. Yet the result was the opposite of what he
   expected: for the chronology did not become clearer but instead
5 more difficult to follow. One can only wonder how it escaped him
   that when many events happened simultaneously in many places, a
   narrative cut up into small portions would not attain that 'pure and
   far-shining light' that is manifest from the deeds themselves.³⁵

6   So, for example, in Book 3 (which alone will suffice) he begins
   by treating the Mytilenaean affair, but before he finishes this
   account, he wanders off to the deeds of the Lacedaemonians. Yet
   he does not even finish these up before he mentions the siege of
   Plataea. But leaving this also incomplete, he then records the war
   of Mytilene, and from there leads the narrative to the events in
   Corcyra, how the people there engaged in civil strife, some bringing in the Lacedaemonians, others the Athenians. Leaving even
   this half-finished, he then makes a few remarks about the earlier
7 Athenian expedition to Sicily. Then, after beginning to talk about
   the Athenian naval expedition against the Peloponnese and the
   expedition of the Lacedaemonians against the people of Doris, he
   moves on to the accomplishments of Demosthenes the general
   around Leucas and the war against the Aetolians. And from there
   he departs for Naupactus. Leaving these land wars also unfinished, he again treats Sicily and after this he purifies Delos, and
   then concludes with Amphilochian Argos which was being warred
   upon by the Ambraciots.³⁶

8   What more needs to be said? The whole book has been chopped
   up in this way and he has destroyed the continuity of his narration. We wander about, and we find it difficult to follow what is

being explained (as one would expect), since our understanding is troubled by events being pulled apart so, and we cannot easily or accurately recall the incomplete memories of what we have heard. But a historical work must be uninterrupted and not drawn from here to there, especially when it is a matter of many events which are difficult to apprehend.[37] It is clear that Thucydides' standard is not correct or appropriate to history: for not one of his successors divided up his history by summers and winters, but all of them pursued the well-worn roads, those which customarily lead to clarity.[38]

Some find fault with his arrangement because he did not choose the beginning that he should have, nor did he fashion an appropriate ending for his work; such critics assert that it is not the least part of good arrangement to choose a beginning for a work to which nothing would seem prior, and an ending to which nothing more would seem needed; and they say that Thucydides has paid appropriate attention to neither.[39] The historian himself has furnished these critics with the basis for their accusation. For having prefaced his work by saying that the Peloponnesian War was greater than previous wars both in its length and in the many sufferings that occurred, he then wishes, at the end of the preface, to give first the causes from which it took its beginning. He then appends two of these, one true but not spoken amongst all (the growth of the Athenians' power) and the other, not true but invented by the Lacedaemonians (the allied force sent to the Corcyraeans from Athens against the Corinthians). And yet he has made the beginning of his narrative by starting not from the reason he thought true, but from the other, writing verbatim as follows:

> The Athenians and Peloponnesians began the war when they dissolved the thirty-year truce, which they made after the seizure of Euboea. As to why they dissolved this truce, I have written first the causes and the grounds for complaint lest anyone ever seek whence so great a war arose for the Greeks. But I consider the truest cause, which was least manifest in speech, to have been that the Athenians, by growing great and frightening the Lacedaemonians, compelled the latter to make war. The charges that were spoken of in the open, however, were as follows.

Epidamnus is a city on the right as you sail into the Ionian gulf. It is inhabited by the barbarian Taulantians, an Illyrian race.⁴⁰

4 After this he goes through events concerning Epidamnus, as well as those about Corcyra and about Potidaea, the assembly of Peloponnesians at Sparta, and the speeches given there against the city of Athens. Having drawn this out for 2,000 lines, he only then gives an account of the other cause, the true one and the one he believed, beginning thus:⁴¹

> The Lacedaemonians voted that the treaty had been violated and that they should go to war against the Athenians, not so much because they were persuaded by the speeches of their allies as that they were afraid of the Athenians, lest they should become even more powerful, seeing that much of Greece was already under their control.
>
> Now the circumstances by which the Athenians grew great occurred in the following way . . .

and he appends to this the deeds of the city, whatever they accomplished from the end of the Persian War to the beginning of the Peloponnesian War, summarily running through them quickly in 5 fewer than 500 lines. Yet remembering that these events were prior to Corcyra and that the war began not from these earlier events but from Corcyra, he then writes this (and I quote):⁴²

> And after these events, there occurred not many years later the aforementioned events, those concerning Corcyra and Potidaea, and all those which formed the pretext of this war. And all these actions, whether the Greeks did them against one another or against the barbarian, happened in an approximately fifty-year period between the retreat of Xerxes and the beginning of this war. And when the Athenians made their rule stronger and themselves grew great in power, the Lacedaemonians perceived it but did not try to prevent it, except for a short period, and they took no action much of the time, being even before this not swift to go to war unless compelled, and at that time somewhat hindered by wars with their own people. But the power of the Athenians was manifestly growing and was starting to impinge upon the Lacedaemonians' allies,

and they considered it no longer endurable, but resolved that they had to act with all eagerness; and that, if they could, they must destroy the Athenians' power by launching this war.

Now since he had begun by seeking the causes of the war, he 11 ought first to have given the true one and the one he believed. For it was only natural that former things begin before later ones and that true things be spoken before false things, and the impact of his narrative would have been far greater if it had employed such an arrangement. Nor would his defenders be able to say that the 2 deeds were minor and not worthy of reckoning or well known and trite thanks to his predecessors, so that he should not have taken his beginnings from these. For he himself has indicated that 3 this period, which deserved inclusion in history, had been omitted by authors of old, writing thus in his own words:

> I have written these things and made this digression in my account because this period was omitted by all those before me, who composed accounts either of Greek history before the Persian Wars or of the Persian Wars themselves. Hellanicus did in fact treat this period in his *Attic History* but he recounted events briefly and inaccurately in terms of chronology. At the same time this digression reveals in what way Athenian rule was established.[43]

This then was evidence that the narrative is not arranged in the 12 best manner by him, I mean that it does not have a natural beginning. Added to this is the fact that the history does not end with 2 the summation it ought to have had. The war lasted twenty-seven years, and although Thucydides lived through the entire period up to its end, he brought his history down as far as the twenty-second year, ending the eighth book with the battle of Cynossema, even though previously he said in the preface that he would treat all the deeds of this war.[44] And in the fifth book he sums up the 3 chronology again, from when the war began to the point at which it ended, writing (and I quote):[45]

> And for those who trusted in any way to oracles, this one alone turned out to be reliable. For I remember how on every occasion,

both when the war was starting and until it ended, many proffered that it was fated to last thrice nine years. I lived through the whole of the war, of an age to perceive it and applying my mind so that I might have some exact knowledge of it. It so happened that I was in exile from my own country for twenty years after my generalship in Amphipolis, and because I was present at events on both sides (and at Peloponnesian events no less, because of my exile), I could better perceive something of them at my leisure. So then I shall narrate the conflict after the ten years, the rupture of the truce, and the subsequent events of the war.

13 Now as to his elaboration of topics, although I could establish by many pieces of evidence that he is less careful and either assigns more words to those that require fewer or that he carelessly treats matters deserving of greater elaboration, I shall cite only a few.
2 Towards the end of Book 2, he begins to write about the first two sea battles between the Athenians and Peloponnesians, in which against forty-seven Peloponnesian ships the Athenians with only twenty <. . .>[46] having battled at sea against the barbarians who were much greater in number, they destroyed some ships, and they captured others with their crews, and in all no fewer than the number they had dispatched for the war. I shall quote him:

> After this there occurred at the Eurymedon river in Pamphylia both a land and a sea battle of the Athenians and their allies against the Persians, and the Athenians were victorious on both in the same day under the command of Cimon, son of Miltiades, and they captured the Phoenicians' triremes and destroyed all 200.[47]

3 Similar are his land battles, which are either extended beyond what is necessary or excessively abbreviated. In Book 4 he begins to narrate the actions of the Athenians around Pylos and the island called Sphacteria on which the Lacedaemonians were shut up and besieged, and then within this battle he narrates some other events alongside it, and then, coming back to the conclusion of this affair, he narrates in detail and forcefully everything that happened in these battles on both sides, devoting more than 300 lines to the battles, although the number of those killed or forced

to surrender was not great. He himself in summing up events in this battle writes thus (and I quote):[48]

> The number of dead and captured on the island was as follows: 420 hoplites in all crossed over to the island; of these 292 were captured alive and the rest perished. 120 Spartiates were captured alive but few Athenians perished.

Yet he has written cursorily in treating Nicias' command, the one 14 when he sailed against the Peloponnese with Athenian forces numbering sixty ships and 2,000 hoplites and shut up the Lacedaemonians in their forts, forced the Aeginetan settlers in Cythera and Thyrea to surrender, ravaged much of the rest of the Peloponnese, and sailed back to Athens bringing a multitude of prisoners. He says as follows:

> When the battle was fought, the Cythereans held out for a little time but then turned and fled to the upper city, but later came to an agreement with Nicias and his fellow commanders, handing themselves over to the Athenians to decide their fate, on condition that it not be death.

Of the capture of the Aeginetans at Thyrea: 2

> And here the Athenians, landing and immediately marching out with their entire force, captured Thyrea and they burned the city and completely plundered its contents, and they brought back to Athens all those Aeginetans who had not died in battle.

When there were great misfortunes in both cities right at the 3 beginning of the war, because of which both sides desired peace, and he writes about the earlier embassy (when the Athenians sent to Sparta asking to obtain peace, because their land was being ravaged, their city was being ruined by the plague, and they had despaired of every other assistance), he does not tell us who the ambassadors were nor the speeches given by them, nor the opposing ones which persuaded the Lacedaemonians to vote against the truce. He has treated these events in a somewhat superficial and careless manner, as if they were small and undistinguished affairs:

> After the Peloponnesians' second invasion, the Athenians, since their land had been ravaged a second time and the plague and war were pressing upon them simultaneously, changed their opinions and they held Pericles responsible because he had persuaded them to go to war and these sufferings had fallen upon them on account of him. They were minded to come to an agreement with the Lacedaemonians and they sent some embassies to them, but these had no success.

4 Concerning the latter attempt at peace, when the Lacedaemonians, wishing to win back the 300 men captured at Pylos, sent an embassy to Athens, he has both given the speeches spoken at that time by the Lacedaemonians and has gone through the reasons why the truce was not made.[49]

15 Now if an exposition touching on the main points of the events was sufficient for the Athenian embassy and there was no need for the speeches and exhortations used by their ambassadors (since the Lacedaemonians were neither persuaded nor accepted the truce), why in the world did he not make the same choice for those who came from Sparta to Athens, since they also departed not having achieved their goal? And if the Lacedaemonian embassy needed a detailed account, why did he carelessly omit the Athenian one? For he was surely not prevented by any weakness in talent from discovering and expressing the inherent arguments on both 2 sides.[50] But if he had some reason for choosing to elaborate the one embassy, I cannot figure out why he preferred the Laconian one to the Athenian, the one later in time to the earlier, the one by a foreign city to the one of his own country, and the one which occurred during fewer sufferings to that which occurred during more.

3 When he has to write about the capture and destruction of cities and enslavements and other such misfortunes he sometimes makes the sufferings so raw and terrible and pitiable that he has left no possibility, either to historians or poets, of surpassing him; but at other times he renders them so slight and small that those reading

him do not perceive even a trace of the horrors. Now concerning 4
his remarks about the city of Plataea and the Mytileneans and the
Melians, I have no need of quoting those passages, in which he is
at the peak of his powers in elaborating the misfortunes of those
people. But when he runs quickly over the sufferings and makes
the sufferings small <. . .>[51] in many passages of his history, these
I *shall* mention.[52]

> Around this same time, the Athenians, having compelled the Scion-
> ians to surrender, killed the men of adult age and sold the women
> and children into slavery, and gave the land over to the Plataeans to
> cultivate.
>
> And the Athenians, under the command of Pericles, crossed back
> over into Euboea and subdued the whole of it. All the rest they set-
> tled by agreement, but they repelled the Histiaeans and themselves
> took possession of their land.
>
> The expelled the Aeginetans from Aegina at this same time, the
> men, women and children, because they charged them with being
> not least responsible for the war they were in; and they thought that
> Aegina, lying as it did off the coast of the Peloponnese, would be
> more secure if they sent colonists of their own to possess it.

One could find many other passages throughout the entire history 16
that either have received the ultimate elaboration (to which nothing could be added and from which nothing could be taken away),
or are carelessly run over and have not the least impress of his
forcefulness, especially in the speeches, dialogues and other rhetorical pieces. It was in taking thought for these that he probably left 2
his history unfinished, as Cratippus, his contemporary, who compiled and wrote up the events omitted by Thucydides, has also
maintained, saying not only that the speeches impeded the action
but were also annoying to the audience. He adds that Thucydides 3
recognized this and thus placed no rhetorical passages in the last
part of his history, even though many events took place in Ionia
and in Athens, all of which resulted from debates and addresses to
the people.[53] If in fact one should set the first and the last book side 4
by side with each other, both would seem to have neither the same

plan nor the same power, since the first treats few and unimportant events and abounds in rhetorical pieces, while the last embraces many important events but contains no public speeches.[54]

17   Now I myself had clearly thought that in the rhetorical pieces the man had the same failing, namely, that when treating the same subject on the same occasion he puts in what ought not to have
2   been said, and leaves out what should have been said. He has done this, for example, in Book 3 in the episode of Mytilene. For after the capture of the city and the arrival of the prisoners dispatched by the general, Paches, there were two assemblies at Athens. The speeches given by the popular leaders in the first assembly he passed over as not being necessary: this was where the people voted to put to death the prisoners and the rest of the men of adult age, and to enslave the women and children; but he considered it necessary to treat the speeches which the same men gave in the latter assembly (when a certain regret came over the majority), even though they were composed on the same theme.[55]

18   And by what calculation did he put the renowned Funeral Oration, of which he gives a detailed account, in Book 2 rather than in some other?[56] For if the dead had to be honoured with the funeral speech's praises, whether in the great misfortunes of the city, when the customary laments had to be spoken for the many brave Athenians who had fought and died, or in great successes from which glorious renown would accrue to the city, it was fitting to have the
2   funeral speech in any book other than this one. In this book the Athenians who fell during the first invasion of the Peloponnesians were altogether few and had not even accomplished any distinguished feat, as Thucydides himself writes. For in speaking of Pericles he says,

> he guarded the city and kept it calm to the extent that he could. He did, however, send out a few cavalry to prevent sudden raids from the army falling upon the fields near the city and doing them harm,

and he says there was a brief cavalry battle

> in Phrygia between the squadron of Athenian horse with their Thessalian allies and the Boeotian cavalry. The Thessalians and Athenians were having the better of it until the Boeotian hoplites brought help

and caused them to retreat. A few Thessalians and Athenians were killed. They took up the bodies, however, on the same day without truce, and the Peloponnesians set up a trophy on the following day.[57]

Now the deeds of Demosthenes and his men at Pylos, in Book 4 – where they fought against the forces of the Lacedaemonians by land and sea, were victorious in both battles, and by their actions filled the city with pride – were much more numerous and greater than those earlier deeds.[58] Why then did the historian open the public graves and bring on Pericles, the most distinguished public speaker, and compose that sublime tragedy, all for a few horsemen who had won neither renown nor power for the city, while not composing a funeral oration for the numerous and better men, who destroyed those who brought war against the Athenians, and who were more suitable to receive this praise? Leaving aside all those battles, both on land and sea, in which many died and which were much more worthy of being adorned with the praises of the funeral oration than the patrols of Attica who numbered ten or fifteen, were not the Athenians and their allies in Sicily with Nicias and Demosthenes who died in the sea battles, land battles and finally in that wretched retreat and who numbered not less than 40,000 and were not able even to receive proper burial – how much more appropriate would it have been for *them* to receive the pity and praise of the funeral oration?[59] But the historian has so ignored these men that he does not even record that the city decreed a period of public mourning, carried out the customary offering for those who die abroad, and designated the most competent orator of that time to make the speeches over them.[60] For it was not likely that the Athenians would have publicly mourned for fifteen cavalrymen, <while those who fell in Sicily>[61] (and there were more than 50,000 of them from the citizen registry) were worthy of no honour. But the historian seems – for I shall say what I think – to have wanted to use the figure of Pericles, and composed the funeral oration as if it had been spoken by him, and because Pericles died in the second year of the war and was not present at any of the misfortunes that the city suffered after this, Thucydides assigned to a minor action not worthy of our interest praise which goes beyond what the event merited.

One could still more see the historian's unevenness in his   19 elaboration when one considers that while omitting many great deeds, he stretches out the preface of his history to 5,000 lines because he wishes to show that the events of Greek history before this war were minor and not worthy to be compared to his war.[62]

2 But it can be shown from many historical events that the truth was otherwise, nor do the rules of art dictate such a degree of magnification (for if something is greater than small things, it is not thereby great, but only if it exceeds great things). Yet his preface, because it contains so many elaborated demonstrations of his thesis, has become a kind of history of its own.[63] The writers of

3 rhetorical treatises recommend that the preface should offer an exposition of one's composition by indicating in advance the chief points of the demonstration to follow; and *this* Thucydides has done in fewer than fifty lines at the end of the preface, just when he is about to begin the narrative. And so it was unnecessary for him to drag in all those remarks that tried to cast down the greatness of Greece, for example that, at the time of the Trojan War, Hellas was not yet called by a single name, or that those who lacked a livelihood first began to cross the sea with ships and 'attacking and plundering unwalled cities and villages, they took the majority of their livelihood from this'. Why was it necessary to talk about

4 Athenian luxury of old, how they plaited their top knots, and wore golden grasshoppers on their heads? Or that the Lacedaemonians 'were the first to exercise naked, taking off their loincloths and anointing themselves with oil while exercising'? Or that the Corinthian Ameinocles was the first to build ships, four triremes for the Samians, or that Polycrates, the tyrant of Samos, captured Rheneia and dedicated it to Delian Apollo, or that the Phocaeans were the ones who settled Massilia when they conquered the Carthaginians in a naval battle or all the rest that is like this – what occasion did he have for telling all this before the narrative proper?[64]

20   If gods and men allow me to say what I think, it seems to me that the preface would have been strongest if he had attached the last part to the introduction, leaving out everything in the middle and arranging it in this way:[65]

Thucydides of Athens composed the war of the Peloponnesians and Athenians, how they fought against each other, beginning as soon as the war broke out, and expecting that it would be a great war and more worthy of account than those which had gone before, taking as evidence the fact that both sides were at their peak[66] in every aspect of their preparation, and seeing that the rest of the Greek world was siding with one or the other, some right away, others intending to do so. This was the greatest upheaval for the Greeks and for some portion of the non-Greek world, and one might even say for the majority of mankind. It was impossible to discover clearly events before this and events even older than those because of the amount of time that had passed. Yet from the pieces of evidence that I have examined as far back as possible and that I find trustworthy, I do not think that those events were great either as regards their wars or the rest.

One should not trust either the poets who celebrate these events by adorning them to make them greater, or the prose-writers who have composed their works to make them more attractive to hear rather than more truthful, given that the majority of these events cannot be refuted because of time, and they have won their way into the realm of the mythical so as to be incredible. But one would not err if one considered that these events, as I have recounted them, have been sufficiently researched using the clearest evidence, at least in light of their antiquity.

And as for all the things which each side said in speech, either when they were about to make war or when they were already in it, it was difficult to remember the detail[67] itself of what was said, both for me, regarding the things I myself heard, and for those reporting to me at one time or another from elsewhere. I have written the speeches as I thought that each would say especially what was necessary for the given occasion, holding as closely as possible to the general purport of what was truly said. But as for that part of the war's actions that had to do with deeds, I did not deem it worthy to write those having learned of them from some chance informant, nor as I thought, but instead I went through each matter in detail – both those at which I was present and those that were reported to me by others – with the greatest accuracy possible. This kept revealing itself to be a difficult matter since those present at each of the events did not give uniform accounts, but gave them as each was affected by partiality for one or the other side, or by their memory. And in the hearing perhaps the lack of a mythic element will seem less pleasurable; but if all those who wish to examine the clarity of events – both those that occurred and those that will occur at some time or another in the same or similar ways in accordance with human nature – will judge this useful, that will be sufficient. The work has been composed as a possession for all time rather than as a competition piece to be heard in the present.

Now of former deeds the greatest was the Persian Wars, yet this nonetheless had a swift resolution through two land and two sea battles. But the length of the present war was greatly protracted, and more sufferings came about in Greece itself than in any equal period of time. For never were so many cities captured and deserted, some by the barbarians, some by the antagonists themselves in their battles with one another, and in some of these they expelled the original inhabitants after they had taken the city. Never were there so many men exiled, some as a result of the war itself, others on account of civil strife. Things which had been spoken of in oral tradition, but had rarely been confirmed as fact, turned out to be credible: earthquakes which occurred over the greatest portion of the earth and were extremely strong, and eclipses which occurred more frequently than those remembered in the time before; and there were great droughts and famines that resulted from them, and that which inflicted not the least damage and destroyed them to some degree, the plague. All these things occurred together with this war.

The Athenians and the Peloponnesians began the war when they dissolved the Thirty Years Peace which they had made after the capture of Euboea. I have prefaced my work with the reasons why they dissolved the peace and the charges they brought against each other so that no one will ever have to seek how such a great war came upon the Greeks.

21 These, then, are the historian's failings and successes in his subject matter.

2   I shall now speak of his style, in which his distinctive character is especially clearest. But perhaps it is necessary first to

speak about the natural divisions of style and what qualities it possesses, and to show in what state it was when Thucydides inherited it from his predecessors, and the innovations that he was the first to make, whether for better or worse, concealing nothing.

Many have noted that style as a whole is divided into two parts: 22 the first concerns the choice of words by which matters are described, and the composition of greater and lesser parts,[68] and each of these is in turn divided into other parts: the choice of the elementary parts of speech (I mean nouns, verbs, and conjunctions) is divided into direct or metaphorical style, while composition 2 is divided into phrases, clauses, and periods.[69] Many before me have noted that for both of these (I mean, of course, for simple and indivisible words as well as for sequences composed from them) there happen to be the so-called figures; and that of the so-called virtues of style, some are essential and ought to be present in all compositions and others are additional; and when the essential virtues support them, then the additional ones have their peculiar force.[70] Since many have noted this, it is not necessary for me to speak about them now nor from what precepts and rules (which are many) each of these qualities arises, since these matters have received very detailed exposition.

I shall now go through, briefly and from the beginning (as I 23 promised), what qualities all those before Thucydides employed and which ones they employed only a little, since in this way one will know more accurately the individual style of the man. I can- 2 not conjecture what sort of style was used by the truly ancient historians, the ones known to us only by name, whether it was plain, unadorned, and without refinement, having only what was useful and necessary, or was, on the contrary, stately, dignified, and elaborate, having also the additional ornaments; the majority 3 of their works have not survived to our times, and those that are preserved are not believed by everyone to be actually the works of those men: these would include the works of Cadmus of Miletus, Aristeas of Proconnesus, and others like them.[71] Those born 4 before the Peloponnesian War whose lives extended into Thucydides' time all had similar aims for the most part, some choosing the Ionic dialect which predominated in those days, others the ancient Attic dialect which had minor differences from Ionic.

5   All these writers, as I said, gave their efforts more towards the direct than the figurative style, though they employed the latter as a seasoning; and all practised a similar composition which was simple and without affectation; and not even in giving shape to their words and thoughts did they depart much from the language that
6   was common, current and familiar to all. The style of all of them displays the necessary virtues (for it is sufficiently pure, clear and concise, each preserving the individual character of the dialect utilized). But as for the additional qualities, where the power of a speaker becomes especially evident, they neither have all of them nor are the ones they have fully developed; they show but a few, and these only slightly developed: I am referring to sublimity, elegance of language, stateliness and grandeur. Their style does not have strength, nor weight nor emotion that rouses the mind, nor that vigorous and competitive breath from which arises what we call
7   intensity. The only exception is Herodotus. In his choice of words, composition and variety of figures he far exceeded the rest, and he fashioned his prose style to be similar to the best poetry for its per-
8   suasiveness, charm and utter pleasure. He in no way fell short in the greatest and most distinguished qualities of style, except for those appropriate to forensic oratory,[72] either because he was not well suited for it by nature or because he deliberately avoided it, reckoning that it was not suitable for histories. He does not have many addresses before the people nor forensic speeches, nor is it his strength to invest his narrative with emotion or forcefulness.

24   Thucydides, coming after such a writer and those others whom I mentioned above, and recognizing the virtues which each of them possessed, was the first to apply himself to bringing into a historical treatise a style that was unique and neglected by all. In his selection of words he chose a style that was figurative, obscure, old-fashioned and foreign in place of the common and familiar
2   style of his contemporaries. In the composition of smaller and larger parts he chose an arrangement that was dignified, austere, sturdy, stately and rough to the ear because of the harshness of the letters, instead of one that was clear, soft, polished and

lacking in roughness. He brought the greatest effort to figures of speech where he especially wished to exceed his predecessors. During the twenty-seven-year period from the beginning to the end of the war,[73] he continually went back and forth through those eight books (which are all he has left behind) and filed down and polished each of the elements of his wording. Sometimes he makes a phrase from a single word and at other times he contracts a phrase into a single word; now he produces a verbal expression in the form of a noun, and then in turn he makes a noun a verb, and even of these he overturns their customary uses, so that a proper noun may become a common noun and a common noun may be spoken as a proper noun. He makes passive verbs active and active verbs passive. He alters the natures of plurals and singulars and he substitutes one for the other. He has feminines agree with masculines, masculines with feminines, and neuters agreeing with both, so that the natural agreement based on gender is lost.[74] The cases of nouns and participles he sometimes diverts to the object from the subject and at other times to the subject from the object. In his use of conjunctions, prepositions, and even more in the parts of speech that articulate the meanings of words, he adopts the independent manner of a poet.

One could find in him a great number of figures which, by changes of person, variations of tenses, and the strained use of expressions of place, depart from customary usage and take on the appearance of solecisms. How many times things are substituted for people and people for things! In his enthymemes[75] and expressions of thought, parentheses abound and being numerous they delay the conclusion for a long time. And there are passages that are tortuous, tangled, difficult to unwind and the like. One would find present in his work not a few ostentatious figures, by which I mean balanced phrases, assonance, wordplay and antithesis, those features that abounded in Gorgias of Leontini, and the followers of Polus and Licymnius and many others who flourished in Thucydides' era.[76] But his most obvious and characteristic features are the attempt to indicate the greatest matters in the fewest words and to put together many thoughts into one, and the fact that he leaves the listener expecting to hear something more, from

11   all of which arises a brevity that is obscure.[77] I may sum up by saying
that there are four instruments, so to speak, of Thucydides' diction:
poetic vocabulary,[78] variety of figures, harshness of arrangement
and swiftness in indicating what he has to say. Its qualities are solidity and compactness, pungency and severity, weightiness, the ability
to inspire awe and fear, and above all these things the power to stir
12   the emotions. Such is Thucydides in the character of his style, by
which he is distinguished from the rest. Whenever his purpose and
his ability coincide, they result in successes that are fully realized
and divine; but when his ability falls short and the intensity is not
maintained to the end, his style becomes unclear because of the
speed of his narrative, and this brings with it some other faults
13   that are not attractive. Throughout his entire history he does not
observe the necessary manner for employing foreign and newly
coined expressions, nor how far to go before stopping, even though
there exist fine precepts which are necessary for every kind of
writing.

25   After these summary remarks, it is now time for me to turn to
detailed proofs of these matters. But I shall not write a separate
account for each feature, arranging Thucydides' style by the discussion of individual points, but rather by certain passages and
topics. I shall take portions of the narrative and the speeches, and
I shall place his successes and failures, whether in subject matter
2   or style, side by side, with the reasons why they are such. I ask
again of you and of any student of literature who will encounter
this treatise to look at the purpose of the examination I have
chosen to make, which is to reveal his style by treating everything
that is characteristic of the man and requires discussion, with the
aim of being useful to those who will want to imitate him.

3   To begin, then, at the outset of his preface he puts forward the
proposition that the Peloponnesian War was greater than all wars
before, writing (and I quote):[79]

> It was impossible to discover clearly events before this and those yet
> older because of the amount of time that had passed. Yet from the
> pieces of evidence that I have examined as far back as possible and
> that I find trustworthy, I do not think that these events were great as
> regards either their wars or the rest.

What is now manifestly called Hellas was not securely settled long ago, but there were changes of population in earlier times and each people easily abandoned their own territory, when they were on any given occasion pressed by those who were more numerous. For trade did not exist nor did they have dealings with one another without fear either on land or sea, but each of them, dwelling in their own land, as much as sufficed, and not having surpluses nor cultivating the land <. . .>

<The Lacedaemonians were no longer able to press the charge vigorously wherever they were being attacked, and the light-armed troops, recognizing that they were now slower in any attempt at defence, and having themselves taken courage by what they saw and themselves manifestly far more numerous, and having become accustomed as well to seeing those no longer as frightening to themselves because they had not straightaway suffered anything worthy of their expectation when they had first landed and in their spirit>[80] were subjugated because they were going against Lacedaemonians, despising them, they raised a shout and set out against them.

This section[81] ought not to have been fashioned by him in this way 4 but in a more normal and useful way, with the last part joined to the first, and the material in the middle following this. Thucydides' expression, figured in the way that it is, is terser and more forceful, but it would have been clearer and more pleasing arranged like this:

When the Lacedaemonians could no longer rush out at the point where the enemy was attacking, the light-armed troops, seeing that they were already more sluggish, formed a compact body and, with a shout, rushed out all together against them. They took encouragement from seeing that they were much more numerous, and they despised them because they no longer appeared to them frightening in the same way, since they had not immediately suffered what they had expected when they had first disembarked, when they were subjugated in spirit because they were going against Lacedaemonians.

When all circumlocution is removed, the rest has been expressed 26 with the most natural words and surrounded with the most suitable figures, and is in need of virtually no excellence of style or subject. And these I do not again need to enumerate.

2   In the seventh book, when he treats the final sea battle between Athenians and Syracusans, he uses the following figures:[82]

Demosthenes, Menander, and Euthydemus (for these had gone on board as generals) weighed anchor from their own camp and sailed immediately to the barricade in the harbour and the exit that remained, wishing to force their way out. But the Syracusans and their allies had already weighed anchor with a similar number of ships as before, and with a portion of them were guarding the exit and the rest of the harbour in a circle, so that they might simultaneously attack the Athenians from all sides. The infantry simultaneously brought assistance in the very place where the ships were in greatest number. In command of the naval forces for the Syracusans were Sicanus and Agatharchus, each holding a wing of the whole force, while Pythen and the Corinthians held the middle.

When the rest of the Athenians reached the barricade, bearing down upon them, in their first charge, they got the better of the ships stationed there and they tried to break the fastenings. After this, when the Syracusans and their allies attacked them from all sides, there was not only a battle at the barricade but also throughout the harbour; and it was more staunchly fought than any that had preceded it. For there was much eagerness from the sailors on both sides in attacking, whenever they were ordered, and there was much counter-manoeuvring of the pilots, and competitiveness with one another, and the marines, whenever ship fell upon ship, gave their effort to ensuring that the actions from the decks would not be inferior to the skill shown by the rest, and every individual was urging himself on to be seen as first in whatever station he had been assigned. And because many ships clashed together in a small space (for this was the greatest number of ships that had ever fought a sea battle in a confined space, the combined number being just short of 200), direct attacks were few because there was little opportunity for backing water or breaking the enemy's line; but collisions were more frequent, as ship happened to fall upon ship, whenever attempting to flee or making for some other ship. For the entire time that a ship was advancing to the charge, the men used javelins,

arrows and innumerable stones against it; but when they reached
the ship, the marines fought hand to hand and tried to board each
other's ships. Because of the narrow space, it happened that everywhere a ship was attacking on one side and being attacked on
another, and two, or sometimes even more, ships were of necessity
joined together, and to the pilots fell the defence in one place and
attack in the other, not one-by-one but in many places and from all
sides, and the great thud of many ships colliding created terror and
simultaneously an inability to hear the orders of their boatswains.

The encouragement and the shouting of the boatswains was quite
different on each side, in accordance with their skill and in order to
deal with the sailors' eagerness for victory: to the Athenians they
cried out to force their way out and now, if ever, eagerly lay hold of
a safe return to their homeland, while on the other side they said to
the Syracusans and their allies that it would be a noble thing to prevent the Athenians from escaping, and, by conquering, for each to
increase his own homeland. In addition the generals on each side, if
they saw anyone backing water not of necessity, called upon them
by name and asked the ships' captains, if Athenian, whether they
were retreating because they considered the most hostile land now
to be more theirs than the sea which they had acquired with no
small effort, while, if they were Syracusans, whether they themselves were fleeing the Athenians whom they knew well to be
minded to escape by any means.

Both sides' armies from the shore had much anxiety and conflict
of spirit so long as the sea battle was equally balanced, the native
soldiers keen for more glory than they already had, while the invad-
ers were afraid that they would fare even worse than their present
circumstances. And since for the Athenians everything depended
on their ships, their fear for the future was like none they had ever
experienced, and because of the irregularity of the shore, they were
constrained in their view of the battle from the land. As they
were looking close to the battle and not seeing everything together
at the same time, those who saw their own men victorious would
take heart and turn to invoking the gods not to deprive them of their
safe return; but those who looked where their men were being
defeated wailed simultaneously with their shouts, and from the
sight of what was transpiring were more dejected in spirit than

those doing the fighting. Others, who looked at some place where the sea battle was evenly matched, were in the most difficult state because of the continued indecisiveness of the battle, in their fear swaying with their very bodies in sympathy with their minds. For they were always just at the point of escaping or perishing.

For as long as the sea battle was nearly equal, every sound could be heard at once, wailing, shouting, 'we are winning', 'we are losing', and others, all those of various kinds that a great camp would be compelled to utter in a great danger. And those upon the boats suffered similarly, until the Syracusans and their allies, after the battle had long remained undecided, routed the Athenians, and charging them brilliantly, while employing much shouting and cheering, pursued them towards the shore. And it was then that the naval force came to land, one in this direction, one in another, and all those who were not captured at sea fell out into the camp. The army, no longer with different cries, but from a single impulse, with wailing and groaning, were greatly vexed at what was happening and some went down to the ships to bring help, others went to what remained of the wall to guard it. Still others, the majority, now began to think about themselves and how they might get safely away. Their shock in the moment was less than none they had ever experienced. They had now suffered very nearly what they had inflicted at Pylos: for when the Lacedaemonians had lost their ships, they lost in addition the men who crossed over to the island.[83] And for the Athenians a safe escape by land was now not at this time to be hoped for unless something unexpected should happen. The sea battle had been fierce and many ships on both sides had been destroyed. The Syracusans and their allies, having recovered the wrecks and the corpses, sailed back to the city and set up a trophy.

27 To me this writing, and writing like this, seemed clearly worthy of emulation and imitation, and I was persuaded that the historian's eloquence, the beauty of the language, the forcefulness and the rest of the qualities in these works are most fully perfected, and I judged this from the fact that every soul is moved by this kind of writing, and neither the irrational critical element of our mind, through which we naturally apprehend what is pleasurable or painful, remains indifferent to it, nor the rational element, by

which in every art the beautiful is recognized.[84] Those who are 2
very inexperienced at political oratory could not identify a word
or figure that displeased them, nor could those who are very fas-
tidious and look down on the ignorance of the masses find fault
with the construction of this style; but the many and the few will
form the same estimate. Those laymen of yours, who are numer- 3
ous, will find no vulgarity, tortuousness, or obscurity to displease
them, while the rare expert, one who has come from no haphaz-
ard training, will find nothing ignoble, humble or inartistic to
fault. But the rational and irrational criteria will be fully in accord, 4
by both of which we deem it worthy to form our judgements about
all works of art. < . . . >[85] the one has been worked out, no longer
does the other exhibit beauty or perfection.

I, however, cannot praise those passages which seem to some to 28
be great and admirable, but which do not have even the first and
most common virtues but have been reduced by elaboration and
fastidiousness to being neither agreeable nor beneficial. I shall furnish a few examples of these, placing immediately next to them
the reasons why they have turned into vices that are the opposite
of virtues.

In Book 3, when he goes through the savage and impious deeds 2
at Corcyra which were done by the commons against the wealthy
on account of civil war, he says everything clearly, concisely and
powerfully as long as he delineates what was done in language
that is common and familiar. But when he begins to adopt a tragic
mode[86] for the common misfortunes of the Greeks, and to depart
from normal usage, he falls short of his own standards by some
measure. The first part, which no one would judge as faulty, is as
follows:[87]

The Corcyraeans, perceiving that the Athenian ships were sailing
towards them and those of the enemy had departed, took the Messenians who had previously been outside the city and brought them
inside, and they ordered the ships that they had manned to sail
around into the Hylaïc harbour; and while these were being brought
around, they killed any of the enemy they had captured, and removing from the ships all those they had persuaded to board, they made
away with them. Going into the sanctuary of Hera, they persuaded

about fifty of the suppliants to stand trial and condemned all of them to death. When the majority of the suppliants, those who had not been persuaded, saw what was happening, they killed one another in the sanctuary, some hanging themselves from trees, others doing away with themselves as they could.

For seven days, from when Eurymedon arrived and during which he remained with sixty ships,[88] the Corcyraeans slaughtered those they considered to be their enemies. Against some they brought a charge of trying to destroy the democracy, while others were killed on account of some private enmity, and still others were killed by their debtors because of the money they owed them. Every form of death occurred and, as is wont to happen in such circumstances, there was nothing that did not occur and still worse. For father even killed son, and men were dragged from sanctuaries or slain at them, and some were even walled up in the temple of Dionysus and died there. To such savagery did this civil strife proceed, and it seemed even more so because it was among the first; later, the entire Hellenic world so to speak was convulsed, and there were disputes everywhere, the leaders of the people attempting to bring in the Athenians, the oligarchs to bring in the Lacedaemonians.

29 What follows this, however, is tortuous and difficult to follow, containing combinations of figures that seem solipsistic, and used neither by those who lived at the time nor by those after, when political eloquence especially was at its height. I shall now quote this:[89]

> The affairs of the cities, then, were in civil strife, and the things that came afterwards somehow, by tidings of what had already happened, carried much further the excess of fashioning novel ideas by the ingenuity of their enterprises and the unusualness of their reprisals.

2 The first of these clauses – 'the affairs of the cities, then, were in civil strife' – is a periphrasis to no purpose; it would have been 3 sounder to say, 'the cities, then, were in civil strife'. And what is said after this – 'the things that came afterwards somehow' – is difficult to interpret and would have been more clearly stated thus: 'the cities that came afterwards'. Then follows: 'by tidings of what had already happened, carried much further the excess of fashioning

novel ideas'; what he wants to say is, 'Those who came later to civil strife, learning what had happened from others, went to excess in fashioning something novel.' Apart from the tangled figures, the shapings of the forms of the units are not pleasing to hear.

He follows this with another phrase, more suitable to poetic, or rather dithyrambic,[90] workmanship: 'by the ingenuity of their enterprises and the unusualness of their reprisals. And they changed the customary signification of words in relation to things, according to their estimation.' Now what he wishes to explicate in this difficult-to-untangle web is as follows: 'They made much improvement in continuing something novel with regard to the skills of their devisings and in the excesses of their reprisals. And changing the customary words used for actions they deemed it worthy to call them differently.' 'Ingenuity', 'unusualness of reprisals', 'customary signification of words' and 'changed estimation in relation to things' are more suited to poetic circumlocution. After this he adds these theatrical figures: 'Illogical daring was thought companion-friendly bravery and cautious hesitation specious cowardice.' Both of these contain assonance and balanced clauses and the adjectives are employed for ornamentation. A figure of expression neither theatrical <. . .>[91] but necessary would be: 'For they called daring bravery and hesitation cowardice.' Similar to this is what follows: 'self-control was a pretext for unmanliness, and understanding towards everything idleness for anything.' It would have been more proper to say it like this: 'Those who had self-control were considered unmanly, and those who were understanding towards all things were idle in all things.'

If, having gone only this far, he had then ceased adorning his diction in some passages and making it harsh in others, he would have been less annoying. But as it is, he adds: 'Safety was treachery, a sensible pretext for desertion. The violent man was always trustworthy, his opponent suspect.' Here again it is unclear whom he has in mind when he says 'the violent man', and in regard to what; likewise, 'his opponent' and what he opposed. He then says, 'that one plotting and succeeding was intelligent, and the one who suspected a plot still cleverer; the one contriving how he might not need plots was a destroyer of his party and afraid of the enemy.' The word 'succeeding' does not make clear the author's

thought; nor can the same man be thought successful and suspicious, in as much as one is successful who has sought after and attained what he expected, whereas the suspicious person is so called because he has a presentiment of some evil that is not yet
4 accomplished but still in the future. The thought would have been 'pure and far-shining'[92] if it had been written thus:

> Those who plotted against others were, if they succeeded, clever, while those who suspected plots were, if they prevented them, still cleverer. The one who foresaw how he would need neither plot nor protections was considered to be destroying his party and petrified of the enemy.

31 He follows this with a single period expressed tersely, powerfully and with clarity:

> In sum, the man who anticipated another in doing harm was praised as was one who urged on another who had not been so minded.

But then once again he will employ poetic substitution:

> And indeed the state of being kin became less near than being of the party because of being readier to dare some act unhesitatingly.

Now 'the state of being kin' and 'being of the party' in place of 'kinship' and 'party' is substitution; as for the phrase 'dare some act unhesitatingly', it is unclear whether it refers here to friends or
2 kin. For in giving the reason why they judged their relations to be less near than their friends, he adds, 'because of being readier to dare some act unhesitatingly'. But the argument would have been clearer if, fashioning it in accordance with his own figure, he had expressed it in this manner:

> And indeed comradeship was more suitable than kinship because of its being readier to dare some act unhesitatingly.

3 What follows also contains circumlocution and is expressed neither strongly nor clearly:

For not with the existing laws, for safety, were there such associations, but with greed, against the established laws.

The thought is as follows:

For it was not with a view towards benefit in accordance with the law that the associations of comrades came about, but for the greedy acquisition of something in violation of the laws.

He continues: 4

And if any oaths of reconciliation somehow came about, they were being given by each for the immediate present in view of their difficulty and they held while they did not have assistance from elsewhere.

There is hyperbaton[93] and circumlocution here: for 'oaths of reconciliation' has the following meaning: 'oaths concerning friendship if somehow they came about'. 'They held' is placed in hyperbaton and goes with 'for the immediate present', for he wishes to say, 'they held for the immediate present'. As for 'being given by each in view   5 of the difficulty, while they did not have assistance from elsewhere', it would have been more clearly expressed like this: 'being given by each in accordance with their difficulty because they had no other help'. The sequence of thought would have been such:

And oaths of friendship, if they somehow came about, were given by each because of a lack of some other pledge, and they held for the immediate present.

More tortuous than these is what he puts next: 32

In the circumstance, the one who anticipated being bold, if he saw something unfortified, was avenged more pleasantly on account of his trust than if foreseen. It was reckoned safety, and because he prevailed by deceit, he received in addition the prize for intelligence.

Now 'in the circumstance' for 'in the moment' and 'unfortified' instead of 'unguarded' and 'being avenged more pleasantly on account of his trust than if foreseen' are obscure circumlocutions, and some part is missing to complete the thought. But it is possible to conjecture that he wishes to say this:

> If somehow an opportunity occurred to someone and he learned that his enemy was unguarded, he was avenged more pleasantly because he attacked one who was trusting rather than on his guard; and he received in addition a reputation for intelligence because he calculated what was safe and because he had prevailed over him by deceit.

2 He then says:

> And the many who were malefactors were called 'skilful' more easily than good men 'ignorant', and they are ashamed of the one and they exult in the other.

This has been expressed intricately and concisely, and what he is trying to indicate lies in obscurity. It would be difficult to know who in the world he thinks the ignorant and the good are. If he is contrasting them with the malefactors, those who were not wicked would not be ignorant. And if he is reckoning the ignorant as senseless and foolish, for what possible reason does he call these men 'good'? And who are the ones who 'are ashamed of the one'? It is unclear whether it is both or only the ignorant. And as for 'they glory in the other', here it is unclear who these are. If he is saying this about both, then he makes no sense, since good men do not glory in being malefactors nor are malefactors ashamed of being considered ignorant.

33   This type of unclear and smitten language, in which the annoyance that obscures the thought is greater than the charm, he extends for a hundred lines. I shall quote what follows without any of my own commentary:[94]

> And of all these things the cause was a desire to rule on account of greed and ambition, and a passion arising from these when they were directed towards contentiousness. For the leaders in the cities on each side, with fine-sounding phrases, in proffering 'political equality of the multitude' or 'restrained aristocracy', while serving

the common interest in word, were setting them up as prizes. Striving to get the upper hand in every manner with each other, they dared the most dreadful things, and they advanced in vengeances yet greater, not stopping at what was just and beneficial for the city but setting the limit at what brought pleasure to each side on every occasion. Either with an unjust vote of condemnation or acquiring power by force, they were ready to fulfil their immediate rivalries. And so neither side made use of piety, but those who managed to hide some malicious act with speciousness of speech were more highly regarded. The citizens in the middle, either because they did not take part in the struggle or because of envy that they had survived, were destroyed by both sides. In this way every form of evil habit arising from civil strife was established in the Greek world. And simplicity, in which nobility of character is the chief element, was ridiculed and vanished. Forming themselves up in opposing lines, untrustingly in their spirit, occurred widely. For there was no speech powerful enough or oath fearsome enough that could end the situation. All, when they gained the upper hand, reckoning on the uncertainty of their security, were contriving that nothing was done against them rather than being able to have trust. Those more lacking in understanding survived for the most part, for they boldly engaged upon actions, fearing that because of their own incapacity and the cleverness of their opponents, they would be defeated in a contest of words and would, because of their opponents' plotting mind, be anticipated in plotting against. Their opponents, thinking in their arrogance that they would foresee what would happen, and that they had no need to take by action what they could take by thought, were off their guard, and for that were more often destroyed.

Lest my treatise progress beyond what is necessary, I shall content 2 myself with these passages, even though I could make clear from still other examples that he is better in his narrative when he remains within the familiar and usual type of language, and worse whenever he turns aside his language from the familiar to strange words and forced figures, some of which have the appearance of solecisms.

Since I promised to make clear as well my views on his speeches 34 (where some think the writer's greatest power lies) I shall now

speak of these as well, separating out as before the content and the
2 style, beginning with the content. Content has two parts, first, the
discovery of arguments and ideas,[95] and second the employment
of these: the former takes its strength more from nature, the latter
more from art. Of these, the former, which is more a matter of
natural ability than of systematic study and which requires less
training, is somewhat admirable in this historian: as if from an
overflowing spring he bears a boundless supply of ideas and argu-
3 ments which are refined, strange and unexpected. The latter,
however, which requires more systematic study and makes the
other appear more illustrious, falls short of what is needed on
many occasions.

Now all those who have admired him beyond measure, and see
him as in no way different from those divinely inspired,[96] seem to
4 feel this because of his abundance of arguments. And if you try to
teach these people by giving an explanation on each matter, that
(for example) a particular argument was not suitable to be spoken
on this occasion and by these characters, or that another was not
suitable for its situation or was excessive, they become angry,
experiencing something like those who, because of some face or
other, have been mastered by a passion that is not so very far from
5 madness.[97] Such people think that all the virtues that are present
in beautiful forms belong also to the virtues that have enslaved
them, and those who attempt to criticize any blemish in them are
6 accused of being slanderers and quibblers. Similarly, these, mes-
merized by the one virtue, claim for him all the virtues, even those
that are not present: for each person thinks that what he wants to
7 be present in something he loves or admires is actually there. But
all those who preserve an impartial mind and make their examination of his speeches according to the proper standards – whether
they have some natural ability at criticism or whether they have
made their critical ability stronger through instruction – will not
praise everything equally, nor will they be critical towards everything; they will give proper recognition to his successes, and if
some part is faulty, they will not offer praise.

35   As for me, I have in all my critical studies not previously hesitated to lay out my standards and set my views out for all, nor
2 shall I desist from doing so now. As I said at the outset, although

I concede to the historian skill in his invention (and I think that anyone who has previously argued otherwise, whether through quarrelsomeness or a lack of critical sensibility, is wrong), I do not concede the other, that is, skill in his arrangements, except in a very few speeches.[98] I see as well that the defects in his style, about which I have already spoken, occur most frequently and are most serious in these forms: rare, strange and poetic expressions abound in these, and tortuous, intricate, and forced figures find their greatest number in these. Whether I have evaluated appropriately you and whoever is led to examine his words will judge. In these matters as well I shall set things out comparatively, analysing side by side those passages that I consider best with those that are not successful in their arrangement or blameless in their phrasing.

In Book 2, when he begins to write about the expedition against Plataea by the Lacedaemonians and their allies, and the Lacedaemonian king Archidamus is on the point of ravaging their territory, Thucydides presents ambassadors from the Plataeans coming to Archidamus and he gives them speeches which are the sort that were probable for both sides to have spoken, both fitting to their characters and appropriate to the occasion, and neither lacking in measure nor going beyond; and he has adorned the speeches with a language that is pure, clear and concise, and has the other virtues as well. He has simultaneously given them so melodious an arrangement that they can be compared with the sweetest compositions:[99]

In the following summer, the Peloponnesians and their allies did not invade Attica, but marched against Plataea. And Archidamus, the son of Zeuxidamas, king of the Lacedaemonians was in command. Encamping his army, he was about to ravage their territory, but the Plataeans immediately sent ambassadors who spoke to him as follows:

'You are not behaving justly, Archidamus, in making an expedition against the land of the Plataeans. For the Lacedaemonian Pausanias, son of Cleombrotus, when he had freed Hellas from the Medes with those Greeks who were willing to join together in the danger and in the battle that occurred in our territory, and when he had sacrificed in the agora of the Plataeans,[100] called together all the allies and handed over to the Plataeans the right to dwell in this land and territory of ours independently, and he stated that no one should ever unjustly march against them or with a view to enslaving them, and if anyone did, the allies present were to defend them with all their strength. Your fathers gave this to us because of our bravery and eagerness in those dangers. But you are doing the opposite of what they did. For you have come with the Thebans, our most hateful enemies, to enslave us. Calling the gods to witness – those who at that time heard the oaths as well as your ancestral and our native gods – we say to you not to act unjustly towards the Plataean land nor transgress your oaths, but to allow us to dwell independently, just as Pausanias thought just.'

2   When the Plataeans had said such things, Archidamus answered as follows:

'You speak justly, men of Plataea, if your actions are congruent with your words. For in accordance with what Pausanias handed over to you, be independent and join in freeing the others, all those who had a share in the dangers of those times and who swore to you but who are now under the rule of the Athenians.[101] This great armament and war have come about to free them and all the rest. Take part in *this*, and you yourselves will be abiding by your oaths. But if not, then do those very things we urged upon you before: remain at peace in the enjoyment of your own property and do not take the part of either side, but receive both sides as friends and neither side if their intent is hostile. And this will be acceptable to us.'

Archidamus, then, spoke in this way. When the Plataean ambassadors heard this, they went into the city. When they had shared Archidamus' remarks with the multitude, they answered him that it was impossible to do what he urged without consulting the Athenians, since their wives and children were with the Athenians; and they were afraid for the whole city as well, lest once the Lacedaemonians had departed, the Athenians should come and not entrust it to them, or the Thebans should attempt again[102] to capture their city on the grounds that the Plataeans were under oath to accept both sides.

And Archidamus, to reassure them, said, 'Then hand over your city and your homes to us Lacedaemonians; mark out the boundaries of the land and the trees and everything else that can be counted. Depart for wherever you wish to dwell as long as the war continues. When it is over, we shall give back to you whatever we received. Until then we shall hold it in trust, working the land and bringing you whatever produce shall be sufficient for your needs.'

When they heard this, they again went back into the city and after they had taken counsel with the multitude, they said that they wished first to take counsel with the Athenians about what he was asking them to do, and if they could persuade the Athenians, they would do it. But until then, they asked him to make a truce and not to ravage the land. He made a truce for the number of days that they would probably need to go and come back, and he did not lay waste the land. The Plataean ambassadors, going to the Athenians, took counsel with them and came back, reporting to those in the city the following: 'In the time before this, men of Plataea, from the time we became allies, the Athenians declare that never have they abandoned you when you were being harmed, nor will they now neglect you, but they shall bring aid with the power they can.[103] And they enjoin you, by the oaths that your fathers swore, not to alter the terms of the alliance.'

When the ambassadors had reported these things, the Plataeans resolved not to betray the Athenians, but to endure even seeing their land devastated if necessary, and anything else that might befall them, and also that no one should any longer leave the city, but that they should answer from the wall that it was impossible to do what the Lacedaemonians were urging.

When they had given this answer, Archidamus then first called the gods and heroes of the land to witness, speaking thus: 'All you gods and heroes who hold the land of Plataea, be witness that since these men had previously abandoned their oath, we have not come at the beginning unjustly into this land in which our fathers, having prayed to you, defeated the Medes, and which you furnished as a favourable place for the Greeks to contend in, nor shall we now be acting unjustly if we take action. For although we have made many reasonable offers, we are not successful. Grant, therefore, that those who first committed injustice should be punished and that those who are lawfully seeking vengeance should obtain it.' Having called the gods to witness with such words, he arrayed his army for war.

37 Let us examine alongside this dialogue, which is so beautifully and remarkably done, another dialogue of his, one which the
2 admirers of his style especially praise. He narrates that when the Athenians dispatched an expedition against the Melians, who were colonists of the Lacedaemonians, the Athenian general and the Melian counsellors, before the battle commenced, met in council concerning how they might avoid war. At the beginning, speaking in his own voice, Thucydides reveals what was said by each side,[104] but he maintains this narrative form for only one set of responses, and thereafter makes a dialogue and has the characters speak in their own person.
3   The Athenians begin by speaking as follows:[105]

> 'Since it is not to the people that we are making our speech – lest the people, no doubt, hearing in a continuous speech things that are attractive and not immediately capable of refutation (for we know this is the reason we are brought before the few) – you who preside over the city must act more safely. And do not make a single speech but render your judgement by answering straightaway to whatever seems not suitably spoken. And first say whether our proposal is acceptable.'
>
> The councillors of the Melians replied: 'The reasonableness of instructing each other undisturbed will not be faulted. But the circumstances of war, present now, and not things about to occur, show that they are different from this.'

4 If someone should claim this last phrase as figurative language, would he not first have to call figures all the solecisms of numbers
5 and cases that are present here? For Thucydides begins with 'The reasonableness of instructing each other undisturbed will not be faulted', but then, joining to this singular and nominative form 'But the circumstances of war, present now and not things about to occur', he joins to these a genitive either of the demonstrative article or pronoun, 'from this'. This agrees neither with the nominative feminine singular nor with the accusative neuter
6 plural. The sentence would be correct if it were constructed as follows:

'The reasonableness of instructing each other undisturbed will not be faulted. But the circumstances of war, present now and not things about to occur, show themselves different from reasonableness.'

He then follows this with an idea which is not absurd but is   7
expressed in a way difficult to follow:[106]

'Now then if you have come here in order to reckon suspicions of what will happen or taking counsel for the safety of your city from anything other than present circumstances and what you see, we shall cease speaking. But if it were for this, we would speak.'

After this he changes the dialogue from narrative to dramatic and   38
he makes the Athenian answer:[107]

'It is reasonable and understandable that men in such a situation will turn to saying and thinking in many different directions.'

Then, after an elegant statement: 2

'The meeting, however, is now concerned with survival, and, if you wish, let the conversation be in the manner you have described',

he first expresses a thought neither worthy of the city of Athens nor fit to be spoken in these circumstances:[108]

'Well, then, we for our part shall not offer a long and unpersuasive measure of speech, saying for example that because we destroyed the Mede we hold our rule justly, or that we have mounted this expedition now because we were treated unjustly.'

This is the same as saying that the expedition is against innocent men, since he is not willing to supply an argument on either of these points. He adds to this: 3

'Nor do we deem it worthy for you to think you will persuade us by saying that although you are colonists of the Lacedaemonians you have done us no wrong; you should try instead to achieve what is possible from those things that each of us truly thinks.'

This means the following:

'Although you think truly that you are being wronged, endure what is necessary and yield. We are not unaware that we are wronging you, but we shall prevail over your weakness by force. For this is what is possible for each side.'

4 Then, wishing to give an explanation of this, he says:

'that justice in human reckoning is judged from equal necessity, and those pre-eminent in power act, and the weak go along.'

39 These things were fitting for barbarian kings to speak to Greeks. But it was not befitting that Athenians, who freed the Greeks from the Medes,[109] should say to Greeks that justice is valid only among equals, whereas it is force that is used by the strong against the
2 weak. When the Melians say a few things in response to this, namely that it would be well for the Athenians to take thought for what is just, lest they themselves, stumbling at some point and coming under the power of others, should suffer the same things at the hands of those stronger, he makes the Athenians reply,[110] 'We are not despondent at the thought of the end of our empire, if in fact it should end', and give as the reason for this that even if the Lacedaemonians destroyed their empire, they would excuse the Athenians because the Lacedaemonians had done many such
3 things themselves. I shall quote his words: 'For it is not those who rule over others, as do the Lacedaemonians, who are terrible to the conquered.' This is similar to saying that tyrants are not hated
4 among tyrants. He adds, 'But as for this, leave it to us to run that risk', a remark that would hardly be made by a pirate or a brigand: 'I have no concern for the vengeance to come if I can satisfy
5 my present desires.' There follow a few exchanges, and the Melians now come to a reasonable proposal: 'And so would you not accept that we refrain from any action and be friends instead of
6 enemies, but allies of neither side?' He makes the Athenians

answer, 'It is not so much that your enmity harms us as that your friendship is a mark of weakness, while your hatred would be seen by our subjects as an example of our power', a wicked idea and tortuously expressed. If someone wishes to examine his thought, it is as follows: 'You will make us appear weak towards the rest if you are our friends, but if you hate us you will make us appear strong. For we do not seek to rule with our subjects' goodwill but with their fear.'

After adding some other answers by the Melians which are 40 overwrought and bitter, Thucydides portrays the Melians as saying that those at war are subject to the same power of fortune, and 'Yielding immediately would be without hope, whereas hope remains while we still take action.' To this he makes the Athen- 2 ians give a reply more convoluted than a labyrinth, to the effect that hope exists for men's destruction, writing (and I quote):[111]

'Hope, which is an encouragement to danger, even if it harms men who employ it when their resources are ample, does not destroy them. But for those who risk all they have – for hope is expensive by nature – she is recognized only when they fall, and once recognized she leaves nothing by which one may guard against her. You who are weak and balanced on a single turn of the scale must not be willing to suffer this, nor must you be like the majority of people, who, when they might still save themselves in a human way and when their visible hopes leave them as they are being hard pressed, have recourse to unseen hopes, divination and oracles and all such things that, accompanied by hopes, do such damage.'

I do not know how anyone could praise this as something fitting 3 for Athenian generals to say, that hope from the gods harms men, and that there is no benefit in oracles or divination for men who pursue a life that is pious and just. For if anything, the chief praise of the city of the Athenians is that in every matter and on every occasion they followed the gods and accomplished nothing without divination and oracles.[112] When the Melians say that with the 4 help of the gods they have put their trust in the Lacedaemonians – who, if for no other reason, then surely for the shame they would suffer, will bring aid to the Melians and not allow them, who are their kin, to be destroyed – Thucydides brings on the Athenian to answer more stubbornly still:[113]

> 'We do not think we are lacking the favour of the divine; for we are claiming and doing nothing beyond the recognized human view of the divine, nor of the wishes that men apply to themselves. For of the gods we suppose and of men it is manifestly clear that everywhere, by nature and from necessity, one rules those over whom one has power.'

The sense of this is difficult to conjecture, even for those who seem adept with this author's work, but it ends with some such conclusion as that all know the divine by supposition but judge what is just in their relations with one another by the common law of nature, and this is to rule over those whom one is able to conquer. These things follow from the first remarks and are fitting to be spoken neither by Athenians nor by Greeks.

41   I could offer much else of this kind of thought, which has an intelligence that is wicked, but in order not to have my essay go beyond measure, I shall cite only one more, the last remark which the Athenian makes as he is leaving the meeting:[114]

> 'But your strengths are hopes to come, while your present resources are slight for prevailing in the face of the forces arrayed against you. And you are displaying great irrationality in your reasoning if, after bidding us withdraw, you do not come to some decision more prudent than what you have offered so far.'

2   And to this he adds:

> 'And do not turn to that sense of shame which most often destroys men in wretched and manifest dangers. For even when they can still foresee into what circumstances they are being borne, this thing called dishonour has led many on by the power of a seductive name, and, defeated by a word, they fall – willingly – into irremediable disasters.'

3   That the historian himself neither was present nor took part in this conference, nor heard these speeches from the Athenians or

Melians who gave them can be easily shown from what he writes about himself in the previous book, namely that he was exiled from his country after his generalship in Amphipolis, and spent the remaining portion of the war in Thrace.[115]

Now then, it remains to examine whether he has fashioned this 4 dialogue with words suitable to the events and fitting to the characters who were present and took part in the conference, 'holding as closely as possible to the general purport of what was truly spoken', as he himself has claimed in the preface of his history.[116] 5 Well, the remarks of the Melians were appropriate and fitting, speaking about freedom and exhorting the Athenians not to enslave a Greek city that had done them no harm, but were those of the Athenian generals similarly fitting, they who would allow the Melians neither to discuss nor even to speak of justice, but rather introduced the law of force and greed, and claimed that for the weak justice was what seemed best to the stronger? I do not 6 think such words were fitting for the leaders from the city with the best laws to speak to foreign cities, nor would I expect that the Melians, who inhabited a small city and had performed no distinguished action, would take greater thought for what was noble than for their safety, and be prepared to endure every sort of horror so as not to be forced to do something shameful; nor indeed that the Athenians, who chose to abandon their territory and their city at the time of the Persian War so that they should endure no shameful injunction,[117] would have charged those who had chosen the same course of action with being fools. I think too that if anyone else had tried to say such things with the Athenians present, the Athenians, who have civilized the lives of all, would have been aggrieved.

For these reasons I cannot praise this dialogue when I compare 7 it with the other. In that earlier speech Archidamus the Lacedaemonian offers the Plataeans equitable treatment and in a language that is pure and clear, without any tortuous figures or anomalous grammar. But in this latter speech, the most thoughtful of the Greeks bring forward the most shameful arguments, and they express them in the most disagreeable language. Perhaps the his- 8 torian bore a grudge against his city for his condemnation and so cast against her these reproaches which would lead everyone to hate her.[118] For the sentiments that the leaders of cities and those entrusted with such great authority conceive and say to other cities on behalf of their own country are universally believed to be those of the city that dispatched them. But let this be sufficient for his dialogues.

42   Of the speeches addressed to the people, I have always admired the one in the first Book spoken by Pericles at Athens about not giving in to the Lacedaemonians, which begins thus: 'My considered opinion, men of Athens, I continue to hold in the same way as ever, not to give in to the Peloponnesians.'[119] The arguments are divinely expressed, and there is nothing to offend the ear, either in the arrangement of parts or by an unusual use of figures that are incorrect or forced; rather, it contains all the virtues that belong to speeches before the people.

2   I admire also the words spoken at Athens by Nicias, the general, about the expedition against Sicily, as well as the letter sent by him to the Athenians, in which he asked them to send another force and relieve him of his command because he was suffering

3   from illness; and the exhortation of his soldiers which he delivered before the last sea battle; and his speech of encouragement when he was about to lead the army away on foot, having lost all his triremes; and any other such public addresses that are pure, clear

4   and suitable for when the stakes are real.[120] But above all the speeches contained in the seven books, I have admired most the defence of the Plataeans, for no other reason than that it is not tortured or too elaborately finished, but is adorned with a colour that is true to life and natural.[121] The arguments are full of emotion and the style does not distract the ear. The composition is elegant and the figures are well suited to the events. These then are the achievements of Thucydides which are worthy of emulation, and I suggest that writers of history take models to imitate from these.

43   I do not praise all of Pericles' defence in the second Book, which he makes on his own behalf when the Athenians are angry that he persuaded them to take on the war; nor the public addresses concerning the city of Mytilene which Cleon and Diodotus give in the third Book; nor that of Hermocrates the Syracusan to the people of Camarina, nor the opposing speech given there by Euphemus,

the Athenian envoy;[122] nor any that are the same type as these: it is not necessary to enumerate all of those that are fashioned in the same type of style. Lest anyone think that I am making unsubstantiated claims, let me offer two public speeches (though I could furnish many other proofs), so that my essay might not become long and drawn out: Pericles' defence and Hermocrates' accusation at Camarina against the Athenians.

To begin, then, Pericles says this: 'I in fact expected your anger 44 against me (for I perceive its reasons) and I called this assembly so that I might remind you and fault you, if you are wrongly angry with me or are yielding to your misfortunes.'[123] It would have been appropriate for Thucydides to write this in the narrative proper but it was not suitable for Pericles to say in defending himself against an angered mob, especially at the beginning of his defence before softening, by means of some different words, the anger of people who were aggrieved with reason in view of their misfortunes: the best portion of their land had been ravaged by the Lacedaemonians and many of the common people had been destroyed by the plague, and the reason for this was the war which they had taken up because of Pericles' persuasion. Chastisement was not the most 2 appropriate stance for what he was trying to accomplish, but humble entreaty instead. It is not fitting for those who address the people to stir up the anger of crowds but to calm it.[124]

To this he adds an idea which is true and cleverly expressed, but 3 which is not, however, useful for the present occasion:[125]

> 'For I consider', he says, 'that when the entire city prospers it is more beneficial to individuals than when each of the citizens is faring well, but the city as a whole is cast down: if a man is doing well individually, while his country is being ruined, he will no less be destroyed along with it, while the man who is unfortunate in a city that is faring well is much more likely to be saved.'

Now if some of the citizens were being personally damaged but the state as a whole were faring well, then this would have been well spoken. But since all of them were in extreme misfortune, it was a poor argument. Nor would the hope that their present sufferings would turn out to be for the good of the city in the future be in any way secure: for the future is unknown to mankind, and the changes of fortune direct our beliefs about the future in light of our present circumstances.

45   He follows this with an even more vulgar sentiment and one least fitting for the occasion:[126]

'And yet you are angry with such a man as I, who am, I think, second to none in knowing what the situation calls for and in being able to explain it, a lover of his city and above bribery.'

2 Now it would be astounding if Pericles, the greatest speaker of that time, did not know what a person of even average intelligence knows, namely that those who do not praise their own virtues sparingly are everywhere manifestly burdensome to their audience, and especially so in trials in the law courts and assemblies,
3 where what is at stake is not honours but punishments. On those occasions they not only are burdensome to others but also bring misfortune upon themselves because they elicit jealousy from the multitude. And whenever someone is in a situation where his judges and his accusers are the same, he needs countless tears and appeals to pity just so that he can first gain a favourable hearing.
4   Yet the speaker is not satisfied with these remarks but he develops them and says in different words what he has already said:[127]

'For the one who knows but cannot clearly explain is the same as one who has not considered things, while the one who has both qualities but is hostile to his city likewise would not say anything appropriate. Whilst if he were favourable to his city but could be won over by money, he would sell everything for this one thing alone.'

5 Although this is true, no one would agree that this was fittingly spoken by Pericles before Athenians who were vexed with him. The discovery of the best arguments and ideas was not in itself worthy of effort unless it was also fitting to the events, characters,
6 occasions and everything else. But just as I said at the beginning, the historian displays his own opinion about Pericles' virtue and seems to have said it in the wrong place. What he should have done was say what he wished about the man but give to one who

was in a dangerous situation words that were humble and sought
to avoid the people's anger: for this was appropriate for the historian who wished to imitate real life.[128]

His juvenile adornments of speech and the intricate figures he 46
uses to express his ideas are annoying:[129]

> '. . . to come to close quarters with the enemy and to ward them off
> not only with contention but also with contempt.[130] For contention
> can come about even from fortunate ignorance and even a coward
> can have it, but contempt arises when someone trusts in his mind
> that he is superior to the enemy. Which is the case with us. Intelli-
> gence gives greater solidity to courage as a result of a consciousness
> of superiority. It trusts less to hope (whose strength is in extreme
> situations) but rather to insights based on the actual situation, and
> this foresight is more secure.'

Now the 'contention <and contempt>' is rather frigid and more 2
appropriate to the taste of Gorgias, and the explanation of the
words is both sophistic and tasteless. And the daring which 'given
equal fortune understanding makes more secure from a sense of
superiority' has a meaning which is more unclear than Hera-
clitean shades,[131] while the remarks about hope, 'whose strength is
in extremity', and about understanding 'from the actual situation
whose foresight is more secure' have been phrased rather poetic-
ally. For what he wants to say is that it is necessary to trust more
to the understanding that we take from present circumstances
than to hopes whose strength is in the future.

And here is something else I just realized: he softens the anger 47
that had taken them in their present misfortunes, most of which
had come about for them contrary to expectation and unforeseen,
and he urges them to bear up under their misfortunes nobly and
not to efface the reputation of the city; he tells them to put away
their private sorrows and to work instead for the safety of the
commonwealth. After this he goes on to say that while they hold
their naval empire securely, they will be overthrown neither by the
King of Persia nor by the Lacedaemonians nor by any other people
whatsoever, the proof of which resides not in the present but in the
future, and which has its secureness not in foresight but in

hopes – but then, forgetting all this, he demands that they not trust to hope whose strength is in extreme situations! These things are contradictory in as much as their suffering was experienced already in the present while the revelation of its utility was still absent.

2   Just as I do not praise these things in terms either of their subject matter or their style, so I admire the following as accurately conceived, finely expressed, and pleasantly constructed:[132]

'Indeed, for those who have a choice, when the rest of their affairs are prospering, it is great folly to go to war. But if it were necessary either to yield to one's neighbours and be subject to them or run the risk and prevail, then the one who flees the danger is more to be blamed than the one who undergoes it. And I in fact am the same and do not change my position, but you are varying your course because it happened that you were persuaded when you were unharmed, but now repent of it because you are suffering.'

And further:

'For what happens suddenly and unexpectedly and most contrary to calculation enslaves the spirit <and this has happened to you, in addition to everything else, especially with the plague.>[133] Nevertheless, it is necessary that those who dwell in a great city and have been brought up in a way of life worthy of her must be willing to undergo misfortunes and not efface her reputation. For men think it equally right that the one who falls short of his existing reputation through cowardice is worthy of blame, and that the one who lays claim to a boldness that is not existent is worthy of contempt.'

3   And again, the following words which arouse the spirits of the Athenians to their ancestral pride:

'It is reasonable for you to assist in the honour of the city that comes from its rule, an honour in which you above all take pride, and not to flee the hardships – or stop pursuing those honours. And do not think that the struggle is for one thing only, slavery rather than freedom, but also over the loss of your empire and the danger from those whose hatred you incurred while you ruled. Nor is it any longer possible for you to step away from your empire, if anyone, fearing this too in the present, is acting bravely – by sitting at home. For you now hold your empire like a tyranny, which seems unjust to have taken up but is dangerous to let go.'

– and everything like this, all the passages that have a modest variation from the usual words and figures and are neither over-wrought nor difficult to follow.

From the public address of Hermocrates I can praise the follow-   48
ing successes of the historian:[134]

'But we have not come here now to reveal to those who know all the injustices that the Athenians (who are easy to accuse) have commit-ted, but much more to blame ourselves, because although we have examples of how the Greeks there[135] were enslaved without even defending themselves and the Athenians are now using against us the same captious arguments – resettlements of the people of Leon-tini, their kinsmen, and assistance to the Egesteans, their allies – we are nevertheless not willing to join together and with greater eager-ness show them that there are not Ionians here nor Hellespontians or islanders, who are always changing rulers (either the Mede or some other), but rather Dorians, free men from the autonomous Peloponnese, dwelling in Sicily. Are we waiting until we are cap-tured city by city, even though we know that only in this way can we be captured?'

This is expressed in a clear and pure manner of speaking and has in addition rapidity, beauty, intensity, magnificence and forceful-ness, and has emotion suitable for oratorical debate. One might use such words in a law court or in the assemblies or even convers-ing with friends.

Here is another in addition to the previous: 2

'If someone feels jealousy or fear towards us (for greater powers suf-fer both these things) and because of those feelings wishes, on the one hand, that Syracuse be harmed so that we might be chastened, but on the other hand that she survive for his own safety's sake, he hopes for a plan that is not characteristic of human power. For it is not possible that the same man simultaneously be the steward of his desire and his fortune alike.'

And that which occurs at the end of the speech:

'We beseech you, therefore, and if we do not persuade you, we call you to witness that we are being plotted against by Ionians who are always our enemy, but we are being betrayed by you, Dorians by Dorians; and if the Athenians subdue us, they will have conquered us by your decisions, but they shall be honoured in their own name; and they shall take as their prize of victory none other than the one who furnished them with the victory.'

I think these passages and those similar to them are indeed worthy of emulation.

3   But I do not know how I could praise this:[136]

'. . . for now into Sicily with, on the one hand, a pretext which you all know but, on the other hand, an intention which we all suspect. And I think they wish not to resettle the people of Leontini but rather to unsettle us.'

4   The play on words is frigid and conveys not emotion but affectation. And what follows are complicated figures which have many convolutions:

'And not for the sake of the freedom of the Greeks, it turns out, did the Athenians oppose the Mede nor did the Greeks for their own freedom, but it was for this: the Athenians so that the Greeks would be enslaved to themselves rather than to the Medes, and the Greeks for a change of master, one who was not more unintelligent but more evilly intelligent.'

5   And further the tiresome substitution of singular for plural and change from plural to singular and from the characters' speech to the speaker's character as here:

'And if anyone has the thought that the Syracusan but not he himself is an enemy of the Athenians, and he considers it terrible to run
the risk for my country, let him consider that he is fighting in my
country not more for my country but equally for his own, and that
he will be safer to the extent that I am not destroyed first, and that
if he takes me as his ally, he will not be fighting in isolation; and that
the Athenian does not wish to punish the enmity of the Syracusan
<but rather, using me as the pretext, secure more greatly the friend-
ship of that one>.'[137]

These constructions are childish and pretentious and are more
obscure than so-called riddles.

And here is another example of this: 6

'And if he errs in his judgement, he might perhaps wish, when he is
mourned over for his own misfortunes, to envy once again my prosperity; but that would be impossible for one who abandoned me and
refused to take on the same dangers not in name but in reality.'

And to this he adds a conclusion that one would expect not even
from a youth:[138]

'For one would in name preserve our power but in fact his own
survival.'

There are in fact other passages in this speech worthy of censure   49
but about them I see no need to say more. I think I have with these
examples made sufficiently clear my thesis that Thucydides' diction is at its best when it departs moderately from customary
usage and maintains the first and essential virtues, and that it is
worse when it turns away greatly from common words and figures
to foreign, forced and ungrammatical constructions whereby
none of the other virtues can display their own power. This type   2
of style is useful neither in assemblies, where cities come together
and debate matters of peace, war, legislation and the proper
order of the state and other communal and important matters,
nor in the law courts, where speeches concerning death, exile,

disenfranchisement, imprisonment and confiscation of property
are addressed to those who have authority in these matters (in
fact, such rhetorical displays annoy the multitude who do not cus-
3 tomarily hear such things), nor in private conversations in which
we speak about daily life when we tell citizens, friends or relatives what happened to us, or discuss one of life's necessities,
admonishing or exhorting them or enjoying with them their successes and grieving with them in their sorrows. I need hardly say
that not even their own mothers and fathers could put up with
people speaking like this on account of its unpleasantness, but
they would need interpreters as if they were listening to a foreign
4 language. These, then, are my opinions about the writer, expressed
with all truth and to the best of my ability.

50   It is necessary that I briefly examine the remarks made by some
about him, so that I may be seen to have omitted nothing. All – or
at least those who are not perverted in their judgement but maintain their sensibilities in accordance with nature – will agree,
then, that this type of style is suitable neither for political contests
2 nor private conversations. But some well-regarded sophists try to
argue that while the style is not suitable for those composing
speeches before the mob or those speaking in court, it is altogether
appropriate for those writing works of history, where magnificence, impressiveness, and amazement are needed, to employ this
recherché, archaic, and figurative style, which departs from cus-
3 tomary figures in favour of that which is foreign and refined: for
they say that Thucydides did not compose his writings for the
man in the street or craftsmen or tradesmen or any others who did
not receive the education befitting a free man, but for those who
have passed through the systematic course of study for philosophy
and rhetoric, to whom none of this kind of language will seem
4 strange. And some have previously tried to argue that the historian composed his history in the way he did because he was not
aiming at posterity but at his contemporaries, for whom this style
of speech <was usual and known to all.> <. . .>[139] This style is not
suitable for either deliberative <or judicial> speeches in which
those who come together in the assemblies and law courts are not
the sorts of people whom Thucydides supposed.[140]

51   Now to those who think that reading and understanding the

language of Thucydides is only for the well educated, I have this to say: such people take away from our common life a work which is necessary and useful for all (for nothing could be more useful or more necessary), making this instead the property of an extremely small number, as if in cities ruled by oligarchies or tyrannies.[141] One can easily number those who understand all of Thucydides, and even these cannot do so without a grammatical commentary for some passages.

To those who would remove the language of Thucydides to 2 archaic times, I need offer but a brief and obvious argument: although many public speakers and philosophers lived in Athens at the time of the Peloponnesian War, not one of them used this language: not the orators Antiphon, Andocides and Lysias, nor Critias, Antisthenes and Xenophon, the followers of Socrates.[142] 3 By comparison with all these, it is clear that Thucydides first practised this means of expression so that he might differ from the rest of the historians. Now whenever he uses this style in a sparing and measured way, he is admirable and comparable to no one else; but whenever he employs it immoderately and tastelessly, observing neither the proper occasions nor the amount of it, he is to be faulted. I would demand that a work of history not be austere or 4 unadorned or lacking in art, but have some poetic quality about it; yet not entirely poetic but rather departing only a little from everyday speech.[143] For excess even of very pleasurable things is vexing, while proportion is in every way useful.

There still remains for me one topic, namely those orators and 52 historians who have imitated the man: now although this topic is as necessary as any for the completion of my treatise, it arouses in us a certain hesitation and a great deal of caution lest we provide an opportunity for attack to those who are accustomed to criticize everything in a manner very different from the fairness which we employ concerning both literature and the authors of literature. 2 To these people we will perhaps seem to be doing something disparaging and malicious if we bring in authors who did not imitate Thucydides well and cite those writings of theirs in which they took pride and because of which they acquired great wealth and were honoured with a distinguished reputation. Lest no such suspicion as this fall upon us, we shall omit criticizing certain people

and recalling their faults. Instead, we shall cite briefly some successful imitations and then conclude our treatise.

4   Of the historians of old, no one, to my knowledge, imitated
Thucydides in those areas in which he seems especially to have
differed from the rest: the recondite, archaic, poetic and strange
language; the transpositions, the convolutions, the ideas that want
to signify much in abbreviated form and take a long time to reach
their conclusions, and in addition to these, the use of figures that
are clumsy, wayward and joined up in a manner far from natural,
and which would be out of place even in poetry – from all of which
results an obscurity in his work which damages all its noble
qualities and casts its virtues into darkness.

53   Of the orators it was Demosthenes[144] alone who emulated
Thucydides just as he emulated all the rest of those who seemed to
have accomplished something great and distinguished in literature. He emulated Thucydides in many respects and added to his
political speeches the virtues which he took from Thucydides, virtues which neither Antiphon, Lysias nor Isocrates – the most
distinguished orators of that time – possessed, namely rapidity,
compression, tension, harshness, solidity and vehemence which
2 arouses emotion. He left aside the recondite language and what
was foreign or poetic because he did not consider them appropriate for real-life cases. He had no fondness for those figures which
wandered from natural sequence and had the appearance of solecisms, but he kept to customary usage, adorning his style with
variations and variety and by never entirely expressing his thought
3 without figures. But he did emulate the intricate thoughts, the
expression of much in a few words, the extension of a train of
thought over a long distance, and the unexpected way of expressing ideas, and he added these to his assembly and law court
speeches, less in his private orations, more abundantly in the public cases.

54   Of the abundant examples from both kinds of speeches, I shall
give only a few, and these will suffice for those who have read the
man. He has one speech before the people whose subject is the
war against the king in which he exhorts the Athenians not to
begin it offhandedly, since their own force is insufficient to battle
that of the king, and their allies will not share in the dangers

reliably and securely. He calls on them to make clear to the Greeks 2 that in outfitting their own force the Athenians will be undergoing the danger on behalf of the freedom of all if anyone attacks them. And he forbids them to dispatch ambassadors to the Greeks, to call them to war before the Athenians themselves have made their preparations, since the Greeks will not heed them. Taking this 3 as his thought, he has fashioned it and shaped it in the following way:[145]

But at that time, if we do what we are now thinking, surely none of the Greeks will have so high an opinion of themselves that when they see a thousand cavalry, as many hoplites as one could wish, and 300 ships, they will not come and beg us, thinking that with such forces their own safety will be most secure. But for you to call on them now is to beg, and, if you are unsuccessful, to fail also to achieve your objective; whereas if you hold off until you have made your own preparations, it is they who will beg you; and be assured that they will all come.

Now this departs from the usual political speech addressed to the masses and it is more powerful than an untrained speaker could do; but it is not obscure nor so unclear as to need interpretation. 4 He adds the following when he starts to talk about the preparations:

The first and most important aspect of preparation, men of Athens, is this: that you direct your thoughts in such a way that each man will do eagerly and willingly whatever needs to be done. For you see, men of Athens, that in all those matters where you ever decided something and afterwards each person thought it was appropriate for himself to take action, nothing ever eluded you; but whenever you decided something and afterwards you looked to others, each person believing that he himself need take no action, but his neighbour would do what was necessary, you have had no success.

Now here the thought in fact has been elaborately interwoven and has been expressed in a way that departs from the usual language, but it guards against over-refinement by its clarity.

5   And in the greatest of his speeches against Philip he has fashioned the very beginning like this:[146]

> Although many speeches, men of Athens, have been given in nearly every assembly about the injustices committed by Philip not only against you but also against the rest ever since he made peace, and although I know that everyone would say (if they do not actually say it) that we must speak and act so that he will cease from his effrontery and render us satisfaction, I see nonetheless that all our affairs have been so betrayed and sacrificed that I fear I may say something ill-omened but nevertheless true: if all those who had come forward wished to urge and have your vote on proposals which would ensure that our affairs be in as terrible a state as possible, I do not think that things could be in worse shape than they now are.

Similar to this is the following:

> And then do you think that the man who chose to deceive those who had done him no harm (but might have guarded against suffering any harm themselves) rather than give them notice before attacking them will make war upon you after giving you warning, especially as long as you are willing to be deceived?

6 In the most powerful of his judicial speeches, the one written on the crown, he mentions the skill with which Philip out-generalled the cities of Greece and fashions his thought in the following way:

> And I no longer add to the reckoning that the cruelty that one could observe in those places over which Philip became master was given to others to experience, while it was yours to enjoy in your good fortune the fruits of the compassion which he feigned for you while he accomplished the rest of his objectives.

7 In the passage where he reveals that those who betrayed their cities to Philip were responsible for all the evils that had come upon the Greeks he writes as follows (to quote exactly):

And yet by Heracles and all the gods, if we examine the matter
truthfully and put aside falsehoods and anything said in hatred, and
ask who were truly the ones on whose head everyone would reasonably and justly lay the blame for what has happened, you would find
that in each of the cities it is men like this one,[147] not those like me:
it was those who, when Philip's affairs were weak and completely
negligible and we were often warning you, urging you and instructing you on the best course, abandoned what was beneficial for the
entire state for the sake of their private lust for gain, deceiving the
citizens in each of their states and corrupting them until they made
them slaves.

I could furnish countless examples from the public and law court   55
speeches of Demosthenes which have been fashioned in the Thucydidean style, displaying departures from the usual way of speaking
in common and ordinary language. But lest my treatise become   2
longer than necessary, I shall satisfy myself with those above which
are suitable for confirming my proposition, and I would not hesitate to suggest to those who study political oratory (those at least
who preserve an undistorted judgement) that they should use
Demosthenes (who we believe was the most powerful of all the
orators) as their counsellor, and that they should imitate those constructions where his brevity, force, strength, tension, magnificence
and the virtues related to these are evident. And further, that they
should neither admire nor imitate those which are riddling, difficult to apprehend, in need of grammatical elucidation and
extremely tortuous, and have the appearance of solecisms.

In sum, it makes no sense to say that the historian's unclearly   3
articulated remarks and those that possess clarity along with all
the other virtues are equally deserving of imitation. One must
agree that what is perfected is better than what is not perfected
and that those things which are clear are better than those which
are unclear. Why in the world, then, do we praise the historian's   4
style as a whole and why are we forced to say that Thucydides wrote
for the men of his time things that were familiar and known to all,
but that he took no account of those of us of a later generation?
Why do we dismiss the language of Thucydides in its entirety from

the law courts and assemblies as being useless, rather than agreeing that the narrative portion of his work, with very few exceptions,
is marvellous and fit and proper for all sorts of uses, while the
speeches are not suitable for imitation in their entirety, but only in
those places where they can be easily understood by everyone,
even if it is not possible for everyone to compose in this way?

5   I could have written pleasanter things for you about Thucydides, my dearest Quintus Aelius Tubero, but not truer ones.[148]

Historians Most Suitable for Imitation

(Letter to Pompeius Geminus 3.1–6.11)

You wished to know what opinion I hold of Herodotus and Xenophon and you wished me to write about them. I have done this in the
treatise I dedicated to Demetrius, entitled On Imitation.[149] The first
book of this work treated the study properly speaking of imitation;
the second covered which writers – poets, philosophers, historians
and rhetors – one should imitate; and the third (not yet completed)
treats how one should imitate. In the second book, I write as follows
about Herodotus, Thucydides, Xenophon, Philistus, and Theopompus
(for I judged that these were the writers most suitable for imitation).

2   If I must speak about Herodotus and Thucydides also, here is
what I think of them.

The first and practically most necessary task for those writing
any kind of history is to choose a subject that is attractive and will
delight those who read it. I think Herodotus has done this better
3 than Thucydides, for Herodotus has produced a common history
of Greek and non-Greek deeds, 'so that neither human events may
become faded nor actions' <. . .>[150] and these very things he himself has said. For this preface is the very beginning and end of his
4 history. Thucydides, on the other hand, writes about one war, one
which was neither attractive nor fortunate: it would have been best
if it had never occurred, or, if it had, it should have been consigned
to silence and oblivion and been ignored by later generations. He
himself makes evident in his preface that he has chosen a poor

topic,[151] for he says that many Greek cities were devastated because 5 of the war, some by the barbarians, some by the Greeks themselves, and that there were exiles and massacres of peoples to an extent that had never occurred before, as well as earthquakes, droughts, plagues and many other misfortunes.[152] And so those reading the proem, since they are about to hear of Greek affairs, find themselves alienated by the subject. Herodotus is more 6 thoughtful than Thucydides in his choice of subject to the same extent that a composition which reveals marvellous deeds of Greeks and non-Greeks is greater than one which narrates the pitiable and terrible sufferings of Greeks. Nor is it possible even to say that Thucydides came to this topic from necessity: that although he knew that those other topics were finer, nevertheless he wished not to write about the same things as others. For inasmuch as he denigrated much earlier deeds in his preface and says that those accomplished in his own times were the greatest and most marvellous, it is evident that he chose his subject willingly.[153] Quite 7 differently did Herodotus behave: for although the earlier historians Hellanicus and Charon had published works on the same topic, Herodotus had the confidence that he would produce something greater. And that is the very thing that he did.[154]

The second task for a historical treatise is to know where to 8 begin and how far to go. Even here Herodotus appears much more thoughtful than Thucydides. For he begins with the reason why the barbarians first harmed the Greeks and having proceeded as far as the chastisement of the barbarians and the vengeance taken against them, he then stopped.[155] But Thucydides made his begin- 9 ning from the point at which the Greek world started to decline. He should not have done this, especially as he was a Greek and an Athenian (and not an Athenian of no account but one whom the Athenians considered among their first men, deeming him worthy of commands and other honours), nor done it so grudgingly as to impute to his own city the manifest causes of the war, even though he could have imputed the causes to many other sources.[156] He should have begun his narrative not from the events at Corcyra but from the greatest deeds that his city accomplished right at the end of the Persian Wars. (He has mentioned these events later in a poor and hasty manner and not in the appropriate place.)[157] He should have narrated these with much goodwill like a man loyal to his city,[158] and then to have added that the Lacedaemonians, as their envy and fear of these deeds progressed, entered into the war, although they alleged other reasons; and at that point he could have told about affairs at Corcyra, the decree against the Megarians and anything else of that sort that he wished to say.[159]

10   The ending has an even greater fault. For although he said that he lived through the whole war and he promised to explicate everything, he ends with the sea battle of the Athenians and Peloponnesians at Cynossema, which occurred in the twenty-second year of the war. It would have been better to have recounted everything and to have made an end of his history that would have been most admirable and especially pleasing to his audience: the return of the exiles from Phyle, which was the point at which the city recovered her freedom.[160]

11   The third task of the historian is to consider which events to encompass in his work and which to omit. In this too, I think Thucydides is wanting. For Herodotus realized that every narration of appreciable length pleasantly disposes the minds of the audience if it has some breathing spaces; while if it remains on the same events, even if it treats these successfully, it pains the reader with its excess; and so he wished to make his writing varied since he was an imitator of Homer.[161] And if we take up his book we are

12   delighted up to the last syllable and we want more. But Thucydides, stretching out one war, goes through battles upon battles and preparation on preparation breathlessly, joining together speech upon speech so as to exhaust the mind of the audience. As Pindar says, 'there is surfeit even of honey and the sweet flowers of Aphrodite'.[162] Thucydides recognized what I say – namely, that change and variety are a sweet thing in the writing of history – and he did this in two or three places, when he explains how the Odrysian kingdom became great and when he treats the cities in Sicily.[163]

13   The next task for the historian is to choose and arrange in its appropriate place each of the matters to be expounded. How then does each historian choose and arrange what he has to say? Thucydides follows the thread of chronology, Herodotus the contours of events. Thucydides can become unclear and hard to follow, because since many events happen in the same summer and winter

but in different places (as you would expect), he leaves the first events half-completed and then takes up other events happening in the same summer or winter. And as you would expect we get lost and we follow what's being described with annoyance, because our train of thought has been disrupted.[164] Herodotus, on the other hand, begins from the empire of the Lydians and comes down to that of Croesus, and then straightaway proceeds to Cyrus, the one who destroyed Croesus' empire, and then begins accounts of Egypt, Scythia and Libya, narrating some as sequences and taking up others as missing links, and still others he introduces to make the narrative more pleasing. And although he narrates Greek and barbarian affairs extending over 220 years[165] and brings it to a close with the retreat of Xerxes, he has not broken up his narrative. So then the result is that the one who took a single subject created many limbs for one body, while the other, who chose many subjects in no way alike, made one harmonious body.[166]

I shall mention one other quality which we seek in all histories no less than the ones already mentioned: the historian's own disposition which he employs towards the events that he narrates.[167] The disposition of Herodotus is equitable throughout, rejoicing with the good and grieving with the bad. The disposition of Thucydides is severe and bitter, grudging towards his city because of his exile. He goes through her mistakes in especial detail, but when events work out according to plan, he either makes no mention at all or as if under compulsion.[168]

On account of this, then, Thucydides is inferior to Herodotus in subject matter. In his style he is worse in some things, better in others, and equal in still others. I shall say what I think about this also.

The first virtue of all, without which none of the other precepts of rhetoric is useful, is a style that observes a purity of vocabulary and preserves Greek idiom.[169] Both writers are exact in this: Herodotus is the best model of Ionic Greek, Thucydides of Attic. <The second virtue is clarity: here Herodotus is incontestably superior to Thucydides.>[170] Third place is held by what is called concision. In this Thucydides is superior to Herodotus, yet one might say that brevity is sweet only when it is arranged with clarity, whereas if clarity is wanting, brevity is harsh. But let Thucydides not be considered inferior in this.

After these, vividness has been accounted first of additional virtues.[171] Both authors are appropriately successful in this.

18   Next comes the imitation of characters and emotions. The historians share this virtue: Thucydides is better at displaying emotion, while Herodotus is cleverer at representing character. After this are the virtues of composition which reveal what is great and marvellous: the historians are equal in these aspects also.

19   Following these are the virtues that produce strength, tension and similar qualities. Thucydides is greater at these than Herodotus. Herodotus, however, is far better at introducing into his work pleasure, persuasion, delight and such virtues as these. In expression Herodotus strives for what is natural, Thucydides for what is brilliant.

20   Of all qualities in literature the most important is appropriateness. Herodotus is more exact in this than Thucydides, for the latter employs a uniform style, even in the speeches more than in the narrative parts. I agree with my friend Caecilius, however, that Demosthenes especially imitated Thucydides' syllogisms.[172]

21   To put it briefly, the poetical compositions – for I would not hesitate to call them that – of both are beautiful, and they differ most from each other in this: the beauty of Herodotus is cheerful, while that of Thucydides is awe-inspiring.[173]

Although much else could be said about these historians, there will be another occasion for it, and this will suffice for now.

4   Xenophon and Philistus, who flourished later than Herodotus and Thucydides, were similar neither in their natures nor their choices. Xenophon imitated Herodotus in both aspects, i.e., subject matter and form. First, he chose subjects for his histories that were attractive and grand and suitable for a philosopher: the *Education of Cyrus*, the model of a good and fortunate king; the *March Up Country* of the younger Cyrus, a campaign in which he himself took part and which contains the greatest encomium of his fellow Greek soldiers; and thirdly the *Hellenica*, the narrative that Thucydides left unfinished, in which the Thirty are overthrown and the walls of Athens, previously torn down by the Lacedaemonians, rise again.[174]

2   Xenophon is worthy of praise not only for his subjects but also for his arrangements. For he has employed the most suitable

beginnings for them and has given each of them the most appropriate ending; he has divided and ordered his material well, and his writing has variety. He displays a character that is pious, just, energetic and accommodating – one, in short, that is adorned with all the virtues. Such is his way regarding subject matter.

His style is sometimes similar to that of Herodotus, sometimes 3 inferior. Like Herodotus', his style is suitably pure in vocabulary, and clear <and vivid>.[175] He selects words that are usual and natural to the subject, and he composes them with much sweetness and grace, the equal of Herodotus. But Herodotus also possesses grandeur, beauty, magnificence and what is called specifically the 'historical cast'.[176] Not only did Xenophon not have the strength to borrow this from him but when he wishes on occasion to elevate his style, he is like an offshore breeze, blowing for a short while and swiftly extinguished. In many passages he goes on longer than is necessary; nor does he, like Herodotus, attain a successful delineation of character, but if one examines rightly he is often negligent.

Philistus would seem to be more like Thucydides and to have 5 fashioned his style in accordance with him. He has chosen a topic that is neither of much use nor contains common achievements of Greeks and non-Greeks, but is single and, what is more, strictly localized. He divided this into two parts, entitling the former On Sicily and the latter On Dionysius. But it is a single subject, which you could recognize from the conclusion of the Sicilian part.[177] He 2 has not given his material the best arrangement but one that is difficult to follow, and is indeed inferior to Thucydides'. He is unwilling to admit extraneous material (just as Thucydides was) and his work is monotonous. He displays a character that is flattering, favourable to tyrants, mean and petty.[178] He has avoided 3 the peculiar and recherché aspects of Thucydides' style but he has imitated the terseness, asperity and argumentative aspect. Yet he falls very far behind Thucydides' beauty of language, solemnity and sheer richness of arguments. This is true not only in style but 4 in his use of figures. While Thucydides' expression is full of figures (and I do not think I need to say more about things that are obvious), that of Philistus is terribly uniform throughout and lacking in figures. One could find many periods one after the other fashioned in the same way by him, as for example in the beginning of his second book of *On Sicily*:[179]

5   The Syracusans, having taken with them Megarians and Eumaeans, and the Camarinaeans, having gathered the Sicels and the rest of their allies except the Geloans (and the Geloans said they would not fight against the Syracusans), and the Syracusans, having ascertained that the Camarinaeans had crossed the Herminus . . .

This seems to me a very unpleasant style.

6   He is petty and ineffectual in every aspect, whether he is narrating sieges or foundations or offering praise and blame. He does not make his speeches equal to the greatness of the speakers but makes even the most powerful speakers frightened, leaving behind their abilities and principles alike. He does, however, bring a certain natural elegance of style and an intelligence that strikes the mean. He is more suitable than Thucydides for actual courtroom cases.[180]

6   Theopompus of Chios was the most distinguished of all of Isocrates' pupils, and composed many panegyrics, many deliberative speeches, letters entitled *Chian* and other treatises worthy of note. As a writer of history he is deserving of praise, first for the subject of his histories (both are attractive, the one treating the conclusion of the Peloponnesian War, the other the deeds of Philip), second for his arrangement (both works are easy to follow and clear) and especially for the care and effort that he put into his writing.[181] For it is evident, even if he had not written anything about it, that he prepared himself by the greatest preparation for
3   the work and incurred the greatest expense in its composition. In addition, he was an eyewitness of many things and met and spoke with many of the leading men of his time – generals, popular leaders, philosophers – all for the sake of his history. For he did not, like some, consider the writing of history to be a secondary activity but rather an activity most necessary of all.[182] One could judge his effort by considering the varied nature of his writing. For he has narrated the foundations of nations, and has gone through the establishment of cities; he has revealed the lives of kings and the peculiarities of their characters; and he has included in his work whatever is marvellous or unexpected in every land and sea.

No one should suppose that he did this only for the purpose of entertainment, since this is not the case; on the contrary, his work offers every kind, so to say, of practical utility.

Leaving aside everything else, who will not agree that those 5 who practise philosophic rhetoric[183] must learn thoroughly the many customs of non-Greeks and Greeks, or hear about many laws and forms of constitutions and the lives of men, their deeds, their deaths, their fortunes? Theopompus has provided all these 6 in abundance and not separate from the events themselves, but alongside them. All these aspects of the historian deserve to be emulated and in addition all the philosophical musings throughout his work concerning justice, piety and the other virtues, on which he has expended many fine words.[184]

Finally and most characteristic of all his accomplishments is 7 something which no other historian, either those previous to him or after him, has elaborated so accurately or powerfully. And what is this? The ability in every action to see and express not only what is evident to the majority of people but also to examine the unseen reasons of deeds and of those doing the deeds, and the emotions of the soul (these are things which it is not easy for most people to know) and to uncover all the mysteries of apparent virtue and undetected vice. I think that perhaps the fabled 8 examination in Hades by the judges there of souls released from their bodies is of the sort that appears in the writings of Theopompus. This is why he has a reputation for slander, because in his reproaches of the famous he included along with what was necessary some things that were not.[185] But here he was acting as physicians do when they apply the knife and fire to the corrupted parts of the body, cauterizing and amputating up to a certain point, but not touching the healthy and normal parts.[186] Such, then, is the character of Theopompus in his subject matter.

His style is especially like that of Isocrates.[187] His diction is 9 pure, usual and clear, elevated and grand, and with much stateliness, arranged according to the middle style and flowing sweetly and softly.[188] His style differs from Isocrates' in its asperity and tension in parts, whenever he gives way to his emotions and especially when he reproaches the wicked plans and unjust actions of cities and generals (and there is much of this in his work). He 10 differs not even a little from the intensity of Demosthenes, as one can see in many of his other writings and especially the *Chian Letters* which he has composed giving vent to his natural feelings. He would have far exceeded himself in expression if in those passages where he expended the greatest effort, he had taken less effort over the blending of vowels, the circular rhythm of periods and the uniformity of figures.

11   There are also places where he is at fault in his subject matter, especially in his digressions: some of them are unnecessary, others are untimely, others display much childishness; for example, the account of Silenus' appearance in Macedonia or the serpent who fought a naval battle against a trireme, and not a few others of that sort.[189]

The historians treated here will suffice to furnish to those who practise civil oratory suitable starting-points in examples of every variety of style.

Purpose, Subject Matter, and Sources for the History

(*Roman Antiquities* 1.1.1–4 + 1.4.1–8.4)

Although I do not wish in the least to give the explanations that authors customarily offer in the prefaces of their histories, I am nevertheless compelled to say something about myself.[190] I do not intend to go on at length in praising myself, which would seem insufferable to my audience, nor do I intend to offer criticisms of other historians, as Anaximenes and Theopompus did in the prefaces of their histories.[191] Instead, I shall explain the reasons that induced me to embark upon this history and give an account of the sources from which I gained the knowledge of the events that I shall relate.

2   I am convinced that those who choose to leave behind to future generations monuments of their intellect which will not perish together with their bodies, and especially those who write histories – works which we all consider to be the very seat of truth, which is the beginning of reason and wisdom – should first choose topics that are noble and grand, and that will bring much benefit

to their readers;[192] and that they should then procure for themselves with great care and effort the sources which are appropriate for the composition of their topic. Those who compose treatises 3 containing matters that are inglorious, wicked or not worthy of our attention, whether they do so because they desire notoriety or to win some sort of name for themselves, or because they want to display the power of their eloquence, are neither admired by posterity for their notoriety nor praised for their talent; instead, they leave behind for those who take up their histories the belief that they approved of the sorts of lives which they treated in their works: for everyone rightly thinks that words are the image of each person's mind. Those, on the other hand, who have chosen 4 the best topics but have composed their accounts without effort and randomly from chance reports,[193] win no approval for their choice; for we do not think it worthy that the histories written about renowned cities and men of power should be written in a careless or lazy way.[194] Because I believe these are the necessary and first principles for historians and because I have taken much care on both counts, I did not wish to pass over them, nor could I place them anywhere other than in the preface.

Dionysius now defends his choice of subject by comparing the Roman empire to previous empires, both Greek and non-Greek, to prove that in writing about the Romans he is treating the 'most illustrious city' and the 'most brilliant actions'. He then argues that the early history of Rome is not well known by the Greeks.

I wish to say briefly that I did not turn to these long-ago events 4 of history without good reason or sensible forethought, lest some of those who like to criticize everything find fault with me (even though they have not yet heard anything that I am going to expound) because I inclined to a history of early times which could offer nothing of distinction about a city so celebrated in our times, but whose first beginnings were without distinction and humble, since it is only a few generations ago that it first acquired distinction and renown when it destroyed Macedonian monarchies and was successful in its wars against Carthage.[195] The history of early 2 Rome is unknown to nearly all Greeks, and certain opinions which are not true but began from chance reports have deceived the majority of them: for example, that Rome boasts of its founders as vagabonds, wanderers and barbarians – and these were not even free men! – or that in the course of time it advanced to world rule not through piety, justice and every other virtue but spontaneously and thanks to an unjust fate that randomly gave the greatest of goods to those who were most undeserving. The more malicious of such critics, moreover, customarily condemn fortune openly on the grounds that it gave the goods of Greece to the most

3 wicked of barbarians. And why should I speak of any others when even some writers have dared to write such things in their histories and leave them behind for posterity? These writers were the slaves of barbarian kings who hated Rome's hegemony, and they spent their whole lives associating with them and gratified them by writing histories neither just nor true.[196]

5   It is these false ideas, as I have called them, that I propose to eliminate from the minds of the majority, and substitute true ones in their place. I shall reveal in this first book who the founders of the city were, and in what eras they came together, and with what changes of fortune they left their native cities. By these means I attempt to show that they were Greeks and that they came from peoples who were by no means the lowest or the most contempt-

2 ible. Beginning with the next book, I shall relate the deeds they accomplished straightaway after the founding and the practices by which their descendants advanced to so great an empire. I shall leave aside nothing, as far as is in my power, of those matters worthy of history, so that I might draw my readers, who at that time will learn the truth, to have an appropriate opinion of the city – unless, of course, they have an unremittingly savage and harsh disposition towards it – and not to grieve at their subjection which has come about in accordance with probability (since it is a universal law of nature, which time shall not destroy, that the stronger always rule the weaker), and not to rail at fortune for having given as a present so great an empire and one which is already of such long duration to

3 a city which does not deserve it. They will learn in this history that Rome from the very beginning, immediately after its founding, produced men with countless virtues; no city Greek or barbarian produced men who were more pious, more just or more prudent throughout their whole life, or who were better competitors in

war.[197] For now, let there be no jealousy attached to my account: for the promise to recount events that turned out contrary to expectation or that are admirable invites just such a reaction. But all those who have brought Rome to such a degree of power are unknown to the Greeks because they have had no writer worth mentioning.[198] Indeed no accurate history of them written in Greek has been published up to our time, with the exception of some summary accounts which have been brief and treated only the high points.

The first as far as I know to have run through Rome's early history was Hieronymus of Cardia in his work on the successors of Alexander.[199] Then Timaeus of Sicily narrated the very early parts in his continuous history and Rome's wars with Pyrrhus in his separate treatise on that topic.[200] Contemporary with them were Antigonus, Polybius, Silenus and countless others,[201] who treated the same events but not in the same way: each of them wrote up just a few matters but even these they did not compile with care or accuracy but only from chance reports. Similar to these and indeed different in no way were all those Romans who published histories in Greek which treated the events of the distant past: the earliest of these were Quintus Fabius and Lucius Cincius, both of whom flourished during the Punic Wars.[202] Each of these men, thanks to his experience, wrote up accurately the events at which he himself was present, but ran through only the highlights of early events after the founding of the city. For these reasons I thought that I should not pass over a noble history, one which had been overlooked and unrecorded by older writers, and one which, if accurately written, will have the best and most just results: on the one hand, the brave men who have accomplished their destiny will obtain immortal renown and will be praised by future generations, something which makes our mortal nature similar to the divine and prevents our deeds from perishing together with our bodies; while present and future descendants of these god-like men, on the other hand, will not choose the most pleasant or easiest life but rather one which is most noble and ambitious, believing that it is appropriate for those who have distinguished lineage to have a high opinion of themselves and pursue nothing unworthy of their ancestors.[203] And I, who have turned to this work not for the sake of flattery but with care for justice and the

truth (for which every history should strive),[204] shall have the
opportunity to show my own intention, that it is beneficent towards
all men who are good and who like the contemplation of noble and
great deeds;[205] and secondly to offer grateful recompense, as far as
is in my power, to this city in remembrance of the education and of
all the other good things I have enjoyed whilst having lived in it.

7   Having offered an account of the reasons for my choice, I wish
to say something about the sources that I used while preparing
this book. For possibly some of those who have previously read
Hieronymus, Timaeus, Polybius, or another one of the historians
whom I mentioned above as slurring over the events, will find
much here written by me that cannot be found in those earlier
authors, and they will suspect that I have invented things and will
demand to know where I got my knowledge of these things. Lest I
acquire such a reputation with some, it would be best to say in this
2 preface which accounts and documents served as my sources. I
arrived in Italy just when Caesar Augustus had ended the civil
war, in the middle of the 187th Olympiad, and I have now been
twenty-two years at Rome.[206] I have learned thoroughly the Latin
language and I have acquired a knowledge of their native writings, and during all that time I have continued to investigate
3 anything that pertains to my subject. I was instructed about some
matters by their most learned men, with whom I met, while others
I gathered from those histories written by the men most praised by
the Roman themselves, namely Porcius Cato, Fabius Maximus,
Valerius Antias, Licinius Macer, the Aelii, the Gellii, the Calpur-
nii, and many others in addition to these, writers by no means
obscure;[207] I based myself on these treatises (they are written in a
manner similar to Greek annals)[208] and then set about writing my
4 history. This, then, is what I have to say about myself, and there
remains for me only to say something about the history itself,
what its chronological limits are, what events the narrative comprises, and what form I have given to the work.

8   I begin this history from the most ancient myths, those which
historians before me have omitted because this material is difficult
2 to discover without a great deal of study.[209] I end my narrative at
the beginning of the Punic War which occurred in the third year
of the 128th Olympiad.[210] I narrate in detail all the foreign wars

which the city waged in those times, and all the internal dissensions that occurred, explaining the causes from which they arose, and in what ways and with what speeches they were resolved. I go through all the forms of constitution that Rome employed, both the monarchical and that following the expulsion of the kings, and what the arrangement of each of them was. I describe their best customs and their most renowned laws, and in short I show the city's entire ancient way of life. The form I give my work is not 3 like that of the authors who have published histories that concerned wars, nor of those who have treated political constitutions in and of themselves, nor is it like those chronicles published by the writers of local histories of Attica – for those are uniform and quickly annoy those who read them – but it is a mixture of every form of public eloquence and theoretical reflection,[211] so that those who dedicate themselves to political eloquence, as well as those who are engaged in philosophical contemplation, and (if there are any) those who want only undisturbed amusement when they read history, will find it advantageous.[212] This, then, will be the subject 4 matter of my history and the form that it will take. I, its composer, am Dionysius, the son of Alexander, from Halicarnassus.[213]

The Need for a Full Contemplation of Historical Events

(*Roman Antiquities* 11.1.1–5)[214]

In the 83rd Olympiad, the one in which Crison of Himera was victorious, and when Philiscus was archon at Athens, the Romans abolished the decemvirate which had managed public affairs for three years.[215] I shall take up from the beginning and go through how they attempted to drive out an oligarchy that had by then taken root, what men were their leaders in liberty, and what their motives and reasons were.[216] I think the knowledge of such events is necessary and noble for everyone, so to speak, but especially for all those who spend their time in philosophical reflection and political activity.[217] For the majority do not consider it sufficient to 2 take only from history that the Athenians and Lacedaemonians, to take an example, won the Persian War in two sea battles and one land battle, themselves and their allies not greater than 110,000 overcoming the barbarian who brought three million troops,[218] but they want to learn from history the locations where the deeds took place, and to hear the reasons why they accomplished these amazing and unexpected deeds, and to inform themselves who the leaders were, both of the Greek and barbarian contingents, and to be uninformed about not a single incident, one might say, of all those that were accomplished in these contests.[219]

3   The mind of every person takes pleasure in being escorted through words to deeds, not only hearing what is being said but also seeing what is being done.[220] Not even when they hear of political actions are they satisfied to learn only the main point and the conclusion of events – for example, that the Athenians, making no effective opposition to the Lacedaemonians, agreed that the latter could destroy the walls of their city, divide up their fleet, set a garrison on their acropolis, and designate an oligarchy for their affairs in place of their ancestral democracy – but they will demand immediately to be instructed about what necessities encompassed the city that they should endure these terrible and wretched miseries, what words persuaded them, and what men

4   spoke those, and everything that pertained to these events.[221] Men engaged in public affairs – and I include among them any philosophers who believe that philosophy is the practice not of words but of noble deeds – take pleasure in a full contemplation of everything that pertains to events, just as the rest of mankind does. But apart from pleasure there is in addition the fact that they can benefit their cities in troublesome times from such experience and they can lead them willingly towards what is beneficial through

5   speech.[222] For people most easily learn what is beneficial and what is harmful when they see such things in many examples, and they testify to the thoughtfulness and great wisdom of those who urge them on to these courses of action. For these reasons I decided to go through in detail the events surrounding the destruction of the oligarchy, all those at least that I consider worthy of account.

Preserved amongst Dionysius' writings is a work entitled Art of Rhetoric, *but it is neither a handbook of rhetoric nor is it by*

Dionysius. It was probably written in the 2nd or 3rd century CE, *and possibly by different hands. Much of it consists of rules for composing different types of epideictic speeches.*[223] *The remark below is included because the thought has been very influential in later ages and is still today regularly cited.*

History is Philosophy by Example

(Pseudo-Dionysius, *On Rhetoric* 11.2 = 376–7 U–R)

Plato says this also, that 'poetry by embellishing countless deeds of the ancients, educates future generations.'[224] And education, you see, is an encounter with characters. Thucydides also seems to say, in speaking about history, that history is philosophy arising from examples:[225] 'but if all those who wish to examine the clarity of events – both those that occurred and those that will occur at some time or another in accordance with human nature in the same or similar ways – will judge this useful' <...> to use ancient histories and examples of characters just as we use history as an example of life.

LIVY

Titus Livius was born in Patavium (modern Padua) in 59 BCE. Little is known of his life. He seems not to have had any sort of political career, though he was on familiar terms with the emperor Augustus and he supposedly encouraged the future emperor Claudius in the latter's attempts at history. He is said to have written philosophical dialogues but his fame rests on the enormous history of Rome that he composed in 142 books, beginning with the foundation of the city and extending to the year 9 BCE. Of these only thirty-five survive, Books 1–10 and 21–45. There are also summaries of each book (except for Books 136 and 137), composed probably in the fourth century CE, but these are brief and unreliable. There is also a summary of Books 37–40 and 48–55 on the so-called 'Oxyrhynchus Epitome' of the early third century CE.

Although considered one of Rome's great historians, modern scholars have frequently found Livy wanting, whether because of his excessive patriotism, simple morality or naïve approach to his sources and to history. More recent scholarship has emphasized the brilliance of his artistry and the detached, sometimes ironic, narrator behind the history. It should be noted that we might have a very different notion of Livy as a historian if the contemporary portions of his work survived rather than the books on early Rome.[1]

The preface below is intended for the entire work, though it is likely that it appeared when the first five books of the history were published. Although it looks to the whole history, the author here also notes (*preface* 5) that the early history allows him, if only temporarily, relief from the consideration of the more violent and discordant history of the late Republic, the times in which Livy himself wrote his history.[2] The passages that follow give some sense of the challenges Livy faced in attempting to write an enormous history that went far back in time.

Preface to *From the Foundation of the City*

(*preface* 1–13)

Whether I shall do something worthwhile in writing a detailed account of the affairs of the Roman people from the origin of the city, I do not rightly know, nor, if I did know, would I dare to say,[3] 2 since I see that the subject is both old and commonplace, in as much as later writers always believe that they will bring more certainty concerning events or will surpass ancient crudeness in their literary style.[4] Whatever it is, it will none the less be a pleasure for 3 me to have given my attention personally to recording the events of the leading people of the world to the best of my ability; and if in such a crowd of writers[5] my own reputation should reside in obscurity, I would console myself with the nobility and greatness[6] of those who will stand in the way of my name.

In addition, the task requires immense labour since it must be 4 traced back more than 700 years, and is something which began from the smallest of origins and has now grown to such a point that it is labouring under its own greatness.[7] I also do not doubt that first origins and their immediate sequel will provide less pleasure for many of my readers, since they will be hastening to recent history,[8] where now for a long time the strength of a preeminent people has been destroying itself. I, on the contrary, shall 5 seek this additional reward for my labour: that for the whole time that I am absorbed in those events of long ago I shall avert my gaze from the evils that our own age has seen now over many years;[9] and I shall be free of that care which can trouble the mind of a historian, even if it cannot deflect it from the truth.[10]

I have no intention of affirming or refuting those things which 6 are handed down about events before or when the city was being founded, and which are more appropriate to the myths of poetry[11] than to the uncontaminated records of history.[12] Antiquity is 7 granted the indulgence of making beginnings of cities more revered by mixing human and divine together; and if it is fitting to permit any people to hallow its own origins and to have recourse to gods as its founders, then such has been the renown of the

Roman people in war that, when it traces its parent and its founder's parent back to Mars above all, then the people of the world endure this with the same equanimity with which they endure Roman rule.[13]

8
9 But I shall think it of no great importance how these and similar things will be judged and evaluated; for me each reader should give his keen attention to the following: what was the manner of life, what was the behaviour, through what men and by what means at home and abroad was empire acquired and increased; then let him follow in his mind how, as discipline faltered little by little, behaviour at first subsided, then became more and more unsteady, and then began to plunge headlong until we arrived at the present age in which we can endure neither our disorders nor the cures for them.[14]

10 In learning of historical events what is especially beneficial and fruitful is this: that you gaze at evidence of every sort of example placed as on a shining monument, from which you can take things to imitate for yourself and your country, and things to avoid, as being foul in their beginnings and foul in their conclusions.[15]

11 For the rest, either love of the task I have undertaken deceives me or no state was ever greater or more scrupulous or richer in good examples, nor was there any state into which greed and luxury migrated so late, nor any place where poverty and thrift were
12 held in such great honour and for so long.[16] So true was it that the less people owned, the less covetousness there was; of late, riches have ushered in greed, while plentiful pleasures have brought a desire for going to ruin and destroying everything through extravagance and licence.

Complaints, however, are perhaps not pleasing even when they are necessary, and they should certainly be absent from the begin-
13 ning of such an undertaking as this one. Instead, if it were the custom for us, as it is for poets, we would begin more willingly with favourable omens and with vows and prayers to the gods and goddesses, that they grant a successful outcome to the beginnings of so great an enterprise.[17]

Conflict in the Sources

(4.23.1–3)

I find in Licinius Macer[18] that the same consuls were re-elected in the next year, Julius for the third time, Verginius for the second.[19] Valerias Antias and Quintus Tubero[20] give Marcus Manlius and Quintus Sulpicium as the consuls for this year. But despite their 2 discrepancy both Tubero and Macer claim they are basing themselves on the Linen Books;[21] nor does either hide that early writers said that military tribunes were elected in this year. Licinius likes 3 following the Linen Books without hesitation; Tubero is uncertain of the truth. Given that everything else is shrouded in antiquity, this too must be left undecided.[22]

New Start to Roman History

(6.1.1–3)[23]

I have recounted in five books, from the founding of the city of Rome to its capture, the Romans' wars abroad and dissensions at home, first under the kings, then with consuls, dictators, decemvirs, and consular tribunes.[24] These matters are difficult to discern 2 given their extreme antiquity, like things that can scarcely be made out from a great distance.[25] Then too writing, the only trustworthy guardian of the memory of events, was brief and rarely used in those times, and as for what did exist in the records of the priests and other public and private monuments, most of it was destroyed when the city was burned. From here on, however, events at home 3 and abroad will be described more brightly and with greater certainty from the second beginning of the city, reborn, as if from the stalk, more prosperously and fruitfully.

Family Traditions and History

(8.40.1–5)

Certain authors say that this war[26] was fought by the consuls and that they triumphed over the Samnites, and that Fabius also advanced into Apulia and led away great spoils from there. There is
2 no disagreement that Aulus Cornelius was dictator in this year, but it is unclear why he was named dictator, whether for the sake of waging war or so that there be someone in the absence of the praetor Lucius Plautius (who was by chance suffering from a serious
3 illness) to give the starting signal at the Roman games[27] for the chariot races, and whether Cornelius, having performed what was hardly a memorable exercise of power, resigned his dictatorship. And it is not easy to choose one account over another or one author-
4 ity over another. I think that the tradition has been corrupted by funeral eulogies and false labels for masks,[28] since each family arrogates to itself the reputation of deeds and honours with a falsehood
5 that deceives. From this it is certain that the deeds of individuals and the public monuments of events are confused; nor is there any writer contemporary with those times on whose authority one can safely base one's account.

23

THE ELDER SENECA

Lucius Annaeus Seneca, the elder, was born at Corduba (modern Córdoba) *c.* 50 BCE. He seems not to have had a political career. He married Helvia, also of Spain, by whom he had three sons, most famously his namesake, the younger Seneca. He was also the grandfather of the poet Lucan. He died around 39 or 40 CE. He wrote a history from the beginning of the civil wars (49 or 43 BCE) up to his own time, and this was published by his son after his father's death. Only two fragments survive that might have been part of the work, but some think even those belong to the son. Seneca's two most famous works are the *Controversiae* (fictional cases, often dealing with difficult or contradictory legal situations) and the *Suasoriae* (fictional speeches directed towards a historical or mythological character urging him for or against a certain action, e.g., should Hannibal invade Italy?). There is much of historical interest in the former (Seneca preserves several historians' accounts of Cicero's death, for example), and the passage below offers a memorable characterization of an outspoken speaker and historian. The passage should be compared with Tacitus' account of the trial of Cremutius Cordus (*Annals* 4.33–4).[1]

The Frank Speech of Titus Labienus

(*Controversiae* 10, preface 4–5, 7–8 = *FR Hist* 62 T 2)

Do you ask about Titus Labienus?[2] He did not declaim before the people but he was extraordinary at declamation.[3] He did not allow the public in both because this custom had not yet been introduced[4] and because he thought it was unseemly, a mark of empty ostentation. He affected a censor's haughtiness,[5] although at heart he was not like that. He was a great orator who struggled against many obstacles, and people had to admit (somewhat against their will) that he had achieved renown for his genius. His poverty was extreme, his notoriety was extreme, his hatred was extreme. But an eloquence which pleases people even against their will must be great eloquence, and since it is people's approval that declares and nurtures genius, how great must that force be which breaks forth amid such obstructions. There was no one who did not, while reproaching everything about the man himself, pay considerable tribute to his genius.

5 His style was that of the oratory of old, his forcefulness that of the new oratory; his refinement was halfway between the previous era and ours, such that each one could claim him for their own. His freedom of speech was such as to exceed the name of freedom,[6] and because he indiscriminately lacerated all ranks and men, he was called 'Rabienus'.[7] Even with such faults, his spirit was enormous, and violent like his genius, and one which had not yet put aside its Pompeian spirit[8] even in an era of such great peace.

For him a new penalty was first devised: his enemies ensured that all his books should be burned.[9] This was a strange and unknown thing, that a penalty should be exacted from literary works . . .

7 How great and how dissatisfied with the rest of its objects is the savagery that sets the flame to literary works and punishes monuments of learning! Thank the gods that those punishments for works of genius began in an age when such works had ceased![10] He who had offered his advice that this punishment be visited on Labienus' writings had his own books burned while he was still alive: no longer a bad example because it was visited on him!

Labienus could not endure this affront, nor did he wish to survive his genius; instead, he ordered that he be carried to the monuments of his ancestors and immured there, afraid no doubt that the fire which had been set to his reputation would be denied his corpse.[11] He not only ended his life, he buried it.

I remember that when he was reciting his history once, he rolled 8 up a big part of the book and said, 'What I pass over here will be read after my death.'[12] What frankness must have been in those passages if even Labienus was afraid of it!

24

POMPEIUS TROGUS

Pompeius Trogus was a slightly younger contemporary of Livy. His family came from Gaul and he himself tells us that his grandfather was given Roman citizenship by Pompey and that his father served under Julius Caesar. He wrote a work entitled *Philippic Histories*, a universal history in forty-four books that began with the Assyrians and Medes and came down to the author's own time. It is a rare instance of universal history written in Latin. The title of the work suggests that he may have been influenced by Theopompus, and he does seem to show the same wide interests in peoples and customs.[1] The work does not survive, however, and we owe our knowledge of it to Marcus Iunius Iustinus (known as Justin) who made a collection of excerpts from the whole work in the fourth century CE; we also have summaries (called 'prologues') of the contents of individual books. It is uncertain to what extent Justin's work is a thoroughly reliable guide to Trogus' work. In the fragments below, we can have some certainty since Justin explicitly attributes the sentiments to Trogus.[2]

Speeches in History

(F 152 = Just. 38.3.10)

Then he [sc. Mithridates][3] calls his soldiers to assembly and urges them with various exhortations to the Roman or rather the Asian wars.[4] This is a speech of which I thought it worthy to insert a copy into the present brief work. Pompeius Trogus expressed the speech indirectly since he found fault with Sallust and Livy for transgressing the scope of history by inserting into their work direct addresses as if they were in their own speech.[5]

Treating the History of Rome

(F 161 = Just. 43.1.1–2)

Having narrated the affairs of the Parthians, the eastern peoples, and those of nearly the whole world as far as the origins of the city of Rome, Trogus returns home, so to speak, as if after a long journey abroad, and he expresses the opinion that he would be an ungrateful citizen if he were to be silent about his country alone,
2 when he had narrated the events of all peoples.[6] And so he merely touches briefly on the origins of the Roman empire so that he neither exceeds the scope of the work he set himself[7] nor, in particular, passes over in silence the origins of the city which is the capital of the whole world.

25

THE YOUNGER SENECA

Lucius Annaeus Seneca, the younger, was born in Spain at Corduba *c.* 4 BCE. By 5 CE he was in Rome, where he studied grammar, rhetoric and philosophy. He won an excellent reputation as an orator, though in 39 he offended the emperor Caligula and was in serious danger. Banished in 41 to Corsica by Claudius (the charge was adultery), he returned to Rome in 49, thanks to the influence of the younger Agrippina, the mother of the future emperor Nero (ruled 54–68) whose tutor Seneca became. In the early years of Nero's reign Seneca was enormously influential, but thereafter his authority declined, and in 62 he requested permission to retire and hand over his vast wealth to Nero. Though the emperor refused, Seneca maintained a low profile, concentrating on writing and philosophy. In 65 he was forced to commit suicide in the aftermath of an unsuccessful conspiracy against Nero (Seneca probably knew of it but was not an active participant); his death, modelled on that of Socrates, is described (not wholly sympathetically) in Tacitus, *Annals* 15.62–4.

Seneca was a vastly prolific author, writing plays (of which nine survive) and philosophical essays and dialogues (many of which survive). The extracts below come from the *Natural Questions*, a work of his later years, which treated (as the title suggests) natural phenomena, and from his satire written after Claudius' death (in 54) called the *Apocolocyntosis* (or *Pumpkinification*). The former passages throw light on the ways in which philosophy dismissed history, while the last shows how easily historiographical conventions could be parodied.[1]

History Inferior to Philosophy

(*Natural Questions* 3, preface 5–10)

Some have worn themselves out while composing the deeds of foreign kings, or reciprocally the sufferings and bold acts of nations. How much better is it to do away with one's own ills than to hand down to posterity those of others? How much better to celebrate the works of the gods rather than the brigandage of Philip and Alexander, and of the rest who, famous for the destruction of the human race, were no less harmful to mortals than a flood which covers every plain or a conflagration that consumes a great part of all living creatures?

6   They write about how Hannibal crossed the Alps, how he unexpectedly brought upon Italy a war that was supported by the disasters in Spain; how tenacious he was even after Carthage, when his affairs were broken, and he wandered amongst the courts of kings, offering himself as a leader against the Romans, asking for an army; and how even as an old man he did not cease to seek war in every out-of-the-way place – so true it is that this man could endure without a country but not without an enemy.[2]

7   How much better is it to seek out what should be done rather than what has been done, and to teach those who have entrusted their own affairs to fortune that nothing fortune bestows is stable, and that her every gift is more fickle than a breeze. She does not know how to be inactive, she rejoices in replacing joys with sorrows, or at least in mixing the two. And so no one should trust her when things are going well, or lose heart when things are going badly.[3] Changes of circum-

8   stance alternate. Why are you happy? You do not know at what point those things that lift you on high are going to leave you: they will have *their* end, not yours. Why are you despondent? You have been brought to the very depths: now is the time to rise again. When things are going against you, they change for the better; when you have what you want, they change for the worse.

9   And so you must grasp in your mind this changeability not only in the private realm (where a slight change in circumstances is enough to cause destruction) but also in public ones. Kingdoms that began from the humblest of circumstances have risen above the ruling

classes, and ancient empires have fallen in the full bloom of their power. One cannot count how many kingdoms have been destroyed by others. At the very moment that the divinity raises some, he brings others low, and he does not put them down gently, but hurls them from their very height with no trace of them remaining.[4]

We believe such matters are great because we are small. In many things 'greatness' comes not from nature itself but from how little *we* are. What is important in human life? Not to fill the seas with fleets, nor to plant one's standards on the shore of the Red Sea,[5] nor, when the land no longer suffices for committing wrongs, to wander over the sea seeking the unknown. It is rather to see everything in one's mind and to have conquered one's faults – there is no greater victory than this. Those who have had dominion over other peoples and cities are innumerable; very few are those who have had it over themselves.

Historians and their Sources

(*Natural Questions* 4b.3.1)

. . . if I assure you that hail is formed in the same way that ice is here on earth,[6] when an entire cloud is frozen, I will have done something too bold. And so count me among those witnesses of a second order who say they have not seen something but have heard it. Or I myself will do what historians do: when they have told lots of lies to their heart's content, they take one item and refuse to vouch for it, and add, 'The responsibility for this must rest with my sources.'[7]

Falsehoods of Historians

(*Natural Questions* 7.16.1–2)

I have refuted the arguments and now I must refute the witnesses.[8] One does not need a lot of effort to destroy Ephorus' credibility: he is a historian.[9] Some historians receive praise because they tell

of unbelievable things, and by using the marvellous they stimulate
a reader who would do something else if he were merely being led
through everyday incidents.[10] Some historians are credulous, some
negligent; falsehood creeps up on some of them unawares, while
others delight in it; the former cannot avoid it, the latter seek it
2 out.[11] What the whole tribe have in common is that they think that
their work will not be approved or popular unless it is sprinkled
with lies. Truly Ephorus is not a man of the most scrupulous
trustworthiness: he is often deceived, he more often deceives.[12]

*In his satire on the emperor Claudius (the title is a play on the
word 'deification') Seneca begins with a parody of historiographical claims, including the remark that he is impartial. He then
quickly reveals the true nature of the work by a pretended show of
silence and then the cheeky remark that since historians do not
have to provide witnesses, neither does he.[13]*

Parody of Historians' Claims

(*Pumpkinification of Claudius* 1.1–2)

I wish to record what happened in heaven three days before the Ides
of October in the new year,[14] at the beginning of a most auspicious
era. No concession will be made to offence or favour.[15] These things
are true just as I state them.[16] If anyone should ask how I know, first
I shall not reply if I do not wish to do so. Who is going to compel
me? I know that I became free from the moment when that man met
his fate who had made the proverb come true that one should be
2 born either a king or an idiot.[17] If I do choose to respond, I shall say
whatever comes into my mouth. Who ever demanded sworn witnesses from a historian?

26

QUINTILIAN

Marcus Fabius Quintilianus was born about 35 CE in Calagurris (modern Calahorra) in Spain. His father was a rhetorician, and at some point the young Quintilian came to Rome where he studied with Domitius Afer (a prosecutor under Tiberius whom Tacitus, at least, has harsh words for at *Annals* 14.19) and presumably had a public career at the Roman bar. He is said to have been the first rhetorician to receive a salary from the state, and he was the first occupant of the Chair of Rhetoric established by Vespasian in 72. He taught for twenty years (the younger Pliny was one of his students) and after he retired he wrote the treatise for which he is known, *The Orator's Training*. An enormous work in twelve books, it is the fullest and most systematic treatment of ancient rhetoric that has come down to us. In the excerpts below, Quintilian explains what the reading of history in general can contribute to the orator's training and which historians in particular the budding orator should read.[1]

The Orator's Reading of History

(*The Orator's Training*, 10.1.31–4)

History too[2] can nourish the orator with a certain rich and pleasant sap; but likewise it must be read in such a way that we realize that many of its virtues must be avoided by the orator. For history is very close to poetry and is in some sense verse without metre, and it is written to tell a story not to demonstrate a point. This whole class of work is composed not for some performance or for an immediate contest,[3] but for the memory of posterity and the renown of the author's ability;[4] and so it seeks to avoid the tedium of narrative by employing more recherché words and somewhat

32 freer figures.[5] And so, as I previously said,[6] we must not seek that famous brevity of Sallust to use on some judge who is occupied with various concerns and himself rather often unlearned, even though nothing could be more accomplished for listeners who have time on their hands and are educated; nor will that milky richness of Livy sufficiently teach one who seeks not beauty of

33 exposition but a trustworthy account. Consider too that Marcus Tullius thinks not even Thucydides or Xenophon are useful for the orator, even though he judges the one to 'sound the war trumpet' and the other to be 'the mouthpiece of the Muses'.[7] We can, however, in digressions sometimes use the historian's sheen, provided we remember that in those matters in which a question is involved, we need not the bulging muscles of the athlete but the sinewy arm of the soldier;[8] nor will that multicoloured garment which Demetrius of Phalerum was said to have used be effective in the dust of the forum.[9]

34 There is also another use for history and it is in fact very important but not pertinent to our discussion here, and that is the familiarity with events and examples with which the orator especially ought to be equipped.[10] The orator should not expect to get all his evidence from his client but he should derive a good deal from his careful knowledge of antiquity, for such evidence is more effective because it alone is free from charges of enmity and from favouritism.[11]

Historians the Orator Should Read

(*The Orator's Training*, 10.1.73–5, 101–4)

Many have written history brilliantly but no one doubts that two   73
are to be preferred far and away to the rest, and though their
excellence is different, the praise they receive is nearly equal.[12]
Thucydides is concentrated, brief and constantly urging himself
on, while Herodotus is charming, lucid and expansive: the former
is better at vehement emotions, the latter at moderate emotions;
Thucydides is better at formal addresses, Herodotus better at
conversations; Thucydides is superior in forcefulness, Herodotus
superior in pleasure. Theopompus is closest to these two, and,   74
though inferior to the aforesaid in history, is more like an orator,
as you would expect from one who was in fact an orator for a long
time before he was spurred on to history.[13] Philistus also deserves
to be singled out from that crowd, however good, of authors after
Herodotus and Thucydides; he is an imitator of Thucydides, much
less forceful but somewhat more lucid.[14] Ephorus, as Isocrates
thought, needs the spur.[15] Cleitarchus' talent is extolled but his
reliability is attacked.[16] Timagenes, born much later, is especially   75
commendable because he revived with a fresh praiseworthiness the
activity of writing history which had lapsed.[17] Xenophon has not
escaped me but he will be treated with the philosophers . . .

But in history[18] we need not be inferior to the Greeks. I would   101
not hesitate to set Sallust against Thucydides, nor would Herodotus resent having Livy matched with himself, for Livy in his narrative
has a marvellous charm and brilliant transparency, and in his
speeches he is eloquent beyond description, so well suited are they
both to the matters at hand and to the speakers;[19] and no historian, if I may speak most moderately, has ever represented more
perfectly the emotions, especially the softer ones. And so by dif-   102
ferent virtues he won an equal renown as Sallust had with his
immortal rapidity. I think Servilius Nonianus[20] spoke admirably
well when he said that the two of them were equal rather than
alike. We ourselves heard Servilius: he was distinguished in the
strength of his talent and his work was packed with maxims, but

103 less concise than the dignity of history demands. Aufidius Bassus,[21] who was a little earlier than Servilius, was exceptional in maintaining that dignity in this genre, at least in his books on the German war, and though he is worthy of commendation in all his
104 writings, he falls short of his own power in some passages. Still alive today and adorning the glory of our era is a man worthy of remembrance through the ages; he will be named one day; for now his name must be inferred.[22] The free speech of Cremutius has its devotees – and not without justification – even though the parts that it had harmed him to utter have been removed from the text; but even in what remains you can catch his proud spirit and his bold maxims.[23]

There are other good writers, but we are dipping into the various genres, not ransacking entire libraries.

27

JOSEPHUS

Flavius Josephus was born in 37/8 CE in Jerusalem. In 64 he visited Rome as part of a delegation; in 66 when Judaea revolted from Rome, Josephus was put in command of the Galilee. He was captured at the siege of Jotapata and became a prisoner, ultimately being freed (he claimed) when he correctly predicted that Vespasian would become emperor (see below, *Against Apion* 1.47–9). He was allied with Vespasian's son Titus during the remainder of the war and was afterwards given Roman citizenship. He was a prolific author, most famous for his account of the Jewish War, which he first published in Aramaic and then in Greek. His sources will have included his own experience as well as the reports and memoranda of Vespasian and Titus (see below, *Life* 359–67). He then published *Jewish Antiquities* in twenty books, modelled on Dionysius of Halicarnassus' *Roman Antiquities* and covering Jewish history from creation to the outbreak of the revolt. Appended to this work is the *Life*, a defence of his actions and history against his detractors, especially Justus of Tiberias who had published a rival account of the Jewish War. There also survives the *Against Apion*, a wide-ranging defence of Judaism which exploits (and criticizes) numerous Greek sources.[1]

Josephus clearly sought to write history in the Thucydidean vein (his style tries to imitate his great predecessor) and he makes the usual proclamations in the prefaces to the *War* and the *Antiquities*. Uniquely valuable, however, are his remarks in the other works which show us (amongst other things) what happened behind the scenes in the composition of a history, the kinds of things historians never mention in their actual histories. He also has much to say of the 'false' traditions of the Greeks.[2]

Preface to the *Jewish War*

(1.1–16)

The war of the Jews against the Romans was the greatest not only of those in our own times but nearly of all the ones that we have received from tradition, either cities against cities or nations against nations,[3] but some have written up these events in an elaborate style, although they were not themselves present at the events and instead gathered random and contradictory informa-
2 tion by word of mouth, while others, who were in fact present, falsified events because of either flattery or hatred towards the Romans, and their writings embrace accusations in some places,
3 encomia in others, but nowhere the accuracy of history.[4] This being the case, I, Josephus – son of Matthias, a man from Jerusalem, a priest, and one who at first fought the Romans and was thereafter present at events by necessity – set myself the task of narrating these events for the inhabitants of the Roman empire, translating into Greek what I had previously put together and published in my native language for the barbarians of the interior.[5]

Josephus now (4–5) speaks of the magnitude of the war, with its vast disturbances throughout the eastern empire, its conflicts between the Romans and their western neighbours, and the death of Nero and subsequent struggle amongst his successors for the throne.

6 I thought it was absurd to allow the truth in such great events to wander off course, and to have Parthians, Babylonians, the furthest-off Arabians and the Adiabanae (their kindred tribe above the Euphrates) know accurately, thanks to my care, the beginnings of the war, through how many sufferings it progressed and the manner of its ending, while the Greeks and those of the Romans who did not take part in the campaign should encounter flattering and fictitious narratives.
7 And yet such writers dare to entitle their works histories, although in them they seem, to me at least, to miss the mark in addition to demonstrating nothing sound. They wish to show the Romans as great while they deprecate and diminish the Jews and

their resources. Yet I do not see how those who conquer the small   8
can have the reputation of being great. These writers have no respect
for the length of the war nor the abundance of sufferings experienced by the Roman army,[6] nor the greatness of the generals, who
despite their many strenuous exertions around Jerusalem are held in
no honour, I think, since their success has been minimized.

And yet I have not decided to strive with those who raise the   9
Romans on high by exalting the resources of my people; instead, I
shall go through the deeds of both sides with accuracy, and I shall
ascribe the remarks about the deeds to my own disposition, giving
my emotions the opportunity to bewail the misfortunes of my
country.[7] Titus Caesar himself, the one who sacked the city,   10
attested that it was destroyed by civil strife, and that the Jews'
own tyrants drew the unwilling hands of the Romans and the fire
to the temple: throughout the whole war Titus took pity on the
people, who were kept in check by the insurrectionists, and he
often willingly postponed the capture of the city, giving time for
those responsible to have a change of heart. And if anyone should   11
be critical of all that we have said in accusation against the tyrants
and their brigands, or in turn of our wailings at the misfortunes of
our country, he must, contravening the law of history, grant pardon to this emotion. For of all the cities under Roman sway it
happened to ours both to advance to the pinnacle of happiness
and in turn to plunge to the extreme depth of misfortune. I think   12
that the sufferings of all people from the beginning of time fell
short by comparison with those of the Jews, and no foreign tribe
was responsible for this, so that one could contrive no way of mas-
tering such griefs. But if one were a judge too inflexible for pity, let
him ascribe the deeds to the history and the laments to the one
writing it.[8]

And yet I myself might justly find fault with those learned   13
Greeks who, when such great events have occurred in our own
times, events which by comparison show that the wars of long ago
were very small, sit in judgement of them and seek to revile those
who aspire to them: even if they somehow have the advantage over
them in literary ability, they nonetheless are inferior to them in
sense. They write up the narratives of the Assyrians and the
Medes as if they had been less well written by historians of old.   14

And yet they are as inferior to them in the power of their writing as they are in judgement. For each of those writers of old gave their efforts to writing events of their own time, where their presence at events would make their narrative vivid, and lying was
15 shameful since one was writing amongst those who knew. Handing down to memory events which have not been recorded previously and composing an account of the events of one's own time for posterity is something worthy of praise and commendation. The hardworking writer is not the one who alters someone else's plan and arrangement but the one who speaks of recent
16 events and fashions a work of history that is his own.[9] And although a foreigner, I nonetheless, at the greatest expense and with the greatest efforts,[10] am offering this record of virtuous actions to Greeks and Romans. For native Greeks, when it is a question of profits or lawsuits, their mouths are agape and their tongues are at the ready;[11] but as for history, where one must speak the truth and gather together events with much effort, they are silent, leaving those who are inferior and do not even know the accomplishments of their leaders to write the history. Let the truth of history be honoured by us at least since the Greeks are unconcerned with it.[12]

Preface to the *Jewish Antiquities*

(preface 1–17)

I see that those who wish to write histories do not have one and the same reason for their interest, but rather many reasons, differ-
2 ing very much from one another. Some wish to demonstrate the virtuosity of their literary skill and in pursuit of the reputation that comes from this they rush into this branch of learning;[13] others, currying favour with those who happen to be the subject of their work, took up the labour it demanded even though it was
3 beyond their powers. Others were compelled by the very necessity of the events at which they were present and took part to set these out in a treatise that narrated the events. The magnitude of important but unknown events impelled many to publish a history of

them for our common benefit.[14] Of the aforementioned reasons   4
the last two are relevant for me. I was compelled by those who had
mistreated the truth in their writings to give a full account of the
war that the Romans waged against us Jews, both of the events in
the war and the way in which it turned out, since I knew these
things by experience.[15] I have taken this present work in hand   5
because I believe that it will seem to all Greeks worthy of their
attention, for it will embrace all of our early history and the constitution of our state translated from Hebrew records.[16] Even   6
before this I was minded, when writing up the war, to set out who
the Jews were in their origins, what their fortunes were, what lawgiver[17] educated them in the ways of piety and the cultivation of
the other virtues, and how many wars they fought in their long
history all the way down to the last one in which they unwillingly
fought against the Romans. But since the breadth of that work   7
was rather large, I separated it out and limited the work by treating that last war's particular beginnings and end. As time went by,
there was a certain hesitation and delay in taking in hand so great
a subject in a language that was foreign and not our own, and this
is something which often happens to those who are minded to
take on great tasks.[18] There were some who, in their desire for that   8
history, encouraged me, and the one who did so most of all was
Epaphroditus, a man devoted to every form of learning, but who
is especially pleased by the experiences which historical events
afford, in as much as he himself has taken part in great deeds of
varying fortunes, and in all of them he has displayed a marvellous
strength of character and an immovable disposition towards virtue.[19] I took his advice, since he is one who always joins with those   9
who have the ability to do something useful or noble in their love
of what is beautiful; and because I would be ashamed of myself if I
seemed to delight in laziness rather than in effort for what is most
noble, I more eagerly took courage.[20] In addition to the aforesaid, I
considered not incidentally whether our ancestors were willing to
share such material and whether some of the Greeks were eager to
know of our affairs.

I found that the second of the Ptolemaic kings, who eagerly   10
gathered knowledge and books, was especially keen to translate
our law and the constitution of our state into Greek.[21] Eleazar,   11

one of the high priests at his court and second to none in virtue,
did not begrudge the aforementioned king the enjoyment of this
useful knowledge, and he would have been wholly opposed unless
12 it were our custom not to leave unsaid anything that was noble.[22]
I considered it fitting for myself too to imitate that high priest's
greatness of spirit, and to suppose that there are many like that
king even now who are desirous of learning, since the king did not
acquire all our records, but the men sent to Alexandria to do
13 the translation transmitted only the parts concerning the law.[23]
The things revealed in our sacred writings, however, are countless, and the history in them embraces 5,000 years, in which are
contained all sorts of unexpected reversals of fortune, many
chance occurrences in wars, brave deeds of military commanders
14 and changes of constitution. In general, one who was willing to go
through it would learn from this history that for those who follow
the will of God and do not dare to transgress laws that have been
well established, all things turn out well, beyond what they could
believe, and their reward from God is good fortune. But to the
extent that they depart from the careful observation of these laws,
possibilities become impossible, and whenever they are eager to
15 do something good, it turns into irremediable sufferings.[24] So now
I call on those who read these books to turn their thoughts to
God, and to test if our lawgiver understood his nature worthily,
and attributed deeds to him that were always fitting to his power,
and took care to speak of him always in a manner that was free of
16 the inappropriate mythical material found in others.[25] And yet he
would have had great freedom to do such a thing given the length
of time and his antiquity, since he was born 2,000 years ago, a
time to which their poets[26] did not even dare to ascribe the births
17 of the gods or the deeds of men or their laws. Now then my
account, as it proceeds, will indicate in its proper order the details
of what is written in the records. I declared that I would do this
throughout my treatise, neither adding anything nor taking anything away.[27]

On the Duty of Historians

(*Jewish Antiquities* 14.1–3)

Now that we have narrated the history of Queen Alexandra and her
death in the previous book,[28] we shall speak of what immediately
followed this, being attentive to ensuring that we not omit any of
the deeds through ignorance or faulty memory. It is necessary that
a history that reveals matters which, because of their antiquity, are
unknown to most people should offer readers a beauty of language
in its narration (the kind that arises from the words and their
arrangement, and all those things that contribute to artistic adornment), so that their instruction may come with a certain amount of
grace and pleasure;[29] but historians must most of all aim at accuracy, preferring nothing to speaking the truth to those who will trust
them for deeds that they themselves do not know.

Failings of historians who wrote on Nero

(*Jewish Antiquities* 20.154–7)

But I shall leave off writing more about these matters.[30] For many
have arranged their history around Nero, some of whom had been
well treated by him and in gratitude cared nothing for the truth,
while others on account of their hatred and enmity with him were
so shamelessly drunk with lies that they themselves deserve condemnation. It occurs to me not to be surprised at those who told
lies about Nero when not even the historians of Nero's predecessors took care for the truth in their histories, even though they
were not the objects of hatred since they lived much later than
those emperors.[31] But let those with no regard for the truth write as
they wish, since they seem to delight in doing so; we, however,
making truth our aim, think it worthy that any matters separate
from the treatise before us receive but slight mention, and instead
we shall reveal, not superficially, what befell the Jews; and we shall
not hesitate to make clear either their misfortunes or their errors.

Defence Against Critics of the *Jewish War*

(*Life* 336–9)

Since I have come to this point in my narrative I wish to say a few things to Justus,[32] the very one who has written an account of these events, as well as to the rest who promise to write history but have little regard for the truth and who, because of either hatred

337   or favour, are not ashamed of falsehood. Such writers are similar to those who compose false documents when making contracts, but unlike those men such writers fear no punishment, and so

338   they despise the truth. Justus, for example, when he attempted to compose an account of the events having to do with these matters, did not tell the truth even about his own country.[33] And so now I, who have had these falsehoods told about me, am compelled to defend myself, and I shall speak on matters about which up to this

339   point I have been silent. And no one should be surprised that I did not make any revelations about this long ago. It is necessary that one who writes history must tell the truth, but one should not reproach people's wicked acts bitterly, and not because of any favouritism towards them but rather on account of one's own moderation.[34]

Reliability and Superiority of Josephus' Account

(*Life* 357–67)

I am amazed at your shamelessness at daring to say that your account is better than all others who have treated this topic,[35] even though you do not know what happened in Galilee (for at that time you were in Berytus with the king) nor did you follow closely all the things that the Romans suffered or did to us in the siege at Jotapata, nor were you able to learn all the things that I accomplished through my own agency during the siege, since everyone who might have informed you perished in the siege.[36]

358   But perhaps you will say that you have written accurately about

what happened at Jerusalem. And how is that possible? You neither happened to be present during the war nor read the memoranda of Caesar. Here is the strongest proof: you have written an account which contradicts Caesar's memoranda.[37]

And if you are confident that your account is the best of all, why 359 did you not publish your work when Vespasian and Titus, the emperors who took charge of the war, were still alive, and while King Agrippa[38] and his family, people with the highest degree of Greek culture, were still living? You had your account 360 written already twenty years before and no doubt I suppose that you were going to obtain evidence of your accuracy from those who knew. But as it is, you have been emboldened because those men are no longer with us and you do not think that you can be refuted.[39]

I was not at all frightened about my own account in the way 361 that you were, but I gave my books to the commanders themselves, when the deeds were almost still in view, because I was conscious that I had taken care to hand down the truth, nor was I disappointed in my expectation that I would receive evidence of this.[40] I immediately gave my history to many others, some of 362 whom had been present in the war, such as King Agrippa and some of his relatives. The emperor Titus wanted the knowledge of 363 these events to be handed down to mankind from my books alone, and so having inscribed them with his own hand, he ordered that they be published. In addition King Agrippa wrote sixty-two let- 364 ters, testifying that I had handed down the truth. Two of them I include here, and from them you may, if you wish, know what he has written:

King Agrippa sends greetings to his dearest Josephus. I went through 365 your book with the greatest pleasure, and you seemed to me to have taken much greater care over your accuracy than others who have written about these matters. Send me the remaining volumes.[41] Farewell.

King Agrippa sends greetings to his dearest Josephus. From what 366 you have written you seem to need no instruction in how we might all learn of events from the beginning.[42] When you meet me, however, I myself shall inform you of many things that are not known.[43]

367 And when my history was completed, then in truth and without
trying to flatter me (for he was not like that) and without speaking
ironically (as you, of course, will claim, but he was far from such
maliciousness), he testified to the truth of my account, as did all
the others who have read my history.

Unreliability of Greek Historians

(*Against Apion* 1.1–27)

I believe, dearest of men Epaphroditus,[44] that in my account of
our earliest history I explained for those reading the work that our
Jewish race is very ancient and its first origins were distinct, and
how it settled the land which it now inhabits; the work covered
5,000 years and I composed it in Greek and based it on our holy

2 books. I now see that quite a number of people are paying attention to the slanders that have been uttered by some against us
because of their ill will, and such men disbelieve what I have written about our early history, citing as proof that our race is so
young that no distinguished Greek historian deemed it worthy to

3 make any mention of us.[45] For this reason I thought I would write
about all this in a concise treatise, so as to refute the hostility and
deliberate falsification of those who have slandered us, to set
straight the ignorance of others, and to instruct all those who

4 wish to know the truth about our antiquity. I shall use as testimony to what I have said those writers judged most trustworthy
by the Greeks on all matters of early history, and I shall show that
those who wrote about us slanderously and falsely patently con-

5 tradict themselves. I shall attempt as well to give the reasons why
few Greeks made mention of our race in their histories, and further I shall make known the writers who did not omit our history
for those who do not know or pretend not to know.

6   First, then, it occurs to me to be utterly amazed at people who
think that when it is a matter of the most ancient deeds, they
should give their attention to the Greeks alone and learn the truth
from them, while disbelieving us and the rest of mankind, since I

see that the opposite is the situation, at least if one does not follow idle opinions but instead gets an appropriate notion from the events themselves.[46] Everything that has to do with the Greeks will [7] be discovered to be new and to have happened yesterday or the day before, one might say, and I mean here the foundings of their cities, their inventions of the arts, and the codification of their laws. And newest of everything pretty much is the care they have taken for writing down their histories. Now the Greeks themselves of [8] course agree that what has been recorded by the Egyptians, the Chaldaeans and the Phoenicians – leaving aside our own history for the moment – has the most ancient and most stable tradition of memory.[47] For these peoples dwell in lands that are least subject [9] to decay from the atmosphere, and they have given the greatest attention to ensuring that none of their accomplishments should be passed over but should be kept in public documents set up by the wisest men. But Greece has experienced countless destruc- [10] tions which erased the memory of events and put in place new peoples who continuously thought of their own era as the begin- ning of everything; and only late and with difficulty did they become literate. They pride themselves on the fact that the people who made the earliest use of letters learned them from the Phoeni- cians and Cadmus.[48] Yet not even from that time could anyone [11] show a written document that has been preserved either in sacred or public storehouses, and this is not surprising since there is so much uncertainty and inquiry about whether those who fought in the Trojan War, which occurred so much later, used writing; the truth that prevails is rather that those men were ignorant of the present-day use of writing.[49] The Greeks unanimously agree that [12] no writing earlier than Homer can be discovered, yet Homer man- ifestly lived later than the Trojan War and they say that he left not even this poem in writing, but that it was remembered in songs that were only later put together, and this is why there are so many contradictions in the poem.[50] Those who first attempted to write [13] history among the Greeks – I mean Cadmus of Miletus, Acusilaus of Argos and any others who are assigned to that era – were only a little earlier in time than the Persian expedition against Greece.[51] [14] And as for those first philosophers of the heavens and the divine amongst the Greeks – Pherecydes of Syros, Pythagoras and

Thales – everyone without exception agrees that they wrote what little they did having studied with the Egyptians and the Chaldaeans.[52] These, then, seem to be the most ancient writings of the Greeks and yet they hardly believe that they were written by these men.

15   How, then, is it not absurd for the Greeks to delude themselves that they alone know ancient history and have handed down the truth of such matters accurately? Who would not learn easily enough from the historians themselves that they wrote their history without knowing a single thing reliably, but instead each of them merely formed conjectures about the events? In fact most of the time in their books they refute one another and they do not hesitate to write the most contradictory accounts about the same

16   events. There is no need for me to instruct others who know better than I all those matters of genealogy where Hellanicus disagrees with Acusilaus or how Ephorus shows Hellanicus has written falsely in the majority of cases, and in turn Timaeus refutes Ephorus, and writers after Timaeus refute *him*, and everyone refutes

17   Herodotus.[53] And not even in Sicilian affairs did Timaeus deem it worthy to agree with what Antiochus, Philistus and Callias had written, nor in turn did the writers of Athenian local history agree about Athenian matters, nor did those who inquired into Argive

18   affairs follow one another.[54] And why should I even mention those who wrote about individual city-states and even smaller entities, when even about the Persian War and its events the most esteemed historians disagree with one another? Even Thucydides is accused by some of often telling falsehoods, and he has the reputation of having written the most accurate history.[55]

19   If one wished to examine the reasons for such differences no doubt many could be found, but I would say the two following are the chief reasons and the former seems to me to be the most import-

20   ant: first, the fact that from the beginning the Greeks took no care that there be public records of what was done on each occasion contributed more than anything to the irregularity and abundance of

21   falsehood faced by later writers of ancient events. And it was not only the rest of the Greeks who had no care for written accounts; not even among the Athenians, who they say are autochthonous and take care for learning, can any such thing be discovered, but their most ancient records are said to be the laws about murder which

Draco wrote for them, and he lived just a little before the tyranny of
Peisistratus.[56] And why even mention the Arcadians who boast of 22
their antiquity? Even later than this they were scarcely literate.[57] So, 23
then, in as much as they did not set down any written account which
would instruct those who wished to know and refute those who
tried to tell falsehoods, there has been much disagreement amongst
historians themselves.

Here is the second reason. Those who felt impelled to write did 24
not pay much attention to truth, even though this is always a common profession, but instead tried to show off their literary ability 25
and they adapted themselves to whatever way in which they thought
they would surpass their predecessors, some turning to legendary
accounts, others praising cities or kings to win their favour, while
still others set out to find fault with deeds or those who wrote them,
thinking that in this way they would win renown.[58] In acting this 26
way, they persisted in doing the thing that most of all is opposed to
history; for the proof of a true history is when everyone says and
writes the same things about the same events, but they have done
otherwise, while thinking that they were showing themselves to be
the most truthful of all. To sum up then, we must yield to the Greeks 27
in eloquence and literary ability, but certainly not in the truth that
their histories of early times offer, especially when the histories
treat their own particular native traditions.[59]

Testimonies to the Reliability of Josephus' Work

(Against Apion 1.44–56)

What Greek would ever have endured that[60] for the same thing?
None would endure even the slightest harm to save all the writings
of his people from disappearing. They consider their accounts to 45
have been invented off-handedly according to the authors' whim.
Such an evaluation is justified for the older authors, since they see
even some of their contemporaries daring to compose accounts of
events at which they were not present nor about which they made
any effort to learn from those who knew.[61] Of course, some who 46

have written histories even about the war that occurred in our life-time have published them without ever investigating the sites or going near the places where the events occurred, but instead put together a few things from chance information and then shame-lessly insulted the name of history.[62]

47 I, on the other hand, having myself been present at all the activ-ities, fashioned an account of the war which was true, both taken
48 as a whole and in its individual incidents. I was the commander of those whom we call Galileans, for as long as resistance was pos-sible, and then was captured and taken prisoner by the Romans, after which Vespasian and Titus kept me under guard and com-pelled me to be at their service constantly. At first I was kept in chains but was then set free and sent to Titus from Alexandria to
49 the siege of Jerusalem. During this time nothing of what was being done escaped my notice, for in fact I saw what was happening in the Roman camp and wrote it down carefully, and I alone learned
50 everything that was told by deserters. Then, when I had uninter-rupted time in Rome, and my entire treatise was prepared, I used some assistants in the Greek language and in this way I fashioned my narrative of events.[63] I had such confidence in the truth of my account that I thought it worthy to make Vespasian and Titus, the
51 commanders of the war, the first of all witnesses. I gave the books to them and then to many of the Romans who had taken part in the war, and I sold copies to many of our acquaintances, men who were versed in Greek wisdom, including Julius Archelaus, Herod, that most eminent man, and that most admirable king, Agrippa
52 himself.[64] These all testified that I had diligently defended the truth, and they would not have held back or been silent if I had changed or omitted any of the events because of ignorance or in a desire to flatter.

53 A few worthless people have attempted to slander my history, thinking that it had been proposed as a rhetorical exercise for boys in school.[65] This is an unexpected accusation and slander, since they ought to know that one who promises to give an account of true events to others must himself first learn these things, either by being present at events or by learning them from those who
54 know.[66] I think I especially have done this with both of my trea-tises. The early history, as I said, I translated from sacred records,

since I am myself a priest and descended from priests, and privy to
the wisdom found in those writings. I wrote the history of the war 55
having myself taken part in many deeds, and having been an eyewitness of the majority of them, and in general I was ignorant of
nothing that was said or done. How then would one not consider 56
reckless those who have dared to contend with me about the
truth? Even if they claim to have read the memoirs of the commanders, they were not present at events that took place on our
side when we fought against the Romans.[67]

PLUTARCH

Plutarch was born c. 65 CE in Chaeronea in Boeotia. He was devoted to his home town (it was a small town, he said, and he did not wish to make it smaller by leaving) although he was a famous man and travelled extensively, including to Athens, Egypt and Rome. He was a student of the philosopher Ammonius from Alexandria, and he remained an ardent Platonist throughout his life. He was honoured with Roman citizenship (his Roman name was Mestrius Plutarchus) and a late source says that he received the consular ornaments and was an imperial procurator of Achaea in the reign of Hadrian (ruled 117–38). Closer to home, he was a priest at the shrine of Apollo at Delphi for the last thirty years of his life, and he wrote several works on the oracle and played a part in its revival under Hadrian. An inscription survives honouring him at Delphi and dedicating a portrait bust of him. The exact date of his death is unknown though it must have occurred before 125.

A fourth-century document known as the 'Catalogue of Lamprias' lists 227 works by Plutarch (though not all will have been by him); what survives today are some seventy-eight essays on various rhetorical, ethical and literary topics (these are grouped together under the term 'Moralia' or 'Moral Essays') and fifty biographies from what is Plutarch's best-known work, the *Parallel Lives*. In the latter Plutarch placed Greek statesmen alongside Roman ones, joining them because of similarities of circumstance or character. These *Lives* have been one of the best-known and most influential works to have survived from classical antiquity, and they were popular almost from their first moment of publication to the present day.[1]

There is no doubt that Plutarch thinks of himself as a moralist, but recent scholarship has emphasized the subtle and nuanced nature of this moralism, especially in the *Parallel Lives*. Plutarch is a careful artist who tries to do full justice to the complexity of human nature and the demands placed upon men in public life, and neither his 'heroes' nor his 'villains' are painted in black and white; he recognizes both virtues and vices and tries to make sense of them as they manifest themselves in unique individuals.

The essay *On the Malice of Herodotus* is both a fully fledged attack on the character of the first historian and an attempt to refute the contents of his history. Because of its harsh tone, its *ad hominem* attacks, and what is often seen as the tendentious nature of its arguments, the essay was long thought to be spurious. Today most scholars accept Plutarch as its author, though it is still sometimes 'excused' as a work of Plutarch's youth or as a sophistic exercise, one of those essays that took on a difficult topic and tried to make a convincing case. Whoever the author, the value of the essay, especially for the present collection, should not be underestimated. Although it might seem naïve or distasteful to modern sensibilities, the essay encapsulates many aspects of historiographical thought in antiquity, especially that approach towards history which saw it as the appropriate medium for the remembrance and promulgation of great deeds and great men, and which encouraged writing on a topic that would ensure glory for its subjects and a desire for emulation in its readers, a sentiment that can be seen in authors as different as Polybius, Diodorus, Dionysius of Halicarnassus and Arrian.

The essay maintains that Herodotus had a fundamentally malicious disposition, not in the obvious way of a Theopompus or Timaeus, but in a much more charming and subtle manner, and it is this very charm that is dangerous and causes readers to miss the malice of the narrative. After enumerating eight 'signs' of a malicious disposition, the author then goes through Herodotus' work Book by Book choosing incidents that reveal the author's approach. The evidence for the counter-arguments is not always full or impressive, although as the essay progresses and approaches the more historical parts of Herodotus' history, Plutarch cites evidence from other writers, including other historians, in an attempt to discredit Herodotus' account. With few exceptions, modern scholars continue to prefer Herodotus' account to that given in this essay.

The other excerpts from Plutarch consist of three methodological remarks from the *Parallel Lives* (space precludes a larger selection) and two important passages from the essays, the first on the relationship of the historian to his history, and the second a much-cited observation on the importance of vivid narration in history.

On the Malice of Herodotus

1 The style of Herodotus <of Halicarnassus>,[2] my dear Alexander,[3] because it is simple and lacking in effort and easily runs over events, has thoroughly deceived many people. And more people have experienced this with regard to his character.[4] For not only is it, as Plato says, the greatest injustice to appear to be just when one is not,[5] it is also an act of the greatest malice to mimic a good nature and simplicity in a way that is hard to detect. <. . .>[6] he has
854F especially employed against the Boeotians and the Corinthians,[7] nor has he refrained from any of the others, I think it is appropriate for us to come to the defence both of our ancestors and of the truth in this very part of his work – since those who wished to go through in detail all the rest of his falsehoods and fictions would require many volumes. But as Sophocles says, 'the face of Persua-
855A sion is fearsome',[8] especially when, in a narrative that has such great charm and power, it is able to cover up all the other absurdities as well as the character of the historian. Philip used to say to those Greeks who were breaking their alliance with him and going over to Titus that they were putting on a collar that was smoother but would last longer.[9] The malice of Herodotus is smoother, to be sure, and softer than that of Theopompus[10] but it fastens on to its object and causes pain more, like winds that blow in secret through a narrow opening compared with those that are dispersed in the open.

Now it seems preferable to me to make an outline of all those
855B things which are in general the footprints and tokens,[11] as it were, of a narrative that is not honest or well disposed, but malicious, and then to test each one of the matters we shall examine to see whether it fits.

2 To begin, then, one who in narrating events uses the harshest words and expressions when milder ones are available[12] – as if one called Nicias 'superstitious' when one could have said 'too devoted to divination',[13] or one spoke of the 'rashness and madness' of Cleon rather than his 'insubstantial talk'[14] – is not well disposed, but takes delight, as it were, in narrating the event in a clever[15] manner.

Second, if there is something discreditable to a person, but it   3
otherwise has nothing to do with the history, and the historian
grabs hold of it and inserts it into his account of the deeds though   855C
there is no need to, lengthening his narrative and coming back to it,
so that he may encompass some misfortune or a deed which is
unusual and of no use, he is clearly taking pleasure in abuse. For
this reason Thucydides did not delineate Cleon's missteps, although
they were innumerable, and merely touching on the demagogue
Hyperbolus in one phrase and calling him 'a scoundrel',[16] he let it
go. Philistus omitted all Dionysius' injustices against the barbarians that were not integral to Greek affairs.[17] For digressions and
diversions in history are best given over to myths and accounts of   855D
earliest times, or yet again to praise;[18] but the one who makes asides
in which he engages in defamation and fault-finding seems to fall
into the tragic curse of 'cataloguing the misfortunes of mortals'.[19]

And then there is the opposite of this, evident to everyone,   4
which is the omission of something fine and noble. This may seem
to be unobjectionable, but it is malicious if in fact what is left out
has a proper place in the history.[20] For praise that is not bestowed
readily is no fairer than taking pleasure in blaming: not only is it
no fairer, it is perhaps even worse.

I identify the fourth sign of a character that is not well minded   5, 855E
in history as one which, when there are two or more accounts of
the same thing, sides with the worse. Sophists are sometimes
allowed, either as practice or in their pursuit of renown, to take up
and adorn the weaker argument,[21] for they are not trying to establish a firm conviction in their thesis, and they often admit that
they fall into paradox when speaking on incredible topics. But the
one who writes history behaves justly if he speaks those things he
knows to be true, and if, where matters are uncertain, he believes
that the better account rather than the worse is spoken truly.[22]
Many omit the worse account entirely, as, for example, Ephorus[23]
in speaking of Themistocles: he says that Themistocles knew
about Pausanias' treason and the latter's activities with respect to   855F
the King's generals, but Themistocles was not persuaded, he says,
nor did he, when Pausanias invited him to share in the plot and
urged him on to such rewards, accept the offer. Thucydides, on
the other hand, has condemned this story by omitting it entirely.[24]

6   Further, when the facts are agreed upon but the reason they were done and the intention of those doing them are unclear, the one who conjectures towards the worse[25] is ill willed and malicious, like the comic poets[26] who portray the war to have been 856A ignited by Pericles on account of Aspasia or Phidias rather than because of rivalry and a wish to lay low the spirit of the Peloponnesians and make no concession to the Lacedaemonians.[27] Now it is thoroughly obvious that a writer falls short of no excess of jealousy and malice if he ascribes a bad reason to deeds that are highly esteemed and actions that are praised, and thus by means of slander leads the reader into inappropriate suspicions about the 'hidden' intention of the historical actor – all because he cannot find fault openly with the deed itself. Such are those who suggest that the murder of the tyrant Alexander by Thebe was not a deed arising from her high-mindedness and hatred of tyranny but rather because of some jealousy and womanish emotion;[28] or 856B those who say that Cato committed suicide because he feared a torturous death at the hands of Caesar.[29]

7   A historical narrative admits of malice if it alters the character of the deed by claiming that it was accomplished by means of money rather than through bravery, as some claim of Philip,[30] or that it was done easily and without effort, as with Alexander;[31] or if it was done not with forethought but by some good fortune, as Timotheus' enemies claim about him, painting pictures that showed the cities themselves crawling into a pot while he slept.[32] It is clear that those who would take away nobility, great effort, 856C excellence and active effort diminish the greatness and the beauty of the deeds.

8   Further, those who openly attack their victims are easily accused of peevishness, brazenness or even madness when they are not measured in their speech. But those who attack from the side, hurling their slanders like weapons under cover, as it were, but then come back around and hesitate by claiming that they disbelieve what they very much want their audience to believe – these writers, in seeking to ward off a charge of malice, incur the additional charge of servility.[33]

9   Similar to these are those who place some praise alongside their criticism, for example, Aristoxenus who said of Socrates that he

was uneducated, ignorant and licentious, and then added, 'but there was no injustice in him'.[34] Just as flatterers sometimes, with a 856D certain skill and cleverness, mix in some light criticisms with their many lengthy praises, as if they were introducing frank speech as a seasoning for their flattery, so maliciousness puts in some praise beforehand to win credence for the criticisms that follow.[35]

One could enumerate more characteristics, but these will suf- 10 fice to furnish a means for observing the disposition and character of the man.[36]

First of all, then, as if from his own hearth, he begins with Io, 11 the daughter of Inachus, a woman whom all the Greeks believe to have been divinized with honours by the barbarians, and who, because of her renown, gave her name to many seas and to the most distinguished harbours, and was the source and origin of the 856E most renowned and most regal families.[37] He says, this excellent writer, that she handed herself over to Phoenician traders because she had been seduced willingly by one of the captains and was afraid that her pregnancy would be revealed.[38] And he falsely attributes this to the Phoenicians, claiming that this is *their* story about her.[39] Citing Persian 'learned men' as his witnesses that the Phoenicians seized Io together with other women, he then imme- diately reveals his opinion that the fairest and greatest deed of Greece, the Trojan War, came about through folly on account of a worthless woman: 'for it is clear', he says, 'that if the women 856F themselves had not been willing', they would not have been stolen away.[40] Well then, are we to say that the gods behave foolishly, since they were angry with the Lacedaemonians for having raped the daughters of Leuktros, and punished Ajax for his assault on Cassandra?[41] For it is evident, according to Herodotus, that unless the women themselves had been willing, they would not have been outraged. And yet he himself says that Aristomenes was taken alive by the Lacedaemonians, and later in time the general of the Achaeans, Philopoemen, experienced this same fate, and the Carthaginians took Regulus, the Roman general, prisoner – and it 857A would be a task to find braver fighters than those men![42] But this is not surprising since men capture alive even leopards and tigers;[43] yet Herodotus condemns the women who were violated and defends the men who violated them.

12   He is so pro-barbarian that he absolves Busiris of the charge of human sacrifice and murder of foreigners, and in bearing witness to the great piety and justice of the Egyptians he turns this defilement and bloodthirstiness against the Greeks.[44] In the second book he says that Menelaus, when he had received back Helen 857B from Proteus[45] and had been honoured with great gifts, proved himself to be the most unjust and wickedest of men: being kept back by bad weather, he contrived an unholy deed, taking two of the native children and cutting them up. Finding himself now the object of hatred because of this act and hunted down, he fled with his ships and arrived in Libya.[46] I have no idea what Egyptian told this story: contrary to this, many honours for Helen and many for Menelaus continue to be observed by the Egyptians.[47]

13   But the historian, continuing the pursuit, says that the Persians 857C learned pederasty from the Greeks.[48] And yet how can the Persians owe their instruction in *this* to the Greeks when it is agreed by practically everyone that they castrated boys before they had ever seen the Greek sea?[49] But we are told that the Greeks learned from the Egyptians how to conduct processions and public festivals and the worship of the twelve gods; that Melampodas learned the name of Dionysus from the Egyptians and taught it to the rest of the Greeks; that the mysteries and the secret rites of Demeter were brought from Egypt by the daughters of Danaus; and that the Egyptians beat their breasts and mourn but for whom, he says, he is unwilling to name, 'maintaining a holy silence about religious matters'.[50] Yet he has displayed no such holy silence at all 857D towards Heracles and Dionysus, whom he shows as being worshipped by the Egyptians, whereas for the Greeks they are mortals who have grown old.[51] He says further that Heracles is of the second generation of gods and Dionysus of the third since they had a point at which they were born and were thus not in existence from the beginning.[52] But at least he declares the Egyptian ones to be gods, whereas he thinks it is necessary to offer honour to the Greek ones as to mortals and heroes but not to offer them sacrifice as to gods.[53] He has said the same about Pan,[54] overturning, by means of the boastfulness and mythic tales of the Egyptians, the most revered and holiest of Greek rites.

14, 857E   And this is not the worst. He traces Heracles' ancestry to

Perseus and says that according to the Persian account, Perseus was Assyrian, and thus 'the leaders of the chiefs of the Dorians would be manifestly Egyptians all the way back if we traced their fathers from Danae and Acrisius'.[55] As for Epaphus and Io, Iasos and Argos, he has completely omitted them, being eager to demonstrate not only other Heracleses – Egyptian and Phoenician – but also to drive that Heracles, whom he says belongs to the third generation, from the land of Greece to the barbarians.[56] And yet none of the learned men of old – not Homer, Hesiod, Archilochus, Peisander, Stesichorus, Alcman or Pindar – has any account of an Egyptian or Phoenician Heracles but all of them know just one Heracles, the one of Boeotia and Argos alike.[57]

857F

Furthermore, of the Seven Wise Men, whom he calls 'sophists',[58] he proclaims that Thales was Phoenician by race and thus originally a barbarian.[59] And slandering the gods in the person of Solon he has him say, 'You ask me – who know that the divine is thoroughly jealous and disruptive – about human affairs.' This is what he himself believed about the gods but he attributed to Solon and thus added malice to blasphemy.[60] He featured Pittacus[61] for small things of no account, yet he passed over the greatest and finest of the man's achievements, although he had occasion to treat the matter.[62] When the Athenians and Mytileneans were fighting over Sigeum, and the general of the Athenians, Phrynon, called for someone to volunteer for single combat, it was Pittacus who took up the challenge, and casting a net around his opponent, who was a strong, tall man, he defeated and killed him. Although the Mytileneans offered him great gifts, he threw his spear and asked only for as much land as was covered by the spearcast. (And to this day the land is called 'Pittaceum'.) And what did Herodotus do when he came to this part of the story? Instead of treating the brave exploits of Pittacus, he mentioned the poet Alcaeus who fled from battle and cast away his weapons.[63] By not treating the fine actions, and by not passing over shameful actions,[64] he bears witness to those who say that jealousy and *schadenfreude* arise from the same vice.

15

858A

858B

After this he lays a charge of treason against the Alcmaeonids,[65] who proved themselves brave men and freed their country from tyranny, by saying that they received Peisistratus back from

16

858C

exile and brought him back on condition that he marry the daughter of Megacles. And he says that she said to her mother, 'Do you see, Mummy? Peisistratus does not have intercourse with me in the normal way.' And he says it was because the Alcmaeonids were indignant at this transgression that they drove out the tyrant.[66]

17   In order that the Lacedaemonians should not experience less of his malice than the Athenians, look at how shamefully he has treated Othryadas, a man who was especially admired and honoured by them. He says, 'But the one survivor of the 300, being ashamed to return to Sparta when the men of his regiment had all perished, did away with himself there on the spot in Thyrea.' Earlier he says that both sides disputed the victory but here he claims the shame of Othryadas as evidence of the defeat of the Lacedaemonians, since to go on living when defeated would be shameful, while to be victorious and survive would be most glorious.[67]

18   I shall pass over the fact that he portrays Croesus as an utterly ignorant, comical braggart, but then says that when he became a prisoner he instructed and admonished Cyrus – Cyrus who has the reputation of having been first amongst kings in intelligence, bravery and greatness of mind.[68] For Croesus he offers no evidence of his doing any good thing other than honouring the gods with many grand dedications – but he indicates that this very thing was the most impious action of all: he says that Croesus' brother, Pantaleon, while their father was still living, contended with him for the throne, and that when Croesus became king, he killed a nobleman who was one of Pantaleon's companions and friends by having him flayed on a carding comb; and it was from this man's possessions that he made dedications and sent them off to the gods.[69] As for Deioces the Mede, who acquired his rule by virtue and justice, he says that he was not like this by nature, but rather made a pretence of justice because he was enamoured of tyranny.[70]

19   But I can dispense with the barbarians, since there is no lack of examples in his treatment of Greeks. He says that the Athenians and most of the Ionians are ashamed of the name 'Ionian' and do not wish to be called by this name but rather shun it; and further, that those men who considered themselves most noble and had set out from the council house of Athens had children by barbarian

858D

858E

858F

women after they had killed these women's fathers, husbands and children; and it was for this, he says, that the women established the custom, by swearing oaths and handing it down to their daughters, never to eat at table with their husbands or to address their husbands by name; and the Milesians of today are descended from these women. He adds that the pure Ionians are those who celebrate the Apatouria festival, 'and all', he says, 'do this except the Ephesians and the Colophonians': in this way he has denied these people their noble birth.[71] 859A

He says that when Pactyes revolted from Cyrus,[72] the Cymaeans 20 <. . .> and the Mytileneans were preparing to hand the man over 'for a certain price, though I cannot say exactly how much': well done this, to claim ignorance of what the amount was and yet to cast such a reproach against a Greek city, as if he knew clearly. He then says that the Chians, when Pactyas was brought to them, removed him from the temple of Athena the City-Guardian and 859B handed him over, and when they had done this they received Atarneus as their reward. Yet Charon of Lampsacus, an older writer, when he comes to treat Pactyes, has attributed no such pollution to the Mytileneans or the Chians. Here are his actual words: 'When Pactyas realized that a Persian army was marching against him, he took flight and went first to Mytilene and then Chios. And Cyrus got hold of him.'[73]

In his third book when he treats the Lacedaemonians' exped- 21 ition against the tyrant Polycrates,[74] he says that the Samians believe and declare that the Lacedaemonians made an expedition to Samos 859C to restore those citizens in exile and make war against the tyrant in gratitude to them for their assistance with Messene.[75] He then says that the Lacedaemonians deny this reason, saying instead that they made the expedition not to help out or to liberate the Samians but to take vengeance against them: for the Samians had stolen a mixing bowl that the Lacedaemonians were sending to Croesus and a linen corselet that was being sent back to the Lacedaemonians from Amasis.[76] And yet we know no city of that time that was more desirous of honour or more hating of tyrants than that of the Lacedaemonians. For what sort of corselet or mixing 859D bowl did they drive out the Cypselids from Ambracia, Lygdamis from Naxos, the sons of Peisistratus from Athens, Aeschines from

Sicyon, Symmachus from Thasos, Aulis from Phocaea, Aris-
togenes from Miletus, and destroy the dynasty of Thessaly by
doing away with Aristomedes and Agelaos through King Leo-
tychidas? These actions have been written about in more detail
elsewhere.[77] But according to Herodotus, the Lacedaemonians fell
short of no excess of wickedness or stupidity if they denied the
fairest and most just explanation for their expedition and instead
859E   agreed that they had attacked men who were unfortunate and in
misery, on account of their vindictiveness and pettiness.

22   Still, he painted the Lacedaemonians in dark colours because
they, in some way or other, fell under the purview of his writing.
But to Corinth, which was outside his path in this matter, he
nevertheless made a detour, so to speak, and infected them with a
terrible charge and a most knavish slander. He says that the Corinthians eagerly took part in the expedition against Samos because
the Samians had previously committed an outrage against them as
follows: Periander, the tyrant of Corinth, was sending 300 boys of
859F   the nobility to Alyattes to be castrated.[78] When they arrived at
Samos, the Samians instructed them to sit as suppliants in the
temple of Artemis, and they brought them each day cakes of honey
and sesame and thereby saved them. This is the 'outrage' of the
Samians against the Corinthians claimed by our historian and it
was on account of this, he says, that the Corinthians urged on the
Lacedaemonians many years later, because the Samians had ensured
that 300 Greek boys should grow up to be men. In attributing this
reproachful act to the Corinthians he makes the city more wicked
than the tyrant. For Polycrates at least protected his own son when
the Corcyraeans were trying to destroy him. But what outrage did
860A   the Corinthians suffer that they wished vengeance on the Samians
who had stood in the way of such savagery and lawlessness – and
why would they do these things three generations later, showing
anger and vindictiveness on behalf of a tyranny that, when it was
finally destroyed, they expended every effort to wipe out and erase
every memory and trace of, because it had been so harsh and burdensome to them?

But let us suppose that this was the Samian outrage against the
Corinthians: what then was the punishment of the Corinthians
against the Samians? If in fact they had been angry with the

Samians, it would have been more appropriate for them not to encourage but to discourage a Lacedaemonian campaign against Polycrates, for then the tyranny would not be destroyed, and the Samians would not become free men nor cease to be slaves. And here is the greatest problem: why in the world were the Corinthians angry with the Samians who wanted to save the boys but could not, while laying no charge against the Cnidians who did save them and sent them home? As it is, the Corcyraeans take little account of the Samians but they remember the Cnidians and have awarded them honours, special privileges and decrees of recognition. For the Cnidians sailed out and drove Periander's guards from the temple and they themselves took up the boys and escorted them back to Corcyra,[79] as Antenor has recorded in his *Cretan Affairs* and Dionysius of Chalcis in his *Foundations*.[80] And one can use the Samians themselves as witnesses that the Lacedaemonians did not make their expedition to take vengeance on the Samians but rather to free them from the tyrant and save them. For they say there is a tomb in Samos, made at public expense for Archias, a Spartiate, who fought brilliantly there and died; and he is honoured by the Samians; and even Herodotus testifies to this at least: that the man's descendants continue to this day to have close ties of friendship with the Samians.[81]

In the fifth book he says that Cleisthenes, a man of the nobility and the highest rank, succeeding in persuading the priestess at Delphi to become a false prophet by continually enjoining the Lacedaemonians to free Athens from the tyrants. In so doing he attaches to this noblest and most just deed the slander of great impiety and fraud while at the same time taking away from the god a prophecy that was fair and noble and worthy of Themis who is said to share in these prophecies.[82] He says that Isagoras went along with Cleomenes' visits to his wife, and, as is his custom, he mingles some praises with his criticisms to win trust for his account.[83] 'Isagoras,' he says, 'was of a distinguished home but I cannot say whence it originated; but his relatives sacrifice to Carian Zeus.' The writer's sneer is graceful and civil, escorting Isagoras away to the Carians as if to perdition.[84] Aristogeiton, however, he attacks not from behind or from the side, but head on and he drives him through the gates to Phoenicia, saying that he is

860B

860C

23

860D

860E

by origin a Gephyraean; and the Gephyraeans, he says, are not from Euboea or Eretria, as some think, but Phoenicians, he himself having learned this by inquiry.[85]

Furthermore, he cannot take away from the Lacedaemonians their liberation of Athens from the tyrants, but he is able to diminish and dishonour this most noble deed by attributing a most shameful reaction: for he says that the Lacedaemonians quickly changed their minds, believing they had not acted rightly because they had been led astray by counterfeit oracles, and had driven out from their homeland the tyrants – men who were friendly to them and had promised to make Athens subservient to them – and had handed the city over to the ungrateful commons. Sending thereupon for Hippias from Sigeum, they were going to restore him to Athens.[86] But the Corinthians opposed them and dissuaded them, Socles going through all those things that Cypselus and Periander had done against the city when they held the tyranny.[87] No wickeder or more savage action is recorded of Periander, however, than the dispatch of those 300 young men; and yet when the Samians seized them and tried to prevent them from suffering this fate, he says the Corinthians were angry and vengeful as if they had been outraged. With such confusion and contradiction does his malice fill his account, sneaking into his account on any pretext.[88]

24   In the account of Sardis that follows, he did everything he could to do away with and despoil the deed.[89] He dares to call the ships which the Athenians sent to the Ionians to assist them in their revolt from the king 'the beginning of evils' because they tried to free so many and such great cities from the king.[90] And remembering the Eretrians only in an aside, he is completely silent about their great and renowned success.[91] For when there was confusion around Ionia and a royal force was sailing against them, the Eretrians went to meet the Cypriots outside, in the Pamphylian sea, and fought a naval battle against them. Then turning back and leaving their ships at Ephesus, they attacked Sardis and besieged Artaphernes who had taken refuge in the citadel, trying thereby to raise the siege of Miletus.[92] They accomplished this and they caused the enemy to withdraw in astonished fear. And when they were then attacked by a great force, they retreated. Others have spoken of this, especially Lysanias of Mallus in his *On Eretria*.[93]

860F

861A

861B

861C

And it would have been a fine thing to have noted this brave deed
and display of prowess if for no other reason than at least to mark
the capture and destruction of the city. But he says that they were
in fact defeated by the barbarians and driven back to their ships,
although Charon of Lampsacus records no such thing, but writes
exactly as follows: 'The Athenians sailed with twenty triremes
intending to bring help to the Ionians, and they marched against
Sardis and captured everything except the royal wall. And having   861D
accomplished these things, they withdrew to Miletus.'[94]

In the sixth book he treats the Plataeans: when they tried to   25
entrust themselves to the Spartiates, the latter bid them instead to
turn to the Athenians since they were their neighbours and could
offer no small assistance, but then he adds, not as a suspicion or
what was believed but as if knowing accurately, that 'the Lacedaemonians suggested this not so much from goodwill towards the
Athenians as from wishing rather to cause trouble to the Athenians who would thereby be at odds with the Boeotians.'[95] So then
if Herodotus is not being malicious, the Lacedaemonians were
plotters and malicious ones at that, the Athenians failed to per-   861E
ceive they were being deceived, and the Plataeans were cast into
the middle not because of goodwill or honour but as a pretext
for war.[96]

And further he has already been clearly convicted of making   26
false accusations against the Lacedaemonians in the matter of the
full moon:[97] he says that they were awaiting this and that was why
they did not bring help to the Athenians at Marathon.[98] But not
only have they made countless expeditions and battles when the
moon was full, but even this battle, which occurred on sixth
Boedromion, they only just missed, such that they in fact could
see the corpses when they arrived at this place.[99] And yet he has   861F
written about the full moon as follows: 'It was impossible for
them to do this immediately because they were unwilling to break
their law. For it was the ninth day early in the month and they said
that they could not march out on the ninth since the moon was not
full. They, then, were awaiting the full moon.'[100] But you are moving the full moon from the middle to the beginning of the month,
and you are confounding the heavens and the calendar and everything![101] And having announced that you were writing up the

affairs of Hellas <so that they might not be lacking in glory>[102]
862A and although you are especially keen on Athens, you have not
recorded the procession to Agras which they send still to this day
on the sixth of the month as a thankoffering. But this at least supports Herodotus against that slander that he received a lot of
money from Athens for flattering them. For if he had read out
these things to the Athenians they would not have allowed it, nor
would they have tolerated an account where Philippides summoned the Lacedaemonians to the battle on the ninth – when he
had just come from the battle[103] – and arrived at Sparta the day
862B after, as Herodotus himself says, unless the Athenians sent for
their allies after having defeated the enemy. It is Diyllus, not a negligible historian, who records that Herodotus received from
Athens, on the motion of Anytus, a gift of ten talents.[104] And when
he reports the battle, Herodotus has, as the majority say,[105] ruined
the deed by the number he records of the corpses. For they say that
the Athenians had vowed to Artemis Agrotera one goat for every
barbarian killed, but then, after the battle, when it became clear
that the number of corpses could not be counted, they passed a
862C decree asking the goddess to accept their sacrifice each year of 500
goats.[106]

27   Even so, we shall let this pass and look at what happens after
the battle:

> With their remaining ships the barbarians set sail and taking up
> from the island the slaves from Eretria that they had left behind,
> they sailed around Sunium, wishing to arrive in the city before the
> Athenians. And there was a charge current among the Athenians
> that the Persians were minded to do this from a contrivance of the
> Alcmaeonids, for the latter had made an agreement with the Per-
> sians and flashed a shield for them when they were already on their
> ships. These, then, were sailing around Sunium.[107]

Let us dismiss his calling of the Eretrians 'slaves', even though
they displayed a daring and eagerness for renown inferior to none
862D of the Greeks, and suffered things unworthy of their courage.[108]
His slander of the Alcmaeonids who boasted the greatest families
and the most distinguished men is also of little import. And the

greatness of the victory has been ruined and the end of this celebrated success has come to nothing: there seems to have been no
struggle or accomplishment of any great sort but a brief skir-
mish[109] with the barbarians as they were landing (just as those
disparaging and envious writers say)[110] if, after the battle, the Persians do not flee, cutting the cables of their ships, giving themselves   862E
over to the wind which carries them far away from Attica, but
instead a shield, a sign of treason, is raised for them as they sail for
Athens expecting to capture it, and when they have sailed around
Sunium they lie off Phalerum, while the first and most renowned
of men in desperation betray the city.[111] For although later he
exonerates the Alcmaeonids, he assigns the treason to others: 'For
a shield was flashed, and this cannot be denied', he says, as if he
himself had seen it![112] Yet this was impossible if the Athenians had
won a decisive victory. And if it had been given, it could not have
been seen by the barbarians for they were being driven to their   862F
ships in flight and with much trouble from wounds and missiles,
each man leaving the land as fast as he could. But when later
Herodotus pretends to be defending the Alcmaeonids from
charges which he was the very first one to make and says, 'It is a
wonder to me, and I do not accept the story that the Alcmaeonids
would ever have by agreement shown a shield to the Persians
because they wanted the Athenians to be under the power of Hippias', I am reminded of a piece of verse: 'Wait, little crab, and I
shall release you.'[113] Why are you so keen to capture something if
once captured you intend to let it go? And you accuse, then defend?   863A
And you compose slanders against pre-eminent men, which you
then take back, clearly distancing yourself.[114] For you have yourself saying that the Alcmaeonids raised a shield to the barbarians
who had been conquered and were in flight. And further, where
you defend the Alcmaeonids, there you reveal yourself to be an
inventor of false charges. For if it's true, as you write here, that
'they are manifestly as much or more hostile to tyrants than Callias, the son of Phaenippus and father of Hipponicus', where will
you put that alliance of theirs which you wrote about in your first
book, when they led Peisistratus back from exile to the tyranny at
Athens so as to make a marriage connection with him, and they
would not have driven him out again until he was accused of   863B

having abnormal intercourse with his wife?[115] Such, then, are the
contradictions in these accounts. And amidst the slander and suspicion cast upon the Alcmaeonids he employs praise for Callias,
the son of Phaenippus, and he adds his son Hipponicus, who was
one of the wealthiest men in Herodotus' time, and in doing so
reveals that although these details were irrelevant to the story he
inserted Callias here as a way of flattering and currying favour
with Hipponicus.[116]

28   Everyone knows that the Argives did not refuse to join the
Greek alliance but demanded to share equally in the command so
that they would not be under the control of the Lacedaemonians,
863C their most hateful enemy, and compelled to follow their bidding
on every occasion.[117] This had to be admitted but he suggests a
most malicious explanation:[118] 'When the Greeks invited them,
they made this demand, knowing full well that the Lacedaemonians would not give them a share in the command so that using
them as an excuse they might take no part.' And he says that later
some Argive ambassadors who were at Susa reminded Artaxerxes
of these things and he replied that 'he considered no city friendlier
than Argos'. And then giving way, as is his wont, and shrinking
back he says he doesn't know exactly about these matters, but he
does know that complaints can be made against all people and
that:

863D   the Argives were not the worst. But I am bound to report what is
      said, although I am not obligated to believe it entirely. And let what
      I've said here apply to my whole work. For indeed this too is also
      said of the Argives, namely, that they invited the Persians into
      Greece since their war with the Lacedaemonians was going badly
      and anything would be preferable to their present suffering.[119]

Well now, Herodotus has the Ethiopian say of the myrrh and purple, 'deceitful are the perfumes, deceitful the garments of the
Persians':[120] could one not say this very thing to him, i.e., deceitful
863E are the words, deceitful the exterior appearance of Herodotus'
account, 'devious and unsound and all twisted'.[121] Just as painters
make the highlights brighter by the use of shadow, so does he not
heighten his slanders by means of denials and does he not make

his suspicions deeper by the expression of uncertainty?[122] Now
one cannot deny that the Argives, by not joining together with the
Greeks and by yielding their reputation for bravery to the Lacedaemonians on account of the command, brought shame upon
Heracles and their own noble heritage;[123] it would have been better to liberate Greece even if Siphnians or Cythnians[124] had been
the leaders rather than, in quarrelling with the Spartiates over the
command, forsake those many great battles. But if they were the   863F
ones who invited the Persians into Greece because their war with
the Lacedaemonians had been going badly, why did they not
medize openly once the Persians had come? Or if they were unwilling to fight together with the Persians, why did they not, when left
behind, ravage Laconian territory or seize Thyrea[125] or in some
other way attack or harass the Lacedaemonians, since they could   864A
have greatly harmed the Greek cause if they had not allowed the
Lacedaemonians to march out to Plataea with so many hoplites?[126]

Well, then, he has here portrayed the Athenians at least as great   29
and called them 'saviours of Greece',[127] which was proper and
just – indeed, except for the many slanderous remarks to be found
amongst the praises! He says that the Lacedaemonians, when
betrayed by the rest of the Greeks and isolated, would have performed great deeds and died nobly, or before this happened, they
would have had to come to an agreement with Xerxes when they
saw the rest of the Greeks taking the Persian side. It is clear that
he says this not to praise the Athenians, but instead praises the
Athenians in order to speak badly of all the others. For why would   864B
one be amazed with him for continually reproaching the Thebans
and Phocaeans in bitter and excessive terms[128] when he convicts
those who actually underwent the risk on behalf of Greece not of
actual treason but of a treason he reckoned they would commit?[129]
And he raises doubts about the Lacedaemonians themselves, making it uncertain whether they would have fallen fighting against
the enemy or handed themselves over: mistrusting, by God, those
minor indications of their character at Thermopylae![130]

When he narrates the story of Ameinocles, the son of Creties of   30, 864C
Magnesia, he says that he profited greatly from the shipwreck that
befell the king's fleet and the many goods that washed ashore,
acquiring an indescribable amount of gold and possessions, but he

doesn't allow this to pass without a biting comment and says, 'He
became very wealthy from his discoveries but in all other respects
he was not fortunate, for he had the horrible misfortune of killing
his own son.'[131]

31   Aristophanes the Boeotian writes that Herodotus failed to
864D obtain money from the Thebans when he demanded it, and when
he tried to converse and engage in philosophy with their young
men, he was prevented by the magistrates because of their boor-
ishness and dislike of argument.[132] There is no other evidence for
this story. And yet Herodotus supports Aristophanes' account by
the charges he himself levels against the Boeotians, narrating
some things falsely, in other matters slandering them, and in still
others writing as if he hated them or had quarrelled with them.[133]
For he declares that the Thessalians medized at first from necessity and here he speaks the truth; and when he prophesies that the
rest of the Greeks would have betrayed the Lacedaemonians, he
adds 'not willingly but from necessity as the cities were captured
864E one by one'.[134] But he does not give the Thebans, who were under
the same necessity, the same indulgence. And yet they sent 500
men with their commander Mnamias to Tempe, and to Thermopylae they sent as many as Leonidas demanded. And only these
and the Thespians remained with him, all the rest departing once
they were encircled.[135]

In fact, the Thebans accepted the king's terms only when they
were hemmed in by great necessity: when the barbarian had control of the passes and was on their borders; when the Spartiate
Demaratus, who was well minded towards Attaginus, the leader
of the Theban oligarchy, because of their guest-friendship, had
offered to make him a friend and guest-friend of the king, and
when the Greeks were on their ships and no land army was com-
864F ing to their aid.[136] For they did not, like the Athenians, have ships
and the sea at their disposal, nor did they dwell far off, like the
Spartiates, in a remote part of Greece, but the Mede was only a
day and a half away when they made their stand at the narrows
and fought with only the Spartiates and the Thespians, and met
865A with misfortune. Now the historian is sufficiently fair to say that
if the Lacedaemonians had been isolated and bereft of their allies
they would have come to an agreement with Xerxes,[137] but he has

only abuse for the Thebans who suffered that very thing on account of the same necessity. Their greatest and finest deed he could not erase as if they had not done it, but he ruins it by attributing a discreditable motive and making it suspect.[138] He has written:

> So then the allies, having been ordered away, departed and they obeyed Leonidas' command. The Thespians and the Thebans alone remained behind with the Lacedaemonians. Of the two the Thebans remained reluctantly and against their will (for Leonidas had held on to them, considering them hostages) but the Thespians were especially willing and said they would never abandon and leave Leonidas and those with him.[139]   865B

Now then is it not clear that he has the same personal anger and ill will against the Thebans, which has caused him not only to slander the city falsely and unjustly but also not even to think out how to make his slander plausible, nor even see clearly that all but a few will realize that he is contradicting himself? For he says of Leonidas, 'when he perceived that the allies were not eager and were not willing to join in the danger, he ordered them to depart', and then a little later he says that he retained the Thebans against their will:[140] but if they were suspected of taking the Persian side, he should have dismissed them even if they were willing. In a situation where he had no need of any who were unwilling, what use could there have been in mixing together men whose loyalty was suspect with the actual fighters? For the king of the Spartiates and the leader of the Greeks could not have been of such a mind as to retain as hostages those 400, who were after all armed, together with the 300, and certainly not when the enemy was now attacking them from the front and behind. For even if previously he had brought them because he considered them hostages, when they were in these final moments, surely they would have given no thought to Leonidas and departed, and he would have had to fear an encirclement by *them* rather than by the Persians. And apart from this, how would it not have been ludicrous for Leonidas to order the rest of the Greeks to depart since death was at hand, but to prevent the Thebans from doing so in order that he – who was   865C   865D about to die – might guard them for the Greeks? For if he were bringing them with him as hostages or rather as slaves, he ought not to have kept them with those who were going to die but rather handed them over to the Greeks who were departing.

The only other explanation – perhaps he kept them with him so that they would be killed – the historian himself has removed by his comments about Leonidas' love of glory. Here is exactly what he says: 'Leonidas, thinking these things over and wishing to lay up glory for the Spartiates alone, dismissed the allies, not because there were differences of opinion.'[141] It was the pinnacle of stupidity to deprive the allies of renown but to allow the enemy to share in it. It is clear, however, from what actually happened, that Leonidas was not suspicious of the Thebans but considered them reliable friends. For when, while leading his army, he had come into Thebes, he asked for and obtained something which no one else has ever obtained, namely to spend the night in the temple of Heracles. And the vision which he saw in his sleep he reported to the Thebans. He seemed to see the most distinguished cities of Greece on a rough and stormy sea, and they were being carried and tossed about capriciously, but the city of Thebes was above all of them and raised to the sky, and then suddenly disappeared. And this was similar to what happened to the city later in time.[142]

In his narrative of the battle Herodotus has obscured Leonidas' great accomplishment, saying that all fell there in the narrows by the hill.[143] But it happened otherwise. When they perceived during the night that the enemy was encircling them, they rose up and made for the camp and nearly reached the king's tent, intending to kill the king himself or die in the attempt. They slaughtered everyone whom they met as far as the tent and caused the rest to retreat as they went forward. But Xerxes was not found, and inasmuch as they were looking for him in a great and immense army and were wandering about, still it was only with difficulty that the barbarians slew them when they had surrounded them from every side.[144] Now all the daring acts in addition to this one and the remarks left behind by the Spartiates will be recorded in a *Life* of Leonidas,[145] but it is not inappropriate even here to mention a few. They celebrated their own funeral games before they left Sparta while their mothers and fathers looked on. To someone who remarked

that he was leading entirely too few men to battle, Leonidas himself said, 'But many enough to die.' To his wife who asked as he
was leaving whether he had something to say, he turned and said,
'Marry good husbands and bear good children.' At Thermopylae,
after the encirclement, he wished to save two men of good family   866C
and gave a letter to one of them, and tried to send him off; but the
other would not accept it and said angrily, 'I came with you as a
fighter, not as a messenger.' He ordered the other of the two to
give a message to the magistrates at Sparta <...> matters,[146]
hoisting his shield he took his place in the ranks.[147] Now one
would find fault with anyone else who omitted these things. But
the man who recorded and memorialized the fart of Amasis and
the thief who drove his asses and gave over his wine,[148] and many
other things of this sort would seem to have omitted fair deeds
and fair words not from carelessness or in oversight but because   866D
he is neither well disposed nor fair minded towards certain people.

   Herodotus says that the Thebans who were with the Hellenes at   33
first fought from compulsion. For not only Xerxes, it seems, but
Leonidas as well had attendants armed with whips and it was by
these that the Thebans were compelled to fight against their will.
Now could any malicious prosecutor be crueller than this man,
who says that those who had the capability of departing and
escaping fought from necessity but that those for whom no support was at hand medized willingly?[149] Right after this he has
written that when the rest:

> were making for the hill, the Thebans split off and were stretching
> out their hands and approaching nearer to the Persians, saying (the   866E
> truest thing they ever said) that they had medized and had given
> earth and water to the king, that they had come to Thermopylae
> under compulsion and that they were not responsible for the dam-
> age done to the king. And by saying this they survived, for they had
> the Thessalians as witnesses of what they had said.[150]

Imagine this pleading being heard as everything was going on
amidst the barbarian cries and the thorough commotion and the
flights and pursuits, and then the examination of witnesses, and
the Thessalians, giving evidence amongst men being slain and

tangled underfoot, saying that until recently they were masters of
866F Greece as far as Thespiae but the Thebans defeated us in battle
and drove us out and they killed our commander Lattamyas. For
that was how things stood with the Boeotians and the Thessalians
at that time: there was nothing fair or friendly between them.[151]
But let us say that the Thessalians did serve as witnesses: how did
the Thebans survive? 'The Persians killed some of them as they
approached,' as he himself says, 'but the majority on Xerxes'
orders were branded with the royal mark, beginning with their
867A general Leontiades.'[152] But it was not Leontiades[153] who was general at Thermopylae but rather Alexander, as Aristophanes in his
Records by Archons and Nicander of Colophon have written.[154]
And nobody at all before that knows of any Thebans being
branded by Xerxes. It would have been the best defence against
such slander, and the city would have done well to be proud of
those brandings since Xerxes would thus have treated Leonidas
and Leontiades as his most hated enemies: the former's body he
mutilated after death and the latter he branded while still alive.[155]
Herodotus considers that the savagery directed against Leonidas
867B revealed that the Persian king was angry with Leonidas (when
alive) more than any other man; but when he says that the Thebans medized at Thermopylae and were branded and that,
although branded, they no less eagerly medized at Plataea, then it
seems to me that just like Hippocleides gesticulating with his legs
on the table, one could say that Herodotus has 'danced away' the
truth and that 'Herodotus doesn't care'.[156]

34   In the eighth Book he says that the Hellenes in fear were plan-
ning a flight from Artemisium to the interior of Greece, and when
the Euboeans begged them to wait a short time so that they could
remove their families and households, they paid no attention until
Themistocles obtained money and shared it with Eurybiades and
867C Adeimantus, the Corinthian general; and only then did they wait
and fight the sea battle. Yet Pindar, who did not come from an
allied city but one which was charged with medism, when he
remembers Artemisium proclaims:

> where the sons
> of the Athenians laid the splendid cornerstone of freedom.[157]

But Herodotus, who some think has glorified Greece, portrays the victory as a work of bribery and theft, and the Greeks as fighting unwillingly, having been deceived by their generals who had taken bribes.

Nor was this the limit of his malice. Nearly everyone agrees 867D that the Greeks were victorious there in the sea battles but that they yielded Artemisium to the barbarians when they learned what had happened at Thermopylae, since there was no benefit to be had by remaining there and guarding the sea, now that the war was south of the Gates and Xerxes was master of the passes.[158] But Herodotus has the Greeks wishing to run away even before announcing the death of Leonidas. He says as follows: 'They had been treated roughly, especially the Athenians, half of whose ships had been damaged, and so they planned to run away into Greece.' Now one can describe or criticize a retreat before battle 867E as 'running away'; but he called it 'running away' before this, and now denotes it as 'running away' and will a little later again speak of 'running away'.[159] With such bitterness does he cling to the term. 'Immediately after this a man from Hestiaea came to the Persians announcing that the Greeks had run away from Artemisium. The Persians, disbelieving him, held him under guard and dispatched swift ships to examine the situation for themselves.'[160] What are you saying? That they ran away as if they had been defeated, but that the enemy after the battle could not believe that they had run off in flight since they had won a convincing victory? And is it worthwhile to trust Herodotus concerning any single man or city when, with one phrase, he takes away the victory from 867F Greece, takes down the trophies and the inscriptions which they set up in the temple of Artemis Facing East, and portrays this as boasting and bombast?[161] The verse reads thus:

> The races of all sorts of men from the land of Asia
>   the sons of the Athenians, once on this sea,
>   subdued in battle, when they destroyed the army of the Medes
>   and offered these tokens to the virgin Artemis.[162]   868A

In his account of the battles he did not note the Greek battle order nor did he reveal what position each city held in the sea battle, and

in their departure, which he himself calls a 'running away', he says
the Corinthians sailed first in the line, the Athenians last.[163]

35   He ought not to have ridden so roughshod over those of the
Greeks who medized, since although he is thought by the rest to
have been Thurian, he himself is really protective of the Halicarnassians, those Dorians who marched against Greece with their
harem accompanying them![164] But he is so far from speaking in
any way mildly when discussing the necessities of those who
868B   medized that when he comes to tell of the Thessalians, who sent
to the Phocaeans, their bitterest enemies, offering to leave their
land unharmed for the price of fifty talents, he writes in these
words: 'For the Phocaeans, alone of the peoples in this part of
Greece, had not medized, and for no other reason, as I calculate,
than for their hatred of the Thessalians. If the Thessalians had
taken the Greek side, the Phocaeans, I think, would have
medized.'[165] And yet a little further on he himself says that thirteen
cities of the Phocaeans were burned down by the Persians, their
868C   territory was laid waste, the temple at Abai was set on fire and all
the men and women who could not reach Parnassus ahead of the
Persians perished.[166] Nevertheless he ascribes the same wickedness
to these people, who underwent the greatest sufferings for not
abandoning what was noble, as to those who most eagerly medized.
And since he could not find fault with these men's deeds, he sat at
his desk and composed ignoble causes and suspicions against them,
bidding us judge their intention not based on what they actually
did but on what they would have done if the Thessalians had not
decided as they had – as if they had to abandon the position of traitor because it was already occupied by others![167]

868D   Now suppose that someone tried to excuse the Thessalians'
medism by saying that they did not want to medize, but did so
against their will because of their differences with the Phocaeans
whom they saw taking the Greek side: would it not seem that such
a writer was engaged in the most shameful flattery and was distorting the truth by fashioning good reasons for bad actions? I
think it would. So then how is it not an absolutely clear case of
false accusation when he declares that the Phocaeans chose the
better cause not because of virtue but because they decided to take
the opposite side to the Thessalians? Nor does he here, as is his

usual way, ascribe the slander to others by saying that he heard it, but rather that he 'calculated' it. He ought to have cited the evidence that persuaded him that those who behaved like the best had the same motives as the worst.   868E

But this charge of mutual enmity is ludicrous. Neither the Aeginetans' differences with Athens nor the Chalcidians' with Eretria nor the Corinthians' with Megara prevented them from joining the Greek alliance.[168] And on the other side, the Thessalians were not dissuaded from taking the Persians' side just because the Macedonians, their bitterest enemy, had done the same. For the common danger made private grievances disappear such that all other feelings were driven out, and men inclined either to noble action because of their character or to what was advantageous because of necessity. And in fact after the danger of destruction at the hands of the Medes had passed, these men again 868F changed back to the Greek side, and Lacrates the Spartiate testified on their behalf.[169] And Herodotus himself, dislodged from his unusual position, admits in his narrative of Plataea that the Phocians were in fact on the Greek side.[170]

But one need not be surprised if he bitterly presses upon the   36 unfortunate when he transforms even those who took the Greek side and shared in the danger into enemies and traitors. The Nax- 869A ians sent three ships as allies to the Persians, but one of the captains, Democritus, persuaded the others to take the side of the Greeks.[171] He does not know how to praise without blaming: to praise one man he has to ruin the reputation of an entire city and people. Of earlier writers Hellanicus, and of later writers Ephorus both bear witness against Herodotus: the former says that the Naxians sent six ships, the latter five ships, to assist in the Greek cause.[172] And Herodotus actually convicts himself of fabrication: the local historians of Naxos say that the Naxians warded off 869B Megabates when he attacked the island with 200 ships and later the Persian general Datis when he sailed against them with a hundred ships after he had burned <. . .>[173] to do harm. But if, as Herodotus has said elsewhere, the Persians burned and destroyed their city and the men survived by fleeing to the mountains, then surely the Naxians had a fine reason for sending help to those who destroyed their country, but not for joining in the fight with those

fighting for the common freedom![174] That he composed this falsehood not to praise Democritus but to bring shame upon the
Naxians is evident from his omission of and silence about the suc-
869C   cess and bravery of Democritus[175] which Simonides has revealed
in his epigram:[176]

> Democritus was the third[177] to join battle, when at Salamis
>   the Greeks clashed with the Medes at sea.
> Five ships of the enemy he captured, and a sixth, a Dorian,
>   he rescued as it was being captured by a barbarian hand.

37   But why should one be annoyed about the Naxians? For if antipo-
dean peoples exist, as some say, dwelling in the underside of the
world, I think even they have not failed to hear of Themistocles,
and Themistocles' counsel, the one whereby he counselled the
869D   Greeks to fight a sea battle at Salamis and after which he built a
temple in Melite to Artemis of the Best Counsel.[178] But this charming historian does everything he can to take away Themistocles'
renown and transfer it to another; here are his exact words: 'And
at that point, when Themistocles had come to his ship, Mnesiphilus, an Athenian, asked him what had been decided. When he
learned from him that the decision was to sail to the Isthmus and
fight there for the Peloponnese, he said, "If you remove the ships
from Salamis, you will not be fighting any longer for a single
869E   country. For each will go home to his own city."' And a little later:
' "But if there is some way, go and try to confound these plans, if
you can somehow persuade Eurybiades to change his mind and
remain here."' Then he adds that 'the proposition pleased Themistocles very much and, making no answer to Mnesiphilus', he went
to Eurybiades and he has written (again his exact words), 'and
sitting beside him Themistocles enumerates all those things he
heard from Mnesiphilus, pretending they are his own and adding
other things in addition'.[179] Do you see that by saying that his plan
was actually Mnesiphilus' he attributes *to Themistocles* a reputation for malice?
38, 869F   In further mockery of the Greeks he says that Themistocles did
not understand what was beneficial but overlooked it (the very
man who was nicknamed 'Odysseus' for his understanding).[180]

But Artemisia, Herodotus' fellow citizen, instructed by no one and thinking it up on her own, could say to Xerxes that:

> the Greeks will not be able to withstand you for long, but you will make them scatter and each will flee to his own city. And if you march the army to the Peloponnese, it is not likely that they will remain, nor will they care to fight on behalf of the Athenians. But if you rush to fight at sea, I fear that the navy, coming to grief, will destroy the army as well.[181]

870A

Her remarks lack only metre for Herodotus to portray Artemisia as a Sibyl prophesying the future so accurately. And so Xerxes handed his own children over to her to lead back to Susa. He seems to have forgotten to bring women from Susa, if the children needed a female escort.[182]

Well, let us take no account of his lies in general but examine instead those lies which are told to someone's detriment. He says that the Athenians claim that Adeimantus, the Corinthian general, when the enemy were at hand, was overwhelmed with terror and fled, not by backing water or quietly slipping through the enemy ships but raising sail openly and turning all his ships around; but then a boat speeding along met up with him as he approached the end of Salamis and from the boat a voice spoke, 'Adeimantus, in your flight you are betraying the Greeks. But they in fact are winning and they have mastered the enemy just as they desired.'[183] This boat, it seems, fell down from heaven: and indeed why should he have spared the tragic crane when everywhere else in his history he surpasses the tragic poets in imposture?[184] And Adeimantus, trusting the voice, returned to camp when it was all over. This is the Athenians' story but 'the Corinthians do not agree but consider themselves to have played a most distinguished part in the sea battle; and the rest of Greece bears witness to them'.[185] The man is like this in many places: he offers different slanders and accusations against different people, with the result that he cannot fail to make someone, at any rate, seem wicked. Just as here the net result for him is that the Corinthians are disgraced if the slander is believed, and the Athenians if it is disbelieved. But I don't think the Athenians ever made this charge

39, 870B

870C

870D

against the Corinthians; I think Herodotus made these false allegations about both at the same time. Thucydides, at least, where
he has an Athenian speaking in opposition to the Corinthians in
Lacedaemon, and the Athenian is taking great pride in Athens'
deeds in the Persian Wars and in the battle of Salamis, has levelled
no charge of treason or desertion against the Corinthians.[186] And
it's not likely that they would defame the Corinthians in this matter when they could see the name of the Corinthians engraved
870E third, after the Lacedaemonians and themselves, on the dedication of spoils taken from the Persians;[187] and on Salamis itself they
gave permission for the men to be buried near the town and to
have this elegy inscribed:[188]

> Stranger, we once dwelt in the well-watered city of Corinth,
>   but now Salamis, the isle of Ajax, holds us.
> Here, capturing the ships of Phoenicians and Persians
>   and Medes, we saved sacred Hellas.

And the cenotaph at the Isthmus has this inscription:[189]

> When all Hellas was standing upon the razor's edge
>   we saved her with our lives, and here lie dead.

870F And the following is inscribed on the dedications of Diodorus, a
Corinthian commander, in the temple of Leto:[190]

> These weapons from the enemy Medes the sailors of Diodorus
>   dedicated to Leto as memorials of the sea battle.

And as for Adeimantus himself, whom Herodotus continually
reproaches for 'being the only general to resist, saying that he would
flee from Artemisium and not remain', look at the renown he held:[191]

> This is the grave of that Adeimantus, through whom
>   all Hellas put on the crown of freedom.

871A Now it was not likely that a coward and a traitor would have
received such honours when he died, nor would he have dared to

name his daughters Nausinike, Acrothinion and Alixibian and his son Aristeus if he had won no renown or brilliance from those deeds.[192]

And further, the Corinthian women, alone of Greek women, made that beautiful and divine prayer, asking the goddess to implant in their husbands a passionate desire to fight against the Persians. It is not credible that Herodotus was ignorant of this; it must have been known even to the remotest Carian,[193] since the matter was widely publicized and Simonides wrote an epigram 871B when bronze statues of the women were dedicated in the temple of Aphrodite, the temple Medea had built either when she was no longer in love with her husband (as some report) or (as others say) when the goddess ended Jason's love for Thetis.[194] This is the epigram:[195]

> Here stand the women who, for the Greeks and their
> > stalwart fighting citizens, prayed to the divine Cypris:
> for shining Aphrodite took care that the citadel of Greece
> > should not be betrayed to the bow-bearing Medes.

It was these things he should have written and remembered rather than throw in the misfortune of Ameinocles killing his son.[196]   871C

Having had his fill of charges against Themistocles, in which he   40 says that Themistocles did not cease to steal and demand more from the islanders unbeknown to the other commanders,[197] he finally takes the crown away from the Athenians and puts it on the Aeginetans, writing as follows: 'The Greeks sent the first fruits of the spoils to Delphi and they asked the god in common if the spoils he had received were sufficient and pleasing. And he replied that those from the rest of the Greeks were but those from the Aeginetans were not. He was demanding from them the prize of valour they had won at Salamis.'[198] So it is no longer to Scythians[199] or Persians or Egyptians that he attributes his fictional 871D speeches (as Aesop had done for crows and monkeys)[200] but now, using the character of the Pythia, he thrusts aside from Athens the first prize won at Salamis.[201] When he told of Themistocles being awarded second prize at the Isthmus because each of the generals had awarded himself first prize and Themistocles second, and of there being no decision in the end,[202] he ought to have found fault with their individual ambition,[203] but he says only that the Greeks sailed away, unwilling to proclaim Themistocles as first because of jealousy.[204]

41   In the ninth and final book, he was keen to pour out as much of his ill will towards the Lacedaemonians that remained, and to the extent he could, he took away from the city its renowned victory
871E   and much-celebrated success at Plataea. He has written that previously the Lacedaemonians were afraid that the Athenians would be persuaded by Mardonius and would leave the Greek alliance, but that when the Isthmus was walled off and they thought the Peloponnese was safe, they no longer took thought for the rest and disregarded them, celebrating a festival at home, detaining the Athenian ambassadors, and wasting time.[205] So how then did 5,000 Spartiates, each served by seven helots, march out to Plataea? How did they take upon themselves so great a danger and then conquer and destroy so many myriads? Listen to this believ-
871F   able explanation: there happened to be at Sparta, he says, a man named Chileos from Tegea, who was visiting there, and some of the ephors were his friends and guest-friends. It was this Chileos who persuaded them to dispatch the army, saying that walling off the Isthmus would be no help to the Peloponnesians if the Athenians should go over to Mardonius.[206] This is what brought
872A   Pausanias and his forces to Plataea. And if some private affair had kept that Chileos back home in Tegea, Greece would not have survived![207]

42   He does not know what to do with the Athenians, shifting up and down, raising the city up sometimes, sometimes casting it down: he says the Athenians disputed with the Tegeans over who would hold second place in the line, and they recalled the children of Heracles and their actions against the Amazons, and they cited their burial of the Peloponnesians who had fallen at the foot of the Cadmeia, and finally they came down in their speech to Marathon − all this in emulous rivalry and with a longing to obtain the command of the left wing.[208] Yet a little later Pausanias
872B   and the Spartiates yield to them the command, exhorting them to take the right wing and be stationed opposite the Persians, and to give themselves the left wing, as if declining the battle against the

barbarians because of their inexperience.[209] And yet it's ridiculous to be unwilling to fight unless the enemy is already familiar.

As for the rest of the Greeks, who were ordered to another camp, he says that when they moved forward, they were happy to flee from the enemy's cavalry to the city of Plataea, and in their flight they came to the Heraion.[210] In this account he has somehow accused all of them simultaneously of disobedience, desertion and treason. And in the end he says that only the Lacedaemonians and Tegeans   872C
met and fought the Persians, and the Athenians the Thebans,[211] and he has deprived absolutely all the other cities of any share in the success. Not one of them joined with the others in battle but all sat with their weapons nearby, abandoning and betraying those who were fighting on their behalf. At a later point, when the Phleiasians and the Megarians learned that Pausanias was winning, they rushed into the fray, fell in with the Theban cavalry, and were shamefully destroyed. The Corinthians did not participate in the battle but after the victory they hastened through the hills so as not to fall in with the Theban cavalry.[212] For the Thebans, when the   872D
rout occurred, brought their cavalry in front of the barbarians and eagerly aided them in their flight – paying them back, no doubt, for the brands they had received at Thermopylae![213] But the Corinthians' place in the line of battle when they fought with the barbarians and the great honour that accrued to them from the battle at Plataea one can learn from Simonides' words about them:[214]

> In the middle the inhabitants of Ephyra of many springs,
>   skilled in every form of bravery in war
> dwelling in Glaucus' city, the town of Corinth,

who   872E

>   established as the fairest witness of their toils
> the gold honoured on high.[215] And it will increase
>   the wide report of themselves and their fathers.

Now Simonides did not teach that to a chorus in Corinth nor did he compose it as a hymn for the city, but he wrote it simply as a narrative of those events.[216]

But Herodotus, anticipating that his lie could be refuted by those who would ask where then the many common graves and great number of tombs and memorials came from – those which up to the present day[217] the Plataeans give offerings to when the Greeks are present – has made an accusation even more shameful

872F than their betrayal of their countrymen: 'Of the rest, all those graves still to be seen in Plataea, these are, so I learn, empty mounds, heaped up by those ashamed of having been absent from the battle and made for the sake of future generations.'[218] Herodotus alone of all men has heard of this absence from battle, this treason, while Pausanias and Aristides and the Lacedaemonians and the Athenians were unaware that the Greeks had abandoned

873A the contest. But neither did the Athenians prevent the name of the Aeginetans, with whom they were at odds, from the inscription,[219] nor did they refute the Corinthians whom previously they had claimed took flight at Salamis, though Greece testified to the opposite. And yet Cleadas of Plataea ten years after the Persian Wars, in order to curry favour with the Aeginetans, built, according to Herodotus, the grave that bears their name.[220] And yet how was it that the Athenians and the Lacedaemonians immediately after the battle nearly came to blows over the erection of the trophy, but still did not deprive of the spoils those Greeks who were cowardly and had run away, but instead inscribed their names on

873B the tripods and the statues, gave them a share of the spoils,[221] and finally, composed and inscribed on the altar:[222]

> The Greeks, once by the power of victory and the work of Ares,
> having driven out the Persians, established for a free Greece
> this common altar of Zeus Eleutherios.

Surely, my dear Herodotus, this was not written by Cleades or someone else in an attempt to flatter the cities? Why then did they need to go through the useless trouble of digging up earth and act fraudulently in fashioning mounds and memorials for the sake of

873C future generations when they could see their renown consecrated on the most distinguished dedications? Indeed Pausanias, so they say, when he already had aspirations to tyrannical power, had inscribed at Delphi:[223]

When he destroyed the army of the Medes, the Greek leader
Pausanias dedicated this memorial to Phoebus.

He called himself 'leader of the Greeks', making them sharers to
some extent of his glory. But when the Greeks would not accept
this and complained, the Lacedaemonians erased this and
inscribed the names of the cities, as was right. And yet how likely   873D
is it that the Greeks would have resented not being included in the
inscription if they knew that they had not been present at the battle, or that the Lacedaemonians would have erased the name of
their leader and general and instead inscribed the names of those
who had avoided and ignored the danger? Isn't it very strange that
Sochares and Aeimnestus[224] and those who fought so brilliantly in
that battle bore no resentment that the names of the Cythnians
and the Melians[225] were engraved on the trophies, while Herodotus ascribes the struggle to three cities alone and all the rest he
uninscribes from the trophies and the sacred dedications?

So, then, of the four contests that were waged at that time   43
against the barbarians,[226] he says that the Greeks ran away from   873E
Artemisium and at Thermopylae their general and king bore the
brunt of the danger, while they stayed home and took no thought
for things, instead celebrating the Olympian and Carneian festivals. In his narrative of Salamis, he has used more words telling
about Artemisia than he has for the entire naval battle. And finally
he has the Greeks at Plataea ignorant of the battle until the end (as
if it were the battle of frogs and mice which Pigres, the son of
Artemisia, described in his jesting nonsense-epic)[227] and they had
made an agreement to fight in silence so the rest would be unaware,
and that the Lacedaemonians were in no way superior to the barbarians in bravery but had won because they were fighting men   873F
who were unarmed and naked. When Xerxes himself was present   874A
and his men were being driven by the whip from behind, the Persians still could hardly bring themselves to attack the Greeks, but
at Plataea, it seems, they had taken on other spirits: 'in spirit and
strength they were not deficient, but their equipment, which
lacked protective armour, hurt them, for they were light-armed
troops fighting against men who were hoplites'.[228] What renown
or grandeur is left to the Greeks from those contests if the

Lacedaemonians fought against unarmed men[229] and the battle
took place without the rest realizing it, and the graves that are
honoured by each man's descendants are empty, and the tripods
874B   and altars erected for the gods are full of false inscriptions, and
Herodotus alone knows the truth and all other men who have
accounts of the Greeks have been deceived by a tradition about
the victories of those times which is overgrown?

What can we say, then? The man knows how to write, his account
is pleasurable and there is charm, force and grace in his narrative,
and he has 'recounted his tale like a poet' not 'knowledgeably' but
instead sweetly and with polish.[230] It is no doubt these aspects that
beguile and win over everyone; but just as one must watch out for
the rose-beetle amongst the roses, so one must be on one's guard
against Herodotus' defamation and abuse, which lie beneath a
smooth and soft appearance, lest we unwittingly accept absurd and
874C   false notions about the best and greatest cities and men of Greece.

Following are several remarks made by Plutarch in his Lives *and
essays which bear on the subject of history.*

On the Difference between History and Biography

(Alexander 1.1–3)

In this Book my subject is Alexander the king and the Caesar who
overthrew Pompey.[231] Because of the abundance of the deeds associated with both men, we shall say nothing by way of preface
other than to ask the indulgence of our readers if we do not narrate all their great deeds or even deal exhaustively with any of
2   the famous ones. For we are composing not histories but biographies and it is not always in the most famous actions that one sees
virtue or vice revealed, but it is often a little thing or remark or
some jest that makes an impression of someone's character, rather
than battles in which countless people die or enormous lines of
3   soldiers or sieges of cities. Just as painters take the likeness from
the face and expression of the eyes where character is revealed and

pay little attention to the rest of the person, so too we must be allowed to penetrate to the signs of the soul, and through these to make a portrait of each man's life, yielding to others the great achievements and the struggles.[232]

On Mythic Material in History

(*Theseus* 1.1–5)

Just as geographers, dear Sosius Senecio,[233] squeeze those parts of the world that they know nothing about in the margins of their maps and explain that 'what lies beyond this are waterless deserts full of monsters', 'trackless swamps', 'Scythian frost' or 'frozen seas', so I too, now that I have in the writing of my parallel lives 2 gone past the period in which one can employ probability and offer a history that relies on events,[234] could say about this earlier 3 time 'what lies beyond this are monsters and material for tragedy, where poets and legend-writers dwell, and where one can no longer find trustworthy or clear accounts'.[235] But when we had 4 published our account of Lycurgus the lawgiver and Numa the king, we thought not illogically to go back further to Romulus,[236] since we were already close to his time period, and when I thought (in the words of Aeschylus)[237]

> Who will meet such a man?
> Whom shall I array against him? Who is capable?

it seemed that the founder of the fair and fabled Athens should be 5 set against and compared to the father of unconquered and far-famed Rome. Our task, therefore, is to purify mythical material and make it obey reason and take on the appearance of history. But where this material arrogantly disdains believability and refuses any admixture of probability, we shall ask our readers' indulgence that they accept affably this account of ancient tradition.[238]

Difficulties in Finding the Truth

(*Pericles* 13.16)

Indeed who would be surprised[239] that men who live debauched lives consistently offer their slanders against their betters in sacrifice to the envy of the multitude as if to some evil spirit, when even Stesimbrotus of Thasos[240] has dared to spread abroad the terrible and abominable impious act of Pericles in regard to his son's wife? It seems that it is always so difficult to track down the truth by research, since later writers find that time obstructs the knowledge of events, while history and biography written contemporary with the events maim and distort the truth, sometimes because of jealousy and hostility, sometimes because of a desire to curry favour or flatter.[241]

Relationship of Historians to their History

(*On the Glory of the Athenians*, 345D–F)

For if you take away those who do the deeds, you will not have the writers of deeds.[242] Take away Pericles' administration of the city, the naval trophies of Phormio at Rhium, the brave deeds of Nicias at Cythera, Megara and Corinth, Demosthenes' actions at Pylos, Cleon's 400 prisoners, Tolmides' circumnavigation of the Peloponnese and Myronides' victory over the Boeotians at Oenophyta – take all these away and you can cross off Thucydides.[243] Take away Alcibiades' daring actions at the Hellespont, those of Thrasyllus at Lesbos, Theramenes' overthrow of the oligarchy, Thrasybulus and Archinus and the seventy men from Phyle who rose up against Spartiate rule, Conon re-embarking the Athenians upon the sea – and Cratippus is done away with.[244]

345E   Now Xenophon became his own history,[245] composing his military exploits and his successes and ascribing the account of them to Themistogenes of Syracuse so that he would be more trustworthy writing about himself as if it were a different person, and giving someone else the renown that accrued to his writings.[246] But all the rest of the historians – Cleidemus, Diyllus, Philochorus, Phylarchus – became for the deeds of others like dramatic actors, arranging the actions of generals and kings and covering themselves with their accounts of those men so that they might share in their light and splendour.[247] For the image of another's renown is reflected 345F from those who do the deeds to those who compose them, and it lights up anew, when the deed is revealed through words as if in a mirror.[248]

Vividness in History

(On the Glory of the Athenians, 347A)

Simonides calls painting silent poetry and poetry painting that speaks.[249] Literature narrates and records as having already happened those actions which painters represent as happening in the moment. They represent the same things, one group with colours and forms, the other with words and phrases; they differ in the medium and manner of their representation but both have one goal, and the best historian makes his narrative like a painting in its emotions and characters. Thucydides, for example, always strives in his account for this vividness,[250] desiring ardently to make the listener like a viewer and to produce in his readers the feelings of surprise and confusion of those who actually saw the events: Demosthenes arranging the Athenians along the very reef at Pylos; Brasidas urging his pilot to beach his ship and hurrying to the gangway, being wounded, fainting and falling forward onto the prow; the Lacedaemonians fighting a land battle from the sea while the Athenians fight a sea battle from land.[251] And again in the Sicilian narrative:[252]

> Both sides' armies from the shore had much anxiety and conflict of spirit so long as the sea battle was equally balanced . . . because of the continued indecisiveness of the battle, in their fear swaying with their very bodies in sympathy with their minds.

In the arrangement and representation of the events <they do not fall short of> pictorial vividness; <but nonetheless>[253] if it is not appropriate to compare painters with generals, let us not compare historians with them either.

Widely considered to be the greatest of Roman historians, Cornelius Tacitus (his first name is given as Gaius or Publius) was born *c*. 56 CE most likely in Narbonese or Cisalpine Gaul. He went to Rome as a young man, and his political career prospered under the Flavians (see *Histories* 1.1.3, below). He was praetor in 88, suffect consul in 97, and proconsul of Asia in 112–13; he held other posts in the state as well. The date of his death is unknown.

Five works of his survive, three entire and two in part. In probable order of composition they are: (1) *Agricola*, a biography of his father-in-law Gnaeus Iulius Agricola, general and governor in Britain from 77 or 78, a work which, while biography, already approaches some of the themes that Tacitus was to explore in his later historical works; (2) *Germania*, a (somewhat idealized) ethnographical account of German society; (3) *Dialogue on Orators*, written in Ciceronian style and examining the decline of oratory under the empire; (4) *Histories*, in twelve or fourteen books (only the first four and a bit of the fifth survive), covering the years 69–96 CE; and (5) *Annals*, in sixteen or eighteen books (nine complete and three partial books survive), an account from the death of Tiberius in 14 CE to 68, thus 'joining up' with the earlier *Histories*. Tacitus' style is closer to that of Sallust than to any other predecessor, and his portrait of imperial Rome is pessimistic and grim. A Senator himself, he was greatly concerned with how the nobility could achieve fame in a system where an Emperor held a monopoly on all claims to glory, while at the same time behaving as honourably as possible, steering a middle course between fawning sycophancy and ineffective independence.[1]

Preface to the *Histories*

(1.1.1–4)

My work will begin with the year in which the consuls were Servius Galba for the second time and Titus Vinius.[2] For many authors have related the 820 years of the earlier era from the foundation of the city, when the deeds of the Roman people were being recorded with equal eloquence and freedom of speech. But after Actium was fought and it was to peace's advantage that all power be conferred on one person,[3] those great talents stopped;[4] at the same time truth was crushed in several ways, first by an ignorance of public affairs as if they were others' concern,[5] and then either by the passion for flattery or by its opposite, a hatred towards those who ruled: neither the hostile nor the submissive[6] had any concern for future gener-

2 ations.[7] Yet whereas you would easily discount a writer's self-interest, disparagement and spite are listened to with ready ears: naturally, since obsequiousness incurs a shameful charge of servitude, while malice gives a false impression of freedom of speech.

3 Galba, Otho and Vitellius were known to me for neither benefit nor injury.[8] I would not deny that our career was begun by Vespasian, improved by Titus, and far advanced by Domitian.[9] But those who promise an uncontaminated trustworthiness must speak of

4 none with affection or hatred. If I live long enough, I have reserved for my old age a history of the principate of the divine Nerva and the rule of Trajan,[10] material which is richer and safer,[11] in the rare good fortune of a time when you are allowed to feel what you wish and say what you feel.

Preface to the *Annals*

(1.1.1–3)

The city of Rome was from the beginning held by kings; Lucius Brutus established liberty and the consulship.[12] Dictatorships were taken up only as needed on occasion; the power of decemvirs

did not last longer than two years and the consular power of military tribunes was of short duration.[13] The despotism of neither
Cinna nor Sulla was long;[14] the power of Pompey and Crassus
quickly passed to Caesar, the military forces of Antony and Lepidus
to Augustus,[15] and he, using the title 'first citizen', took everything,
which was by this time exhausted by civil dissensions, under his
command.

The successes and setbacks of the Roman people of old have 2
been recorded by distinguished writers, and distinctive talents were
not lacking in recording the times of Augustus, until they were
deterred by increasing obsequiousness. The affairs of Tiberius,
Gaius, Claudius and Nero were falsified because of fear while they
were alive, and, after they had died, were compiled with hatreds
still fresh.[16] My plan, therefore, is to record a few things concerning 3
Augustus, and matters concerning the end of his reign, and then the
principate of Tiberius, and the rest, without anger or partisanship,
the reasons for which I keep far off.[17]

Commemoration of Virtues and Vices

(Annals 3.65.1)[18]

It has not been my practice to rehearse the opinions of senators
unless such opinions are distinguished by their honesty or are of
noteworthy shamefulness (this is a paramount task, I believe, of
history), and I do this lest virtuous actions be passed over in
silence, and so that the fear of infamy from posterity should attach
to debased words and actions.[19]

Republican versus Imperial Historiography

(Annals 4.32.1–35.5)[20]

I am not unaware that much of what I have recorded and shall
record may perhaps seem unimportant and trivial to relate; but let

no one compare our annals with the writing of those who composed the Roman people's affairs of long ago.[21] *They* related enormous wars, sieges of cities, kings laid low and captured, or, when they turned their attention to domestic events, disagreements between consuls and tribunes, agrarian and grain laws, the struggles of the plebs and the aristocracy – and they did so free to explore where they

2 wished. *Our* labour is restricted and without glory: peace was unbroken or only moderately disturbed; the affairs of the city were gloomy; and there was an emperor who cared nothing for extending the empire.[22]

And yet it will not be without benefit to look into those matters which on first view seem trivial but from which the movement of

33 great events often arises.[23] To illustrate: the rulers of all cities and nations are either the people, the foremost men or individuals. (A form of government which is made up of a blending of these is more easily praised than realized, and, if it is realized, it can hardly

2 last long.)[24] And so just as formerly when the common people were strong or the Senate exerted influence, one needed to know the nature of the crowd and the means by which it could be restrained, and those who had thoroughly learned the natures of the Senate and the aristocrats were considered clever and wise in their time, in the same way, now that the political situation has changed and there is no safety for our affairs other than rule by one man, it will be advantageous to investigate and record these things,[25] because few can distinguish with proficiency what is honest from what is worse, or what is useful from what is harmful; and the majority are taught by the experiences of others.[26]

3 But, although such things are beneficial, they offer the least amount of pleasure.[27] It is the topographies of nations, the fluctuations of battles, the noble deaths of leaders which hold and refresh readers' minds; we for our part join together savage orders, a continuous series of charges, deceitful alliances, the ruin of the innocent, and identical reasons for death, the sameness and the satiety of these matters always thrown in my way.[28]

4 There is also the fact that writers of old rarely find a detractor, and it makes no difference to anyone if you praise Punic or Roman armies more floridly; by contrast, the descendants of many who were punished or disgraced in Tiberius' reign are still alive. And

even if those families are now extinct, you will find people who, because of a similarity of character, think the evil deeds of others are being ascribed to themselves.[29] Even glory and virtue make some hostile, because they seem to condemn too closely their opposites. But I return to my task.

In the year in which Cornelius Cossus and Asinius Agrippa 34 were consuls, Cremutius Cordus was charged with a new crime that was then heard for the first time:[30] namely, that in the annals that he published he praised Marcus Brutus and called Gaius Cassius 'the last of the Romans'.[31] His accusers were Satrius Secundus and Pinarius Natta, clients of Sejanus.[32] That meant destruction 2 for the accused, as did Caesar's savage look while listening to the defence, which Cremutius, his mind made up to end his life, began in this way:

My words, conscript fathers, are on trial; so blameless am I as far as deeds go. But these words have not been spoken against the *princeps* or the *princeps'* father, who are covered by the law on treason. I am said to have praised Brutus and Cassius, and no one has recorded their deeds without honour, even though very many have written of them.

Livy, renowned for his eloquence and reliability, elevated Pompey 3 especially with such praises that Augustus called him 'the Pompeian'.[33] He nowhere describes Scipio, Afranius, Cassius and Brutus[34] as brigands and parricides – the names which are now imposed on them – but often as pre-eminent men. The writings of 4 Asinius Pollio hand down the distinguished memory of these same men; Messalla Corvinus continually referred to Cassius as his 'commander'; and both Pollio and Messalla flourished in wealth and honours.[35] When Marcus Cicero in his book raised Cato to the heavens, what did the dictator Caesar do other than respond with his own speech, as if he were arguing his case in court?[36]

The letters of Antony, and Brutus' speeches before the people, are 5 full of charges, false of course but expressed with much bitterness, against Augustus;[37] the poems of Bibaculus and Catullus, replete with insults against Caesar, are still read.[38] Yet divine Julius himself, divine Augustus himself bore those remarks and disregarded them, and it would be difficult to say if they did so more because of restraint

or wisdom: for things that are scorned fade away; if you grow angry,
35   they seem recognized. I will not even mention the Greeks, for whom
not only freedom of speech but even licence went unpunished; or if
someone did notice, he avenged words with words.

But what was considered especially exempt and beyond criticism
was to write about those whom death had set free from hatred or
2   favouritism.[39] And surely I am not, with Cassius and Brutus armed
and holding the fields of Philippi, inciting the people to civil war
through public speeches? Is it not the case that they, who perished
seventy years ago, although they are still known by their images
(which not even the victor destroyed), retain a part of their memory
3   in writers?[40] Posterity assigns each his honour; if destruction falls
upon me, there will be no lack of those who remember not only Cassius and Brutus but also me.

4   He then walked out of the Senate and ended his life by starvation.
The Senate declared that the aediles should ensure that his books
were burned; but the books survived, concealed and published.[41]
And so one might all the more laugh at the dull wits of those who
believe because of their present power that the memory of the future
can also be extinguished. Far from it: when talents are punished,
their prestige increases, and foreign kings and those who behave in
the same savage way beget nothing except dishonour for themselves
and glory for their victims.

Wearying the Reader

(Annals 6.7.5)[42]

I am not unaware that the trials and punishments of many men
were omitted by the majority of writers, since they grew weary of
the abundance of them, or because they feared that a similar aversion might affect potential readers of the topics which had been too
numerous and grim for themselves. We, however, have come upon
many things worthy to be known,[43] even though they have been
unrecorded by others.

Wearying the Author

(16.16.1–2)[44]

Even if I were recording external wars and deaths on behalf of the state in such similar circumstances, satiety would have overcome me, and I would expect others to feel disgust and aversion towards deaths of citizens which were honourable, to be sure, but sorrowful and continuous. But as it is, this servile passivity and the vast waste of blood at home wear out the spirit and constrict it in grief. 2 And from those who will learn of these events I ask no defence other than that they[45] not hate those who died so feebly. It was divine anger directed against Roman affairs, and one cannot, as with the slaughter of armies or the capture of cities, pass over it with a single mention. Let it be granted, then, to the posthumous renown of distinguished men that just as in their funerals they are separated out from common burial, so too in the recording of their moment of death they may receive and possess their own remembrance.

30

THE YOUNGER PLINY

C. Plinius Caecilius Secundus, known as Pliny the Younger, was born *c.* 61 CE and died *c.* 112. He was born at Comum (modern-day Como) and adopted by his uncle, Pliny the Elder, the prolific polymath who died in the eruption of Vesuvius in 79. Pliny studied rhetoric with Quintilian and had a distinguished career under Trajan, knowing many of the major figures of his time, including the historian Tacitus. An accomplished orator, he had great success in the courts. His fame rests today on the collection of letters that he published in his lifetime, nine books published *c.* 100 CE, to a variety of correspondents, and a tenth containing Pliny's letters, while provincial governor in Bithynia-Pontus (*c.* 110–12), to the Emperor Trajan and the emperor's replies.[1]

The three letters below come from the early 100s CE. In the first, Pliny muses on the possibility of writing a history in a letter which bears a number of resemblances to Cicero's letter to Lucceius (above, p. 127). The second, expressing Pliny's desire that one of his actions be included in Tacitus' *Histories*, shows both the way in which a historian could receive 'raw material' (Pliny had already provided Tacitus with an account of his uncle's death in the eruption of Vesuvius) as well as the pressures likely to be experienced by any who wrote history well; in this sense it also bears comparison with the Lucceius letter. The third concerns, as so often under the empire, the constraints felt by historians when recording the actions of contemporaries, although here the letter's emphasis is on the (rare) assurance of the historian's freedom of speech.

Pliny Debates Whether He Should Write History

(*Letters* 5.8)

Pliny sends greetings to Titinius Capito:
You urge me to write history and you are not alone in doing so: many have often advised me to do this and I myself am willing, not because I am sure that I will do it properly (one would scarcely think that unless one were an amateur), but because it seems to me an especially noble thing not to allow events that deserve immortality to die, and also to increase the renown of others along with

2 one's own.[2] Nothing so stimulates me as the love of and desire for lasting fame, something which is most worthy of a man, especially one who is conscious of no fault in himself and so does not fear the

3 memory of posterity. And so day and night I think if 'I too could somehow raise myself from the earth': this would suffice for my prayer; it would be beyond my prayer 'to move as victor upon the lips of man'. 'Although O, if I could' – but what history alone seems

4 to promise is enough.[3] A speech or a poem is held in little esteem unless it shows the greatest eloquence; history gives pleasure however it is written.[4] For men are curious by nature and are fascinated by knowledge of events, however unadorned, given that they are charmed by gossip and anecdotes. For me there is also a family

5 precedent that directs me to this pursuit. My uncle (and, by adoption, my father) wrote histories and in a most conscientious manner.[5] I find it said by wise men that it is most honourable to follow in the footsteps of one's ancestors, provided only that they travelled before us on a right road.

6 Why, then, do I delay? I have conducted great and important cases, and I intend to revise these speeches (even if I have little expectation of them), to prevent all my hard work from perishing at the same time as myself if I do not add the remaining effort they

7 need.[6] For if you consider posterity, whatever has not been thoroughly finished is held in the same regard as if it had never been begun. You will say, 'You can revise your speeches and compose a history at the same time.' If only! But both tasks are so great that

8 it would be enough and more to complete *one* of them.[7] I began to

speak in the forum in my nineteenth year and only now do I see, though still dimly, what an orator should be responsible for.[8] What if a new burden were to be added to the other?

Oratory and history have many things in common but they differ in those very things which they seem to have in common. Oratory has a narrative, history has a narrative, but they are different: in oratory most of the matters are unimportant and trivial and drawn from ordinary situations, while in history everything that is abstruse, glorious and lofty comes together; what befits oratory is leanness, modest muscles, sinews; history has bulging muscles and a full mane of hair;[9] for oratory gives pleasure most of all by its power, acrimony and concentrated force, history by its drawn-out style, its sweetness and even charm; finally, their vocabulary differs, their tone differs, their arrangement differs. For it makes the greatest difference, as Thucydides says, whether it is a 'possession' or a 'performance-piece': one of these is oratory, the other history.[10]

For these reasons I am not induced to mingle and mix two very different things which differ in the very quality which gives them greatness, lest, misled by such a jumble, as it were, I might do in one place what I ought to do in the other. And so, to use the language familiar to me, I ask for an adjournment.

Nevertheless you can already consider now what era it would be best for me to attempt. Older events which have already been written up by others? Here the investigation has already been done, but the comparison of accounts is burdensome.[11] Recent events that have not been treated? Here offences are serious, gratitude slight.[12] For beyond the fact that in the numerous faults of mankind there are more things to blame than to praise, it is also the case that you will be called sparing in praise and excessive in criticism even though you are most generous in the former and most restrained in the latter.[13]

But all this does not discourage me: I have enough spirit to give me confidence. I ask that you prepare the road towards which you urge me, and select the material, so that, when I am at last ready to write, some other legitimate reason for hesitation or delay will not arise. Farewell.[14]

Raw Material for Inclusion in a History

(*Letters* 7.33)

Pliny to Cornelius Tacitus:

I predict – and I am not deceived in my prediction – that your histories will be immortal,[15] and I candidly confess that this is the

2 reason I desire to be included in them.[16] If we usually care that our likeness be rendered by the best artist possible, should we not wish

3 that our actions find a writer and publicist similar to yourself?[17] So I am giving an account here although it cannot have escaped your attention since it is in the public records,[18] but I am giving it nonetheless so that you may be more assured that it will please me if you embellish, with your talent and your testimony, this deed of mine, the credit for which has grown on account of its risk.

4 The Senate had assigned me together with Herennius Senecio[19] as counsel for the province of Baetica[20] against Baebius Massa, and, when Massa was convicted, the Senate had decreed that his property should be held in public custody.[21] When Senecio had ascertained that the consuls would be open to appeals,[22] he called me and said, 'Let us approach the consuls with the same spirit of cooperation in which we conducted the prosecution assigned to us,

5 and ask them that they not allow the property to be dispersed.' I replied, 'Since we were assigned to the case by the Senate, consider whether you think our roles have been played, now that the Senate has completed its case.' He replied, 'You may choose whatever boundary you wish for yourself, since you have no bond with the province except for that service of yours – and that recent, as well;

6 whereas I was born there and held office as quaestor there.' Then I said, 'If that's your decision and your determination, I shall go along with you, so that if any ill will arises, it won't be only yours.'

7 We went to the consuls.[23] Senecio explained the matter and I added a few things. We had scarcely fallen silent when Massa complained that Senecio had employed not the good faith demanded of an advocate but the bitterness of personal hostility, and he arraigned

8 him as defendant on a charge of dereliction of duty.[24] Everyone was in shock. I said, 'I fear, most distinguished consuls, that Massa, by

not arraigning me as defendant as well, has by his silence charged
me with collusion.' This remark was immediately taken up and
afterwards much talked about.[25] The divine Nerva himself (for   9
even before he was emperor he noticed anything that was done for
the benefit of the state)[26] sent me a most thoughtful letter in which
he congratulated not only me but also our own times, which (so he
wrote) have found an example similar to those of olden days.

These matters, such as they are, you will make better known,   10
more distinguished, more important. I do not ask, however, that you
go beyond what was actually done. For history should not depart
from truth, and truth suffices for honourable deeds.[27] Farewell.

The Historian's Freedom

(*Letters* 9.19)

Pliny to Cremutius Ruso:
   You say that you read in a certain letter of mine[28] that Verginius
Rufus[29] had ordered this inscription to be put on his tomb:

> Here lies Rufus, who once, when he had defeated Vindex,
>   claimed power not for himself but for his country.

You fault him for ordering this and you add that Frontinus[30]
behaved better and more justly because he forbade any monument
at all to be constructed for himself; and finally you ask what I
thought of each man.

   I loved each of them but I admired more the one whom you fault,   2
and indeed I admired him so much that I did not think he could ever
be praised enough; and yet I must now defend him. It is my judge-   3
ment that all who have accomplished some great and memorable
deed[31] are worthy not only of indulgence but also of praise if they
seek an immortality which they have merited, and strive to prolong
the glory of an enduring name even with their epitaphs. And I can-   4
not easily think of anyone except Verginius whose modesty in
promoting himself was equal to his glory in the actual deed.

5   I myself can testify to this: he was a genuine friend and he approved of me, and yet only one time in my presence was Verginius ever brought to make a remark about his actions, when he was once with Cluvius[32] who said to him, 'Verginius, you know the truth that is owed to history,[33] and so I ask your pardon if you read anything in my history which is not to your liking.' To which Verginius replied, 'Cluvius, do you *not* know that I did what I did so that you would be free to write whatever you wished?'[34]

31

ARRIAN

Flavius Arrianus (his first name is given as either Lucius or Aulus) was born in Nicomedia in Bithynia *c.* 86 CE. He studied with the philosopher Epictetus whose discourses he published in the *Encheiridion*. Arrian's father or grandfather had received Roman citizenship, and Arrian himself was supported by the emperor Hadrian who enrolled him in the Senate. Arrian was consul possibly in 129 and was also legate to Cappadocia. He was archon at Athens in 145/6 and died probably *c.* 160.[1]

Arrian was a prolific writer and styled himself as a second Xenophon. He wrote a manual on hunting (updating Xenophon's earlier treatment of that topic) and essays on battle tactics, as well as a local history of Bithynia in eight books. He also wrote a Parthian history in seventeen books, which included the campaigns of Trajan, but his fame rests on his account of Alexander, which he called the *Anabasis* (in imitation of Xenophon's account of the Ten Thousand) and which covered from Alexander's accession to his death in Babylon in 323 BCE.[2] As Arrian makes clear, he based his work on Ptolemy and Aristobulus, two early historians of Alexander, whom he considered the most reliable sources. He also composed a work on India, based on that of Megasthenes, one of Alexander's generals.[3]

Preface to the *Anabasis*

(*preface* 1–3)

Where Ptolemy, son of Lagus, and Aristobulus, son of Aristobulus,[4] have both agreed in their accounts of Alexander, son of Philip, I have written the same here as being entirely true;[5] where they disagree, I have selected what seems more reliable to me and at the same time more worthy of telling.[6] Different writers have written of Alexander in various ways, and there is no person about whom more people have written nor more divergent accounts. But to me Ptolemy and Aristobulus seem more reliable in their narratives, Aristobulus because he campaigned together with King Alexander, and Ptolemy because in addition to having campaigned with Alexander he was a king and it would have been more disgraceful for him to tell falsehoods than for any other. In addition, both men wrote when Alexander was already dead, and there was no constraint or reward for writing anything other than what happened.[7] I have also written here some things that were composed by others because these too seemed worthy of telling and not entirely untrustworthy, though I have recorded them only as what is said about Alexander. If, when there are already so many writers about Alexander, anyone is surprised that I decided to write this history, he should be so only when he has read everything written by my predecessors and then read our work as well.[8]

The 'Second Preface'

(*Anabasis* 1.12.1–5)[9]

In the intervening passages Arrian has taken Alexander from his accession on the death of Philip in 336 to his early campaigns in the north and his invasion of Greece and destruction of Thebes. When Alexander crosses over into Asia in spring 334, he is the first man to disembark and he immediately visits Troy, at which point Arrian returns to some themes from the opening preface.

When Alexander arrived at Troy, Menoetius the pilot crowned him with a golden crown, and after this Chares the Athenian also arrived, coming from Sigeum, and some others, Greeks and natives, <. . .>[10] but others, that he garlanded the tomb of Achilles as well; and they say that Hephaestion garlanded the tomb of Patroclus.[11] Alexander, so the story is told, called Achilles fortunate because he had Homer as the herald of his future fame.[12] Indeed, Alexander was right to call Achilles happy, not least 2 because for Alexander himself, unlike for the rest of his good fortune, this one field was left free, and there is no worthy account of Alexander's deeds, either in prose or in verse.[13] Not even any choral poetry was composed for Alexander as it was for Hiero, Gelon, Theron and many others[14] who were in no way like Alexander, so that Alexander's actions are far less well known than the most trivial deeds of long ago.[15] Much better known than Alexander 3 and his deeds are the march inland of the Ten Thousand with Cyrus against King Artaxerxes, their journey back to the sea under the command of Xenophon, and the sufferings of Clearchus and of those captured with him, all thanks to Xenophon's account.[16] Yet Alexander did not share the command with any- 4 one, nor did he, in flight from the great king, merely conquer those who were blocking his way back to the sea; on the contrary, there is no other man who displayed so many great deeds, either in number or in magnitude, amongst Greeks and barbarians.[17] It is for this reason that I set myself to writing this treatise, and I do not think I am unworthy to make Alexander's deeds known to mankind.

5   As for who I am who have composed this account, I see no need to write my name (since it is not unknown to people) or my country or family, or any offices I may have held in my native land. Instead I write this: that my country, family and offices are these very writings, and they have been so from my youth. For this reason I consider myself not unworthy of first place in Greek literature, just as Alexander was first in arms.[18]

Including an Event that is Possibly True

(*Anabasis* 2.12.8)

Now I have included this in my account neither as true nor as entirely unreliable.[19] If in fact it did occur in this way, then I praise Alexander for the pity that he showed the women and for the trust and honour he bestowed on his comrade. If it did not happen, I still praise Alexander because it seemed credible to those who wrote about him that he would have done and said such things.

Inclusion of Material about the Gods

(*Anabasis* 5.1.2)

I am unable to decide whether the Theban Dionysus set out from Thebes or Tmolus in Lydia when he led his campaign against the Indians,[20] and whether he attacked so many warlike tribes unknown to the Greeks at that time, conquering by force none of them except the race of Indians. But it is not right to make a minute examination of the tales told about divine figures from long ago. For these matters are not trustworthy to one who composes in accordance with probability; but when one adds the divine element to a story, these matters do not seem wholly untrustworthy.[21]

Appropriateness of Ethnographical Material in History

(*Anabasis*, 5.5.1–2)

I am going to write a separate work on the Indians, which will include the most reliable material recorded by those who campaigned with Alexander, by Nearchus, who made a voyage in the great sea on the Indian coast, and by Megasthenes and Eratosthenes, reputable men: the customs of the Indians, unusual flora and fauna that grow there, and the voyage along the coastline of the outer sea.[22] In this work, however, I shall record only what 2 pertains to Alexander's deeds.[23]

From the Conclusion

(*Anabasis* 7.30.1–3)

Whoever reproaches Alexander should do so not by bringing forward only those things that were worthy of reproach, but should collect all the evidence together[24] and then calculate who he is himself and what sort of fortune he has enjoyed that he reproaches a man such as Alexander who achieved such measure of human success and was unambiguously king of two continents,[25] and whose reputation went everywhere – whereas the one criticizing is himself a rather insignificant person engaged in insignificant tasks, performing not even these with any distinction. I think that 2 there was no race of men, no city at that time, not even any individual who had not heard of Alexander. I do not believe that a man like no other man could have been born without the assistance of the divine. This is shown by the oracles that are said to have been reported at his death, as well as the visions and dreams that have been seen by many different people at different times, and his honour and memory amongst men, which is greater than human: even now after so many years,[26] new oracles continue to be reported amongst the Macedonians on how they should honour Alexander. Although I too have found fault with Alexander 3 sometimes in the course of this account of his deeds, I am not ashamed to express my admiration for Alexander himself.[27] I censured those actions for the sake of truth and to make my work useful amongst mankind.[28] And I too embarked on this work not without the agency of the divine.[29]

APPIAN

Appian was born in Alexandria towards the end of the first century BCE; he became a Roman citizen probably during Hadrian's reign and later, thanks to his friend Fronto (see below, p. 357), he became a procurator under Antoninus Pius (see below, *preface* 62). His history of Rome in twenty-four books began with early Rome and the kings, and thereafter was organized by theatre of action (e.g., Sicily, Gaul, Carthage, Spain). After the treatment of the Mithridatic wars in the east, he treated the Roman civil wars in Books 13–17 and in 18–21 the wars in Egypt (where Octavian and Antony clashed). Eleven books survive, while the others are fragmentary. Appian saw Roman virtue as the reason for their success, while greed and ambition led to the civil wars. Despite this moralizing approach, Appian is more interested in social and economic issues than almost any other ancient historian. The passages below offer Appian's explanation of his arrangement, and his reasons for treating the civil wars.[1]

From the Preface

Many Greeks and Romans have written of these events, and their history is much greater than that of Macedon, which was previ-
46 ously the greatest. In my interest to see the empire in its entirety, people by people, my treatise has often carried me from Carthage to Spain and from Spain to Sicily or Macedonia, or to embassies and alliances made with other nations; then in turn it has carried me back to Carthage or Sicily and back again, like a wanderer, while everything was still in its unfinished state, until I gathered
47 the portions together.[2] I treat all their expeditions, embassies and actions in Sicily, until they brought it to its present arrangement; and all the battles and agreements with Carthage, and the embassies they sent or received from them, and whatever they did to them or suffered at their hands, until they razed Carthage,[3] took in addition the Libyan nation, and then settled Carthage and
48 Libya with their own people, bringing it to its present state. I have arranged what follows people by people, because I wished to examine Roman actions against each of them, in order that I might learn the weakness or endurance of these nations, and the bravery or fortune of the conquerors, and any other circumstance
49 that contributed to the victory. Because I thought that others too might wish to learn Roman history in this way, I have written my account nation by nation; if there are events taking place simultaneously concerning other nations, I omit them and place them in
50 the relevant nation's history.[4] I thought it unnecessary to give the chronology for all the events, but I shall occasionally record those for the most famous events . . .

Appian now lists each of the books of his history, beginning with the early history of Rome and Italy, and then proceeding to the others according to the theatre of conflict (Gaul, Spain, Macedon, etc.); after these he will treat the Roman civil wars beginning with Marius and going down to Octavian, after which Egypt became part of the empire and the government became a monarchy.

So in this way each of the books is divided either by country or,   61
in the case of the civil wars, by general. The last book will also
contain an account of the extent of the army, the revenues which
the Romans receive from each nation, what they expend on naval
garrisons and other things of that sort.

It is fitting that one who writes about the Romans' brilliance   62
should begin with his own family. Many know who I am who
have written these things and I have previously indicated it,[5] but
to speak more clearly, I am Appian of Alexandria: I have achieved
the first rank in my country and have argued cases at Rome before
the emperors until they deemed me worthy of being named their
procurator. If anyone has an interest in learning the rest, I have
written a treatise on this as well.[6]

Purpose of Narration of Civil Wars

(Civil Wars 1.24)

In this way, then, from manifold civil wars the state of the Romans
ended up in harmony and monarchy. I have written up and brought
together the material on how this happened, material that is worthy
of wonder for those who wish to see the limitless ambition of men,
the frightening love of power, their untiring perseverance and the
forms of countless evils, and especially because it was necessary for
me to write up these events as preceding the portion of my work
devoted to Egypt, where this history will conclude.

33
FRONTO

Marcus Cornelius Fronto was born around 95 CE at Cirta (modern Constantine) in north Africa. Educated at Rome, he was a leading advocate under Hadrian and was appointed by Antoninus Pius to be the tutor of his heir Marcus Aurelius and Marcus' adopted brother Lucius Verus. He remained on close terms with both his students until his death c. 166. While a few fragments of speeches have survived, Fronto is best known today for his correspondence, including letters between him and his erstwhile pupils. Fronto was a lover of old-style Latin, and his archaizing tendencies can be seen in his preference for the early writers Cato and Ennius and for Sallust, himself an imitator of early Latin prose.

In the first of the two passages below, Lucius Verus, co-emperor with Marcus, writes to Fronto from the east in 166 CE where he is finishing up his campaigns against the Parthians, and promises him materials which can then be worked up into a fully fledged account of the war. The second passage, long known as the *Principia Historiae* ('Sketch of History'), though this is not Fronto's title, is a letter to Marcus Aurelius (written before the materials promised by Verus had arrived) giving an idea of the way in which he would write up the deeds of Marcus' brother, Verus. The comparison of Homer and Achilles shows that Fronto was ready to pull out all the stops in his history, and what is found in the letter is often used to indict Fronto for craven fawning and for producing the kind of eulogistic history against which Lucian was later to inveigh. The history, however, was never written, and it cannot now be known whether that was because Fronto had a change of heart or died before writing it.[1]

Offering Materials for History

(*Letters to the Emperor Verus* 1.2)

<Lucius Verus to my teacher, Fronto . . . >[2] they appended to their letters. But what was done before my own departure[3] you will learn from the letters written to me by the leaders entrusted with each particular matter.[4] Our staff Sallust, who is now Fulvianus,[5] will give you copies of them. And so that you can record the reasons for my decisions, I shall send you my own letters as well, in which whatever had to be done is explained. But if you also want some paintings,[6] you can get those from Fulvianus. And so that I can bring you, as it were, right on the spot, I have ordered Avidius Cassius and Martius Verus[7] to compose some memoranda for me, which I shall send to you. From them you will become familiar with those men's way of life and thought.

If you wish me too to write up any memorandum, let me know: I shall compose whatever kind you like and I shall do as you order. For I am prepared to undergo anything provided that our actions are embellished by you. Obviously you won't disregard my speeches to the Senate[8] and the harangues I delivered to the troops. I shall send you as well the conversations I had with the barbarians: these will help you a great deal.

2 One thing I wish not to point out to you (I the student to his teacher!) but ask you to consider, namely that you spend a good deal of time on the causes and beginnings of the war, and also the setbacks that occurred before we arrived:[9] take your time in getting to us. Furthermore, I think it's necessary to clarify how greatly superior the Parthians were before my arrival, so that the magnitude of what we have done will be evident. Whether you should, therefore, cover all that material rapidly, as Thucydides did in his 'Fifty Years',[10] or rather speak in a little more detail (though not, of course, to the same degree that you will expatiate upon our actions subsequently), you must decide for yourself.

3 In sum, my accomplishments, of whatever kind, are only as great as they actually are; they will, however, *seem* as great as you wish them to seem.[11]

'Sketch of History'

(*Letters to the Emperor Verus*, 2.1)[12]

<Fronto to my Lord Antoninus Augustus>[13]

<. . .>[14] and for the great deeds of your brother[15] a history writ-
ten intelligently and carefully will add something of interest and
celebrity, just as a light breeze will blow and fan a fire however
great.

As soon as your brother sends me the memoranda of his accom-   2
plishments, we shall start to write, but only if this sketch which we
are sending as an hors d'oeuvre is not displeasing . . . I fear, nevertheless, that . . . we are starting on deeds as great as Achilles wished
he had accomplished and Homer wished he had written.[16] . . .

What am I to add? Distinguished as you are, you must allow that   3
we seek out those things that are to be defined . . . I follow matters
that have been prepared . . . with the greatly unbridled customs of
foreign Antioch . . . it will remain, if you come, to visit and afterwards to stop . . . great and despairing grievous slaughters on this
side of the Taurus, were told afterwards through pleasing tall
tales.[17] Indeed, their exceedingly rich talents would have been for
nothing had they not occupied themselves in writing up magnificent deeds, and likewise had the talents also of the writers not
matched up to the magnitude of the events (or, if you will, had not
adapted themselves to the events).[18] The poems of Homer would be
ruined if there were no battles, which he showed in the second book
as a whole but also in the opening lines of the first book.[19] Certainly
Xenophon of Athens, a worthy custodian of the experience of the
Greeks, served as a voluntary soldier in the army of Cyrus . . .[20] And
the labours of Hercules are famous, if not for the deeds themselves,
then nevertheless for Hercules' disciplined conduct.[21]

. . . but truly the one who has received far and away the greatest   4
praises both for his oratory and his actions is Cato Porcius the
Censor[22] . . . the free time he was given away from his work he
occupied in hunting . . .

. . . his friends despairing, Alexander had washed his body . . .   5
the empire of the Roman people was extended by Trajan beyond

the enemy's rivers[23] . . . *no blame attaches to the lover who is silent . . . For the rest of mankind lies when the moment presents itself, but the lies of historians merit a blame as long-lasting as their memory.*[24]

6   I call you to witness . . . is present . . . Pollio[25] . . . nations which have brought about defeats through plundering and pillaging I consider brigands rather than enemies. The Parthians alone of mankind have borne a reputation for hostility against the Roman people that must never be despised. Not only do the slaughter of Crassus and the shameful flight of Antony demonstrate this, but also the destruction of the legate with his army under the leadership of that bravest emperor Trajan; and indeed when that prince left for his triumph, his retreat was hardly free from fear or unbloodied.[26]

7   And so I will proceed to compare the two greatest wars fought in our time and with the same result against the Parthians by the two greatest emperors,[27] in the light of the forces of each leader on each occasion. I am not unaware that the brave deeds of the living are received in a more grudging manner, while those of the dead more appreciatively; we favour the past and envy the present.[28] For jealousy always . . .

8   As soon as the state demanded a great leader, that is, a man equal to responsibilities put before him, one appeared who was braver and more warlike than all the leaders who came from poor Arpinum and hard Nursia[29] . . . *the Parthians, stained with Roman blood . . .* [30.]

9   . . . once against the Romans <an enemy?> strong and hostile and well-prepared, trained in war and to such a degree from the ambushes of the Romans . . . since he was being led headlong into daring every crime, with no more audacious crime that he might dare being left.

10   Then in addition . . . he set out for war with proven soldiers who despised the Parthian enemy, and considered the impact made by their arrows contemptible after the enormous wounds inflicted by the scythe-like swords of the Dacians.[31] The emperor would call many of the soldiers each by his own name or would jokingly use the nickname they had received in camp. A good many he advanced to the rank of centurion or *cornicularius*, or

gave double pay, and many he advanced to centurion *primipilus* or *hastatus*[32] ...

By contrast, Lucius in his campaign against the Parthians had [11] either to take new recruits chosen by a levy or to retain those who were broken by the harsh terms of their military service, the soldiery having been corrupted by grim and lax conditions.[33] For after the emperor Trajan they had become nearly entirely without discipline, since Hadrian as emperor had plenty of energy for going around and addressing the armies eloquently but avoided actual battle.[34] Indeed, he preferred to abandon provinces that had been captured by Trajan by force (the Dacian provinces were still not pacified) rather than retain them with his army. You can see the monuments of his travels that he set up in many cities of Europe and Asia, both many other kinds and tombs built of stone.[35] He set out not only for frozen lands but also twice for those in southern areas because of his concern for the safety of those provinces which lay beyond the Euphrates and the Danube and which Trajan had annexed ...[36] to the Roman empire in the hope of adding them as provinces to Moesia and Asia. By contrast, Hadrian on his own initiative gave back these provinces – Dacia and the parts lost by the Parthians – in their entirety. The army in Asia amused themselves with jokes in their tents instead of with shield and swords: they never again saw a commander of that sort.

Aurelius Antoninus, that sacred emperor, is said to have [12] restrained himself by abstaining from bloodshed, and is to be put on a level only with King Numa of all Roman rulers.[37] ... after Hadrian towards similar works and the state should be administered by himself ... nor was there any initiator of war against the Parthians, because the Roman soldiery had been reduced to cowardice from the long unaccustomedness of fighting; since inactivity is harmful both for all other skills and especially for warfare. It matters a very great deal that soldiers should experience changing fortunes and diligent training in the field.

The soldiers in Syria were the most depraved of all: seditious, [13] insolent, absent from their unit without leave, wandering in front of their prescribed posts, going about like scouts, drunk from noon to the next day, not even practised in taking up their armour; but because they could not endure labour, they were half-armed like skirmishers or slingers, one man after another failing to take up his arms. In addition to such disgraces, they were so demoralized by their unsuccessful battles that at the first sight of the Parthians they turned their backs as if they heard the trumpets indicate the signal for retreat.[38]

14   Lucius checked this great collapse in military discipline as the situation demanded, offering his own purposeful activity as an example of how to be a soldier.[39] He himself at the head of the column was more often worn out from walking than from riding his horse; he bore the burning midday sun as easily as the clear morning air; the swirling dust he endured as if it were fog; the sweat running down his armour he took no notice of, as if he were playing some sport; his head was uncovered to the sun, storms, hail and snow, and was unprotected even against weapons; he gave his efforts to inspecting the soldiers in the field and going to visit those who were ill; with great interest he visited the soldiers' quarters, but casually examined the refinements of the Syrians and the stupidity of the Pannonians, getting from each man's conduct an idea of his character. After the day's business was done, he himself would take his bath, and then dine at a simple table, eating the same food as the soldiers, drinking the local wine and whatever water was available for the occasion. He himself took the first watch obligingly, and was already long awake as he awaited the last watch; he took pleasure in toil rather than leisure, and he used up his free time in working; the time free of military duties he occupied in transacting administrative matters. On occasions of sudden deprivation he used branches and leaves simply for his bedding and the ground sometimes for his pillow. He took sleep earned by labour, not obtained in silence.[40] Only serious misdeeds did he punish severely, while less serious ones, though he was aware of them, he pretended not to notice: he offered an opportunity for repentance; for many correct their own faults when they think they have not been seen, but persist in their shameless behaviour when their faults are clearly revealed.

15   . . . through so many provinces, through so many open dangers of sieges, battles, and the destruction of citadels, garrisons and outposts, he[41] distributed tokens of care and counsel, not of luxuries; he nevertheless freely gave a thousand spoils . . .

... Lucius in the cleverness of his counsels <was> far superior   16
to Trajan ... *he knew that mail-clad soldiers were like fishy
beasts, and that they pop out of the deep sea, and, somersaulting,
leap about on the great plains*[42] ... to send legates repeatedly; the
deed was well done: a few days previously Lucius had of his own
accord sent letters to Vologaesus,[43] offering to end the war, if he
wished, by agreement. Because the foreigner rejected the peace
that was offered, he was roughly treated.

This makes very clear how deep-seated Lucius' care for the sol-   17
diers was, since he desired to purchase at the cost of his own glory
a peace won without bloodshed. As for Trajan, many conclude
from the rest of his actions that he believed his own glory would
be greater in the blood of his soldiers, since he sent back disappointed the ambassadors of the Parthians who came to him
begging for peace.

Amongst the barbarians Lucius had a hallowed reputation for   18
justice and clemency; Trajan was not equally blameless in the eyes
of all. No one ever regretted handing over his kingdom or his fate
to Lucius' trustworthiness, whereas Trajan can hardly be excused
for the slaughter of king Parthamasirus who came to him as a suppliant.[44] Even if that king was justly killed when turmoil arose
(given that he had begun the violence), nonetheless the reputation
of the Romans would have been better served if, as a suppliant, he
had been allowed to depart without punishment rather than suffer
the punishment he justly deserved. In such actions the cause of the
deed lies hidden, while the deed itself is seen, and it is greatly preferable to ignore an injury and have public opinion be favourable
than to avenge it and have that opinion be hostile.

In each of the two Parthian wars, two men of consular rank   19
each leading an army were butchered – Severianus when Lucius
had not yet set out from the city;[45] whereas Appius Santra was
slain by Arsaces[46] on his return to Balcia in the Taurus Mountains, when Trajan was in fact present in the east increasing the
ferry dues for horses and camels on the Euphrates and the Tigris.

That also ... an actor to have been summoned to Syria from   20
Rome. But undoubtedly, just as we see the highest trees to be shaken
more violently by the winds, so jealousy pursues more viciously the
greatest virtues. I leave it undecided whether the emperor Trajan

should be judged more distinguished in war or peace, except to note
that even Spartacus and Viriathus[47] had a certain degree of ability
in war: in the arts of peace, however, hardly anyone has been more
agreeable than Trajan to the people, and perhaps no one has even
been as agreeable. These very things, together with criticisms of his
earlier life, provoke criticism.[48] They seem to be derived from the
highest principle of civic wisdom, namely, that the emperor did not
fail to take care even of mime artists and the other practitioners
whether on stage, in the circus or in the arena, being one who knew
that the Roman people were controlled by two things above all, the
grain dole and spectacles;[49] that one's rule was approved no less by
amusements than by serious things, and that the neglect of serious
matters brought greater harm but that of amusements a weightier
resentment; cash donatives are weaker incentives than public spectacles because the former pacify individually and by name only
those who are on the grain-register, while the latter delight the
entire population[50] . . . or was placated <more?> by purificatory
sacrifices than the games and the rites that are part of the circus
performances. For that reason processions, carriages, religious carriages and attributes of the gods were dedicated by our ancestors,
and elephants in peacetime (the Roman people never used them in
battle) they made use of in night-time spectacles[51] . . . such a fuss to
make of you or they enunciate mischief by all sorts of idle stories: I
have recorded these things for the sake of refuting those who are my
detractors.

21   . . . Lucius himself, however, wherever he accomplished something, sent missives to the senators, his letters eloquently
composed to indicate the situation, in as much as he desired with
lavish effort to rehabilitate eloquence . . . if anyone reads what has
been written, whether the great-grandfather or the great-grandson
will be seen as superior in virtue, the result of the comparison will
remain in the family.[52]

34

LUCIAN

Lucian was born in Samosata in the Roman province of Syria sometime between 115 and 125 CE. In his work *The Dream*, which is possibly autobiographical, he says that his father originally apprenticed him to a sculptor but he proved no good at the work and wished to pursue a literary education. Trained in rhetoric in Ionia, he became a powerful and popular speaker, travelling throughout the Mediterranean, including to Rome and Gaul. Around the age of forty he settled in Athens and spent the 160s and 170s there. Towards the end of his life he was given an imperial post in Egypt, where he most probably died, sometime in the late 180s or early 190s. Some eighty works have come down under his name, in a variety of genres: dialogues, diatribes, rhetorical exercises and brief introductions, to name just a few. Lucian's satirical wit shines through consistently, and *How to Write History* is no exception, especially in its first half where the author pillories a series of named and anonymous historians.[1]

How to Write History can be dated to 166 CE, given the references to the Parthian campaign of Lucius Verus (reigned 161–9) and the mention of a plague (15) which occurred during Verus' attack on Seleucia in 166; the remarks about future events related to the war (31) suggest that the war was still being fought when the treatise was written. There has been debate on whether the names of the offending historians (15–16, 30, 32) are those of real historians or invented by Lucian himself, but the former seems more likely.[2]

The work is often thought to be influenced by Cynic philosophy and to have something of the form of a Cynic diatribe, and indeed Diogenes the Cynic is invoked at the beginning of the essay, while

Lucian identifies himself with this same thinker at the end. Whether or not Lucian belonged to a particular philosophical school, his writing is protean, and many different strands of thought come together in his works. It is perhaps safest to say that he disliked and derided excessively theoretical and abstract philosophical approaches, and favoured instead a pragmatic approach to life.

Because *How to Write History* is the only surviving work from classical antiquity to treat historiography generally and not with reference to a particular author, there has been a tendency to see it as a kind of handbook or guide that encapsulates the opinions of previous critics. While there is certainly much to be said for this view, it would be wrong to treat this essay as a handbook of ancient 'theory' about the writing of history in antiquity for several reasons. First, Lucian's essay is a satire, albeit a brilliantly funny one, which spends half its space parodying contemporary historians of the emperor Lucius Verus' wars in Parthia. Satire can be serious, of course, but it is also its nature to be exaggerative and one-sided. Second, Lucian is particularly obsessed with the blurring in his day of panegyric and historiography, and much of his criticism is focused on the absurd ways in which his historians embellished and augmented the emperor and his achievements while denigrating his opponents. The emphasis on encomium (not simply praise) and exaggeration and the desire to please the ruling power can certainly find parallels in earlier historiographical criticism, but in no other work does it play so important a role. Nor is Lucian's belief that some think that encomium is the part of history that gives pleasure (9) attested in earlier writings. Although exaggeration and bias are important areas of historiographical criticism, the heavy concentration on these features is a result of the conditions of Lucian's own time. Nor is it coincidence that a good portion of the essay satirizes poor performances in history, since polemic was an important part of the ways in which the writing of history was discussed. Finally, Lucian's ideas and interests cannot be separated from the literary milieu in which he worked, the so-called Second Sophistic, in which Greek authors affected a classicizing style and looked back to the writers of the fifth and fourth centuries BCE; that meant above all exalting the early historians Herodotus, Thucydides and Xenophon. In sum, much of what Lucian says is indeed paralleled in the earlier tradition, but in nearly every case Lucian gives it his own particular spin.[3]

The essay can be divided into the following sections:[4] the Introduction (1–6) explains the topic of the essay and its purposes; the body of the essay comprises 7–60, divided into two parts, the former consisting of the delineation between history and encomium and offering examples of wretched historical compositions (7–32) and the latter offering positive guidelines in the writing of history (33–60); the final chapters (61–3) offer recapitulation and an anecdote illustrating the author's main point.

How to Write History

1 They say that when Lysimachus[5] was king, my dear Philo,[6] a plague fell upon the people of Abdera[7] of the following sort: the entire population suffered at first from a strong and persistent fever and around the seventh day some had a great deal of blood run from their noses while others had profuse sweating, and in either case this broke the fever.[8] But the disease affected their minds in a rather ridiculous way: all of them were violently stirred to tragedy and uttered iambic lines and wailed greatly. They sang solo parts especially from Euripides' *Andromeda*, and in particular they went through the entire speech of Perseus with its musical accompaniment.[9] The city was full of pale, thin, seventh-day[10] tragic performers declaiming, 'You, Eros, tyrant over gods and men',[11] and crying out all the rest in a great voice. And it went on for a long time too, until winter came on and a great frost put an end to their prattling. The reason for such behaviour, I think, was Archelaos,[12] the tragic actor who was famous at that time and who had performed the *Andromeda* for them in mid-summer in sweltering heat, such that the majority caught fever from the theatre, and when they later recovered, they slipped into tragedy, the *Andromeda* greatly occupying their minds and Perseus with Medusa still flying around in each one's thoughts.

2 So then, to compare one thing with another (as they say), that plague of Abdera has now come upon the majority of the well-educated, such as to make them not declaim tragedy (they would be less delirious if they were possessed by the fine iambic lines of another) but rather, ever since our current disturbances began – I mean the war against the barbarians with the defeat in Armenia and the subsequent victories – there is no one who is not writing history.[13] We have all Thucydideses[14] and Herodotuses and Xenophons,[15] and so it seems indeed that the remark that 'war is the father of all'[16] was true, if at any rate it sired so many historians at a stroke.

3 Well then, my friend, in seeing and hearing these things, that famous story of the man from Sinope[17] came into my mind: when Philip was said to be already on the march against the Corinthians, they were all in an uproar and all were busy at their tasks: one

man was fashioning shields, another transporting stones, another repairing the city wall, one reinforcing the battlements, and others doing other useful things. All this was being watched by Diogenes who had not been assigned any task, since no one considered him of use for anything. He, however, eagerly girding himself in his threadbare cloak, began rolling his barrel (the one in which he lived) up and down the Craneion hill.[18] When one of his acquaintances asked, 'Why are you doing this, Diogenes?', he replied, 'I am rolling this barrel so as not to seem to be the only one doing nothing among so many who are working.'

And so, dear Philo, lest I alone be mute at such a moment of 4 cacophony and, like a comic bodyguard, roam about openmouthed in silence, I too supposed that it would be good for me to roll my barrel to the best of my ability, not to the point of composing history or narrating the deeds themselves – I am not so enamoured of my own abilities as that, and you need have no fears about me on that account.[19] I know how great the danger is if one should roll down from the rocks, especially as such a little winejar as mine has not been very sturdily made by the potter: it would immediately strike against some tiny stone and I would have to gather up the sherds. No, I shall tell you what I have decided and how I shall myself stand safely out of the range of the missiles and yet have a part in the war. I shall keep myself away from 'this smoke and surge',[20] and all the cares that weigh on a historian, and rightly so.[21] But I shall offer a little advice and some few suggestions for historians so that I might have a share with them in the building, if not in the inscription on it, then at least touching my fingertip to the mortar.[22]

And yet the majority think they need no advice for this task, any 5 more than they need some technical manual for walking or seeing or eating; they think it's quite simple and easy to write history, and anyone can do it, provided one can express whatever one thinks.[23] But, my friend, you yourself know, I suppose, that this is not one of those things that is easily manageable or can be put together carelessly; on the contrary, it requires, if anything in literature does, a great deal of thought – at least if one wishes, as Thucydides says, to compose a possession for all time.[24] Now I know that I shall not convert many of them, and indeed I shall seem very annoying to some of them, especially to the very many whose histories have already been completed and exhibited in public. And if their history has been praised by those who heard it at the time, it is madness even to expect that such men will rework or rewrite any part of what has once been officially approved and stored up in the royal halls, as it were.[25] Nevertheless, it's not a bad idea if what follows is addressed to those men as well, so that if ever another war should occur[26] between Celts and Getae or Indians and Bactrians – no one would dare to fight against us since they have already all been conquered – they will be able to compose their works in a better way, following this ruler, provided it seems straight to them. Otherwise, let them continue to measure their work with the same yardstick as they now use.[27] The physician cannot very well be blamed if all the people of Abdera declaim the *Andromeda* of their own free will.

6   Since giving advice is a two-fold task, that is, teaching what to choose and what to avoid,[28] let us first discuss what those who write history must avoid and especially what faults must be eliminated, and then what the historian needs to use so that he does not fail to travel the correct road which is straight: what sort of beginning he should make; what arrangement is appropriate for the events, and what proportion for each; what should be passed over in silence, what should be treated in detail, and what it is better to treat briefly; and how to express it all and put it all together.[29] These and similar matters we shall come to, but now let us begin with all the faults that attend those who write history badly. Now it would be a lengthy task and not germane to the present essay if I were to go through all the errors – in diction, expression and arrangement of thought – that are common to all literary endeavour, and all such failures of technique (for these are, as I said,

7   common to all literature). Instead, I shall treat those errors that are made in the writing of history, and if you give your attention to them, you will find them to be just the ones that I have often thought of when I am listening to historians, especially if you open your ears to all of them.

To begin with, then, let us look at how great a mistake the following is. Most writers have no concern with investigating what happened,[30] but linger fondly on praises of rulers and generals, raising their own on high and casting down the enemy's beyond measure: they are unaware that history is separated and walled off from encomium not by a narrow isthmus but by a great wall that is set between them, or, to use musical terminology, that they are two full octaves apart.[31] The writer of an encomium has one concern only, to praise and gladden the recipient by any means necessary, and if he needs to lie to reach that goal, he will think little of it. But history cannot allow any falsehood to intrude,[32] not even a momentary one, any more than a windpipe, as physicians say, can take in a foreign object.

Such men seem not to know in addition that the principles and rules of poetry and poems are specific to them, while history has different ones.[33] In poetry freedom is unbounded and there is one law: the poet's imagination. For the poet is divinely inspired and possessed by the Muses,[34] and no one will begrudge him if he wishes to yoke a chariot to winged horses or if he portrays other horses running over the water or on the tops of asphodel. And when his Zeus draws up and holds aloft earth and sea together from one thread, they will not fear that it will be severed and everything will fall down and shatter.[35] No, and if they wish to praise Agamemnon, no one will prevent them from making his head and eyes be like those of Zeus, or his chest like Poseidon's, the brother of Zeus, or his waist like Ares'; indeed, the son of Atreus and Aeropë must be put together from all the gods since Zeus or Poseidon or Ares alone would not be suitable for fulfilling his beauty.[36] But if history admits any flattery, what does it become if not a poetic work in prose, devoid of the exalted language of poetry but displaying the rest of poetry's marvels without metre and more noticeable because of that? It is a great, indeed beyond great, fault if one does not know how to distinguish history's properties from poetry's, and instead introduces into history the embellishments of poetry: mythical material[37] and encomium and the excesses that come with these. It's as if one put purple garments and prostitutes' finery on one of those strong and sturdy athletes, and applied rouge and white lead to his face. By Heracles, how utterly ridiculous one would make him, shaming him with that adornment.[38]

I am not saying that one should not give praise in history 9 sometimes; but one must praise at the appropriate moment and in a measure appropriate to the deed,[39] so that it not be offensive to later readers of these matters; and one must measure these things entirely with a view towards the future, as we shall show a little later.[40]

Do you see how far from the truth those people are who think it right to divide history into two parts, the pleasurable and the useful, and because of this introduce encomium into history as something which gives pleasure and delights readers? To begin with, they make a false distinction: for there is one task and one purpose of history, the useful, and this comes from truth alone.[41] It is better if the pleasurable accompanies truth, like beauty on an athlete. But if not, nothing will prevent Nicostratus, the son of Isidotus, a noble man and braver than any of his opponents, from being a successor to Heracles, even if Nicostratus is hideous in appearance and the handsome Alcaeus of Miletus is his opponent (and the lover, so they say, of Nicostratus).[42] So too if pleasure is a by-product of history, then history would attract many lovers to herself, as long as she maintains unblemished the one thing that is particularly hers – I mean the revelation of truth – and takes little thought for beauty.

10   It is worth saying further that the mythical[43] is not at all pleasurable in history, and praise of either side is especially repugnant to the listeners – assuming you are thinking not of the crowd and rabble but of those who will listen like judges and even, by Zeus, like nit-pickers: they would not fail to notice anything you passed over, since they see more keenly than Argos[44] and from all over their body, and they examine carefully each individual phrase like a money-changer, such that they will immediately cast off anything counterfeit but accept what is genuine and legal and bears an accurate stamp. It is towards *these* that you should look when you write history, and think little of the rest, even if the latter are filled to bursting with praises.[45] If, on the other hand, you pay no attention to the former and you sweeten your history beyond measure with mythical material, panegyrics and all that other flattery, you will quickly make your history resemble Heracles in Lydia. You've probably seen the painting somewhere, in which Heracles is enslaved to Omphale, fitted out in very strange dress,

while Omphale wears his lion skin and holds his club in her hand, as if indeed she were Heracles. He, on the other hand, is carding wool and dressed in saffron and purple, and is being struck by Omphale with her sandal. The most shameful sight is that his clothing is falling away from his body, not clinging to it, and the manliness of the god is being feminized in an unseemly way.[46]

The majority will perhaps praise you even for this but the few, 11 those whom you despise, will laugh long and hard when they see how unsuitable, incongruous and loosely constructed your work is. Each thing has its peculiar beauty: if you change this, it becomes ugly, by being used wrongly. I need hardly say that praises are perhaps pleasurable only to one – the person being praised – and annoying to everyone else, especially if the praises contain monstrous exaggerations. These are the very sorts of praises that the majority of writers work away at, striving for the goodwill of those they praise, and lingering over it until they have made their flattery obvious to all.[47] They do not know how to do this with skill, nor do they shade their flattery, but they simply go at it, jumbling together improbabilities with plain facts. The result is that 12 they do not even achieve what they most want. For those who are praised by them hate them even more and turn away from them as flatterers; and in doing this they are acting rightly, especially if they have a manly spirit. <Aristobulus, for example, wrote in his history an account of the battle between>[48] Alexander and Porus,[49] and when he read this particular passage to Alexander – for he thought he would win favour from the king by inventing false episodes of his great prowess in battle and fashioning deeds greater than the truth – Alexander took the book, and, as they happened to be sailing on the Hydaspes river, threw it straight into the water and said, 'I should have treated you in the same way, Aristobulus, for fighting single-combats on my behalf and for slaying elephants with a single throw of the javelin.'[50] Alexander would have been angry like this, given that he had not been able to endure the effrontery of the builder who promised to make Mount Athos in Alexander's image and reshape the mountain into a likeness of the king; but Alexander immediately recognized the man as a flatterer and no longer employed him, not even for the tasks he had performed before.[51]

13   Where, then, is the pleasure in these matters unless one is so
foolish as to enjoy being praised for something that can immediately be refuted? It is the same as when ugly people, and women
especially, command painters to paint them so that they look as
beautiful as possible. Such people think that they will have a better appearance if the painter adorns them with more rouge and
mixes more white into his pigment. Many historians are like this,
attending to the concerns of the present day, their individual
goals, and the profit that they expect to get from history. It would
be well to despise them, since to the present generation they are
obvious and incompetent flatterers, and to future generations they
demonstrate that their entire history is suspect because of their
exaggerations. But if someone thinks that pleasure absolutely
must be mixed in with history, there are other things that are
pleasurable in those other kinds of embellishments that are congruent with truth;[52] yet the majority ignore them and pile up those
which are completely inappropriate.

14   So then I am going to tell you all the things I remember hearing
just now from some historians in Ionia and, by Zeus, from some
others in Achaea the day before yesterday who were narrating this
same war.[53] And by the Graces, let no one disbelieve what I shall
say. If it were tasteful to have an oath in a literary essay, I would
swear they are true.[54]

One historian began straightaway from the Muses, invoking
the goddesses to join with him in his history.[55] Do you see how
harmonious this beginning is, how it fits history so snugly, and is
appropriate for this type of literature? Then a little further on he
compared our commander to Achilles and the Persian king to
Thersites, not realizing that Achilles was a better name for our
commander if he were to destroy a Hector rather than a Thersites,
and if a noble man was fleeing 'and a much greater man was pursuing'.[56] Then he introduced some praise of himself, saying that he
was worthy to compose these deeds because they were so distinguished. And then, as he was coming to the preface's conclusion,
he praised also his city, Miletus, adding that he was here acting
better than Homer, who did not mention his native land at all.[57]
Then at the end of the preface he promised explicitly and
clearly that he would exalt our own affairs more greatly while

conquering the barbarians to the best of his ability.[58] He began the
history like this: 'The foulest and most accursed Vologaesus
began the war for the following reason.'[59]

Well, that was his work. Another one, a keen imitator of Thucyd-   15
ides, who moulded himself very well to his model, began as that
one did, with his own name, the most graceful of all beginnings
and smelling of Attic thyme.[60] Consider it: 'Crepereius Calpurni-
anus, a Pompeiopolitan, wrote up the war of the Parthians and the
Romans, how they fought against each other, beginning as soon as
the war broke out.'[61] After such a beginning why would I need to
tell you the rest: the kinds of things he represented the Corcyraean
speaker in person in Armenia as saying to the people, or the sort
of plague, taken from Thucydides, which he introduced among
those people of Nisibis who had not taken the Roman side, using
the whole thing in its entirety except the Pelasgian oracle and the
long walls where those who were suffering from the plague lived?
And the rest of it, how the plague began in Ethiopia and spread
down into Egypt and much of the king's territory – and there it
remained and good that it did! For my part I left him while he was
still burying the wretched Athenians in Nisibis and when I
departed I knew accurately in fact everything that he was going to
say after I left.[62] For now this is pretty well the thing, thinking that
you are speaking like Thucydides if you use Thucydides' words
with slight changes <. . .>[63] By Zeus, I nearly forgot this other
thing: this same historian described many of the weapons and the
contrivances for war using the Latin terms for them, for example,
the Latin word for a trench, and bridge and such things. Consider,
if you please, the great value this history has and how appropriate
it is to Thucydides to place these Italian words in amongst the
Attic ones, as if adorning it with the purple, making it so suitable
and entirely harmonious with it.[64]

Another person put together a memorandum of events in a lan-   16
guage quite prosaic and flat, such as a soldier or craftsman or
merchant who accompanied the army might compose, recording
events day by day.[65] At least this amateur was more measured,
and he revealed immediately what sort of writer he was, one who
had done the preliminary work for someone else who is accomplished and would be able to write history. With one thing alone

I found fault, namely that he entitled his books in a more dramatic fashion than they could bear – 'Of Callimorphus, Surgeon to the Sixth Company of Pike-Bearers, The Parthian History, Book Such-and-such' – and beneath this he inscribed each book number. And by God he also made his preface terribly frigid by arguing that it was appropriate for a physician to write history since Asclepius was the son of Apollo, and Apollo was leader of the Muses and ruler over all learning.[66] Also, although he began his work in the Ionian dialect, for some reason or other he straightaway changed into everyday language and thus used the Ionic forms of 'physician', 'attempt', 'how much' and 'plague', but the rest was the common language of the crowd – and the majority of *that* was vulgar.[67]

17   Now if I must mention a philosopher, let me leave his name unspoken,[68] but let me tell you his thoughts and his recent compositions in Corinth, which surpass all expectation. Right at the outset, in the first sentence of his preface, he posed to his readers a series of questions, keen to prove a thoroughly clever argument, namely that it was fitting for the philosopher alone to write history. Then, just a little after, there was another syllogism, then another. His proem entirely consisted of argument-by-question in every form.[69] There was flattery to excess, and the encomia were vulgar and rather lewd, but not without syllogisms, though even those were full of questions and conclusions. Another thing that seemed vulgar to me and least suited to a philosopher and a long grey beard was his remark in the preface that our leader will consider it a remarkable thing that philosophers now deem it worthy to write up his deeds. Even if such a thing were true, it would have been better to leave this to be deduced, rather than say it oneself.[70]

18   Indeed it would not be right to forget the one who began his preface thus: 'I am going to speak about Romans and Persians', and a little later wrote, 'For it was necessary that the Persians should come to a bad end', and again, 'Osroës, whom the Greeks call Oxuroës', and lots more like that.[71] Do you see? This writer was like that earlier one, but this one resembled Herodotus just as that other resembled Thucydides.

19   There is another writer, famous for his literary ability, who also is similar to Thucydides or even a little better since he has described all the cities, all the mountains and plains and rivers in

the clearest and most powerful manner – so he thinks. May the
divinity who wards off evil turn his composition against our
enemy: the frigidity of his writings was greater than Caspian snow
and Celtic ice! Just to describe the emperor's shield needed nearly
an entire book: the Gorgon on the boss, with her eyes of dark
blue, white and black, and her girdle rainbow-like and the serpents whirling around in spirals and curls. And, by Heracles, how
many words were needed for Vologaesus' trousers and the bridle
of his horse, and for what Osroës' hair looked like when he swam
across the Tigris, and what sort of a cave he fled into, with ivy,
myrtle and laurel all entwined together in it and making it completely shaded. See how necessary such things are for history:
without these we would not have known any of the events in that
part of the world![72]

Writers turn to such descriptions of places and caves either   20
from weakness in dealing with essential matters or from ignorance of what should be said;[73] and whenever they happen upon
numerous and great events, they are like a newly rich slave who has
just inherited his master's property and who knows neither how to
dress nor how to eat normally, often gorging himself greedily
(sometimes to bursting) on some soup or smoked fish, although
birds, swine and hares have been set before him. The writer whom
I just mentioned also described wounds that were really unbelievable and odd deaths, for example, how someone wounded in his
big toe immediately died, or how twenty-seven of the enemy fell
dead when the general Priscus merely shouted.[74] Furthermore, this
writer falsified the number of the dead even beyond what had been
written in the dispatches of the commanders: he recorded that at
Europus 70,326 of the enemy perished, while of the Romans only
two were killed and nine wounded. I don't know how any sane
person could put up with that.[75]

Here is another thing that, though small, should be noted.   21
Because he was an Atticist and had purified his language most
exactly,[76] he thought it right to change even the names of the
Romans and to 'translate' them into Greek: so Saturninus he called
Kronios and Fronto[77] Phrontis and Titanus Titianos; and there
were others much more ridiculous.[78] This same man wrote further
about the death of Severianus,[79] saying that all the rest had been

deceived in thinking that he had died by a spear point, when instead he had starved himself to death, thinking that this was the least painful way to die. But the writer doesn't know that Severianus suffered his fate within, I think, three days while the majority of those who starve themselves hold out until the seventh day – unless one should assume that Osroës stood around and waited until Severianus died of starvation, and that this was the reason he made no attack for a week.

22   And where, my dear Philo, would one put those who use poetic words in history?[80] Those who say, for example, 'the crane was shaken, the wall in falling greatly thudded' and again in another part of this fair history, 'Edessa thus was rattled round with weapons and all was din and clashing', and 'the general pondered in his mind how best he should assault the wall'.[81] And this writer stuffed in alongside this many low, common and beggarly words: for example, 'the stratopedarch sent a dispatch to the master' and 'the soldiers were purchasing the needful', 'now washed, they were doing their business', and others like that.[82] And so the work resembled a tragic actor who has one foot in his high boot and the other in a sandal.[83]

23   Indeed you will see others composing prefaces that are distinguished and dramatic and excessively long, so that you fully expect to hear the same sort of marvellous stuff thereafter; but they attach to this the main body itself of the history which is so small and ignoble that it resembles a child, as if somehow you saw Eros playing whilst wearing an enormous mask of Heracles or a titan.[84] The audience will immediately utter in response to this, 'the mountain is in labour'.[85] It should not be this way, I think, but everything should be similar and of like colour, and the rest of the body should be appropriate to the head, lest the helmet be gold and the breastplate quite ridiculously cobbled together from rags and rotten hides, and his shield be of wicker and with pigskin for his greaves. You might see a plentiful number of such histories as these, who place the head of the Colossus of Rhodes[86] on the body of a dwarf.

Others again in turn will introduce bodies without heads, works that have no preface and move straight to the events: these claim as their fellow practitioner Xenophon – who begins in this

way: 'Darius and Parysatis have two children' – and other writers
of long ago, because they do not know that there are virtual prefaces, which the majority fail to recognize as such; we shall
demonstrate this point later.[87]

Yet all these errors, of either expression or any other aspect of 24
arrangement, are bearable. But what good can there be when writers tell falsehoods about the places themselves, not merely by
furlongs but by whole miles?[88] One writer so lazily put together
his history – he had never met a Syrian, nor even, as the saying
goes, heard those who tell such tall tales in the barbershop – that
he said: 'Europus is situated in Mesopotamia, two days' journey
distant from the Euphrates, and it was settled by Edessaean colonists'.[89] As if this wasn't enough for him, this distinguished
gentleman in the same book lifted up my home town, Samosata,
with its very acropolis and walls, and put it down in Mesopotamia, so that it was surrounded by two rivers, which flowed closely
on either side and all but touched the walls. It would be absurd,
dear Philo, if I now should have to defend myself to you as not
being a Parthian or Mesopotamian, which is where this admirable
writer brought and settled me.[90]

By Zeus, this same writer has said something else quite persua- 25
sive about Severianus: he swore that he had heard from one of those
who escaped that Severianus had not wished to die by the spear nor
by drinking poison nor by the noose, but rather he contrived a dramatic death, strange in its daring.[91] Severianus happened to have
some enormous cups made of the finest glass and when he had
absolutely decided to die, he shattered the largest of the cups and
used one of the shards to cut his throat – as if he could not come up
with even a little sword or spear so that he might have a manly and
heroic death.

And then, since Thucydides had a funeral oration spoken over 26
the first dead of his war,[92] he also considered it necessary for Severianus to speak one as well – all this in his rivalry with Thucydides
who was in no way responsible for the suffering in Armenia! Having buried Severianus in magnificent style, he then has a certain
Afranius Stilo,[93] a centurion, stand upon the tomb, and rivalling
Pericles, has him declaim about so many things and at such great
length that, by the Graces, I was nearly weeping from laughter,

especially when the rhetor Afranius, in tears at the end of his speech and with pathetic wailing, remembered the lavish dinners and toasts, after which he capped it off with a finish worthy of Ajax:[94] drawing his sword (and nobly, as you would expect from a frantic man)[95] he slew himself upon the tomb, with everyone looking on – though, by Ares, he had deserved to die long before this for having declaimed such things. This writer continues, saying that all those present who saw these events marvelled and praised Afranius to the skies. I, however, condemned him both in general and for practically recalling soups and shellfish and for weeping at the remembrance of cakes; but I blamed him most for not slaying the writer and producer of this drama before he killed himself.[96]

27   Many others like these I could enumerate for you, my friend, but having named a few I shall proceed now to my second promise: advice on how one might write history better.

There are some who leave aside or rush over great events, those worthy of memory,[97] and from lack of education[98] or want of taste or ignorance of what to say and what to ignore, describe the most insignificant things richly and with great effort, dwelling on them: it is just as if someone did not see the entire beauty of the Zeus at Olympia, although it is so great and so fine, or didn't praise it or describe it to those unfamiliar with it, but instead saved his amazement for the breadth and the polish of the footstool and the fine proportions of the foundation, and described all those things with much care.[99]

28   I have heard someone run through the battle of Europus[100] in not even seven lines but spend twenty or more measures of the water clock[101] on a narrative that was frigid and of no relevance to this: how a certain Moorish horseman, Mausacas by name,[102] wandered from thirst through the mountains and came upon some Syrian peasants who were setting out their morning meal and who at first were afraid of him but thereafter, learning that he was a friend, received him and feasted him, since one of them had actually travelled to Mauretania[103] when his brother was serving in the army there. After this there were long, drawn-out tall tales and narratives of how he himself had hunted in Mauretania and seen many elephants feeding together in the same place, and how he was almost gobbled down by a lion and how big the fish that he bought in

Caesarea[104] were. This admirable historian decided to omit the enormous slaughter that occurred in Europus, the cavalry charges, the imposed truces, the watches and the counter-watches, and instead to stand looking until well into the evening at Malchion the Syrian in Caesarea, purchasing enormous fish at a bargain price.[105] If night had not overtaken him, he would have perhaps dined with him, the fish having already been cooked. Now if all these things had not been carefully written down in a history, we would have been in great ignorance, and it would have been an unbearable loss to the Romans if Mausacas the Moor had not found something to drink when he was thirsty but had had to return to the camp without having had supper.[106]

And yet how many other matters, even more essential than these, do I willingly now pass over: how a flute-girl from a nearby village came to them and how they exchanged gifts with one another, the Moor giving Malchion a lance while Malchion gave Mausacas a brooch, and many other similar 'main events' of the battle of Europus. Well then, one might reasonably say that such men do not look at the rose itself but examine in minute detail the thorns around the roots.

There was another writer, dear Philo, one who was especially 29 ridiculous, who had never even set foot out of Corinth or wandered as far as Cenchrea,[107] far less seen Syria or Armenia, and who began thus (for I remember it): 'Ears are more untrustworthy than eyes: I write, therefore, what I saw, not what I heard.'[108] And so accurately had he seen everything that he said that the serpents in Parthia – they are actually the creatures on their standards,[109] and each 'serpent' is at the head of, I believe, a thousand men – are enormous living serpents that are born in Persia a little above Iberia,[110] and they are wound around large poles and raised on high, and when the Persians advance, these serpents cause fear, and when the Persians come to actual combat, they release the serpents and these lay hold of the enemy. No doubt many of our men were swallowed down in this way while others were suffocated and mangled when the serpents coiled round them. And he says that he himself was nearby and saw this, although he made his observation in safety from a tall tree. He did well not to meet up with these wild beasts, since we would not now have this amazing

historian who offhandedly accomplished great and brilliant deeds
in this war. Indeed, he ran many risks and was wounded around
Sura, evidently when he was walking down from the Craneion to
Lerna.[111] He read all this out to the Corinthians who listened and
knew precisely that he had never seen even a wall painting of a
battle. He didn't even know what weapons or siege engines were,
nor the proper terms for companies or muster-rolls. But he cared
very much about calling a column formation a 'line' and saying
'column' when he meant 'front line'.[112]

30   One really distinguished writer squeezed together into less than
500 lines all the events from beginning to end, I mean everything
done in Armenia, Syria and Mesopotamia, all the events at the
Tigris and in Media; and in doing this claimed that he had composed a history.[113] The title that he gave his book was nearly as
long as the book itself: *A Description by Antochianus, victor at
the Sacred Games of Apollo* – I think perhaps he won the boys'
long-race – *of the Recent Actions of the Romans in Armenia,
Mesopotamia and Media.*

31   I also listened recently to someone composing a history of the
future: the capture of Vologaesus and the death of Osröes – how
he will be thrown to the lions, and, to top it off, our much longed-
for triumph![114] Possessed like a seer, he is in this way already
hastening to the end of his work. He has already established a city
in Mesopotamia, 'greatest in greatness and most beautiful in
beauty',[115] but he is still considering and turning over in his
mind whether it should be called Victoria (from our victory) or
Concord or Peaceful. That beautiful city, then, is still in name
undecided and anonymous to us, though it teems with much nonsense and writerly drivel. But he has promised that he will now
write an account of future events in India and the circumnavigation of the outer sea, and these are not just promises: the preface
of the *Indian Matters* has already been composed, and the third
legion, the Celts and a small portion of Moors with Cassius have
all crossed over the Indus river.[116] What they will achieve and how
they will withstand the attack of elephants our admirable writer
will shortly report to us from Mouziris or Oxydracae.[117]

32   These writers, because of their lack of education,[118] write a lot
of nonsense like this, neither seeing what is worthy to see nor, if

they did see it, expressing it as it deserves; they invent and fashion 'whatever comes to an inopportune tongue', as the saying goes,[119] and they further take pride in the number of their books and especially in the titles. Even these are ludicrous: 'So-and-so's Parthian Victories in so-many books', and again, 'First *Parthis*', 'Second *Parthis*' – just like an *Atthis*, of course.[120] Another, much more refined (I read it): 'Parthian History of Demetrius of Sagalassus'[121] <. . .> not so as to laugh at and make fun of these historians who are so fine, but for the sake of doing something useful, since whoever avoids these and similar faults has already anticipated a significant part of correct composition; but even so, a few things are still needed for that proposition that people say is true: namely, that when there are two opposites, the destruction of the one makes way inevitably for the other.

Well now, someone might say, the ground has been very carefully cleared by you, and the thorns and brambles have been uprooted and the debris from the rest has been carried away; whatever was rough is now smooth, and so now you yourself must build something in order to demonstrate that you are not only generous at subverting the works of others but can contrive something clever and something which no one, not even Momus, could fault.[122]   33

Well then, I assert that the best writer of history is one who comes to the task bringing at the outset two chief attributes: understanding of how public life works and powers of expression.[123] The former cannot be taught and is a gift of nature, while the latter is acquired by much practice, continuous effort and emulation of the writers of old.[124] The former cannot be reduced to rules and thus requires no advice from me, for this book of ours does not claim to make men of perception and understanding out of those who are not so endowed by nature. It would be worth a lot – indeed it would be worth everything – if it were possible to reshape and refigure things to such an extent that one could reveal gold from lead, or silver from tin, or fashion a Titormus from a Conon or a Milo from a Leostrophidos.[125]   34

But where are rules and advice useful? Not in the creation of qualities but in the appropriate employment of them. For example, Iccus, Herodicus, Theon[126] and any other trainer would not promise to take a Perdiccas (if it was really he who was enamoured of   35

his stepmother and wasted away because of this, and not Antiochus, the son of Seleucus, who was enamoured of the famous
Stratonice)[127] and turn him into an Olympian victor who was a
match for Theagenes of Thasos or Polydamas of Skotoussai;[128] but
if he were given a nature that was well disposed towards undergoing training, he could make him much better by the application of
systematic study. Let no grudge be borne against us, then, if we
promise that we have devised a set of rules for a task so great and
difficult; for we do not say that we can take anyone and make him
into a historian. We claim, rather, that we can point out to someone who has natural intelligence and has been very well trained in
literary composition, some straight paths (if indeed they shall be
seen as such) by which one might reach one's goal more swiftly and
more easily.

36   Indeed, you would not say that even an intelligent person does
not also need rules and instruction in matters of which he is ignorant: were that the case, one could play the lyre or flute without
instruction and one would know everything; in reality, one can't
do any of those things without instruction; but if someone shows
the way, he would learn easily and pursue them well on his own.[129]

37   So then let such a student be given to us now, one who has understanding and is not incapable of expression but is sharp sighted,
able to administer affairs if they were entrusted to him, and who
had an understanding of the military, and also matters of state, and
who had experience as a general and, by Zeus, had even once been
in a camp and seen soldiers training and arraying themselves for
battle, and knew something about weapons and contrivances and
what 'in a column' and 'in a line' mean, the how, when and why of
a troop or cavalry marching or manoeuvring, and in general not a
stay-at-home who can only rely on his informants.[130]

38   Especially and before everything else let him be free in giving
his view and neither fear anyone nor expect anything, since in that
case he will be like worthless judges who for a price render a decision based on favour or enmity.[131] He is not to care for Philip
who had his eye put out by Aster of Amphipolis, the archer at
Olynthus – he will be shown such as he was – nor Alexander who
will be distressed if his brutal murder of Cleitus at the banquet
should be narrated clearly; nor will Cleon, who had such great

power in the assembly and dominated the speaker's platform, frighten him from saying that he is a destructive and crazy person; nor for that matter would even the entire city of Athens intimidate him into failing to record the disaster in Sicily, the capture of Demosthenes, the death of Nicias and how the soldiers in their thirst were drinking the water and the majority of them were slaughtered as they drank.[132] For he will consider – and this is most just – that no right-thinking person will believe him to be responsible if he narrates unfortunate and ill-conceived events as they occurred, since he did not create the events but only reported them.[133] And so even if they are then being defeated in a sea battle, he is not the one sinking the ships, nor if they are in flight is he the pursuer – unless he omitted to utter a prayer when he should have. For of course if he could have made it a success, either by not mentioning it or by describing it in the opposite way, then Thucydides could have easily, with a single pen-stroke, torn down the cross-wall at Epipolae, sunk Hermocrates' trireme, transfixed the accursed Gylippus while he was blockading the road with walls and ditches, and finally thrown the Syracusans into the quarries and have the Athenians sail around Sicily and Italy, as Alcibiades had first hoped.[134] But what has already been done not even Clotho, I think, can unspin nor Atropos turn back.[135]

The historian's sole task is *this*: to recount how it was done.[136] 39 And he could not do this if as physician to Artaxerxes he either feared him or expected that he would receive a purple garment or golden bracelet or Nisaean horse as a reward for the praises in his history.[137] But Xenophon, a just historian, will not do that, nor will Thucydides. But even if the historian bears private grievances against certain people, he will consider the common good more necessary, and he will consider truth of greater importance than private enmity; and if he has friendly feelings towards someone, nevertheless he will not hold back when that person makes mistakes.[138] For this is the one thing, as I said, that is particular to history, and one must sacrifice to truth alone if one is going to embark on writing a history. Nothing else is to be of concern to the historian: in short, there is one rule and one accurate measure: to keep one's eye not on one's present audience but on those who will read one's history in the future.[139]

40   If someone paid court to the present, he would reasonably be considered to be a flatterer, those whom history long ago and right from the start rejected, just as athletic training rejected cosmetics.[140] Alexander, for example, is remembered as having said, 'I should like to come back to life for a little while, Onesicritus,[141] after my death, so that I might learn how men of that time are reading these accounts. If they now praise and welcome them, don't be surprised; for each thinks that he will draw forth our favour with this large bait.'[142] Homer is another example: even though the majority of what he wrote about Achilles tended towards the mythical, some people today give it credence, offering one thing only as a strong piece of evidence of its truth: that Homer wrote about Achilles after his death; this being the case, they can discover no reason why he would have lied.[143]

41   So then my historian is to be this kind of man: fearless, above bribery, free, a friend of frank speech and truth, one who calls figs figs and a trough a trough,[144] as the comic poet says, indulging neither in hatred or friendship nor holding back because he feels pity, shame or embarrassment; he will be an impartial judge, well minded towards all,[145] to the point of not apportioning to one side or the other anything more than their due, a stranger among his books, a man without a country, self-governing, not ruled by a king, nor taking into account what someone or other will think, but rather stating what has been done.[146]

42   It was Thucydides who laid down the laws very well and distinguished between what was good and bad in historiography; he saw that Herodotus was especially admired, to the point that his individual books were named after the Muses.[147] He says both that he is composing a possession for all time rather than a competition piece for the present, and that he does not welcome the mythic but instead is leaving behind the truth of what happened. He introduces the notion of usefulness and what any right-thinking person would assume was the goal of history, namely, that if ever again similar circumstances should occur, readers would be able, he says, by looking at what happened before to deal well with the things at hand.[148]

43   My historian is to come, then, with such an intellectual stance. As for his language and his powers of expression, let him begin his

work not by honing that vehement and jagged style, with unremitting periods intricate with dialectical reasoning, and the rest of that rhetorical-type forcefulness, but with a more peaceful disposition.[149] His thought is to be coherent and compact, his language clear and ordinary, of a kind that will reveal most conspicuously the subject matter.[150]

Just as we set frank speech and truth as the aims in the historian's intellectual approach, so in his language he has one main goal, to expound the matter accurately and to explain it in the clearest way possible, not with uncommon and out-of-the-way words nor with the language of the marketplace and merchants, but such as the majority will understand and the educated praise. Indeed let it be adorned with figures that are not irksome or affected, since otherwise he is displaying words that resemble finely prepared sauces.[151] **44**

His thought should have a share in, and employ, some poetic elements, in as much as that too is lofty and elevated, especially whenever he is involved with the marshalling of troops and with land and sea battles. For at that time he will need a poetic wind wafting over the boats and bearing the ship along high upon the crests of the waves. Let his language nonetheless walk upon the ground, raised up by the beauty and greatness of what is being described, adapting itself in this one thing alone and not using unusual expressions or inspired beyond what the occasion warrants.[152] For otherwise there is the danger that the style will be violently excited, and possessed by the Corybant of the poetic art; so he must at that time especially trust to the bridle and show restraint, knowing that excessive pride even in one's literary creation becomes a sickness, and not a slight one at that.[153] It is preferable, therefore, that one's thought goes on horseback but one's expression follows alongside on foot, holding on to the saddle so as not to get left behind in the onrush. **45**

He is to employ an arrangement of words that is well mixed and moderate, neither separating the words too much or detaching them (for that results in harshness) nor connecting them practically in rhythm: for the latter is blameworthy, while the former gives the audience no pleasure.[154] **46**

The events themselves must be gathered together not at random **47** but with the historian making repeated inquiries about the same matters, with industriousness and painstakingly;[155] best of all he should be present and be an eyewitness of events, but if not, he should give his attention to those who tell of the events more impartially, and those whom one would reckon least likely either from favouritism or from enmity to add to or detract from events. And at that point let him be skilful at perceiving and putting together the more probable account.[156]

48   When he has gathered all his material or at least the majority of it, he should weave together a preliminary sketch of events and form a body of material which is still without beauty and disjointed. Then he should impose an arrangement on it and add colour to it by means of diction, and add figures and rhythm.[157]

49   In general he is to be like Homer's Zeus, looking now at the land of the horse-herding Thracians, now at that of the Mysians:[158] for in just this same way the historian himself must look now separately at the actions of the Romans and, gazing from on high, reveal what their plans were; then at the actions of the Persians, and then at both together if they join battle. In the line of battle itself, he is to look not at one part only or one cavalryman or foot soldier – unless some Brasidas were to spring forward or a Demosthenes were to drive back the attack.[159] He is to look to the generals first and any order they give should be heard also by the audience,[160] as well as how they arrayed their troops and for what reason and with what intention. When they join together in battle, his view is to be of both sides, and, as if with a pair of scales, he is to weigh the events in the balance,[161] and he is to pursue with the pursuers and flee with those fleeing.

50   In all these things he is to impose a sense of proportion without excess, vulgarity or youthful folly; and he should leave the scene effortlessly. When he has established one set of events, he is now to move over to others if such events are urging him on; then when he is freed from those events, he is to return whenever they summon him. Let him exert himself for all of them, to the extent possible; he is to deal with simultaneous events together and to fly from place to place, from Armenia to Media, and from there with one rush to Iberia, and then into Italy, so that he does not leave behind any crucial moment.[162]

Above all he is to bring to the task a mind like a mirror: undis- 51
turbed, gleaming and accurate in its focus, and whatever the
forms of the deeds he receives are the forms in which he should
show them, not distorting, colouring or reshaping them in any
way.[163] For historians do not write like orators: what the historian
is going to narrate already exists and is what will be said; for it has
already happened. But they do have to arrange and express it. And
so historians do not need to seek *what* they are to say but *how*
they are to say it.[164] In short, let us consider that the writer of history must resemble Phidias, Praxiteles, Alcamenes or another of
that sort: these men did not make the gold, silver, ivory or other
material, but the material was already in existence and ready to
hand, since the Eleians, Athenians or Argives had procured it; the
artists only shaped and sawed the ivory, polished, glued, propor-
tioned and gilded it: their skill was in treating their material to the
extent necessary.[165] Such is also the task of the historian, to arrange
the actions in good order and to show them as clearly as his ability
allows. And whenever someone in the audience thinks that he is
seeing what is being said,[166] and thus offers praise, then and only
then will the work of our Phidias of history have been accurately
wrought, and received its due praise.

When everything has now been prepared, the historian will 52
sometimes begin his history without a preface whenever the matter does not demand a preliminary treatment. Even then, though,
he will use a virtual preface, which will make clear what will be
narrated.[167]

Whenever he does use a preface, he will begin with two points 53
only, not three like orators: he will make his audience attentive
and ready to learn, but he will omit a request for their goodwill.[168]
They will be attentive to him if he shows that he is going to speak
of matters that are great, necessary, appropriate or useful.[169] He
will make what follows clear and easy to comprehend, laying out
beforehand the causes and outlining the main events.

The best historians have used prefaces such as these: Herod- 54
otus, on the one hand, writes so that the events should not become
faded in time since they were great and marvellous, and they
revealed Greek victories and barbarian defeats; on the other hand,
Thucydides says that he himself expected that that war would be

most worthy of account and greater than those that had gone before, for it happened that the sufferings in it were great.[170]

55   After the preface, which should be proportionately lengthened or shortened according to the events, the transition to the narrative is to be unforced and easy to follow, since the remaining body of the history is simply a long narrative; so let it be adorned with the virtues of narrative, moving forward smoothly, evenly and consistently, so as to be neither excessive nor deficient.[171] And let it bloom with a clarity that will be achieved by the diction, as I said,[172] and by the interconnectedness of the events. He will separate out the parts and finish each of them individually, and having elaborated the first unit he will bring in the second and join it, like a chain, fitting it together in such a way that it neither is broken up nor has many narratives laid alongside each other; rather, the first will always be neighbour to the second and will also have something in common with it and be blended in at the end-points.[173]

56   Speed is useful everywhere and especially if there is no shortage of events to be told. This must be brought about not so much from the words or phrases as from the events. What I mean is, if you set aside minor and less important events, you could more effectively narrate great ones.[174] Many things can be left out. If you invite your friends to dinner and everything has been prepared, you will not, in the midst of the pastries, birds, shellfish, wild boars, hares and tunny fish, also serve the perch and the legume soup just because these too have been prepared; you will instead take no thought for the cheaper foods.

57   Be especially restrained in the descriptions of mountains, walls and rivers, lest you appear to make a vulgar display of your literary talent, and neglect history while showing off what you can do.[175] Instead, treat these things briefly if they are useful or for clarity's sake, and then move on, avoiding the snares in the material and all such self-indulgence, just as you see Homer behave so high-mindedly: although a poet, he runs quickly past Tantalos, Ixion, Tityos, and the rest. If Parthenius or Euphorion or Callimachus were to speak of these men, how many words do you think they would need just to get the water to Tantalus' lips or to turn Ixion on his wheel?[176] Look rather at how Thucydides himself uses a few words for this type of description and then immediately

moves on, once he has described a contrivance or revealed the arrangement of a siege, one that is necessary and useful, such as the layout of Epipolae or the Syracusan harbour. When he describes the plague it may seem lengthy, but just look at what he actually does, and you will recognize his speed, and although he seems to be in flight from them, he nevertheless lays hold of the events, numerous as they were.[177]

If you ever need to introduce someone to give a speech, make 58 sure that more than anything he speaks words appropriate to the character and the matter at hand, and then that his speech is as clear as can be. Only then is it permitted to play the orator and display the virtuosity of your writing.[178]

Praises or criticisms should be sparing, circumspect and unex- 59 ceptionable, provided with proofs,[179] brief and not inappropriate, since historical figures are not on trial; otherwise, you will incur the same charge as the one levelled against Theopompus who was fond of accusing most of his characters in a quarrelsome spirit and busying himself with it to such an extent that he prosecuted events rather than narrated them.[180]

Furthermore, if some mythical material should fall your way, it 60 must be recounted, but certainly not wholly trusted; suspend judgement so that your readers can make conjectures about it however they wish. You should run no risk nor incline to either side.[181]

In general remember this one thing (for I shall say it often): you 61 should write not looking to the present only or so that contempor- aries will praise and honour you; instead, aim at all of time, and compose your history with a view to men of the future, and demand from *them* the reward for your writing, so that it will be said of you, 'he for his part was a free man and abundantly frank, with no flattery or servility; but truth was in everything he wrote'. If someone is wise, he would place this above all present-day expectations which are so short-lived.[182]

Do you see the sort of thing the Cnidian architect did?[183] He 62 built the lighthouse at Pharos, the greatest and most beautiful work of all, so that the beacon-signals from it could go out a great distance to sailors on the sea there, and keep them from being borne down into Paraetonia, a very harsh place, they say, and impossible to escape from, should one fall into the reefs.[184] Having built it, he inscribed his own name inside on the stones, and then put a facing of gypsum over this, and when he had covered it all over, he inscribed on the gypsum the name of the king at that time. He knew – and this is in fact what happened – that with the passing of just a little time, that inscription would fall off together with the gypsum, and what would be revealed was, 'Sostratus, son of Dexiphanes, of Cnidus dedicated this to the saviour gods on behalf of sailors.'[185] So in this way he too was looking not at that particular moment nor his own short lifetime but to our time today and to all future time, as long as that tower shall stand and his own skill abide.

63   That's the way history should be written, with truth and with an expectation about the future, rather than with flattery and with a view towards making it pleasurable to one's contemporaries who are being praised. Let this be your standard and ruler for an impartial history.[186] If some people measure themselves by it, that would be good and our treatise will have been written to good purpose. If not, then at least I've rolled my barrel on the Craneion hill.[187]

35

GRANIUS LICINIANUS

The remains of the history of Granius Licinianus are preserved on a palimpsest (now largely illegible) of the eleventh century, first discovered in 1847 and published in 1853. Although possibly mentioned by a few other Latin writers (though scholars disagree about this), nothing is known of him. His work seems to have been annalistically arranged and he probably wrote sometime in the second century CE after Hadrian's reign (117–38). What survives of his work concerns events from the 160s to the 70s BCE, but where it began and where it ended is not known.[1]

Marvels in History

(28.22–3)

I am of the opinion that many marvels should be omitted in these histories, and its pages should not be filled with investigations of this sort,[2] since it was of sufficient use and . . . about the brothers[3] there was the need to have sense in knowing just how much we could entrust to memory and how much we could hold back.

23

Sallust More of an Orator than a Historian

(36.30–32)

Here we encounter the work of Sallust,[4] but as we have resolved, we shall omit anything that delays us or is not pressing. For they say that Sallust should be read not as a historian but as an orator: he reproves his own times, he criticizes faults, he inserts speeches, he gives here and there locations, mountains, rivers and other things of this sort,[5] and in discussions he assigns blame and makes comparisons.[6]

31
32

36

SEXTUS EMPIRICUS

The dates of Sextus Empiricus' birth and death are unknown, although most scholars today believe that his works were written towards the end of the second century CE. Sextus counted himself a Sceptic, a school which based itself on the teaching of Pyrrho of Elis (c. 360–270 BCE), who purportedly argued that nothing could be known for certain (our senses and our judgements are neither true nor false), and that one must therefore suspend judgement. The suspension of judgement leads to tranquillity.[1]

Against the Grammarians is the first book in Sextus' *Against the Professors*, a wide-ranging polemic against the liberal arts (others are *Against the Rhetoricians, Geometers, Mathematicians, Astrologers*, etc.). The work is in some ways an answer to the Stoics who claimed that they alone could provide an understanding of how to speak properly and interpret texts correctly. Sextus launches a wholesale assault on this approach, and holds that no special knowledge is needed to understand one's own language. The present passage is valuable for what it reveals of philosophical attacks on historiography (it thus complements some of the younger Seneca's remarks) and also for its delineation of the traditional division of narratives.[2]

True, As if True, and False History

(*Against the Grammarians*, 1.252–69)³

252 Asclepiades⁴ in his *On Grammar* says that the first parts of grammar were three: the technical, the historical and the grammatical (the last of which comprehends both of the others, i.e., the technical and the historical), and the historical is further divided into three parts: he says that one is true, one is false and one is as if true. True history is concerned with actual events, false history is concerned with fictions and myths, and as if true history is such as

253 comedy and mime.⁵ And of true history in turn there are three parts: one concerns the persons of gods, heroes and men; one concerns places and times; and one concerns actions. Of false, that is, mythic, history, he says that there is one form only, the genealogical. And he says, as does Dionysius,⁶ that 'glosses' are generally assigned to the historical. For that branch discovers by inquiry that *krēguon* means 'true' or 'good'.⁷ And so too with the part concerning proverbs and definitions. So it is clear from this that they want the historical to be part of grammar.⁸

254 But it follows that since the majority of them are agreed that it is non-technical and consists of material that is without method, they have freed us from the need to respond to them any further. Let us, nevertheless, ask this question so that we do not pass over this topic without mention. Either Grammar is an expert skill or it is not. If it is not, the matter at hand has been resolved. But if it *is* an expert skill, then the historical would not be a part of grammar since the parts of such a skill must be technical, and the historical, it has been agreed, is without method.

255 That this is really the case is practically self-evident. For whereas the physician speaks from some universal method and expert ability, when he notes that this particular thing is healthy and this thing diseased, or the musician says that this part is in harmony but that part is not, and that this is harmonic in accordance with this chord but not in accordance with that one, the grammarian, by contrast, is in no way able to make a pronouncement from some scientific and universal theory that (for example)

Pelops' shoulder was ivory, because it had been eaten by Ares or
Demeter, or that Heracles' head went bald, because his hair fell
out when he was swallowed by the sea-monster attacking Hes-
ione;[9] in order to make an exposition of these, one would have had   256
to read the individual accounts about these matters. But simply to
repeat the particular events by reading these very accounts is not
an expert craft. So then the historical part is not systematized by
the grammarians on the basis of some expertise.

And indeed since one part of history is about places, another   257
about times, another about persons and another about actions, it
is clear that if the description of places and times is not a technical
skill, then neither will that concerning persons and deeds be so.
For how would it differ to master the latter rather than the former? In fact, there is nothing expert in offering a history of a place
by saying, for example, that Brilesus and Aracynthus are mountains in Attica, or that Acamas is a promontory in Cyprus; or in a
chronological history to say that Xenophanes of Colophon was
born in the fortieth Olympiad.[10] For one who is not a grammarian
but is nevertheless exceedingly curious will be able to do this. Nor,   258
let me tell you, will an account of persons and deeds be a technical
skill, such as that Plato the philosopher was previously called Aris-
tocles, and that when he was young he had his ear pierced and wore
an earring; or that Pythias, the daughter of Aristotle, was married
three times, first to Nicanor of Stageira (a relative of Aristotle), then
to Procles (a descendant of the Lacedaemonian king Demaratus),
by whom she had two children (Procles and Demaratus, students
of Theophrastus), and finally to the physician Metrodorus, a pupil
of Chrysippus of Cnidus, and a teacher of Erasistratus who had a
son Aristotle. These things and things like them, in addition to   259
being completely useless, reveal no expert ability, and so the
expounding of historical inquiry is also not a technical skill.

In addition, as we showed above,[11] there is no expert knowledge
of things that are infinite or that happen in constantly different
ways. Individual histories are infinite because of their multitude,   260
and unstable because the same things are not recorded about the
same matters by everyone. To take an example (since it is not out of
place for us to use familiar examples), historians, basing themselves
on a false premise, say that the founder of our science, Asclepius,[12]

was struck by lightning, but they are not satisfied with this false-
261 hood but must add to it various fictions: Stesichorus says in his
Eriphyle that it was because he raised up some of those who had
died at Thebes; Polyanthus of Cyrene in his *On the Origin of the
Asclepiads* because he healed the daughters of Proteus who had
been driven mad by the anger of Hera; Panyassis says it was
because he raised up the corpse of Tyndareus; Staphylus in his *On
the Arcadians* says that he healed Hippolytus when he fled Tro-
ezen (in accordance with the stories handed down about Hippolytus
262 in the tragedians), Phylarchus in his ninth book because he restored
the sons of Phineus who had been blinded, wishing to gratify their
mother, Cleopatra, the daughter of Erechtheus; and Telesarchus in
his *Account of the Argolid* because he tried to bring Orion back to
life.[13] So then there could be no technical investigation of a subject
that begins from so false a basis, that is infinite in its variants,
and that is fashioned according to the preference of each writer.

263   Let us remember too that there are three parts of history: history, myth and fiction. History is the exposition of things that are
true and have happened, for example that Alexander died at Babylon, having been poisoned by plotters;[14] fiction is the exposition
of things that have not happened but are told like things that have,
264 for example, the plots of comedies and mimes; myth is the exposition of things that have not happened and are false, for example
when they say that the race of poisonous spiders and snakes was
born alive from the blood of the Titans, or that Pegasus emerged
out of the head of the Gorgon when her throat was cut, or that the
companions of Diomedes were turned into sea-birds or Odysseus
into a horse, or Hecuba into a dog.[15]

265   Since, then, there is such a variety of histories and since there
can be no technical skill concerning what is false and non-existent,
and since myths and fictions (with which the grammar of the historical part is especially concerned) are false and non-existent,
there would not be a technical skill for the historical portion of
266 grammar. From this one can justifiably laugh at those who say
that even if the material for history is without method, nonetheless there will be a technical judgement of history by which we
267 will know what has been falsely recorded and what truly. To begin
with, the grammarians have not handed down to us any criterion

for true history, such that we may judge when it is true and when it is false. Second, since there is no true history amongst the grammarians, the criterion for truth is also non-existent: when one says that Odysseus was killed by the son of Telegonus in ignorance, and another that he died when a seagull dropped a ray's sting on his head, and still another that he was transformed into a horse – how would it not be a difficult task to try to discover the truth in such absurd matters? For it would be necessary first to establish who in these discordant accounts is telling the truth, and then seek what the truth is. But when everyone speaks unbelievable and false things, there is no point of entry for a technical criterion. 268

And indeed the grammarians do not even tell us by what means history is written well, so that by reference to such propositions we might say that there exists some technical part amongst them; for this is the task of the rhetoricians.[16] And so since even they themselves agree – and we have argued – that history is some kind of account without method, and since they have not otherwise handed down any technical precept for the knowledge and composition of history, we must say that the historical portion of grammar is non-existent. 269

37

CASSIUS DIO

Cassius Dio was born *c.* 164 CE in Nicaea in Bithynia (modern Iznik in Turkey); he followed in his father's footsteps as a statesman and was praetor in 194, suffect consul *c.* 204 and later served as proconsul of Africa and legate of both Dalmatia and Upper Pannonia. In 229 he was consul with the emperor Severus Alexander (see below, 80.4.2), after which he retired to Nicaea. His *Roman History* in eighty books began with the foundation of the city and went to 229 CE; it survives only partially. Dio used various sources for the early part of the history, while the latter parts are particularly valuable for Dio's accounts based on his own or contemporaries' eyewitness.[1]

From the Preface

(1.1.2)

I have read everything, one might say, that has been written by anyone about them [sc. the Romans], but I have written up not everything but as much as I selected out.[2]

Difficulties of Writing History under the Empire

(53.19.1–6)[3]

In this way, then, the constitution was changed at that time towards what was better and safer, since somehow or other it had been completely impossible for the Romans to have their democratic form of government and survive.[4] But of course the events that occurred from that time on could not be written about in the same
2 way as previous events. Previously everything was referred to the Senate and the people, and if something occurred far away, reports about it were brought to the city. Because of this, everyone knew what was happening and many wrote about the events, and the truth could be discovered from this in some way or other, for even if things were written from fear and favour or in friendship or enmity,[5] one could go to other writers who covered the same events
3 or to the public records.[6] But from this time onwards, the majority of activities began to take place without people's knowledge and secretly, and whenever something was made public, it could not be tested and was thus disbelieved, for there is the suspicion that everything is done and said in accordance with the wishes of the
4 men who are in power at the time and their associates. As a result, many things that do not occur are repeated over and over again, while much that in fact does happen is unknown, and everything so to speak is reported in a way other than how it actually occurred. And indeed the vast size of the empire and the multitude of events in it means that accuracy in reporting them is extremely
5 difficult. Much is going on at Rome and much in the provinces,

and against the enemy something happens all the time and every day, one might say, and in these matters no one can easily ascertain the truth apart from the actors; indeed, the majority of people never hear of them at all. So then in what follows I will recount 6 everything that will be necessary to say, on the grounds that it has been given out to the public, whether in fact it happened in that way or in some other.[7] I shall add something of my own conjecture,[8] to the extent it is possible, in those cases where I was able to infer more than what was publicized, based on the great amount of evidence that I read, heard or saw.

Avoidance of Repetitive Events

(72.7.3)

I would make my history thoroughly annoying if I were to record in detail one by one those whom he [Caracalla] put to death, either through false informants or suspicions that were not true, or because the person had great wealth, was from a distinguished family, was pre-eminent in learning or had some other distinction.[9]

Possibly Inappropriate Subject Matter for History

(72.18.3–4)

Dio has just narrated an event in the amphitheatre at which the emperor Commodus slew single-handedly in one day a hundred bears by casting javelins down from the railing of the balustrade; being weary, he took from a woman some wine in a cup shaped like a club, at which all the senators there shouted out 'Long live the Emperor'. Dio, recognizing the somewhat trivial and sycophantic nature of this event and narrative writes as follows:

No one should think that I am defiling the lofty nature of history by narrating these events.[10] Ordinarily I would not have written such things, but since this was done by the Emperor, and I was

present, saw, heard and discussed the events, I thought it was
right to conceal none of it, but to record for future generations all
4 these things as if they were great and indispensable events. The
rest of the deeds that occurred in my lifetime I shall take particular care over and treat in greater detail than previous events,
because I was present at them, and because I know of no one as
capable of writing an account worthy of record as I.[11]

How the Author Came to Write History

(72.23.1–5)

Wars and great conflicts occurred after this,[12] and I composed a
treatise on them for the following reason. I had written and published a little book on the dreams and signs by which Severus had
2 expected he would become emperor.[13] I sent it to him and when he
had read it, he wrote back to me with many compliments. I received
this letter when it was already getting towards evening, and when I
3 fell asleep, the divine power commanded me to write history, and it
was in this way that I came to write what I am now setting down.[14]
Since what I had written pleased others and especially Severus himself, I became eager to compose everything that had to do with the
Romans, and for this reason I no longer left that treatise as a separate composition but placed it within this larger narrative, so that I
might leave behind in a single treatise everything that I have written
4 from the beginning to whatever point Fortune deems best. This goddess strengthens me when I am cautious and hesitant about writing,
and by means of dreams she revives me when I am hard pressed and
want to give up, and she gives me fair hopes that the future will preserve my history and never fail to give it renown. I have received her,
so it seems, as the guardian of the conduct of my life, and for this
5 reason I am dedicated to her.[15] I took ten years to gather together all
the material for my Roman history from the beginning to the death
of Severus, and another twelve years to compose it.[16] Remaining
events will be written to whatever point they progress.

The Author's Dream

(78.10.1–2)

Such then were the events surrounding this man, however one chooses to call him.[17] For me, even before he came to the throne, I had been given somehow by his father the foreknowledge that I would write about him too. For just after he died I had a dream in which I saw the entire military force of the Romans in a great plain, and Severus was speaking with them seated on a hill on a high platform. He saw me standing there and so that I might hear what was being discussed, he said, 'Come closer, Dio, so that you may learn accurately and write up what is being said and done.'[18]

Conclusion of the History

(80.4.1–5.3)

He has become frightening to us and with his great army is threatening not only Mesopotamia but also Syria, and he threatens that he will reclaim everything that the Persians of old held, all the way up to the Aegean Sea.[19] He himself is of no account but our soldiers are so disposed that some of them are actually joining his side whilst others are simply unwilling to defend themselves. So great is their wantonness, arrogance and licence that those in Mesopotamia dared to kill their commander Flavius Heracleo, while the Praetorian Guard accused me to Ulpian of having commanded the soldiers in Pannonia forcefully; they also demanded my surrender, because they feared that someone might compel them to be disciplined in the same way as the Pannonians.[20] Alexander[21] did not in fact pay them any attention, instead giving me special honour and choosing me for a second consulship jointly with himself, and he himself even paid the expenses associated with my consulship.[22] When the soldiers became aggrieved at this, he became frightened that they might kill me when they saw me in the insignia of my office, and so he ordered me to spend the time

of my consulship outside Rome somewhere in Italy. Afterwards
I went to Rome and Campania to see him and we spent some days
2 together. The soldiers saw me but did me no harm. I left for home,
obtaining permission because of the weakness of my feet, so that
I might live the remainder of my life in my native country, just as
the divine had revealed most clearly to me when I was still in
Bithynia: for I once dreamed that the divine had ordered me to
3 place at the conclusion of my work the following verses:

Zeus led Hector out from the missiles and the dust,
from the slaughters of men, and the blood, and the tumult.[23]

38
HERODIAN

Herodian was born possibly in Syria or eastern Anatolia in the late second century CE. He tells us that he held offices, but we do not know what they were, and it is unlikely that he came from a distinguished background. His history in eight books treated events from the death of Marcus Aurelius to the accession of Gordian III (180 to 238 CE). He is one of only two historians writing in Greek (the other is Cassius Dio) who survive from the third century.[1]

From the Preface to the History

(1.1.1–3)

The majority of those who have occupied themselves with the harvesting of history and who have sought to renew the memory of deeds of long ago have strived for an everlasting renown for their learning (lest if they were silent they would remain unknown being numbered among the great rabble), and have held the truth in slight regard in their narratives, while concerning themselves greatly with language and euphony: they were emboldened by the belief that even if they said something wildly exaggerative, they themselves would nonetheless profit from the pleasure in their recitations, while the accuracy of their investigation would not be examined.[2] There are some as well who, because of their hatred and hostility towards tyrants, or in turn because of flattery or a desire for honour from cities and individuals, have handed down to posterity worthless and unimportant deeds giving them a renown greater than the truth.[3] I, on the other hand, have not taken any information that was not established and corroborated by witnesses; rather, while the memory of those who will read these events is still fresh, I gathered together the material for my treatise with all accuracy. And I expect that even for future generations a knowledge of these events, which, although great and numerous, occurred within a short span, will not be without pleasure.[4]

Herodian then goes on to argue that no similar span of time as that embraced by his history would be found to contain so many natural and man-made disasters.

Appropriate Treatment of Events

(2.15.6–7)

Many historians and poets, making the life of Severus[5] the subject of their entire history,[6] have recorded more extensively than is appropriate the stages of his march, the things he said in each city he visited, the signs that appeared frequently which seemed to indicate the divine will, and the numbers of soldiers who fell on each side in the battles.[7] But my aim is to write up systematically [7] the deeds accomplished by many emperors in a period of seventy years, deeds which I myself know. I shall, therefore, in what follows treat the most important and distinguished deeds of Severus' separate actions in the order in which they happened, neither elevating him on high in any way because of favouritism (as previous writers have done) nor omitting anything that is worthy of account or of remembering.[8]

39

AMMIANUS MARCELLINUS

The last great pagan historian of the classical world, Ammianus Marcellinus was born around 330 CE in Syrian Antioch, at that time one of the most brilliant cities of the eastern Roman empire. As a young man he was a member of the *protectores domestici*, an elite corps that served as bodyguard for the emperor. In 353 he joined the staff of Ursicinus, the commander-in-chief of Rome's armies in the east, and he saw service over the next years in both the eastern and the western provinces of the empire. He escaped from the capture of Amida by the Persians in 359 (he himself tells the story at 19.8) but his service seems to have come to an end in the following year with Ursicinus' dismissal. Shortly thereafter, he participated in the emperor Julian's disastrous Persian campaign of 363, but we do not know in what capacity. In later years he travelled widely and seems to have settled at Rome sometime in the 380s. He died around 395.

Ammianus' first language was Greek, and we do not know why he chose to write in Latin, but his history in thirty-one books represents the only serious historical effort in that language since the time of Tacitus, to whose *Histories* (which ended in 96 CE) Ammianus joined his own work. The first thirteen books are lost, and the history as we have it commences with events of 353; it ends with the events of 378. The work has had many admirers from Gibbon on.[1]

The loss of the opening of his work has deprived us of a full understanding of why Ammianus wrote and what he thought the value of history was. The extracts below come from throughout the history and give some sense of his interests and concerns.

Preface to Book 15

(15.1.1)

As far as I have been able to investigate the truth, we have narrated those matters which we were able to witness in our life or to know of by carefully examining those who were centrally engaged, setting forth the order of the different events.[2] The remainder, which the following text will make clear, we shall discharge to the best of our ability in a more polished manner, in no fear of those detractors of the length (as they conceive it) of my work. Brevity is only to be praised when it cuts short untimely delays but in no way diminishes our understanding of events.[3]

Praise Approaching Panegyric

(16.1.1–3)

While the order of the fates was joining together these events in the Roman world, the Caesar at Vienne was admitted into the college of magistrates by the Augustus who was then consul for the eighth time.[4] With his native energy urging him on, he was dreaming of the din of battle and the slaughter of the barbarians, ready to gather up the fragments of the province, if only fortune should
2 be at hand with a favourable breeze at last. Because the great deeds and improvements which he effected by his bravery and good fortune throughout Gaul surpass many brave deeds of the ancients, I shall display them one by one in a progressive sequence, employing all my modest talents if only they prove adequate. What
3 I shall narrate, however, will come close to panegyric, yet it is not concocted by clever falsehood, but rather is based on a faithful reliance on events, supported by clear proofs.[5]

Exaggeration in History

(18.6.23)

How long, fable-loving Greece, will you continue to tell us the story of Doriscus, the town in Thrace, where armies were counted regiment by regiment within the confines of a fenced enclosure?[6] We, however, because we are cautious or (rather more truthfully) timid, magnify nothing apart from those things which have been shown by evidence – and reliable at that – to be trustworthy.[7]

Propriety in History

(20.8.18)

With this letter he[8] sent another, a more confidential one, to be delivered secretly to Constantius, which was reproachful and biting. It was not permitted to investigate the contents of this letter, and if it had been, it would not have been fitting to publish it.[9]

Brevity in History

(23.6.1)

Having reached this point, the subject requires a demonstration, as in a swift digression, of the topography of Persia, with the descriptions of their peoples carefully arranged, about whom very few have recorded anything true and that only with difficulty.[10] Yet my text, which will be somewhat detailed, will contribute to a fuller knowledge of them. In narrating matters that are unknown, the one who affects an excessive brevity is on the lookout not for what he might explain more clearly but what he ought to pass over.[11]

Dangers of Contemporary History;
History's Appropriate Subject Matter

(26.1.1–2)

Having narrated the course of events with quite considerable care up to the boundaries which are nearer to our own memory, it would have been appropriate now to step aside from matters more widely known both so that those dangers which are often closely connected with the truth might be avoided,[12] and so that we might not thereafter endure the untimely critics of the work we are composing,[13] clamouring as though injured if one passes over what the emperor said at dinner, or omits why the common soldiers were punished before the standards, or because it was inappropriate in a complex description of geographical areas to say nothing about some trivial forts, or because the names of all those who greeted the urban praetor on his assumption of office were not listed;[14] and very many things like these which are at odds with the rules of history, for history is accustomed to range over lofty matters, not to track down the minutiae of lowly subjects.[15] If anyone wishes to know these, he can also hope to be able to count those tiny indivisible bodies which we call 'atoms' flying through the void.

2   It was in fear of these things that some writers of old did not publish in their lifetime their accounts of various events which were composed in rich style, as Cicero, a witness who deserves respect, affirms in a letter to Cornelius Nepos.[16] So then let us disregard the crowd's ignorance and proceed to narrating the remaining events.

Arrangement in History

(26.5.15)

So then because at one and the same time storms bringing the greatest grief broke out on both sides, we shall recount individual events separately in their relevant place, narrating first a part of what took place in the east and then the wars with the barbarians. Most of the events which took place in the west and the east occurred in the same months,[17] and I fear that by going jumpily from one place and then returning to it, we would confuse everything and entangle the order of events in the greatest neglect.[18]

Summary Accounts of Difficult Matters

(29.1.24 + 31.5.10)[19]

And since we have seen many disappear after agonizing tortures, and everything blends together in confusion (as happens when matters are in the dark), we shall discharge more briefly what we can recall, since the complete memory of events eludes us.[20]

And since we have come to this point after many events, we   31.5.10
must ask whoever will be our readers not to seek from us a detailed account or demand the exact number of those killed, which could not be discovered in any way; for it will be enough to lay out a summary of the events, not veiling the truth with any falsehood, since a faithful integrity is everywhere owed to explaining the recollection of the events.

Conclusion of the History

(31.16.9)

A former soldier and a Greek,[21] I have narrated these events to the best of my ability, starting with the principate of Nerva Caesar all the way to the death of Valens. The work professed the truth, and I have never (or so I believe) dared to corrupt it either knowingly by silence or by falsehood.[22] Let those who are in the prime of life and learning compose events which follow these; if they wish to make the attempt, I advise them to forge their tongues to the grander style.[23]

40

ANONYMOUS
EVALUATION OF
HISTORIANS

(*Oxyrhynchus Papyrus* 4808)

Oxyrhynchus Papyrus 4808 was written sometime in the late first or (more likely) early second century CE. The beginning of this excerpt (the beginning of the treatise is lost, nor do we know how much would have been written before what we have) is part of a discussion of the Alexander historians, followed by longer entries on Hieronymus of Cardia, the best-regarded historian of Alexander's successors, and Polybius (see above, p. 51). As can be seen from what appears here, even though fragmentary, the author says something of the character of each historian and his work and also gives some biographical details. It is striking that for none of the historians does the author give a sense of the contents of each author's work: even for Hieronymus, the fact that he 'wrote about the Diadochs' is mentioned only to distinguish him from other men of the same name.[1]

... having been a student of Diogenes the Cynic.[2] And Chares,[3] in addition to having lied a great deal (for he has narrated the majority of things in a unique manner[4]), displays malice; for example, you catch him blackening Parmenio and his followers.[5] Cleitarchus[6] has also written his history in a boastful manner but his disposition is faultless.[7] He was ... just as ... says ... and the teacher ... of Philopator.[8] col. 1

Hieronymus, the one who wrote about the Diadochs[9] ... fair ... having practical skill ... for he has in fact written about those whom ... he followed [*or*: in whose retinue he was] ...

arbiter . . . he furnished himself . . . with favour[10] . . . having written. And if . . . with speeches . . . benefits . . . of no one . . . of
col. 2   historians . . . First then . . . of Alexander . . . twenty-<five> . . .
trustworthy . . . Antigonus . . . many . . . Dem<etrius> . . . Antigonus . . . he lived more than ninety years[11] . . . a model of sober
behaviour . . . from all of which . . . historian and serious man.

Polybius[12] . . . was himself engaged in affairs, and he went on
military campaigns together with <Scipio>; he was an eyewitness
of very many things and he composed his history with love for
<the truth>[13] . . . <he was rather learned> both in . . . and espe-
cially in political matters . . . learned . . . history . . . but also . . .

41

ANONYMOUS
COMMENTARY ON
THUCYDIDES

(*Oxyrhynchus Papyrus* 853)

Oxyrhynchus Papyrus 853, a commentary on Book 2 of Thucydides, is to be dated sometime in the second century CE, and this portion is a discussion of Dionysius' criticisms (*Thuc.* 9–12) of Thucydides' arrangement of his history. The papyrus thus takes up the issues of arrangement in history that we see in Dionysius and elsewhere, and especially the challenge for the historian in narrating simultaneous events.[1]

It has been written in order, as each event transpired, by summers and winters.[2] Dionysius of Halicarnassus in his treatise *On Thucydides* finds fault with Thucydides for a few things, treating three in the greatest detail: first, that unlike all other authors he did not arrange his history by archon dates or by Olympiads, but uniquely by summers and winters;[3] second, that he separated and divided his history and breaks up events by not completing his accounts of each of them, but going back and forth from one to the other before bringing them to a conclusion;[4] and third, that he said, from his own exhaustive examination, that the true cause of the war was the Lacedaemonian concern about the power of the Athenians, and not, by god, events around Corcyra or Potidaea or for the reasons offered by the majority of people; but Thucydides did not begin from the events – the growth of Athenian power after the Persian Wars – that he himself believed, but turns to the commonly spoken causes.[5] That's what Dionysius says.

Yet one might reasonably <counter> Dionysius who has made such precipitate criticism . . .[6] For the <arrangement> by archons

col. 1

col. 2

and Olympiads <had not yet become> widespread[7] . . . nor as
Herodotus . . . going through Plataean affairs <from the first> up
to the end, and then to go back and write about all the invasions
of the Peloponnesians one after the other, and then next the Corcyrean affairs, though these did not happen at the same time.[8] For
he would have confounded everything by repeatedly going back to
the same periods of time inappropriately and illogically. For this
was not a single subject nor did it occur at a single time or location; rather, these were several subjects occurring at many times
and in many places. And indeed if he had composed according

col. 3 to archon years, he would have had to divide up events anyway,
because some occurred under one archon, others under a different
one; only when one writes about an individual topic does one
compose a continuous narrative.

Dionysius thus contradicts himself. For if Thucydides should
have written according to archon years, as Dionysius states, then
he would similarly have had to break up events according to the
archons. If the events are connected and the chronology does not
impose an obstacle, then Thucydides does narrate in order, for
example . . . in the seventh book . . .

In regard to the beginning of the history and the fact that he did
not start from the growth of Athens' power which he considered
the truest cause of the war, it must first be noted that he did not
intend, in setting out to write up the Peloponnesian War, to introduce in a digression many wars that began almost at the end of the
Persian Wars themselves, at which point the Athenians first began
to increase their power.[9] For that was wholly outside his topic.
Second, one must consider that every historian ought to explain
accurately the obvious and commonly held causes of events at the
outset, and if he suspects other, more hidden reasons . . .[10]

Notes

1. HECATAEUS

1. The fragments of Hecataeus' work can be found in *FGrHist* 1 and, with English translation and updated bibliography, at *BNJ* 1 (F. Pownall). Still fundamental is F. Jacoby, 'Hekataios', *RE* VII (1909) pp. 2666–769 (in German); good introductory treatments in English are Pearson (1939), chapter 2; Brown (1973) pp. 7–12; Drews (1973) pp. 11–19; *Nature* pp. 4–12; see also L. Bertelli, 'Hecataeus: From Genealogy to Historiography', in N. Luraghi, ed., *The Historian's Craft in the Age of Herodotus* (Oxford, 2001) pp. 67–94; for Hecataeus' relationship with H., S. West, 'Herodotus' Portrait of Hecataeus', *JHS* 111 (1991) pp. 144–60.
2. This opening remark is notable for its absence of any sense of divine guidance as had been found in earlier writers, both poets and prose-writers; the suggestion is rather that everything will depend on the author's own investigation and reason. See Intro. §3.

2. HERODOTUS

1. Still fundamental on H. is Jacoby's massive article (in German) in *RE* Suppl. II (1913) pp. 205–520. Important works on H.'s historical method and approach include: H. Immerwahr, *Form and Thought in Herodotus* (Cleveland, 1966); D. Lateiner, *The Historical Method of Herodotus* (Toronto, 1989); J. Gould, *Herodotus* (London, 1989) pp. 19–41; Duff (2003) pp. 13–24; four essays by H. van Wees, P. Cartledge and E. Greenwood, S. Hornblower and J. Cobet, in E. J. Bakker et al., *Brill's Companion to Herodotus* (Leiden, 2002) pp. 321–412; N. Luraghi, 'Meta-*historie*: Method and Genre in the *Histories*', in C. Dewald and J. Marincola, eds., *The Cambridge Companion to Herodotus* (Cambridge, 2006)

pp. 76–91; and D. Asheri, 'General Introduction', in D. Asheri et al., *A Commentary on Herodotus Books I–IV* (Oxford, 2007) pp. 1–71. See also *GH* pp. 19–60; Scanlon (2015) pp. 26–68. For different reactions to him in antiquity see D.H. *Pomp.* 3.2–21 and Pl. *Malice.*

2. This is clear from L. *Hist.* H.'s influence in antiquity can be studied through K.-A. Riemann, *Das herodoteische Geschichtswerk in der Antike* (diss. Munich, 1967); J. A. S. Evans, 'Father of History or Father of Lies: the Reputation of Herodotus', *CJ* 64 (1968), pp. 11–17; O. Murray, 'Herodotus and Hellenistic Culture', *CQ* n.s. 22 (1972), pp. 200–213; S. Hornblower, 'Herodotus' Influence in Antiquity', in Dewald and Marincola (n. 1) pp. 306–18; J. Priestly, *Herodotus and Hellenistic Culture* (Oxford, 2014).

3. The Greeks divided the world into themselves (*Hellenes*) and everyone else (*barbaroi*), and the latter is the term that H. uses here; for H. at least, the term maintains its originally neutral sense, without the pejorative overtones (as in the English use of 'barbarian') that it was later to have.

4. The emphasis on glory (*kleos*) links H. to the epic world of Homer and the world of Pindar's odes in praise of victorious athletes: see Intro. §7.

5. The final clause shows that part of H.'s wider aim was to establish causes; see Intro. §7; for more on causes see P. 3.6.1–7.

6. The passages show the importance of 'great deeds' as the subject matter of history (see Intro. §2); note too that in the last passage the phrase 'did or suffered' anticipates Aristotle's definition of history (*Poetics*, chapter 9).

7. For the Athenian tyrants see T. 1.20.2 with n. 10. Athenian liberation took place in 514; Ionia revolted from the Persian empire in 499.

8. This is the earliest recognition we have of the tendency to exalt rulers by composing false accounts of them; see Intro. §6.

9. This passage comes from H.'s account of Egypt, in which he discusses amongst other things the gods of the Egyptians. He learns that there is an Egyptian Heracles which does not seem to have much in common with the Greek accounts of Heracles, and this passage is his attempt to reconcile the two traditions. This is the clearest account that H. gives us of particular travels made to discover material for his history; nowhere else is he so detailed about his actual inquiries. For a full discussion of the passage see A. B. Lloyd, *Herodotus Book II: Commentary 1–98* (Leiden, 1976) pp. 200–212.

10. A hero was a semi-divine figure, having a god as one parent; in Hesiod's *Theogony* they are an intermediate race between gods and men. They received cult from the Greeks though not exactly the same kind offered to the gods.

11. Cf. Hecataeus' remark, F 1a.

12. H. has been describing the geography of Egypt (including the sources of the Nile) and the customs of the Egyptians; he is now about to relate the history of their early kings.

13. Having now related the history of the Egyptians' early kings, H. moves on to their later kings; this period was better known since it encompassed the time when Greeks had business in Egypt (thus he says 'the Egyptians and everyone else').

14. These two passages show H. aware of earlier accounts, though we cannot assume that this was a procedure universally followed in the rest of the history.

15. There are a number of such intentional silences in H., especially when dealing with religious matters in Book 2. This remark, however, indicates H.'s desire not to glorify the Samian (for glory as one of the purposes of his history see H.'s preface, above and n. 4).

16. H. is describing the naval battle of Lade in 494, which ended the Ionian Revolt against Persia.

17. H. here recognizes the role that partiality plays in history: cf. Intro. §6 and T. 1.22.4 for a more explicit expression of the idea.

18. H.'s principle of *legein ta legomena* – 'to say what is said' – is one of the hallmarks of his history, for he very much sees himself as someone whose job is to gather together for the reader those traditions that he discovered in his inquiries. Such a principle could be interpreted by later generations negatively: see Pl. *Malice*; for criticism of historians' tendency to include something and not take responsibility for it, see Seneca, *Natural Questions* 4b.3.1.

3. ANTIOCHUS OF SYRACUSE

1. On Antiochus see Pearson (1987) pp. 11–18; R. Vattuone, *CGRH* pp. 191–3. His fragments are at *FGrHist* 555, now with English translation and excellent commentary in *BNJ* 555 (N. Luraghi); see also the edition of C. Cuscunà, *I frammenti di Antioco di Siracusa. Introduzione, traduzione e commento* (Alexandria, 2003).

2. Whereas Hecataeus, H. and T. all begin by giving their names and country, Antiochus gives the name of his father, as do D.H. *Rom. Ant.* 1.8.4 and Josephus, *Jewish War* 1.3.

3.   The word used here for 'most reliable', *saphesteta*, is the superla-
tive of the adjective *saphes*, which means 'manifest' or 'clear', and
so this literally means here 'the clearest'; *saphes* is used by T. at
1.22.4 (and cf. 1.9.2, for oral informants who know (as here) the
saphestata); see the commentary of Luraghi at *BNJ* 555 F 2.

4. THUCYDIDES

1.   For T. see J. H. Finley, Jr., *Thucydides* (Cambridge, Mass., 1942);
id., *Three Essays on Thucydides* (Cambridge, Mass., 1967); W. R.
Connor, *Thucydides* (Princeton, 1984); S. Hornblower, *Thucydides* (London and Chapel Hill, 1987); T. Rood, *Thucydides:
Narrative and Explanation* (Oxford, 1998); Duff (2003) pp. 25–38;
and the essays collected in A. Rengakos and A. Tsakmakis, eds.,
Brill's Companion to Thucydides (Leiden and Boston, 2006), and
J. S. Rusten, ed., *Thucydides* (Oxford Readings in Classical Studies; Oxford, 2009). The bibliography on T.'s historical method is
vast, and is perhaps best explored by the use of the two standard
commentaries in English: A. W. Gomme, A. Andrewes and K. J.
Dover, *A Historical Commentary on Thucydides*, 5 vols. (Oxford,
1945–80); S. Hornblower, *A Commentary on Thucydides*, 3 vols.
(Oxford, 1997–2008). The essays to be found in Rengakos and
Tsakmakis, op. cit., especially those of Rood, Kallet and all those
in Part III, are also helpful in giving some sense of T.'s methods of
inquiry. *GH* pp. 61–104 provides a bibliographic guide up to about
the year 2000.

2.   On T.'s influence in antiquity see R. Nicolai, '*Ktêma es aei*: Aspects
of the Reception of Thucydides in the Ancient World', in Rusten (n.
1) pp. 381–404; and the essays in part IV of Rengakos and Tsakmakis (n. 1).

3.   For full commentary on this passage see *HCT* vol. 1 pp. 89–91; *CT*
vol. 1 pp. 3–7; for its imitation of H.'s preface, Moles (1993) pp.
98–100.

4.   The war today is known as the Peloponnesian War, thus betraying
the Athenian point of view, but for T. it is always 'the war of the
Peloponnesians and Athenians'; note that in the opening sentence
he says not that he composed an *account* of the war but rather the
war itself.

5.   For the notion of what is 'worthy of account' (*axiologon*) see Intro. §2.

6.   T. follows this with a long 'proof' of this remark, using literary
sources and tradition to argue that the times leading up to the

Peloponnesian War were not comparable to his own era and the power of Athens and Sparta in the mid fifth century. This passage (1.2–19) is sometimes referred to as the 'Archaeology'.

7. This extract contains some of the most important and influential discussion of method in historiography: for detailed commentary see *HCT* vol. 1 pp. 135–50; *CT* vol. 1 pp. 56–62.

8. T. has now concluded his discussion of earlier times (see n. 6) and has a few more remarks to make before giving his method.

9. T. adds this last clause because it was usually assumed that the natives of a place were the best source of information about that place (see *ATAH* pp. 283–4) and he wishes to make the point that they are no more reliable than anyone else.

10. Peisistratus was tyrant of Athens in the sixth century BCE. His sons were Hippias and Hipparchus, and in Athenian popular tradition (as known from contemporary drinking songs that are quoted by later authors) the tyranny was ended when two young noblemen, Harmodius and Aristogeiton, killed Hipparchus, after which his brother Hippias went into exile. H. too records that Hippias was tyrant when Hipparchus was murdered (5.55) but neither historian seems to have changed popular belief.

11. The remarks here seem to be an implicit criticism of H. who mentions both things (6.57; 9.53).

12. For the notion of the 'mythical' see below, 1.22.4 and Intro. §9.

13. Here begins the statement of methodology proper, carefully structured by a series of antitheses: T. divides the events of the war (*ta prachthenta*, literally 'the things done') into words (*logoi*) and deeds (*erga*), and offers the procedure that he followed for each.

14. 'Said in speech' may sound pleonastic, but T. thinks of speeches as an important part of history (see n. 13).

15. Literally, 'the necessary things' (*ta deonta*), i.e., necessary to that particular situation; see C. Macleod, 'Rhetoric and History (Thucydides 6.16–18)' in id., *Collected Papers* (Oxford, 1983) pp. 68–70.

16. Vast amounts of ink have been spilt on this passage, not least because T. seems to be suggesting two contradictory things, first that he presumed that the speakers would say things necessary for the occasion (see n. 15) but then that he held as closely as possible to what was actually (*alēthōs*, 'truly') said. T.'s speeches have a high degree of stylistic uniformity so whatever the relationship is between what was said on a particular occasion and what T. has written, it is nonetheless the case that the words for all of them are, quite literally, those of T. himself. See further Hornblower, *Thucydides* (n. 1) pp. 45–72; Rusten and Pelling in Rusten, ed. (n. 1) pp. 4–6

and 176–87 (respectively); *GH* pp. 77–85; for speeches in history, Intro. §11.

17. For P.'s echo of this see 3.31.12; for utility in history, Intro. §7.

18. The so-called 'second preface' appears after T.'s narration of the first ten years of hostilities between Athens and Sparta (431–421) followed by the years of broken ceasefires and treaties. Later historians will imitate this use of a second preface usually at some definable break in the narrative. For detailed commentary see *HCT* vol. 4 pp. 9–17; *CT* vol. 3 pp. 44–53.

19. T. here is narrating an attempt by the Athenians to seize the heights around Syracuse so as to regain control of them. They decide to make a daring attempt by night and have a certain amount of success before they are driven back by the Boeotians. It is at this point that T. makes the remarks below. Descriptions of night battles after T. are fairly frequent, and are usually based on T.'s account and written in imitation of him. See *HCT* vol. 4 pp. 422–4; *CT* vol. 3 pp. 618, 626–7.

20. See Euripides, *Suppliant Women* 846–56 for similar sentiments about participants in battle scarcely knowing what is going on.

5. CTESIAS OF CNIDUS

1. Ctesias' fragments are at *FGrHist* 688; a new edition with French translation and copious notes is D. Lenfant, *Ctésias de Cnide: La Perse, L'Inde, Autres Fragments* (Paris, 2004); English translation of the *Persica* with notes in L. Llewellyn-Jones and J. Robson, *Ctesias' History of Persia: Tales of the Orient* (London and New York, 2010). For Ctesias' life and career see T. S. Brown, 'Suggestions for a Vita of Ctesias of Cnidus', *Historia* 27 (1978) pp. 1–19; for his historical activity, Drews (1973) pp. 103–18; J. M. Bigwood, 'Ctesias as Historian of the Persian Wars', *Phoenix* 32 (1978) pp. 19–41; ead., 'Ctesias' *Indica* and Photius', *Phoenix* 43 (1989) pp. 302–16; D. Lenfant, *CGRH* pp. 202–8.

2. The 'I' here is the Byzantine patriarch Photius (*c.* 810–893) who compiled for his brother a work entitled *The Library*, which contained capsule summaries of some 279 books from classical antiquity, many of which are now lost.

3. This is the historian Xenophon.

4. For Cyrus' attack on his brother Artaxerxes II, see the introduction to X. (below, p. 21).

5. Ctesias' claim to have consulted royal records is generally disbe-
    lieved; there is no other testimony to the existence of these works
    and his history does not read as if it is based on official accounts:
    see the discussion of Lenfant (n. 1) pp. xxxvi–xxxix.

6. XENOPHON

1. On X. see J. K. Anderson, *Xenophon* (London and New York,
    1974); H. R. Breitenbach, *Historiographische Anschauungen Xeno-
    phons* (Freiburg in der Schweiz, 1950); P. J. Rahn, 'Xenophon's
    Developing Historiography', *TAPhA* 102 (1971) pp. 497–508; V. J.
    Gray, *The Character of Xenophon's* Hellenica (London and Chapel
    Hill, 1989); ead., ed., *Xenophon* (Oxford Readings in Classical Stud-
    ies; Oxford, 2010); C. Tuplin, *The Failings of Empire* (Stuttgart,
    1993); id., ed., *Xenophon and his World* (Stuttgart, 2004); J. Dillery,
    Xenophon and the History of his Times (London and New York,
    1995); Pownall (2004) pp. 65–112; M. A. Flower, *Xenophon's* Anaba-
    sis, *or* The Expedition of Cyrus (New York and Oxford, 2012);
    Scanlon (2015) pp. 126–59.
2. Theramenes, although originally one of the Thirty oligarchs set up
    by the Spartans to rule Athens after they were defeated in the Pelo-
    ponnesian War (404 BCE), fell out with the other oligarchs,
    especially Critias, and was condemned in a sham trial and exe-
    cuted. Satyrus is one of the Eleven, the board at Athens charged
    with carrying out executions.
3. *Kottabos* was a game at drinking parties in which one threw the
    dregs of wine into a bowl or disc whilst saying the name of one's
    love, divining by the sound made whether one's chances might be
    successful or not. Theramenes inverts the game by speaking the
    name of his enemy and casting hemlock rather than wine.
4. For 'worthy of account' see Intro. §2.
5. X. is narrating events of 389 BCE; he has just described campaigns
    of the Spartans against Acarnania and Argos.
6. See n. 4.
7. X. is detailing events concerning the Spartan fleet in the year 389
    BCE, and the change of command from the previous year's admiral,
    Teleutias, to the current one Hierax.
8. See above, n. 4. The terms 'expense', 'danger' and 'contrivance'
    may be thought to give specific examples of the kind of thing usu-
    ally thought to be worthy of account.

9.   For X.'s interest throughout all of his works in the qualities of great leadership, see V. J. Gray, *Xenophon's Mirror of Princes: Reading the Reflections* (Oxford, 2011).

10. Phlius in the north-east Peloponnese had long been a Spartan ally, and X. here praises them in particular for their loyalty in the aftermath of the Spartan defeat at Leuctra in 371, when many other Spartan allies defected.

11. X. has just narrated the indecisive battle of Mantinea in 362. On the tradition of continuators, see Intro. §2. X. had begun his work with 'and after these events' (1.1.1), so the words here form a kind of ring-composition. See also Agatharchides, *On the Red Sea* 5.112; Ammianus 31.16.9.

7. EPHORUS OF CYME

1.   Isocrates (436–338 BCE) was the most important rhetorician of his day, and one of the most influential writers on succeeding generations. Twenty-one of his orations survive, all of which are display pieces, i.e., not meant for delivery in actual trials or assemblies (even though this is the fiction that is adopted in many of them). Isocrates was renowned especially for the care that he took over his writing, and he sought to make prose the equal of poetry in beauty. He is usually thought to have bequeathed to historiography the 'rhetorical' style, not least through his supposed pupils, Ephorus and Theopompus (who are, however, not likely to have been his pupils: M. A. Flower, *Theopompus of Chios: History and Rhetoric in the Fourth Century BC* (Oxford, 1994) pp. 42–62); and although he was certainly interested in the past, his influence on the genre of historiography is likely to be small: see J. Marincola, *BTP* pp. 39–61.

2.   Ephorus' fragments are at *FGrHist* 70; English translation with updated bibliography at *BNJ* 70 (V. Parker). On Ephorus see E. L. Barber, *The Historian Ephorus* (Cambridge, 1935) and the comprehensive work of G. Parmeggiani, *Eforo di Cuma: studi di storiografia greca* (Bologna, 2011; English translation forthcoming). On the arrangement of his work, R. Drews, 'Ephorus and History Written *kata genos*', *AJPh* 84 (1963) pp. 244–55; on his historical method there is much of value throughout Parmeggiani's book; see also G. Schepens, 'Éphore sur la valeur de l'autopsie (*FGrHist* 70 F 110 = Polybe XII 27. 7)', *Ancient Society* 1 (1970) pp. 163–82; id., 'Historiographical Problems in Ephorus', in *Historiographia Antiqua:*

Commentationes . . . in honorem W. Peremans (Leuven, 1977) pp. 95–118; Pownall (2004) pp. 113–42; V. Parker, 'The Historian Ephorus: His Selection of Sources', *Antichthon* 38 (2004 [2006]) pp. 29–50; J. Marincola, *CGRH* pp. 172–4; N. Luraghi, *BTP* pp. 133–51; J. Tully, ibid. pp. 153–95. For Ephorus' arrangement see Diod. 5.1.4 with n. 32.

3.   On this fragment see Parmeggiani (n. 2) pp. 99–110 and Schepens, 'Historiographical Problems' (n. 2).

4.   See Parmeggiani (n. 2) pp. 93–5.

5.   See Schepens, 'Éphore sur la valeur' (n. 2); Parmeggiani, *Eforo* (n. 2) pp. 114–23; on eyewitness, Intro. §3.

8. ARISTOTLE

1.   For discussion of this passage see G. F. Else, *Aristotle's Poetics: The Argument* (Cambridge, Mass., 1957) pp. 301–9; G. E. M. de Ste Croix, 'Aristotle on History and Poetry (*Poetics*, 9, 1451a36–b11)', in A. Rorty, ed., *Essays on Aristotle's Poetics* (Princeton, 1992) pp. 23–32; and S. Halliwell, *Aristotle's Poetics* (London and Chapel Hill, 1986) pp. 78–80; for Aristotle's approach to history more generally see R. Zoepffel, *Historia und Geschichte bei Aristoteles* (Heidelberg, 1975); L. Bertelli, *BTP* pp. 289–303.

2.   The reference is to chapters 7–8 of the *Poetics* where Aristotle discussed the construction of plots, and argued that there must be a unity of action rather than a unity based on an individual character, since a single person can perform many actions which do not necessarily have a unity of action.

3.   At *Poetics* 1447b18 Aristotle says that Homer and Empedocles are not doing the same thing simply because they both write in verse.

4.   The term used here, *ta katholou*, is also employed by P. in describing his 'universal' history (1.4.3–6), but he compares it not to individual things (*kat' hekaston*) as does Aristotle, but to 'individual' (*kata meros*) histories.

5.   In other words, the fact that a play is about Oedipus does not limit its universality.

6.   Alcibiades was perhaps the most notorious figure of classical Athens. Born *c.* 450, he was a ward of Pericles, and clearly alienated some people by his ostentatious lifestyle. He figures largely in Thucydides' history: wealthy and flamboyant, he urged the Athenians to conquer Sicily and was appointed one of the generals in command of the expedition. When he was recalled to Athens to

stand trial for possible sacrilege (almost certainly engineered by his political enemies), he escaped instead to Sparta where he encouraged the Spartans in their war against Athens. He was eventually forced to leave Sparta and found himself in the retinue of the Persian governor Tissaphernes, whom he advised to defeat both Athens and Sparta by a war of attrition. Eventually recalled to Athens, he almost as suddenly was again forced into exile. He died in 403; the traditions about his death vary. He is an excellent point for Aristotle's example here, since he can be said to have lived a life of many actions but actions that in no way pointed to a single goal. For more on him see H. D. Westlake, *Individuals in Thucydides* (Cambridge, 1968) pp. 212–60; D. Gribble, 'Individuals in Thucydides', in A. Rengakos and A. Tsakmakis, *Brill's Companion to Thucydides* (Leiden, 2006) pp. 439–68, with references to earlier discussions.

7. The term here is *mimesis*, often translated as 'imitation'.

8. At this point Aristotle has ceased talking about tragedy and moves on to epic poetry.

9. For the metaphor of the living creature in a possibly similar context, see P. 1.3.4.

10. There were, of course, many histories like that of X.'s *Hellenica* which treated a particular period of time, without necessarily trying to impose a single 'plot' on the events of that period. Aristotle either ignores or does not think relevant T.'s attempt to narrate a single, 'unified' war with beginning, middle and end. Cf. Else (n. 1) pp. 304 n. 9: 'There is no really satisfying explanation of Aristotle's absolute neglect of Thucydides . . . It seems to be a genuine blind spot – or a deliberate omission.' P. attempts to argue the unified nature of his 'universal' history, which tended 'to one goal' at 1.3.3–4, 1.4.1.

11. The naval battle of Salamis, in which the Greeks defeated the Persians, occurred in 480; the Carthaginian battle referred to here is the battle of Himera (also 480) in which the forces of Gelon of Syracuse and Theron of Agrigentum defeated the Carthaginians. H. 7.166 says that the two battles were fought on the same day; in the later tradition the two events were 'joined' by the proposition that the Persians and Carthaginians were allied against the Greeks: Xerxes made common cause with the Carthaginians, the Persians choosing to invade the Greek mainland, the Carthaginians ordered to attack the western Greeks in Italy and Sicily: see Diod. 11.1.1–5.

9. THEOPOMPUS OF CHIOS

1.   Ancient appraisals of Theopompus at P. 8.9–11; D.H. *Pomp.* 6.1–9;
     Pl. *Malice* 1; L. *Hist.* 59. His fragments are at *FGrHist* 115 and,
     with English translation and updated bibliography, at *BNJ* 115
     (W. S. Morison). For his work, W. R. Connor, 'History without
     Heroes: Theopompus' Treatment of Philip of Macedon', *GRBS* 8
     (1967) pp. 133–54; Pédech (1989) pp. 19–254; G. S. Shrimpton, *Theo-*
     pompus the Historian (Montreal and Kingston, 1991); M. A.
     Flower, *Theopompus of Chios: History and Rhetoric in the Fourth*
     Century BC (Oxford, 1994); Pownall (2004) pp. 143–75.
2.   The Greek text here is problematic, but the general sense is prob-
     ably as rendered in the translation. The phrase 'even if he had not
     written anything about it' is the basis for assuming that Theopom-
     pus actually did say these things in his history.
3.   It is not clear that this is a methodological pronouncement; Jacoby
     in his commentary ad loc. thinks it comes from a speech; Pédech,
     Polybe: Histoires Livre XII (Paris, 1961) p. 146 connects this
     with D.H.'s remark (previous passage), and it is just possible that
     both passages formed part of Theopompus' methodological
     remarks in his preface. For a fuller context for P.'s remarks see
     below, p. 107.
4.   Theopompus devoted Book 8 (often referred to simply as 'Mar-
     vels') of his *Philippica* to this sort of material.
5.   For Ctesias, above, p. 19; for Hellanicus, D.H. *Thuc.* 5.2 with n. 18.
     On myths see Intro. §9. The fragment is often translated 'says
     he will tell myths in his history better than Herodotus, Ctesias,
     Hellanicus and the writers on India', but see Flower (n. 1) pp. 34–5
     (followed by Morison, *BNJ* ad loc.) for the correct interpretation.
     For the fuller context of Strabo's remarks see below, p. 175.

10. CALLISTHENES

1.   Callisthenes' fragments are at *FGrHist* 124; there is an English
     translation of them in C. A. Robinson, Jr., *The History of Alexan-*
     der the Great (Providence, 1953) vol. 1 pp. 45–77. For Callisthenes'
     life and works see Pearson (1960) pp. 22–49; A. B. Bosworth, 'Aristotle
     and Callisthenes', *Historia* 19 (1970) pp. 407–13; P. Pédech, *Histo-*
     riens compagnons d'Alexandre (Paris, 1984) pp. 15–69; L. Prandi,
     Callistene: uno storico tra Aristotele e i re macedoni (Milan, 1985);

D. Golan, 'The Fate of a Court Historian: Callisthenes', *Athenaeum* 66 (1988) pp. 99–120; A. Zambrini, *CGRH* pp. 219–20. The inscription honouring Aristotle and Callisthenes is *SIG*³, no. 275.

2.   The author is discussing the necessity for concision in technical treatises (this quotation appears in the preface of a work on machines); for the context see D. Whitehead and P. H. Blyth, *Athenaeus Mechanicus: On Machines* (Stuttgart, 2004) pp. 47 and 73.

3.   For Isocrates see Ephorus n. 1 See Quintilian, *Orator's Training* 10.3.4 for Isocrates' *Panegyricus* being overtaken by events.

4.   This seems to be the earliest explicit remark by a historian on the need for appropriateness in history. It is usually thought that Callisthenes here is referring to rhetorical elaboration and, as in rhetorical training, demanding that the speaker use words and sentiments appropriate to the characters and situation; for how this may have affected the truth of history see Intro. §10. For discussion of this fragment see Pearson (1960) p. 31; *SP* pp. 246–7; Fornara, *Nature* pp. 145–6, who compares D.H. *Thuc.* 41.4; Marincola, *CGRH* pp. 122, who connects this remark with T.'s above on *ta deonta* (1.22.1 with n. 15).

5.   I adopt the interpretation of Whitehead and Blyth (n. 2) p. 73 who see the second part of this sentence as adversative.

6.   This shows that the remark was not part of Callisthenes' history; the story may have arisen in the hostile attitudes towards Callisthenes after his death.

7.   The usual notion amongst historians is that a glorious subject reflects glory on them: see P. 12.23.7, Sallust *Catiline* 3.2; Pl. *On the Glory of the Athenians* 345D–F; cf. L. *Hist.* 17; Intro. §2.

8.   For the supposedly divine circumstances of Alexander's birth and Olympias' role in them see Pl. *Life of Alexander* 3.3–4.

11. TIMAEUS OF TAUROMENIUM

1.   The fragments of Timaeus are at *FGrHist* 566; English translation, with updated bibliography, at *BNJ* 566 (C. Champion). On Timaeus' life and work see T. S. Brown, *Timaeus of Tauromenium* (Berkeley, 1958); L. Pearson, *The Greek Historians of the West* (Atlanta, 1987), *passim*; R. Vattuone, *Sapienza d'Occidente: il pensiero storico di Timeo di Tauromenio* (Bologna, 1991); id., *CGRH* pp. 196–9; *PRHW* pp. 165–77; C. A. Baron, *Timaeus of Tauromenium and Hellenistic Historiography* (Cambridge, 2013), especially good on P.'s treatment of Timaeus; Scanlon (2015) pp. 197–200. For Cic.'s

evaluation of him see *On the Orator* 2.58, and for his *Wars against Pyrrhus* see Cic. *Letters to Friends* 5.12.2.

2. Jacoby suggests that Book 6 of Timaeus' history began the history proper, after his treatment of the geography and foundations of Sicily in Books 1–5.

3. *FGrHist* 566 F 7. Given the close connection between rhetoric and historiography (see Intro. §10), it is not surprising that a historian would have discussed the relationship. Epideictic ('display') rhetoric was used on ceremonial occasions and particularly for praise and blame, and as such could be seen to overlap with history's emphasis on great and glorious deeds. Cf. the brief discussion in Cic. *On the Orator* 2.43–6; on history and epideictic, *RICH* pp. 95–8; Zangara (2007) pp. 135–74.

4. On this stage of history-writing see L. *Hist*. 48.

12. DURIS OF SAMOS

1. Duris' fragments are at *FGrHist* 76, and, with English translation and updated bibliography, *BNJ* 76 (F. Pownall). On Duris' life and works see R. B. Kebric, *In the Shadow of Macedon: Duris of Samos* (Wiesbaden, 1977); P. Pédech (1989) pp. 257–389; and, most comprehensively, F. Landucci Gattinoni, *Duride di Samio* (Rome, 1997).

2. Discussions of this remark are legion, but there is little agreement amongst scholars about its exact meaning. 'Representation' here is the Greek *mimēsis*, often translated as 'imitation' and very important in Aristotle's *Poetics* (above, p. 28); but the sense is probably 'not representation *tout court* . . . but a certain kind of quality of representation, one that exhibits the objects of representation with imaginative directness or immediacy' (S. Halliwell, *The Aesthetics of Mimesis* (Princeton, 2002) pp. 290–91); cf. *SP* p. 226: 'dramatic *mimesis* with its associated pleasure in the narrative' and Halliwell, *Aesthetics* p. 290: 'It is reasonable to assume that Duris's complaint pertains to a perceived lack of dramatic qualities and therefore implies a positive esteem for bringing historical scenes alive with the kinds of narrative technique and artistry that traditionally belonged to poetry'. Pownall at *BNJ* 76 F 1 suggests 'exactness of representation'. Taking a very different tack, V. J. Gray, 'Mimesis in Greek Historical Writing', *AJPh* 118 (1987) pp. 467–86, argues that *mimēsis* has to do with stylistic propriety and Duris' remark is an indictment not of the content but of the *style* of

Ephorus and Theopompus which failed to be appropriate to the
characters and actions (as recommended by Callisthenes, above, p. 34).
For additional discussion see *SP* pp. 226–8; Halliwell, *Aesthetics*
pp. 289–91; *Nature* pp. 124–30; B. Gentili and G. Cerri, *History
and Biography in Ancient Thought* (Amsterdam, 1988) pp. 105–6;
Pédech (1989) pp. 368–82. See further Intro. §7.

13. CATO THE ELDER

1.   The first Roman historian, Quintus Fabius Pictor (see P. n. 16),
      wrote in Greek, although a Latin version of the work was also
      known; the relationship between the two is a vexed issue (see *LH*
      pp. 4–22), so perhaps to be more precise we should say that Cato's
      history seems to have been the first that was *composed* in Latin.

2.   Cato's fragments, with English translation and commentary, are at
      FRHist 5 (T. J. Cornell). On Cato's life and work see A. E. Astin,
      Cato the Censor (Oxford, 1978); E. S. Gruen, *Culture and National
      Identity in Republican Rome* (Ithaca and London, 1992) pp. 52–
      83; U. Gotter, *CCRH* pp. 108–22; masterful discussion at *FRHist*
      vol. 1 pp. 195–217 (T. J. Cornell).

3.   This omission of the names of commanders is confirmed by the
      fragments, where Cato identifies people by their title, 'consul',
      'praetor', and so on; even Hannibal is referred to as 'the dictator of
      the Carthaginians' (F 78); see further *FGrHist* I.213–14.

4.   It is noteworthy that Cato seems to have introduced in his preface
      the notion of the historian's pleasure at recounting events; we do
      not have an earlier example of this; for another 'personal' remark
      of this sort see Livy, *preface* 5.

5.   From another testimonium (T 9) we know that Cato praised the
      value of history also in his preface. On the preface of the work see
      J. B. Churchill, 'On the Content and Structure of the Prologue to
      Cato's *Origines*', *ICS* 20 (1995) pp. 91–106.

6.   Cato here seems to link the absence of writing (they are illiterate)
      with an inability to get at the truth. Cato was praised for his indus-
      try in investigating traditions: see *FRHist* 5 TT 1 and 14.

7.   For the tablet of the Pontifex Maximus, see Cic. *On the Orator* 2.52
      with n. 49. This remark is thought to come from the beginning of
      Book 4, where Cato would have begun his narrative of Roman his-
      tory proper. Although we lack the context of the remark (Gellius
      quotes it in a discussion of the interest of the early Romans in the
      causes of eclipses), it is usually assumed that Cato is defining here

what the subject matter of his history will be, and does so in contrast with the records of the Pontifex. For discussion, see *FRHist* vol. III pp. 127–9 (T. J. Cornell).

14. AGATHARCHIDES OF CNIDUS

1. Agatharchides' historical fragments (but not *On the Red Sea*, which Jacoby considered a geography) are at *FGrHist* 86; English translation, with commentary and updated bibliography, at *BNJ* 86 (S. Burstein); English translation of *On the Erythraean Sea* with notes can be found in S. Burstein, *Agatharchides of Cnidus: On the Erythraean Sea* (London, 1989). On Agatharchides' life and works see P. M. Fraser, *Ptolemaic Alexandria* (Oxford, 1972) vol. 1 pp. 515–17, 539–50 and Burstein, op. cit. pp. 1–36; for his history, see W. Ameling, 'Ethnography and Universal History in Agatharchides', in T. C. Brennan and H. I. Flower, eds., *East & West: Papers in Ancient History Presented to Glen W. Bowersock* (Cambridge, Mass., and London, 2008) pp. 13–59.

2. This passage comes from the *Library* of Photius, the patriarch of Constantinople: see Ctesias n. 2.

3. On myth in history see Intro. §9.

4. The passage is somewhat elliptical but Agatharchides seems to be saying that unless one engages in such refutation of poetic licence in history, the genre of history loses its value because it can no longer be considered reliable.

5. Here Photius moves to direct quotation, and the 'I' is Agatharchides.

6. The quarrel of Zeus and Poseidon is a reference to events told in *Iliad* Books 13–15; the reference to Hesiod (*c.* eighth century BCE) is to his *Theogony*, a poem that narrates the births and descendants of the gods; the criticism of Aeschylus may be to the fantastic plots and situations that his dramas sometimes had (for example, the necromancy in his *Persians*); Euripides spent his last years at the court of Macedon, where he enjoyed the patronage of its king, Archelaus; Temenos was an Argive hero and ancestor of the inhabitants of Argos and Macedonia. Teirisias was the famous Theban prophet who appears in many plays of Sophocles and Euripides.

7. Agatharchides here follows in the footsteps of Eratosthenes, the great scholar at Alexandria (*c.* 285–*c.* 194 BCE), who had argued that 'every poet strives for amusement, not instruction' (Strabo

1.1.10, C6; 1.23, C15). For Agatharchides' views on this topic see H. Verdin, *Purposes* pp. 1–15.

8.   For the way in which a historian might deal with emotional narratives see Intro. §7. See P. 2.56.13 for a similar demand that emotional narratives need to be accompanied by causes and consequences.

9.   Philip destroyed Olynthus in 348 BCE, Alexander razed Thebes in 335.

10. The incident resonated even many centuries later: see Arrian, *Anabasis* 1.9.1–8 for the reaction to Alexander's destruction of Thebes.

11. For the importance of imitation see Intro. §1.

12. This is first explicitly demanded by Callisthenes, F 44.

13. 'Force' translates *energeian*; an alternate reading has *enargeian*, which would mean 'vividness' (on which see Intro. §10).

14. The great hero of the Theban hegemony: see Cic. *Letters to Friends* 5.12.5 with n. 11.

15. For flattery as the enemy of history see Intro. §6.

16. The word *pathos* ('disaster') can also mean here 'emotion [sc. of the situation]'. For *enargeia*, 'bringing things before the eyes' see Intro. §10.

17. With 'periods' Agatharchides is referring to the rhetorical period, 'a circular construction . . . such that at the beginning of the period incomplete idea elements occur which are in need of integration, and which are only integrated into a complete idea at the end of the period, while the middle parts are embraced and orientated towards the whole by this procedure. The end is thus expected . . . and is in sight' (H. Lausberg, *Handbook of Literary Rhetoric* (Leiden, 1998) p. 414). The sentence thus from its beginning is structured so as to look to a foreseen ending, and this kind of composition is often contrasted with the 'loose' or 'strung-out' style where the clauses simply follow one another without particular direction. For a discussion of periodic composition see L. P. Wilkinson, *Golden Latin Artistry* (Cambridge, 1963) pp. 167–88.

18. Cadmus, the legendary founder of Thebes, was said to have killed a dragon and cast its teeth into the ground, out of which sprang the *Spartoi*, the 'Sown Men'.

19. Demosthenes (384/3–322), famous for his opposition to the Macedonian kings Philip II and Alexander, was held to be the greatest of the Attic orators. See D.H. *Thuc.* 53. This particular item is not found in Demosthenes' surviving works; the orator is alluding to the story that agriculture first appeared in Attica, and the Athenians then shared it with the rest of the world.

20. Hermesianax (third century BCE) wrote amatory poems and possibly a *Persian Matters* (fragments at *FGrHist* 691).

21. The pun is based on the story that Athena had sprung full-grown from the head of Zeus.

22. The next two that follow to the end of this paragraph are assumed by Jacoby to come from Hermesianax; other scholars think they belong to Hegesias.

23. There is a pun here, between 'Cyrus' (*Kourou*) and 'invalid' (*akuron*), which I have tried to give a sense of; the sentence means literally, 'Who could make a gift of Cyrus' invalid?'

24. Again a pun here on 'inviolable' (*abaton*) and 'bramble' (*baton*).

25. Agatharchides goes on to give some examples from the orators Stratocles and Aeschines.

26. This and the previous are clearly inappropriate metaphors.

27. The 'I' here is most likely Agatharchides.

28. According to Photius, Agatharchides then went on to give some examples of good expressions from orators including Demosthenes and Aeschines.

29. Troglodytice (Berenice) is on the eastern coast of Africa on the Red Sea and was an important commercial port (Strabo 16.4.14).

30. On effort in history see Intro. §4.

31. This could refer either to Ptolemy VIII's purge of intellectuals in the 140s BCE or to the year 132 when this same Ptolemy was driven from Egypt by a rebellion of the Greek population in Alexandria: see Burstein (n. 1) p. 16.

32. A reference to the style demanded for history: see Intro. §12.

33. For other endings of histories where the speaker encourages later writers to take up the cause see X. *Hellenica* 7.5.27; Ammianus 31.16.9.

15. POLYBIUS

1. Fundamental on all aspects are K. Ziegler, 'Polybios', *RE* XXI.2 (1952) pp. 1440–578 (in German) and *HCP*. On P.'s life and times see *Polybius* 1–31. On P.'s history and historical methodology, amongst the most important studies are: I. Devroye and L. Kemp, *Over de historische Methode van Polybios* (Brussels, 1956); Pédech (1964), a magisterial work; K.-E. Petzold, *Studien zur Methode des Polybios und zu ihrer historischen Auswertung* (Munich, 1969); K. Meister, *Historische Kritik bei Polybios* (Wiesbaden, 1975); *Polybius* 32–156; Sacks (1981); B. McGing, *Polybius' Histories* (New York

and Oxford, 2010). See also Duff (2003) pp. 56–60; *GH* pp. 113–49; *PRHW* pp. 1–27; J. Davidson, *CCRH* pp. 123–36 and his article cited at Intro. n. 85. There are a number of important articles in *Purposes*, and also in G. Schepens and J. Bollansée, eds., *The Shadow of Polybius* (Leuven, 2005).

2.   Here at the outset P. emphasizes what will be a persistent theme in his history, i.e., the didactic and pragmatic value of history. See also 1.35.6–10, 2.61.6–12.

3.   Much of Greek historiography before P. is lost, and we do not know, therefore, to whom he is referring. Such sentiments as these, at least in this form, are not to be found in H., T. or X., although they are certainly implicit in many of those historians' observations. But P. seems to be envisaging an explicit praise of history as a genre, such as we find later with Diod. 1.1–2.

4.   Although addressing himself primarily to men in public life, P. here expresses the belief that ordinary people benefit from history as well.

5.   The years are 220 to 167 BCE. Just two books later (3.1.4–5) P. explains that he will extend his history down to the year 146 (an epochal year, in which the Romans razed both Corinth and Carthage). On P.'s reasons for this extension see *HCP* vol. 1 pp. 292–7 and *Polybius* pp. 13–31.

6.   The phrase translated here as 'political history' is *pragmatikē historia* (sometimes *pragmatikos tropos*), which means for P. a narrative of events (*pragmata*) as opposed to accounts of genealogies or foundings of cities and colonies (see 9.1.2–4, 12.25e.1). It does not by itself need to mean 'pragmatic' in the English sense, though the adjective can sometimes connote the sense of skilful, shrewd or practical activity: see further *Polybius* pp. 56–8.

7.   The Olympiad, named from the quadrennial games, was a unit of four years. It was useful as a way of showing simultaneous actions in the Greek world by transcending the individual calendars of Greek city-states. The first Olympiad coincides with the traditional date for the establishment of the Olympic games and thus covers the years 776–772 (i.e., summer 776 to spring 772); the 140th Olympiad comprises summer 220 to spring 216 BCE. See further P. Christesen, *Olympic Victor Lists and Ancient Greek History* (New York and Cambridge, 2007) pp. 8–15.

8.   The Social War was fought from 223 to 217, pitting a coalition of Greek states under the Macedonian king Philip V against the Aetolian League (P. treats it in Books 4 and 5); the war between

Antiochus and Philopater is the Fourth Syrian War (221–217), one of a series fought between the Ptolemies and Seleucids for possession of southern Syria; the Hannibalic War is the Second Punic War (218–202) fought by the Romans against Hannibal. 'Most people' here probably means the Greeks, since they tended to write the war from the Carthaginian point of view; we know the names of a few of them: Silenus of Caleacte, Sosylus of Lacedaemon, Chaereas and Eumachus of Naples (*FGrHist* 175–8 respectively), but only the merest of fragments survive from these works. Cf. below, n. 56.

9. Aratus of Sicyon (271–213 BCE) was an important general for the Achaean League; a *Life* of him by Pl. survives. See further F. W. Walbank, *Aratos of Sicyon* (Cambridge, 1933). Aratus' treatise, his *Hypomnēmata* (usually translated *Memoirs*) was more than thirty books in length; for the fragments see *FGrHist* 231, and, with English translation and updated bibliography, *BNJ* 231 (H. Beck). It was common in antiquity to join one's work to that of a respected predecessor: see Intro. §2.

10. For 'organic' P. says literally 'body-like' (*somatoeidēs*), and the sense is 'like an organic whole': cf. below, 1.4.7–9, where P. compares his universalizing history to a living, as opposed to a dismembered, creature; cf. Cic. *Letters to Friends* 5.12.4; for the motif of weaving, see below, 3.32.2, and *SP* pp. 313–24. The notion that it tends 'towards one end' (mentioned also below at 1.4.1) may be a tacit allusion to Aristotle's *Poetics* chapter 23.

11. The first Roman incursion into Asia occurred in 191 BCE.

12. 'Fortune' here translates *tychē*, a word that also covers the English 'chance' or 'fate' either good or bad; it is an important concept in P. who views it sometimes as an impersonal force, sometimes (as here) as a force directing history (see especially 1.4.5, below). From the fourth century onwards, there is evidence that she was worshipped as a goddess with cult activities and sacrifices. For *tychē* in P. see *Polybius* pp. 58–65; Walbank, *CGRH* pp. 349–55.

13. Fortune is here presented almost as a theatrical producer putting on a show; see *HCP* vol. 1 p. 4. The term 'show-piece' (*agōnisma*) is used elsewhere by P. at 3.31.12, where its meaning is closer to that of T. 1.22.4.

14. See P. 12.25e.7 for another comparison of paintings with history.

15. For additional praises of universal history and condemnations of individual histories, 3.31.1–32.10, 5.33.1–8, 7.7.6, 8.2.1–11, 9.44.2, 12.23.7, 12.25g.3, 16.14.1 and 29.12.1–12; for utility and pleasure in history, Intro. §7.

16. Philinus (*FGrHist* 174) of Acragas in Sicily was probably a contem-
     porary of the events and wrote an account of the war in Greek; its
     title and length are unknown and only five fragments survive;
     Quintus Fabius Pictor was active in the late third century; he was
     sent as an envoy to Delphi by the Romans in the aftermath of
     their tremendous defeat at Cannae in 216 (Livy 22.57.5). The first
     Roman historian, he wrote a history in Greek (there was also a
     Latin version, but its relationship to the Greek version is unclear)
     that went from the city's founding to his own times: fragments,
     with translation and commentary, at *FRHist* 1 (E. H. Bispham,
     T. J. Cornell).

17. Deliberate vs. accidental lying is a theme that permeates P.'s discus-
     sion of the writing of history. See 12.5, 12.7.6, 12.11.4, 12.12.4–6,
     12.25a.2, 16.14.7–8, 16.20.8–9 and 29.12.12; discussion in Luce,
     ORGRH pp. 291–313; *ATAH* p. 222.

18. Cf. 16.14.6 where P. takes this up in connection with Zeno of
     Rhodes, but there he seems to suggest that partisanship is some-
     what acceptable.

19. For impartiality see Intro. §6; P. stresses it repeatedly: 2.56.2,
     2.56.12, 3.47.6, 8.8.5–9, 10.21.8, 12.7.3–6, 12.11.8, 12.27–8.

20. See 12.12.3 for a repetition of the sentiment; for P.'s insistence on
     truth and impartiality as indispensable elements of history, see also
     2.56.2, 2.56.12, 3.47.6, 8.8.5–9, 10.21.8, 12.7.3–6, 12.11.8, 12.12.3,
     12.27–8, 34.4, 38.4.5.

21. This is a consistent refrain amongst not only ancient historians but
     also the majority of Greek and Roman writers.

22. From a lost play, the *Antiope*: see *TrGF* F 200, where the lines are
     quoted in a fuller version.

23. See P. 1.1.2 for the sentiment; likewise Diod. 1.1.1–2.

24. On 'political' history, above, n. 6.

25. On the importance of this passage see Intro. §7.

26. Phylarchus was from Athens or Naucratis, and was active in the
     third century BCE. His history, in twenty-eight books, began with
     Pyrrhus' invasion of the Peloponnese in 272 and ended with the
     death of Cleomenes III of Sparta in 221. Other writers as well,
     including Pl., fault him for dramatic exaggeration. About sixty
     fragments of his work survive: see *FGrHist* 81. For discussion of his
     life and historical work (the latter inevitably treated through P.'s
     lens) see T. W. Africa, *Phylarchus and the Spartan Revolution*
     (Berkeley, 1961), and for a recent treatment, A. Eckstein, 'Polybius,
     Phylarchus, and Historiographical Criticism', *CPh* 108 (2013) pp.
     314–38.

27. This refers to the Spartan king Cleomenes' aggressive campaigns in the Peloponnese in the 220s; he was opposed by Aratus and the Achaean League, and Aratus eventually called in the Macedonian king Antigonus to assist in defeating Cleomenes, which he did in 223. Aratus' action was long remembered as having given Macedon an opening for becoming involved in the affairs of Greece.

28. P.'s language here echoes T. 1.22.2.

29. For vivid narration in a history, see Intro. §12.

30. Ignoble because that is not how one should bear sufferings: see 1.1.2 for history teaching noble endurance; 'womanish' because marked by love of the marvellous and excessive emotional display: cf. 12.24.4 on Timaeus.

31. For P.'s demands about proper speech-writing in history see 12. 25a–b, 12.25i.4–26d.6 and 36.1.1–7.

32. P. here makes the case for history against tragedy; he employs many of the terms Aristotle uses in the Poetics (above, p. 28), but he changes the context and in so doing asserts the superiority of history, based as it is on real events, to tragedy, which for P. is inferior because it portrays invented events and fictitious people.

33. See Agatharchides, On the Red Sea 5.21 on the need to provide reasons for emotional accounts.

34. It was not uncommon at the sack of a city to kill the adult men and sell the women and children into slavery.

35. For criticism of sensationalism in history see also 2.58.12, 2.59.3, 3.47.6–9, 3.48.8–12, 7.7.1–8, 12.24.5, 15.34.1–36.11, 16.12, 16.18.2 and 29.12.

36. An 'improbable lie' represents a particularly embarrassing low point, since it suggests that the author lacked the ability even to come up with a plausible invented scenario.

37. Aristomachus took over the tyranny of Argos after his brother's death in 235, supported by the troops of Demetrius II of Macedon. After Demetrius' death in 229, Aratus offered him a large sum of money to disband his army and join the Achaean League which he did in 229, at which point he joined Argos to the Achaean League. Initially entrusted with action against Sparta for the League, he was removed from command and eventually took Cleomenes' side, allowing him to take Argos. P. is strongly biased against Aristomachus and is basing his account here on the hostile narrative that would have been in Aratus' Memoirs.

38. For additional criticisms of exaggeration in history see 7.7.1–8.

39. See 12.15.9 for another place where P. likewise demands that history record noble actions as well as base ones.

40. Cleomenes captured Megalopolis in 223; some of the citizens escaped to Messene and it is these Megalopolitans to whom P. refers here.

41. For one of history's functions as the incitement to emulate noble deeds, see Intro. §7.

42. The targets here are unknown; see below, n. 56.

43. Saguntum in Spain was besieged by Hannibal in 219 BCE. The city was almost certainly not a formal ally of Rome's, but the circumstances surrounding its status are unclear, not least because Hannibal's action against it, as we can see here, became one of the actions related to the beginnings of the Second Punic War and was used by the Romans as a justification to begin hostilities against the Carthaginians. The treaty concerning the Ebro (modern Ebre) river is given by P. at 2.13.7 and it stated that the Carthaginians were not to cross the Ebro with the intent of making war. Saguntum was on the Carthaginian side of the river.

44. Alexander the Great crossed over to Asia in 334, marking the start of his war against Persia; the Aetolians summoned King Antiochus III of Syria to assist them in Greece, and he crossed from Asia to Demetrias in Thessaly in 192; the action precipitated war with Rome.

45. P. is fond of comparisons of medicine with history: see 12.25d.

46. See 3.32.6–7 (next passage), 12.25i.9 and 22.18.6–7 for brief restatements of the importance of a knowledge of causes.

47. See n. 12 for P.'s focus on chance and reversals.

48. A rare acknowledgement of the difficulties of knowing the true intentions or purposes of men in public life; for the more usual recognition of the difficulties of knowing what is transpiring amongst those in power, see Cassius Dio 53.19.2–4.

49. This is the clearest allusion in the surviving text of P. to T.'s methodological statement at 1.22.4. See 38.4.8 for a similar sentiment.

50. P. reverts here to the image of weaving that he used for his universal history in 1.3.4.

51. A reference to where Timaeus' history ended.

52. That is, from 222 to 146; the latter date is that of the Roman destruction of Corinth.

53. Diod. 1.3.8 uses a similar argument but in a different context.

54. P. echoes here his beliefs about the desirability of universal history and its appropriateness for his own times: see 1.3.3–4, 1.4.1–11. The wars (in reverse order, as P. gives them here) are: First Syrian War, 192–188; Second Macedonian War, 200–197; Second Punic War, 218–202; First Punic War, 264–241. Cf. n. 10 above.

55. The difference between hearsay and eyewitness is a frequent feature of historiographical criticism: see Intro. §3. See also P. 3.48.12.

56. It is not certain to whom P. is referring here. Hannibal had at least two historians with him: Sosylus of Lacedaemon, who wrote a work *On Hannibal* in seven books (*FGrHist* 176 T 2), and Chaereas, both of whom published works on his campaigns. P. elsewhere criticized their work as 'having the disposition and quality not of history but of a barber's gossip and vulgar chatter' (3.20.5). P. may also be thinking of Silenus of Caleacte, in whose history a god appears to Hannibal in a dream and reveals to him the future destruction of Italy (*FGrHist* 175 F 2); the Latin historian Coelius Antipater followed Silenus and likewise recounted the dream: see *FRHist* 15 F 8.

57. For P.'s opposition to startling the reader and to marvels see 2.56. 10–13.

58. For contradiction as the mark of falsehood, see P. 8.9 on Theopompus' portrait of Philip.

59. P. refers here to the mechanical crane used in Greek drama by which a god or hero was raised above the stage; in several surviving plays (see Euripides' *Heracles* for an especially good example) the god appears and resolves the issues in the play that have become deadlocked; and he or she often gives orders to the characters and/ or makes predictions about their futures. For an earlier reference to tragedy and history see 2.56.10–11.

60. I.e., the hopes of defeating the Romans; the Alpine tribes, like Hannibal, were hostile to the Romans.

61. It is not known exactly when P. made his crossing of the Alps, but possibly in 150 when returning from Spain; see *HCP* vol. 1 p. 382.

62. The objects of P.'s attack here are unknown.

63. On Ephorus see above, p. 25; P. has more to say of him below at 12.25f.

64. Three or four columns of a papyrus role would comprise only a few pages of a printed text. Cf. L. *Hist.* 30.

65. The war for Sicily is the First Punic War (264–241 BCE).

66. This is extremely obscure: see *HCP* vol. 1 pp. 563–4, where Walbank, following Jacoby (1949) p. 356 n. 20, thinks that the words 'in chronological records' may originally have been an explanatory note in the margins which has crept into the text. In any case, it is clear that these 'memoranda' are merely short notices of events and could not be called 'history', much less 'universal history'.

67. Hieronymus, the son of Gelon, became king at Syracuse in 215 when he was only fifteen years old. For his tyrannical conduct, which led to his assassination, see Livy 24.4–7 (probably based on

the lost portions of P.'s history). The writers P. is thinking of here may include Baton of Sinope (*FGrHist* 268) and Eumachus (*FGrHist* 178 F 1).

68. For P.'s dislike of sensationalism in history, see above, n. 35.

69. These are tyrants famous for their cruelty (see Seneca, *On Anger* 2.5.1 where the two are joined as here). Phalaris ruled Agrigentum in Sicily *c.* 571–555 and was famous for his construction of a bronze bull in which he roasted alive his enemies (see P. 12.25.1–5), while Apollodorus was a popular leader in Cassandreia who seized power probably in 279 and ruled with the help of Galatian (i.e., Celtic) mercenaries.

70. For universal history, above, 1.4; similar remarks at 12.23.7, 29.12.4–5.

71. Hiero II was born in 306 BCE, seized power in Syracuse in 275/4 and adopted the title of 'king' in 269. Originally an ally of the Carthaginians in the lead-up to the First Punic War, he quickly changed sides and remained a loyal ally to Rome until his death in 215. He is fondly remembered in the Roman tradition, and P. thinks of him as an excellent example of a 'pragmatic' ruler: see 1.8.3–9.8. His son Gelon was made co-regent with his father but died a year before his father.

72. See 1.3.3–4; 1.4.11; cf. 3.32.

73. It seems odd that P. should ascribe to Fortune (on which see above, n. 12) a 'form of constitution'; presumably he is using Fortune's deed here as a synonym for Roman success, and the constitution is clearly the Romans': see below at §7.

74. See 1.1.5.

75. See 1.4.1–11, 3.31.1–32.10 for the notion that true understanding and knowledge can come only from universal history.

76. The reference is to Philip V's attack on Messenia in 213 BCE.

77. The reference is to 7.11–14, where P. talks of the change in Philip's character and the importance for a king to surround himself with good counsellors.

78. For the influence of favour and fear in the writing of history see Intro. §6.

79. On the differences between history and encomium, see Intro. §6; see also 10.21.7–8; L. *Hist.* 7–13, where there is extensive treatment of the theme.

80. For Theopompus of Chios, see above, p. 32.

81. *FGrHist* 115 F 27.

82. *FGrHist* 115 F 225, where Athenaeus' (slightly different) version can also be found.

83. The term here, *lastauros*, is somewhat obscure but I follow the interpretation of T. K. Hubbard, in id., ed., *Homosexuality in Greece and Rome* (Berkeley and Los Angeles, 2003), who sees the word as a strengthened form of *stauros*, 'an upright stake used especially for impalement', and which here 'seems to be a metaphorical term for those characterized by habitual sexual excess' (p. 74). It would have been a vulgar, or at the very least, a colloquial word, in keeping with what P. says here about Theopompus' language, and so I have used the term 'stud' to try to get across the dual meaning.

84. Homoerotic desire in Greece was most often directed towards young men just before or around the time of puberty; Theopompus says here literally that 'they fornicated with men who were bearded', and thus were engaging in an activity that ought to have been abandoned long before.

85. There are a series of puns here, including the last which plays on *androphonoi* vs. *andropornoi*; this particular phrase was criticized by the later literary critic Demetrius (*On Style* 5.247 = *FGrHist* 115 T 44), who found its artificiality pretentious and frigid. These lines smack too of the punning found in Hegesias and criticized by Agatharchides, *On the Red Sea* 5.21.

86. The centaurs, known from Homer onwards, were half-man and half-horse, and stories of their conflicts with the Lapiths of Thessaly were especially popular with artists (they figure on the Parthenon frieze, amongst other places) and were often interpreted as struggles between civilization and barbarism. The Laestrygonians were a mythical race of giants (later localized in Sicily: see T. 6.2.1) who in the *Odyssey* (10.77–132) destroy all Odysseus' ships and men except his own.

87. On bitterness as a cause for the distortion of history see also 12.4a. 1–4d.8, 12.7.1, 12.15.1–10, 12.23.1, 12.25.5–6, 12.25c.

88. For similar strictures against using harsh language, see P. 12.8.4–6; Pl. *Malice* 2.

89. King of Nineveh in Assyria, he was famous for his wealth and lifestyle: see H. 2.150 (his treasures), and, for the fullest account where he can be seen to be a type for effeminate and luxurious behaviour, Diod. 2.23–5 (most likely based on Ctesias); the Greek form of the name is a transliteration or adaptation of Ashurbanipal, king of Assyria 668–627, but the portrait found in Greek writers is wholly invented.

90. Diod. 2.23.3 gives a longer version, Athenaeus 8.336A a slightly different one; Cic. translated the lines into Latin (*Tusculan Disputations* 5.101), saying that he found them in Aristotle.

91.   P. refers here to the struggles of Alexander's successors after his
       death, both those of the first generation (called the Diadochs, i.e.,
       the receivers) and those of the second and later generations (the
       Epigoni, i.e., the descendants).

92.   For more on Agathocles, see P. 12.12b.1–15.12; for Timaeus and
       Agathocles, above, p. 35.

93.   Cf. Tacitus *Histories* 1.1.4, for the notion that criticism suggests
       reliability.

94.   Theopompus' *Hellenica* ended in 394, twenty-three years before
       the battle of Leuctra; in that battle the Thebans for the first time
       soundly defeated the Lacedaemonians, an event that heralded the
       end of Spartan power in Greece; it is not surprising that P., an
       inveterate opponent of Sparta, and a citizen himself of Megalopolis
       (which was founded by the Thebans in the aftermath of Leuctra),
       would think of these events as 'the most renowned of Greek
       accomplishments'.

95.   For individual-centred history see Intro. §2.

96.   The suggestion is that by writing for a king Theopompus would
       have won material advantage for himself; the notion is a popular
       one: see Intro. §6.

97.   *FGrHist* 70 T 18b; Jacoby thinks it comes from Ephorus' preface;
       for Ephorus, see above, p. 25.

98.   For 'pragmatic' history see above, n. 6; cf. Intro. §2.

99.   This explanation of P.'s preference must have been in one of the lost
       sections of his history; but cf. 1.1.1–5 and 3.31 for mention of polit-
       ical history and its benefits.

100.   For the contrast between utility and pleasure see Intro. §7.

101.   Philopoemen (253–182 BCE), cavalry-commander and eight-time
       general of the Achaean League, was devoted to increasing the power
       of the Achaean League, and this brought him into conflict first with
       other powers in Greece and eventually with Rome. His staunch anti-
       Roman programme sharply divided the League, since others (but not
       P.) desired a more accommodating position. He was captured in 182
       in a campaign against Messene, was taken prisoner, and eventually
       died, possibly by poisoning. Pl.'s *Life* of him, probably highly
       dependent on P.'s biography, survives; for modern studies see espe-
       cially R. M. Errington, *Philopoemen* (Oxford, 1969).

102.   For the fragments of P.'s biography of Philopoemen, see *FGrHist*
       173 and, with English translation and updated bibliography, *BNJ*
       173 (F. Pownall).

103.   On biography see A. Momigliano, *The Development of Greek
       Biography* (Cambridge, Mass., 1971; expanded edition 1993); on

the relationship between history and biography see P. A. Stadter, *CGRH* pp. 528–40. On the divide between encomium and history see L. *Hist.* 7 and Intro. §6. For a different suggestion on where history and biography differ see Pl. *Life of Alexander* 1.1–3.

104. The Table of Contents (*prographē*) referred to here was a list attached to the end of a scroll or inside the scroll preceding the text, which gave a capsule summary of the events to be found in that book. Although none of those that P. refers to in 11.1a.5 survives, we do have examples from some of the books of Diod.'s history: for example, at the beginning of Book 17, his account of Alexander, we find: 'How Alexander, having succeeded to the throne, disposed the affairs of his kingdom. How he recovered the tribes which revolted. How he razed Thebes to the ground and terrified the Greeks and was elected plenipotentiary general of Greece', etc.

105. Interestingly enough, P. here ascribes to the mere table of contents what other writers ascribe to the fully developed (i.e., rhetorically amplified) preface of a work, which was considered to have three functions: to make the audience receptive, well disposed and attentive (Pseudo-Aristotle, *Rhetoric to Alexander* 29; Pseudo-Cic., *Rhetoric to Herennius* 1.7).

106. As noted previously, none of P.'s tables of contents survive.

107. Here begins Book 12, which was devoted virtually in its entirety to attacking Timaeus of Tauromenium, on whom see above, p. 35. For the structure of the book, G. Schepens, *Purposes* pp. 39–61.

108. *FGrHist* 566 F 3; some of Timaeus' account of Corsica remains in Diod. 5.13–14.

109. P. introduces a theme here that he will cover more fully below, 12. 9–11 and 12.27–28a.

110. *FGrHist* 115 F 341. The events referred to occurred in 344 when Dionysius the younger had surrendered Syracuse to Timoleon in 344, and was then brought back to Corinth; see Diod. 16.70.3 for the journey.

111. The elder Dionysius was born around 431/0 and died in 368/7, although there is some dispute about the chronology of the events in his life.

112. Proverbial dullards, joined together also by L. on several occasions; Margites was the subject of a mock epic ascribed to Homer.

113. This is Timaeus' separate work on Pyrrhus: see above, p. 35.

114. The Romans did have a horse race each October in which one of the horses of the winning chariot was sacrificed to Mars but nothing connects this with the Trojan horse or the fall of Troy.

115. The importance of personal inquiry and presence at events is developed below, 12.27–28a. This summary remark is echoed by L. *Hist.* 47.

116. Errors about one's own land would be particularly embarrassing since it was usually thought that the natives were the most reliable sources for their own history; cf. T. 1.20.1 with n. 9.

117. The spring Arethusa is on the north side of the island of Ortygia at Syracuse; the notion that its waters flowed underground from the Peloponnese is found in a number of early authors including Ibycus (*PMG* 321) and Pindar (*Nemean Odes* 1.1).

118. A stade was approximately 600 feet, though its exact length is uncertain; so the distance here is *c*. 450 miles; the actual distance is *c*. 330 miles. The Sicilian Sea is the Ionian Sea.

119. *FGrHist* 566 F 41b.

120. P. now begins a long refutation of Timaeus. Locris is located in central Greece but is actually three areas, the Epicnemidian Locrians inhabiting the north-eastern areas, the Opuntian Locrians the south-eastern, and the Ozolian Locrians to the west, separated from the eastern Locrians by the areas of Doris and Phocis. The Epizephyrian ('western') Locrians were a colony in the toe of south Italy, and the settlement had been founded in the seventh century BCE by the Opuntian Locrians. The discussion that follows concerns what relationship the city in Italy had to the Locrians in Greece, in particular the circumstances surrounding the colony's foundation. For Timaeus' arguments see *HCP* vol. 2 pp. 330–31. P. in general eschews writing about earlier history, including foundations and colonies (see 9.2.1–3) but here the desire to refute Timaeus has overcome his reluctance.

121. P.'s services to the Locrians would have occurred around 156/5 BCE (the date of the Dalmatian campaign) and he was probably able to assist them by using his influence with Scipio Aemilianus: *HCP* vol. 2 p. 331.

122. P. here invokes the usual reasons why a historian would offer praise, e.g., because of benefits received: see Intro. §6.

123. Aristotle probably treated the Locrians in his collection of the various constitutions made by himself and the members of his school (only one of which, that on the Athenians, survives).

124. Presumably P. means that these arguments were raised with him in his discussions with the Epizephyrian Locrians, not that they were present in Aristotle's account.

125. P. is referring to an oracle given to the Locrians requiring them (in atonement for the rape of Cassandra at Troy by Ajax, son of Oileus)

to send two maidens chosen by lot to Troy each year for a thousand years; the women once there could be killed with impunity by any Trojan man; in historical times the Locrians sent two maidens annually to serve in Athena's temple at Ilium.

126. 'Sicels' was the term used by the Greeks to denote the native populations of Sicily whom they encountered when they colonized the island; the Sicels were assumed to have recently arrived from Italy, which explains their presence in the story of Epizephyrian Locri's foundation. Not surprisingly, there were numerous hostilities between Greeks and Sicels over the centuries.

127. Similar tricks can be found elsewhere, including colonial foundations at Metapontum and Tarentum (Strabo 6.265), and Callipolis (D.H. *Rom. Ant.* 19.3).

128. This passage, though not following directly from what has gone before, is printed here in texts of P. because it must be part of P.'s refutation of Timaeus and his defence of Aristotle. Texts of P. print alongside this paragraph the similar testimonium from Athenaeus which reads, 'Timaeus of Tauromenium, forgetting himself (Polybius of Megalopolis refutes him on this in the twelfth book of his histories), says that it was not the custom amongst Greeks to possess slaves.' *HCP* vol. 2 pp. 337–8 has further information on P.'s arguments on this topic.

129. In autumn 426, during the Peloponnesian War, the Athenian general Laches attacked Locris, a staunch ally of the Peloponnesians; see T. 3.103.3 for the campaign.

130. A famous story: the Spartans had bound themselves not to return home until they had captured Messenia; in the tenth year of the war they allowed the young men who had not sworn the oath to return to Sparta to father children by the unmarried women; see Strabo 6.279; Diod. 15.66.3; Athenaeus, *Learned Banqueters* 6.271C–D.

131. Sparta certainly differed in her customs from other Greek citystates, but this passage of P. is the only evidence of Spartan polyandry.

132. See Pl. *Malice* 2 and L. *Hist.* 59 for similar strictures against excessive abuse.

133. On deliberate vs. accidental falsehood, see above, n. 17.

134. For favour and enmity as reasons for historians' false accounts, see Intro. §6.

135. P. actually discusses the battle mentioned here, at which Alexander defeated the Persian king, below, 12.17.2–22.7; why Timaeus chose this battle is unknown, but the point is that Aristotle seems to

speak with the assuredness of an eyewitness and participant. Aristotle's father was a surgeon and the remark is a slight at Aristotle's social standing, suggesting that he had become a philosopher only after abandoning a mercantile career; the abuse is uttered by a number of people in antiquity. The evidence is surveyed by I. Düring, *Aristotle in the Ancient Biographical Tradition* (Göteborg, 1957). The term *sophistēs* originally meant something like 'wise man', but came to have a pejorative sense during the fifth-century enlightenment when itinerant teachers claimed to be able to teach the young important skills for public life, including clever speaking. They are satirized in Aristophanes and condemned in Plato. See further W. K. C. Guthrie, *History of Greek Philosophy* III (Cambridge, 1969) pp. 3–319.

136. See P.'s comments above, 8.10.1–3 on inappropriate language and below, 12.14.1–4 on appropriate 'retaliation'. The courts Aristotle is supposed to have frequented were those of Themison of Cyprus, Hermias of Atarneus and Philip II of Macedon. We do not know of any generals whose tents he frequented but the point again must be that he flattered those in power.

137. See above, n. 120; the two Locri, western and eastern.

138. We are not certain who this Echecrates is; it has been suggested that he was a Pythagorean (mentioned by Diogenes Laertius 8.46) and the recipient of Phaedo's account of Socrates' death (Plato, *Phaedo* 57a); further details at *HCP* vol. 2 p. 346. Echecrates' father is mentioned as an ambassador by Timaeus so as to indicate the high social status (and thus presumed reliability) of his source; on social status as a mark of authority see *ATAH* pp. 141–7.

139. The groups mentioned here were used in a variety of chronographical works, the synchronism being necessary since each Greek city-state maintained its own calendar (with different year-beginnings). For Timaeus' interest in chronology see above, p. 35.

140. It is not known where Theophrastus would have discussed this matter, although he did write extensively on laws, customs and constitutions; see *HCP* vol. 2 p. 330 for some suggestions.

141. P. means that he did not wish to have digressions throughout his work arguing against this or that point in Timaeus; at 12.7.1 he accuses Timaeus of just such neglect of duty.

142. On truth as essential to history, Intro. §5.

143. See 1.14.6; P. is not being deliberately vague in using the words 'somewhere in my work'; ancient books were written on scrolls which did not have page numbers, and consultation of them was a

much more difficult matter than for a modern printed book, let alone for an electronic book.

144. See above, n. 17.

145. In the proverb some word such as 'transgressed' or 'betrayed' is elided. This passage on the Locrians and their agreements was, as Walbank suggests (*HCP* vol. 2 p. 351), possibly part of Timaeus' defence of the Italian Locrians. The origin of the proverb was debated even in antiquity.

146. The return of the descendants of Heracles (the Heracleidae) to the Peloponnese to reclaim the land of their fathers from those who had expelled Heracles was the founding myth of the Spartan state and the basis for its claim to rule the Peloponnese. Rhion is either the promontory in Achaea on the Corinthian Gulf or the straits by that name, which are where Rhion faces Anti-Rhion across the water in Aetolia. The Isthmus is the Isthmus of Corinth.

147. The opening of this passage is missing some words.

148. For Callisthenes see above, p. 33. The reference to the ravens concerns Alexander's visit to the oracle of Ammon, where two ravens were said to have indicated the proper route when Alexander got lost (*FGrHist* 124 F 14); the raving women are not mentioned in any surviving fragments of Callisthenes; the reference may be to Athenais of Erythrae, a woman who testified to Alexander's divine birth, or to some other prophetess.

149. Sometime after the death of his companion Hephaestion in autumn 324, Alexander sent back a request to the Greek cities that they set up divine honours for him and also for himself as the son of Zeus (though the exact nature of the request for himself is somewhat uncertain); this provoked the opposition of Demosthenes and others, and Timaeus clearly praised such men as being above flattery of the powerful, unlike Callisthenes (who is called a 'philosopher' because he is Aristotle's nephew). For Demosthenes see Agatharchides n. 19.

150. Born around 350 BCE, Demochares was Demosthenes' nephew; he maintained Demosthenes' policy of political independence for Athens from strongmen and kings, and was famous for his freedom of speech (Seneca, *On Anger* 3.23.2); he also wrote histories of at least twenty-one books, though little is known of these; fragments and testimonia at *FGrHist* 75. Cic. says they were written 'not so much as history but as oratory' (*Brutus* 286).

151. Botrys was said to be from Messana and is perhaps to be dated to the fifth century BCE, while there are several references to Philaenis as being from Leucas or Samos; her date is unknown.

152. Archedicus, as we learn below; he was obviously a contemporary of Demochares', but little else is known of him: see *PCG* vol. 2 pp. 533–6.

153. Antipater was left behind in Macedonia as Alexander's regent and general for Europe, his mission to keep peace in the Greek city-states while Alexander was away in Persia. Demetrius of Phalerum (a township in Attica) was a statesman and pupil of Theophrastus. He ruled Athens from 317 to 307 BCE, having been installed by the Macedonian general Cassander to keep Athens from causing trouble to Macedon. He wrote on a wide variety of topics, including rhetoric (fragments at F. Wehrli, *Die Schule des Aristoteles IV*, 2nd edn (Basel, 1968) pp. 34–7). See C. Habicht, *Athens from Alexander to Antony* (Cambridge, Mass., 1997) pp. 37–47 for the former, pp. 53–66 for the latter.

154. *FGrHist* 75 F 4.

155. A similar demand for this kind of propriety by the historian is made by Pl. *Malice* 2.

156. For Timaeus' hatred of Agathocles see above, p. 35, and P. 8.10.12.

157. *FGrHist* 566 F 124b.

158. P. remarks on this again at 15.35.2; Diod. 20.63.4 mentions Agathocles' work as a potter.

159. See the similar remarks made about narrating good and bad at 2.61.3.

160. The words in angled brackets are supplements by Büttner-Wobst; for the historian's responsibility to offer both praise and blame see 1.14.4–5; for his obligation not to conceal anything that is pertinent to the subject, Cic. *On the Orator* 2.62; Pl. *Malice* 4.

161. The criticism of Callisthenes in these chapters was probably a digression from P.'s larger criticism of Timaeus, though its exact relationship cannot now be determined. The arguments are likely to strike one as arid and forced, and Walbank has aptly noted that 'the criticism of Callisthenes shows P. at his worst ... His points are almost all trivial or fallacious ... and his mathematical calculations are marred by egregious errors of logical reasoning' (*HCP* vol. 2 p. 364). In the summation to this section (22.7) P. mentions a treatment of Ephorus as well but this does not survive; for remarks about Ephorus' battle narratives see below, 12.25f.1–5.

162. *FGrHist* 124 F 35. P. is referring to the battle of Issus, fought in November 333; Callisthenes' account does not survive; for accounts of the battle see Arrian, *Anabasis* 2.6–12; Diod. 17.32.4–37; Curtius 3.7–11 and Pl. *Alexander* 20.1–5.

163. For the length of a stade see above, n. 118.

164. The Macedonian sarissa was a spear or pike some four to six metres long; P. here notes that such a weapon would have necessitated even greater space than for the traditional hoplite spear which was about two metres long.

165. Homer, *Iliad* 13.131.

166. In the lacuna was probably something on the order of 'and of these same fourteen stades the cavalry occupied nearly three, half of it placed alongside the sea, half on the right' (*HCP* vol. 2 pp. 374–5).

167. The reference is to 12.12b.2 above, where Timaeus said that Callisthenes received a just punishment from Alexander for his flattery.

168. During the tyranny of the younger Dionysius, the opposition party asked for help from Corinth, its mother-city (Syracuse had been founded by Corinthian colonists *c*. 733 BCE); they sent Timoleon, who quickly defeated Dionysius and had him sent back to Corinth as a political hostage (see above, 12.4a.2, on the boat which brought him there); Diod.'s praise of Timoleon (16.82–3) may go back to Timaeus, who is also an important source for Pl.'s *Life of Timoleon*.

169. For the importance of the subject matter of a history and its reflection on the historian's own greatness, see Intro. §2.

170. For the accusations against the elder Dionysius' luxury see *FGrHist* 566 F 40 with Jacoby's commentary.

171. See *FGrHist* 566 FF 29, 43, 46, 84–90 and 95 for dreams and marvels in Timaeus' history; at 2.56.9 P. accuses Phylarchus of having a 'womanish' disposition.

172. For further development of this argument see below, 12.28a.10, where P. suggests that one needs experience to understand what one sees.

173. For Phalaris and the bull see above, n. 69.

174. There are contradictory testimonia about what Timaeus actually said concerning the bull; we are also told that Timaeus said the bull was sunk in the sea by the people of Acragas after Phalaris' death (*FGrHist* 566 F 28(c)); for recent discussions of the issue see two articles by G. Schepens, 'Polybius on Timaeus' Account of Phalaris' Bull: A Case of *Deisidaimonia*', *Ancient Society* 9 (1978) pp. 117–48, and 'Timaeus *FGrHist* 566 F 28 Revisited: Fragmenta or Testimonia?', *Simblos* 2 (1997) pp. 71–84.

175. P. uses the term 'disposition' here in a similar way to D.H. *Pomp.* 3.15.

176. Diod. mentions two speeches of Timoleon's to his troops (16.78.2, 16.79.2) which may be based on Timaeus. Since the ancients

usually divided the known world into three continents (as Timoleon does here), the point of P.'s criticism is probably not the content of the speech, but the fact that Timoleon's remarks are unsuitable for someone addressing soldiers. For Margites, see above, n. 112.

177. The text breaks off here.

178. For P.'s views on speeches in history see the fuller discussion below, P. 12.25i.4–9 with notes there. When P. says 'in his addresses to the people', he does not mean Timaeus' own addresses but the ones that he gives his characters; ancient critics sometimes ascribe the views of speakers in historical texts to the authors themselves: see Pl. *Malice* 15, an extreme (but not isolated) example.

179. See above, 2.56.10 for such a procedure as being characteristic of tragedy.

180. An echo of what he has said elsewhere: see 3.31.11–12; on the importance of causes, 3.6.1–7, 3.7.4–7; for similar thoughts, Sempronius Asellio, FF 1–2.

181. See 1.1.2 for the benefits of history. The thought goes back to T. 1.22, but T. promises knowledge from history, not necessarily improvement of one's own life or assistance in avoiding mistakes in the future.

182. On Timaeus' later reputation see the testimonia assembled at *FGrHist* 566 TT 11–23.

183. Strato of Lampsacus (*c.* 335–*c.* 269 BCE) became head of the Peripatos after Theophrastus' death: see Diogenes Laertius 5.58–64.

184. See 12.25h.1 and n. 198.

185. The traditional division of medicine was diet, drugs and surgery; P. compresses the latter two into one and introduces the theoretical group, who will provide the comparison with Timaeus (see 25e).

186. Herophilus of Chalcedon lived in the early third century BCE and is one of the two great names in Hellenistic medicine (the other, Erasistratus of Ceos, is not mentioned by P.); his students were numerous and famous. Callimachus' date is uncertain; he was a doctor in Herophilus' school. For both men see H. von Staden, *Herophilus: The Art of Medicine in Early Alexandria* (Cambridge, 1989) pp. 445–71 and 480–83 respectively.

187. There are echoes here of Plato's criticism of fine speakers able to defeat actual experts: see, e.g., *Gorgias* 458e3–459c5.

188. No such division occurs in earlier writings about history and P. is trying here to argue his own view on the importance of real-life experience for historians.

189. For history's esteem see Diod. 1.1.1, 1.3.1; Pliny, *Letters* 5.8.4.

190. On Ephorus, see above, p. 25.

191. *FGrHist* 70 T 20. The first battle took place in 391/0 and ended in Persian victory (see Diod. 14.98, 15.2–4 and 8–9; X. *Hellenica* 4.8.24); the famous battle of Cnidus, which put an end to Spartan supremacy after the Peloponnesian War, took place in 394; the Persians and the Athenians, with Conon as commander, defeated the Peloponnesian forces under Peisagoras (*Hellenica* 4.3.11–12; Diod. 14.83.4–7).

192. The battle of Leuctra was fought in 371; Spartan forces were defeated by the Thebans under Epaminondas and in its wake the Thebans established the city of Megalopolis (P.'s home town) as a refuge for the Messenians; the battle marks the beginning of the end of Spartan power: see X. *Hellennica* 6.4.3–15; Diod. 15.52–6). Mantinea, the battle with which X. ended his *Hellenica* (7.5.1–17; cf. Diod. 15.82.1–84.2) was fought in 362 and marked the end of Theban dominance; for Epaminondas' death see Cic. *Letters to Friends* 5.12.5 with n. 11.

193. On Theopompus, above, p. 31.

194. Presumably P. went on to give a more detailed refutation, but the excerptor did not select it.

195. P. has hinted at the importance of the historian's experience before this but he now brings the notion front and centre, and will make the case that it is the most desirable quality in a historian. Although many of the historians before P. had political and military experience we have no direct evidence that anyone before P. thought this a sine qua non for writing history. While P. almost certainly believed what he was writing, there was a benefit to taking this approach, since such an emphasis on practical experience had to reflect badly on Timaeus, who otherwise was, as P. himself concedes (12.27a.3), a serious researcher and writer; see further *ATAH* pp. 133–48.

196. See 3.31.12 for similar sentiments. For vividness, see Intro. §12 and below, 25h.1–25i.1.

197. P. has brought this charge against writers of individual history as well: see 7.7.6; 29.12.6.

198. The date of Timaeus' exile is uncertain, but he was expelled from Sicily by Agathocles sometime after 216. The words probably come from the preface to his books on Agathocles, but as Walbank (*HCP* vol. 2 p. 395) points out P. is not giving an exact quotation here, and Timaeus' words are likely only to have been that he spent fifty years in exile continuously at Athens; the rest, about experience, is P.'s own spin on the remarks.

199. See 1.4.7–10 for similar remarks about living creatures.

200. See 12.25e.7 for the comparison to painting; cf. L. *Hist.* 50–51.

201. On this matter see Schepens cited at Intro. n. 86.

202. The 'predecessors' here may be Ephorus and Theopompus, whom P. cites below, 12.27.7–8.

203. On vividness in history see Intro. §12.

204. The following discussion of speeches offers the most comprehensive treatment of the topic that we find in ancient historiography. T. had given some thought to this (1.22.4) but, as noted there, his manner of expression makes it difficult to understand exactly what he was doing. Callisthenes' brief remark (F 44) suggests the necessity for congruence between character, circumstance and speech, but his remark is often understood to justify the wholesale invention of speeches (though this is not necessarily what he is saying). P., by contrast and in his usual manner, spells things out clearly, and reaffirms in no uncertain terms that the historian is to give the reader what was actually said on the occasion. For discussion of P.'s approach to speeches see *SP* pp. 242–61; Pédech (1964) pp. 254–302; Sacks (1981) pp. 79–95; J. Marincola, *CGRH* vol. 1 pp. 23–6.

205. At 2.56.10 P. suggests that such a procedure is appropriate to tragedy.

206. The remarks here introduce the notion of 'appropriateness' (the word P. uses is *prosientai*, 'to be fitted/disposed to') for various groups, which might seem to be in conflict at times with what was actually said: did no one ever give a speech in which he said something unexpected? But cf. T. 1.22.2 for a similar balancing of what was appropriate with what was actually said. For P., it is probably the case that there is no contradiction, for he believes that in this regard at least appropriateness and truth are one.

207. Again, note the emphasis on personal experience (n. 195).

208. For earlier remarks on causation see 3.6.1–7, 3.7.4–7; see also below, 22.18.6–7.

209. Hermocrates, son of Hermon, was a Syracusan leader who came to prominence in 424 BCE when he encouraged the Sicilians to unify in the face of Athenian aggression during the Peloponnesian War; later he was instrumental in the Syracusan defeat of Athens. He features prominently in T.'s history, where he is given three speeches (4.59–64, 6.33–34, 6.76–80) and plays a fatal trick on the Athenians which ensures their destruction (7.73.3). After the Syracusan victory he fought on the Spartan side against Athens, until 410 when he was banished. He died in 407 (Diod. 13.75.6–9). The elder Gelon ruled *c.* 491 to his death in 478/7, and amongst his

accomplishments was the great victory over Carthage at the battle of Himera in 480; for Timoleon, see n. 168; for Pyrrus, above, p. 35.

210. The Athenian general Eurymedon arrived in Sicily in 424 BCE, but Hermocrates frustrated his wish to set the Sicilian cities against one another by successfully urging the Sicilians to band together. T. gives a version of the speech at 4.59–64, and Timaeus must have 'rewritten' this speech for his history, something that he is attested as doing elsewhere by Pl. who criticizes his puerile efforts (*Nicias* 1.1–2).

211. *FGrHist* 566 F 22.

212. On Hermocrates and the Athenians, see above, n. 209; P. is wrong that Hermocrates fought at Aegospotami, which occurred in 405. He has perhaps confused that battle with the battle of Cyzicus fought in 410 where Hermocrates was present alongside the Spartans.

213. *FGrHist* 566 F 22; the three quotations are (respectively) *Iliad* 5. 890–91, 9.63 and the lost *Cresphontes*, *TrGF* F 453.

214. The speech was clearly full of antitheses of the kind often associated with another Sicilian, Gorgias of Leontini; for the possible relationship between one of Gorgias' speeches and the one ascribed to Hermocrates by Timaeus see *HCP* vol. 2 pp. 400–401; for a discussion of this speech and Timaeus' speeches in general, see C. A. Baron, *Timaeus of Tauromenium and Hellenistic Historiography* (Cambridge, 2013) pp. 170–201.

215. The reference here must be to a custom similar to that mentioned by X., who says that the Persians always thrust their hands into their sleeves in the presence of the king (*Hellenica* 2.1.8).

216. The text breaks off here. The speech is *FGrHist* 566 F 31b.

217. A reference to the Persian Wars when the Greeks in 480 asked the Syracusans for assistance: see H. 7.153–7. The numbers here agree with those in H.'s account (though H. mentions others), but the replies given there come from the Athenians and Spartans, not the Corinthians. Also, in H.'s account Gelon refuses the request because the Greeks will not give him a share in the command; Timaeus' story in which the forces were sent was thus more favourable to the Sicilians.

218. *FGrHist* 566 F 94.

219. Both of these were the kinds of paradoxes set to speakers to test their ability at persuasion since according to Homer, Thersites was the ugliest and most useless man that went to Troy, while Penelope, of course, was renowned for her loyalty and chastity.

220. The Academy was the school set up at Athens by Plato, but in later years, especially under the influence of Arcesilaus (*c.* 315–241/0

BCE) and Carneades (214/3–129/8), the so-called 'New Academy' was renowned for its extreme scepticism: see the texts and commentary in A. A. Long and D. N. Sedley, *The Hellenistic Philosophers* (Cambridge, 1987) vol. 1 pp. 438–67.

221. Ephesus is in Asia Minor (western coast of modern Turkey) and so across the Aegean from Athens.

222. P. is being sarcastic in suggesting that Timaeus' readers become like Timaeus himself.

223. The 'political part' means where Timaeus actually comes to historical deeds and actions, as opposed to his earlier treatment of 'colonies, foundations of cities and genealogies' just mentioned above (26d.2): see P.'s division of history at 9.1.2–4.

224. A famous remark by the pre-Socratic philosopher (*VS* 22 B 101a), it appears already in the opening story of H.'s history, though in somewhat different form: 'for amongst men ears happen to be more untrustworthy than eyes' (1.8.2).

225. A reference, perhaps, to the choice of Heracles, ascribed to the early fifth-century philosopher and sophist Prodicus and told by X. in his *Memories of Socrates* (2.1.21–34): Heracles is offered, in the guise of two women, the choice of two roads, one leading to a life of pleasure without hardship, the other toil and eventual virtue. For another reference to the story see Cic. *Letters to Friends* 5.12.3.

226. Because the ancients read aloud, 'hearing' also includes reading.

227. See above, 12.25d.1–25e.7 for excessive reliance on books.

228. See on Ephorus, above, p. 25.

229. Theopompus, *FGrHist* 115 F 342, on which see above, p. 32.

230. The quotations are (respectively) *Odyssey* 1.1–2, 1.3–4 and 8.183. On Odysseus as a model for historians here and elsewhere see Marincola (2007) (P. is treated at pp. 16–20).

231. Plato, *Republic* 5.473c–e.

232. On these remarks of Timaeus see above, p. 37.

233. Epideictic oratory was 'display' oratory, and usually comprised praise or blame. It was distinguished from dicanic oratory (in the courtroom where a legal case was argued) and probouleutic speech (that before an assembly where a decision had to be made).

234. See Diod. 5.1.4 for similar sentiments about Ephorus. For 'amplification of the narrative' (*epimetrounta logon*) see 7.7.7 above, where the same phrase is used (in a critical context). Jacoby connects P.'s evaluation of Ephorus here with what he sees as the tradition of praise and blame in moralistic historiography; *Nature* p. 148 has 'critical appraisal'.

235. Cf. Pliny, *Letters* 5.8.12, where just such collation is considered 'burdensome'.

236. P. now qualifies even further the way in which a historian should conduct his inquiries, since he suggests that only an experienced man will know *how* to question witnesses.

237. In other words, an inquirer must guide the recollections of his informant; otherwise the latter 'will drift along at the mercy of a train of associations' (*HCP* vol. 2 p. 412).

238. P. is discussing affairs in Egypt, specifically the accession of Ptolemy V Epiphanes in 204/3 or 203/2 (when still a child) at the death of his father, Ptolemy IV Philopator. It is not certain to which historians P. is here referring; for some possibilities see *HCP* vol. 2 p. 493.

239. As *HCP* vol. 2 p. 494, points out, P. elsewhere admits these qualities of Fortune (8.20.10, 30.10.1) but objects here to the exaggerated role these historians ascribed to it.

240. P. means he avoided writing a lengthy and detailed account of these events.

241. Agathocles (called 'of Alexandria' to distinguish him from the more famous Syracusan of the same name: see n. 242) and Sosibius had played an important part in Egyptian affairs since *c.* 219 BCE; both became regents for Ptolemy V on his accession (see n. 238) until they were overthrown by Tlepolemus in 203. The tradition against this Agathocles was uniformly hostile.

242. For Agathocles of Sicily, see 12.15.1–8; for Dionysius see 12.4a.3.

243. Publius Cornelius Scipio, later surnamed Africanus, born in 236, defeated Hannibal in 202 at the battle of Zama, thus bringing an end to the Second Punic War (218–202). P. may have learned this remark from Africanus' adopted grandson, Scipio Aemilianus, the conqueror of Carthage in the Third Punic War (149–146), and P.'s companion and confidant.

244. P. began his history by noting the importance in it of reversals of fortune (1.1.2, 1.35.1–10); here he makes clear that not all reversals are worthy of being included but only those that can benefit the reader.

245. See Intro. §7.

246. For P.'s views on tragedy, see 2.56.11–12.

247. P. has in the earlier part of this book treated Philip V's aggressive actions in the eastern Aegean, including his attack on Pergamum and the sea battles of Chios and Lade, and the activities of the Spartan king Nabis in 202/1 against Messene.

248. Little is known of Antisthenes (late third century BCE) to whom both a Rhodian history (fragments at *FGrHist* 508) and a

Successions of Philosophers were ascribed; see the discussion at *BNJ* 508 (C. Champion). Zeno (late third/early second century BCE) is better known: his *Chronological History* seems to have treated early Rhodian history as well as contemporary events: for the fragments see *FGrHist* 523 and, with English translation and updated bibliography, *BNJ* 523 (C. Champion); for a good recent treatment of his work, see H.-U. Wiemer, 'Zeno of Rhodes and the Rhodian View of the Past', in R. Gibson and T. Harrison, eds., *Polybius and His World: Essays in Memory of F. W. Walbank* (Oxford, 2013) pp. 279–306.

249. See 16.14.9 below, for the reason that one would distrust someone who wrote for pay.

250. The island of Rhodes was a naval and commercial power from the fourth century BCE onwards, and was a dominant force in the Hellenistic world until the mid second century BCE.

251. P.'s statement here comes very close to contradicting what he says at 1.14.1–8 about partiality towards one's country.

252. On style see Intro. §12. See Livy, *preface* 2 and Josephus, *Jewish Antiquities* proem 2, both of whom mention stylistic superiority as a reason for historians to compose their works.

253. Part of the Fifth Syrian War (202–198 BCE) between Antiochus III and Ptolemy V, these events probably took place in 202. 'Hollow Syria' or Coele-Syria was an area embraced by the modern Beqaa Valley, with territory that today is part of Syria, Lebanon and Israel.

254. See above, 12.25e, 12.27.1–7, for inquiry and eyewitness as the most important aspects of writing history.

255. Laconia is the area of the Peloponnese where Sparta is located. This must have to do with Zeno's treatment of Nabis' activities (n. 247) in and around Sparta.

256. For Timaeus' tendency to behave in this way see 12.25c.

257. For deliberate vs. accidental lying, see above, n. 17.

258. The context of this remark is not known. For the importance of eyewitness, see 12.4c.4.

259. See P.'s earlier discussion of the matter, 3.6.1–7 and 3.7.4–7.

260. There is a gap at the beginning of the text. P. seems to be referring to the Sixth Syrian War (170–168 BCE) between Antiochus IV and Ptolemy VI.

261. For criticisms of writers of individual history see 1.4.3–11.

262. Walbank, *HCP* vol. 3 p. 374, thinks that this refers to brief notices in sources or in an early draft, but I think P. here is referring to the elaboration of speeches.

263. The siege of Phanote is possibly that by Appius Claudius Centho in 169; of Coronea that of Titus Quinctius Flamininus in 196; for other possibilities see *HCP* vol. 3 pp. 374–5.

264. As Walbank, *HCP* vol. 3 p. 375 notes, the subject after the gap has to have changed to P. himself, who is contrasting his own procedure with those he has just criticized.

265. Tarentum was captured by Hannibal in 213/12; Corinth was besieged by Lucius Flamininus and others in 198; Antiochus III besieged Achaeus in Sardes in 215/14 and Gaza in 201, and Bactra in 208. Carthage was besieged by Scipio Aemilianus in 147–6.

266. There is a gap of a few words in the text here, but the sense seems clear.

267. For deliberate lying see above, n. 17.

268. The island of Jerba, some 26 miles off the coast of Tunisia. The Lotus-Eaters are the fabulous creatures whom Odysseus meets on his travels and who offer him the Lotus which promises forgetfulness of all cares (*Odyssey* 9.82–104).

269. The 'Catalogue of Ships' is a lengthy passage in the *Iliad* (2.484–760) where Homer details all the Greek contingents who fought in the war; the references here are to *Iliad* 2.496, 2.508, 2.502, 2.640.

270. The subject is the Third Punic War (149–146 BCE), the war that destroyed Carthage; it is clear from other sources that some historians provided lengthy debates before the Roman decision: see *HCP* vol. 3 pp. 651–2.

271. See 12.25i.4 for criticism of this procedure.

272. This echoes P.'s remarks on speeches at 12.25a.8; 12.25b.1; 29.12.10.

273. The remarks here should be compared with Diod. 5.1.4 and 16.1.1–2; D.H. *Thuc.* 9; Appian, *preface* 12; and L. *Hist.* 49.

274. On digressions see Intro. §12.

275. Jacoby prints this passage as *FGrHist* 115 F 28 and assumes that it comes from Book 1 of Theopompus' *Philippica*, where he gave a background survey before commencing his history proper. Alexander of Pherae was tyrant of Thessaly 369–358; Peloponnesian and Theban activity seems to refer to the years after the battles of Leuctra (371) and Mantinea (362); Iphicrates was an Athenian general but later became a mercenary in the service of Persia, leading a campaign against Egypt in 374/3; Clearchus, a student of Plato and Isocrates, became tyrant of his home town of Heraclea Pontica and was renowned for his harsh treatment of his fellow citizens.

276. P. divided up events first by Olympiads (n. 7) and then followed a consistent procedure of treating separately events in Europe, Asia and Africa.

277. Both events probably took place in the 360s.

278. Aulus Postumius Albinus was consul in 151 BCE and wrote a history of Rome in Greek (as had earlier Romans, including the first, Quintus Fabius Pictor); testimonia and fragments are at *FRHist* 4 (S. Northwood).

279. For Cato the Elder, see above, p. 41. The remark became famous: see also Aulus Gellius 11.8.4, Pl., *Life of Cato the Elder* 12.5, and Macrobius, *Saturnalia*, preface 14. The criticism is perhaps not wholly disinterested, since Cato is attested as having written the first history of Rome in Latin.

280. A council that administered the shrine of Apollo at Delphi and that was made up of representatives of the surrounding states; 'mentioned simply as a body of great authority' (*HCP* vol. 3 p. 727).

281. The pankration was a mixture of wrestling and boxing.

282. On effort in history, Intro. §4.

283. The battle took place in 146 BCE.

16. SEMPRONIUS ASELLIO

1. For full treatment of Asellio, see *FRHist* vol. 1 p. 274–7; vol. 2 pp. 446–57 (fragments with English translation), and vol. 3 pp. 277–83 (commentary).

2. On the term *annales*, see Intro. n. 27. Similar attempts to distinguish the words are found at Servius ad *Aeneid* 1.373 and Isidore, *Etymologies* 1.44.4.

3. *Cognitio* here could also mean 'knowledge of'.

4. One might compare a passage in Ammonius' *On the Differences of Similar Words* (250 Nickau), where such a distinction is made in Greek but not in the way that Verrius Flaccus indicates: ' "Historiographer" (*historiographos*) differs from "composer" (*sungrapheus*), because a historiographer is one who writes about events earlier than his own time (like Herodotus) while a composer writes up events of his own time (like Thucydides).' As pointed out by Scheller (1911) pp. 13–14, this distinction is based simply on the language that H. and T. used in their prefaces, and we find no actual Greek historian ever making such a distinction.

5. We do not know to which specific historians (if any) Asellio was referring: see *FRHist* III.278.

6. This might also mean 'only what deed was accomplished in each year' (*LH* p. 30 n. 68).

7.   The text of this fragment is problematic: see *FR Hist* vol. 3 pp. 278–81 and *LH* pp. 28–37; I am much indebted to the discussion in the latter.

8.   Accepting Woodman's emendation (*LH* p. 34) *ab re perperam faciunda* for Marshall's *ad rem perperam faciundam*; for the notion of motivating readers, Intro. §7.

9.   Reading Woodman's (*LH* p. 36) *quae<que> in bello gesta sint iterare, non praedicare aut interea* for Marshall's *et eo libro, quae in bello gesta sint, non praedicare autem*.

10. This is a fairly close echo of P. 3.6.1–7 and 3.7.4–7, where similarly causes and consequences are considered essential; for the connection between not knowing history and being a child see Cic. *Orator* 120.

17. CICERO

1.   See below, n. 21, for the works he wrote on his consulship and exile.

2.   Much has been written on Cic.'s approach to and view of what historiography is and what it demands: see D'Alton (1931) pp. 519–20; Leeman (1963) pp. 168–73; P. A. Brunt, *ORGRH* pp. 207–40; *Nature* pp. 101–2; *RICH* pp. 70–116 (= *ORGRH* pp. 241–90); Nicolai (1992) pp. 164–76; M. Fleck, *Cicero als Historiker* (Stuttgart, 1993); Potter (1999) pp. 135–8; A. Feldherr, 'Cicero and the Invention of "Literary" History', in U. Eigler et al., eds., *Formen römischer Geschichtsschreibung von den Anfängen bis Livius* (Darmstadt, 2003) pp. 196–212; E. Fantham, *The Roman World of Cicero's De Oratore* (Oxford, 2004) pp. 146–60; Matthew Fox, *Cicero's Philosophy of History* (Oxford, 2007).

3.   Discussions of this letter are numerous, not least because it is thought that it provides important evidence for theories of Hellenistic historiography: see references in n. 2.

4.   Presumably this means that the narrative of the events of the Social and Civil Wars from 91 to 88 was now complete and Lucceius was moving on to subsequent events.

5.   For continuous histories, see Intro. §2.

6.   Cf. P. 7.7.6 for criticism of writers of monographs who exaggerate the importance of their topics.

7.   *FRHist* 30 F 1; for Heracles' choice see P. n. 225.

8.   On Cic.'s exile and return see above, p. 125.

9.   A commonplace, first found in Euripides, *TrGF* F 133, translated by Cic. at *On Moral Ends* 2.105. See P. 1.1.2 for reversals of fortune as the subject matter of history.

10.   Cf. P. 1.35.1–10 for the benefit to readers of history in observing the errors and sufferings of others.

11.   Epaminondas was the great general during Thebes' decade-long hegemony after he smashed Spartan power at the battle of Leuctra (371); his own death at the battle of Mantinea in 362 BCE put an end to Theban dominance, but he was well remembered in the tradition (he was the subject of Pl.'s first (now lost) parallel life), and it is clear from this letter that his death scene must have been embellished by later writers: see Diod. 15.87.5–6.

12.   Themistocles of Athens, victor at Salamis and architect of the Athenians' great naval power in the fifth century. In his later career, he was ostracized and then exiled by the Athenians, and eventually fled to the Persian court, in some versions promising the Persian king that he would lead a new expedition against Greece, but died before he could carry this out, perhaps by suicide (the accounts of his death were already problematic in T.'s time: see his account 1.138.4–6, and Cic. *Brutus* 41–4) and was buried in Asia. Most editors think that either Cic. has made a mistake in speaking of Themistocles' 'return' (*reditu*) or that the manuscripts are corrupt and some such word as 'death' (*interitu*) originally appeared there. But Cic. may be thinking of the later romanticized story (told at Pl. *Themistocles* 32.5–6) in which Themistocles' bones are brought back home and he is given a tomb overlooking the Athenian harbour.

13.   Cic. is referring here, most likely, to the *Annales Maximi*: see below, n. 49.

14.   On this notion of pleasure in reading of changes of fortune by great men, see Marincola (2007) pp. 37–47.

15.   Much has been made of the ways in which historians (especially Roman ones) frame their narratives as if they were dramas: see especially E. Burck, *Die Erzählungskunst des T. Livius*, 2nd edn (Berlin and Zurich, 1964) pp. 177–233; D. A. Pauw, 'The Dramatic Elements in Livy's History', *Acta Classica* 34 (1991) pp. 33–49.

16.   For the close connection between the author's renown and the deeds he narrates see Intro. §2.

17.   Apelles and Lysippus were amongst the most renowned of Greek artists. Horace, *Epistles* 2.1.239 tells the same story of the former.

18.   The text is uncertain here. Agesilaus was king of Sparta from 400 to 359; he figures largely in the works of X. who included his deeds

at length in his *Hellenica* and wrote a eulogy of him as well (the 'one little book' of the next sentence), where this story appears: see *Agesilaus* 2.7. For the opposite approach see Callisthenes T 8.

19. For Timoleon see P. 12.23.4 with n. 168; for Themistocles, above, n. 8. Gnaeus Naevius, poet and dramatist, served in the First Punic War (264–241). Some thirty-two titles of comedies and six of tragedies are known, but none survive. Likewise lost is his poem on the First Punic War, possibly the earliest treatment of Roman history (if it precedes the work of Quintus Fabius Pictor, which is not certain) and an important influence on Virgil's *Aeneid*. This quotation is *TrRF* F 14. For Alexander at Sigeum see Arrian, *Anabasis* 1.12.1.

20. Cic. is thinking here probably above all of Marcus Aemilius Scaurus, Publius Rutilius Rufus and Quintus Lutatius Catulus (*FRHist* 18, 19 and 21, respectively), all of whom were born in the mid second century and composed works with titles such as *On his own Life*. On the genre of memoir-writing see A. M. Riggsby, *CGRH* pp. 266–74.

21. On the difficulties of self-praise see *ATAH* pp. 175–82. Cic. did in fact write up accounts of his own actions: a memoir of his consulship in Greek (fragments and testimonia at *FRHist* 39) and a poem in Latin on his consulship and one on his exile and return (fragments at *FLP* pp. 156–74).

22. In a letter to his friend Atticus later this same year (*Letters to Atticus* 1.340), Cic. refers to a 'book' that he is to give Lucceius, and it is presumably the notes here promised.

23. For commentaries on *On the Orator*: A. S. Wilkins (Oxford, 1892); A. D. Leeman, H. Pinkster and H. L. W. Nelson, vol. 2 (Heidelberg, 1985); for an up-to-date translation of the entire work see J. Wisse and J. May, *Cicero on the Ideal Orator* (New York and Oxford, 2001).

24. On the second day of the discussion Cic. brings in two new characters. Quintus Lutatius Catulus (*c.* 150–87 BCE) was consul in 102; in 101 he and Marius defeated the Gauls at the battle of Vercellae; he was forced to commit suicide in 87, when Marius fled Rome and his followers were attacked by Lucius Cornelius Sulla. He was an accomplished poet and was especially well versed in Greek literature. Gaius Julius Caesar Strabo Vopiscus (*c.* 130–87 BCE) was Catulus' half-brother and well regarded as an orator of especially effective wit. He too was killed in the circumstances of 87.

25. There is a play on words here between *os, oris* ('mouth') and *orator* ('speaker').

26. They laugh at the pretension of Antonius in describing himself as a professional, at his claim to be telling them something he has *not* learnt and perhaps also at the pun (n. 25) he has just made.

27. An *ars* (in Greek, *technē*) is what we might call a discipline or systematic study with its own rules and techniques, something that can be taught to another.

28. For 'periods' see Agatharchides n. 17.

29. The word translated here as 'ideas', *sententiae*, can also have the sense of 'general observations', 'reflections' or 'maxims'.

30. Cic. is here thinking of matters of state.

31. There is an echo here of T.'s evaluation of Pericles at 2.65.9, where he praises the latter particularly because he could rouse the people when they were despondent and rein them in when they were excessively confident.

32. That is, a speech of prosecution will bring the guilty to punishment, while a speech of defence will protect the innocent.

33. The phrase *lux veritatis* can also mean 'illumination of reality'.

34. For similar praise of history see Diod. 1.1.1–2.

35. *On the Orator* 1.65–9.

36. Cf. P. 12.25d, where a comparison is made between doctors good at speaking and those good at the actual task of medicine.

37. The quotation is from line 705 of Plautus' play, which is similarly an interruption and praise for what has just been said.

38. See *On the Orator* 1.260, 263 for Antonius' earlier description of the orator as a labourer. Caecilius Statius was an early Roman writer of comedies, none of which survive. This particular quotation is F 246 (Guardì).

39. See above, n. 24.

40. See *On the Orator* 1.137–45.

41. It is usually assumed that Aristotle was the first to divide rhetoric into three types: forensic (court-room speeches before a jury or judges), deliberative (political speeches before the people or the magistrates) and epideictic (speeches of praise and blame before any audience): see Aristotle, *Rhetoric* 1.3 and 2.18.1. Only the first two aimed at receiving a particular verdict or course of action; the third was sometimes dismissed as 'show' rhetoric.

42. P. (6.53) gives a description of the funeral oration spoken before the public by a relative of the deceased at his funeral. Before Catulus' speech in honour of his mother Popilia (the date of which we do not know) only men received such an honour. For the *laudatio funebris* (as it was called), see W. Kierdorf, *Laudatio Funebris* (Meisenheim am Glan, 1980).

43. The speech does not survive; the colleague was Gnaeus Domitius Ahenobarbus and the year was 92 BCE. For the fragments, ORF^4 66 FF 34–40.

44. Tribune of the plebs in 99 BCE, he attempted to pass an agrarian law but was prevented from doing so by bad omens and the vetoes of his fellow tribunes; he was tried for treason in 98 (this is presumably the occasion for Antonius' testimony), convicted, and went into exile. Cic. has a persistent dislike of plebeian tribunes, since he saw them as often inciting discord amongst the orders; and perhaps also because one had been responsible for Cic.'s own exile.

45. See above, 2.35.

46. Here begins the main discussion of the role of the orator in writing history. It is generally assumed that Antonius' opinions here are Cic.'s own; for similar remarks see On the Laws 1.5–7 (there voiced by Atticus).

47. For Marcus Porcius Cato, see above, p. 41; for Quintus Fabius Pictor see P. 1.14.1–3 with n. there; Lucius Calpurnius Piso Frugi was tribune of the plebs in 149 BCE; his history seems to have begun with the founding of Rome and continued to his own day; he might be the first to have written Roman history in this comprehensive way. For futher discussion, see FRHist vol. 1 pp. 233–9 (M. P. Pobjoy); G. Forsythe, The Historian L. Calpurnius Piso Frugi and the Roman Annalistic Tradition (Lanham, Md., New York and London, 1994).

48. That is, from approximately 753 BCE to 130 or 115 BCE (the possible dates of Publius Mucius Scaevola's pontificate). See n. 49.

49. The name means Greatest Annals, though it is possible (but less likely) that the Maximi refers to the Pontifex Maximus, and indicates something like The Annals of the Pontifex Maximus. The Annales Maximi are one of the most vexed problems in Roman historiography, and the testimonia about them seem impossible to reconcile. There is no doubt that the Pontifex Maximus kept a record and that these records ceased at the time of Publius Mucius (n. 48), but the form that these records took thereafter is unclear, although in Cic.'s time there must have been some way to read these records still. Later authors refer to an eighty-book edition, but this seems difficult to square with Cic.'s characterization of the annals as brief and dry. For discussion of the numerous issues involved see FRHist vol. I pp. 142–58 (J. W. Rich), an exemplary treatment; cf. B. W. Frier, Libri Annales Pontificum Maximorum (Rome, 1979, reprinted with new introduction, Ann Arbor, 1999). See below, On the Laws 1.6 for more on the pontifical annals.

50. Acusilaus of Argos and Pherecydes of Athens are important early mythographers and genealogists (*FGrHist* 2 and 3, respectively); for Hellanicus see D.H. *Thuc.* 5.2.

51. Lucius Coelius Antipater wrote sometime in the mid second century BCE and was the first in Roman historiography to write a monograph, in his case on the Second Punic War (218–201) in seven books. Antipater is also mentioned below, *On the Laws* 1.5. At *Orator* 229–30 (= *FRHist* 15 F 1) Cic. mocks his style for its obsessive concern with the transposition of words.

52. See D.H. *Thuc.* 24.7–10 and Quintilian 10.1.73 for similar evaluations.

53. For his exile see T. 5.26.

54. On Philistus see D.H. *Pomp.* 5.1 with n. 177.

55. For Ephorus and Theopompus see above, pp. 25 and 31 (respectively).

56. For X. and Callisthenes see above, pp. 25 and 31 (respectively).

57. On Timaeus see above, p. 35.

58. A reference to Antonius' self-deprecation above, 2.28–29.

59. Misenum (modern Miseno) is on the Bay of Naples; the country villa Antonius refers to here was later owned by his grandson, the famous Mark Antony.

60. 'Your' philosophers because Catulus and Caesar were both devotees of Greek literature.

61. For the requirements of content here and their connection with rhetorical precepts and teaching see *RICH* pp. 83–95 (= *ORGRH* pp. 259–278).

62. Cf. P. 3.32.6; Sempronius Asellio, FF 1 and 2.

63. See *RICH* pp. 94–5 (= *ORGRH* pp. 276–8) for the style desiderated by Cic. for historiography.

64. For the fragments of the *Marius*, with commentary, see *FLP* pp. 174–8.

65. For discussions of the opening passage see A. R. Dyck, *A Commentary on Cicero, De Legibus* (Ann Arbor, 2004) pp. 46–88; C. B. Krebs, 'A Seemingly Artless Conversation: Cicero's *De Legibus* (1. 1–5)', *Classical Philology* 104 (2009) pp. 90–106; A. J. Woodman, 'Poetry and History: Cicero, *De Legibus* 1.1–5', in id., *From Poetry to History: Selected Papers* (Oxford, 2012) pp. 1–16; T. P. Wiseman, 'History, Poetry and *Annales*', in id., *Unwritten Rome* (Exeter, 2008) pp. 243–70.

66. Cic.'s brother Quintus was also a poet: *FLP* pp. 179–81.

67. *FLP* F 1 (= Cic. FF 15–16); for the identity of this Scaevola see Courtney's commentary, ibid.

68. *FLP* FF 15–16; Odysseus (Ulysses) calls the Delian palm 'tall and slender' at *Odyssey* 6.162–3.

69. The story of Iulius Proculus is told by Livy 1.16.5–8; that of the north wind (*Aquilo* in Latin, *Boreas* in Greek) abducting Orithyia, the daughter of the Athenian king Erechtheus, is found in a variety of Greek poets and prose-writers, including Simonides (*PMG* 534) and Acusilaus, *FGrHist* 2 F 30 = *EGM* F 30.

70. Numa was the second king of Rome after Romulus; Egeria was a goddess of springs, who is often described as Numa's 'wife' or 'consort' who in some accounts gives him the laws that he promulgates amongst the Romans: Livy 1.19.3; Pl. *Numa* 4.2, 8.10–21. For Tarquinius and the eagle, see Ennius, *Annals* 139–40 Skutch.

71. For H. see above, p. 5; for Theopompus' tall tales see his F 381.

72. A reference to Cic.'s suppression of the Catilinarian conspiracy.

73. For the priestly annals see above, n. 49. 'More pleasurable' (*iucundius*) is the reading of all the manuscripts, but this is usually emended to 'drier' (*ieiunius*) to bring Atticus' statement here in accord with C.'s view of them elsewhere (e.g., *Letters to Friends* 5.12.5; *On the Orator* 2.52). For a defence of the manuscript reading, see J. Marincola, 'Cicero, *Leg.* 1.6: "Pleasurable" Annals?', *CQ* 65 (2015) pp. 401–7.

74. For Fabius, Cato and Piso see above, n. 47. The identity of Gaius Fannius is uncertain: see *FRHist* vol. 1 pp. 244–9 (T. J. Cornell) for discussion; testimonia and fragments at *FRHist* 12. Practically nothing is known of Vennonius: see *FRHist* 13 for the meagre testimonia and fragments; discussion at *FRHist* vol. 1 pp. 250–51 (S. J. Northwood).

75. For Coelius Antipater see above, n. 51.

76. Gaius Licinius Macer was tribune of the plebs in 73. For Gellius, see D.H. n. 207; Clodius is perhaps Paulus Clodius (*FRHist* 16) but this is uncertain; for Asellio, above, p. 121; whether he is identical with the historian is uncertain; for testimonia and fragments see *FRHist* 27, with discussion at vol. 1 pp. 320–31 (T. J. Cornell).

77. Cic. means here the speeches in his history, not the speeches he may have given in real life.

78. Cleitarchus was a historian of Alexander the Great: see Pearson (1960) ch. 8. His reliability is frequently impugned: see Quintilian 10.1.74; *Oxyrhynchus Papyrus* 4808, col. 1. L. Cornelius Sisenna wrote a history from the Social War to Sulla's death: see *FRHist* 26.

79. Cf. Pliny, *Letters* 5.8.12 for similar indecision.

80. Cf. Pliny, *Letters* 5.8.7.

81. For Themistocles see above, n. 12; the person he followed is Peisistratus, who was tyrant of Athens in the sixth century.

82. Cic. is referring here to the second Persian invasion of 480–479 BCE. The Volscians fought a series of wars with the Romans in the fifth century BCE. Gnaeus Marcius Coriolanus had fought against the Volscians, receiving his cognomen from his capture of the Volscian town of Corioli in 493 BCE. Spurned by the plebeians because of his opposition to a grain law and his generally haughty behaviour, he went into exile amongst the Volscians, and led an attack by them against the Romans, but was persuaded to turn back by his mother and sister. In at least one version of his death he was killed by the Volscians. There is an extant *Life* of him by Pl.

83. Atticus' *Chronicle* (*Liber Annalis*), mentioned again in *Orator* 120, brought together events from both the Roman and the non-Roman world in a single chronological scheme, so that one could see which events occurred simultaneously. The testimonia and fragments of his historical works are at *FRHist* 33; for full discussion see *FRHist* vol. 1 pp. 344–53 (A. Drummond).

84. For Cleitarchus see above, n. 78. Stratocles was an Athenian orator of the fourth century BCE; nothing is known of his historical work (if indeed Atticus is here referring to a history).

85. These characteristics of T. – that he was a 'native', a nobleman and a near-contemporary – are noted here as marks of his authority and reliability.

86. Marcus Cornelius Cethegus was consul in 204 BCE. Cato was consul in 195.

87. In 149; Cic. was consul in 63.

88. Appius Claudius Caecus ('the Blind'), consul in 307 and 296, was long remembered for a speech he gave in the Roman senate, advising his colleagues not to ransom prisoners taken by Pyrrhus (*ORF*[4] 1 FF 1–11). On funeral orations see above, n. 42.

89. Cf. Livy 8.40 with notes there.

90. Manius Tullius Longus was consul in 500 BCE.

91. For Cato see above, p. 41.

92. Cf. above, *On the Orator* 2.35 for these qualities in an orator.

93. On Philistus see D.H. *Pomp.* 5.1; for Demosthenes, the great fourth-century orator, see D.H. *Thuc.* 41.1; for Lysias, below, p. 148.

94. These are, of course, Caesar's famous *Commentaries* on his campaigns in Gaul.

95. On Cic. and Atticism, D'Alton (1931) pp. 208–65; Leeman (1963) pp. 136–67.; E. Narducci, '*Brutus*: the History of Roman Eloquence', in J. May, ed., *Brill's Companion to Cicero: Oratory and Rhetoric* (Leiden, 2002), pp. 401–25 at pp. 408–12.

96. For the Athenians as the first to receive the knowledge of agricul-
     ture from Demeter see Agatharchides, *On the Red Sea* 5.21 with n.
     18.

97. For similar sentiments about the unsuitability of Thucydides for
     would-be orators see Cic. *On the Best Kind of Orator* 15–16; for
     X.'s style see Cic. *On the Orator* 2.58.

98. For 'epideictic' (the word means 'display') oratory see Timaeus F
     152 with n. 3; Isocrates' *Panegyric*, published in 380 BCE, was a call
     for a pan-Hellenic campaign against Persia under the joint leader-
     ship of Athens and Sparta. His *Panathenaicus*, mentioned below,
     published shortly before 338, was his last work and an unapolo-
     getic paean to Athenian greatness.

99. Thrasymachus of Chalcedon is perhaps best known as the speaker
     in Book 1 of Plato's *Republic* who argues that justice is might; for
     his contributions to rhetoric see Kennedy (1963) pp. 68–70; Gorgias
     (*c.* 480–380 BCE) was sent by his city Leontini (in Sicily) to Athens
     in 427 to ask for an alliance, and his speech on that occasion
     became famous for the dazzling language that he used: he was par-
     ticularly fond of wordplay and balanced clauses; see Kennedy
     (1963) pp. 61–8. Theodorus is satirized in Plato's *Phaedrus* for his
     over-refined articulation of a speech; for 'cunning speech-wrights'
     (*logodaidalos*) see *Phaedrus* 266d5.

100. The phrase *canit . . . bellicum* means 'to sound the war trumpet',
     i.e., to give the signal for attack. This may be a comment on his
     vivid narrative style: see Pl. *On the Glory of the Athenians* 347A.

101. In his work *On Style*, now lost but much used by Cic.; on the work
     see Kennedy (1963) pp. 273–84.

102. See above, n. 83.

103. For a similar sentiment, Sempronius Asellio FF 1–2.

104. Cic.'s term here is *exempla*, not just 'examples' but examples from
     the past of appropriate or inappropriate behaviour: see Intro. §8.

18. DIODORUS

1. Good brief treatment of Diod. in Scanlon (2015) pp. 241–5; the trad-
    itional view of Diod. can be well seen in P. Stylianou, *A Historical
    Commentary on Diodorus Book 15* (Oxford, 1998) pp. 1–17; for the
    more recent 'positive' approach, see K. Sacks, *Diodorus Siculus and
    the First Century* (Princeton, 1990); P. Green, *Diodorus Siculus, Books
    11–12.37.1* (Austin, 2006) pp. 1–34. See also D. Ambaglio, *La* Biblioteca
    Storica *di Diodoro Siculo: Problemi e metodo* (Como, 1995).

2.   For the idea of history as vicarious instruction, P. 1.1.2, 1.35.1–10.

3.   Homer, *Odyssey* 1.4: see P. 12.27.10–11 with n. there.

4.   The sentiments expressed here are generally thought to be Stoic, although it is possible that several philosophies have been blended together: for discussion see A. Burton, *Diodorus Siculus Book I: A Commentary* (Leiden, 1972) pp. 35–8; Sacks (n. 1) pp. 36–7.

5.   For similar sentiments, see Sempronius Asellio, F 2.

6.   For the idea that history treats noble deeds, see Intro. §2.

7.   For similar praises of history, see Cic. *On the Orator* 2.36.

8.   On myths in history see Diod. 4.1.1–4 and Intro. §9.

9.   On the importance of benefactions to mankind as an element of Diod.'s thought see Sacks (n. 1) pp. 61–82.

10. A play here on *axiologos*, literally 'worthy of speech' but used also as in the sense of 'worthy of account', i.e., meeting the standard of important historical deeds: see Intro. §2.

11. On the contrast between pleasure and benefit see Intro. §7.

12. On this notion see below, 20.2.2; Sallust, *Catiline* 3.2; Intro. §4.

13. See Cic. *On the Orator* 2.35 for these same qualities ascribed to oratory.

14. For 'self-contained' events and accounts see below, 16.1.1–3.

15. Chief amongst them would have been Ephorus (above, p. 25); the shortcomings that Diod. ascribes to his predecessors are structured in such a way as to make his own work seem the culmination of a tradition: *ATAH* pp. 241–2.

16. Again, Ephorus is meant here: see below, 4.1.3; Ephorus is not likely to have passed over 'mythical' times because of the effort involved, but rather because he did not believe that the tradition was reliable: see his F 9.

17. The Diadochs were the immediate successors of Alexander, the Epigoni the generation after them. To which historians Diod. is referring here is unknown.

18. Compare this expression with P.'s 'lovers of learning' (1.2.8).

19. See Livy, *preface* 10, for a somewhat different metaphor with a similar idea.

20. Diod. seems here to be using arguments advanced by P. (3.32.1–5) in a different context.

21. See D.H. *Rom. Ant.* 1.7.2 and Dio 72.23.5 for remarks on numbers of years spent on their work.

22. Apart from Egypt, scholars are reluctant to concede such wide-ranging travels to Diod.; if he took them, they have not left much

of a mark on his history. For the importance of eyewitness, Intro. §3.

23. Diod. is presumably referring to the availability of books in Rome but also 'native' records such as the *Annales Maximi* (for which see Cic. n. 49).

24. This seems to be a reference to pirated editions of Diod.'s work, published before he could bring out his entire history.

25. An echo again of P.'s request for correction when one is unwittingly in error: see P. 1.14.2 with n. 17.

26. For myth in history see Intro. §9.

27. For Ephorus, see above, p. 25.

28. For Callisthenes, see above, p. 33; for Theopompus, see above, p. 31; note too that Theopompus did include myths in his history: F 381.

29. The benefactions (n. 9) of mythical figures are thus of the same importance to Diod. as those of the more 'historical' figures.

30. On the importance of arrangement in history see below, 16.1.1–3, and Intro. §12.

31. On Timaeus and his nickname see above, p. 35. For Timaeus' harsh disposition see P. 12.26d. For a similar play on names with a Latin author see Pliny the Elder, *Controversiae* 10, preface 5.

32. The arrangement 'topic by topic' (*kata genos*) means most likely that events were grouped according to their geographical area rather than in a strict chronological order. See Sacks (n. 1) p. 18 n. 31 and Marincola, *CGRH* p. 172, both with further references. Diod. 16.76.5 notes that Ephorus gave each book an individual introduction, and this may have contributed to a sense of each book's unity.

33. Diod. seems to have been speaking about the philosopher Pythagoras and his followers.

34. Diod. largely follows the lead of P. here: see P. 1.14.2 with n. 17.

35. For another remark on arrangement see above, 5.1.1–4; see also D.H. *Thuc.* 9.4–10, *Pomp.* 3.13.

36. Diod. is narrating the events of 318 BCE. Eumenes of Cardia had been secretary to Philip and Alexander; after the latter's death he was part of the struggles over Alexander's kingdom, and in the changing alliances of chieftains that marked those years, he was in 320 condemned to death but fled and later allied with Polyperchon, one of Alexander's generals.

37. For this notion of fortune's inconstancy (though not there allied with history) see the Younger Seneca, *Natural Questions* 3, preface 7–9.

38. On speeches in history see Intro. §11. For the argument that this passage comes from Duris of Samos (above, p. 39) see *Nature* pp. 146–50; Sacks (n. 1) pp. 95–6 defends Diod.'s authorship. There is an edition, Italian translation, and comprehensive discussion of this passage in I. Achilli, *Il Proemio del Libro 20 della* Bibliotheca Storica *di Diodoro Siculo* (Lanciano, 2012).

39. For similar criticisms of speeches see Cratippus (at D.H. *Thuc.* 16.2); Pompeius Trogus F 152; Granius Licinianus 36.30–32.

40. For the notion that the historian can display his own rhetorical prowess in his speeches see L. *Hist.* 58.

41. Again, Diod. borrows a metaphor from P. (1.4.7–9; cf. 1.3.4 with n. 10) but uses it in his own way.

42. This remark suggests that Diod. believed the speeches in previous historical accounts to have some element of truth in them.

43. See Intro. §4.

44. For the historian's need to explain events see P. 12.25b.1–4; Cic. *On the Orator* 2.63.

45. This passage is also sometimes ascribed to Duris (above, p. 39) and connected with his F 1: see Intro. §7; *Nature* p. 150 n. 9; *contra*, Sacks (n. 1) pp. 95–6.

46. The occasion for these remarks is the attempt by the Carthaginian Bormilcar to become tyrant at Carthage in 308 BCE. Diod. has been shifting his narrative back and forth between Bormilcar's actions and those of Agathocles, each of whom would have benefited from the other but each of whom acted in ignorance of the other.

47. On bias in history see Intro. §6. Timaeus here is faulted for bitterness, Callias for indulgence: they represent the twin extremes to which history could go.

48. On Timaeus' bitterness see P. 8.10.12, 12.8.1, 12.11.4. This entire passage has much in common with P.'s criticisms of Timaeus throughout his Book 12.

49. See P. 12.15.9–10 on Timaeus' failure to record Agathocles' good deeds.

50. Points made by P. as well: 12.15.7–8, 12.35.2–6.

51. This passage immediately follows on from the previous one in the standard text of Diod., but it comes in fact from a separate passage; for all that, it is likely that the criticism of Timaeus and Callias went together. Callias of Syracuse wrote a favourable history of Agathocles (ruled 316–289 BCE) in twenty-two books; his work seems to have left little influence on the tradition, probably because of the attacks on it by Timaeus. Callias' fragments are at *FGrHist*

564 and, with English translation and updated bibliography, at
BNJ 564 (D. W. Roller).

52. The point of this last sentence is obscure.

19. SALLUST

1. For a treatment of all aspects of Sallust's career and works see
R. Syme, *Sallust* (Berkeley and Los Angeles, 1964); on Sallust's his-
torical thought and method see: D. C. Earl, *The Political Thought
of Sallust* (Cambridge, 1961); Leeman (1963) pp. 179–87; G. M.
Paul, 'Sallust', in T. A. Dorey, ed., *Latin Historians* (London and
New York, 1966) pp. 85–113; Duff (2003) pp. 66–71; *LatHist* pp.
10–50. Commentaries on the *Catiline*: K. Vretska, *C. Sallustius
Crispus De Catilinae Coniuratione*, 2 vols. (Heidelberg, 1976);
P. McGushin, *Bellum Catilinae: A Commentary* (Leiden, 1977);
J. T. Ramsey, *Sallust's* Bellum Catilinae, 2nd edn (New York and
Oxford, 2007). For the *Jugurtha* see: E. Koestermann, *C. Sallustius
Crispus Bellum Jugurthinum* (Heidelberg, 1971) (in German);
G. M. Paul, *A Historical Commentary on Sallust's Bellum Jug-
urthinum* (Liverpool, 1984). For the *Histories*: P. McGushin,
Sallust: The Histories, 2 vols. with translation (Oxford, 1992, 1994);
R. Funari, *C. Sallusti Crispi Historiarum fragmenta* (Amsterdam,
1996); A. LaPenna and R. Funari, *C. Sallusti Crispi Historiae I:
fragmenta* 1.1–146 (Berlin, 2015). There is an excellent translation
of the two monographs and the more substantial fragments from
the *Histories* by A. J. Woodman (Harmondsworth, 2007); see also
the new Loeb Classical Library edition of J. T. Ramsey, 2 vols.
(Cambridge, Mass., 2014).

2. For the sentiment see also Diod. 1.2.7, 20.2.2, and Intro. §4.

3. This observation is adapted from Pericles' Funeral Oration in T.
2.35.2, where Pericles speaks of the difficulty of praising the dead to
the living; for the reluctance of people to hear praise of others, see
Intro. §4.

4. There is some resemblance here between Sallust's account of his
foray into public life and the seventh letter of Plato, where a similar
desire to benefit one's country finds little success: *Epistles* 7.
324b–326b.

5. The words *servilibus officiis*, translated here as 'the duties of
slaves', are often taken in apposition with agriculture and hunting,
such that Sallust might be seen to be equating them with the work
of slaves, a viewpoint difficult to maintain since agriculture was

considered a noble occupation for a free man: see, e.g., Cic., *On Duties* 1.151. For the translation here see J. Delz, 'Verachtete Sallust die Beschäftigung mit der Landwirtschaft?', *Museum Helveticum* 42 (1985) pp. 168–73. (I thank A. J. Woodman for calling this to my attention.)

6.   For the notion of a monograph on an individual subject, see Intro. §2; cf. Cic., *Letters to Friends* 5.12.4; for 'worthy of memory', Intro. §2.

7.   For the importance to the historian of freedom from bias, see Intro. §6.

8.   For the Catilinarian conspiracy see above, p. 125.

9.   For a similar remark passing over the praise of history because others have already done so, see P. 1.1.1.

10.   This is a reference to the canvassing that Roman politicians did before elections.

11.   The two great heroes of the Second Punic War (218–201): Quintus Fabius Maximus, whose strategy of delay kept Hannibal at bay during the latter's fourteen-year occupation of Italy, and Publius Cornelius Scipio, the man who finally brought the war to Carthage and defeated Hannibal at the battle of Zama in 202.

12.   These images (*imagines*) were wax masks of distinguished ancestors kept by noble families in the atrium (entrance-way) of their houses and brought out on public display at the funeral of a distinguished family member (see Cic. n. 42 for the ceremony). Labels (*tituli*) recording the achievements of the individual appeared beneath the wax images: for a comprehensive treatment, H. I. Flower, *Ancestor Masks and Aristocratic Power in Roman Culture* (Oxford, 1996), especially pp. 145–50, 180–84.

13.   On history's ability to inspire great actions, see Sempronius Asellio, FF 1–2; Diod. 1.1.5–2.1.

14.   A 'new man' was the first in the history of his family to achieve the 'curule' offices, i.e., those that allowed their holder to sit in the ivory chair of state, such as the praetorship and the consulship; examples of new men from the late republic include Marius and Cic.

15.   It is generally assumed that this statement of impartiality appeared in the preface of the *Histories*.

20. STRABO

1. For Strabo's life and times see Bowersock (1965) pp. 126–34;
    G. Aujac, *Strabon et la science de son temps* (Paris, 1966);
    K. Clarke, 'In Search of the Author of Strabo's *Geography*', *JRS*
    87 (1997) pp. 92–110; D. Dueck, *Strabo of Amaseia* (London
    and New York, 2000); and the essays collected in D. Dueck et al.,
    eds., *Strabo's Cultural Geography: The Making of a* Kolossourgia
    (Cambridge, 2005). Strabo's historical fragments are at *FGrHist*
    81; see also the Italian edition of D. Ambaglio (Milan, 1990) with
    introduction and commentary.
2. Cf. P. 1.1.1 for similar thoughts, and cf. Intro. §7 on utility; see also
    J. Engels, '*Andres endoxoi* or "men of high reputation"', in Dueck
    et al. (n. 1), pp. 129–43.
3. Cf. Intro. §2 for the 'great' subject matter of history.
4. On Strabo's *Geography* as a 'colossus' see S. Pothecary, '*Kolos-
    sourgia*: "A Colossal Statue of a Work"', in Dueck et al. (no. 1) pp.
    5–26.
5. For Hecataeus see above, p. 3; for Pherecydes see Cic. n. 50. Cad-
    mus of Miletus is said here and at Josephus *Against Apion* 1.13 to
    have been the earliest prose writer in Greece; works on Miletus and
    Ionia were ascribed to him, but he is a shadowy (if even genuine)
    figure: see further *FGrHist* 489. For Hellanicus see D.H. *Thuc.* 5.2
    with n. 18. This sketch of the development of Greek prose can be
    usefully compared with D.H. *Thuc.* 5.1–4.
6. The mythical figure Andromeda was chained to a rock in the sea
    and was to be sacrificed to a sea-monster until Perseus came along,
    slew the beast, and then married Andromeda. The location of Iope
    is uncertain.
7. On myth in history see Intro. §9.
8. Apollodorus of Athens (born *c.* 180 BCE) was a scholar who pro-
    duced a number of works, including a commentary on Homer's
    Catalogue of Ships in twelve books, where he discussed Homeric
    geography. His fragments are at *FGrHist* 244.
9. For similar remarks see Agatharchides, *On the Red Sea* 1.8 with
    notes there. The references are: Hesiod, F 153 (Merkelbach-West);
    Alcman, *PMGF* F 148; Aeschylus, *TrGF* FF 431, 441, 434a. Alc-
    man was a lyric poet, active at Sparta in the mid to late seventh
    century BCE.
10. *FGrHist* 115 F 381; see above, p. 32.

11. H., Ctesias (above, p. 19) and the Indian writers were often grouped together as being especially famous for their tall tales. See a similar correlation in the following passage.

12. Historians of Alexander frequently come in for criticism; see, e.g., Arrian, *Anabasis* 1.12.2–4; L. *Hist.* 12.

13. On bias in history see Intro. §6.

14. 30,000 stades is *c.* 5,500 km; the actual distance is *c.* 4,100 km.

15. Prometheus, having violated Zeus' orders by giving fire to mankind, was punished by being chained to a rock and having his liver eaten by an eagle; he was ultimately freed by Heracles.

16. Dionysus' expedition to India was an early subject for Greek poets, and was treated by Diod. 3.63.3–5.

17. There is a gap in the text here.

18. On H., above, p. 5; on Ctesias, above, p. 19; for Hellanicus see D.H. *Thuc.* 5.2. For myth in history, Intro. §9.

21. DIONYSIUS OF HALICARNASSUS

1.   There have been many studies of D.H. as a critic: fundamental is S. F. Bonner, *The Literary Treatises of Dionysius of Halicarnassus: A Study in the Development of Critical Method* (Cambridge, 1939); other important studies include Grube (1965) pp. 207–30; Kennedy (1972) pp. 342–63; D. C. Innes, 'Dionysius of Halicarnassus' in G. A. Kennedy, ed., *The Cambridge History of Literary Criticism I: Classical Criticism* (Cambridge, 1989) pp. 267–72; C. C. de Jonge, *Between Grammar and Rhetoric: Dionysius of Halicarnassus on Language, Linguistics, and Literature* (Leiden, 2008); and N. Wiater, *The Ideology of Classicism: Language, History, and Identity in Dionysius of Halicarnassus* (Berlin, 2011). D.H.'s approach in favour of classical writers is clearest in the essay 'On the Ancient Orators', which introduces his critical assessments of the orators; it has been called a 'manifesto of classicism': for German translation and full commentary see T. Hidber, *Das klassizistische Manifest des Dionys des Halikarnass: Die* praefatio *zu* De oratoribus veteris (Stuttgart, 1996); see also E. Gabba, *Dionysius and* The History of Archaic Rome (Berkeley, 1991) pp. 23–59. For D.H. as historian, see C. Schultze, 'Dionysius of Halicarnassus and his Audience' in I. Moxon, J. D. Smart and A. J. Woodman, eds., *Past Perspectives: Studies in Greek and Roman Historical Writing* (Cambridge, 1986) pp. 121–41 and Wiater (above).

2.   For *Thuc.* see G. Pavano, *Saggio su Tucidide* (Palermo, 1958); and Pritchett (1975), which contains a translation and very full notes.

3.   Commentary by S. Fornaro, *Dionisio di Alicarnasso: Epistola a Pompeio Gemino* (Stuttgart, 1995).

4.   See especially Wiater (n. 1). On the *Rom. Ant.* see especially Gabba (n. 1); on D.H.'s envisaged audience see *Rom. Ant.* 1.8.3 with n. 212; 11.1.1.

5.   This treatise does not survive except for a summary of its Book 2 and an excerpt in *Pomp.* 3.

6.   Tubero is also named at *Letter to Ammaeus* 2.1, and is almost certainly the Roman historian Q. Aelius Tubero, whom D.H. claims to be following in his *Roman Antiquities* at 1.80.1 (= *FRHist* 38 T 3), where he is described as 'clever and careful in the compilation of his history'. He came from a noble family and was a well-known jurist; only slightly more than a dozen fragments of his history survive: see further Bowersock (1965) pp. 129–30; *FRHist* vol. 1 pp. 363–4; vol. 2 pp. 746–59.

7.   On the importance of imitation in historiographical criticism, see Intro. §2.

8.   This is probably not the *On Demosthenes* by D.H. that survives (which most likely was published before *Thuc.*), but a different work, which does not survive.

9.   There is a gap in the text here; for T. as the greatest historian see L. *Hist. passim.*

10. Like P. before him and Pl. after him, D.H. uses the term 'theatrical' here and elsewhere (see below, chapters 5.3, 7.3, 29.5) in a disparaging sense, to mean overly dramatic, exaggerated, or simply false: see Intro. §9.

11. D.H. wants his readers to know that he does not have the character of someone such as Timaeus (above, p. 35), and he wishes to ensure that his work is not seen in the highly critical spirit of something like Pl.'s *Malice.*

12. For the commonplace that virtues and vices are neighbours, see Horace, *Ars Poetica* 24–31; Pseudo-Longinus, *On the Sublime* 3.3; Quintilian 8.3.7.

13. D.H. returns to this theme below, chapter 34.

14. The first three were generally held to be the three finest painters, the latter the three finest sculptors. D.H. uses these men as examples elsewhere (e.g., *On Demosthenes* 50.4); the comparison between literature and painting is an old one, already seen in Simonides (Pl. *On the Glory of the Athenians* 346F), and plays a large role in Horace's *Ars Poetica*; cf. also Strabo 1.1.23.

15. For D.H.'s views on aesthetics, see D. M. Schenkeveld, 'Theories of Evaluation in the Rhetorical Treatises of Dionysius of Halicarnassus', in A. Laird, ed., *Ancient Literary Criticism* (Oxford, 2006) pp. 284–99; C. Damon, 'Aesthetic Response and Technical Analysis in the Rhetorical Writings of Dionysius of Halicarnassus', *Museum Helveticum* 48 (1991) pp. 33–58.

16. The words in angled brackets are added by Jacoby, *FGrHist* 332 T 2.

17. There has been a great deal of discussion about this passage and its reliability: Jacoby thinks it full of errors and untrustworthy as a reliable indicator of 'early' historians (see *FGrHist* 330, Notes, p. 488), but cf. T. S. Brown, 'Herodotus and his Profession', *American Historical Review* 59 (1954) pp. 835–8; S. Gozzoli, 'Una teoria antica sull'origine della storiografia greca', *Studi Classici e Orientali* 19–20 (1970–71) pp. 158–211. The identity of most of these historians is uncertain. Eugeon (or Euagon: see Jacoby, *FGrHist* 535) of Samos wrote a history of Samos and is cited as an authority in an inscription of the third century BCE recording a territory dispute by Samos and Priene. Deiochus of Cyzicus (*FGrHist* 471; the supplement in the text is that of Jacoby) is frequently cited in the scholia to Apollonius' *Argonautica*. For Bion of Proconessus, see *FGrHist* 332. For Eudemos of Paros, see *FGrHist* 497 (where T 2 cites a historian Eudemos of Naxos). Democles of Phygela (Pygela in Strabo 14.1.20) was said to have recorded earthquakes that had occurred in Lydia, Ionia and the Troad (Strabo 1.3.17). Hecataeus of Miletus is considered the most important of H.'s predecessors: see above, p. 3. Acusilaus of Argos (*FGrHist* 2) is an important early mythographer. Charon of Lampsacus wrote a *Persica*, *Hellenica* and *Voyage outside the Pillars of Heracles*; see K. von Fritz, *Die griechische Geschichtsschreibung* (Berlin and New York, 1967), vol. 1, pp. 519–22; Pl. cites him against H. at *Malice* 17 and 20; his fragments are at *FGrHist* 262 and, with English translation and updated bibliography, at *BNJ* 262 (P. Ceccarelli). Melesagoras of Chalcedon is not otherwise known, and some think the historian Amelesagoras (*FGrHist* 330) is here meant; but Amelesagoras has problems of his own (he is otherwise cited as an Athenian, for one) and Jacoby thought that a name and ethnic had fallen out between 'Amelesagoras' (as he read it) and 'of Chalcedon': see further Pritchett (1975) pp. 52–3.

18. Hellanicus of Lesbos (*FGrHist* 4) was a prolific early historian, and, according to Jacoby, the inventor of the genre of Athenian local history; T. 1.97.2 is critical of his chronology; cf. Strabo 10.2.6, 11.6.2, etc. For Damastes of Sigeum see *FGrHist* 5;

Xenomedes of Ceos' fragments are at *FGrHist* 442; the manuscripts of D.H. read 'of Chios' but this was emended by Wilamowitz:
cf. *P.Oxy.* 1011.54, where a 'Xenomedes of Ceos' is cited. Xanthus
of Lydia (*FGrHist* 765) wrote a *Lydian Matters* (*Lydiaca*). It has
been noted that Pherecydes of Athens, an early historian for whom
D.H. elsewhere expressed admiration (*Rom. Ant.* 1.13.1), is a surprising omission from these lists.

19. For 'neither adding anything nor taking anything away' as a marker
     or claim of truth, see Josephus, *Jewish War, preface* 17; L. *Hist.* 47;
     LS 44–5; and cf. below, 16.1, for a different application of the
     saying.

20. Although Attic was to become the most literary of the Greek dia-
     lects, early writers, including H., wrote in Ionic.

21. The manuscripts read '240 years' but are corrected on the basis of
     Pomp. 3.14, which has '220 years'. H.'s work ends in 479 BCE with
     the siege of Sestos, so either 719 or 699 would be the starting point:
     the Lydian king Gyges, the first historical figure to appear in H.,
     reigned *c.* 716–678.

22. For D.H.'s appreciation of H. as the best of all historians, see
     Pomp. 3–5.

23. D.H. here uses several passages from T. himself in giving this infor-
     mation (1.1.1, 1.22 and 5.26.5) but other parts of it (e.g., all of 6.1)
     are inferences of his own.

24. For T.'s claim that his work lacks *to mythōdes*, see 1.22.4 and n.
     there.

25. The term 'Lamian' could be used of any monstrous woman: see
     Strabo 1.2.8; Naiads is a general term for water nymphs of all
     kinds, and Tartarus is another name for the underworld.

26. As did D.H. himself when writing the history of early Rome: see
     *Rom. Ant.*1.8.1; cf. Diod. 4.1.1–4.

27. See above, n. 10.

28. T. 1.22.4, though the first sentence is slightly different: for the ori-
     ginal see above, pp. 16–17.

29. See Diod. 1.2.2 for history as 'the prophetess of truth'.

30. For the importance to the historian of praising fairly and without
     jealousy see P. 1.14.5, Diod. 15.1.1, L. *Hist.* 59.

31. See, e.g., T. 1.138 (Themistocles), 2.65 (Pericles), 6.15 (Alcibiades),
     7.86 (Nicias). The general Demosthenes (not the famous orator)
     was responsible for several Athenian successes in the Peloponne-
     sian War; Nicias' greatest fame came in the disastrous Sicilian
     expedition in which he lost his life; for Alcibiades see Aristotle,
     Poetics chapter 9 with n. 6.

32. A sentence follows in the manuscripts: 'And best of all is that he nowhere deliberately speaks falsely or sullies his own conscience.' This is likely to be an interpolation and is deleted by all editors.

33. On arrangement, see Intro. §12.

34. See *Pomp.* 3.13–14 for similar sentiments about the way H. and T. structured events; for the arrangement of 'local' history see *Nature* pp. 16–23, with references there.

35. The quotation is from an unknown lyric poet.

36. For these events of Book 3 see (respectively) 2–14, 15–19, 20–26, 27–50, 69–85, 86–8, 89–93, 94–9, 100–102, 103, 104 and 105–14. D.H. omits 51 (Nicias' seizure of Minoa), 52–68 (the conclusion of the siege of Plataea), and 115–16 (an Athenian raid on Himera in Sicily and an eruption of Mount Etna).

37. T.'s division ran counter to the later school of thought that believed individual events should be narrated in a manner that was 'self-contained': see *Pomp.* 3.13–14 and Diod. 16.1–2 for similar sentiments. But cf. *Oxyrhynchus Papyrus* 853 for a refutation of D.H. and defence of T.'s procedure. Cf. Intro. §12.

38. This is not exactly true: the so-called Oxyrhynchus historian of the fourth century BCE, who covered events after those of T., followed his division by summer and winter, at least in part (cf. 19.1 of that work). It is usually inferred that D.H., therefore, did not know the Oxyrhynchus historian (and quite a lot has been built on this) but that is to take his dismissiveness here too literally.

39. Cf. *Pomp.* 3.8–9 for comparison on this score between H. and T. The critics referred to here are unknown.

40. T. 1.23.4–24.1; as often in D.H.'s quotations there are some slight changes from what the manuscripts of T. read. D.H.'s discussion (and my translation) elides T.'s distinction between *aitiē* (charge) and *prophasis* (cause), and he treats both words as if they mean the same thing; see *CT* I.64–6 for the importance of the distinction to T.; for a discussion of the differences between causes and pretexts see P. 3.6–7.

41. D.H. joins here T. 1.88.1 and 1.89.1.

42. T. 1.118.1.

43. T. 1.97.2. For the fragments of Hellanicus' *Attic History* see *FGrHist* 323a; Jacoby (1949) *passim*, and especially pp. 215–25, argues at length that Hellanicus invented the genre of Athenian local history.

44. T.'s history breaks off in mid-sentence in the year 411; it is generally assumed that he died before he could finish it, but D.H. here and at *Pomp.* 3.10 seems to think that T. ended his history where he did deliberately.

45. T. 5.26.3.

46. There is a large gap in the text here; the words before the gap refer
     to events of 429 (T. 2.83–92), those after the gap to events of *c*. 465
     (T. 1.100.1).

47. The Eurymedon river in Pamphylia (modern Antalya in Turkey) was
     the site in 469 or 466 BCE of a double victory by Cimon and the Athen-
     ians against the Persians on land and sea: see Pl. *Cimon* 12–13.

48. The following three passages are T. 4.38.5, 4.54.2 and 4.57.3.

49. The passage quoted is T. 2.59.1; the later narrative referred to is 4.
     15–22.

50. D.H. refers here to the idea that the historian in writing up his
     speeches is expected to 'discover' the arguments that were inherent
     in the situation; see P. 12.25i.4, with the notes there, and on
     speeches in general, Intro. §11.

51. There is a gap in the text here.

52. The three passages that follow are T. 4.32.1, 1.114.3 and 2.27.1.

53. *FGrHist* 64 F 1; for similar criticism of the inclusion of speeches see
     Diod. 20.1.1–2.2, Pompeius Trogus F 152 (= Justin 38.3.10) and
     Granius Licinianus 36.30–32. For Cratippus see n. 54.

54. Even in antiquity Book 8 seemed different to readers from the other
     seven books: Marcellinus, *Life of Thucydides* 43, says, 'Some say
     that the eighth book is not genuine, nor by Thucydides', and notes
     that even those who think it is by T. find it unadorned and rough
     (44). As for Cratippus, Jacoby thought he was a later forger; the bal-
     ance of scholarly opinion these days, however, inclines to agree with
     D.H.; for discussion see Pritchett (1975) pp. 67–8. Cratippus has
     often been proposed as the Oxyrhynchus historian (i.e., the author
     of the papyrus fragments discovered in the last century and known
     as the *Hellenica Oxyrhynchia*), but this remains controversial.

55. For Paches see T. 3.36 and for the debate, 3.36–49.

56. The speech, possibly the most famous in all of classical historiog-
     raphy, is T. 2.35–46; see 2.34 for the custom of the funeral and the
     funeral speech.

57. T. 2.22.1–2; Phrygia is a (unknown) place in Attica.

58. T. 4.9–23, 26–40.

59. D.H. is referring to the destruction of the Athenian forces in Sicily,
     narrated in detail in T.'s Book 7.

60. Pritchett (1975) p. 70 suggests that the orator Antiphon may have
     been the source of this information (which is not in T.).

61. The reference to 'those who fell in Sicily' alludes to the massive
     losses of the Athenians in their campaign of 415–413 there, the sub-
     ject of T.'s Books 6–7.

62. D.H. here considers 1.1.1–21.2 to be the preface; this comprises about 17 pages in a standard modern edition.

63. T.'s preface contains a number of arguments designed to demonstrate that early affairs in Greece were in no way comparable to those of his war; in doing so he ranges over a number of historical topics, such as tyranny, trade and political upheaval.

64. The individual passages to which D.H. refers are (respectively) T. 1.3, 1.5, 1.6.3, 1.6.5, 1.13.3, 1.13.6 and 1.13.6.

65. D.H. here rearranges T.'s text such that 1.21–3 follow immediately after 1.1.1–2.

66. D.H. read here *ēsan* ('they were') while most manuscripts of T. read *ēisan* ('they went into').

67. The word used by T. here is *akribeia*, which for him would have meant 'accuracy' in accordance with objective reality (see *CT* I.60); by D.H.'s time, however, as we can see from the way he himself uses the term, the word just as often meant 'detail' (see Schultze, n. 1), and since I think that is how D.H. would have read the word, that is how I translate it here.

68. D.H. wrote separate works on both these aspects but only *On the Composition of Words* survives.

69. For 'periods' see Agatharchides of Cnidus n. 17.

70. The essential virtues are generally reckoned by D.H. as purity of language, clarity and brevity; the additional virtues include vividness, representation of emotion and character, grandeur, vigour, charm and propriety: see further Bonner (n. 1) pp. 18–20.

71. For Cadmus see Strabo n. 5; Aristeas of Proconessus is discussed by H. 4.13ff. where we are told that he wrote a poem, the *Arimaspea*, on the tribes of the far north.

72. For forensic oratory see Cic. *On the Orator* 2.43 with n. 41.

73. 431–404 BCE, although T.'s history only gets as far as the year 411.

74. Greek as a highly inflected language had different endings for the masculine, feminine and neuter forms of nouns and adjectives.

75. An enthymeme is a syllogism in which one of the premises is supressed.

76. For Gorgias see Cic. n. 99. Polus, possibly a pupil of Gorgias, came from Agrigentum and features in Plato's *Gorgias* (461b–481b). Licymnius of Chios flourished in the late fifth century BCE and was a dithyrambic poet (see n. 90) and rhetorician.

77. Cf. Cic. *Orator* 30.

78. In *On Literary Composition*, 25.7 D.H. equates poetic vocabulary with rare, foreign, figurative and coined words.

79. What follows are T. 1.1.2 and 1.2.1; there is then a lacuna of some length, in which D.H. would have discussed these passages (and perhaps others), and when the text resumes D.H. is quoting T. 4.34.1.

80. The passage in angled brackets is not in the manuscripts of D.H. and has been added from the text of T.

81. This refers only to the immediately preceding 4.34.1.

82. T. 7.69.4–72; the description of the final battle in the harbour of Syracuse was much admired by the ancient critics: see, e.g., Pl. *On the Glory of the Athenians* 347A–C.

83. A reference to the battle of Pylos in 425, when the Spartans crossed over to the island of Sphacteria but were eventually blockaded by the Athenians and forced to surrender.

84. See above, n. 15.

85. There is a gap here of indeterminate length.

86. For tragedy in history, see Intro. §7. See also above, n. 10.

87. 3.81.2–82; T.'s description of civil strife on Corcyra was much imitated by later historians.

88. Eurymedon was the Athenian general sent to Corcyra who took control after the Spartans left the island.

89. The quotations here and to the end of chapter 32 come from 3.82. 3–7. For an analysis of D.H.'s rewritings of T. here, see C. Macleod, 'Thucydides on Faction (3.82–83)', in id., *Collected Essays* (Oxford, 1983) pp. 123–40 at 131–5.

90. A dithyramb was a choral hymn in honour of Dionysus, known for its ecstatic character.

91. There is a short gap in the text here.

92. On the phrase see above, n. 35.

93. Hyperbaton is the removal of a word from its normal or ordinary position.

94. T. 3.82.8–83.3.

95. See P. 12.25i.4 and notes there.

96. That is, no different from poets who often claimed poetic inspiration from the Muses.

97. For a similar comparison where passion affects judgement see P. 1.14.

98. On invention see Intro. §11.

99. T. 2.71.1–75.1.

100. Plataea was the site in 479 of the final battle of the Persian Wars in mainland Greece; the victor was the Spartan regent Pausanias leading a group of allied forces. H. describes the battle in his Book 9 but he does not mention these particular details.

101. A reference to the subjects of the Athenian empire whom Athens had subjugated in the aftermath of the Persian Wars. Plataea as an Athenian ally was thought to be complicit in Athenian acts of imperial aggression.

102. The Thebans had attempted in 431 to take over the city of Plataea; for T. this incident marked the beginning of the Peloponnesian War.

103. The Athenians did not bring help to the Plataeans.

104. Much has been written on the Melian Dialogue (T. 5.84–113), which is considered one of T.'s most brilliant pieces: see the comprehensive notes in CT III.216–25; C. W. Macleod, 'Form and Meaning in the Melian Dialogue', in id., Collected Papers (Oxford 1983) pp. 52–67 treats both aspects well.

105. 5.85.

106. 5.87.

107. The quotations in this chapter come from 5.88 and 5.89.

108. For the notion of the appropriateness of speeches see Intro. §11. D.H. holds a view of Athens that makes this particular set of speeches, with its harsh characterization of the Athenian spokesmen, particularly offensive to his sensibilities.

109. D.H. here accepts the tradition that the Athenian contribution to the war against the Persians was the greatest, a claim which Athenian writers and orators consistently proffered and which diminished the contributions of other states, particularly Sparta.

110. The passages referred to in this chapter are from T. 5.90–91.2 and 94–95.

111. T. 5.102–103.

112. Again, D.H. assumes an idealized Athens.

113. 5.104–105.

114. This and the following passage are from T. 5.111.2.

115. T. 5.26.5; the remark that he spent his exile in Thrace is an inference by D.H. from T.'s remarks elsewhere that he had mining concessions in Thrace; T. says only that his exile allowed him the opportunity to be with both sides, especially the Peloponnesians.

116. T. 1.22.1 for the quotation; for the notion of suitability see Callisthenes F 44.

117. The 'shameful injunction' was the demand by the Persian king to give earth and water as tokens of their submission to him.

118. See Pomp. 3.15 for a similar thought.

119. T. 1.140–44.

120. Nicias' speeches are T. 6.9–14 and 20–23; his letter is 7.11–15, his address at the last naval battle 7.61–4, and his final address 7.77.

121. The speech of the Plataeans is 3.53–9.
122. T. 2.60–64 (Pericles), 3.37–40 (Cleon), 3.42–48 (Diodotus), 6.76–80 (Hermocrates), 6.82–7 (Euphemus).
123. T. 2.60.1.
124. This is perhaps the best example of the distance between D.H. and T.: D.H. follows standard rhetorical teaching about dealing with the people; T. (presumably) followed Pericles' actual arguments, or at least his general stance. Cf. n. 128.
125. T. 2.60.2.
126. T. 2.60.5.
127. T. 2.60.6.
128. Again, D.H. is working with the concept, above all, of propriety: see Intro. §10.
129. T. 2.62.3.
130. T. uses wordplay in the Greek, contrasting *phronēma* ('fighting spirit') and *kataphronēma* ('contempt'); I have tried to get the wordplay across by using, somewhat archaically, 'contention' for the former.
131. Heraclitus of Ephesus (late sixth century BCE) was a philosopher renowned for his obscure pronouncements; his nicknames included 'the Dark' and 'the Riddler'. For Gorgias, see Cic. n. 99.
132. T. 2.61.1; the two following passages are T. 2.61.3 and 2.63.1.
133. The words in brackets have been added by Usher from the text of T.
134. The three passages that D.H. admires are T. 6.77.1, 6.78.2 and 6.80.3.
135. That is, on the mainland and the islands.
136. The four displeasing passages are T. 6.76.2, 6.76.4, 6.78.1, 6.78.3.
137. The words in brackets are added by Usher from the text of T. 'That one' refers to the person mentioned at the beginning of the passage, the one who thinks that the Syracusan and not he himself is not an enemy of the Athenians.
138. Cf. P.'s criticism of Timaeus' speeches as those of a schoolboy: 12.25k.8–11.
139. There is a gap in the text here.
140. There was much discussion about the suitability of T.'s speeches for real-life assemblies and law courts: see, e.g., Cic. *Orator* 30–31; *Brutus* 287.
141. For history as helpful to our common life, see Diod. 1.1.1.
142. Cf. Cic.'s remarks (*Orator* 30–32) on the unsuitability of T. for courtroom speakers.
143. Cf. Quintilian, *Orator's Education* 10.1.31 for poetry and history.

144. For Demosthenes see Agatharchides n. 19. D.H.'s *On Demosthenes* offers a full treatment of his style; T. is mentioned in that essay in chapters 1–2, 4, 6 and 9–10 (the last of which contains examples of Demosthenes' imitation of T.).

145. The first two quotations are from Demosthenes' *On the Symmories*, sections 13 and 14–15 (respectively). The king is Philip II.

146. The following two excerpts are from *Third Philippic* 1 and 13 (respectively); there follow *On the Crown* 231 and 294.

147. A reference to Aeschines, Demosthenes' main political opponent and a proponent of rapprochement with Macedon.

148. Here at the end D.H. makes an allusion to T.'s own distinction (1.22.4) between truth and pleasure; see further, Intro. §§5, 7; there may also be an echo of Nicias' letter to the Athenians recorded by T. at 7.14.4. See *Thuc.* 2.1 for Tubero as lover of truth.

149. Only fragments of *On Imitation* survive. The dedicatee Demetrius is unknown.

150. There is a gap in the text here; the quotation that precedes is from H.'s preface.

151. For D.H.'s belief that history should treat noble subjects see *Rom. Ant.* 1.1.3.

152. T. 1.23.1–3.

153. See *Thuc.* 6 for more on T.'s choice of subject.

154. See *Thuc.* 5.5 for Hellanicus and Charon, and the ways in which H. surpassed his predecessors.

155. H. 1.5.1 for Croesus as the first to begin injustices against the Greeks; in Book 9 H. treats the victories at Plataea (chapters 31–85), the inglorious retreat of the last Persian remnant under Artabazus (89) and the battle of Mycale (90–107) which liberated the Greek city-states in Asia Minor.

156. See *Thuc.* 10–11.1 for T.'s approach to causes. Cf. D.H.'s own grateful disposition towards the subject of his history: *Rom. Ant.* 1.6.5.

157. On T.'s arrangement see *Thuc.* 9.

158. Cf. P. 1.14.4 and 16.14.16 for how a historian should behave towards his native city.

159. For similar sentiments see *Thuc.* 10.2–11.1.

160. See *Thuc.* 12.2 for similar sentiments about the ending, although D.H. does not suggest there the conclusion that he does here. At the end of the Peloponnesian War the Spartans installed a garrison and an oligarchy of thirty rulers at Athens. Their behaviour was at first moderate but then turned lawless and bloody. A group of Athenian exiles, with active help from the Thebans and the passive

assistance of one of the Spartan kings, using Phyle as their base, managed to evict the oligarchs, and democracy was restored in 403, approximately eighteen months after the war had ended.

161. For Homer and historiography see Intro. §2. For variety in historical narration see P. 38.5.1–6.6.

162. Pindar (late sixth to mid fifth century BCE) was the most renowned of epinician poets; this line is *Nemean Odes* 7.52.

163. T. 2.97; 6.2–5; the latter passage is an introduction to the great Athenian expedition against Sicily in 415–413 and serves as a kind of Sicilian 'archaeology': see *CT* III.262–3.

164. See *Thuc.* 9 for detailed criticisms of this.

165. See *Thuc.* 5.5 with n. 21.

166. Naturally, H. must move from event to event just as T. does, and so of course in some sense he breaks up his narrative, but D.H. here is suggesting that H. completes his accounts of individual events before moving on in a way that allows the reader to maintain the thread of the action. Cf. *Thuc.* 9 with the notes there for similar remarks about T.'s arrangement. For 'self-contained' events see D.H. 16.1.1–3; for history and the 'body' see P. 1.3.4 with n. 10.

167. On disposition see Scheller (1911) pp. 34–6; Meijering (1987) pp. 30–35, 238 n. 77; Fornaro (n. 3) pp. 210–11; R. Nünlist, *The Ancient Critic at Work* (Cambridge, 2009) pp. 246–8; on the favourable/critical dichotomy see *RICH* pp. 40–44.

168. See the similar remark at *Thuc.* 41.8.

169. For D.H.'s essential and additional virtues, see *Thuc.* 24ff.

170. This sentence is added by Aujac, based on the fragments of D.H.'s *On Imitation.* 3.1.

171. On vividness see Intro. §12.

172. For Demosthenes' imitation of T. see *Thuc.* 53–4; Caecilius is the critic from Caleacte (in Sicily), mentioned in the beginning of the pseudo-Longinus *On the Sublime*; he was, after D.H., the most important critic of his era: see Kennedy (1972) pp. 364–71.

173. For D.H.'s view of poetical language see *Thuc.* 24.11 with n. 62.

174. On X., see above, p. 21; on Philistus, see below. X.'s *Cyropaedia* (*The Education of Cyrus*) is generally not considered a historical subject: it is an idealized biography of the Persian king Cyrus the Great, which consists largely of advice that he gives on a host of issues relating to effective rule; Cic. says it was written 'not according to historical truth but as an image of a just ruler' (*Letters to Quintus* 1.1.23). The *Anabasis* (*March up Country*) tells the story of a group of mercenaries who accompanied Cyrus the younger in his bid to wrest the kingship from his brother, Cyrus' defeat and

death at the battle of Cunaxa, and the long, adventurous return of the Greek mercenaries to the safety of their homeland, with X. as their leader. The *Hellenica* covers events from 411 to 364, thus significantly later than D.H. suggests here with the rebuilding of Athens' walls (which occurred in the years following 394).

175. The words in angled brackets were added by Usener from the fragments of a parallel passage of the *On Imitation*.

176. The 'historical cast' (*plasma historikon*) seems to be a particular kind of arrangement which was thought especially suitable to history. In *On Literary Composition* (4.8–9) D.H. alters the arrangement of words in H.'s celebrated opening (1.6) of the story of Croesus and Candaules, and having done so says, 'I alter the arrangement of the words and the cast becomes no longer historical and drawn out but rather excited and forensic.'

177. Philistus began with earliest times, then moved through early Sicilian history, becoming more expansive as he reached his own day; *On Sicily* ended with the year 406/5, treating 800 years in seven books; *On Dionysius* continued the story from that date, treating the elder Dionysius in four books (Diod. 13.103.3 = *FGrHist* 556 T 11a), ending with the year 367, and then in two further books the rule of Dionysius the younger to 363/2 (Diod. 15.89.3 = 556 T 11b); the history was probably left unfinished at his death in 357/6; see further Pearson (1987) pp. 23–9; R. Vattuone, *CGRH* pp. 194–6.

178. 'Favourable to tyrants' because Philistus was clearly a partisan of the elder Dionysius, assisting him in his rise to power by his financial support (Diod. 13.91.4 = *FGrHist* 556 T 3); on impartiality, Intro. §6.

179. For periods, see Agatharchides n. 17. The translation of what follows tries to get across the (excessively) long string of clauses and the use of one participial phrase after another.

180. On appropriateness for speeches see Callisthenes F 44 and Intro. §11. For Thucydides' unsuitability for the courtroom see Cic. *Orator* 30–32.

181. For Theopompus see above, p. 31.

182. Cf. P. 12.28.3–4.

183. For D.H.'s notion of 'philosophic rhetoric' see Wiater (n. 1) pp. 65–92; at p. 73 he defines this as 'not simply a certain rhetorical style among others, but [one which is] coupled with a well-defined set of political and moral values. [It] implies respect for the moral and political tradition of the *progonoi* [ancestors] . . . commitment to the *polis* and its citizens . . . and the will to achieve political excellence'.

184. For Theopompus' moralizing see above, p. 31 and next note.

185. It is surprising, given his preference for history that extols great deeds and does so largely in a positive light, that D.H. should accord praise to Theopompus for this aspect of his history. For the usual characterization of him as malicious and spiteful see P. 8.9–11; Pl. *Malice* 2; L. *Hist.* 59.

186. Cf. P. 12.25d for the comparison of historians with physicians, although the points there are rather different.

187. For Isocrates see Ephorus n. 1.

188. Cic. *Orator* 75–99 discusses the three styles, plain, middle and grand, a distinction that may go back to Theophrastus. Which one was appropriate to history was the subject of much discussion: D.H. here and in *Thuc.* 51 suggests that history should be written in the middle style, as does L. *Hist.* 43, 46, whereas Cic. (*Orator* 66; 207; *On the Orator* 2.64) and Quintilian (9.4.18, 129; cf. 2.4.2–3) advocated a more Isocratean style, while still others demanded the grand style for history: Pliny, *Letters* 5.8.9–11; Hermogenes, *On Types of Style* 408–11. See Intro. §12.

189. For Theopompus' fondness for digressions see *FGrHist* 115 TT 30–31. For Theopompus' marvels see F 381 with n. there; those mentioned by D.H. here are FF 74b and 296. Silenus is a satyr-like figure; according to H. (8.138) the Macedonians maintain that he was captured there in a place called the Gardens of Midas; possibly Theopompus was speaking of the same incident: see further the commentary at *BNJ* 115 F 75b. Nothing is known about the serpent episode.

190. D.H. adopts here a defensive posture, one that was often reserved for the law courts where speakers would only indulge in self-praise if they could plead necessity. Note that in the next sentence he speaks of praising himself.

191. Anaximenes was a fourth-century orator and historian who wrote works on Philip and Alexander and was said to have accompanied Alexander on his conquests: testimonia and fragments at *FGrHist* 72 and, with English translation and updated bibliography, *BNJ* 72 (M. F. Williams); for Theopompus see above, p. 31 and for D.H.'s praise of him, *Pomp.* 6.1–11.

192. On the importance of a 'noble' topic, *Pomp.* 3.2.

193. An echo of T. 1.22.1.

194. For claims of effort in the writing of history, see Intro. §4.

195. The 'few generations ago' is a vague reference to the years 264–146: the earlier date saw the opening of hostilities with Carthage, the latter date the destruction of both Carthage and Corinth. A preference for more recent history is also mentioned at Livy *preface* 4.

196. There has been much speculation over who these Greeks are who so maligned Rome; one persistent candidate is Timagenes of Alexandria, a contemporary of D.H.'s, and outspoken in his hostility to Rome and the emperor Augustus. Timagenes came to Rome as a prisoner in 55 BCE, but was ransomed and subsequently set free by Sulla's son. He was originally friends with Augustus but his frankness led to an estrangement, and he lived at the house of Asinius Pollio. Of his many writings we know the title of only one, *On Kings*, an attempt at universal history that began from earliest times and went to Julius Caesar. The work was hostile to Rome. His fragments are at *FGrHist* 88 and, with English translation and updated bibliography, at *BNJ* 88 (J. MacInerney and D. Roller).

197. For a similar sentiment, see Livy, *preface* 11.

198. This kind of dismissal of one's predecessors, so common in historiography, should not be taken at face value: see *ATAH* pp. 225–36.

199. Hieronymus of Cardia wrote a history of the wars of Alexander's successors (testimonia and fragments at *FGrHist* 154). The work was generally esteemed in antiquity and modern scholars, reconstructing it from Diod.'s Books 18–20, where Hieronymus is a main source, have similarly estimated it highly: see J. Hornblower, *Hieronymus of Cardia* (Oxford, 1981). Hieronymus is praised at *Oxyrhynchus Papyrus* 4808, col. 1.

200. On Timaeus see above, p. 35.

201. Practically nothing is known of Antigonus who wrote on Italian history (see *FGrHist* 816 and the commentary at *BNJ* 816 (H. Beck)) sometime possibly in the third century BCE. For P. see above, p. 51; for Silenus, P. 3.47.6 with n. 56.

202. For Fabius see P. 1.14.1–3 with n. 16; Lucius Cincius Alimentus (*FGrHist* 810; *FRHist* 2), praetor in 210 BCE, wrote a history of Rome in Greek (and possibly one also in Latin); for his importance see G. Verbrugghe, 'L. Cincius Alimentus: His Place in Roman Historiography', *Philologus* 126 (1982) pp. 316–23.

203. For very similar sentiments about history see Diod. 1.2.1–4, 10.12, 11.38.

204. For the universal demand that history be impartial, Intro. §6.

205. D.H. here seeks to assure his audience that he has a nature appropriate for the writing of history: see *Pomp.* 3.15.

206. The year of arrival was 30 or 29 BCE and thus the date of composition of this passage is 7 BCE.

207. For Marcus Porcius Cato, see above, p. 41; Fabius Maximus Servilianus (consul in 142 BCE) wrote a history in Latin (*FRHist* 8); for Valerius Antias and Licinius Macer see Livy 4.23.1–3 with nn. 19,

21; the Aelii are Q. Aelius Tubero, friend of D.H. and dedicatee of the *Thuc.* (above, n. 6) and his father Lucius (both *FRHist* 38); the Gellii are Gnaeus Gellius (*FRHist* 14) and probably Sextus Gellius (see *FRHist* vol. 1 p. 640 for his possible identity); we know of only one Calpurnius who was a historian, Lucius Calpurnius Piso Frugi: see Cic. *On the Orator* 2.51 with n. 47.

208. See below, 1.8.3, for D.H.'s rejection for his history of this 'monotonous' style of writing

209. On myth in history see Intro. §9; for similar remarks about the 'difficulty' of myths see D.H. 4.1.1–4.

210. 264 BCE, the date at which P.'s history commenced.

211. For local history see Intro. §2.

212. D.H.'s claims here for his audience both those who will follow an active life in politics as well as those who are of a more philosophical or scholarly bent. See V. Fromentin, 'La définition de l'histoire comme "mélange" dans le prologue des *Antiquités Romaines* de Denys d'Halicarnasse (I, 8, 3)', *Pallas* 39 (1993) pp. 177–92, who observes that D.H.'s words here 'designate not so much the content of the history as the use and employment that his readers (political men, orators, philosophers) can make of the content' and that D.H. 'conceives of his work simultaneously as instruction and a work of art, written as much for the pleasure of his readers as for their improvement' (pp. 181, 185). For a different delineation of history's genres and audiences see P. 9.1.1–4.

213. For other historians who give their father's name see Antiochus of Syracuse, F 2 and Josephus, *Jewish War* 1.3.

214. These remarks come at the beginning of the second half of D.H.'s history, and form a kind of second preface.

215. The 83rd Olympiad comprised the years 448–445 BCE; the synchronism which D.H. offers here with the athletic victor Crison and the eponymous archon at Athens, Philiscus, was a common way in historical accounts to bring into line the disparate calendars of individual states.

216. The 'oligarchy' to which D.H. is referring is the rule of the Decemvirs (Board of Ten) in Rome in 451–449 BCE. They were originally chosen to compose a law code for the Romans but having done so, they became more tyrannical in their behaviour and refused to abdicate until they were violently overthrown.

217. For D.H.'s philosophic rhetoric see above, n. 183; for his presumed audience, n. 212.

218. A reference to the Persian Wars of 480–479 BCE; the two sea battles are Artemisium and Salamis (both 480) and the land battle that of

Plataea (479). Both sets of troop numbers are unreliable, that for the barbarians especially so.

219. See Cic. *On the Orator* 2.63 for similar sentiments.

220. On vividness see Intro. §12.

221. For these events see above, n. 160.

222. On the utility of history see Intro. §7.

223. On this work see Kennedy (1972) pp. 634–6.

224. Plato, *Phaedrus* 245a.

225. The quotation that follows is from T. 1.22.4; it is hard to know how much was quoted since there is a gap in the text following and in fact the text that follows is uncertain. The notion, however, that history is philosophy by example is merely this author's interpretation of what T. says in speaking of the recurrence of events; T. himself nowhere either utters such a sentiment or discusses the value of examples. For examples in historiography see Intro. §8.

22. LIVY

1. For Livy's relationship with Augustus, see Tacitus, *Annals* 4.34.3; for Claudius, see Suetonius, *Claudius* 41.1. Important treatments of Livy include: P. G. Walsh, *Livy: His Historical Aims and Methods* (Cambridge, 1961); Leeman (1963) pp. 190–97; T. J. Luce, *Livy: the Composition of his History* (Princeton, 1977); *LatHist* pp. 51–81; A. Feldherr, *Spectacle and Society in Livy's History* (Berkeley, 1998); M. Jaeger, *Livy's Written Rome* (Ann Arbor, 1997); Duff (2003) pp. 79–89; J. D. Chaplin, *Livy's Exemplary History* (Oxford, 2000); D. S. Levene, *Livy on the Hannibalic War* (Oxford, 2010); and the excellent collection of essays in J. D. Chaplin and C. S. Kraus, *Livy* (Oxford, 2009). S. P. Oakley's monumental commentary on Books 6–10 of Livy (Oxford, 4 vols., 1997–2005), especially the long introduction in vol. 1, is illuminating on all aspects of Livy's work and artistry.

2. On the preface, J. L. Moles, 'Livy's Preface' in Chaplin and Kraus (n. 1) pp. 49–90 is indispensable.

3. Livy's diffident beginning, no more than a rhetorical pose, is in strong contrast with the confident openings of other historians.

4. For the reasons for writing non-contemporary history see Intro. §2; both of these are commonplaces but note that Livy does not claim either, again observing only that this is what writers believe.

5. There is something a bit dismissive about Livy's reference to his predecessors as a 'crowd' (*turba*); the phrase may be modelled on

Sallust, *Histories* 1.3 ('we in so great an abundance of learned men'), where that author too may have been comparing himself to his predecessors.

6. A nod to the fact that Livy's important predecessors in Roman history had mainly been statesmen and senators.

7. Livy plays here on the labour involved in writing history (Intro. §4) and the Roman empire labouring under its own weight.

8. A preference for the new can be found as far back as Homer's *Odyssey* (1.325–8, 336–52) where Telemachus says that the audience always prefer the new songs. Cf. D.H. *Rom. Ant.* 1.4.1.

9. A reference to the long series of civil wars that Rome had endured for nearly a century, ending with (in Livy's lifetime) the conflict first of Caesar and Pompey and then of Octavian and Antony.

10. Livy alludes here to the 'danger' of writing contemporary history: see Intro. §6. For the cares of the contemporary historian see Tacitus, *Annals* 4.33.4 and Pliny, *Letters* 5.8.12.

11. For myth and history, see Intro. §9.

12. In the first five books Livy treats the origins of the city to its conquest by the Gauls in 390 BCE. See 6.1.1–3, below.

13. This is a brilliantly understated sentence, suggesting simultaneously an understanding of the deficiencies of the early tradition of Roman history and the dissatisfaction of Rome's subject states.

14. It is unclear to what times in particular Livy is referring here. The reference to disorders and their remedies has been much discussed, most scholars seeing here a reference to the emperor Augustus' attempts at moral reformation in Rome; for the idea that 'remedy' refers to the one-man rule of Augustus as a cure for the state's ills, see Moles (n. 2) pp. 67–74, who suggests also that Livy's history is part of the remedy.

15. Diod. 1.1.2–4; Tacitus, *Annals* 3.65.1 for similar notions. For examples in history, see Intro. §8.

16. Cf. D.H. *Rom. Ant.* 1.5.3.

17. The last sentence is a clever *praeteritio*, Livy claiming that historians do not ask the gods for success (cf. L. *Hist.* 14 with n. 55) while getting the notion across anyway. We have no record of any historian before Livy invoking the gods at the beginning of his history.

18. Gaius Licinius Macer, tribune of the plebs in 73 BCE, wrote a history of Rome from its founding in at least sixteen books; testimonia and fragments at *FR Hist* 27 (S. P. Oakley).

19. The year is 434 BCE.

20. Valerius Antias, a first-century BCE predecessor of Livy's wrote a history of Rome in at least seventy-five books and was frequently

criticized by him for exaggeration. Testimonia and fragments: *FRHist* 25 (J. W. Rich); Quintus Aelius Tubero (*FRHist* 38) wrote a history of Rome in at least fourteen books in the 30s BCE.

21. Little is known of the 'Linen Books', found in the temple of Juno Moneta, on which Macer (above, n. 18) claimed to have based his history: see *FRHist* vol. 1 pp. 324–6 (S. P. Oakley).

22. The remark is sometimes cited to indicate Livy's lack of interest in determining the truth but more likely reveals a shrewd sense of the hopelessness of trying to disentangle contradictory testimonies for events so far in the past.

23. For this important passage of Livy's see the commentary of C. S. Kraus, *Livy: Ab Urbe Condita Book VI* (Cambridge, 1994) pp. 83–8.

24. The capture and burning (mentioned below) to which Livy refers occurred during the sack of Rome by the Gauls in 390 BCE. Two consuls were elected every year in the early Roman Republic, though occasionally a dictator was chosen to rule during a crisis, after which he retired from the office; decemvirs were boards of ten men chosen to rule in times of crisis (most famously such a group traditionally formed the early law code, the XII Tables: see D.H. n. 216); boards of consular tribunes (from four to eight men) first replaced consuls in 445 BCE and occasionally thereafter until 367.

25. See Feldherr (n. 1) p. 2 for the visual metaphor.

26. The war between Rome and the Samnites in 322 BCE.

27. The Roman games were traditionally instituted by Tarquinius Priscus, Rome's fifth king.

28. On funeral orations see above, Cic. *Brutus* 62; for the labels and masks see Sallust, *Jugurtha* 4.5 with n. 12.

23. THE ELDER SENECA

1. For the elder Seneca's historical activity see *FRHist* vol. 1 pp. 506–8 (B. M. Levick); the testimonia and fragments (such as they are) can be found at *FRHist* 74.

2. Most of what we know about Labienus comes from this account; for the few other pieces, see *FRHist* 62 (T. J. Cornell), with discussion at *FRHist* vol. 1 pp. 472–3; cf. Leeman (1963) p. 247.

3. On declamation, the employment of practice speeches to train for the courtroom or the assembly, see S. F. Bonner, *Roman Declamation* (Liverpool, 1949).

4. For the development of declamation into a social event, Bonner (n. 3) pp. 27–50.

5. Amongst the other duties of the Roman censors were their charge over public morals.

6. Freedom of speech was considered an essential characteristic of the historian: see Intro. §6.

7. A play on his name with *rabies*, madness, rage or fury. Cf. above, p. 35, for Timaeus' nickname *Epitimaios*.

8. The suggestion is that even under Augustus, he retained his sympathies for the lost cause headed by Pompey (not surprising since a relative, possibly his father, had defected from Caesar to Pompey at the outbreak of the civil war); the term could also be used of someone with 'republican' sympathies, i.e., hostile to the one-man rule of Augustus. See Tacitus, *Annals* 4.34.3 on Cremutius Cordus.

9. See an echo of this language at Tacitus, *Annals* 4.34.1.

10. Seneca is referring to earlier 'classic' writers such as Cic. The notion of decline in the contemporary arts, especially oratory, is a noticeable feature in the early imperial period. The man referred to is probably Cassius Severus.

11. That is to say, he was afraid that he would be denied proper burial rites.

12. Labienus is reading from a scroll, of course. Deferred publication was not unknown in the early Empire, and was meant to guarantee the reliability of the author's account. It is said that Livy's later books (121–42) were published after the death of Augustus (Livy, *Periochae* CXXI), and the Elder Pliny remarked that his history was entrusted to his heir for publication after his death, 'lest my life be judged to have conceded anything to ambition' (Pliny, *Natural History* preface 20 = *FRHist* 80 T 5). Cf. Josephus, *Life* 360–62.

24. POMPEIUS TROGUS

1. R. Develin, 'Pompeius Trogus and Philippic History', *Storia della Storiografia* 8 (1985) pp. 110–15 has argued that by 'Philippic' history Trogus meant to indicate that he followed in Theopompus' tradition of caustic moralizing, as described by D.H. *Pomp.* 6.7–8.

2. There is no complete commentary on either Trogus or Justin but for a complete and excellent recent translation of Justin see *Justin: Epitome of the Philippic History of Pompeius Trogus*, translated by J. C. Yardley, with introduction and explanatory notes by R. Develin (Atlanta, 1994). Important scholarly treatments of Trogus include Otto Seel, *Eine römische Weltgeschichte* (Nuremburg, 1972); F. R. D. Goodyear, 'On the Character and Text of Justin's

Compilation of Trogus', in id., *Papers on Latin Literature*, ed. K. M. Coleman et al. (London, 1992) pp. 210–33 (orig. pub. 1982); Develin, art. cit. (n. 1); J. M. Alonso-Núñez, 'An Augustan World History', *Greece & Rome* 34 (1987) pp. 56–72; id., *La historia universal de Pompeyo Trogo* (Madrid, 1992); J. C. Yardley, 'The Literary Background to Justin/Trogus', *Ancient History Bulletin* 8 (1994) pp. 60–70; id., *Justin and Pompeius Trogus: A Study of the Language of Justin's Epitome of Trogus* (Toronto, 2003); D. S. Levene, *CGRH* pp. 287–9.

3. Mithridates VI, king of Pontus, born *c.* 120 BCE, battled the Romans in a series of wars lasting intermittently from 89 to 63; in that last year he was soundly defeated by Pompey and forced to commit suicide. His fierce anti-Roman feelings are captured not only in the speech Trogus goes on to record here (38.4–7) but in a very similar 'letter' in Sallust's *Histories* (4.69 = 4.60 Ramsey).

4. Justin's wording here suggests that Trogus referred to them as the 'Roman' wars, i.e., from the point of view of Mithridates, whereas Justin assumes his readers will know them better as the 'Asian' wars.

5. 'As if they were in their own speech' might mean instead 'composed in their own style'. Whatever the meaning, Trogus cannot be finding fault with lengthy speeches (the speech that Justin goes on to quote is more than four full pages) but rather with the attempts by historians to impersonate the characters in their history. For similar criticism of speeches see Diod. 20.1.1–2.2; Granius Licinianus 36.30–32.

6. Cf. P. 1.14.4–8 and 16.14.6 on the historian's relationship to his native country. Cf. D.H. *A.R.* 1.6.6 for similar gratitude.

7. Because Trogus' history covered so vast a time in a relatively small compass, he cannot give the kind of detailed treatment of early Roman history that someone such as Livy or D.H. can.

25. THE YOUNGER SENECA

1. For Seneca's life and times see M. T. Griffin, *Seneca: A Philosopher in Politics* (Oxford, 1976); for discussion of Seneca and historiography see J. Master, 'The Shadow of Sallust: History-Writing in the *Natural Questions* of Seneca', *CPh* 110 (2015) pp. 333–52.

2. After the defeat of Carthage in the Second Punic War, Hannibal remained in Carthage and helped the city recover. His reforms, however, were unpopular and he went into exile at the Seleucid court where he encouraged Antiochus III to challenge Rome.

When Antiochus was defeated at the battle of Magnesia in 190, Hannibal fled to Bithynia. Betrayed to the Romans, he committed suicide before he could be captured.

3. See P. 1.35.2 and Diod. 18.59 on fortune's mutability.

4. The theme of rise and fall of empires is common in historiography beginning with H. 1.5.

5. The term 'Red Sea' in antiquity comprised the Red Sea, Indian Ocean and Persian Gulf.

6. It is likely that the first part of this sentence is lost.

7. The phrase is used by Sallust, *Jugurtha* 17.7; cf. *Pumpkinification* 1.2.

8. Seneca has been talking about the formation of comets.

9. On Ephorus see above, p. 25.

10. For strictures against marvels in history, see Intro. §9.

11. This recalls P.'s strictures about deliberate and intentional lying: P. 1.14.2 with n. 17.

12. Cf. P.'s praise (12.28.10) of Ephorus' history.

13. On this work see O. Weinreich, *Senecas Apocolocyntosis* (Berlin, 1923) pp. 13–25; Griffin (n. 1) pp. 129–33; P. T. Eden, *Seneca: Apocolocyntosis* (Cambridge, 1984) pp. 62–5.

14. The date is 13 October, the date of Claudius' death; the year is 54 CE; the term 'new year' already indicates that this is a joke since the Roman new year began in January.

15. For freedom from fear or favour as a historiographical trope see Intro. §6.

16. A. J. Woodman suggests that the words *haec ita uera* might be *haec ita<que> uera*, in which case the meaning would be 'and so these things are true', i.e., because they are written without fear or favour: for the close connection between truth and impartiality, see Intro. §6.

17. This is similar to the Greek proverb, 'for a fool and a king the law is unwritten'; Eden (n. 13) p. 64 observes that Claudius was both since he was considered a fool by his mother and was also a king in that he was a member of the imperial family (and eventually emperor, of course). But the text here is very uncertain and some think corrupt.

26. QUINTILIAN

1. On Quintilian see D'Alton (1931) pp. 464–6; Leeman (1963) pp. 329–32; Kennedy (1972) pp. 487–514; id., *Quintilian* (London and New York, 1969).

2. In addition to poetry, which Quintilian has just been discussing.

3. In a double sense: the contest in the court, but an echo too of the rejection of history as a 'competition piece' in T. 1.22.4.

4. For this notion see Pliny, *Letters* 5.8.1. Cf. Intro. §2.

5. Cf. Cic. *Orator* 65–6.

6. *The Orator's Training*, 4.2.45.

7. See Cic. *Orator* 30–32.

8. For the same metaphor see Pliny, *Letters* 5.8.10.

9. For Demetrius of Phalerum see P. n. 153. The 'multicoloured garment' suggests 'a style too ornamental for the forum' (W. Peterson, *M. Fabi Quintiliani Institutionis Oratoriae Liber Decimus* (Oxford, 1891) p. 37).

10. Cf. Cic. *Orator* 120.

11. It is free from enmity and favouritism because it already belongs to history and is not part of the contemporary world: see Intro. §6.

12. Cf. Cic. *On the Orator* 2.55–8; D.H. *Pomp.* 3–6.

13. For Theopompus see above, p. 31. It is usually assumed by ancient critics that he was 'spurred on' by his supposed teacher, Isocrates; and see n. 15. Cf. D.H. *Pomp.* 6.9–10 for Theopompus' style.

14. On Philistus, see D.H. *Pomp.* 5.1.

15. Cf. Cic. *Brutus* 204: ' . . . as Isocrates is supposed to have said about the very impetuous nature of Theopompus and the very mild nature of Ephorus, that he applied the spur to the one, the reins to the other.'

16. For Cleitarchus see Cic. *On the Laws* 1.7 with n. 78.

17. For Timagenes see D.H. *Rom. Ant.* 1.4.3 with n. 196.

18. As opposed to tragedy, Quintilian's previous topic, where the Romans were judged much inferior to the Greeks.

19. Cf. Callisthenes, F 44.

20. A prominent orator and statesman, Servilius wrote *Annals* but their scope and subject matter are unknown. His birthdate is unknown; he died in 59 CE. He and Aufidius Bassus (n. 21) are coupled together by Tacitus in his *Dialogue on Orators* 23.2–3. He is usually assumed to be a source for Tacitus in his *Annals*. Testimonia and fragments at *FRHist* 79; discussion *FRHist* vol. 1 pp. 522–4 (B. M. Levick).

21. Aufidius Bassus was slightly older than Servilius; he seems to have suffered from ill health and did not have a public career. He died *c.* 64 CE. He wrote a *German War* (scope and subject matter controversial) and a history of his own times, which may have begun with the civil wars. Testimonia and fragments at *FRHist* 78; discussion *FRHist* vol. 1 pp. 518–21 (B. M. Levick).

22.   We do not know to whom Quintilian is referring. It is usually assumed
      to be Fabius Rusticus, whose work does not survive and about whom
      there is much controversy. Testimonia and fragments are at *FRHist*
      87; discussion, *FRHist* vol. 1. pp. 568–72 (B. M. Levick).
23.   For Cremutius see Tacitus, *Annals* 4.34.

27. JOSEPHUS

1.   On Josephus' life and times see T. Rajak, *Josephus: the Historian and
     his Society*, 2nd edn (London, 2002); S. J. D. Cohen, *Josephus in Gali-
     lee and Rome* (Leiden, 1979); and the vast annotated edition of the
     Life by S. Mason, vol. 9 in the Brill Josephus project (Leiden, 2001).
2.   On Josephus' historiographical activity see R. J. H. Shutt, *Studies
     in Josephus* (London, 1961); P. Villalba i Varneda, *The Historical
     Method of Flavius Josephus* (Leiden, 1986); Z. Rodgers, ed., *Mak-
     ing History: Josephus and Historical Method* (Leiden, 2007);
     H. Chapman, *CCRH* pp. 319–31; J. C. Edmonson et al., eds., *Fla-
     vius Josephus and Flavian Rome* (Oxford, 2005) and H. Chapman
     and Z. Rodgers, eds., *A Companion to Josephus* (Malden, Mass.,
     2016), ch 5,.1–5, 11.
3.   For the greatness of events as incentive to write history, Intro. §2.
4.   On falsification because of favouritism see Intro. §6.
5.   Josephus' first account of the war was written most probably in
     Aramaic. For other historians who give their patronymic see Anti-
     ochus of Syracuse, F 2 and D.H. *Rom. Ant.* 1.8.4. For historians
     citing their status as priests, see *ATAH* pp. 109–12.
6.   The length of the war and its sufferings are also used by T. (1.23.2)
     as evidence of the greatness of the Peloponnesian War.
7.   Josephus walks a tightrope here, for he wishes both to ensure the
     accuracy of his account and to let his audience know his grief at the
     destruction of his country. The latter might seem to compromise
     the former (although see P. 16.4.6 for understanding of a historian's
     indulgence towards his country) and so Josephus must assert that
     his feelings will be kept separate from the narrative of the actions
     in the war. See also his request for indulgence in 11, below. There
     are some similar remarks in the Roman historians at the grief felt
     in light of the civil wars: see, e.g., Velleius Paterculus' remark that
     'no one has lamented the fortune of this entire era [sc. that of the
     civil wars] in a sufficiently worthy manner' (2.67.1) or the remark
     about Cremutius Cordus' 'spirit with which he lamented the civil
     wars' (*FRHist* 71 T 3).

8.   Again, Josephus assures his audience that any emotional indul-
      gence on his part is not done at the expense of truth.
9.   Some of Josephus' remarks here echo those of P. (9.2.1–3) on the
      superiority of contemporary to non-contemporary history.
10.   On expense and effort as essential to writing history see Intro. §4.
11.   The Greeks, especially the Athenians, were often characterized as
      excessively litigious.
12.   Such exaggerated claims about predecessors are common in Greek
      historiography and should not be taken at face value: *ATAH* pp.
      225–36.
13.   Cf. Livy, *preface* 2.
14.   For common benefit from history see Diod. 1.1.1 and Intro. §7.
15.   This refers, of course, to his *Jewish War*.
16.   For the (scant) use of written records in the historians see Intro.
      §3; for translating from native records see *Against Apion* 1.9 with
      n. 47.
17.   He is referring to Moses. Calling him a 'lawgiver' puts him in terms
      that a Greek audience could understand, and makes him similar to
      the Athenian Solon or the Spartan Lycurgus.
18.   For hesitation in undertaking to write history see Cic. *On the Laws*
      1.8 and Pliny, *Letters* 5.8.5–8.
19.   All Josephus' works except the *War* are dedicated to this Epaph-
      roditus but his identity is uncertain: see J. M. G. Barclay, *Flavius
      Josephus: Translation and Commentary Volume 10: Against
      Apion* (Leiden, 2007) pp. xxvi–xxviii, 3–4.
20.   For the labour of history see Intro. §4.
21.   Ptolemy II (Philadelphus), reigned 283–245 BCE.
22.   Ptolemy requested from Eleazar that he send six elders from each of
      the Jews' twelve tribes to translate the Pentateuch into Greek (*Let-
      ter to Aristeas* 33).
23.   That is, the Pentateuch; Josephus now will better that by treating
      everything that is in the Jews' sacred scriptures.
24.   This is a decidedly un-classical notion of the benefits of history: see
      Intro. §7, and cf. P. 1.1.1 where history's purpose is to teach people
      to bear changes of fortune nobly.
25.   Josephus here, following T., disavows 'the mythic' (*to mythōdes*),
      which was especially important to do when one was narrating early
      history: see Intro. §9.
26.   The Greek poets, that is.
27.   For the notion of neither adding nor detracting as an indication of
      fidelity to historical truth, see D.H. n. 19.

28. She came to the throne on the death of her husband Alexander Jennaeus and ruled from 76 to 67 BCE; her exploits are treated by
Josephus at *Antiquities* 13.405–32.

29. It is rare for historians to discuss style and language in their histories (unless they are dismissing style as of no importance), but
Josephus here acknowledges that good style was essential in writing history: see Intro. §12.

30. Josephus has just mentioned Nero's crimes, including that of murdering his mother.

31. For the falsification of history of emperors, see especially Tacitus,
Histories 1.1.1–2; *Annals* 1.1.2.

32. Much of what we know of Justus of Tiberias and his account of the
war comes from Josephus and so must be treated cautiously. Photius knew of a work entitled *The Jewish Kings in Genealogical
Order* which went down to the year 100 CE, but it is generally
thought that this cannot be the work Josephus refers to, since it does
not sound like a narrative history. Testimonia and fragments, with
English translation, at *BNJ* 734 (R. Bloch). See further T. Rajak,
'Justus of Tiberias', *Classical Quarterly* 23 (1973) pp. 345–68;
Mason (n. 1) pp. xxvii–xxxiv.

33. Josephus explains that Justus was in Berytus during events in his
home country (next passage), but Josephus may also be tapping
into the notion that ignorance about one's own land was a particularly egregious kind of error, indicating utter incompetence: see P.
12.4d.4.

34. Reminiscent of P.'s strictures: 12.14.4.

35. He is addressing Justus; the technique of direct address is common
in polemic: cf. Pl. *Malice* 26.

36. The siege of Jotapata is described in Book 3 of the *War*.

37. 'Caesar' is the emperor Titus. Josephus' appeal to the authority of
the emperor might seem a particularly dangerous tack, given the
obvious opportunities for abuse by those in power, but it is just possible that he is playing on the same sentiment that Arrian expresses
(*Anabasis* 1.1.2) whereby it is especially shameful for a king to lie.

38. Marcus Iulius Agrippa II succeeded his uncle, Herod the Great, as
king in 50; his palace was next to the temple in Jerusalem, but he
was driven out with his sister Berenice in 66, after which he supported the Romans in the war and was present with Titus in its
later stages.

39. Josephus is being sarcastic in the previous sentence, but he must
have been aware that deferred publication was often seen as an

indication that a history was more, not less, reliable: see Elder Seneca n. 12.

40. It is valuable to compare what Josephus says here about the composition of his history with how he presents the work in the preface to the *War*. Such remarks as we find here, if put into the preface of the *Jewish War*, would have immediately raised the reader's suspicion of favouritism: see Intro. §§3 and 6.

41. Presumably the king has read the first Book or two of the history.

42. It is not quite certain what the text means here.

43. The ability to write history under autocratic regimes was often dependent on access to highly placed sources, but this carried its own dangers: see Intro. §6.

44. See above, n. 19.

45. Who exactly these people are is unknown.

46. Josephus takes the kinds of criticisms that Greek historians had uttered against their predecessors and contemporaries over the centuries and cleverly exploits them so as to suggest that all of them are unreliable.

47. The notion that Egyptian history is much older than Greek is found already in H. 2.143, but Josephus here may be thinking of the Hellenistic historians Manetho of Egypt and Berossus of Babylon (both are mentioned elsewhere in the work: 1.73, 1.129). The Phoenician that Josephus is thinking of is probably Philo of Byblos, born *c*. 70 CE and an author who claimed ancient texts as the basis for his history: see *FGrHist* 790 and, with English translation and updated bibliography, *BNJ* 790 (A. Kaldellis and C. López Ruiz); not coincidentally perhaps these authors all claimed, like Josephus, to be translating native texts into Greek.

48. Cadmus was the legendary founder of Thebes.

49. Cf. D.H. *Thuc.* 5.3 who says that the earliest Greek historians did write up what was in temple archives.

50. The reference is to the *Iliad*; Josephus here anticipates the arguments of eighteenth- and nineteenth-century scholars about the oral nature of Homeric poetry: see F. A. Wolf, *Prolegomena to Homer*, translated with introduction and notes by A. Grafton et al. (Princeton, 1985) pp. 94–5 with n. 38

51. For Cadmus see Strabo n. 5; for Acusilaus see D.H. *Thuc.* 5.2 with n. 17.

52. Pherecydes of Syros (mid sixth century BCE) composed a cosmogony, believed to be the first treatise written in prose; he was said to be the teacher of Pythagoras.

53. On the ubiquity of polemic in historiography, see Intro. §1.

54. For Timaeus, see above, p. 35; Antiochus, above, p. 11; Philistus, D.H. *Pomp.* 5.1; for Callias, Diod. 21.17.4.

55. For T. as the supreme historian see D.H. *Thuc.* 2.2.

56. Draco's lawcode is usually assigned to the late seventeenth century BCE. The Athenian tyrant Peisistratus began his rule in *c.* 560.

57. Arcadia is in the Peloponnese and had the reputation in antiquity of being a particularly ancient settlement.

58. See *Jewish War* 1.1; *Jewish Antiquities, proem* 1–3.

59. Although T. (1.20.1) thought native informants no more reliable than others, most Greek and Roman historians thought native sources best knew their own countries: see, e.g., P. 12.4d.4 with n. 116.

60. Josephus has just mentioned that many Jews died rather than disobey the laws and sacred writings.

61. Josephus is suggesting that one should have the same attitude towards older writers as contemporary ones, since the latter are only following in the footsteps of the former.

62. See *Jewish War* 1.1.

63. Josephus here suggests a preliminary working-up of events which was then used as the basis for the fully fledged literary treatment of the sort described by L. *Hist.* 48.

64. Julius Archelaus was the brother-in-law of King Agrippa II; the Herod mentioned is unknown; for Agrippa see above, n. 38.

65. Cf. P. 12.25a.5, 12.25k.8–11 for schoolboy exercises.

66. Cardinal points for historiographical reliability: Intro. §3.

67. See P. 12.27 for a similar devaluation of reading sources as compared to personal presence and participation.

28. PLUTARCH

1. For all aspects of Pl., K. Ziegler, *RE* XXI.1 (1951) pp. 636–92 should be consulted. On Pl.'s life and times, C. P. Jones, *Plutarch and Rome* (Oxford, 1971) is fundamental. For Ammonius see the same author's 'The Teacher of Plutarch', *HSCPh* 71 (1967) pp. 205–13. D. A. Russell's *Plutarch* (London and New York, 1973) has much of value in its background information and insightful readings. For Pl.'s *Lives* see: A. Wardman, *Plutarch's Lives* (London, 1974) and the studies of C. Pelling in his *Plutarch and History: Eighteen Studies* (Swansea and London, 2000). Important collections of essays are: *ANRW* II.33.6 (1991); P. Stadter, ed., *Plutarch and the Historical Tradition* (London and New York, 1992);

B. Scardigli, ed., *Essays on Plutarch's* Lives (Oxford, 1995); and J. Mossman, ed., *Plutarch and his Intellectual World* (Swansea and London, 1997). On Pl.'s *Malice* and his attitudes towards history see C. Theander, *Plutarch und die Geschichte* (Lund, 1951); P. A. Stadter, *Plutarch's Historical Methods* (Cambridge, Mass., 1975); J. W. Boake, *Plutarch's Historical Judgment with Special Reference to the De Herodoti Malignitate* (diss. Toronto, 1975); the studies of Pelling just mentioned and the same author's 'De Malignitate Plutarchi: Plutarch, Herodotus, and the Persian Wars', in E. Bridges et al., eds., *Cultural Responses to the Persian Wars* (Oxford, 2007) pp. 145–65. There is a very useful edition of the *Malice* with Greek text, English translation and copious historical notes in A. J. Bowen, *Plutarch: The Malice of Herodotus* (Warminster, 1992); see also M. Grimaldi, *La malignità di Erodoto* (Naples, 2004).

2. There is a gap in the text: the supplement as printed here would have Pl. echo the opening of H.'s own text.

3. A number of Pl.'s works are dedicated (e.g., the *Parallel Lives* to Sosius Senecio, a high-ranking Roman official); the identity of this Alexander is not certain but it is likely that he is Alexander the Epicurean, known from Pl.'s *Table Talk* (2.3.1) and two honorary inscriptions from the Athenian agora. Boake (n. 1) pp. 390–96 suggests it is Alexander of Kotyaeon, the teacher of Marcus Aurelius, but this has generally not been accepted.

4. For the importance of the historian's character in evaluating his work see *ATAH* pp. 128–74. Style and character are often seen as closely related, but Pl. seems to be making two separate points, i.e., that neither H.'s style nor his character is what it seems.

5. Plato, *Republic* 361a.

6. There is a gap in the manuscripts here of three or four lines. The object of the phrase that follows, 'he has especially employed', must be something like 'this malice'.

7. See chapters 31, 33 for his defence of the Boeotians; 22, 39, 42 for the Corinthians.

8. The quotation is from a lost play (*TrGF* F 865).

9. Philip V, king of Macedon from 221 to 179, claimed to be liberating the Greeks from Roman control, but his manner and actions alienated some of them, who then defected to the Romans. He was defeated by the Romans at the battle of Cynoscephalae in 197, after which Titus Quinctius Flamininus proclaimed 'the freedom of the Greeks' at the Isthmian games. This line recurs in slightly altered form in Pl.'s *Life of Flamininus* (10.2), where it is ascribed in a slightly different context to the Aetolians.

10. On Theopompus' malice see above, p. 31; at *Lysander* 30.2 Pl. says that one trusts Theopompus more when he praises than when he criticizes.

11. 'Tokens' here are those employed in recognition scenes in Greek tragedy.

12. For similar concerns about the historian's lexical choices, see P. 8. 10–11, 12.25; L. *Hist.* 59.

13. Nicias, the Athenian general in command of the expedition against Sicily during the Peloponnesian War, was famed for his piety and devotion to divination; the latter phrase here comes from T. 7.50.4, at the point where Nicias refuses to move his troops after an eclipse (with disastrous results); Pl. treats the story at *Nicias* 23, where he does refer to Nicias' 'superstition' (*deisidaimonia*) but with a term different from the one here (*theolēptos*).

14. Athenian leader in the late fifth century, consistently reviled in our sources, especially by the comic poets. The phrase here is from T. 4.28.5, where the characterization of Cleon is ascribed to the Athenians in light of Cleon's promise to finish off the campaign against the Spartans on Sphacteria within twenty days (which, despite their contempt, he in fact does).

15. The reading here is uncertain; there may be a lacuna in the text.

16. Hyperbolus, like Cleon a popular leader, was prominent in the later phases of the Peloponnesian War, and is, like Cleon, much criticized in the comic poets; the last victim of the Athenian practice of ostracism, he was forced to leave Athens in 417 or 416 BCE and was killed in 411 on the island of Samos: T. 8.73.3, where he is called 'a scoundrel'; cf. *HCT* vol. 5 pp. 257–64; *CT* vol. 3 pp. 968–72.

17. For Philistus see D.H. *Pomp.* 5.2, where his character is defined as, among other things, that of a tyrant-lover, since he portrayed Dionysius' rule as tyrant in Syracuse in a favourable light.

18. On digressions see Intro. §12.

19. The line, from an unknown play (*TrGF* Adespota 388), is quoted by Pl. at *On Curiosity* 520B, with the addition of 'damn you' at the beginning.

20. For a similar sentiment see Cic. *On the Orator* 2.62, and the places where historians claim 'neither to have added anything nor taken anything away': D.H. n. 19.

21. For sophists, see P. n. 135. Pl. is here thinking of two aspects that came to be seen as characteristic of them: the ability to speak at length even on trivial subjects (e.g., 'praise of salt') and their notorious ability to 'make the stronger case the weaker'. Cf. below, 15, 857F, where Pl. objects to H.'s characterization of Solon as a *sophistēs*.

22. The expression here is ambiguous and it is not clear what exactly 'the better' and 'worse account' are: does Pl. mean 'more/less credible' or 'more/less favourable'? The latter might seem to display a certain naïveté for which Pl. has often been faulted; but in light of his remark at *Cimon* 2.4–5 this is almost certainly what he means: see further Russell (n. 1), pp. 61–2.

23. On Ephorus, see above, p. 25; this fragment is *FGrHist* 70 F 189.

24. For Themistocles see Cic. n. 12. Pl. tells this story at *Themistocles* 23, clearly basing himself on Ephorus there (though he does not name him). For Pausanias see D.H. n. 100. Although Themistocles and Pausanias were the architects of the two greatest victories of the Persian Wars, both men shortly thereafter fell out with their respective cities. Pausanias was accused of collaborating with the Persians and recalled to Sparta, where he fled to a temple and was starved to death; Themistocles was ostracized and then exiled from Athens and eventually made his way to the Persian court, but died before doing anything in partnership with the king. The fates of both men are treated at T. 1.128.3–138, where, as Pl. notes, no mention is made of collusion between Themistocles and Pausanias.

25. Similarly, Aristotle in the *Rhetoric* says that malice is 'always assuming the worse interpretation' (1389b20).

26. By the comic poets Pl. means specifically the poets of Old Comedy, chief amongst them Aristophanes; in the *Comparison of Aristophanes and Menander*, Pl. faults him for malice (854A, 854D *bis*) and argues that he 'imitates towards the worse' (854D), just as H. here 'conjectures towards the worse'.

27. The war is the Peloponnesian War, the responsibility for which is almost always laid at Pericles' door; in T. Pericles is portrayed as saying that the Athenians must maintain their empire and not yield to the demands of the Spartans, but in the comic poets Aspasia, Pericles' concubine, and Pheidias, who was commissioned to make the chryselephantine statue of Athena for the Acropolis but was indicted for embezzlement (Philochorus, *FGrHist* 328 F 121), were both cited (how seriously we cannot tell) as the causes of the war: see Aristophanes, *Acharnians* 524–37 (itself possibly a parody of the opening of H.'s *Histories*) and *Peace* 605–14 (respectively).

28. Alexander ruled over Pherae in southern Thessaly and was assassinated by Thebe and her brothers *c.* 359: the earliest source is X. *Hellenica* 6.4.35–7; Pl. tells the story also at *Pelopidas* 28 and 35 and refers to it at *Moralia* 256A; cf. Diod. 16.14.

29. Cato the Younger, lionized by later generations as the indomitable defender of the Roman Republic, committed suicide after the

battle of Utica in 46 BCE when his and Brutus' forces were defeated by Caesar's. Pl. offers the opinion at *Cato the Younger* 72.3 that Caesar would have spared his life.

30. A number of sources refer to the use of bribery by Philip II (king of Macedon 359–336 and father of Alexander the Great); in one of the more famous, Philip is told that a town is impregnable and he then asks if even gold could not scale its walls (Diod. 16.54.3–4); see also *Moralia* 178A–B, *Aemilius Paullus* 12.10.

31. The debate about whether bravery or fortune was more responsible for Alexander the Great's success seems to have been a stock debating theme. Pl. himself touches on it in his *On the Fortune or Virtue of Alexander*.

32. Timotheus, an Athenian general active in the 370s and 360s, was extremely successful in winning cities over to Athens' side (see X. *Hellenica* 5.4.63–6, 6.2.11–13; Diod. 15.36.5–6). Eventually prosecuted for bribery or treason, he fled to Chalcis where he died in 355/4. Pl. tells the same story of him in *Moralia* 187B–C and at *Sulla* 6.3–4.

33. Pl. clearly has in mind here statements such as H. 7.152.3 (above, p. 9). The charge of 'servility' comes from the fact that a free man is expected to be able to speak freely (see Intro. §6), and the historian who behaves as Pl. describes is hiding behind someone else's account and failing to take responsibility for his statements.

34. Aristoxenus of Tarentum, born *c.* 376, was a pupil of Aristotle, and wrote works on musical theory (some of which survive). He also wrote on the philosophers Archytas, Socrates and Plato (highly critically of the latter two). See F. Wehrli, *Die Schule des Aristoteles V: Aristoxenos*, 2nd edn (Basel/Stuttgart, 1967). This particular passage is F 55.

35. Cf. *Moralia* 51C–D for similar sentiments about flatterers; in his essay *On Praising Oneself Inoffensively*, Pl. suggests that one should admit to minor faults in order to claim the larger virtues (543F–544B).

36. On the importance of the historian's disposition see also P. 12.24 and D.H. *Pomp.* 3.15 with the notes there.

37. Io was especially known from Aeschylus' *Suppliant Women* 291–324, where the story is told how Zeus mated with her, and Hera in jealousy turned her into a cow, and thereafter set a gadfly to drive her away; she eventually arrives in Egypt where she begets a son by Zeus, Epaphus. She is a character in *Prometheus Bound*, encountering the chained Prometheus as she makes her way to Egypt. The

Ionian Sea takes its name from her, and the Bosphorus ('Cow-ford') is said to commemorate her wanderings. Her son Epaphus was said to be the ancestor of both Aegyptus and Danaus, rulers of Egypt and Argos respectively. Further details in Gantz (1993) pp. 199–203; *LIMC* V.1.661–78.

38. In H. 1.1, the seizing of Io 'explains', according to the Persians, the reason for the conflict between Asia and Europe, and forms part of a demythologized version of earlier poetic and tragic accounts.

39. H. actually says that the Persians attribute this story to the Phoeni-cians (1.1.1). There is reason to doubt that H. is referring here to any genuine local tradition; his opening stories smack of Greek rationalization.

40. The notorious remark of H. occurs at 1.4.2 where he dismisses all such stories as explanatory for the later Greek/Persian conflict. Pl. realizes that if Io went willingly with the Phoenicians, then the Greeks have no moral justification for their retaliation, and this ultimately affects the Trojan War because Io's abduction is part of a series that culminates in the abduction of Helen, the usual cause given for the Trojan War.

41. The former story appears in X. *Hellenica* 6.4.7 and Pausanias 9.13. 5–6; Pl. tells it at 773B–774D; the latter story of the rape of Cas-sandra by Ajax son of Oileus (not the more famous Ajax son of Telamon) was told in the (now lost) epics on the sack of Troy: see Gantz (1993) pp. 650–55.

42. Aristomenes was a leader of the Messenians in their revolt against Sparta, possibly in the early seventh century BCE (though the trad-itions are confused and he may belong to a later time). Pl. wrote his biography, though it does not survive; his exploits, including his capture, are told by Pausanias 4.14.6–24.3 (possibly basing himself on Pl.'s lost work). Aristomenes is not mentioned by H., and this is an odd mistake for Pl. to make: on possible reasons see D. Ogden, *Aristomenes of Messene* (2004), who suggests that a Herodotean-style treatment of Aristomenes' exploits was in circulation and that this might be the cause of Pl.'s error. For the Achaean leader Philo-poemen, see P. 10.21.2 with n. 101 (his last days are recounted at Pl.'s *Philopoemen* 18). For Regulus see P. 1.35.1–10.

43. In other words, the fact that one is captured is no indication of one's strength.

44. In the early Greek poetic tradition Busiris was a king of Egypt who sacrificed strangers who landed in Egypt, until Heracles arrived and killed him and his assistants (see *EGM* II.317–8). H. (2.45) ascribes the story to 'the Greeks', and rejects it as silly,

incompatible with actual Egyptian religious practices, and improbable; he does not mention Busiris by name, but the story was very well known.

45. H. 2.113–15 presents, as part of his rationalized version of the Trojan War, a series of events told to him by the Egyptian priests, in which Paris is blown off course to Egypt, and there his crime against his host, Menelaus, is revealed. The Egyptians are horrified and their king, Proteus, does not allow Paris to take Helen or the goods he took from Sparta to Troy, and they detain her in Egypt for the duration of the conflict, to be reclaimed by Menelaus after the war's end.

46. H. 2.119.2–3; as with the earlier parts of the story (see n. 45), H. ascribes the story to the Egyptian priests themselves.

47. There is no evidence that they were in fact honoured by the Egyptians.

48. H. makes the remark in the context of the Persians' openness to cultural borrowings (1.135). Pederastic relationships were common amongst the elite in classical Greece, and are known from all periods; heterosexual and homosexual love are both treated in Pl.'s *Erotikos*, with positive arguments made for both.

49. Pl.'s point here is not clear: he might be suggesting that castration would ruin the possibility of male love, or (conversely) that because the Persians castrated boys from the beginning, they were already aware of the erotic charms of beardless youths.

50. For these four religious items see (respectively) H. 2.4.2 and 58; 2.49.1; 2.171.2–3 and 2.61.1. The final quotation is at 2.171.1.

51. H. 2.43–4, 145–6.

52. H. 2.43, 145–6.

53. H. 2.44–5.

54. H. 2.46.1, 145.1.

55. H. 6.53–4. The Dorians claimed descent from the sons of Heracles.

56. H. 2.43–4.

57. Heracles was born in Thebes (and was thus Boeotian), while his maternal grandfather was Electryon, king of Mycenae in the Argolid (and was thus Argive).

58. On the term 'sophist' see above, n. 21; P. n. 135. The first list of the Seven Wise Men appears in Plato, *Protagoras* 343A, but the membership is not fixed: although Thales of Miletus, Solon of Athens, Pittacus of Mytilene and Bias of Priene are always included, the remaining three vary widely over more than a dozen names, including Pythagoras, Chilon of Sparta and Periander of Corinth (a

particular surprise in that H. at least portrays him as a violent tyrant). They all lived in the late seventh to early sixth century BCE.

59. H. 1.170.3; the tradition of his Phoenician origin (which may mean a descendant of those Phoenicians who came to Greece with Cadmus) was not unique to H. since his contemporary, the philosopher Democritus, also recorded it (*VS* 55 B 115).

60. The remark comes in a famous encounter between Solon and Croesus when Croesus asks Solon about prosperity and Solon warns that one's current lot is not necessarily permanent (1.32.1). The belief about the 'jealousy' of the gods is common in early Greek literature, but for Pl., who as a Platonist believed that only good things come from the gods, the sentiment was intolerable, and it is markedly absent in Pl.'s own version of the meeting (*Solon* 27).

61. Considered an 'elected tyrant' by Aristotle (*Politics* 1285a35–40), Pittacus ruled over Mytilene in the early sixth century BCE. He is the object of bitter attacks by the poet Alcaeus who claims he was destroying the city and its people. H. mentions a tradition that he visited Croesus' court (1.27.2, though this is chronologically unlikely) and dissuaded the king from mounting an expedition against the islands off the coast of Ionia.

62. Strabo 13.1.38 mentions that Pittacus was commander at this battle (*c.* 607/6) and tells the same story told by Pl. here. Pl.'s source for the story is unknown, but the battle (which was ultimately mediated by Periander) is likely to have been treated in the poems of Alcaeus: see D. L. Page, *Sappho and Alcaeus* (Oxford, 1955) pp. 152–61.

63. H. 5.94–5.

64. For these as signs of malice see chapters 3–4. For a similar complaint about focusing on bad deeds and overlooking good ones, see P. 12.15.11.

65. The Alcmaeonids were one of the most prominent clans at Athens, and the one to which Pericles belonged. Pl. takes up their story again at chapter 27 where he emphasizes their role as opponents of tyranny. Here he refers to the early incidents in H.'s narrative of Athenian history (1.59–61), where Athens is described as being beholden to three factions, two of which (led by Megacles the Alcmaeonid and Lycurgus) combined to drive out the tyrant Peisistratus. The two parties then fell out and Megacles made overtures to Peisistratus and promised to restore him on condition that he marry his daughter.

66. H. 1.61.2; the 'abnormal' way was perhaps designed to avoid pregnancy and in that sense could be taken to be an affront.

67. Thyrea was a source of conflict between Sparta and Argos for many years until they decided to have a battle in which each side had 300 selected warriors. At the end, only two Argives and Othryadas survived, but the two, assuming the victory by their numbers, left the battlefield, while Othryadas stayed and stripped the enemy dead (the usual indication of claiming victory). The next day a fresh dispute arose with new combatants and in this battle the Spartans were victorious. The story of Othryadas' suicide is mentioned at the end, possibly as a Spartan tradition (H. 1.82.8, where the quotation appears).

68. Croesus is so characterized presumably because he shows off his wealth to Solon and fails to understand Solon's warnings about prosperity (1.29–33). Upon his capture by Cyrus Croesus is indeed portrayed by H. as a 'wise adviser' (a common figure in H. whose advice is sound but ignored) to the king (1.88–91). Pl., however, accepts this role of Croesus' in *Solon* 28. The view of Cyrus as a great and wise monarch can be found in H., but Pl. has almost certainly been influenced by X.'s idealistic portrayal of him in his *Cyropaedia*.

69. On Croesus' gifts see H. 1.92, where he distinguishes the gifts Croesus sent to Delphi and the shrine of Amphiaraus (which were his own) from those to other shrines taken from the property of Pantaleon's supporter.

70. For the story of Deioces the Mede see H. 1.96–100.

71. Pl.'s summary here combines two passages, 1.143.3 and 1.146.2–3; H.'s claim that the Ionians are ashamed of the name probably dates from his own era when the Greeks of Asia Minor had a reputation for softness and servility. The notion that the Athenians and Ionians are connected is at least as old as Homer (*Iliad* 13.685–90).

72. Pactyes was entrusted by Cyrus with the task of conveying the Lydian booty to the Persian court, but he induced the Lydians to revolt, and then fled to Cyme where Pl. picks up the story; the lacuna in the text following 'the Cymaeans' makes it somewhat unclear: as H. tells it (1.153–60), the Persians demanded Pactyes from the Cymaeans, who sent him to Mytilene where the Mytileneans intended to hand him over; but the Cymaeans took him from there and brought him to Chios, where the Chians dragged him from the temple and surrendered him to the Persians; Pl.'s quotation is at 1.160.2. Atarneus was a fertile site on the island of Lesbos east of Mytilene. The 'pollution' referred to by Pl. would be the defilement of the temple arising from the forcible removal of the god's suppliants.

73. *FGrHist* 262 F 9; Charon (also cited below in chapter 24) wrote a work cited as *Chronicles of the Lampsacenes*. His date is uncertain

and it is not clear that he wrote before H., though he is almost certainly a contemporary; his plain style may have led Pl. and other critics to date him as an early writer: see D.H. *Thuc.* 5.2 with n. 17.

74. Polycrates, tyrant over Samos *c.* 540–522, is often portrayed as cunning and violent in the tradition. H. tells the story of his ring, which he flung away but which miraculously returned to him, as a warning of the dangers of prosperity. Initially supportive of Persia, his ambitions and naval power eventually brought him into conflict; lured into a trap by the Persian governor Oroetes, he was captured and crucified: see H. 3.41–3 (ring), 120–25 (capture and death).

75. H. 3.47.1; the war is probably the Second Messenian War in the mid seventh century BCE.

76. Amasis was king of Egypt *c.* 570–526; H. has many stories to tell of him (2.172–4).

77. Pl. tries to make his case by a piling-up of names. The Spartans had the reputation of being anti-tyrant in the decades leading up to Marathon (possibly because tyrants, like the Peisistratids at Athens, often supported Persia). It is not clear if Pl. is thinking of a single account where the Spartans' actions against tyrants were narrated or is merely saying that other writers have treated these expulsions in their separate works.

78. Alyattes, the penultimate king of the Lydian dynasty, reigned *c.* 610–560. Periander inherited the tyranny from his father Cypselus *c.* 625. The story of the boys is told at H. 3.48, where the action is explained as retaliation for the murder of Periander's son, Lycophron (3.49–53).

79. H. says only that the boys were taken by the Samians back home to Corcyra (3.48.4).

80. Antenor of Crete wrote a history of the island (date unknown), of which only this (*FGrHist* 463 F 2) and two other fragments survive; Dionysius of Chalcis wrote a work entitled *Foundations* in five books: testimonia and fragments at *FGrHist* 1773 (D. Engels); this fragment is F 9.

81. H. mentions Archias (whose grandson, also named Archias, he claims to have met and spoken with) at 3.55.

82. The story of the liberation of Athens from the tyrants is told at 5. 62–5; Cleisthenes is mentioned as the one who bribed the priestess at 5.66.1. Themis is said by Aeschylus (*Eumenides* 1–6) to be the second to hold the seat at Delphi after Earth, her mother, and before Apollo. (Themis is also the personification of law or right action.)

83. For this technique as a sign of malice, see above, chapter 9.

84. H. 5.66. Isagoras, son of Tisander, is portrayed as Cleisthenes' opponent, who, when bested by Cleisthenes, appeals to the Spartans for their support; they come but meet resistance from the Athenians and eventually depart (5.66, 72). Caria was an area of south-west Asia Minor that, while Hellenized, was not quite Greek. The last sentence contains a pun on the phrases *eis Karakas* ('to the Carians') and *eis korakas* ('to the crows', often used in the sense of 'to hell').

85. H. 5.55, 57.1.

86. H. 5.90–91.1. Hippias, the deposed tyrant of Athens, had fled to Sigeum on the Scamander river: 5.68.3.

87. H. 5.92, the longest speech in H. and noteworthy for its extended narrative of Corinthian history under the tyrants.

88. For the story of the boys see above, n. 78. Pl.'s point seems to be that Socles' speech indicated an inconsistent character for the Corinthians since in his speech he finds fault with tyranny but the Corinthians themselves, in the incident of the boys, had shown great cruelty and support for the actions of the tyrant.

89. Pl. moves here to H.'s account of the Ionian Revolt (499–494 BCE); Sardis, the capital of Lydia, was a wealthy and important city in the Persian empire.

90. H. 5.97.3: 'these ships were the beginning of evils for Greeks and barbarians'; H.'s phrase (*archē kakōn*) is meant to recall Homer, *Iliad* 5.62, 11.604; and Pl. clearly caught the allusion since he actually uses the adjectival form *archēkakous* employed by Homer.

91. H. 5.99, 102.3.

92. Miletus, the 'ornament of Ionia', was a wealthy and powerful city at the mouth of the Maeander. Its recapture in 494 BCE and subsequent destruction at the hands of the Persians marked the end of the Ionian uprising against Persia.

93. *FGrHist* 426 F 1; once again Pl. uses a local history to correct and improve H. Nothing is known of Lysanias who is mentioned only here: see the discussion at *BNJ* 426 (C. J. Tuplin).

94. *FGrHist* 262 F 10; for Charon see above, n. 73 and D.H. *Thuc.* 5.2; for the Eretrians' defeat, H. 5.102.3.

95. H. 6.108.1–4, where the story is told to account for the Plataeans' presence in assisting Athens at Marathon. Plataea, while in Boeotian territory, refused to be part of the Boeotian alliance headed by Thebes, and this led to perpetual friction between Athens and Thebes.

96. Pl. seems to be reading ahead here, knowing, as he does, that the attack on Plataea by the Thebans was the opening event of the Peloponnesian War (T. 2.1).

97. It is not clear if by 'already convicted' Pl. is referring to a particular refutation of this incident by a predecessor.

98. H. 6.105–6 for the dispatch of Philippides to Sparta and the Spartans' reply.

99. The Attic month Boedromion, the second of the year, fell in late summer; the Athenians held a festival to Artemis on the sixth of this month, at which they commemorated Marathon (which Pl. mentions just below), and Pl. supposes this to have been the actual day of the battle. For the Spartans' viewing of the Persian corpses, H. 6.120.

100. H. 6.106.3.

101. Greek calendars were lunar, the middle of the month (i.e., the fourteenth) being the full moon; the Spartans thus could not have gone out until the fifteenth day of the month. But Pl. assumes, from the date of the festival (n. 99), that the Spartans would have arrived at Marathon around the tenth or so of the month, well before the full moon.

102. There is a gap in the text here: the supplement, by Pearson, would have Pl. echo H.'s own words about his purpose as they appear in the preface.

103. Again, Pl. assumes that the battle was on the sixth.

104. *FGrHist* 73 F 3. Diyllus wrote a history in twenty-six books, covering events from the outbreak of the Third Sacred War (357/6) to the death of Philip, son of Cassander, in 297/6. Diod. 16.76.6 says that he treated some of the same events as Ephorus and that his second part continued from where Ephorus left off. The total of ten talents, a sizeable fortune, is out of all proportion to similar grants and can hardly be genuine; the story arose in a different (later) milieu where historians began to be rewarded for their efforts in composing histories for individual cities: see chapter 31 below.

105. Again, it is not known to whom Pl. is referring here.

106. H. 6.117.1 records 192 Athenian, 6,400 Persian dead; the latter number became greatly magnified in the later tradition; the story of the 500 goats vowed to Artemis was already known to X. who mentions it in a speech to his troops (*Anabasis* 3.2.12).

107. H. 6.115–16.

108. For the use of harsh words as an indication of malice see above, chapter 2 (855B).

109. H. 6.113.1 says in fact that the battle lasted a long time, but Pl. is probably thinking of the general brevity of his account.

110. Pl. is probably thinking here of Theopompus whom he mentioned earlier (chapter 1) and who specifically criticized the Athenians for magnifying that nature of their struggle with the Persians: see, e.g.,

FGrHist 115 F 153: 'The Hellenic oath, which the Athenians say the Hellenes swore against the barbarians before the battle of Plataea, is falsified, as is the treaty of the Athenians with King Darius. Moreover, the battle of Marathon did not happen in the way that all celebrate it, and all the other things that the city of Athens brags about and uses to dupe the Hellenes.'

111. In *Aristides* 5.5 Pl. has the Persians after the battle blown by the winds 'inwards, towards Attica'; he clearly is using a different tradition here which has them blown far away from Attica.

112. H.'s exoneration of the Alcmaeonids is part of a long digression at 6.121–31 after his narrative of the battle; the claim quoted by Pl. is 6.124.2.

113. H. 6.121.1; the 'little crab' perhaps derives from a fable of a crab and snake: see E. Diehl, ed., *Anthologia Lyrica Graeca*, vol. 2 (Leipzig, 1964) p. 184.

114. For this technique as a sign of malice, see chapter 8.

115. The quotation is at 6.121.1; the alliance: 1.60.2–61.2, and above, chapter 16.

116. H. mentions these three at 6.121.1, but he does not mention their wealth; the assertion that H. wished to curry favour with Hipponicus is Pl.'s own inference.

117. H.'s story of the Greeks' attempt to enlist Argive assistance is at 7. 148–52.

118. For malice as putting a sinister cast on matters that cannot be denied, see chapter 6.

119. The quotations are from (respectively) H. 7.150.3, 7.151, 7.152.2–3; for the technique see H. n. 18.

120. At 3.20–22 the Persian king Cambyses sends gifts to the Ethiopians; the Ethiopian king, suspecting that the Persians were spies, refutes Cambyses for the deceptiveness of the clothing (because it had been dyed and was thus 'false') and the perfume (because it masked a real odour with a false one).

121. The quotation is from Euripides, *Andromache* 448.

122. See chapter 8 for this technique as a sign of malice.

123. On Heracles as Argive, above, chapter 14.

124. The Siphnians and Cythnians are both attested as having fought against the Persians but they were tiny towns, the former providing but one (8.48), the latter two (8.46.4) ships for the Greek fleet.

125. For Laconia, above, P. n. 255; for Thyrea, above n. 67.

126. H. (9.12) has the Argives tell the Persians that they were unable to keep the Spartans from marching out, but he does not detail any effort by them to do so.

127. Pl. here takes on one of the most famous passages in H., his lengthy argument (7.139) that the Athenians were most responsible for the Greek victory over the Persians; the phrase 'saviours of Greece' occurs at 7.139.5.

128. See below, chapters 31, 33, 35 for Pl.'s attack on H.'s portrayal of the Thebans and Phocaeans.

129. H. uses a series of counterfactuals to argue that the other Greeks could not have withstood Persian power without the Athenians (7.139.2–4), and it is this 'imaginary' history that Pl. attacks.

130. Pl.'s point being, of course, that since the Spartans fought to the last man at Thermopylae, they would have done likewise in any other battle.

131. H. 7.190. Pl. suggests that the comment was gratuitous and thus indicative of malice (see chapter 3 where the introduction of an irrelevant misfortune is specifically mentioned).

132. *FGrHist* 379 F 5. Aristophanes wrote *Theban Chronicles* (possibly called *Boeotian Matters*) but little is known of him; of the nine fragments that survive Pl. cites two (here and in chapter 33); he probably wrote in the late fifth/early fourth century BCE (so Jacoby ad loc.; further discussion at *BNJ* 379 (A. Schachter)). Again, the demand for money (above, n. 104) suggests a much later milieu than H.'s.

133. Cf. above, chapter 1, for Pl.'s claim that a defence of the Boeotians was an important part of his essay. The suggestion that H. 'hated' the Boeotians would indicate an inappropriately biased approach to the writing of history: Intro. §6.

134. An amalgamation of 7.172.1 and 7.139.3.

135. Tempe was the first place the Greeks determined to make their stand against Persian land forces but they withdrew when informed of an alternative path (7.173.4, offered as H.'s opinion). H. mentions the total forces sent to Tempe as 10,000 (7.173.2) but says nothing of the Theban contingent in particular, nor does he name their commander Mnamias; Pl. must have got this information elsewhere.

136. Pl. presumably here is referring to the Greek decision to abandon the mainland and entrust their fortunes to their navy. He writes as if the Thebans decided to medize only when the rest of the Greeks took to their ships, while in H. the decision to take to the ships is in part because the Thebans and others had medized (see 8.34.1 where the Boeotians are described as already having medized when Xerxes enters their territory). Guest-friendship (*xenia*) was a reciprocal relationship whereby men offered hospitality to those visiting

from different countries and served as their sponsors and protectors when their guest-friends visited.

137. Pl. had just attacked him for saying so: see chapter 29 (865A) above.

138. See above, chapter 6, for this technique as an indication of malice.

139. H. 7.222.

140. H. 7.220.2 and 7.222.

141. H. 7.220.4.

142. Given that the dream foretells the later rise and swift fall of the Theban hegemony (371–362 BCE), it must come from a time after those events, and is thus, of course, post-Herodotean. (It presents no problem for Pl. because he believes in prophetic dreams.)

143. H. 7.225.2–3.

144. This story is recorded by Diod. (11.9.4–10.4) and Justin (2.11.5–18); it may go back to Ephorus.

145. If Pl. wrote this life it does not survive; there is a collection of sayings of Leonidas at *Moralia* 225A–E; some of the remarks here are also found there.

146. There is a gap in the text here and the word 'matters' must follow from what has gone before. No suitable supplement has been suggested. At *Moralia* 225E, Leonidas tries to save three men, the second of whom replies, 'I would be a better man if I remained here', but it is not certain that this is any help for the present passage.

147. The celebration of the funeral games while still at Sparta must belong to the tradition (again, post-Herodotean) that the Spartans (or at least Leonidas) knew that they were going to certain death. As to the two Spartans Leonidas tried to dismiss, H. mentions alternative traditions about two Spartans at Thermopylae (7.229–32), one of whom is sent as a messenger, but those have little in common with Pl.'s account here.

148. H. 2.162.3, 2.121δ.

149. H. 7.233.1 for the Thebans fighting under compulsion; the whips refer to the method used by Xerxes' commanders for driving the Persian allies forward against the Spartans (7.223.3).

150. H. 7.233.1–2.

151. H. does not mention this battle but Pl. mentions it at *Camillus* 19.4, where it is dated 'more than 200 years before Leuctra', i.e., before 571, and so hardly 'until recently'.

152. H. 7.233.2.

153. The son of Leontiades, Eurymachus, played a role in the Theban attack on Plataea that opened the Peloponnesian War (T. 2.2.3), and it has been suggested that contemporary hostility against the son resulted in the accusation of medism against the father.

154. *FGrHist* 379 F 6: for Aristophanes see above, n. 132; *FGrHist* 271–2 F 35: Nicander was active in the late third/early second century BCE and was honoured by the Delphians for composing a song for them (*SIG*³ 452, dated between 225 and 210 BCE); a number of historical works are attributed to him: see *BNJ* 379 (F. Jenkins).

155. For Xerxes' mutilation of Leonidas' corpse, H. 7.238, which H. sees as the greatest evidence that Xerxes hated Leonidas more than all others. Pl. is trying to suggest that the branding of Leontiades was a similar action from a similar motive.

156. H. 6.129.4; Hippocleides was a guest at the home of Cleisthenes of Sicyon who was holding a contest for his daughter's hand. Hippocleides was the leading candidate until one evening he got carried away and began to dance on the table; Cleisthenes in anger told him he had 'danced his marriage away' to which Hippocleides gave the response, 'Hippocleides doesn't care!'

157. For Pindar see D.H n. 177; this is F 77 Snell, quoted several other times by Pl. In another fragment Pindar refers to Athens as the 'bulwark of Hellas' (F 76), but his attitude towards the Persian Wars is not easy to discern.

158. Artemisium takes its name from a temple of Artemis (Artemis Prosēoa, i.e., 'facing east') on the north-west corner of the island of Euboea. The Greek navy had been sent there as part of the advance strategy, which included Thermopylae (the 'Gates' referred to here): H. 7.175–7.

159. H. 8.18. For the use of harsher terms when milder ones are available as an indication of malice, see chapter 2; the objection here may seem overdone, but it is an essential part of Pl.'s characterization of H.

160. H. 8.23.1.

161. On the temple of Artemis 'Facing East', see above, n. 158.

162. *FGE* XXIV; the lines are also quoted at *Themistocles* 8.4. If the poem really did refer to the battle of Artemisium, the phrase 'destroyed the army of the Medes' would seem exaggerated, since the Persian navy was far from through.

163. H. 8.21.2.

164. Thurii was a pan-Hellenic colony in Italy founded in 443 under the leadership of Athens (Diod. 11.90.3–4), and there was an ancient tradition that H. joined this (Aristotle, *Rhetoric* 3.9.2 says that H.'s work began 'H. of Thurii', although our manuscripts begin 'H. of Halicarnassus'); Pl. discussed the question in his *On Exile* (604F). Pl. rejects Thurii here so that he can sneer at the Halicarnassians; it is not clear why he thought H. 'protective' of them: perhaps

because of the role that H. assigns to Artemisia (see below, n. 181; whence also the references to 'harem'). On the Halicarnassians as Dorian see H. 7.99.3.

165. H. 8.30.1–2.

166. H. 8.32–3, where twelve, not thirteen, cities are named.

167. For the suggestion of bad motives as a mark of malice, see chapter 6.

168. When the Greeks formed their alliance against the Persians, a major condition was to end any fighting between members of the confederacy (H. 7.145.1), the chief offenders being Athens and Aegina; H. does not mention reconciliation between Chalcis and Eretria (though the two had been inveterate enemies) or Corinth and Megara (who often clashed over the land on the borders).

169. Nothing is known of Lacrates; he is unlikely to be a historian and Pl.'s words make it sound more as if he gave some kind of oral testimony after the Persians' retreat.

170. H. does not list the Phocians when he gives the Greek battle order (9.28.2–6); he does mention 1,000 Phocians serving for Persia where he also notes that not all had medized and some Phocians were making raids from Parnassus on the Persian army (9.31.5).

171. H. says that Naxos sent four ships (8.46.3).

172. *FGrHist* 4 F 183 and 70 F 187. For Hellanicus see D.H. *Thuc.* 5.2 with n. 18; for Ephorus see above, p. 25.

173. The gap in the text has not been plausibly emended.

174. H. 6.96. Pl. is again being sarcastic.

175. For silence about noble actions as a marker of malice, see chapter 4.

176. *FGE* XIX; cf. Page's comment ad loc.: 'probably a short piece designed for recitation at symposia'. Simonides of Ceos was the most famous poet of his time, being renowned already in the late sixth century BCE, and becoming known eventually as the great poet of the Persian Wars. None of his poems survives entire, but he was proficient at virtually every genre of poetry, and in some traditions he was seen as a wisdom figure.

177. The Aeginetans and Athenians claimed first and second place: see H. 8.84.

178. For Themistocles see Cic. *Letters to Friends* 5.12.5 with n. 12. H. does not mention Themistocles' erection of a temple to Artemis: see Pl. *Themistocles* 22.2; Themistocles had his house at Melite, which lay west of the Athenian agora.

179. The passages are (respectively) H. 8.57.1–2, 8.57.2, 8.58.1, 8.58.2. The belief that Themistocles was the architect of the winning naval

strategy is everywhere in the tradition, appearing already in the speech that T. gives the Athenians at Sparta when they are defending themselves (1.72–78). Mnesiphilus was prominent enough to have been a candidate for ostracism, but only H. gives him the credit for this strategy. Pl. in *Themistocles* 2.6 has Mnesiphilus as an early and influential teacher of Themistocles, a way of both maintaining his presence in the tradition as known from H. and not taking any credit away from Themistocles for his winning strategy. See further Pelling, 'De Malignitate Plutarchi' (n. 1) 158–9.

180. Although even in H. Themistocles shows Odyssean cunning, no one other than Pl. says that he had this nickname, nor does Pl. use it in his own *Themistocles*.

181. H. 8.68β–γ. Artemisia took over the rule of Halicarnassus after the death of her husband Mausolus. H. clearly found her a fascinating figure, not least because she was a woman fighting against men; she here plays a role common in H.'s work, that of the 'wise adviser' (above, n. 68).

182. Sibyls were inspired female seers who usually gave their prophecies in verse; they were not associated with oracles (as was, for example, the Pythia at Delphi) and were of indeterminate number, although the most famous ones were at Erythrae and Cumae. Xerxes hands over his children to Artemisia to escort back to Susa after his defeat at Salamis (H. 8.103).

183. H. 8.94.2–3.

184. For the tragic crane see P. 3.48.8–9 with n. 59; for the stage as a locus for improbabilities and falsehoods, see Intro. §9.

185. H. 8.94.4; it is often pointed out in H.'s defence that he gives this only as an Athenian version; but Pl. will have recognized that H. tacitly accepted the Athenian account since in his narrative of the battle H. gives the Corinthians no actual role.

186. T. 1.73.2–74.4; an argument from silence, of course, but given Athenian hatred for Corinth in these years, it's hard to imagine they would not have brought up so powerful a charge if it were to hand.

187. H. 9.81 says that the Greeks, after their final victory at Plataea, made dedications to Apollo, Zeus and Poseidon; the one to Apollo was a golden tripod atop a bronze column in the shape of a three-headed snake. The tripod was melted down by the Phocians in the fourth century (Pausanias 10.13.9) but the column (called the 'Serpent Column') survived and was eventually taken by Constantine to Constantinople and placed in the Hippodrome (where a part of it survives to this day). On this monument the Corinthians do

indeed come third, after the Lacedaemonians and the Athenians: see C. W. Fornara, *Archaic Times to the End of the Peloponnesian War*, 2nd ed. (Cambridge, 1983), no. 59, coil 2.

188. *FGE* XI; the first two lines partly survive on stone: *Inscriptiones Graecae*, vol. 1, 3rd edn (Berlin, 1981), no. 1143; at least one source attributes it to Simonides.

189. *FGE* XII; further lines of this are quoted by Aelius Aristides and the Palatine Anthology: see Page ad loc., who points out that the verb *keimetha* ('lie dead') seems inappropriate for a cenotaph.

190. *FGE* XIII.

191. *FGE* X; the ascription to Simonides is 'not to be taken seriously' (Page ad loc.).

192. It was not uncommon for the Greek elite to name their children so as to commemorate their own achievements. The children's names mean (respectively) 'victory with ships', 'best of the spoils', 'averter of violence' and 'champion'.

193. See above, n. 84 for Caria.

194. See Pausanias 2.5.1 for the temple, which was dedicated on the citadel to the 'armed' Aphrodite. The story of Jason's love for Thetis is not directly attested elsewhere.

195. *FGE* XIV. Cypris is an alternative name for Aphrodite. The lines are also quoted by Theopompus (*FGrHist* 115 F 285), Timaeus (556 F 10), Athenaeus 13.32, 573C–E and the scholion to Pindar, *Olympian Odes* 13.32; see the full discussion at *FGE* 207–10, where Page concludes that Theopompus' version is probably the correct one and that the verses accompanied a painting, not a statue.

196. See above, chapter 30; and for omission of noble actions as an indicator of malice, chapter 4.

197. H. 8.112.

198. H. 8.122. H. notes (8.93.1) that the Aeginetans were regarded as the best fighters at Salamis and the Athenians were second. Apollo's demand in H. is ambiguous: either he means he wants a dedication commensurate with the Aeginetans' having fought best overall or he wants the Aeginetans to award their prize of valour to him. H. says that in response to the god's demand they dedicated three gold stars on a bronze mast (8.122).

199. Pl. has not previously mentioned the Scythians (a nomadic people who resided in what is now Ukraine and southern Russia), even though H. devoted more than half a book to them (4.1–142) and to Darius' ultimately unsuccessful attempt to conquer them.

200. Aesop, probably from the early sixth century BCE, was famous for his animal stories and is often mentioned by Pl. The point here is

that H.'s speeches have as much truth value as speeches assigned to animals.

201. Pl. here follows the tradition largely developed by the Athenians themselves, that they were the ones most responsible for the victory at Salamis; the viewpoint is pervasive especially in Athenian oratory of the fourth century BCE (see M. Nouhaud, *L'utilisation de l'histoire par les orateurs attiques* (Paris, 1982) pp. 155–61), which Pl. knew well.

202. H. 8.123.

203. A rather surprising remark from Pl. here, given that he has been criticizing H. throughout for being such a fault-finder.

204. H. 8.124.1.

205. H. 8.144 (Spartan fear concerning Athens); 9.6–9 (Spartan delay).

206. H. 9.9; for guest-friendship see above, n. 136.

207. Cf. chapter 37 for Pl.'s objections to H.'s portrayal of Mnesiphilus who likewise communicated essential strategy; as in that previous passage, the introduction of an external adviser robs the main characters of the renown that ought to be theirs.

208. H. 9.26–7 has the Tegeans and the Athenians rehearse their great deeds before the Spartans as a way of determining who would hold the left wing (the right always being held by the Spartans); the Athenians mention several deeds from their past, including Marathon, after which the Spartans award them command of the wing (9.26–7).

209. H. 9.46, one of the oddest incidents in H.'s account of Plataea, the more so in that it comes to nothing, for the Persians, seeing the switch, then switch their own lines, after which the Greeks go back to their original formation. Pl. treats the incident in *Aristides* 12.

210. H. 9.52; the Heraion is the temple of Hera; scholars have assumed that some tactical manoeuvre, misunderstood by H., lies behind this, but H.'s account of the fighting at Plataea, as is usual in his battle narratives, focuses on just a very few cities.

211. H. 9.59.1, 9.67.

212. H. 9.69.2 for the Phleiasians and Megarians, 9.69.1 for the Corinthians.

213. H. 9.68 for the Boeotian (not only Theban) cavalry; see above, chapter 33 (866F and 867B) for the branding of the Thebans.

214. *IEG*² FF 15–16; the lines are often printed as a single six-line unit, but it is clear that the last three lines are part of a separate poem, and I have translated them as they are presented in *IEG*². Ephyra is mentioned by Homer as a city in Argos (*Iliad* 6.152) and is later equated with Corinth. Glaucus, son of Sisyphus and Merope, was king in Corinth.

215. The 'gold honoured on high' is the sun.

216. Pl. clarifies this in this way because if Simonides had written it for a chorus or as a hymn, it would have had a largely panegyrical tone, and could thus be judged as not wholly trustworthy; so he suggests that Simonides wrote it in the more straightforward language of a simple account, an argument he can make because the lines are not written in a hymnic metre.

217. See Pl., *Aristides* 21.2–3, Pausanias 9.2.6 and Strabo 9.2.31 for the ceremonies still celebrated at Plataea in Pl.'s own day; given that Plataea had been destroyed more than once between the Persian Wars and Pl.'s own time, it is unlikely that the celebrations that Pl. knew were part of an unbroken chain going back to the fifth century BCE.

218. H. 9.85.3.

219. The Serpent Column (n. 187), where the Aeginetans appear on coil 3.

220. H. 9.85.3.

221. For the Athenians and Spartans nearly coming to blows (not in H.) see *Aristides* 20.1–4.

222. *FGE* XV; the three lines appear also in Pl. *Aristides* 19.7; *Palatine Anthology* 6.50 (ascribing the poem to Simonides) has an additional verse between Pl.'s first and third ('trusting to the daring strength of their spirit'), but this is not likely to be part of the original: see *FGE* pp. 211–12. On the altar to Zeus Eleutherios ('Zeus of freedom'), see Pausanias 9.2.5.

223. *FGE* XVII(a); the story is told at greater length by T. 1.132, who states that the inscription was on the 'tripod' (see above, n. 187) and that, as Pl. says in the next sentence, the Spartans had these offensive lines immediately erased and replaced with the names of all the cities that had jointly fought and defeated the barbarians. On Pausanias' actions after the war, see above, n. 24.

224. Sochares is probably the Sophanes of H. 9.73.1 (called Sochares also in Pl.'s *Cato the Elder* 29.2); for Aeimnestus see H. 9.64.2.

225. On the Cythnians see above, n. 124; the Melians provided two ships at Salamis: H. 8.48; for their names on the monument see coils 10 and 7 (respectively).

226. In beginning his summation Pl. now mentions his previous complaints; for the incidents he refers to here see: H. 8.18 (Artemisium); 7.206 (Thermopylae); 8.68–9, 87–8, 93, 101–103 (Artemisia); 9.69–70.1 (Plataea).

227. A 300-line 'battle of frogs and mice' survives attributed to Homer, although this can hardly be accepted. The Byzantine lexicon

known as the Suda says Pigres was Artemisia's brother (though neither son nor brother is likely), and the work is also ascribed to a Tigres.

228. H. 9.62.3 and 9.63.2; this is a new point not previously made by Pl.

229. H. does not say they were 'unarmed', though the phrase could be read that way; but it is clear that he means without the heavy protective armour of the hoplite.

230. Pl. alludes here to and alters *Odyssey* 11.368 where Alcinous compliments his guest, Odysseus: 'you have recounted the tale knowledgeably, like a poet'; although the remark 'like a poet' in Homer has a positive sense, Pl. here follows Plato in believing that poetry is marked by its agreeable nature, but that poets themselves tell many falsehoods.

231. Pl. has to identify Julius Caesar in this way since many of the emperors were also called 'Caesar'.

232. For another remark comparing history and biography see P. 10.21. 2–8.

233. This is the dedicatee of Pl.'s *Parallel Lives*.

234. This is P.'s 'pragmatic' history: 9.1.4 with n. 98.

235. For the treatment of mythical material in history see Intro. §9.

236. Lycurgus was the (almost certainly legendary) early lawgiver of Sparta. Numa was Rome's second king, Romulus its first. Theseus, though here called the 'founder', was not (even in legend) Athens' founder in the way that Romulus was for Rome; rather he was credited by the Athenians with unifying Attica, a move that signalled the first steps in Athens' rise to greatness. See T. 2.15.

237. *Seven Against Thebes* 435, 395–6.

238. For other remarks 'excusing' incursions into early history see Diod. 4.1.1–4 and Livy, *preface* 6–7 (which suggests a similar indulgence for early accounts).

239. Pl. has been discussing rumours against Pericles, including that he had relations with his son's wife.

240. A writer of the fifth century BCE whose works are lost to us; he wrote a political pamphlet on some of the politicians of his time, including Themistocles, Pericles and Thucydides, son of Melesias (not the historian). Testimonia and fragments at *FGrHist* 107 and, with English translation and updated bibliography, at *BNJ* 107 (S. Dmitriev).

241. On flattery and hostility see Intro. §6.

242. In this essay, also known as *Were the Athenians More Renowned in War or Wisdom?*, Pl. argues that doers of deeds are always the most important members of the community and that it was they

who made Athens great. We pick up his argument here (the beginning of the treatise is lost) at a point where he is saying that without great deeds there are no historians. For the notion of the historian's glory being dependent on his subject see Callisthenes, T 8 with n. 2 and Intro. §2.

243. The references to T.'s work are (respectively): 2.65, 2.86–92, 4.53–7, 3.51, 4.42–5, 4.3–16, 4.30–39, and 1.108.

244. On Cratippus (whose work does not survive), see D.H. *Thuc.* 16.2. Some of these events are known from other historians.

245. This is an unusual phrase; Pl. seems to suggest that the historian and his theme became one.

246. On X. see above, p. 23. In the *Hellenica* (3.1.2) X. says that a certain Themistogenes of Syracuse has written up an account of the retreat of the 10,000 after the battle of Cunaxa, an obvious reference to X.'s own *Anabasis*. Though scholars have argued on both sides, the general consensus today is that expressed here by Pl., namely that X. used a pseudonym, though not all agree with Pl.'s reasons for why X. did so.

247. The first three are all Athenian historians (*FGrHist* 323, 73 and 328, respectively), chosen no doubt not because they were famous but because they were Athenian; on Phylarchus, see P. 2.56.

248. See Sallust, *Catiline* 3.2 for a different reflection on the historian's renown. For the historian as mirror, L. *Hist.* 51.

249. On Simonides see n. 176.

250. Cf. D.H. *Rom. Ant.* 11.1.3; on vividness, Intro. §12.

251. These events are narrated at T. 4.9–12; for the paradox of the reversal of Athenian and Spartan roles see 4.12.3.

252. The full quotation of this passage (there are gaps here in the manuscripts of Pl.) can be found at D.H. *Thuc.* 26.2.

253. The text here is very uncertain.

29. TACITUS

1. For Tacitus' life and times, R. Syme, *Tacitus*, 2 vols. (Oxford, 1958), is exhaustive and somewhat overwhelming; more readable are R. H. Martin, *Tacitus* (London and Berkeley, 1981; rev. edn, Bristol, 1994) and R. Ash, *Tacitus* (London, 2006). For Tacitus' methods and notions of history see B. Walker, *The Annals of Tacitus* (Manchester, 1962); Leeman (1963) pp. 337–60; J. Ginsburg, *Tradition and Theme in the Annals of Tacitus* (New York, 1981); R. Mellor, *Tacitus* (London and New York, 1993); *LatHist*

pp. 88–118; R. Ash, *Ordering Anarchy: Armies and Leaders in Tacitus' Histories* (London and New York, 1999); Duff (2003) pp. 93–101; E. C. O'Gorman, *Irony and Misreading in the Annals of Tacitus* (Cambridge, 2000); and H. Haynes, *The History of Make-Believe: Tacitus on Imperial Rome* (Berkeley and Los Angeles, 2003). Three excellent collections of essays are: T. J. Luce and A. J. Woodman, *Tacitus and the Tacitean Tradition* (Princeton, 1993); A. J. Woodman, ed., *Cambridge Companion to Tacitus* (Cambridge, 2009); and R. Ash, ed., *Tacitus* (Oxford Readings in Classical Studies, Oxford, 2012).

2. The year is 69 CE.

3. Actium, where Octavian (the future Augustus) defeated Antony and Cleopatra, was fought in 31 BCE and marked the end of nearly a century of civil war; over the next decades Octavian consolidated his power to become the 'first citizen' (*princeps*) of Rome.

4. Tacitus is most probably referring here to republican historians, ending with Livy.

5. For the importance of political experience see P. 12.25d–28a; cf. Dio 53.19.2–3.

6. This must refer to the writers of the early empire, though it is difficult to tell which ones specifically Tacitus has in mind.

7. For the dangers of flattery and hostility, Intro. §6.

8. These three were all short-lived emperors in the year of civil war (68–69 CE) which followed on the death of Nero, the last of the Julio-Claudians.

9. The Flavian emperors ruled (respectively) 69–79 CE, 79–81, 81–96.

10. Nerva ruled 96–8, Trajan, 98–117. Tacitus seems never to have written such a history, since in his next work, the *Annals*, he went further back in time to the Julio-Claudians, beginning with Tiberius.

11. Richer perhaps because of Trajan's conquests (cf. *Annals* 4.32.1–2) and safer because of the tolerance of free speech shown by Nerva and Trajan.

12. The opening of the *Annals* moves from the original sole power of the kings of Rome through the divided powers of the consuls and other magistrates of the Republic to the return of sole power under Augustus.

13. For these offices, see Livy, 6.1.1 with n. 24.

14. A reference to the troubles of the 80s BCE. Lucius Cornelius Cinna marched with Marius on Rome in 87, and both men followed with a purge of their political enemies; Cinna was again consul in 85 and

84, intending to fight a civil war with Sulla but before he could do
so, his army mutinied and killed him. Lucius Cornelius Sulla on his
return from the east defeated Cinna's partisans and had himself
appointed dictator in 81, after which he engaged in the proscriptions, the murder of his political opponents and confiscation of
their property. Having passed a legislative programme in 81 and
80, he retired from the dictatorship and wrote his memoirs (the
fragments of which are at *FR Hist* 22).

15. References to the (unofficial) First and (official) Second Triumvir-
ates: in 60 BCE, Caesar, Pompey and Crassus formed an unofficial
alliance to advance each of their interests; the alliance was under
repeated strain, and eventually Caesar and Pompey fought against
each other, Pompey's decisive defeat coming at Pharsalus in 48.
Antony, Lepidus and Augustus were officially proclaimed 'trium-
virs for the restoration of the republic' in 43 BCE; like Sulla, they
engaged in proscriptions; the growing dissension between the two
leading men, Antony and Augustus, was only resolved at Actium
(n. 3).

16. This offers a slight contradiction with what Tacitus said in the earlier *Histories* (1.1.1). Cf. Josephus, *Jewish Antiquities* 20. 154–7.

17. For the importance of impartiality, see Intro. §6.

18. For this passage see the important discussions of T. J. Luce,
'Tacitus on "History's Highest Function": *praecipuum munus
annalium (Annals* 3.65)', *ANRW* II.33.4 (1991) pp. 2904–27, and
A. J. Woodman, '*Praecipuum Munus Annalium*: The Construction, Convention and Context of *Annals* 3.65.1', in id., *Tacitus
Reviewed* (Oxford, 1998) pp. 86–103. I follow the latter's interpretation of the parenthesis; in the more usual translation, Tacitus is
seen as saying that he has recorded certain senatorial opinions
because he thinks that history's greatest function is not to pass over
noble actions and to ensure that debased words and actions may
have the fear of posterity.

19. For history's protreptic function in both virtue and vice see Diod.
1.1.5; 15.1.1.

20. This is one of the most commented upon sections of Tacitus' work,
important for his understanding of the historian's role and his own
history. For discussion see: H. Cancik-Lindemaier and H. Cancik,
'Zensur und Gedächtnis: zu Tacitus, Annales IV.32–8', *Der alt-
sprachliche Unterricht* 29.4 (1986) pp. 16–35; *RICH* 180–86;
R. Martin and A. J. Woodman, *Tacitus: Annals IV* (Cambridge,
1989) pp. 169–84; J. L. Moles, 'Cry Freedom: Tacitus, *Annals* 4.
32–35', *Histos* 2 (1998) pp. 95–184.

21. For history as the record of 'great' events see Intro. §2; Tacitus' remark here stands in strong contrast to the usual claims made by historians of the greatness of their events, but as the passage continues it is clear that he believes he has chosen the right approach to the very different possibilities afforded by imperial history.

22. Tiberius (14–37 CE), who followed the directives that Augustus left at his death that the empire's boundaries not be extended.

23. Tacitus here defends the inclusion of 'small' matters because, he argues, they have an effect on 'great' ones and are thus instructive to the reader.

24. There are allusions here to P.'s famous discussion of the Roman constitution as 'mixed' (6.3–10) and Cic.'s implicit rejection of it at *On the Republic* 1.53–4.

25. For an alternative approach to the challenges offered by an autocratic government see Dio 53.19.

26. See P. 1.35 and Diod. 1.1.1–5 for the vicarious experience afforded by history.

27. On the dichotomy between pleasure and utility see Intro. §7.

28. Cf. below, *Annals* 6.7.5 and 16.16.1–2.

29. It had been common from the early days of the Republic to infer contemporary references from remarks made by characters on stage, but the issue took a much more serious turn under the empire, where caution was constantly needed lest offence be given. In Tacitus' *Dialogue on Orators*, one of the characters, Curiatius Maternus, had given offence during the recitation of his *Cato* (presumably Cato the Younger, the opponent of Julius Caesar) because he was thought to be covertly criticizing the ruling regime: see *Dialogue* 2.1 with R. Mayer, *Dialogus de Oratoribus* (Cambridge, 2001) pp. 91–3 and, more generally, F. Ahl, 'The Art of Safe Criticism in Greece and Rome', *AJPh* 105 (1984) pp. 174–208.

30. The year is 25 CE; for the 'new crime' cf. Seneca the Elder, *Controversiae* 10, preface 5 on Titus Labienus.

31. Well into the early empire, Caesar's assassins, Marcus Junius Brutus and Gaius Cassius Longinus, continued to be invoked as figures of resistance to monarchical power: see E. Rawson, 'Cassius and Brutus: the Memory of the Liberators', in ead., *Roman Culture and Society* (Oxford, 1991) pp. 488–507.

32. Lucius Aelius Sejanus, the prefect of the Praetorian Guard, had risen to power during Tiberius' absence from Rome, during which he ruled virtually unopposed; he was eventually charged with treason and executed in 31 CE.

33. See above at the Elder Seneca, *Controversiae* 10, preface 5 with n. 8.

34. Quintus Caecilius Metellus Pius Scipio and Lucius Afranius were partisans of Pompey who died when the latter was defeated by Julius Caesar at the battle of Pharsalus in 49 BCE. For Cassius and Brutus, above, n. 31.

35. Asinius Pollio, a supporter of Caesar and then Antony, is perhaps best known as the patron of Virgil; orator and poet, he also wrote *Histories*, beginning with the year 60 (the work is referred to in a famous poem of Horace's, *Odes* 2.1) and going down to at least 42 and possibly beyond; he was especially famous for his independence: testimonia and fragments at *FR Hist* 56; discussion at *FR Hist* vol. 1 pp. 435–45 (A. Drummond). Messala Corvinus was originally a supporter of Brutus and Cassius but later supported Augustus; little is known of his history: testimonium and fragments at *FR Hist* 61 (A. Drummond).

36. In response to Cic.'s *Cato* Caesar wrote an *Anticato*.

37. Neither the letters of Antony nor the speeches of Brutus survive.

38. Marcus Furius Bibaculus wrote an epic poem, *Annals of the Gallic War*, in at least eleven books, where (presumably) his insults of Caesar were to be found; for the fragments see *FLP* pp. 192–200; for Catullus' invectives against Caesar see poems 29, 54, 57 and 93.

39. Cf. Quintilian 10.1.34 with n. 11.

40. The 'images' referred to here are their ancestral masks: see Sallust, *Jugurtha* 4.5 with n. 12.

41. Though with some parts lost: see Quintilian, *Orator's Training* 10.1.104.

42. The context for this remark is a series of attacks on various members of the Senate in 32 CE; what follows as an example of what was unrecorded but worthy to be known is an exceptionally brave and straightforward speech by Marcus Terentius (6.8.1–6).

43. For this notion as important to the subject matter of history, Intro. §2.

44. This remark comes after Tacitus' narration of Antistius Sosianus' false charges against Publius Anteius and Ostorius Scapula, both of whom committed suicide before they could be condemned. The year is 66 CE.

45. The passage is difficult to interpret. An alternate reading is 'I hate'; those who adopt this reading see it either as an expression of impartiality by Tacitus (so E. Koestermann, *Cornelius Tacitus: Annalen*, vol. 4 (Heidelberg, 1968) p. 366) or as a defence offered by Tacitus for describing each death individually (so A. J. Woodman, *Tacitus: The Annals* (Indianapolis, 2004) p. 347 n. 39.

30. THE YOUNGER PLINY

1. On Pliny's life and career see R. Syme, *Tacitus*, 2 vols. (Oxford, 1958) pp. 75–85; A. N. Sherwin-White, *The Letters of Pliny* (Oxford, 1966) pp. 69–82. For Pliny and history see Leeman (1963) pp. 332–7; F. Gamberini, *Stylistic Theory and Practice in the Younger Pliny* (Hildesheim, 1983) chapter 2; R. Ash, '"Aliud est enim epistulam, aliud historiam . . . scribere"' (Epistles 6.16.22): Pliny the Historian?', *Arethusa* 36 (2003) pp. 211–25; I. Marchesi, *The Art of Pliny's Letters* (Cambridge, 2008) pp. 144–206.

2. For the historian's renown, Intro. §2.

3. The first quotation comes from Virgil's *Georgics* (3.8–9); the second is a modification of the poet Ennius' epitaph, *Epigrams* 17–18 (Vahlen): 'Let no one adorn me with tears or furnish my funeral with weeping. Why? Alive, I fly upon the lips of men.' The third comes from Virgil's *Aeneid* 5.195.

4. There is perhaps some slight devaluation of history here, compared as it is to poetry and oratory (see Intro. §1); Cic. *On the Orator* 2. 62–4 and *On the Laws* 1.5–7 notes the need for careful composition in history.

5. Pliny catalogues the Elder Pliny's writings at *Letters* 3.5; his major historical works were a history of Rome's wars with Germany (twenty books), and a continuation of the history of Aufidius Bassus (thirty-one books), possibly covering the years from about 50 to 71 CE. The scant fragments are at *FRHist* 80, and discussion is at vol. 1 pp. 428–34 (B. M. Levick).

6. Roman orators often wrote up their speeches after their actual delivery, sometimes in the process giving them, as Pliny suggests here, greater polish.

7. On the labour involved in writing history see Intro. §4.

8. Pliny was probably in his late thirties when this letter was written.

9. For the same metaphor see above, Quintilian 10.1.33.

10. Pliny here refers to T. 1.22.4, although his context could not be more different; whereas T. saw the value of his history in its factual content, Pliny here seems to suggest that it is the style that will determine the work's enduring value. Cf. P. 3.31.12 for another echo of this passage with yet a different take on the reference.

11. It was usually assumed that a historian writing non-contemporary history would read his predecessors and create his own account based on them, offering a variety of 'improvements': see Intro. §3.

For similar indecision about older or more recent history, Cic. *On the Laws* 1.8.

12. For the dangers of writing contemporary history see Intro. §6.

13. Cf. Sallust, *Catiline* 3.2 for similar reflections.

14. Pliny is not known to have ever written a history.

15. Pliny is referring here to Tacitus' *Histories*, which were in the process of composition; no doubt he had heard or read one of the earlier books. The events described here took place in 93–4 CE, a point which Tacitus was approaching in his writing of the work.

16. Cf. Cic.'s desire to be in a history written by Lucceius (*Letters to Friends* 5.12.7).

17. Cf. Cic. *Letters to Friends* 5.12.7 on Alexander and the artists he desired for his portraits.

18. Pliny is referring to some sort of archives here, perhaps the *acta diurna*, which were records of events, celebrations and other important matters at Rome; the *acta Senatus*, the official records kept of the Senate's business, could not really be described as 'public', though Tacitus, as a senator, would have had access to them.

19. He was a junior senator at the time; shortly after the events of this letter, Senecio was charged with treason, found guilty, and executed.

20. Baetica was the province of southern Spain; the province brought a charge against Massa (for malversation of funds during his time as governor there in 92–3 CE) and Pliny and Senecio were assigned by the Senate to assist the province in its prosecution. Conviction carried a penalty of exile.

21. His goods were not confiscated per se but held by the state treasury so as to ensure repayment of the monies he had extorted.

22. The fear was that Massa might conceal his assets, thereby defrauding the province of the money owed to it.

23. This would have been a public meeting of the consuls sitting on their tribunals as ministers of justice, which is why Massa would be there as well.

24. Roman law prescribed penalties for advocates who prosecuted with excessive zeal. If Senecio had been convicted, the case against Massa would have been thrown out.

25. Pliny was turning the tables on Massa by suggesting that his arraignment of Senecio was also motivated by personal hostility.

26. Marcus Cocceius Nerva, emperor 96–8 CE; he calls him 'divine' because by the time this letter was published Nerva was already dead and had been deified by the Senate.

27. Here Pliny seems to contrast himself with Cic. who had asked Lucceius to bend the laws of history (5.12.3).

28. The letter is 6.10. Virtually nothing is known of Cremutius Ruso, though he might be connected with Cremutius Cordus, the historian mentioned by Tacitus at *Annals* 4.34.

29. Governor of Upper Germany in 63 CE, he became embroiled in the civil wars of 68–9 that followed the death of Nero, the last of the Julio-Claudians. Having defeated the rebel Gaius Iulius Vindex, Verginius nonetheless refused to accept his troops' attempts to declare him emperor, handing it to the Senate to decide. He died shortly after 97, and his funeral oration was given by Tacitus.

30. Sextus Julius Frontinus, consul in 73, 98 and 100, a friend of Pliny's, and author of works on military stratagems and the water supply of ancient Rome (both of which survive). He was governor of Britain from 73 to 78.

31. The language echoes that of the subject matter of history: see Intro. §2.

32. Cluvius Rufus, consul, orator and historian, was a provincial governor of Tarraconensis Spain in 68, first supporting Otho in the struggles over the throne and then Vitellius, and he served in the negotiations between Vitellius and the future emperor Vespasian. Although Tacitus mentions him as a source for his own account of Nero (*Annals* 13.20.2), the starting point of his history is unknown as is the end date, though some think it concluded with the year 68. Text and fragments at *FRHist* 84 with discussion at vol. 1. pp. 549–60 (B.M. Levick).

33. On history and truth see Intro. §7.

34. For the sentiment cf. Tacitus, *Histories* 1.1.4.

31. ARRIAN

1. For Arrian's career see P. A. Stadter, *Arrian of Nicomedia* (Chapel Hill and London, 1980); R. Syme, 'The Career of Arrian', *HSCPh* 86 (1982) pp. 181–211.

2. It is an example of individual-centred history: Intro. §2.

3. On Arrian's historical method see G. Schepens, 'Arrian's View of his Task as Alexander-Historian', *Ancient Society* 2 (1971) pp. 254–68; Stadter (n. 1); A. B. Bosworth, *From Arrian to Alexander* (Oxford, 1988); id., *A Historical Commentary on Arrian's History of Alexander*, 2 vols. (Oxford, 1980–95), especially vol. I. pp. 16–34.

4. We have no other work of ancient historiography that so clearly marks itself out as being dependent on earlier sources (see, however, P. 1.14.1 for his remark that he will base his account of the

First Punic War on Fabius and Philinus). At the partitioning of Alexander's empire after his death, Ptolemy took Egypt, and he and his descendants ruled Egypt for the next three centuries (the last Ptolemy was Cleopatra); his history (fragments and testimonia at *FGrHist* 138) is mainly known through Arrian and has been subjected to the most disparate evaluations: see Pearson (1960) chapter 7; A. Zambrini, *CGRH* pp. 217–18; Scanlon (2015) pp. 192–3. Aristobulus of Cassandreia also served with Alexander, and according to one source at least he began writing his history in his eighty-fourth year. Fragments and testimonia at *FGrHist* 139 and, with English translation and updated bibliography, at *BNJ* 139 (F. Pownall): see Pearson (1960) chapter 6; Zambrini (art. cit.) pp. 218–19; Scanlon (2015) pp. 193–5. He is criticized as a flatterer at L. *Hist.* 12.

5. For the notion that agreement equals truth see Josephus, *Against Apion* 1.26.

6. These seem to be two separate categories; for a possible example of the sort of thing Arrian means by 'worthy of telling' (without actually being true) see below, 2.12.8.

7. For the importance of eyewitness and participation, see Intro. §3; for impartiality, §6.

8. Arrian is suggesting that his account will be superior in both accuracy and style. See next passage.

9. On this passage see P. A. Stadter, 'Arrian's Extended Preface', *ICS* 6 (1981) pp. 157–81; J. L. Moles, 'The Interpretation of the "Second Preface" in Arrian's *Anabasis*', *JHS* 105 (1985) pp. 162–8; V. Gray, 'The Moral Interpretation of the "Second Preface" to Arrian's *Anabasis*', ibid. 110 (1990) pp. 180–86.

10. There is a gap in the text here.

11. Hephaestion was Alexander's beloved companion, much like Achilles' Patroclus.

12. The story was well known and frequently told: see, e.g., Pl., *Alexander* 15.8.

13. This is an assertion Arrian needs to make to justify his history, but it plays into a long-standing tendency to denigrate Alexander's historians (e.g., Cic. *Brutus* 42; Strabo 11.5.5, 11.6.2–4; Quintilian 10.1.74).

14. All fifth-century tyrants in Sicily: for Hiero and Gelon see P. 7.7.7 with n. 72; Theron was tyrant at Acragas in Sicily 485–466 BCE.

15. This is the kind of exaggeration so often made in historiographical prefaces so as to justify a new work, and it should not be taken at face value.

16. All incidents from X.'s *Anabasis*.

17. The 'display of deeds' recalls H.'s preface; Arrian echoes these words at the conclusion, 7.30.2.

18. Arrian's elaborate refusal to give his name is in stark contrast to many other historians; for possible reasons see *ATAH* pp. 146–7, 274–5. His claim to 'first place' is based on the importance of his subject: see Intro. §2.

19. The reference is to Alexander's actions after he defeated Darius III and came into possession of his goods and also his womenfolk. Arrian has detailed Alexander's care for them; and when one of the women mistook Hephaestion for Alexander, Alexander did not reprove her but said of his companion that he was 'another Alexander'.

20. For Dionysus' expedition to India see Strabo 11.5.5 with n. 16.

21. For another argument about including the divine in history see Diod. 4.1.1–4.

22. Arrian's *Indikē* survives; there is an up-to-date English translation by M. Hammond (Oxford, 2013). Nearchus was Alexander's friend from boyhood; testimonia and fragments at *FGrHist* 133 and, with English translation and updated bibliography, *BNJ* 133 (M. Whitby); for his work see Pearson (1960) chapter 5. Megasthenes was sent on several embassies to the Indian king and his work on India, based on first-hand knowledge, became the standard account in antiquity: testimonia and fragments at *FGrHist* 715 and, with English translation and updated bibliography, *BNJ* 715 (D. W. Roller). Eratosthenes is the famous geographer (see Agatharchides n. 7)

23. The limitation to Alexander's 'deeds' (*erga*) shows that Arrian recognizes a kind of generic limitation on subject matter: see Intro. §2.

24. Arrian has been discussing Alexander's character and some of his more controversial actions, such as claiming to be the son of a god and adopting Persian dress.

25. Europe and Asia; since the ancients thought there were only three continents (Africa the third), Arrian can make it seem as if Alexander conquered two-thirds of the entire world.

26. Arrian writes some 400 years after Alexander's death.

27. The phrasing is Herodotean and Arrian shows himself as having a favourable disposition towards Alexander, i.e., that his history is to be seen in the tradition of glorifying the events it treats; see Intro. §7.

28. For the utility of history, Intro. §7.

29. It is rare for a historian to claim divine inspiration: Livy skirts it (*preface*, 13), but see Dio 73.23.1–5 for the strong presence of the divine in encouraging him to write history.

32. APPIAN

1. On Appian see A. M. Gowing, *The Triumviral Narratives of Appian and Cassius Dio* (Ann Arbor, 1992), *passim*; K. Brodersen, 'Appian und sein Werk', *ANRW* II.34.1 (1993) pp. 339–63; G. S. Bucher, *CGRH* pp. 454–60; and K. Welch, ed., *Appian's Roman History: Empire and Civil War* (London and Swansea, 2015). For the civil war books in particular, see E. Gabba, *Appiano e la storia delle guerre civili* (Florence, 1956), and the same author's commentaries on Books 1 and 5 of the *Civil Wars* (Florence, 1967 [2nd edn] and 1970 respectively).

2. The travels here seem to be figurative, not actual. The gathering of portions suggests perhaps the kind of preliminary sketch mentioned by L. *Hist*. 48.

3. In 146 BCE at the end of the Third Punic War. The phrase 'whatever they did to them or suffered' is reminiscent of Aristotle, *Poetics*, chapter 9.

4. Appian's work in some sense represents the undoing of P.'s notion of universal history where events come together to form a unified whole (P. 1.3.3–4.6) and is perhaps closer to Diod.'s notion of self-contained events (16.1.1–3).

5. Whatever hints there were in the preface that the writer was Appian are lost to us; with Appian's remarks here compare Arrian's self-conscious anonymity at *Anabasis* 1.12.5.

6. Presumably an autobiography, but the work does not survive.

33. FRONTO

1. For Fronto's life and times see E. Champlin, *Fronto and Antonine Rome* (Cambridge, Mass., 1980); Fronto's text is problematic in the extreme; the standard edition, followed here, is that of M. P. van den Hout (Leipzig, 1988); see also van den Hout's massive commentary, *A Commentary on the Letters of M. Cornelius Fronto* (Leiden, 1999). There is a very useful translation of some letters of Fronto with notes by C. Davenport and J. Manley, *Fronto: Selected Letters* (London and New York, 2014). For discussions of Fronto and historiography see M. Leroy, 'La conception de l'histoire chez Fronton', *Musée Belge* 32 (1928) pp. 241–52; D'Alton (1931) pp. 318–21 (on his style) and pp. 522–3; Champlin, op. cit., pp. 55, 115–16; P. V. Cova, *I Principia Historiae e le idee storiografiche di*

Frontone (Naples, 1970); R. Poignault, 'Historiographie et rhétorique dans la correspondance de Fronton', in G. Lachenaud and D. Longrée, eds., *Grecs et Romains aux prises avec l'histoire* (Rennes, 2003) pp. 459–77; A. M. Kemezis, 'Lucian, Fronto, and the Absence of Contemporary Historiography under the Antonines', *AJPh* 131 (2010) pp. 285–325.

2. The beginning of this letter is lost.

3. Verus here refers to the actions of his predecessors in the Parthian campaigns; he himself set out for Parthia in the summer of 162.

4. These would have been Marcus Statius Priscus, Gaius Avidius Cassius and Publius Martius Verus. For Priscus see L. *Hist.* 20; for the latter two, below, n. 7.

5. The reference to 'our staff Sallust' is meant to be humorous; on his possible identity see van den Hout's *Commentary* (n. 1) p. 266.

6. van den Hout believes 'maps' to be the meaning of *picturas*; for the argument that the word means paintings (i.e., of the battle) see Davenport and Manley, op. cit., p. 170.

7. Gaius Avidius Cassius was a legate in the third legion and sacked the Parthian cities of Seleucia and Ctesiphon; Martius Verus was a legate of the fifth legion. Cassius is also mentioned by L. *Hist.* 31.

8. These would be not actual speeches he delivered in the Senate, but reports from him to the Senate that would have been read out in that body.

9. Cf. Cic.'s suggestions to Lucceius (*Letters to Friends* 5.12.4). Marcus Sedatius Severianus was governor of the Roman province of Cappadocia. In 161 he invaded Armenia and was defeated by Osroës at Elegeia near the headwaters of the Euphrates; he subsequently committed suicide. In that same year the Syrian governor, Lucius Attidius Cornelianus, was killed during a Parthian invasion.

10. On T.'s *Pentekontaetia* (50-year period) see above, D.H. *Thuc.* 10.5.

11. It is hard to read this as anything other than pressure on Fronto to elaborate his account.

12. In this extract, words in italics indicate that they come from notes made in the margins of the text by a certain Caecilius; some of this material may derive from other manuscripts, and thus represent what Fronto wrote. For Caecilius' activity see J. E. G. Zetzel, 'The Subscriptions in the Manuscripts of Livy and Fronto and the Meaning of *Emendatio*', *CPh* 75 (1980) pp. 38–59 at pp. 49–55.

13. The opening of this letter, addressed to Marcus Aurelius (his full titulature: Marcus Aurelius Antoninus Augustus), is lost.

14. The beginning is quite mutilated and only a few words or phrases can be made out.

15. Lucius Verus, Marcus' adoptive brother.
16. Alexander above all was famous for being compared to Achilles: see Arrian, *Anabasis* 1.12.1–2; see also L. *Hist.* 14 for the historian who compared Lucius Verus to Achilles and himself to Homer (though as van den Hout, *Commentary* (n. 1) pp. 463–5, points out, that is not evidence that L. knew this work of Fronto's).
17. On the avoidance of tall tales in historiography see Intro. §9.
18. On history's great deeds, Intro. §3; for words matching deeds, Intro. §4.
19. Book 2 of the *Iliad* contains the false dream of Agamemnon, his attempt to test the spirit of the Achaeans, and a long catalogue of Greek forces (as well as a somewhat shorter one of Trojan). The opening lines of the Book 1 outline the theme of the work.
20. For X. see above, p. 21; van den Hout, *Commentary* (n. 1) p. 466 suggests that something on the order of 'but he was a fighter not a soldier' followed; Fronto is making the transition from Homer, an author but not a fighter, through X. to Cato, both an author and a fighter.
21. For Hercules' labours see Gantz (1993) pp. 381–466.
22. On Cato see above, p. 41.
23. The rivers are the Tigris and Euphrates; the reference is to Trajan's short-lived conquests of Parthian territory subsequently abandoned by Hadrian.
24. For the consequences of deliberate lying see P. 1.14.2 with n. there.
25. Perhaps Gaius Asinius Pollio (on whom see Tacitus, *Annals* 4.34.4 with n. 35).
26. The disasters referred to here are those of Marcus Licinius Crassus in 53 BCE at Carrhae; Mark Antony's disgrace and retreat in 36 BCE; and (perhaps) Appius Santra, mentioned below, chapter 19.
27. The two greatest emperors are Trajan (his Parthian campaigns lasted from 114 to 116) and Lucius Verus; given Trajan's demonstrated competence as a general, the comparison is, to say the least, absurd.
28. Cf. Sallust, *Catiline* 3.2 with n. 3.
29. The great Republican general Gaius Marius (see Cic. *On the Laws* 1.1) was born near Arpinum, while Nursia was the home town of Quintus Sertorius, the great Roman general famous for his conquests in Spain (80–72 BCE) and his battles with Pompey. For the details of their careers see the *Lives* of each man by Pl.
30. An additional marginal note reads 'extracts from a panegyric of Vologaesus', which suggests that Fronto would have included a magnification of the enemy (below, n. 43) to make Verus look greater.

31.   Trajan headed for the east in 114 after his conquest of Dacia.

32.   On these ranks see Davenport and Manley (n. 1) pp. 182–3.

33.   As part of the praise of Verus, Fronto is suggesting that he did not have the trained and excellent soldiers of Trajan.

34.   This is meant to be derogatory, but Dio (69.9.1–6) praises Hadrian in this regard.

35.   Most famously, perhaps, Hadrian's own mausoleum, still standing in Rome.

36.   There is a short gap in the text here, but only one word or so is missing.

37.   Antoninus Pius (ruled 138–61 CE), the adoptive father of Marcus Aurelius and Lucius Verus. Numa, the second king of Rome, was distinguished for his peace-loving ways.

38.   The trumpet was sounded both to commence battle and to signal its end; the former is deliberately interpreted by these soldiers to be the latter.

39.   The praises that follow are full of commonplaces used to describe the good general: see van den Hout, *Commentary* (n. 1) p. 477.

40.   It is not clear what this means.

41.   Fronto is probably still talking about Verus.

42.   A reference to the *kataphraktoi*, the mailed cavalry of the Parthians.

43.   Vologaesus III was the king of Parthia, 148–93 CE; in 161 he invaded Armenia, a client kingdom of Rome's, expelled its king, and replaced him with his own man. This particular event probably occurred in 163.

44.   King of Armenia; according to Dio (68.17–20) Trajan refused to acknowledge him as king and annexed Armenia as a province; in other accounts (e.g., Arrian's *Parthica*, *FGrHist* 156 F 51), he was executed by Trajan.

45.   According to Dio 71.2.1, Marcus Sedatius Severianus was slain by the Parthians, but L. *Hist.* 21 says that he committed suicide.

46.   Appius Santra is usually identified with the Maximus mentioned by Dio (68.30.1) who was sent by Trajan to put down revolts in Parthia. Arsaces is unknown.

47.   Spartacus was leader of the famous slave revolt in 73–71 BCE; Viriathus led a series of revolts against Roman rule in Spain in the years 147–139 BCE. The suggestion seems to be that even slaves can be skilled at warfare, whereas this is not the case with the arts of peace.

48.   Dio (68.7.4) says that in his youth Trajan was fond of young boys and wine.

49. Strongly reminiscent of Juvenal's 'bread and circus' as the main
     concerns of the Roman lower classes (*Satires* 10.80–81).

50. Distributions either of grain or of cash were usually made on spe-
     cial occasions such as the accession of a new emperor.

51. A reference probably to Julius Caesar's night-time triumph over the
     Gauls in 46 BCE (Suetonius, *Julius Caesar* 37.2).

52. The emperors of this era were all adopted by their predecessors,
     but they would still be seen as being of the same family: Trajan
     adopted Hadrian, Hadrian adopted Antoninus Pius, Antoninus
     adopted Marcus Aurelius and Lucius Verus; thus Verus was the
     great-grandson of Trajan.

34. LUCIAN

1.   On L.'s life, often difficult to establish because it is not clear how
     accurate his 'autobiographical' writings are, see C. P. Jones, *Cul-
     ture and Society in Lucian* (Cambridge, Mass. and London, 1986).
     On L.'s enormous literary output see J. Bompaire, *Lucien écrivain:
     imitation et création* (Paris, 1958); B. Baldwin, *Studies in Lucian*
     (Toronto, 1973); G. Anderson, *Lucian: Theme and Variation in the
     Second Sophistic* (Leiden, 1976); J. Hall, *Lucian's Satire* (New
     York, 1981). For an excellent overview of L.'s era, the so-called
     'Second Sophistic', see T. Whitmarsh, *The Second Sophistic*
     (*Greece & Rome* New Surveys in the Classics, no. 35; Oxford,
     2005).

2.   See Jones (n. 1) pp. 61–4.

3.   For *Hist.* see the commentary of H. Homeyer, *Lukian: wie man
     Geschichte schreiben soll* (Munich, 1965); *LS* offers a collection of
     testimonia giving the background to *Hist.* but the author often
     overlooks what is distinctive about L.'s treatment. There is an Eng-
     lish translation with notes in M. D. Macleod, *Lucian: a Selection*
     (Warminster, 1981) pp. 198–247, 283–302 and a French translation
     with notes by A. Hurst, *Lucien: comment écrire l'histoire* (Paris,
     2010). Two important recent works are: R. Porod, *Lukians Schrift:
     'Wie man Geschichte schreiben soll': Kommentar und Interpret-
     ation* (Vienna, 2013), which is particularly valuable for emphasizing
     the influence of Hellenistic historiography on L. (a point over-
     looked by earlier scholars who tended to focus nearly exclusively
     on T.'s influence), and A. Free, *Geschichtsschreibung als Paideia:
     Lukians Schrift 'Wie man Geschichte schreiben soll' in der Bil-
     dungskultur des 2. Jhs. n. Chr.* (Munich, 2015), who places the

work within the context of L.'s other works and (just as importantly) of the competitive culture in which L. wrote and performed.
See also Porod's 'Lucian and the Limits of Fiction in Ancient Historiography', in A. Bartley, ed., *A Lucian for Our Times* (Newcastle,
2009) pp. 29–46; Baldwin (n. 1) pp. 75–95; and for L.'s *True Histories*, a work that has much in common with *Hist.*, see A. Georgiadou
and D. H. J. Larmour, *Lucian's Science Fiction Novel* True Histories (Leiden and Boston, 1998) and J. Hall, *Lucian's Satire* (New
York, 1981) chapter 3.

4.   I follow the delineation of Homeyer (n. 3) pp. 13–14.

5.   Lysimachus was one of Alexander's generals and ruled Macedonia
      286–281 BCE; there is no evidence to suggest that this incident is
      historical.

6.   Philo is not otherwise known.

7.   The people of Abdera in Thrace were proverbial for their
      stupidity.

8.   This description seems to be a parody of T.'s famous account (2.
      47–53) of the plague at Athens in 430 BCE; see below, chapter 15,
      for the attempt by Crepereius Calpurnianus to adopt the plague
      wholesale for his own history.

9.   The play, which does not survive, treated Perseus' rescue of
      Andromeda from a sea-monster: see *TrGF* FF 114–56; it was paro-
      died in Aristophanes' *Women at the Thesmophoria* of 411.

10.   T. 2.49.6 says that the victims of the plague died on either the sev-
      enth or ninth day of the fever.

11.   For these lines from the *Andromeda* see *TrGF* F p. 136, where six
      further lines are quoted.

12.   He is otherwise unknown. In L.'s time recitations of individual
      passages from tragedy were all the rage.

13.   The reference is to Rome's eastern wars against the Parthians, spe-
      cifically the defeat at Elegeia in Armenia in 162 CE. They are called
      'barbarians' because in H. and other Greek writers of the fifth cen-
      tury BCE the term is frequently used of the Persians, and the
      Parthians were often assimilated to the Persians.

14.   See Cic. *Brutus* 287 and *Orator* 30–32 for an earlier generation of
      T.-imitators.

15.   As becomes clear in the course of the essay, it is not authors' desire
      to model themselves on the three great historians which is the prob-
      lem, but rather the inept and wholesale unimaginative copying,
      combined with a failure to do the preliminary work of investiga-
      tion, which makes the works of these writers wholly worthless. On
      imitation see Intro. §2.

16. The remark goes back to the pre-Socratic philosopher, Heraclitus of Ephesus: VS 22 B 53.

17. The man is Diogenes (named below), the Cynic philosopher; the story is set in the time of Philip of Macedon, after his victory over the Greeks at Chaeronea in 338, but the details about Diogenes are probably invented so as to give point to his witty saying.

18. Diogenes was famous for his poverty; the Craneion hill was where he usually resided.

19. For similar hesitation and recognition of the effort required by history, see Cic. On the Laws 1.9 and Pliny, Letters 5.8.1–2.

20. From Homer's Odyssey, 12.219, spoken of the Wandering Rocks that Odysseus must avoid.

21. For the historian's cares cf. Livy, preface 5.

22. L. returns to the building metaphor at the end of the essay, chapter 60.

23. Cic. suggests a similar belief amongst the early Roman historians: On the Orator 2.51; and cf. Sextus Empiricus, Against the Grammarians 1.256, for the notion that history is not an expert craft.

24. T. 1.22.4, often cited by later writers, e.g., P. 3.31.12; D.H. Thuc. 7.3; Pliny, Letters 5.8.11. For the care required in history, see Intro. §4.

25. The language here suggests an 'official' version; cf. Josephus, Life 361–7 for validation of one's works by the powerful.

26. An echo perhaps of T. 2.54.3 where he says that he will give a description of the plague in case it should ever recur.

27. For the same image, linking the carpenter's rule with truth, see Timaeus, F 151.

28. For the notion that one learns as much from poor composition as from correct see the story often told by Pl. (e.g., Antony 1.6) of the Theban musician Ismenias, who would show his pupils good and bad flute players with the admonition to play like the former and not to play like the latter.

29. The first part of the work, 7–32, covers what not to do; the second part, 33–61, what one should do.

30. Although eyewitness and inquiry were thought to be fundamental to the writing of history (Intro. §3) they are rarely discussed in historiographical discussions, and L.'s work is no exception: he has one paragraph (47) treating the topic.

31. The issue of praise, especially inordinate praise, is one of the most insistent in L.'s treatise; it is true, of course, that a concern with the proper use of praise and blame is a long-standing concern of historiography (Intro. §6), but no earlier author treats it with the detail and emphasis seen here. This may be not only a function of

the actual histories written in L.'s time but also the tendency in theoretical writers to make history a branch of epideictic (see Timaeus n. 3): see Cic. *Orator* pp. 37, 66 with *RICH* pp. 95–7.

32. For history's devotion to truth, see Intro. §5.

33. For the differences between poetry and history see P. 2.56.10–11; Cic. *On the Laws* 1.5; Diod. 1.2.7; but cf. Quintilian, *Orator's Education* 10.1.31 for the suggestion that poetry and history have close affinities.

34. The notion is a long-standing one, going back to earliest Greek thought, and finding its classic statement in Plato's *Ion*: see P. Murray, *Plato on Poetry* (Cambridge, 1996) pp. 6–12. It is clear that L. is thinking of poetry mainly as the domain of the mythic in which impossible matters occur: see Intro. §9; for the division of narratives by probability and possibility see Sextus Empiricus, *Against the Grammarians* 1.252, 263.

35. Horses running over water: *Iliad* 20.226–9; Zeus drawing up earth and sea: *Iliad* 8.18–26.

36. Homeric references again: *Iliad* 2.477–9; the son of Atreus and Aeropë is Agamemnon.

37. For 'myth' in history, see Intro. §9.

38. Ancient cosmetics included the application of white lead to women's faces to brighten their complexions. This is one of several places where L. laments the 'emasculation' of history: see also 10–13, 25; and for an earlier attacks on 'effeminate' historians see P. 2.56.9 (Phylarchus) and 12.24.4 (Timaeus); cf. *CC* p. 5.

39. See P. 1.14.7 and Intro. §6 for praise in history.

40. Future readers and the discerning few as one's ideal audience is a prominent theme in the essay: see 10, 11, 13, 32, 39, 44, 59, 61–2.

41. See Intro. §7 for utility and pleasure in history.

42. Nicostratus was an Olympic victor twice over in the games of 37 CE. Nothing is known of Alcaeus.

43. The word here is *mythōdes*, with L. again allying the 'mythical' to excessive praise.

44. Argos was the hundred-eyed guardian sent by Hera to watch over Io after the latter's transformation into a heifer.

45. See above, n. 40.

46. For effeminacy see above, n. 38. This incident was a famous one, found frequently in literature and art (Gantz (1993) pp. 439–42; *LIMC* VII.1. 45–52), and had even been treated by historians: Ephorus, *FGrHist* 70 F 14; Diod. 4.31.5.

47. The attempt at ingratiation with the subjects of one's history is a long-standing concern: see Intro. §6.

48.   There is a brief gap in the text here, but the words are likely to be as represented in the angled brackets. For Aristobulus see Arrian, *Anabasis*, preface 1, where a very different attitude towards the historian is evident.

49.   Porus was an Indian king of enormous size, defeated (and later honoured) by Alexander; none of our surviving sources mentions a single combat between him and Alexander.

50.   The Hydaspes river is the modern Jhelum in Kashmir; the story here is almost certainly invented, though whether by L. or some predecessor cannot be known; see Pearson (1960) pp. 150–51. Flatterers of Alexander were a staple of the tradition: see Strabo 11.5. 5–6, 11.6.2–4.

51.   The name of the builder is given as Stasicrates in Pl. *Alexander* 72.5; as Dinocrates by Vitruvius, *On Architecture* 2, preface 1–4 (where a different version is found).

52.   L. means stylistic adornment: see below, chapters 43–6.

53.   That is, the war of Lucius Verus against the Parthians.

54.   See the similar jibe against historians by Seneca, *Pumpkinification of Claudius* 1.2.

55.   As if he were a poet; for the different method of the historian see Hecataeus, F 1a with n. 2; Intro. §3.

56.   The quotation is *Iliad* 22.158, from the final chase of Hector around the walls of Troy by Achilles. Thersites was the 'most shameless man to come to Ilion', physically repulsive and hated and reproved by all the leaders there (*Iliad* 2.212–21).

57.   Several cities laid claim to Homer, the three chief being Chios, Colophon and Smyrna; L. satirized the entire matter in his *True Histories* 2.20, making Babylonia Homer's true city: see L. Kim, *Homer between History and Fiction in Imperial Greek Literature* (Cambridge, 2010) pp. 162–8.

58.   The historian here, as so often, mimics the actual deeds of the characters whose actions he is narrating.

59.   The criticism here is that the historian did not maintain the kind of impartiality in the narrative that history demanded; see Intro. §6; for Vologaesus see Fronto, *Sketch of History* 16 with n. 43.

60.   Thyme had been associated with the inhabitants of Attica from early on; it is already a stereotype in Theophrastus' *Characters* 4.3.

61.   A fairly exact copying of the opening of T.'s history, replacing T.'s name with the comically awful and alliterative Crepereius; the offence here, apart from mindless imitation, is the lack of euphony. Pompeiopolis was a city in Cilicia; for more on Crepereius see Jones (n. 1) pp. 161–6.

62. These are all events taken wholesale out of T.: 1.32–6 (Corcyrean speaker), 2.47–53 (plague), 2.17 (Pelasgian oracle and long walls); 2.48.1 (the beginning of the plague); the public burial (2.34); Pericles' oration (2.35–46); for another appropriation of Pericles' oration see Afranius Stilo mentioned below, chapter 26.

63. There is a gap in the text here.

64. For the proper language in history see below, chapters 43–8 and Intro. §12. The 'purple' is a reference to the purple stripe of the toga worn by Roman senators.

65. For memoranda (Greek *hypomnēmata*, Latin *commentarii*) see Cic. *Brutus* 262; for day-by-day accounts, Sempronius Asellio, FF 1–2.

66. For frigidity arising from arguments that are too clever or ingenious in the wrong way, see Agatharchides, *On the Red Sea* 5.21.

67. Ionic was the dialect in which H. (and some of his imitators) wrote; the fault here is to write a work lacking stylistic unity.

68. Why L. does this is unclear; Arrian, *Anabasis* 1.12.5 ostentatiously refuses to name himself, but that does not seem to be what is going on here.

69. For the inappropriateness of writing history in a philosophical way, see Cic. *Orator* 65–6.

70. Compare the story told of Callisthenes and his claim that Alexander owed his fame to him rather than the other way around: T 8, with n. 7.

71. The three passages are near-exact verbal repetitions from H.: 1.5.3, 1.8.2 and 1.7.2. Osroës (Chosroes) was the commander of Vologaesus' army. See further below, n. 114.

72. For the exalted subject matter demanded by history see Intro. §3 and below, n. 73.

73. For descriptions and digressions, Intro. §12. Ammianus 26.1.1–2 offers a similar complaint about overlong digressions.

74. Marcus Statius Priscus was from Cappadocia: see *Augustan History Verus* 7.4; the shout is probably meant to recall the cry of Ares at *Iliad* 5.859.

75. There are, of course, disparate numbers for casualties in some surviving historians, though none quite so absurd as this one. For Europus, see below, n. 89.

76. The term 'Atticist' here does not mean what it did in Cic.'s time (e.g., *Orator* 30–32 with introductory note); in L.'s era Atticists were Greek writers who sought to mimic painstakingly the language and style of the earliest Athenian writers, partly as a marker of cultural identity: see S. Swain, *Hellenism and Empire: Language,*

Classicism, and Power in the Greek World, AD 50–250 (Oxford, 1996) pp. 17–64; L. himself practised a modified form of Atticism and derided the excessive zealousness of purists in his *Lexiphanes* and *Teachers of the Rhetoricians*.

77. This is not Fronto the writer (above, p. 357), but a general named Marcus Claudius Fronto.

78. The usual way for Greek writers to treat Roman names was simply to transliterate them.

79. For Marcus Sedatius Severianus see Fronto, *Letters to Verus* 1.2, with n. 9.

80. For the use of poetic words in history cf. D.H. *Thuc.* 24.11 with n. there.

81. The author here is imitating Homeric language: see *Iliad* 1.530, 4.504, 12.199, 21.199; *Odyssey* 10.122.

82. The author is here faulted both for using inappropriately technical language (though 'stratopedarch', which means camp-commander, does appear, if rarely, in other historians) and for including 'humble' activities in history: see Intro. §2 on history's grand subject matter.

83. Tragic actors in Athens wore high boots (*kothornoi*) and the boot itself is often used as a metaphor for tragedy or other high poetry.

84. The question here is of proportion; for the notion of a literary work as a body, see Plato, *Phaedrus* 264c.

85. A famous proverb, perhaps best known from Horace's *Art of Poetry* 139: 'the mountain is in labour, and a silly mouse is born'.

86. Built between 302 and 290 to a height of nearly thirty metres, the Colossus of Rhodes was one of the great engineering feats of antiquity; it collapsed in an earthquake of 226, yet several centuries later the elder Pliny (*Natural History* 34.41) finds even its remains amazing.

87. The reference is to the opening of X.'s *Anabasis*; L. returns to the topic at chapter 52.

88. The Greek says literally 'not merely by parasangs but by whole stathmoi': the former is a Persian term, indicating about one-fifth of the usual daily marching distance for an army; the latter was about a day's march.

89. For a barbershop as the location of idle gossip, see P. n. 56. There were two towns in Syria named Europus, both on the Euphrates: one was Dura-Europus (where spectacular archaeological remains have been found) and the other located further north. Edessa was in northern Mesopotamia.

90. Samosata was the capital of the Roman province of Commagene; it was on the Euphrates, not the Tigris.

91. For Severianus, see above, n. 79. The dramatic death has suggested
     to some that this historian wrote in a tragic manner, somewhat as
     Phylarchus is said to have done by P. 2.56.
92. This refers to Pericles' famous funeral oration: T. 2.35–46.
93. Nothing is known of this Afranius, if indeed he was a real person
     and not a character conveniently created by the historian.
94. The legendary hero Ajax committed suicide by falling on his sword
     when driven mad after losing to Odysseus in the contest for the
     arms of Achilles.
95. I follow here MacLeod's suggestion that L. is punning on the name
     Afranius and the Greek term *aphron*, which means senseless or
     foolish or mad (just as Ajax was); he suggests 'frantic' to get across
     something of the pun. The line is, of course, sarcastic.
96. In classical Athens the playwright not only composed the play but
     also served as its producer, instructing the chorus and teaching
     them their lines. For the connection of history with drama, see
     Intro. §9.
97. For this as the touchstone for history, Intro. §2.
98. See above, n. 40.
99. The statue of Zeus at Olympia was sculpted by Phidias *c.* 430 BCE,
     and was considered his masterpiece. It is described by Pausanias
     5.11.1–9.
100. For Europus see above, n. 89.
101. Athenian courtrooms used water clocks, so many measures of water
     being allotted to particular speeches and placed in one vessel which
     then drained into another; when the water ran out, time was up.
102. Nothing is known of him, and that is probably the point: not only
     are his 'adventures' worthless, but he himself is of no importance
     to history.
103. Mauretania comprised much of what is modern-day Morocco.
104. A number of ancient cities were called 'Caesarea': this one, as one
     can see from the story, is in Cappadocia, modern Kayseri, the chief
     city of the province.
105. In other words, the historian omitted what should have been the
     actual subject matter of his history. Malchion was presumably one
     of Mausacas' hosts during his visit.
106. Again, the errors are of suitability and proportion.
107. The eastern harbour of Corinth.
108. A claim of eyewitness is one of the oldest historiographical tropes:
     see Intro. §3; there is also an allusion here to the proverb about eyes
     and ears, versions of which are found at H. 1.8.2 ('ears are more
     untrustworthy than eyes') and P. 12.27.1.

109. Arrian, *Tactics* 35.3–7 describes these as 'Scythian standards' and says that they were made from painted rags; the point is that the historian being derided is so inexperienced that he fails to understand that they are only images on the standards, not actual snakes.

110. Iberia is here not Spain but an area in the middle of the Caucasus east of the Black Sea.

111. Sura is a town in Syria on the Euphrates; for the Craneion, a hill in Corinth, see above, chapter 3; Lerna is a district in Corinth.

112. For the demand that the historian needs military experience see especially P. 12.25g.1.

113. See a similar complaint by P. concerning writers who boast of composing universal history (5.33.1–8).

114. A triumph was celebrated in 166; Vologaesus was not captured nor was Osroës thrown to the lions; in L.'s *Dialogues of the Dead* (12.4), Philip accuses Alexander of throwing men to the lions.

115. Presumably a quotation from the author's history.

116. For Avidius Cassius see Fronto, *Letters to Verus* 2.3.1.

117. Mouziris is a port on India's south-west coast; the Oxydracae were an Indian tribe conquered by Alexander (Arrian, *Anabasis* 6.4.3, etc.).

118. See above, n. 40.

119. The words are also quoted by Strabo (1.2.14) with minor variants but the poet is unknown: see *PMG* 1020.

120. *Atthis* was a title of local histories of Attica: see D.H. *Rom. Ant.* 1.8.3.

121. This is the sole mention of Demetrius: for recent discussion of him see *BNJ* 209 (J. P. Stronk). Sagalassus was a city in Pisidia in Asia Minor. A gap follows in the text.

122. Momus was a proverbial fault-finder; were L. to offer only criticism he would be open to the charge of bitterness or fault-finding: Intro. §6.

123. The two features, as Macleod has noted, owe something to Pericles' characterization of himself in T. 2.60.5 (quoted by D.H. *Thuc.* 45.1) as one 'who knows both what is necessary and how to communicate it'. L.'s notion of political understanding has a few things in common with P.'s claims (12.25d–28a) that one needs political experience to write history well, although L. suggests here that it is something innate; yet chapter 37 suggests much the same kind of experience as P. desiderated. L.'s demand that the historian be a capable writer has much in common with Cic.'s demands about historiographical style: *On the Orator* 2.28–64. L. speaks further of the former at chapter 37, of the latter at chapters 44–6, 48.

124. On the importance of imitating previous writers, see Intro. §1.

125. Titormus was a shepherd of exceeding strength, Conon was known for his tiny physique; Milo of Croton was a famous sixth-century BCE wrestler, while Leostrophidos was an Athenian general known for his thinness.

126. The first two trainers are mentioned together by Plato (*Protagoras* 316e), the third was a contemporary of L.'s and known to Galen.

127. The love of Perdiccas, one of Alexander's generals, for his step-mother is mentioned by Pl. *Demetrius* 38; the story of the love of Antiochus, the son of Seleucus I, for his father's wife Stratonice is a favourite of L.'s: see *Icaromenippus* 15, *On Dancing* 58.

128. Theagenes was a prolific victor in the early fifth century BCE; Poly-damas is also mentioned by Plato.

129. Cf. Cic. *On the Orator* 2.62 for a complaint that the rules for his-toriography are nowhere written up.

130. For 'in a column' and 'in a line' see the inept historian of chapter 29. For political and military experience as desiderata in a histo-rian see P. 12.25d–28a.

131. For impartiality as necessary to the historian's reliability see Intro. §6.

132. Philip II, the father of Alexander the Great, lost his right eye in an attack on the city of Methone in 354 BCE; Cleitus 'the black', who had saved Alexander's life at the battle of the Granicus in 334 BCE, was killed by him in 328 during a drinking party: the incident exer-cised Alexander apologists who strained to justify the action (traces of this can still be seen in Arrian, *Anabasis* 4.8–9; Pl. *Alex-ander* 50–52); Cleon was a leading politician in Athens after the death of Pericles; he is much criticized by T., who does not in fact speak of him as 'crazy' (a point made by Pl. *Malice* 2 with n. 14); the final reference is to Athens' expedition against Sicily in 415–413 BCE, narrated by T. in his Books 6 and 7: the scene of the Athen-ians' final destruction, where the soldiers are slain as they are drinking at the Assinarus river, is at 7.84.

133. Cf. chapter 51 for the historian as only recorder, not inventor of deeds.

134. The cross-wall built by the Syracusans on the high ground called Epipolae put an effective end to Athenian attempts to circumvallate the city (T. 7.4–6); Hermocrates and Gylippus encourage the Syracu-sans not to give up in the fighting of the Athenians (7.21); the latter had been sent by the Spartans to assist the Syracusans and proved an effective commander, but it is Hermocrates, not Gylippus, who

blocks the roads (7.73); Athenian prisoners thrown into the quarries: 7.86; Alcibiades' hopes: 6.15.

135. In Greek myth Clotho, Lachesis and Atropos are the three Fates, the sisters who determine human destiny: see Gantz (1993) pp. 7–8.

136. The sentence is often compared with the famous remark of Leopold von Ranke that the historian's duty is to narrate the past 'as it actually was' (*'wie es eigentlich gewesen ist'*); L. further explains in chapter 51 that the historian is not to engage in the kind of invention that the orator might.

137. The reference is to Ctesias of Cnidus (above, p. 19).

138. For the common good as the aim of history see Diod. 1.1.1–2 etc.; the sentiments about impartiality are very close to those at P. 1.14.1–9.

139. See above, n. 40.

140. See above, chapter 8, for the metaphor of cosmetics.

141. Onesicritus was a historian of Alexander, frequently criticized by later writers: see Pearson (1960) chapter 4; A. Zambrini, *CGRH* pp. 211–15.

142. These remarks of Alexander are recorded by none of his surviving historians, and they are likely to be unhistorical.

143. On impartiality, Intro. §6; cf. Arrian, *Anabasis* preface 2, for the claim that Ptolemy and Aristobulus were both reliable because they wrote after Alexander's death.

144. Like our 'call a spade a spade'; the line probably comes from Menander: see *PCG* F 507 with additional citations of the line, including by L. in his other works.

145. That is to say, without a hostile temperament: see Intro. §6.

146. This is a very condensed way of expressing a number of sentiments that were uttered by L.'s predecessors about the need for a historian to be impartial.

147. T. nowhere mentions H. by name in his history and the division of H.'s work into nine books, each with the name of one of the Muses, took place after both H.'s and T.'s time.

148. This is a capsule summary of T. 1.22, but T. does not promise there that one can 'deal well with the things at hand'.

149. For similar stylistic suggestions see Cic. *Orator* 37–9.

150. For the appropriate language and style for history see Intro. §12.

151. See D.H. *Thuc.* 26–7 for similar thoughts about historiographical style.

152. L.'s advice here is very close to Aristotle's to orators in the *Rhetoric*: see 3.1406a18–19; for praise of an 'elevated' passage that is not excessive see D.H. *Thuc.* 27.

153. Corybants were priests of Cybele known for their ecstatic rites. For criticism of an excessively elaborate style see Agatharchides, *On the Red Sea* 5.21.

154. The arrangement of words was a special interest of D.H., who devoted an entire treatise, *On the Arrangement of Words*, to the topic; some of his thoughts on the matter can be found at *Thuc.* 24.

155. An echo of T. 1.22.3–4.

156. In the entire essay this is all that L. has to say on the actual business of inquiry by the historian; his remarks emphasize eyewitness and participation (Intro. §3), as one would expect, and the suggestion that one should inquire from the more reliable (i.e., less partial) sources echoes P.'s remarks at 12.4c.4–5. It is noteworthy how much personal evaluation goes into deciding what sources are the more impartial. R. Porod, 'Von der historischen Wahrheit und dem Ende historiographischer Fiktionalität: Überlegungen zu Lukians Schrift *pōs dei historian suggraphein*', *Antike und Abendland* 53 (2007) pp. 120–40, shows the importance of this chapter and how it is connected to other methodological pronouncements, especially those by P. For adding to or detracting from events see D.H. n. 17.

157. For the preliminary sketch, see above, chapter 16 with n. 65.

158. The reference is to *Iliad* 13.1–9. On seeing like Zeus, Zangara (2007) pp. 21–39.

159. Brasidas and Demosthenes (not the famous orator) are both commanders in T.'s history: L. may be thinking of T. 4.9–12 where the two men confront each other during the fighting at Pylos.

160. Strategy could be conveyed via speeches, either full-blown harangues before the battle or shorter remarks made in passing.

161. Here again a reference to Zeus in the *Iliad* (e.g., 8.69, 19.223), who balances the scales of individual warriors' destinies.

162. This is, of course, to make sure that the historian gives a full picture of the war, and is obviously in contrast with the historians criticized earlier who dwelt on individual (and often unimportant) matters at length: above, chapters 27–8. But it also seems like a defence of T.'s arrangement (criticized by D.H. *Thuc.* 9.4–10) and a repudiation of Diod.'s demand for 'self-contained' events (16.1.1–3).

163. Speech is compared to a mirror often by Plato (*Theaetetus* 193c, 206d; *Cratylus* 414c; *Republic* 402b).

164. This is perhaps the clearest statement that we have from ancient authors that the historian's task is not to invent material but only to form and shape it; L. is no doubt thinking of the ridiculous inventions, bordering on mythical, that he criticized in the earlier part of

the essay: see chapter 9 and the invented story by Aristobulus in chapter 11.

165. For Phidias, see D.H. *Thuc.* 4.2 with n. 14; above, n. 99. Praxiteles, sculptor of the fourth century BCE, was most famous for his Aphrodite of Cnidus. Alcamenes was a pupil of Phidias' and famous in his own right, but since L. mentions the Argives as commissioners, it is usually assumed that Alcamenes is an error for Polyclitus who created the famous chryselephantine statue of Hera at her great sanctuary in Argos.

166. L. here encourages the historian to employ vividness (*enargeia*) to bring things before the eyes of the audience: see Intro. §12.

167. See above, chapter 23, for those historians who imitate X. without understanding how his prefaces work.

168. The notion that the introduction of a speech should make the audience attentive, receptive and favourable is found already in Aristotle's *Rhetoric* 3.14, 1414b–1416a, and is a commonplace of rhetorical theory: see Cic. *On Invention* 1.20; pseudo-Cicero, *Rhetoric to Herennius* 1.6; Quintilian 4.1.5.

169. These are typical claims for the subject matter of a history: see Intro. §2.

170. L. refers to H.'s preface and to T. 1.1.1; T. does not, however, mention sufferings at the very outset of his work; he only does so at 1.23.1, though this might still be considered his (somewhat extended) preface.

171. The narration (Greek *diēgēsis*; Latin *narratio*) is the second part of a speech (after the introduction) in which the facts of the case are set out: Aristotle, *Rhetoric* 3.16, 1416b–1417b; quite a number of the narrations of surviving speeches in both Greek and Latin read very similarly to historical narratives.

172. See above, chapter 43.

173. Cf. D.H. *Thuc.* 9.6–8 for criticism of T.'s way of narrating events.

174. See L.'s criticism above, chapter 28, of the historian who spent all his time on a minor and personal incident, thereby ignoring the important events of the war.

175. Compare the historians criticized at chapters 19–21 and 27–8 for just this failing. On digressions in history see Intro. §12.

176. Eternally punished for their impious actions, Tantalos was 'tantalized' by waters that receded whenever he tried to drink, Ixion was crucified on a wheel of fire that rotated eternally, and Tityos had vultures tear at his liver forever. Homer mentions the first and third at *Odyssey* 11.576–92; for Ixion (whose torture is not mentioned by Homer) see Gantz (1993) pp. 718–21. Parthenius (first century

BCE), Euphorion and Callimachus (both third century BCE) are all
poets known for the refinement of their style and a love of learned
allusion and detail.

177. L.'s examples from T. refer to the following (respectively): 4.100,
6.75, 7.43.1ff., 7.25.5ff., and 2.47–54.

178. On speeches in history see Intro. §11; for the appropriateness of
speech to character see Callisthenes, F 44.

179. For the notion that praise and blame must be based on proofs, see
Aristotle, *Rhetoric* 2.22, 1396a.

180. On Theopompus see above, p. 31; for similar sentiments about him
see P. 8.10.1–2; Pl. *Malice* 1; but cf. D.H. *Pomp.* 6.7.

181. On mythical material in history see Intro. §9.

182. L. repeats here at the end what he has been saying throughout the
essay: chapters 9, 13, 39.

183. Sostratus, who is named just below.

184. Pharos is the name both of the lighthouse and of the island off the
coast of Alexandria on which it was located; it was built around
280 BCE; the 'king of that time' is Ptolemy II Philadelphus. Paraetonia (modern Mersa Matruh) is a seaport about 240 km west of
Alexandria.

185. The saviour gods are Castor and Pollux, patrons of sailors. The
inscription is also mentioned (but not quoted) by Strabo 17.1.6,
791C.

186. For the ruler metaphor, see Timaeus, F 151.

187. A reference to the opening story (chapter 3) about Diogenes.

35. GRANIUS LICINIANUS

1. For discussion of the man and his work (to the extent that it can be
known), see N. Criniti, 'Granio Liciniano', *ANRW* II.34.1 (1993)
pp. 119–205; there is an Italian commentary on the work by
B. Scardigli (Florence, 1983).

2. On the avoidance of marvels in history see Intro. §9.

3. The reference is to Tiberius Gracchus (tribune of the plebs, 133
BCE) and his brother Gaius (tribune, 123 and 122 BCE).

4. Scardigli (n. 1) thinks that Granius is referring to the use of Sallust
as a source for his account of the revolt of Marcus Aemilius Lepidus in 78–77 BCE.

5. Sallust had a reputation later for severity of judgement: see the famous
remark of Macrobius (3.13.9): 'a most harsh critic and censor of
other people's luxury'; for criticism of his speeches see above,

Pompeius Trogus F 152 with n. there; Granius also seems to suggest that Sallust perhaps had too many topographical digressions.

6. The last phrase here is difficult and the exact point of Granius' criticism is not clear; for a good example of Sallust's ability to make comparisons see *Catiline* 53.2–54.6.

36. SEXTUS EMPIRICUS

1. For a brief overview of Scepticism see A. A. Long, *Hellenistic Philosophy*, 2nd edn (London and Berkeley, 1986) pp. 75–106.

2. For a full translation and commentary on this work see D. L. Blank, *Sextus Empiricus: Against the Grammarians (Adversus Mathematicos I)* (Oxford, 1998).

3. For discussion of this passage see: K. Barwick, 'Die Gliederung der Narratio in der rhetorischen Theorie und ihre Bedeutung für die Geschichte des antiken Romans', *Hermes* 63 (1928) pp. 261–87; Meijering (1987) pp. 76–90; *SP* pp. 233–6; *Nature* pp. 10–11; W. J. Slater, 'Asklepiades and *Historia*', *GRBS* 13 (1972) pp. 317–33; T. P. Wiseman, *ORGRH* pp. 320–22; E. Gabba, *ORGRH* pp. 337–64; G. Rispoia, *Lo spazio del verisimile* (Naples, 1988) pp. 170–204.

4. Asclepiades of Myrlea in Bithynia (north coast of modern Turkey) was active in the first century BCE; he wrote a history of Bithynia (testimonia and fragments at *FGrHist* 697 and *BNJ* 697 (A. Trachsel)) but also works of scholarship, including on Homer. The tradition about him is vexed because he is often confused with other men of the same name.

5. One sees here the capaciousness of the term 'history', since it seems to embrace any narrative of actions in the past or presented as past. Compare P.'s very different way of dividing up historical narratives: 9.1.2–7.

6. Dionysius the Thracian (Dionysius Thrax), lived *c*. 170–90 BCE, and despite his name was from Alexandria; a teacher of grammar and literature at Rhodes, he wrote extensively on Homer as well as commentaries on other poets. Most relevant here is his *Grammatical Craft*, a work that summarized thoughts on grammar going back to the earliest Greek times and itself became a much-used handbook. The book opens with his definition of grammar: 'Grammar is the empirical knowledge of what is for the most part said by poets and prose-writers.' He thereafter distinguished six parts of grammar. See further R. Pfeiffer, *History of Classical*

Scholarship: From the Beginnings to the End of the Hellenistic Age (Oxford, 1968) pp. 266–72.

7. *Krēguon* was a rare Homeric word.

8. In other words, that part of grammar which inquires into things so as to give explanations (following from the root meaning of *historiē*, 'inquiry') can be called 'historical'.

9. These are common stories in the Greek mythographical tradition.

10. Xenophanes of Colophon was a philosopher of the late sixth and early fifth century BCE.

11. A reference to chapter 256, above.

12. Asclepius, the divine patron of physicians, is first mentioned in Homer's *Iliad* as a 'blameless physician' (*Iliad* 4.405); he is the son of Apollo and Coronis, raised by the centaur Chiron who teaches him the skills of healing.

13. Stesichorus was a lyric poet of the late seventh/early sixth century BCE: this is *FGrHist* F 92e (Davies/Finglass); Polyanthus of Cyrene is known only from this passage, though Jacoby includes a related fragment ascribed to Polyarchos of Cyrene: *FGrHist* 37 F 1 and *BNJ* 37 (M. Horster); Panyassis was said to be the uncle or cousin of H. and to have written a well-regarded epic on Heracles (*PEG* F 26); Staphylus of Naucratis lived in the second century BCE and wrote a number of local histories: see *FGrHist* 269 and *BNJ* 269 (L. V. Pitcher); for Phylarchus, see P. 2.56 with notes there; Telesarchus, possibly of the third century BCE, wrote on Argos; not much else is known of him: see *FGrHist* 309 and *BNJ* 309 (A. V. Mori).

14. As Walbank (*SP* p. 233) points out, this is perhaps not the best example since Alexander's death was much debated even in antiquity, and most modern scholars do not think he was poisoned.

15. In other words, myth is the realm of the impossible: see Intro. §9.

16. In other words, the grammarians cannot claim to have any knowledge of the proper way to write history because the writing of history is left to rhetoricians, not grammarians. Cf. Cic. *On the Orator* 2.64, on the absence of precepts for writing history.

37. CASSIUS DIO

1. On Dio's life and times see F. Millar, *A Study of Cassius Dio* (Oxford, 1964); on his historiographical methods see Millar, op. cit.; A. M. Gowing, *The Triumviral Narratives of Appian and Dio* (Ann Arbor, 1992); Hose (1994) pp. 356–451; id., *CGRH* pp. 461–7; Kemezis (2014) pp. 90–149; Scanlon (2015) pp. 265–9.

2. This must refer mainly to the non-contemporary parts of Dio's history, where the reading of one's predecessors would have been expected (see Intro. §3); the sources for his contemporary portions he explains at 73.23.1–5.

3. The passage stands as one of the few explicit remarks from the historians on the actual difficulty of finding out what happened; see further Intro. §3.

4. This remark comes in the context of the events of 27 BCE, where Dio has described Octavian's arrangements for the consolidation of his power into the principate, and his adoption of the name 'Augustus'; thereafter, Rome became a monarchy rather than an oligarchy (despite the fact that Dio says 'democratic form') as it had been since the early sixth century.

5. The usual suspects that corrupted history: Intro. §6.

6. The idea that one could eliminate bias by comparison of accounts may go back to T. 1.22.4, although he does not say that explicitly; cf. P. 12.4c.5 and L. Hist. 47.

7. Dio tries here to fulfil the responsibility of the historian while simultaneously removing any personal responsibility from himself as to the accuracy of what he reports.

8. The words echo H. 2.99.1 and 2.147.1, where he is talking of Egypt.

9. Cf. Tacitus' similar remarks, Annals 16.16.1–2 about the wearying nature of a narrative that must treat many deaths at the hands of the Emperor.

10. On great deeds as the subject matter of history, see Intro. §2.

11. The remarks touch on a number of common tropes in historiography: the author's presence at events as guarantee for their accuracy; the concern that future generations know what happened; the claim to be writing an account worthy of record; and the historian's own competence (Intro. §§2, 3 and 7).

12. Dio has just recorded the death of Commodus in 192 CE.

13. The emperor is Septimius Severus who came to power in 193; cf. Josephus' prediction of Vespasian's reign which he mentions at *Against Apion* 1.47–9. The work mentioned here does not survive.

14. For Dio's further dreams see below, 78.10.1–2, 80.5.3. The Elder Pliny said that he had been motivated to write his account of the German wars by a dream (see *FRHist* 80 T 1 with *ATAH* pp. 47–9), but Dio's claim that his history was the result of a divine command finds scant parallel in earlier Greek or Roman historians; the closest one comes is Arrian, *Anabasis* 7.30.3, but that can be understood differently from Dio's approach here.

15. The goddess *Tychē* (Fortune) plays an important role in P.'s history but as one of the forces that drives history, not as the spur to any individual to take a particular action. For dreams in historiography see *ATAH* pp. 43–51.

16. Claims of effort are common in the historians; for other mentions of the number of years it took to compose a history see Diod. 1.4.1; D.H. *Rom. Ant.* 1.7.2.

17. Dio has just narrated the death of Caracalla, the son of Septimius Severus, in 217.

18. This suggests the kind of privileged access to power that was more or less required for writing history under the empire: see Josephus, *Life* 366 and Intro. §3.

19. Dio is speaking of the Persian Artaxerxes, who had conquered the Parthians in three battles, killed their king Artabanus, and made an attempt on the city of Hatra in 227 CE to use as a base against the Romans (though he was repulsed). The 'Persians of old' is a reference to the fifth century BCE for according to H. 1.4.3, the Persians claimed everything in Asia as their own.

20. For similar complaints about soldiers in the empire, see Fronto, *Sketch of History* 12.

21. The emperor Severus Alexander, who ruled from 208 to 235.

22. Dio's second consulship occurred in 229.

23. For Dio's previous dreams see the previous two extracts; the quotation is from *Iliad* 11.163–4.

38. HERODIAN

1. On Herodian see G. W. Bowersock, 'Historical Writing of the High Empire', in P. E. Easterling and B. M. W. Knox, eds., *Cambridge History of Classical Literature I: Greek Literature* (Cambridge, 1985) pp. 710–12; C. R. Whittaker, *Herodian: History of the Empire*, vol. 1 (London and Cambridge, Mass., 1969) pp. ix–lxxxii; Pitcher (2009) pp. 40–44; Kemezis (2014) pp. 227–72; Scanlon (2015) 268–9.

2. This is strongly reminiscent of Josephus, *Jewish War* 1.1 and *Jewish Antiquities*, preface 2.

3. On flattery as the enemy of truth, Intro. §6.

4. On pleasure and utility in history, Intro. §7.

5. Septimius Severus, reigned 193–211.

6. Who these writers are is unknown; for some possibilities, Whitaker (n. 1) p. 246 n. 2.

7.   Cf. Ammianus, 26.1.1 on inappropriate details in a history.

8.   On the need to avoid flattery in history, Intro. §6; on omission as
      equally injurious to history as falsehood see P. 12.15.12; Cic. *On
      the Orator* 2.62; Pl. *Malice* 4; on 'worthy of account' as defining
      history's subject matter, Intro. §2.

39. AMMIANUS MARCELLINUS

1.   On Ammianus' life and times see J. F. Matthews, *The Roman
      Empire of Ammianus* (London and Baltimore, 1989); on his history
      and historiographical thought see: E. A. Thompson, *The Historio-
      graphical Work of Ammianus Marcellinus* (Cambridge, 1947);
      R. C. Blockley, *Ammianus Marcellinus: A Study of his Historiog-
      raphy and Political Thought* (Brussels, 1975); G. Sabbah, *La
      méthode d'Ammien Marcellin: Recherches sur la construction du
      discours historique dans les 'Res Gestae'* (Paris, 1978); C. W. For-
      nara, 'The Prefaces of Ammianus Marcellinus', in M. Griffith and
      D. J. Mastronarde, eds., *Cabinet of the Muses: Essays . . . Thomas
      G. Rosenmeyer* (Atlanta, 1990) pp. 163–72; id., 'Studies in Ammi-
      anus Marcellinus II: Ammianus' Knowledge and Use of Greek and
      Latin Literature', *Historia* 41 (1992) pp. 420–38; J. den Boeft et al.,
      eds., *Cognitio Gestorum: The Historiographic Art of Ammianus
      Marcellinus* (Amsterdam, 1992); T. D. Barnes, *Ammianus Marcel-
      linus and the Representation of Historical Reality* (Ithaca, 1998);
      D. Hunt and J. W. Drijvers, *The Late Roman World and its Histo-
      rian: Interpreting Ammianus Marcellinus* (London and New
      York, 1999); G. Kelly, *Ammianus Marcellinus: The Allusive Histo-
      rian* (Cambridge, 2008).

2.   Books 1–14 covered events from 96 CE to 354. For the reliance on
      autopsy and inquiry see Intro. §3; on this passage see the discussion
      of Barnes (n. 1) pp. 29–30.

3.   Brief histories and biographies in Latin were very popular in Ammi-
      anus' time; his own history was an attempt to go back to an older
      style of more detailed history-writing, which, as with earlier histor-
      ians, could explain and delineate the ways in which events occurred
      rather than simply mention them or give only a brief account. See
      also below, 23.6.1.

4.   Ammianus has just been narrating events at Rome and in Gaul and
      the Persian invasions of Armenia and Mesopotamia in the east. The
      'Caesar' is the (future) emperor Julian (reigned 361–3), the 'Augus-
      tus' is the emperor Constantius II (reigned 337–61).

5.   The passage shows Ammianus' recognition of the widespread use of history for panegyric, as can be seen, for example, in L. *Hist*. 7, and Fronto's correspondence with Lucius Verus (above, p. 357). See Intro. §6. For proofs and panegyric see L. n. 159

6.   A reference to H. 7.59–60 where he claims that Xerxes counted his massive army by gathering 10,000 men together, making an enclosure around them, and in this way numbering the remaining men, which H. put at 1,700,000.

7.   Again, a recognition of the exaggerative nature of battle reports: for a particularly ludicrous example see L. *Hist*. 20.

8.   The reference is to Julian.

9.   On the notion of what is worthy of account in history see Intro. §2.

10.   The occasion is Julian's invasion of Persia in 363.

11.   On brevity see above, n. 3.

12.   On the 'danger' of contemporary history see Intro. §6.

13.   Cf. Tacitus, *Annals* 4.33.4 on detractors.

14.   The praetors entered office on 1 January; presumably they, like other Roman magistrates, were offered formal congratulations by their peers and fellow citizens.

15.   For Ammianus' strictures here about the appropriate subject matter for history cf. P. 29.12.1–4; L. *Hist*. 27; Herodian 2.15.6.

16.   The letter does not survive.

17.   These are the events of September 365 to May 366.

18.   For different ways of arranging one's history see Intro. §12. A. J. Woodman has called my attention to 'jumpily' (*saltuatim*), a rare word also used by Sisenna in discussing his history's arrangement: *FRHist* 26 F 130, quoted above, Intro. n. 110.

19.   The context of the first passage is the aftermath of Theodorus' attempt to seize the throne in 371–2; he and many accomplices were executed by the emperor Valens. The second is Lupicinus' campaign against the Theruingi in 376.

20.   On this passage see Kelly (n. 1) pp. 72–4. One might compare T. 7.44.1 on the difficulties of narrating the night battle at Epipolae. And cf. the next passage as well.

21.   In identifying himself in this way, Ammianus, though writing in Latin, lays claim to the long tradition of Greek historiography and of the Polybian ideal of a man versed in political and military affairs. For discussion see Barnes (n. 1) pp. 65–6; *ATAH* pp. 256–7; Kelly (n. 1) p. 103: 'The phrase is pregnant and multivalent, allusive to rather than identical with the simple and precise description of origins and status which one might expect to find in earlier historians.'

22.   Cf. Cic. *On the Orator* 2.62.

23. A call, most likely, to his successors to continue to write detailed history in the elevated style which Ammianus himself practised: cf. X., *Hellenica* 7.5.27; Agatharchides, *On the Red Sea* 5.112.

40. ANONYMOUS EVALUATION OF HISTORIANS

1. The papyrus was first edited by A. G. Beresford, P. J. Parsons and M. P. Pobjoy, '4808. On Hellenistic Historians', *Oxyrhynchus Papyri* 61 (2007) pp. 27–36 with Plate IV.

2. The author must here be talking of Onesicritus of Astypalaea (*FGrHist* 134; *BNJ* 134 (M. Whitby)), who wrote a work on Alexander, possibly modelled on X.'s *Education of Cyrus*. See further Whitby at *BNJ* 134 T 1 who has a full discussion of the title. On Onesicritus see Pearson (1960) chapter IV. On Diogenes see L. *Hist.* 3.

3. Chares of Mytilene was Alexander's chamberlain and wrote a history of Alexander in at least ten books: see Pearson (1960) pp. 50–61; testimonia and fragments are at *FGrHist* 125 and, with English translation and updated bibliography, at *BNJ* 125 (S. Müller), although this passage is not included.

4. This probably means that he tells events differently from all the other historians, not that he had a peculiar style.

5. Parmenio was Alexander's second-in-command during the early stages of his invasion of Asia, but he later had a falling-out with Alexander; when Parmenio's son, Philotas, was executed for alleged participation in a conspiracy, Parmenio too was executed.

6. For Cleitarchus see Cic. *On the Laws* 1.7.

7. Although the first editors took this 'disposition' to mean the arrangement of his work, the general tendency of this treatise to evaluate character and biography suggests that the term here is equivalent to character: see, e.g., D.H. *Pomp.* 3.15.

8. A reference to Ptolemy IV Philopator, ruler of Egypt from *c*. 244 to 205 BCE.

9. For Hieronymus see D.H. *Rom. Ant.* 1.6.1 with n. 199.

10. These and what follow are probably references to Hieronymus' career and work.

11. According to the pseudo-Lucianic *Long-Lived Men* 22, he lived to be 104.

12. On P. see above, p. 51.

13. The words 'the truth' are not in the text, but they seem likely given P.'s reputation and his frequent exhortations to historians to cultivate truth.

41. ANONYMOUS COMMENTARY ON
THUCYDIDES

1.   For arrangement in history see Intro. §12.
2.   Just as in a modern commentary, the commentator begins with a lemma, i.e., a passage on which to comment, here T.'s remark at 2.1.
3.   D.H. *Thuc.* 9.4.
4.   D.H. *Thuc.* 9.5–10.
5.   D.H. *Thuc.* 10–11.
6.   Here and elsewhere the dots indicate gaps in the text.
7.   On Olympiad dating, see P n. 7. The arrangement of events by archon dates is characteristic of Athenian local history; the archonship was an annual Athenian magistracy, but because of Athens' cultural importance it was used by other historians (e.g., Diod. in his universal history) in synchronisms.
8.   The commentator here is discussing events to be found in Books 2–4 of T.'s history.
9.   The commentator here must be referring to the attacks made by the Athenians against fellow Greeks and briefly treated by T. at 1. 98–117.
10. The text breaks off here. For the importance of the historian's analysis of causation see P. 3.6.1–7 and further references there.

Bibliography

The bibliography does not contain works listed in the Abbreviations. Bibliographies for individual historians can be found in the relevant chapters.

Bowersock, G. W. (1965) *Augustus and the Greek World* (Oxford)

Brown, T. S. (1973) *The Greek Historians* (Lexington, Mass.)

D'Alton, J. F. (1931) *Roman Literary Theory and Criticism: A Study in Tendencies* (London and New York)

Drews, R. (1973) *The Greek Accounts of Eastern History* (Cambridge, Mass.)

Duff, T. E. (2003) *The Greek and Roman Historians* (Bristol)

Gantz, T. (1993) *Early Greek Myth: A Guide to Literary and Artistic Sources* (Baltimore and London)

Gill, C. and T. P. Wiseman, eds. (1993) *Lies & Fiction in the Ancient World* (Exeter and Austin)

Grube, G. M. A. (1965) *The Greek and Roman Critics* (London)

Hose, M. (1994) *Erneuerung der Vergangenheit: die Historiker im Imperium Romanum von Florus bis Cassius Dio* (Stuttgart)

Jacoby, F. (1909) 'Über die Entwicklung der griechischen Historiker und den Plan einer neuen Sammlung der griechischen Historikerfragmente', *Klio* 9: 80–123; English translation by M. Chambers and S. Schorn, *On the Development of Greek Historiography and the Plan for a New Collection of the Fragments of the Greek Historians* (*Histos* Supplement 3; Newcastle, 2015). Cited from the English translation

—— (1949) *Atthis: The Local Chronicles of Ancient Athens* (Oxford)

Kemezis, A. (2014) *Greek Narratives of the Roman Empire under the Severans* (Cambridge)

Kennedy, G. (1963) *The Art of Persuasion in Greece* (Princeton)

—— (1972) *The Art of Rhetoric in the Roman World* (Princeton)

Leeman, A. D. (1963) *Orationis Ratio: The Stylistic Theories and Practice of the Roman Orators, Historians, and Philosophers*, 2 vols. (Amsterdam)

Marincola, J. (2007) 'Odysseus and the Historians', *Syllecta Classica* 18: 1–79

Meijering, R. (1987) *Literary and Rhetorical Theories in Greek Scholia* (Groningen)

Moles, J. L. (1993) 'Truth and Untruth in Herodotus and Thucydides', in Gill and Wiseman (1993) pp. 88–121

Nicolai, R. (1992) *La storiografia nell'educazione antica* (Pisa)

Pearson, L. (1939) *Early Ionian Historians* (Oxford)

—— (1960) *The Lost Historians of Alexander the Great* (New York and Oxford)

—— (1987) *The Greek Historians of the West: Timaeus and his Predecessors* (Atlanta)

Pédech, P. (1964) *La méthode historique de Polybe* (Paris)

—— (1984) *Historiens Compagnons d'Alexandre: Callisthène, Onésicrite, Néarque, Ptolémée, Aristoboule* (Paris)

—— (1989) *Trois Historiens Méconnus: Théopompe, Duris, Phylarque* (Paris)

Pelling, C. (2000) *Literary Texts and the Greek Historian* (London and New York)

Pitcher, L. V. (2009) *Writing Ancient History: An Introduction to Classical Historiography* (London and New York)

Potter, D. S. (1999) *Literary Texts and the Roman Historian* (London and New York)

Pownall, F. (2004) *Lessons from the Past: The Moral Use of History in Fourth-Century Prose* (Ann Arbor)

Pritchett, W. K. (1975) *Dionysius of Halicarnassus: On Thucydides* (Berkeley)

Rutherford, R. B. (1994) 'Learning from History: Categories and Case-Studies', in R. Osborne and S. Hornblower, eds., *Ritual, Finance, Politics* (Oxford) pp. 53–68

Sacks, K. (1981) *Polybius on the Writing of History* (Berkeley)

Scanlon, T. F. (2015) *Greek Historiography* (Malden, Mass., Oxford and Chichester)

Scheller, P. (1911) *De hellenistica historiae conscribendae arte* (diss., Leipzig)

Zangara, A. (2007) *Voir l'histoire: théories anciennes du récit historique* (Paris)

Thematic Index

Index of Passages Translated

General Index

Pisidia 549
Pitanate regiment 16
Pittaceum 301
Pittacus 301, 511, 512
pity l, lxviii, 45, 47–8, 57, 58–60,
    65, 114, 128–9, 194, 197, 228,
    241, 279, 350, 386,
plague, at Athens 375, 391, 542, 546
plasma (fiction) liii
plasma historikon (historical
    cast) 490
Plataea/Plataeans 188, 195, 217–9,
    226, 307, 311, 316, 319, 324–6,
    327, 482, 485–7, 488, 494, 515,
    519, 522, 524–5
Plato 108, 140, 184, 255, 293, 296,
    397, 454, 457, 461, 471, 475,
    509, 544, 550
Plautius, Lucius (praetor 322 BCE)
    262
Pliny the Elder (Gaius Plinius
    Secundus) xxxvi, 341, 342, 497,
    532, 557
Pliny the Younger (Gaius Plinius
    Caecilius Secundus) xlv, 273,
    341–6, 532–4
Plutarch xxix, xxxviii, l, lvii, 19,
    293–332, 506–27
polemic xxxii, xxxiii, xxxv, lix,
    lxiv, 366, 395, 503, 504
political history (*pragmatikē
    historia*) 75, 99, 106, 438, 458,
    526
political oratory 209
political philosophy 183
Pollux 554
Polus 203, 484
Polyanthus of Cyrene 398, 556
Polyarchos 556
Polybius xxx, xxxiii, xxxvi,
    xxxvii, xxxix, xl, xli, xliv, xlv,
    xlvii, xlviii, xlix, l, lii, liii, lvii,

lix, lxii, 13, 27, 35, 36, 51–119,
    127, 173, 180, 251–2, 294, 418,
    437–62, 492, 537
Polyclitus 184, 553
Polycrates 198, 303, 304, 514
Polydamas 384, 550
Polyperchon 473
Pompeiopolis 375, 545
Pompeius Geminus 240
Pompeius Trogus 267–8, 497–8
Pompey (Gnaeus Pompeius) 125,
    126, 143, 264, 267, 328, 335,
    337, 495, 497, 529, 531, 539
Pontifex Maximus xxxvi, 43, 137,
    434–5, 467
Pontus 118, 498
Popilia 135, 466
Porus 373, 545
Poseidon 46, 371, 435, 522
Postumius Albinus, Aulus 119, 462
Potidaea 190, 419
'pragmatic' history: *see* political
    history
Praxiphanes lxiii
Praxiteles 389, 553
preface, of a historical work 22,
    198–200, 241, 376, 378–9,
    389–90, 553; virtual 389
preliminary sketch: see
    hypomnēma
Priene 480
priests 278, 291, 501
princeps ('first citizen') 528
Priscus 377
probability xlii, liii, lv–lvi, lxviii,
    lxx, 11, 26, 28, 56, 59, 60, 63,
    67, 68, 75, 82, 83, 84, 88, 103,
    106, 110, 217, 250, 329, 350,
    388, 441, 511, 544
Procles 397; his son, 397
Proconessus 480
Prodicus 458